End-to-End QoS Network Design

Tim Szigeti, CCIE No. 9794, Christina Hattingh

Copyright © 2005 Cisco Systems, Inc.

Published by:
Cisco Press
800 East 96th Street
Indianapolis, IN 46240 USA

Printed in the United States of America   5 6 7 8 9 0

Fifth Printing March 2007

Library of Congress Cataloging-in-Publication Number: 2003111984

ISBN: 1-58705-176-1

Trademark Acknowledgments

All terms mentioned in this book that are known to be trademarks or service marks have been appropriately capitalized. Cisco Press or Cisco Systems, Inc., cannot attest to the accuracy of this information. Use of a term in this book should not be regarded as affecting the validity of any trademark or service mark.

Warning and Disclaimer

This book is designed to provide information about Quality-of-Service network design best-practice recommendations. Every effort has been made to make this book as complete and as accurate as possible, but no warranty or fitness is implied.

The information is provided on an "as is" basis. The authors, Cisco Press, and Cisco Systems, Inc., shall have neither liability nor responsibility to any person or entity with respect to any loss or damages arising from the information contained in this book or from the use of the discs or programs that may accompany it.

The opinions expressed in this book belong to the author and are not necessarily those of Cisco Systems, Inc.

Corporate and Government Sales

Cisco Press offers excellent discounts on this book when ordered in quantity for bulk purchases or special sales.

For more information please contact:
U.S. Corporate and Government Sales   1-800-382-3419   corpsales@pearsontechgroup.com

For sales outside the U.S. please contact: **International Sales** international@pearsoned.com

Feedback Information

At Cisco Press, our goal is to create in-depth technical books of the highest quality and value. Each book is crafted with care and precision, undergoing rigorous development that involves the unique expertise of members from the professional technical community.

Readers' feedback is a natural continuation of this process. If you have any comments regarding how we could improve the quality of this book or otherwise alter it to better suit your needs, you can contact us through e-mail at feedback@ciscopress.com. Please make sure to include the book title and ISBN in your message.

We greatly appreciate your assistance.

Publisher	John Wait
Editor-in-Chief	John Kane
Cisco Representative	Anthony Wolfenden
Cisco Press Program Manager	Nannette M. Noble
Executive Editor	Christopher Cleveland
Acquisitions Editor	Michelle Grandin
Production Manager	Patrick Kanouse
Development Editor	Howard A. Jones
Copy Editor	Krista Hansing
Technical Editors	Frank Knox
	Anna To
	Connie Varner
Team Coordinator	Tammi Barnett
Cover Designer	Louisa Adair
Composition	Octal Publishing, Inc.
Indexer	Eric Schroeder
Proofreader	Tonya Cupp

CISCO SYSTEMS

Corporate Headquarters
Cisco Systems, Inc.
170 West Tasman Drive
San Jose, CA 95134-1706
USA
www.cisco.com
Tel: 408 526-4000
    800 553-NETS (6387)
Fax: 408 526-4100

European Headquarters
Cisco Systems International BV
Haarlerbergpark
Haarlerbergweg 13-19
1101 CH Amsterdam
The Netherlands
www-europe.cisco.com
Tel: 31 0 20 357 1000
Fax: 31 0 20 357 1100

Americas Headquarters
Cisco Systems, Inc.
170 West Tasman Drive
San Jose, CA 95134-1706
USA
www.cisco.com
Tel: 408 526-7660
Fax: 408 527-0883

Asia Pacific Headquarters
Cisco Systems, Inc.
Capital Tower
168 Robinson Road
#22-01 to #29-01
Singapore 068912
www.cisco.com
Tel: +65 6317 7777
Fax: +65 6317 7799

Cisco Systems has more than 200 offices in the following countries and regions. Addresses, phone numbers, and fax numbers are listed on the
Cisco.com Web site at www.cisco.com/go/offices.

Argentina • Australia • Austria • Belgium • Brazil • Bulgaria • Canada • Chile • China PRC • Colombia • Costa Rica • Croatia • Czech Republic
Denmark • Dubai, UAE • Finland • France • Germany • Greece • Hong Kong SAR • Hungary • India • Indonesia • Ireland • Israel • Italy
Japan • Korea • Luxembourg • Malaysia • Mexico • The Netherlands • New Zealand • Norway • Peru • Philippines • Poland • Portugal
Puerto Rico • Romania • Russia • Saudi Arabia • Scotland • Singapore • Slovakia • Slovenia • South Africa • Spain • Sweden
Switzerland • Taiwan • Thailand • Turkey • Ukraine • United Kingdom • United States • Venezuela • Vietnam • Zimbabwe

About the Authors

Tim Szigeti, **CCIE No. 9794**, attended the University of British Columbia, where he majored in management information systems. After graduating, Tim joined Cisco Systems and soon after began to specialize in Quality-of-Service technologies, supporting technical marketing initiatives for the Cisco Class Data acquisition, which led to the Cisco QoS Policy Manager (QPM) product. After supporting QPM through several generations and serving as product manager for the Cisco Quality of Service Device Manager (QDM) product, Tim joined the Enterprise Solutions Engineering team and led large-scale testing initiatives of campus, WAN, and VPN QoS designs. Tim now belongs to the newly formed Technology Solutions Engineering team within the Cisco Central Technical Marketing organization. There, he continues to define and drive strategic QoS solutions across Cisco technology groups and business units while working with many Fortune 500 companies—both enterprise and service providers—providing QoS design expertise.

Christina Hattingh is a member of the technical staff in the Multiservice Customer Edge Business Unit of Cisco Systems. These products, including the Cisco 2600, 3600, and 3700 series access router platforms, were some of the first Cisco platforms to converge voice and data traffic onto an IP network by offering TDM voice interfaces, WAN interfaces, and critical QoS features, while later integrating call control elements into the router-based platform itself. In this role, she trains Cisco sales staff and advises customers on voice network deployment and design.

About the Technical Editors

Frank Knox has more than 37 years of telecommunications experience. During his career at IBM, Frank held positions in field service, field support, service planning, and education; his final position before retirement was curriculum manager for IBM's Network Education in North America. After leaving IBM, Frank held the position of network engineering manager for GTE Directories, where he was responsible for the company's voice and data network design and support. Concurrent with his work at IBM and GTE, Frank taught as an adjunct professor for the University of Dallas MBA program. For the past six years, Frank has worked for Skyline Computer as a senior instructor and consultant; he is currently Skyline's chief technical officer (CTO). Frank holds two CCIE certifications (R&S and SNA/IP); he also has a master's degree in telecommunications from Pace University.

Anna To has worked with Cisco for more than three years as a software/deployment engineer on the ITD QoS team. One of Anna's key tasks is to promote QoS deployment and increase the understanding of QoS technology in the field. Anna works on the Modular QoS CLI (MQC) solution team to bring consistency in QoS configuration across various Cisco platforms. In addition, Anna is involved with the AutoQoS project to simplify QoS deployment.

Connie Varner is a technical marketing engineer in the Cisco Enterprise Systems Engineering group. She has extensive experience designing and testing large-scale networks based on customer requirements, in part based on four years of experience with the Cisco Customer Proof of Concept Labs. Connie specializes in QoS designs that meet the needs of converged data, voice and video networks, and designs that involve IPSec VPNs.

Dedications

Tim: This book is obviously dedicated to my wife; otherwise, of course, she'd kill me. It amuses me to think that if others are actually reading this, they probably think I'm only joking—but, alas, the Greek capacity for vengeance is no laughing matter. I cancelled far too many dates, stayed in my office and labs far too many weekends, and stared blankly into space (thinking about these designs) far too many times (while she was talking to me) to ever allow the thought of *not* dedicating this work to her to even cross my tiny xeno-brain.

I know, I know, it's not a work of literature or a collection of poetry: It's just a technical book—boring to tears for any not interested in the subject (and probably just boring to yawns for the rest). But, for whatever it's worth, I'm dedicating it to you, Lella. I love you with all my heart.

Christina: To Robert Verkroost and Ria and Willie Hattingh, who unfailingly support my various forays into the publishing world.

Acknowledgments

Off the top, I'd like to thank my friend and co-worker Dave Barton, who—although he was extremely busy downing beers at Chicago's Navy Pier—gallantly managed to sic Brett Bartow onto me, which got the ball rolling on this whole project. (Dave, did you make it back okay to the hotel that night?)

Many thanks to Todd Truitt, one of the top talents at Cisco, for inviting my collaboration on the original *AVVID QoS Design Guide*, hiring me onto his design team, and recommending Christina as a co-author for this project. Do you ever get tired of being right, Todd?

Thanks also to Neil Anderson, Joel King, Ted Hannock, and Steve Ochmanski for guidance and collaboration on IPSec V3PN designs. Thanks for letting me leverage your excellent and thorough work so that I did not to have to reinvent the wheel on these designs.

Thank you, Mike Herbert, for your brilliant flash of using QoS for DoS/worm mitigation via the Scavenger class. Though you derailed and postponed many whitepapers and publications (including this one), you opened up a whole new scope of application for QoS technologies—and we're all better off for it.

Thank you, too, Alex Dolan, for building out multiple large-scale MPLS VPN testbeds for me and continually tweaking them to suit my mood-of-the-day. I don't know where your patience or your good nature comes from, but they're most appreciated. Thanks, too, for nudging me back into playing ice hockey. Next time I break a leg or chip a tooth, I'll think of you and grimace.

Muchos gracias, Arlindo Callejas, for being much more than my awesome lab administrator. You always went out of your way for me and got me everything I ever needed—instantly. Sometimes I'm afraid to ask where you sourced the gear you did. (I'm not sure whether those 10GE linecards "fell off the back of a Cisco truck" or what, but they sure came in handy at just the right time.)

A round of applause is merited by the technical reviewers. Having done this before myself, I can genuinely appreciate the time, effort, and painstaking attention to detail that goes into this process. Frank, your comments were right on and helped make this a better book. Anna, is there anything you don't know about Cisco QoS? I'm very thankful you took time out of your extremely busy schedule, developing code while helping anyone and everyone on planet Earth (and some nearby systems) that are having QoS problems. And Connie, if you hadn't reviewed this work, I would not have submitted it for publication. You're simply the best technical reviewer—and one of the sharpest engineers—I've ever had the pleasure of working with.

Thank you Howard Jones for your excellent editing and coordinating the complex content review and copy review processes. And thank you, too, Patrick Kanouse for managing the production of this publication and allowing me to make hundreds of last-minute edits in the galley-review phase (when edits are to be kept at a minimum). How you put up with me I'll never know, but I truly appreciate your patience and desire to help make this book as correct and as current as possible. Also thank you Chris Cleveland for your fine recommendations and guidance during the course of production.

I need to extend thanks also to Debbie Morrison, who is, in my opinion, the best technical writer—period. Debbie, as I've said over and over again, you polish my ugly little chunks of coal into beautiful diamonds. I love how I can barely recognize my own work once you've done your magic. I'll truly miss working with you now that you've gone on to bigger and better things. (I'm so terrified of the future—who's going to make me look good now?)

Brett Bartow, what can I say? This would never have happened without you. Time and time again, it seemed to fall by the wayside, but your persistence, perseverance, and patience kept it all going. Thank you. You didn't back off, and I'm glad for it. Your guidance has been uncanny, and your vision has paid off. Thanks also to your production team.

And lastly, thank you, Christina. You made it fun. Right when I read your first draft of your first chapter, I knew you were the best person to embark on this project with (even though you write like an engineer!). Thank you for sacrificing so many weekends on this (thank Robert for me too). I know this is only one of many publishing projects you're pursuing; all I ask is that you save me an autograph before you move to Hawaii and start on your best-seller!

Contents at a Glance

Table of Contents

Icons Used in This Book

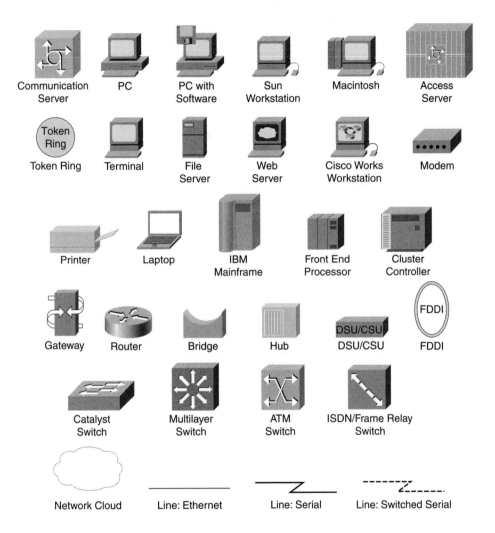

Command Syntax Conventions

The conventions used to present command syntax in this book are the same conventions used in the Cisco IOS Command Reference. The Command Reference describes these conventions as follows:

- **Boldface** indicates commands and keywords that are entered literally as shown. In actual configuration examples and output (not general command syntax), boldface indicates commands that are input manually by the user (such as a **show** command).

- *Italics* indicates arguments for which you supply actual values.

- Vertical bars (|) separate alternative, mutually exclusive elements.

- Square brackets [ ] indicate optional elements.

- Braces { } indicate a required choice.

- Braces within brackets [{ }] indicate a required choice within an optional element.

Introduction

QoS is a maturing technology, one that many networking professionals, to a greater or lesser extent, are already familiar with. This is both a blessing and a curse. It is a blessing because more administrators are enabling QoS on their networks, which allows for the convergence of voice, video, and data onto a single IP network, among other business advantages. It is a curse because almost every individual with whom I've ever discussed QoS designs has a slightly different opinion on how QoS should be enabled.

The result often has led to confusing babble from the customer's perspective, especially for customers seeking QoS design guidance for non-VoIP applications. For example, a customer might ask the local Cisco Systems engineer how best to enable QoS for networks and receive one answer. Later, the customer might attend an Executive Briefing session in San Jose and receive a different answer (even receiving multiple different answers within the same day from different presenters). Later, while attending a Networkers conference, the customer might be told something else entirely. Finally, when the customer gets home and picks up a Cisco Press book, he or she might get still another story. Confused and frustrated, many customers decide to enable minimal QoS, if any, despite the touted benefits that they were sold on. Therefore, in my opinion, presenting such inconsistent recommendations is a major disservice to our customers and a considerable barrier to the widespread deployment of QoS.

The Cisco Technology Baseline committees were created to remedy the situation and help unify various technologies across Cisco products and platforms. To this end, a series of Technology Baselines were developed internally by our leading experts (many of whom likewise developed the related IETF RFCs and other standards) to which all Cisco products and features must conform. Additionally, these documents provide uniform, strategic recommendations (that can be shared with customers) to help ensure that QoS recommendations are unified and consistent, for both enterprises and service providers. Specific to QoS, the QoS Baseline strictly defines the Cisco strategic direction in QoS technologies from now into the foreseeable future.

Thus, a unique feature of this book is that it is the first Cisco Press publication to present design recommendations that are compliant with the QoS Baseline.

Another huge advantage of this publication is that it is one of the first documents to present a detailed, cohesive strategy that shows how QoS can extend beyond its traditional role (of prioritizing important applications) and be used to provide deferential services to DoS/worm-generated traffic, thus mitigating and containing the collateral damage caused by such attacks. This is a fresh perspective and context for a technology that many considered baked and done. Yet in such a role, the critical interdependency of Quality of Service, High-Availability, and Security technologies becomes manifest and holistically promotes the "Self-Defending Networks" business objective.

However, having a strategic direction and tactical approaches for QoS designs is only half the solution. An important motto that I like to emphasize is: "In theory, theory and practice are the same." It's one thing to make a design recommendation based on an assumption that something "should work." It's something completely different to make a design recommendation that has been verified in large-scale, complex lab scenarios, such as provided by one of the largest Cisco labs: the Enterprise Solutions Engineering testbeds in Research Triangle Park, North Carolina.

Notwithstanding, it should be noted that designs presented in this book are not infallible. While all due diligence has been done to present working, tested configurations—including a rigorous technical reviewing process by some of the sharpest Cisco QoS engineers—hardware/software/platform-specific issues that didn't surface during our tests may nonetheless exist, as may issues introduced in newer releases of hardware/software dating from our time of testing.

Furthermore, the recommendations presented in this book are not to be taken as commandments or dictates ("Thou shalt configure this or that"), but are simply best-practice design recommendations that are the result of extensive lab testing and customer deployments. They should be viewed as templates that can be modified and tweaked to customer-specific requirements. Following the 80/20 Pareto Rule, these design recommendations should be viewed as 80 percent of the solution, to which the remaining 20 percent is up to each customer to complete and tailor to their individual needs and constraints.

Here's an analogy of how to view these design recommendations: Given a business objective (for example, to hammer a nail into a wall), you will have certain tools at your disposal—tools that may or may not be optimally suited to the task (let's say, a hammer and a banana). Our lab testing presents the optimal tool to use for the given objective (normally, a hammer tests better than a banana, but you never know—I've seen some pretty funky frozen bananas that might do the trick). It's still up to the customer to pick the tool that best suits their objectives, situations, and comfort levels. These recommendations are not mandates; they are simply suggestions based on extensive lab testing and customer deployments.

Who Should Read This Book?

Some might ask, "Why should I read this book? Especially when I have AutoQoS?"

Certainly, AutoQoS-VoIP is an excellent tool for customers whose objective is enabling QoS for VoIP (only) on their campus and WAN infrastructures, and AutoQoS-Enterprise is a fine tool for enabling basic WAN-edge QoS for voice, video, and multiple classes of data. For customers who have basic QoS needs and don't have the time or desire to learn or do more with QoS, AutoQoS is definitely the way to go.

However, it's important to remember where AutoQoS came from. AutoQoS tools are the result of QoS design guides that Cisco Technical Marketing Engineers (including myself) put together based on large-scale lab testing. AutoQoS-VoIP is the product of our first "AVVID QoS Design Guide," one of the most popular and most downloaded technical whitepapers ever produced within Cisco. AutoQoS-Enterprise is the result of the QoS Baseline coupled with our second-generation QoS Design Guide. This book represents our third-generation QoS Design Guide. And it is the goal of the authors to drive these designs (including DoS/worm-mitigation strategies) into future releases of AutoQoS. So, basically, what you are reading is the proposed blueprint for the next version of AutoQoS.

When it comes to any given technology, there are really only two types of people: those who are interested in the technology and seek a thorough understanding of the relation of the parts to the whole, and those who just want to "turn it on" and walk away. The former are the ones who will confidently unleash the true power of the technology and push it to its limits; the latter are the ones who are usually hesitant, timid, and conservative in their use of the technology, typically accompanied with mediocre results.

For example, there are those who enjoy looking under the hood of a Ferrari and want to know all the details about how the engine generates its beautiful purring and power, and there are others who want only to turn it on, drive away, and look sexy. The former group will drive more confidently, boldly unleashing the engine's tremendous power and, thus, pushing the car to its limits.

This book is intended for the former type of QoS networking professional—those looking for a thorough understanding of what makes them move so fast, sound so good, and look *so sexy* as they confidently harness their technology.

Goals and Methods

The main goal of this book is to present templates that address 80 percent or more of a customer's requirement of QoS in a particular context and architecture (LAN, WAN, VPN). Additionally, the rationales and considerations behind the recommendations are explained in detail so that as tweaking is required, network administrators are well informed of the trade-offs involved.

A key approach that we've used throughout this configuration-rich book is to incorporate inline explanations of configurations. In this way, the QoS-relevant commands are highlighted and detailed line-by-line to illustrate the function of each element and how these parts make up the whole solution.

To complement these line-by-line design recommendations, related verification commands are detailed. These verification commands are presented in context with the design examples, and specific details of what to look for in the resulting output are highlighted. These verification examples are, therefore, significantly richer in relevance than most such examples presented in Cisco documentation, and they allow network administrators to confirm quickly whether the recommended designs have been deployed correctly.

Finally, each design chapter has a case-study example at the end that ties together many of the design elements presented in the chapter and presents a bigger-picture detailed example for the infrastructure architecture being discussed (LAN/WAN/VPN). These examples are indicative of what can be expected in production environments. Often these case-study examples span several devices and, thus, highlight critical interrelationships.

How This Book Is Organized

This book is divided into three main parts: an introduction and overview section, a QoS toolset review section, and (the heart of the book) a QoS design section.

- **Chapter 1, "Introduction to QoS,"** is an introduction and brief history of the development of QoS technologies, showing where these came from and the direction they're headed in.

- **Chapter 2, "QoS Design Overview,"** is an overview of QoS design. It begins by detailing the service-level requirements of voice, video, and data applications, and it presents the Scavenger-class DoS/worm-mitigation strategy and high-level QoS best practices that will be detailed in the design chapters to follow.

To set proper context for the design chapters, various QoS tools are reviewed. This review is not indented to serve as feature documentation, but it supplements Cisco documentation to highlight various inter-dependancies or caveats for these tools that at times impact the recommended QoS designs that follow. The QoS toolset review section, Chapters 3 through 11, covers the following topics:

- **Chapter 3, "Classification and Marking Tools"**—This chapter reviews Layer 2 marking mechanisms (such as 802.1Q/p, Frame Relay Discard Eligibility, ATM Cell Loss Priority, and MPLS Experimental Values) and Layer 3 marking mechanisms (such as IP Precedence and Differentiated Services Code Points).

- **Chapter 4, "Policing and Shaping Tools"**—This chapter reviews the token bucket algorithm, which is the basis for most policers and shapers. Both two-rate and three-rate policers are covered as are ATM and Frame Relay traffic shaping.

- **Chapter 5, "Congestion-Management Tools"**—This chapter reviews the evolution of queuing mechanisms and focuses on Low-Latency Queuing and Class-Based Weighted Fair Queuing. This chapter highlights the interoperation and interdependencies of these mechanisms with other QoS mechanisms, such as link-fragmentation and shaping tools.

- **Chapter 6, "Congestion-Avoidance Tools"**—This chapter reviews the Weighted Random Early Detection mechanism and shows how this can be used to provide Differentiated Services within an (RFC 2597) Assured Forwarding traffic class. This chapter also shows how this mechanism can be used to set (RFC 3168) IP Explicit Congestion Notification bits.

- **Chapter 7, "Link-Specific Tools"**—This chapter reviews header-compression techniques (such as TCP and RTP header compression) and link-fragmentation and interleaving techniques (such as Multilink PPP Link Fragmentation and Interleaving [MLP LFI] and Frame Relay fragmentation [FRF.12]).

- **Chapter 8, "Bandwidth Reservation"**—This chapter reviews the Resource Reservation Protocol (RSVP) and shows how it can be applied to admission control and MPLS Traffic Engineering.

- **Chapter 9, "Call Admission Control (CAC)"**—This chapter reviews local, resource-based, and measurement-based call admission control (CAC) mechanisms, including the use of RSVP for CAC. The tools reviewed in previous chapters can protect voice from data, but only CAC tools can protect voice from voice.

- **Chapter 10, "Catalyst QoS Tools"**—This chapter reviews the main classification, marking, mapping, policing, and queuing tools available on the current Cisco Catalyst platforms (including the Catalyst 2950, 2970, 3550, 3560, 3570, 4500-Supervisors II+ to V, and Catalyst 6500 Supervisor 2 and Supervisor 720).

- **Chapter 11, "WLAN QoS Tools"**—This chapter reviews QoS mechanisms available for wireless access points, including the 802.11e Enhanced Distributed Coordination Function (EDCF) and the QoS Basic Service Set (QBSS).

When the QoS toolset is reviewed, the context is set for the detailed design recommendations that follow. The next chapters—which comprise the heart of this book—cover the QoS design recommendations for protecting voice, video, and multiple classes of data while mitigating DoS/worm attacks for the following network infrastructure architectures:

- **Chapter 12, "Campus QoS Design"**—This design chapter details access, distribution, and core layer considerations and designs for Cisco Catalyst 2950, 2970, 3550, 3560, 3570, 4500-Supervisors III-V, and Catalyst 6500 Supervisor 2 and Supervisor 720 series switches. Five separate access-edge models are presented, along with detailed queuing/dropping recommendations on a per-platform basis. Platform-unique features, such as the Catalyst 3550 per-Port/per-VLAN policing feature, the Catalyst 6500 PFC2 Dual-Rate Policing feature, and the PFC3 Per-User Microflow Policing feature, are highlighted in context.

- **Chapter 13, "WAN Aggregator QoS Design"**—This design chapter details considerations and designs for low-speed (≤ 768 kbps), medium-speed (> 768 kbps and ≤ T1/E1), and high-speed (> T1/E1) private WAN topologies, such as leased lines, Frame Relay, ATM, ATM-to-Frame Relay service interworking, and ISDN.

- **Chapter 14, "Branch Router QoS Design"**—This design chapter details branch-specific considerations and designs, such as unidirectional applications, and branch-to-campus traffic classification through access lists and Network-Based Application Recognition (NBAR). Branch-specific designs include Cisco SAFE recommendations for using NBAR for known worm identification and policing.

- **Chapter 15, "MPLS VPN QoS Design"**—This design chapter details considerations and designs for both enterprises (that are mapping into MPLS VPN service-provider [edge] classes of service) and service providers (that are provisioning edge and core classes of service). Service provider designs also include details on how to provision MPLS DiffServ Tunneling Modes (Uniform, Short-Pipe, and Pipe) and an introduction to MPLS Traffic Engineering (demonstrating per-customer traffic engineering and per-customer/per-application traffic engineering through MPLS DiffServ Traffic Engineering).

- **Chapter 16, "IPSec VPN QoS Design"**—This design chapter details the considerations and designs for deploying site-to-site IPSec VPNs and for teleworker IPSec VPNs (which traverse broadband media, such as cable and DSL).

- **Appendix, "At-a-Glance" QoS Summaries**—Single-page summaries of key QoS concepts presented throughout this the book for ready-reference, including
  - QoS Tools
  - The Cisco QoS Baseline
  - QoS Best Practices
  - Scavenger-Class QoS Design
  - Campus QoS Design
  - WAN QoS Design
  - Branch QoS Design
  - MPLS VPN QoS Design (for Enterprise Subscribers)
  - MPLS VPN QoS Design (for Service-Providers)
  - IPSec VPN QoS Design

Introduction to QoS

Part I of this book provides a brief background of the evolution of QoS technologies and overviews various currently available QoS features and tools. The QoS requirements of voice, video, and multiple classes of data applications are presented, along with an overview of the nature and effects of various types of DoS and worm attacks. QoS design principles are introduced to show how QoS mechanisms can be strategically deployed to address application requirements while mitigating such attacks.

The chapters in this part of the book are as follows:

This chapter provides a brief history of both voice and data network evolution, illustrating the background of the concept of Quality of Service (QoS). It introduces the fundamental QoS concepts of IntServ and DiffServ to set the stage for the later discussion of individual QoS mechanisms. The following topics are introduced and briefly discussed:

- IntServ and DiffServ
- QoS tools categories
- Modular QoS CLI
- QoS Baseline
- QoS classes
- Automatic QoS

CHAPTER 1

Introduction to QoS

A fair amount has been written in the industry about quality of service (QoS), but it seldom is explained why QoS has become a topic of concern in modern networks when it was something relatively unheard of only a few years ago. It is instructive to review briefly a small amount of networking history that puts QoS technology in perspective.

A Brief Historical Perspective

A century ago, the public switched telephone network (PSTN) started building out a worldwide, circuit-switched network. This network consisted of fixed-bandwidth, dedicated circuits and ideally was suited to carrying real-time traffic, such as voice. Some five decades later, networking experts from military and educational environments introduced packet-switched networks to circumvent any single points of failure, common in circuit-switched networks. Packet switching chops the information flow into small chunks of data, which can be routed over independent paths to the same destination, analogous to the operation of the postal system.

The resiliency of packet-switched networks caused a shift toward connectionless communication protocols that can handle packets that might arrive out of order. However, for many data applications, this was not only complicated to design around, but it also was insufficient in meeting application needs. Thus, connection-oriented protocols such as X.25 and Systems Network Architecture (SNA), and later Frame Relay and Asynchronous Transfer Mode (ATM), were developed. In these protocols, a circuit (permanent or switched virtual circuit, PVC or SVC) is defined over the underlying connectionless packet-switched network to handle a session of communication between two devices or endpoints.

In theory, real-time communications such as voice can use virtual circuits regardless of the underlying networking technology. Several universities conducted many experiments to this effect in the 1970s. However, voice over virtual circuits did not become a commercial or practical reality until the routers and switches used in packet-switched networks gained the CPU and memory power required to drive packet streams at real-time speeds at cost-effective prices.

When processing power became available at affordable cost points, other issues with carrying real-time communications over a packet-switched network manifested themselves. For example, when packets are delayed or dropped en route because of buffer overflows or other momentary failures, the intelligent protocols in the seven-layer International Organization for Standardization (ISO) model recover the "session" through the use of error-detection and correction capabilities, such as timeouts and retransmissions. Although these recovery methods work well for data applications, they fall far short of satisfying the needs of real-time information streams.

ATM was the first general data-networking technology to include a class of service concept at the lower layers of communications transport protocols—that is, offering different treatments for different types of traffic (protocols such as SNA already had this concept at higher layers in the stack). ATM minimizes latency by defining fixed-length cells, which can be switched in hardware. ATM also uses the familiar concepts of PVCs and SVCs to eliminate routing delays by doing an initial connection setup, after which all other packets that belong to the stream can be forwarded to the destination without additional routing.

It has been said—only partly facetiously—that packet switching has been a 30-year failed experiment. The attributes that the ATM architecture strived for are none other than those of the original circuit-switched PSTN: low latency, fixed circuit-based routing, predictable service levels, and information-order preservation. Then why not just use the PSTN? Options for transmitting data over the voice network met with equally limited success. The PSTN simply is not optimized for data networks: The equipment is expensive, the architecture is rigid, the bandwidth allocations are wasteful, and the infrastructure as a whole is ill suited to applications in which sessions are short, variable, multipoint, or connectionless.

In an effort to find a more effective solution to support a combination of voice and data, integrated services offerings were introduced. The term *integrated services* (as in Integrated Services Digital Network [ISDN] or the IETF Integrated Services [IntServ] model) refers to the mixing of different types of traffic, such as voice, video, and data, over a single packet-switched network. ISDN, which is considered by some to be the first foray into an architecture for converged networks, defines how data protocols can be carried over a circuit-switched infrastructure that natively supports voice. The PSTN evolved slightly with the introduction of ISDN. However, with the exception of a handful of countries in Europe, ISDN never really took off. This was primarily because of nontechnical reasons, such as the pricing strategies that the providers adopted.

In the late 1990s, IP won out as the technology of choice for converged networks because of its ease of use, ubiquity, and advances in handling real-time traffic.

The key enablers for IP networks to converge successfully voice, video, and data over packet-switched infrastructures were QoS technologies. QoS allows for the differentiated treatment of data traffic versus voice and other delay-sensitive traffic. In other words, it allows the network to include a system of "managed unfairness." As QoS technologies evolved, increasing numbers of enterprises saw the value of a single-network infrastructure and began planning toward deploying converged networks.

QoS Evolution

IP networks of the mid-1990s were invariably best-effort networks, and the Internet, as a whole, remains so today. Privately owned enterprise and service provider networks, though, have been widely transformed from best-effort models to more complex differentiated services models, meaning that the network gives different applications differing levels of service.

Figure 1-1 shows the broad steps in the evolution of QoS concepts since the early 1990s.

Figure 1-1   *QoS Evolution*

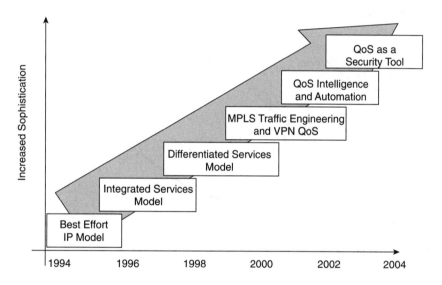

The first attempt to standardize QoS came in the mid-1990s, when the Internet Engineering Task Force (IETF) published the Integrated Services Request For Comments (IntServ RFCs—starting with RFC 1633 in June 1994). These RFCs centered on a signaling protocol called the Resource Reservation Protocol (RSVP). RSVP signals bandwidth and latency requirements for each discrete session to each node along a path (logical circuit) that packets would take from the sending endpoint to the receiving endpoint. Initially, RSVP required every node to heed its reservations, which was highly impractical over the Internet, on which servers, switches, and routers of every description, vintage, and vendor coexist.

To address this challenge, another set of standards—the DiffServ model—emerged as a second attempt at standardizing QoS. The DiffServ model describes various behaviors to be adopted by each compliant node. The nodes could use whatever features (proprietary or otherwise) were available, as chosen by the vendor, to conform. Packet markings, such as

IP Precedence (IPP) and its successor, Differentiated Services Code Points (DSCPs), were defined along with specific per-hop behaviors (PHBs) for key traffic types.

As the IntServ and DiffServ models have evolved, the general popularity of one method versus the other has swung back and forth (as shown in Figure 1-2), and their coexistence has become an ever-increasing struggle, with committed advocates on both sides. Today the debates over the advantages of each continue without a clear, industry-wide agreed-upon resolution. The realization has begun that neither method offers a complete solution and that elements of both should be combined to provide the most general method applicable to the widest range of traffic and application types.

Figure 1-2   *IntServ and DiffServ*

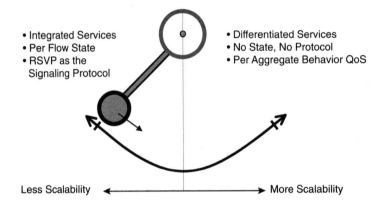

A short definition of IntServ and DiffServ follows:

- IntServ uses a flow-based concept coupled with a signaling protocol along the packet path. The signaling protocol guarantees that adequate resources are available (at each hop) for the flow before admitting the flow onto the network. In initial deployments, the IntServ model suffered from scalability issues because of the many flows that needed management on network backbones.

- DiffServ uses packet markings to classify and treat each packet independently. Although this scales well (which is probably why enterprises and service providers deploy it more frequently), it offers no specific bandwidth guarantees to packets that belong to a flow and, therefore, fails to provide admission control to new flows.

With no clear advantage to either model, QoS mechanisms continue to use a mix of IntServ and DiffServ technologies to offer the breadth of services required on networks. IntServ and DiffServ are discussed further in the section "QoS Models" later in this chapter.

In the late 1990s, QoS techniques became more sophisticated and were adapted to advanced networking technologies, such as Multiprotocol Label Switching (MPLS) and Virtual Private Networks (VPNs).

The most recent trend in QoS is simplification and automation, with the goal of simply and efficiently provisioning "intelligent" QoS on IP networks. When viewed as individual features, QoS technologies offer a myriad of "nerd knobs" that can be turned. In the hands of capable administrators, these can be used to build very sophisticated networks. However, they also can result in very complex configurations. Many administrators do not have the time or the desire to delve into QoS technologies to this expert level and instead would prefer to define high-level policies and have the network simply "do the right things" to implement them.

User Network Expectations

The perception of how the network behaves, or how well it behaves, depends on how you look at it. End users, or consumers, of the network might have a very different view of network quality of service than the staff managing the network.

End User

An end user's perception of QoS is typically subjective and relative, and not easily measurable.

End users perceive the network quality through their end device and have certain expectations of appropriate service levels. For example, typical users expect a voice call on a standard phone to be of toll quality. Yet they do not expect that same quality level from a cell phone or a voice call spoken into a microphone on a personal computer. This is the general expectation, regardless of the fact that all three calls might be carried by the same network in the same manner.

The end user has no concept of and typically very little interest in the capabilities of the networks in between—unless, of course, the quality of the network response is lacking. Therefore, end users' perception of the quality of the service that they receive is based on previously observed behavior on similar devices (examples include a PSTN phone call, a PBX phone call, a bank teller application, and the refresh of a web page display) and the cost of the service (which, in an enterprise network, the general end user perceives as $0).

Information Technologies Management

IT management perceives the network quality through management statistics such as throughput, usage, percentage of loss, and user complaints. Expectations and "quality problems" from an IT perspective tend to be more absolute and measurable. (For example, the one-way latency of more than 150 ms is unacceptable for a voice call, or a transaction refresh time for a bank teller application must be fewer than 5 seconds.)

Service providers formalize these expectations within service-level agreements (SLAs), which clearly state the acceptable bounds of network performance. Corporate enterprise networks typically do not have such formal SLAs, but they nevertheless manage their networks on some form of measurement and monitoring. Some enterprise networks indeed might use SLAs of various levels of formality between the IT department and the customer departments that they serve.

User complaints might result even though the network met the SLA (formal or otherwise). For example, the packet loss statistics over a certain period of time might be within bounds, but the user whose file transfer session timed out or whose print job was lost during a period of momentary congestion would most likely perceive it as a "network problem."

Understanding QoS

Appreciating what QoS tools and methods do to packets in a network is fundamental to appreciating the effect of individual QoS tools discussed in later chapters, and ultimately understanding the network designs and methods that constitute the material in this book.

End-to-End QoS

Regardless of how it is measured, QoS is a vital element in any converged network. To ensure the highest level of quality, however, QoS must be implemented across all areas of the network.

QoS is described aptly by an age-old cliché: It's only as strong as the weakest link. Optimally, every device (host, server, switch, or router) that handles the packet along its network path should employ QoS to ensure that the packet is not unduly delayed or lost between the endpoints. It is a popular myth that QoS is applicable only to slow-speed wide-area networks (WANs) or the Internet. Testing has shown that delay-sensitive applications, such as voice, suffer quality loss when QoS is not enabled on campus devices, such as Cisco IP phones and Cisco Catalyst switches.

Figure 1-3 shows the segments of the network where QoS must be deployed in the typical IP telephony enterprise network and what QoS techniques are common in each segment.

Figure 1-3 *Enabling QoS in an Enterprise Network*

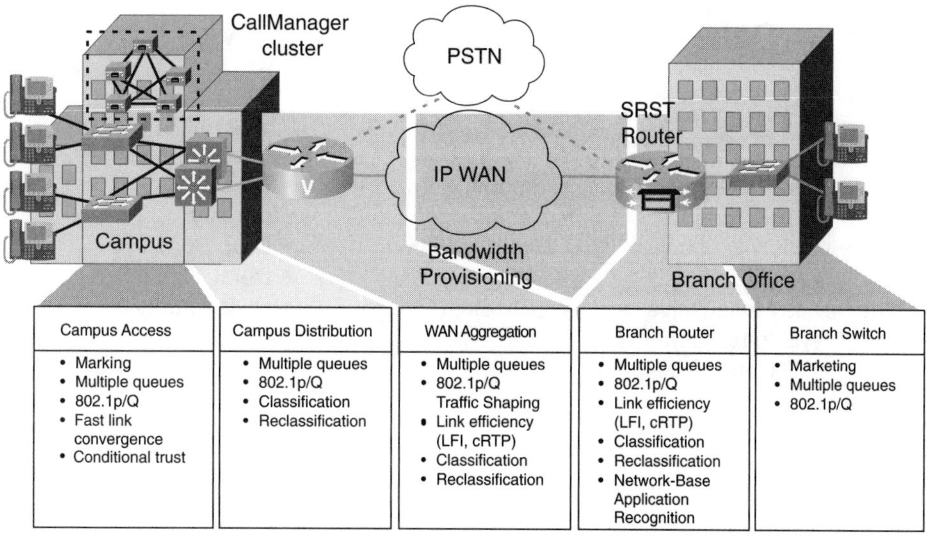
CallManager cluster
PSTN
SRST Router
IP WAN
Campus
Bandwidth Provisioning
Branch Office
Campus Access
• Marking
• Multiple queues
• 802.1p/Q
• Fast link convergence
• Conditional trust
Campus Distribution
• Multiple queues
• 802.1p/Q
• Classification
• Reclassification
WAN Aggregation
• Multiple queues
• 802.1p/Q Traffic Shaping
• Link efficiency (LFI, cRTP)
• Classification
• Reclassification
Branch Router
• Multiple queues
• 802.1p/Q
• Link efficiency (LFI, cRTP)
• Classification
• Reclassification
• Network-Base Application Recognition
Branch Switch
• Marketing
• Multiple queues
• 802.1p/Q

All Packets Are (Not) Equal

Networks without QoS enabled are described as *best-effort* networks. Best-effort network designs treat all packets as equally important. Such networks work well if there is enough CPU, memory, and bandwidth to handle immediately all the packets traversing the network as they arrive (in other words, at line rate). However, because this is rarely the case, the following scenarios tend to emerge:

- User-based contention occurs when packets from different users, user groups, departments, or even enterprises contend for the same network resources.
- Application-based contention occurs when different applications from the same user or user group contend with each other for limited network resources. These applications might have different service requirements from the network, as illustrated in Figure 1-4.

Figure 1-4 *Application-Based Contention*

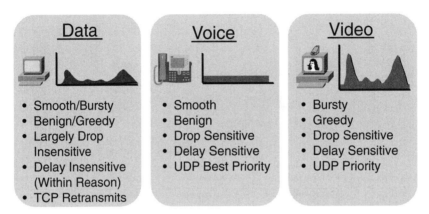

To obtain the appropriate levels of service from often scarce network resources experiencing contention, the fundamental concept of QoS must be applied—namely, that all packets are not equal. In other words, to resolve the contention, packets must be treated with managed unfairness (either preferentially or deferentially). In other words, administrative policies must be defined and deployed throughout the network infrastructure to ensure that each node makes consistent decisions about the relative importance of an individual packet (or flow) and adjusts its packet-handling behavior accordingly.

This concept of unfairness applies equally to traffic for which higher levels of priority must be maintained (for example, to voice and video traffic) and traffic that is undesirable in the network (denial-of-service [DoS] or worm-generated traffic, or even general web surfing to destinations unrelated to the goals of the enterprise). The latter category of traffic introduces the concept of less than best-effort service, also referred to as *Scavenger* service (based on an Internet 2 draft specification). Best-effort or better service is provided to all desirable traffic on the network, but there is no sense in providing even best-effort service to unwanted traffic. Such Scavenger traffic, if not dropped outright, is carried only when spare capacity is available.

The Challenges of Converged Networks

The high-level goal of QoS technologies in a converged network is to abstract the fact that there is only one network and to make voice, video, and data convergence appear transparent to the end users. To achieve this goal, QoS technologies allow different types of traffic to contend inequitably for network resources. Real-time applications, such as voice or interactive video, can be given priority or preferential services over generic data applications—but not to the point that data applications are starving for bandwidth.

QoS is defined as the measure of a system's service availability and transmission quality. Service availability is a crucial foundation element of QoS. Before any QoS can be implemented successfully, the network infrastructure should be designed to be highly available. The target for high availability is 99.999 percent uptime, with only 5 minutes of downtime permitted per year. The transmission quality of the network is determined by the following factors:

- **Packet loss**—This is a comparative measure of the number of packets faithfully transmitted and received to the total number transmitted, expressed as a percentage. Packet loss in the context of QoS does not relate to drops because of network outages or link flaps (because these are a function of a high-availability network design), but instead relates to drops because of network congestion.

- **Delay (or latency)**—This is the finite amount of time that it takes a packet to reach the receiving endpoint after being transmitted from the sending endpoint. In the case of voice, this equates to the amount of time that it takes for speech to leave the speaker's mouth and be heard by the listener's ear. This time period is termed *end-to-end* delay and is comprised of two components: fixed network delay and variable network delay.

  In data networks carrying voice, *fixed network delay* further is broken down into the following:

  - **Packetization delay**—The time required to sample and encode voice or video signals into packets.

  - **Serialization delay**—The time required to transmit the packet bits onto the physical media, based on the clocking rate of the interface.

  - **Propagation delay**—The time required for the electrical/optical pulses to traverse the media en route to their destination, based on the laws of physics.

- **Delay variation (or jitter)**—Also known as interpacket delay, this is the difference in the end-to-end delay between sequential packets. For example, if one packet requires 100 ms to traverse the network from the source endpoint to the destination endpoint, and the following packet requires 125 ms to make the same trip, the delay variation would be calculated as 25 ms, as illustrated in Figure 1-5.

Figure 1-5 *Delay Variation*

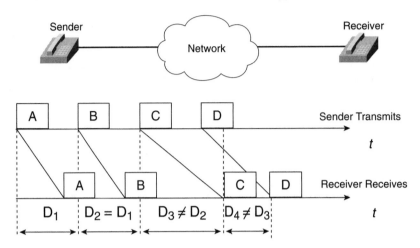

Each end station in a VoIP or video over IP conversation has a jitter buffer, which is used to smooth out the variation in arrival times of data packets that contain voice. Jitter buffers can be fixed or adaptive.

Instantaneous changes in arrival times of packets that exceed the jitter buffer's capability to compensate result in jitter buffer overruns and underruns.

— A jitter buffer underrun occurs when the arrival times of packets increase to the point that the jitter buffer has been exhausted and contains no packets for the digital signal processors (DSP) to process when it is time to play the next piece of voice or video, resulting in clips.

— A jitter buffer overrun occurs when packets containing voice or video arrive faster than the jitter buffer can accommodate. When this happens, packets are dropped when it is time to play the voice or video samples, resulting in degraded voice quality.

Variable network delay generally is caused by congestion within the network.

QoS Models

As briefly introduced earlier, there are two models for providing the differentiated levels of network service required in converged networks: IntServ and DiffServ.

IntServ Overview

Think of best-effort IP service in terms of the regular mail (snail-mail) service. The mail is delivered if and when it can be, but it also might be lost (arriving at some undetermined time in the future or not at all). By comparison, IntServ is analogous to a custom mail service, such as diplomatic mail or courier services, with certain parameters regarding loss and delivery guaranteed.

More specifically, IntServ is a specification of the following:

- What the sender is sending (rate, maximum transmission unit [MTU], and so on), as described by the Transmission Specification (TSpec)
- What the receiver needs (bandwidth, MTU, and so on), as described by the Receiver Specification (RSpec)
- How the signaling is performed on the network by the sender and receiver (that is, the use of RSVP)

The framework of IntServ preserves the end-to-end semantics of QoS for IP. Key endpoints are the sender and receiver applications that request a desired service from the network for a set of flows, as defined by the source address, destination address, transport protocol, source port, and destination port.

IntServ describes three main classes of service that an application can request:

- **Guaranteed services (RFC 2212)**—Provides firm (mathematically provable) bounds on end-to-end packet-queuing delays, making it possible to provide a service that guarantees both delay and bandwidth
- **Controlled load (RFC 2211)**—Provides the application flow with a quality of service closely approximating the QoS that the same flow would receive from an unloaded network element, but uses capacity (admission) control to ensure that this service is received even when the network element is overloaded
- **Best-effort service**—Provides no service guarantees of any type

The advantages of the IntServ model include the following:

- Conceptual simplicity, facilitating the integration with network policy administration
- Discrete per-flow QoS, making it architecturally suitable to voice calls
- Call admission control (CAC) capabilities, which can indicate to endpoints whether the desired bandwidth is available

The disadvantages of the IntServ model include these:

- All network elements must maintain state and exchange signaling messages on a per-flow basis, which might require a significant amount of bandwidth on large networks.
- Periodic refresh messages are used, which might require protection from packet loss to keep the session(s) intact.
- All intermediate nodes must implement RSVP.

DiffServ Overview

Continuing the analogy of mail services, DiffServ can be compared to different tiers of mail service, such as regular, registered, priority, and express mail. Each service offers particular parameters of delivery, and the piece of mail is stamped at each intermediate handling point to ensure that it gets the required service. However, there is no specific connection between the sender of the piece of mail and the treatment that the mail receives.

The premise of DiffServ is very simple: It offers different network service levels to a packet, thereby "enable[ing] scalable service discrimination in the Internet without the need for per-flow state and signaling at every hop" (RFC 2474). Packets of a particular service belong to a particular "class," and the treatment of each "class" is described by PHBs with which the network node must comply. Meaningful services can be constructed by a combination of the following:

- Setting a field in the IP header upon network entry or at a network boundary (IPP or DSCPs)
- Using this field to determine the nodes inside the network forward the packets
- Conditioning the marked packets at network boundaries in accordance with the requirements or rules of each "class" or service

The essence of DiffServ is the specification of PHBs that an application can receive from the network:

- **Expedited forwarding (RFC 3246, previously RFC 2598)**—Provides a strict-priority service (compare this to express mail service)
- **Assured forwarding (RFC 2597)**—Provides a qualified delivery guarantee (compare this to registered mail service) and makes the provision for oversubscription to this service (specifically, markdown and dropping schemes for excess traffic)
- **Class selectors (RFC 2474)**—Provides code points that can be used for backward compatibility with IP Precedence models
- **Best-effort service**—Provides a "delivery when possible" service (compare this to regular mail service)

DiffServ constructs services from the PHBs by classifying packets into "classes" at the edge, or boundary, of the network and marking the packets accordingly. Optionally, the packets can be metered with policing or shaping techniques. The core of the network implements the PHBs and uses the packet markings to make queuing and dropping decisions.

The DiffServ model include these advantages:

- **Scalability**—No state or flow information is required to be maintained.

- **Performance**—The packet contents need be inspected only once for classification purposes. At that time, the packet is marked and all subsequent QoS decisions are made on the value of a fixed field in the packet header, reducing processing requirements.
- **Interoperability**—All vendors already are running IP.
- **Flexibility**—The DiffServ model does not prescribe any particular feature (such as a queuing technique) to be implemented by a network node. The node can use whatever features optimize its hardware and architecture, as long as it is consistent with the behavior expectation defined in the PHBs.

The disadvantages of the DiffServ model include the following:

- No end-to-end bandwidth reservations are present; therefore, guarantees of services can be impaired by network nodes that do not implement the PHBs appropriately over congested links or by nodes that are not engineered correctly for the expected traffic volume of a specific class.
- The lack of a per-flow/per-session CAC makes it possible for applications to congest each other. (For example, if only enough bandwidth for 10 voice calls exists and an 11th call is permitted, all 11 calls suffer call-quality deterioration.)

Introduction to the QoS Toolset

A fair amount of literature exists on QoS concepts, technologies, and features. The purpose of this book is not to reiterate in depth how these tools work, but rather to show how these tools interact with each other and what combination of tools can be used to achieve the overall design objectives of a network. However, to lay the context for the designs set forth in this book, a brief overview of the toolset follows.

Generally, QoS tools fall into the following categories:

- Classification and marking tools
- Policing and shaping tools
- Congestion-avoidance (selective dropping) tools
- Congestion-management (queuing) tools
- Link-specific tools

Figure 1-6 illustrates the relationship and overall cohesiveness of different QoS tools.

Figure 1-6 *QoS Toolset*

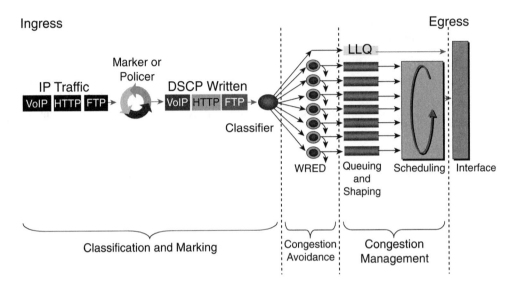

Packets or frames entering a network device must be analyzed to determine the treatment that they should be given. This analysis is referred to as *classification*. Classification is the first QoS function to occur for any given QoS policy, and it can occur repeatedly at various stages of policy enforcement. To reduce the requirement for detailed recursive classification, it generally is recommended that traffic types be classified as close to their sources as possible and that their packets be marked accordingly.

Marking establishes a distinct trust boundary that demarcates the point where the packet markings are set properly and, therefore, detailed classification (Layer 4 through 7 analysis) no longer is required.

When packets enter a network device, three generic marking possibilities exist:

- Packets are unmarked.
- Packets are marked, but the markings are not trusted.
- Packets are marked and the markings are trusted.

In the first two scenarios, it is recommended that the packets be marked or re-marked.

After marking, the next step is another classification process based on packet markings. At this point, packets might be discarded by a policer (for example, if they exceed an SLA) or a congestion-avoidance mechanism (for example, early dropping because buffers reached the maximum limit). Packets that are not discarded are subject to congestion management (queuing) to prioritize and protect various traffic types when congestion happens to the transmission link. Finally, these packets are scheduled for transmission on the egress link, where shaping might occur to control bursts and ensure that outgoing traffic conforms to any SLA that is in effect on the ingress of the next hop.

Link-specific tools usually are required only at WAN edges and include mechanisms for compression or fragmentation to reduce delay and jitter.

Some QoS tools (such as marking and policing) can be applied in both the ingress and egress directions of the traffic flow on an interface. Other tools (such as queuing) can be applied only in the egress direction (with some platform-specific exceptions).

The QoS mechanisms (primarily DiffServ) described previously are applicable to packets already admitted to the network. Such tools are very effective in protecting real-time (voice) from non-real-time (data) traffic, but they are completely ineffective in protecting real-time applications from other real-time applications (that is, protecting voice traffic from other voice traffic). Such protection can be achieved only through call admission control (CAC) mechanisms, which decide whether to allow or disallow new packet streams onto the network. IntServ mechanisms, such as RSVP, can be used to implement discrete CAC.

Simplifying QoS

In the late 1990s, Cisco spent significant development effort to implement an extensive QoS tool and feature set. The portfolio of QoS mechanisms and options became very rich and, simultaneously, very complicated to deploy. During the early 2000s, the predominant customer feedback relating to QoS was the request to simplify QoS deployment. In response to this feedback, a series of QoS simplification and automation projects was initiated. The result included the following:

- The creation of a Modular QoS Command-Line Interface (CLI)
- The establishment of a QoS Baseline
- Default behavior (conforming to the QoS Baseline)
- Cross-platform feature consistency
- Automatic QoS (AutoQoS)

Modular QoS Command-Line Interface

The first step toward simplification was to modularize the configuration of QoS and make it consistent across platforms. To this end, a new configuration syntax, termed Modular QoS Command-Line Interface (MQC), was introduced in Cisco IOS Release 12.0(5)T.

Three main components make up the MQC:

- **class-map**—A classification filter defined within the policy map to identify traffic for preferential or deferential treatment. Traffic can be identified by IPP or DSCP, named or numbered access control lists (ACLs), Network-Based Application Recognition (NBAR), Layer 2 parameters (CoS, FR DE, ATM cell loss priority [CLP], MPLS Experimental [EXP] value), or a combination of these.

- **policy-map**—A statement that defines how each traffic type, as identified by the class map(s), should be serviced. Options include marking/re-marking, policing, shaping, low-latency or class-based weighted fair queuing, selective dropping, and header compression.

- **service-policy**—A statement that binds the policy to an interface and specifies direction.

Example 1-1 demonstrates a sample MQC policy. This is just an example of a possible configuration; the significance of the commands used in this example is explained in subsequent chapters.

Example 1-1   *MQC Policy*

```
Router(config)# class-map match-any CRITICAL-DATA
Router(config-cmap)# match protocol http url "*customer*"
Router(config-cmap)# match protocol citrix
Router(config)# policy-map WAN-EDGE
Router(config-pmap)# class CRITICAL-DATA
Router(config-pmap-c)# bandwidth 1000
Router(config)# interface Serial 0/0
Router(config-if)# service-policy output WAN-EDGE
```

QoS Baseline

Although MQC was a major step in simplifying QoS features, it addressed only the user interface element of QoS deployment. Another factor in the complexity of QoS deployment is the inconsistency of QoS features across specific hardware platform releases or software releases.

In 2002, a series of internal Cisco initiatives, dubbed Technology Baselines, was launched to address the inconsistency of which features exist on which platforms. Specific to QoS, the QoS Baseline is a strategic internal document written by Cisco's most qualified QoS experts, each of whom had contributed to multiple QoS RFCs and so was best qualified to interpret these standards in additional detail. The QoS Baseline was developed with two primary goals:

- To document which QoS features are required on platforms that are considered QoS-enabled products

- To provide a gap analysis of which features, deemed important by the baseline, existed on what platforms

In part, the Cisco QoS Baseline is aimed at producing higher-quality new products, predictable QoS feature sets across products, and improved consistency of QoS features across platforms. To that end, it provides engineers who are developing new products with a reference list of QoS features that they must include and test. For existing platforms, it provides a gap analysis that is used to steer product roadmaps to achieve QoS baseline compliance.

Beyond its engineering influence, the overall objective of the QoS Baseline is to unify QoS within Cisco: from service provider to enterprise, from engineering to marketing. For example, the concept of traffic classification inevitably begs the question of how many classes of traffic there should be. MQC supports up to 256 different traffic classes within a policy map. Although adept QoS administrators might see this as desirable, those who are new to QoS and have no idea how many classes of traffic they need in their networks might view it as daunting.

To address the needs of the both expert and casual QoS users, the QoS Baseline defines a set of class template recommendations that can be either be implemented "as is" or customized to individual needs. It gives a starting point for network design and implementation, and it provides a basis for comparable product testing and performance reporting—both of which significantly simplify the implementation of QoS in a network.

The QoS Baseline defines up to 11 classes of traffic that are used in all Cisco design guides, configuration examples, and testing suites. The QoS Baseline does not dictate that every enterprise deploy all these traffic classes immediately. The set of 11 classes is designed to accommodate the QoS needs of an enterprise not only for today, but also for the foreseeable future. Even if an enterprise needs only a handful of these 11 classes today, following the QoS Baseline recommendations will enable it to smoothly implement additional traffic classes in the future.

Table 1-1 gives a summary of the QoS Baseline recommendations.

Default Behavior

The next step in the trend toward simplification was for the network nodes "to do the right thing." Through a series of changes in Cisco IOS Software and selected non–Cisco IOS products (such as IP phones), voice packets now are marked by default to the recommended value of DSCP EF. These adjustments in the default behavior eliminate the need for access lists and explicit marking configurations that were required in earlier software releases. These changes are discussed in more detail in Chapter 3, "Classification and Marking Tools."

Table 1-1 *QoS Baseline Recommendations*

PHB	DSCP	DSCP Binary Value	Reference	Intended Protocols	Configuration
EF	EF	101110	RFC 3246	Interactive voice	Admission control = RSVP Queuing = priority
AF1	AF11 AF12 AF13	001010 001100 001110	RFC 2597	Bulk transfers, web, general data service	Queuing = rate based Active queue management = DSCP-based WRED
AF2	AF21 AF22 AF23	010010 010100 010110	RFC 2597	Database access, transaction services, interactive traffic, preferred data service	Queuing = rate based Active queue management = DSCP-based WRED
AF3	AF31 AF32 AF33	011010 011100 011110	RFC 2597	Locally defined; mission-critical applications	Queuing = rate based Active queue management = DSCP-based WRED
AF4	AF41 AF42 AF43	100010 100100 100110	RFC 2597	Interactive video and associated voice	Admission control = RSVP Queuing = rate based Active queue management = DSCP-based WRED
IP routing	Class 6	110000	RFC 2474 section 4.2.2	BGP, OSPF, and so on	Queuing = rate based Small guaranteed minimum rate Active queue management = WRED

Table 1-1 *QoS Baseline Recommendations (Continued)*

PHB	DSCP	DSCP Binary Value	Reference	Intended Protocols	Configuration
Streaming video	Class Selector 4	100000	RFC 2474 section 4.2.2	Often proprietary	Admission control = RSVP Queuing = rate based Active queue management = WRED
Telephony signaling (voice and video)	Class Selector 3	011000	RFC 2474 section 4.2.2	SIP, H.323, and so on	Queuing = rate based Small guaranteed minimum rate Active queue management = WRED
Network management	Class Selector 2	010000	RFC 2474 section 4.2.2	SNMP	Queuing = rate based Small guaranteed minimum rate Active queue management = WRED
Scavenger	I2SS or Class Selector 1	001000	Internet 2 usage	User-selected service	Queuing = rate based No bandwidth guarantee Active queue management = WRED
Other	Default or Class Selector 0	000000	RFC 2474 section 4.1	Unspecified traffic	Queuing = rate based Minimal bandwidth guarantee Active queue management or Per-flow fair queuing Active queue management = WRED

Cross-Platform Feature Consistency

An additional objective in the simplification of QoS (beyond syntax and automation) is to improve the operational and semantic feature consistency across platforms.

As part of this effort, Cisco is consolidating and improving the QoS code bases of the distributed router architectures (such as the Cisco 7500 series of routers) and the nondistributed router families (such as the Cisco 7200 to 1700 series routers). This initiative is called *Consistent QoS Behavior* code and should remove most (if not all) of the traditional QoS idiosyncrasies between the distributed and nondistributed platforms.

Such projects are ongoing, as the application drivers for QoS continue to demand unique features for specific scenarios, but administrators generally prefer QoS consistency and simplicity.

Automatic QoS

Automatic QoS (AutoQoS) is essentially an intelligent macro that enables an administrator to enter one or two simple AutoQoS commands to enable all the appropriate features for the recommended QoS settings for an application on a specific interface.

For example, in its first release, AutoQoS VoIP would provide best-practice QoS configurations for VoIP on Cisco Catalyst switches and routers. By entering one global or one interface command (depending on the platform), the AutoQoS VoIP macro then would expand these commands into the recommended VoIP QoS configurations (complete with all the calculated parameters and settings) for the platform and interface on which the Auto-QoS is applied.

AutoQoS is available on both LAN and WAN Cisco Catalyst switches and Cisco IOS routers. In its initial version, however, AutoQoS applies only to VoIP deployments.

For campus Catalyst switches, AutoQoS performs the following automatically:

- Enforces a trust boundary at Cisco IP phones
- Enforces a trust boundary on Catalyst switch access ports and uplinks/downlinks
- Enables Catalyst strict priority queuing for voice and weighted round-robin queuing for data traffic
- Modifies queue admission criteria (such as CoS-to-queue mapping)
- Modifies queue sizes and queue weights, where required
- Modifies CoS-to-DSCP and IP precedence-to-DSCP mappings

For Cisco IOS routers, AutoQoS is supported on Frame Relay, ATM, HDLC, Point-to-Point Protocol (PPP), and Frame Relay-to-ATM links. It performs the following automatically:

- Classifies and marks VoIP bearer traffic (to DSCP EF) and call-signaling traffic (originally to DSCP AF31, but more recently to CS3)
- Applies scheduling:
    - Low-latency queuing (LLQ) for voice
    - Class-based weighted fair queuing (CBWFQ) for call signaling
    - Fair queuing (FQ) for all other traffic
- Enables Frame Relay traffic shaping with optimal parameters, if required
- Enables Link Fragmentation and Interleaving (either MLPPP LFI or FRF.12) on slow links (those less than or equal to 768 kbps), if required
- Enables IP RTP header compression (cRTP), if required
- Provides RMON alerts of VoIP packets that are dropped

The first phase of AutoQoS on the Cisco IOS router platforms is available in Cisco IOS Release 12.2(15)T.

In its second release—for Cisco IOS routers only—AutoQoS Enterprise detects and provisions for up to 10 (of the 11 QoS Baseline) traffic classes. (The only class that is not assigned automatically is Locally-Defined Mission-Critical because it is defined subjectively by network administrators and varies from one enterprise to the next.)

The AutoQoS Enterprise feature simplifies QoS implementation and speeds the provisioning of QoS for voice, video, and data over a Cisco network. It reduces human error and lowers training costs. AutoQoS Enterprise creates class maps and policy maps on the basis of Cisco experience and best-practices methodology, such as that documented in this book. Customers also can use existing Cisco IOS commands to modify the configurations that automatically are generated by the AutoQoS Enterprise feature, to meet specific requirements.

The AutoQoS Enterprise feature consists of two configuration phases, completed in the following order:

1 **Autodiscovery (data collection)**—The autodiscovery phase uses protocol discovery based on Network-Based Application Recognition (NBAR) to detect the applications on the network and perform statistical analysis on the network traffic.

2 **AutoQoS template generation and installation**—This phase generates templates from the data collected during the autodiscovery phase and installs the templates on the interface. These templates then are used as the basis for creating the class maps and policy maps for the network. After the class maps and policy maps are created, they are installed on the relevant interface(s).

Table 1-2 shows the classes of traffic automatically detected and provisioned for by AutoQoS Enterprise, complete with their QoS Baseline recommended markings.

Table 1-2   *AutoQoS Enterprise Class Definitions and Marking*

AutoQoS Class Name	Traffic Type	DSCP Value
IP Routing	Network-control traffic, such as routing protocols	CS6
Interactive Voice	Interactive voice-bearer traffic	EF
Interactive Video	Interactive video-data traffic	AF41
Streaming Video	Streaming media traffic	CS4
Telephony Signaling	Telephony signaling and control traffic	AF31 or CS3
Transactional/Interactive	Database applications transactional in nature	AF21
Network Management	Network-management traffic	CS2
Bulk Data	Bulk data transfers, web traffic, general data service	AF11
Scavenger	Casual entertainment, rogue traffic (traffic in this category is given less-than best-effort treatment)	CS1
Best Effort	Default class, all noncritical traffic, HTTP, all miscellaneous traffic	0

This second phase of AutoQoS became available in Cisco IOS Release 12.3(7)T.

If I Have AutoQoS, Why Should I Be Reading This Book?

It is important to keep in mind not only the evolution of QoS, but also, more specifically, that of AutoQoS.

In the late 1990s, critical QoS features for enabling the convergence of voice and data networks, such as low-latency queuing (LLQ), Link Fragmentation and Interleaving (LFI), Catalyst queuing, and trust were developed and released within Cisco IOS and within Catalyst hardware/software.

Despite the recognition that these features could enable network convergence, many customers were slow to adopt and deploy these technologies. Mainly, this was because they were at a loss for how best to deploy such QoS mechanisms to achieve the end-to-end service levels that VoIP required. Many "nerd-knobs" within the QoS toolset could be turned and tuned, and overall the tools were complex and disparate, and required an in-depth understanding to be used effectively.

To address this barrier to adoption, a small group of dedicated technical marketing engineers within a Cisco solutions engineering team was tasked with figuring out how best to deploy QoS for converged voice and data networks and publishing a best-practices design guide that customers could use as a reference. To accomplish this mandate, they built the largest networking lab within Cisco to run extensive scale tests of QoS features on various hardware and software platforms.

Unlike conventional regression testing of QoS features, this team used a different approach: They tested QoS features not in isolation, but in conjunction with the many other features that typically would be deployed within a large enterprise environment. For example, QoS tools were enabled simultaneously with availability tools, multicast tools, and security and encryption tools. The objective was to make the tests as representative of real-life enterprise environments as possible.

The results from these extensive tests were summarized and published in late 1999 as the QoS Design Guide. This document quickly became one of the most downloaded technical documents ever published by Cisco. Customers finally had not only the tools to achieve convergence of their voice and data networks, but also the verified design guidance to do so with confidence.

Nonetheless, at around 200 pages, the configuration-rich QoS Design Guide was a serious read that took a long time for most network administrators to fully absorb. Furthermore, it indirectly highlighted how difficult it was to enable end-to-end QoS across a single vendor's (Cisco's) products. There were far too many platform-specific idiosyncrasies to keep in mind, as far as most network administrators were concerned.

Thus, to simplify the process, the solutions engineering team engaged with various technology groups and business units within Cisco to drive the automation of these best-practice recommendations. The response was very favorable, and the result was AutoQoS VoIP for the campus and WAN. AutoQoS VoIP is a cross-platform feature that is targeted to customers who want to deploy QoS for VoIP quickly and accurately, without the requirement of extensive knowledge of QoS.

As with all technical papers, the QoS Design Guide needed to be updated and expanded after a couple years. During this time, customers increasingly were struggling with how best to deploy QoS for videoconferencing and different types of data applications. Therefore, the scope of the original design guide was expanded to include these applications, and a second version of the document was released in August 2002. At the time, all design guides originating from the solutions engineering team were rebadged as Solution Reference Network Designs (SRNDs), to set them apart from the many (often unverified and not scale-tested) design guides available on Cisco.com. Thus, the second version of this document was titled the Enterprise QoS SRND.

Shortly thereafter, the QoS Baseline was completed and released internally. Because the QoS Baseline conflicted with some of the (DSCP marking) recommendations published in the QoS SRND, it took precedence and required the Enterprise QoS SRND to be rewritten to be compliant with the QoS Baseline. This caused changes in the document because the marking recommendations put forward in the Enterprise QoS SRND reflected the best practices for an enterprise, but not necessarily for a service provider. As the lines between enterprise and service provider are not only blurring but also requiring a level of cooperation previously unprecedented (as discussed in additional detail in Chapter 15, "MPLS VPN QoS Design"), it is important for a single set of marking recommendations to be used for both enterprise and service provider design guides.

Following this, Cisco IOS development combined the best practices put forward in the QoS design guides with the classification and marking recommendations defined in the QoS Baseline, and released AutoQoS—Enterprise for the WAN. AutoQoS Enterprise, similar to AutoQoS VoIP, is targeted at customers who want to enable QoS for voice, video, and multiple classes of data quickly and accurately over their WANs, without requiring an extensive knowledge of QoS configuration and operation.

So why is this relevant? This brief history was given to describe the cycles required in AutoQoS evolution, illustrated in Figure 1-7.

Figure 1-7   *AutoQoS Evolution*

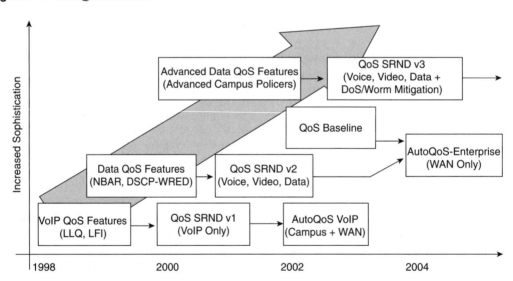

Specifically, AutoQoS evolution depends on two prerequisites:

- QoS feature development
- Verified network design guides

The Continuing Evolution of QoS

As a technology, QoS is still evolving, with new features continually being developed. Likewise, the role of QoS is evolving.

Specifically, following the development of advanced hardware policers within the Catalyst switching platforms, such as per-port/per-VLAN policers, dual-rate policers, and user-based microflow policers, new contexts for the use of QoS tools have become possible. These include the use of QoS as a technology not only to enable convergence, but also to increase security—especially in relation to the exponentially increasing number of DoS and worm attacks experienced by customers since 2000.

Therefore, this book, which represents the third generation of the Cisco QoS design guides, details the role of QoS technologies in protecting voice, video, and critical data, and how these tools can be used to mitigate DoS and worm attacks.

As QoS continues to evolve, it is the goal of the authors that as networks increasingly adopt these recommended designs, they will be automated through a future release of AutoQoS.

Therefore, the value in reading this book is to learn the rationale behind the best practices that went into AutoQoS VoIP and AutoQoS Enterprise development, and to go beyond these contexts and see the next-generation strategic role of QoS technologies.

Summary

This chapter briefly reviewed the fundamental concepts of QoS, such as IntServ and DiffServ; the categories of QoS tools that exist, and why they are categorized in this way; the Modular QoS CLI that pulls together the use and configuration of various QoS tools, making it clearer how and where they interact; the QoS Baseline; and Automatic QoS Cisco initiatives. This chapter also introduced the QoS Baseline 11 classes of traffic, including the less-than best-effort Scavenger class.

You are now ready to get into the principles of QoS design and then review salient details of the QoS toolset. Chapter 2, "QoS Design Overview," introduces QoS design principles and objectives. Chapters 3 through 9 provide a more in-depth discussion of the various QoS tool categories, the specific tools in each, and how and where these should be applied. Chapters 10 through 16 provide design examples of how these tools are deployed in specific types of networks. These network types are included in these discussions:

- LAN QoS design
- WAN QoS design, covering both remote office and WAN aggregator designs
- MPLS and IPSec VPN QoS design

The objective of this book is not to discuss every QoS feature in isolation—plenty of material available in the industry accomplishes this. The goal instead is to show how these techniques are used in a holistic network design to achieve end-to-end QoS for the entire network. Another objective of this book is to show how to deploy QoS not only for purposes such as maintaining voice quality for VoIP calls, but also to show how QoS can be used to achieve such goals as protecting the network against denial-of-service (DoS) attacks and managing traffic flows to keep unwanted traffic (such as copyright-infringing music file-sharing applications) off the network.

Further Reading

General

- *IP Quality of Service.* Srinivas Vegesna. Indianapolis: Cisco Press, 2001.
- *Cisco Catalyst QoS: Quality of Service in Campus Networks.* Michael Flannagan and Kevin Turek. Indianapolis: Cisco Press, 2003.
- *Cisco DQOS Exam Certification Guide.* Wendell Odom, Michael Cavanaugh. Indianapolis: Cisco Press, 2003.
- Communications Convergence.com: http://www.cconvergence.com.
- CommWeb Tech Library: http://techlibrary.commweb.com/data/web/cweb/cweb_index.jsp.
- Cisco.com QoS page: http://www.cisco.com/go/qos.

IntServ

- IntServ is described by a series of RFCs from the IntServ IETF working group.
- RFC 1633, "Integrated Services in the Internet Architecture: An Overview": http://www.ietf.org/rfc/rfc1633.txt.
- RFC 2205, "Resource Reservation Protocol (RSVP) Version 1 Functional Specification": http://www.ietf.org/rfc/rfc2205.txt.
- RFC 2210, "The Use of RSVP with IETF Integrated Services": http://www.ietf.org/rfc/rfc2210.txt.
- RFC 2211, "Specification of the Controlled-Load Network Element Service": http://www.ietf.org/rfc/rfc2211.txt.
- RFC 2212, "Specification of Guaranteed Quality of Service": http://www.ietf.org/rfc/rfc2212.txt.
- RFC 2215, "General Characterization Parameters for Integrated Service Network Elements": http://www.ietf.org/rfc/rfc2215.txt.

DiffServ

- DiffServ is described by a series of RFCs from the DiffServ IETF working group.
- RFC 2474, "Definition of the Differentiated Services Field (DS Field) in the IPv4 and IPv6 Headers": http://www.ietf.org/rfc/rfc2474.txt.
- RFC 2475, "An Architecture for Differentiated Services": http://www.ietf.org/rfc/rfc2475.txt.
- RFC 2597, "Assured Forwarding PHB Group": http://www.ietf.org/rfc/rfc2597.txt.
- RFC 2598, "An Expedited Forwarding PHB": http://www.ietf.org/rfc/rfc2598.txt.
- RFC 2697, "A Single Rate Three Color Marker": http://www.ietf.org/rfc/rfc2697.txt.
- RFC 2698, "A Two Rate Three Color Marker": http://www.ietf.org/rfc/rfc2698.txt.
- RFC 3168, "Explicit Congestion Notification (ECN) to IP": http://www.ietf.org/rfc/rfc3168.txt.
- RFC 3246, "An Expedited Forwarding PHB" (replacing RFC 2598): http://www.ietf.org/rfc/rfc3246.txt.

AutoQoS

- AutoQoS VoIP for Cisco IOS router platforms, Cisco IOS Release 12.2(15)T documentation: http://www.cisco.com/univercd/cc/td/doc/product/software/ios122/122newft/122t/122t15/ftautoq1.htm.
- AutoQoS Enterprise for Cisco IOS router platforms, Cisco IOS Release 12.3(7)T documentation: http://www.cisco.com/univercd/cc/td/doc/product/software/ios123/123newft/123t/123t_7/ftautoq2.htm.
- AutoQoS VoIP, Catalyst 2950, Catalyst IOS version 12.1(19)EA1: http://www.cisco.com/univercd/cc/td/doc/product/lan/cat2950/12119ea1/2950scg/swqos.htm#1125412.
- AutoQoS VoIP, Catalyst 2970, Catalyst IOS version 12.1(19)EA1: http://www.cisco.com/univercd/cc/td/doc/product/lan/cat2970/12119ea1/2970scg/swqos.htm#1231112.
- AutoQoS VoIP, Catalyst 3550, Catalyst IOS version 12.1(19)EA1: http://www.cisco.com/univercd/cc/td/doc/product/lan/c3550/12119ea1/3550scg/swqos.htm#1185065.
- AutoQoS VoIP, Catalyst 3750, Catalyst IOS version 12.1(19)EA1: http://www.cisco.com/univercd/cc/td/doc/product/lan/cat3750/12119ea1/3750scg/swqos.htm#1231112.
- AutoQoS VoIP, Catalyst 4500, Catalyst IOS version 12.2(18): http://www.cisco.com/univercd/cc/td/doc/product/lan/cat4000/12_2_18/config/qos.htm#1281380.
- AutoQoS VoIP, Catalyst 6500, Catalyst CatOS version 8.2: http://www.cisco.com/univercd/cc/td/doc/product/lan/cat6000/sw_8_2/confg_gd/autoqos.htm.

This chapter provides an overview of the QoS design and deployment process. This process requires business-level objectives of the QoS implementation to be defined clearly and for the service-level requirements of applications to be assigned preferential or deferential treatment so that they can be analyzed.

These enterprise applications with unique QoS requirements are discussed in this chapter:

- Voice
- Call-Signaling
- Interactive-Video
- Streaming-Video
- Best-Effort Data
- Bulk Data
- Transactional Data
- Mission-Critical Data
- IP Routing traffic
- Network-Management traffic
- Scavenger traffic

Additionally, key QoS design and deployment best practices that can simplify and expedite QoS implementations are presented, including these:

- Classification and marking principles
- Policing and markdown principles
- Queuing and dropping principles
- DoS and worm mitigation principles
- Deployment principles

CHAPTER 2

QoS Design Overview

More than just a working knowledge of QoS tools and syntax is needed to deploy end-to-end QoS in a holistic manner. First, it is vital to understand the service-level requirements of the various applications that require preferential (or deferential) treatment within the network. Additionally, a number of QoS design principles that extensive lab testing and customer deployments have helped shape can streamline a QoS deployment and increase the overall cohesiveness of service levels across multiple platforms.

This chapter overviews the QoS requirements of VoIP, Video (both Interactive-Video and Streaming-Video), and multiple classes of data. Within this discussion, the QoS requirements of the control plane (routing and management traffic) are considered. The Scavenger class is examined in more detail, and a strategy for mitigating DoS and worm attacks is presented.

Next, QoS design principles relating to classification, marking, policing, queuing, and deployment are discussed. These serve as guiding best practices in the design chapters to follow.

QoS Requirements of VoIP

VoIP deployments require the provisioning of explicit priority servicing for VoIP (bearer stream) traffic and a guaranteed bandwidth service for Call-Signaling traffic. These related classes are examined separately.

Voice (Bearer Traffic)

The following list summarizes the key QoS requirements and recommendations for voice (bearer traffic):

- Voice traffic should be marked to DSCP EF per the QoS Baseline and RFC 3246.
- Loss should be no more than 1 percent.
- One-way latency (mouth to ear) should be no more than 150 ms.
- Average one-way jitter should be targeted at less than 30 ms.
- A range of 21 to 320 kbps of guaranteed priority bandwidth is required per call (depending on the sampling rate, the VoIP codec, and Layer 2 media overhead).

Voice quality directly is affected by all three QoS quality factors: loss, latency, and jitter.

Loss

Loss causes voice clipping and skips. Packet loss concealment (PLC) is a technique used to mask the effects of lost or discarded VoIP packets. The method of PLC used depends upon the type of codec. A simple method used by waveform codecs such as G.711 (PLC for G.711 is defined in G.711 Appendix I) is to replay the last received sample with increasing attenuation at each repeat; the waveform does not change much from one sample to the next. This technique can be effective at concealing the loss of up to 20 ms of samples.

The packetization interval determines the size of samples contained within a single packet. Assuming a 20-ms (default) packetization interval, the loss of two or more consecutive packets results in a noticeable degradation of voice quality. Therefore, assuming a random distribution of drops within a single voice flow, a drop rate of 1 percent in a voice stream would result in a loss that could not be concealed every 3 minutes, on average. A 0.25 percent drop rate would result in a loss that could not be concealed once every 53 minutes, on average.

NOTE   A decision to use a 30-ms packetization interval, for a given probability of packet loss, could result in worse perceived call quality than for 20 ms because PLC could not effectively conceal the loss of a single packet.

Low-bit-rate, frame-based codecs, such as G.729 and G.723, use more sophisticated PLC techniques that can conceal up to 30 to 40 ms of loss with "tolerable" quality when the available history used for the interpolation is still relevant.

With frame-based codecs, the packetization interval determines the number of frames carried in a single packet. As with waveform-based codecs, if the packetization interval is greater than the loss that the PLC algorithm can interpolate for, PLC cannot effectively conceal the loss of a single packet.

VoIP networks typically are designed for very close to 0 percent VoIP packet loss, with the only actual packet loss being due to L2 bit errors or network failures.

Latency

Latency can cause voice quality degradation if it is excessive. The goal commonly used in designing networks to support VoIP is the target specified by ITU standard G.114 (which, incidentally, is currently under revision): This states that 150 ms of one-way, end-to-end (from mouth to ear) delay ensures user satisfaction for telephony applications. A design should apportion this budget to the various components of network delay (propagation delay through the backbone, scheduling delay because of congestion, and access link serialization delay) and service delay (because of VoIP gateway codec and dejitter buffer).

Figure 2-1 illustrates these various elements of VoIP latency (and jitter because some delay elements are variable).

Figure 2-1   *Elements Affecting VoIP Latency and Jitter*

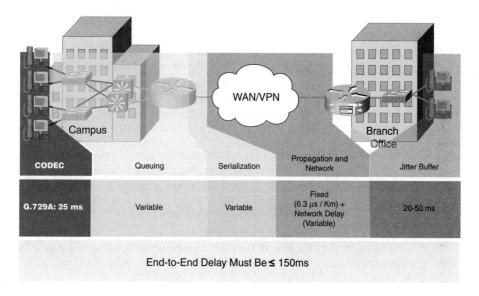

CODEC	Queuing	Serialization	Propagation and Network	Jitter Buffer
G.729A: 25 ms	Variable	Variable	Fixed (6.3 µs / Km) + Network Delay (Variable)	20-50 ms

End-to-End Delay Must Be ≤ 150ms

If the end-to-end voice delay becomes too long, the conversation begins to sound like two parties talking over a satellite link or even a CB radio. The ITU G.114 states that a 150-ms one-way (mouth-to-ear) delay budget is acceptable for high voice quality, but lab testing has shown that there is a negligible difference in voice quality mean opinion scores (MOS) using networks built with 200-ms delay budgets. Thus, Cisco recommends designing to the ITU standard of 150 ms. If constraints exist and this delay target cannot be met, the delay boundary can be extended to 200 ms without significant impact on voice quality.

NOTE   Certain organizations might view higher delays as acceptable, but the corresponding reduction in VoIP quality must be taken into account when making such design decisions.

Jitter

Jitter buffers (also known as playout buffers) are used to change asynchronous packet arrivals into a synchronous stream by turning variable network delays into constant delays at the destination end systems. The role of the jitter buffer is to trade off between delay and the probability of interrupted playout because of late packets. Late or out-of-order packets are discarded.

If the jitter buffer is set either arbitrarily large or arbitrarily small, it imposes unnecessary constraints on the characteristics of the network. A jitter buffer set too large adds to the end-to-end delay, meaning that less delay budget is available for the network; hence, the network needs to support a tighter delay target than practically necessary. If a jitter buffer is too small to accommodate the network jitter, buffer underflows or overflows can occur. In an underflow, the buffer is empty when the codec needs to play out a sample. In an overflow, the jitter buffer is already full and another packet arrives; that next packet cannot be enqueued in the jitter buffer. Both jitter buffer underflows and overflows cause voice quality degradation.

Adaptive jitter buffers aim to overcome these issues by dynamically tuning the jitter buffer size to the lowest acceptable value. Well-designed adaptive jitter buffer algorithms should not impose any unnecessary constraints on the network design by doing the following:

- Instantly increasing the jitter buffer size to the current measured jitter value following a jitter buffer overflow

- Slowly decreasing the jitter buffer size when the measured jitter is less than the current jitter buffer size

- Using PLC to interpolate for the loss of a packet on a jitter buffer underflow

When such adaptive jitter buffers are used—in theory—you can "engineer out" explicit considerations of jitter by accounting for worst-case per-hop delays. Advanced formulas can be used to arrive at network-specific design recommendations for jitter (based on maximum and minimum per-hop delays). Alternatively, because extensive lab testing has shown that voice quality degrades significantly when jitter consistently exceeds 30 ms, this 30 ms value can be used as a jitter target.

Because of its strict service-level requirements, VoIP is well suited to the expedited forwarding per-hop behavior, defined in RFC 3246 (formerly RFC 2598). Therefore, it should be marked to DSCP EF (46) and assigned strict-priority servicing at each node, regardless of whether such servicing is done in hardware (as in Catalyst switches through 1PxQyT queuing, discussed in more detail in Chapter 10, "Catalyst QoS Tools") or in software (as in Cisco IOS routers through LLQ, discussed in more detail in Chapter 5, "Congestion-Management Tools").

The bandwidth that VoIP streams consume (in bits per second) is calculated by adding the VoIP sample payload (in bytes) to the 40-byte IP, UDP, and RTP headers (assuming that cRTP is not in use), multiplying this value by 8 (to convert it to bits), and then multiplying again by the packetization rate (default of 50 packets per second).

Table 2-1 details the bandwidth per VoIP flow (both G.711 and G.729) at a default packetization rate of 50 packets per second (pps) and at a custom packetization rate of 33 pps. This does not include Layer 2 overhead and does not take into account any possible compression schemes, such as Compressed Real-Time Transport Protocol (cRTP, discussed in detail in Chapter 7, "Link-Specific Tools").

For example, assume a G.711 VoIP codec at the default packetization rate (50 pps). A new VoIP packet is generated every 20 ms (1 second / 50 pps). The payload of each VoIP packet is 160 bytes; with the IP, UDP, and RTP headers (20 + 8 + 12 bytes, respectively) included, this packet become 200 bytes in length. Converting bits to bytes requires multiplying by 8 and yields 1600 bps per packet. When multiplied by the total number of packets per second (50 pps), this arrives at the Layer 3 bandwidth requirement for uncompressed G.711 VoIP: 80 kbps. This example calculation corresponds to the first row of Table 2-1.

Table 2-1   *Voice Bandwidth (Without Layer 2 Overhead)*

Bandwidth Consumption	Packetization Interval	Voice Payload in Bytes	Packets Per Second	Bandwidth Per Conversation
G.711	20 ms	160	50	80 kbps
G.711	30 ms	240	33	74 kbps
G.729A	20 ms	20	50	24 kbps
G.729A	30 ms	30	33	19 kbps

NOTE   The Service Parameters menu in Cisco CallManager Administration can be used to adjust the packet rate. It is possible to configure the sampling rate above 30 ms, but this usually results in poor voice quality.

A more accurate method for provisioning VoIP is to include the Layer 2 overhead, which includes preambles, headers, flags, CRCs, and ATM cell padding. The amount of overhead per VoIP call depends on the Layer 2 media used:

- 802.1Q Ethernet adds (up to) 32 bytes of Layer 2 overhead (when preambles are included).
- Point-to-Point Protocol (PPP) adds 12 bytes of Layer 2 overhead.
- Multilink PPP (MLP) adds 13 bytes of Layer 2 overhead.
- Frame Relay adds 4 bytes of Layer 2 overhead; Frame Relay with FRF.12 adds 8 bytes.
- ATM adds varying amounts of overhead, depending on the cell padding requirements.

Table 2-2 shows more accurate bandwidth-provisioning guidelines for voice because it includes Layer 2 overhead.

Table 2-2   *Voice Bandwidth (Including Layer 2 Overhead)*

Bandwidth Consumption	802.1Q Ethernet	PPP	MLP	Frame Relay with FRF.12	ATM
G.711 at 50 pps	93 kbps	84 kbps	86 kbps	84 kbps	106 kbps
G.711 at 33 pps	83 kbps	77 kbps	78 kbps	77 kbps	84 kbps
G.729A at 50 pps	37 kbps	28 kbps	30 kbps	28 kbps	43 kbps
G.729A at 33 pps	27 kbps	21 kbps	22 kbps	21 kbps	28 kbps

Call-Signaling Traffic

The following list summarizes the key QoS requirements and recommendations for Call-Signaling traffic:

- Call-Signaling traffic should be marked as DSCP CS3 per the QoS Baseline (during migration, it also can be marked the legacy value of DSCP AF31).

- 150 bps (plus Layer 2 overhead) per phone of guaranteed bandwidth is required for voice control traffic; more may be required, depending on the Call-Signaling protocol(s) in use.

Originally, Cisco IP Telephony equipment marked Call-Signaling traffic to DSCP AF31. However, the assured forwarding classes, as defined in RFC 2597, were intended for flows that could be subject to markdown and aggressive dropping of marked-down values. Marking down and aggressively dropping Call-Signaling could result in noticeable delay to dial tone (DDT) and lengthy call-setup times, both of which generally translate into poor user experiences.

Therefore, the QoS Baseline changed the marking recommendation for Call-Signaling traffic to DSCP CS3 because Class-Selector code points, defined in RFC 2474, are not subject to such markdown and aggressive dropping as Assured Forwarding Per-Hop Behaviors are.

Some Cisco IP Telephony products already have begun transitioning to DSCP CS3 for Call-Signaling marking. In this interim period, both code points (CS3 and AF31) should be reserved for Call-Signaling marking until the transition is complete.

Most Cisco IP Telephony products use the Skinny Call-Control Protocol (SCCP) for Call-Signaling. Skinny is a relatively lightweight protocol and, as such, requires only a minimal amount of bandwidth protection (most of the Cisco large-scale lab testing was done by provisioning only 2 percent for Call-Signaling traffic over WAN and VPN links). However, newer versions of CallManager and SCCP have shown some "bloating" in this signaling protocol, so design recommendations have been adjusted to match (most examples in the design chapters that follow have been adjusted to allocate 5 percent for Call-Signaling traffic). This is a normal part of QoS evolution: As applications and protocols continue to evolve, so do the QoS designs required to accommodate them.

Other Call-Signaling protocols include (but are not limited to) H.225 and H.245, the Session Initiated Protocol (SIP), and the Media Gateway Control Protocol (MGCP). Each Call-Signaling protocol has unique TCP and UDP ports and traffic patterns that should be taken into account when provisioning QoS policies for them.

QoS Requirements of Video

Two main types of video traffic exist: Interactive-Video (videoconferencing) and Streaming-Video (both unicast and multicast). Each type of video is examined separately.

Interactive-Video

When provisioning for Interactive-Video (video conferencing) traffic, the following guidelines are recommended:

- Interactive-Video traffic should be marked to DSCP AF41; excess videoconferencing traffic can be marked down by a policer to AF42 or AF43.

- Loss should be no more than 1 percent.

- One-way latency should be no more than 150 ms.

- Jitter should be no more than 30 ms.

- Assign Interactive-Video to either a preferential queue or a second priority queue (when supported); when using Cisco IOS LLQ, overprovision the minimum-priority bandwidth guarantee to the size of the videoconferencing session plus 20 percent. (For example, a 384-kbps videoconferencing session requires 460 kbps of guaranteed priority bandwidth.)

Because IP videoconferencing (IP/VC) includes a G.711 audio codec for voice, it has the same loss, delay, and delay-variation requirements as voice—but the traffic patterns of videoconferencing are radically different from those of voice.

For example, videoconferencing traffic has varying packet sizes and extremely variable packet rates. These are illustrated in Figures 2-2 and 2-3.

Figure 2-2 *Videoconferencing Traffic Packet-Size Breakdown*

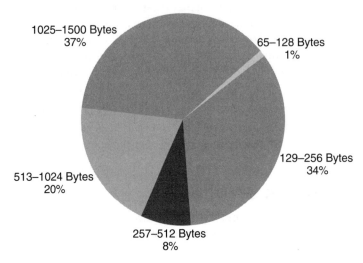

Figure 2-3 *Videoconferencing Traffic Rates (384-kbps Session Example)*

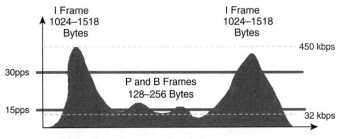

- I frame is a full sample of the video.
- P and B frames use quantization via motion vectors and prediction algorithms.

The videoconferencing rate is the sampling rate of the video stream, not the actual bandwidth that the video call requires. In other words, the data payload of videoconferencing packets is filled with 384 kbps of voice plus video samples. IP, UDP, and RTP headers (40 bytes per packet, uncompressed) need to be included in IP/VC bandwidth provisioning, as does the Layer 2 overhead of the media in use. Because (unlike VoIP) IP/VC packet sizes and rates vary, the header overhead percentage also varies, so an absolute value of overhead

cannot be calculated accurately for all streams. However, testing has shown that a conservative rule of thumb for IP/VC bandwidth provisioning is to assign an LLQ bandwidth equivalent to the IP/VC rate plus 20 percent. For example, a 384-kbps IP/VC stream adequately is provisioned with an LLQ of 460 kbps.

NOTE   The Cisco LLQ algorithm has been implemented to include a default burst parameter equivalent to 200 ms of traffic. Testing has shown that this burst parameter does not require additional tuning for a single IP videoconferencing (IP/VC) stream. For multiple streams, this burst parameter can be increased as required.

Streaming-Video

When addressing the QoS needs of Streaming-Video traffic, the following guidelines are recommended:

- Streaming-Video (whether unicast or multicast) should be marked to DSCP CS4, as designated by the QoS Baseline.

- Loss should be no more than 5 percent.

- Latency should be no more than 4 to 5 seconds (depending on the video application's buffering capabilities).

- There are no significant jitter requirements.

- Guaranteed bandwidth (CBWFQ) requirements depend on the encoding format and rate of the video stream.

- Streaming-Video is typically unidirectional; therefore, remote branch routers might not require provisioning for Streaming-Video traffic on their WAN or VPN edges (in the direction of branch to campus).

- Nonorganizational Streaming-Video applications (either unicast or multicast), such as entertainment video content, may be marked as Scavenger—DSCP CS1, provisioned in the Scavenger traffic class and assigned a minimal bandwidth (CBWFQ) percentage. For more information, see the "Scavenger Class" section, later in this chapter.

Streaming-Video applications have more lenient QoS requirements because they are not delay sensitive (the video can take several seconds to cue up) and are largely not jitter sensitive (because of application buffering). However, Streaming-Video might contain valuable content, such as e-learning applications or multicast company meetings, in which case it requires service guarantees.

The QoS Baseline recommendation for Streaming-Video marking is DSCP CS4.

An interesting consideration with respect to Streaming-Video comes into play when designing WAN and VPN edge policies on branch routers: Because Streaming-Video is generally unidirectional, a separate class likely is not needed for this traffic class in the branch-to-campus direction of traffic flow.

Nonorganizational video content (or video that's strictly entertainment oriented in nature, such as movies, music videos, humorous commercials, and so on) might be considered for Scavenger service, meaning that these streams will play if bandwidth exists, but they will be the first to go during periods of congestion.

QoS Requirements of Data

Hundreds of thousands of data applications exist on the Internet, in all shapes and sizes. Some are TCP, others are UDP; some are delay sensitive, others are not; some are bursty in nature, others are steady; some are lightweight, others are bandwidth hogs—the list goes on.

Data traffic characteristics vary from one application to another, as illustrated in Figure 2-4, which compares an enterprise resource planning (ERP) application (Oracle) with another (SAP).

Figure 2-4 *Data Application Differences*

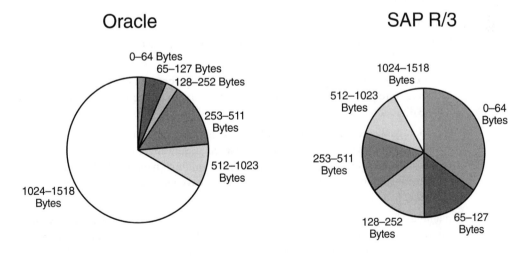

To make the matter even more complicated, it is crucial to recognize that, just as applications vary one from another, even the same application can vary significantly from one *version* to another.

A brief anecdote speaks to this point: After a southern California semiconductor company provisioned QoS for Voice and Mission-Critical Data (SAP R/3), everything went well for about six months. At that point, users began complaining of excessive delays in completing basic transactions. Operations that previously required a second or less to complete were taking significantly longer. The application teams blamed the networking teams, claiming that "QoS was broken." Further investigation produced the information in the following graph, shown in Figure 2-5.

Figure 2-5   *Data Application Version Differences*

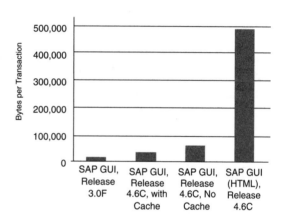

SAP Sales Order
Entry Transaction

Client Version	VA01 # of Bytes
SAP GUI Release 3.0 F	14,000
SAP GUI Release 4.6C, No Cache	57,000
SAP GUI Release 4.6C, with Cache	33,000
SAP GUI for HTML, Release 4.6C	490,000

The Mission-Critical Data application—in this instance, SAP—had been upgraded from version 3.0F to 4.6C. As a result, a basic order-entry transaction required 35 times more traffic than the original version. Additional provisioning and policy tuning was required to accommodate the new version of the same application.

Given this reality, the question on how best to provision QoS for data is a daunting one. After wrestling with this question for several years, the authors of the QoS Baseline came up with four main classes of data traffic, according to their general networking characteristics and requirements. These classes are Best-Effort, Bulk Data, Transactional Data/Interactive Data and (Locally-Defined) Mission-Critical Data. Each of these classes is examined in more detail in the following sections.

Best-Effort Data

When addressing the QoS needs of Best-Effort traffic, the following guidelines are recommended:

- Best-Effort traffic should be marked to DSCP 0.

- Adequate bandwidth should be assigned to the Best-Effort class as a whole because the majority of applications default to this class. It is recommended to reserve at least 25 percent for Best-Effort traffic.

The Best-Effort class is the default class for all data traffic. Only if an application has been selected for preferential or deferential treatment is it removed from the default class.

In 2003, one Wall Street financial company did an extensive study to identify and categorize the number of different applications on its networks. It found more than 3000 discrete applications traversing its infrastructure. Further research has shown that this is not uncommon for larger enterprises. Therefore, because enterprises have several hundred—if not thousands of—data applications running over their networks (of which the majority default to the Best-Effort class), adequate bandwidth needs to be provisioned for this default class to handle the sheer volume of applications that are included in it. Otherwise, applications that default to this class easily are drowned out, typically resulting in an increased number of calls to the networking help desk from frustrated users. It is therefore recommended that at least 25 percent of a link's bandwidth be reserved for the default Best-Effort class.

Bulk Data

When addressing the QoS needs of Bulk Data traffic, the following guidelines are recommended:

- Bulk Data traffic should be marked to DSCP AF11; excess Bulk Data traffic can be marked down by a policer to AF12 or AF13.

- Bulk Data traffic should have a moderate bandwidth guarantee but should be constrained from dominating a link.

The Bulk Data class is intended for applications that are relatively noninteractive and not drop sensitive, and that typically span their operations over a long period of time as background occurrences. Such applications include FTP, e-mail, backup operations, database synchronizing or replicating operations, video content distribution, and any other type of application in which users typically cannot proceed because they are waiting for the completion of the operation (in other words, a background operation).

The advantage of provisioning moderate bandwidth guarantees to Bulk Data applications (instead of applying policers to them) is that Bulk Data applications dynamically can take advantage of unused bandwidth and thus can speed up their operations during nonpeak periods. This, in turn, reduces the likelihood that they will bleed into busy periods and absorb inordinate amounts of bandwidth for their non-time-sensitive operations.

Transactional Data/Interactive Data

When addressing the QoS needs of Transactional Data and Interactive Data traffic, the following guidelines are recommended:

- Transactional Data traffic should be marked to DSCP AF21; excess Transactional Data traffic can be marked down by a policer to AF22 or AF23.

- Transactional Data traffic should have an adequate bandwidth guarantee for the interactive, foreground operations that it supports.

The Transactional Data/Interactive Data class is a combination of two similar types of applications: Transactional Data client/server applications and interactive messaging applications. For the sake of simplicity, this class is referred to as Transactional Data only.

The response-time requirement separates Transactional Data client/server applications from generic client/server applications. For example, with Transactional Data client/server applications (such as SAP, PeopleSoft, and Oracle), the user waits for the operation to complete before proceeding (in other words, the transaction is a foreground operation). E-mail is not considered a Transactional Data client/server application because most e-mail operations happen in the background, and users usually do not notice even delays of several hundred milliseconds in mailspool operations.

Locally Defined Mission-Critical Data

When addressing the QoS needs of Locally-Defined Mission-Critical Data traffic, the following guidelines are recommended:

- Locally-Defined Mission-Critical Data traffic should be marked to DSCP AF31; excess Mission-Critical Data traffic can be marked down by a policer to AF32 or AF33. However, Cisco IP Telephony equipment currently is using DSCP AF31 to mark Call-Signaling traffic; until all Cisco IPT products mark Call-Signaling to DSCP CS3, a temporary placeholder code point, DSCP 25, can be used to identify Locally-Defined Mission-Critical Data traffic.

- Locally-Defined Mission-Critical Data traffic should have an adequate bandwidth guarantee for the interactive, foreground operations that it supports.

The Locally-Defined Mission-Critical class is probably the most misunderstood class specified in the QoS Baseline. Under the QoS Baseline model, all traffic classes (with the exclusion of Scavenger and Best-Effort) are considered "critical" to the enterprise. The term *locally defined* is used to underscore the purpose of this class: for each enterprise to have a premium class of service for a select subset of its Transactional Data applications that have the highest business priority for it.

For example, an enterprise might have properly provisioned Oracle, SAP, BEA, and Siebel within its Transactional Data class. However, the majority of its revenue might come from SAP, so it might want to give this Transactional Data application an even higher level of preference by assigning it to a dedicated class (such as the Locally-Defined Mission-Critical class).

Because the admission criteria for this class is nontechnical (being determined by business relevance and organizational objectives), the decision about which application(s) should be assigned to this special class easily can become an organizationally and politically charged debate. It is recommended to assign as few applications to this class (from the Transactional Data class) as possible. In addition, it is recommended that executive endorsement for application assignments to the Locally-Defined Mission-Critical class be obtained: The potential for QoS deployment derailment exists without such an endorsement.

For the sake of simplicity, this class is referred to simply as Mission-Critical Data.

Based on these definitions, Table 2-3 shows some applications and their generic networking characteristics, which determine what data application class they are best suited to.

Table 2-3   *Data Applications by Class*

Application Class	Example Applications	Application/Traffic Properties	Packet/Message Sizes
Interactive PHB: AF2	Telnet, Citrix, Oracle Thin-Clients, AOL Instant Messenger, Yahoo! Instant Messenger, PlaceWare (Conference), Netmeeting Whiteboard.	Highly interactive applications with tight user-feedback requirements.	Average message size < 100 bytes. Max message size < 1 KB.
Transactional PHB: AF2	SAP, PeopleSoft—Vantive, Oracle—Financials, Internet Procurement, B2B, Supply Chain Management, Application Server, Oracle 8i Database, Ariba Buyer, I2, Siebel, E.piphany, Broadvision, IBM Bus 2 Bus, Microsoft SQL, BEA Systems, DLSw+.	Transactional applications typically use a client/server protocol model. User-initiated, client-based queries are followed by server response. The query response can consist of many messages between client and server. The query response can consist of many TCP and FTP sessions running simultaneously (for example, HTTP-based applications).	Depends on application; could be anywhere from 1 KB to 50 MB.

Table 2-3 *Data Applications by Class (Continued)*

Application Class	Example Applications	Application/Traffic Properties	Packet/Message Sizes
Bulk PHB: AF1	Database syncs, network-based backups, Lotus Notes, Microsoft Outlook, e-mail download (SMTP, POP3, IMAP, Exchange), video content distribution, large FTP file transfers.	Long file transfers. Always invokes TCP congestion management.	Average message size 64 KB or greater.
Best-Effort PHB: Default	All noncritical traffic, HTTP web browsing, other miscellaneous traffic.		

DLSw+ Considerations

Some enterprises support legacy IBM equipment that requires data-link switching plus (DLSw+) to operate across an enterprise environment.

In such cases, it is important to recognize that DLSw+ traffic, by default, is marked to IP Precedence 5 (DSCP CS5). This default marking could interfere with VoIP provisioning because both DSCP EF and DSCP CS5 share the same IP Precedence, 802.1Q/p CoS, and MPLS EXP value (of 5). Therefore, it is recommended to re-mark DLSw+ traffic away from this default value of IP Precedence 5.

Unfortunately, at the time of writing, Cisco IOS does not support marking DSCP values within the DLSw+ peering statements; it supports only the marking of type of service (ToS) values using the **dlsw tos map** command.

NOTE   To explain this behavior from a historical perspective, when DLSw+ was developed, *ToS* was a term loosely used to refer to the first 3 bits (the IP Precedence bits) of the IP ToS byte, as defined in RFC 791. For many years, these were typically the only bits of the ToS byte in use (the others almost always were set to 0), so it seemed to make sense at the time.

However, with the development of newer standards defining the use of the first 6 bits of the IP ToS byte for DiffServ markings (RFC 2474) and the last 2 bits for IP explicit congestion notification (RFC 3168), using the term *ToS* to refer to only the first 3 bits (the IP Precedence bits) of the IP ToS byte has become increasingly inaccurate.

However, marking DLSw+ to an IP Precedence/class selector value could interfere with other QoS Baseline recommended markings. For example, if DLSw+ is marked to IPP 1, it would be treated as Scavenger traffic; if it is marked to IPP 2, it could interfere with Network-Management traffic; if it is marked to IPP 3, it could interfere with Call-Signaling; if it is marked to IPP 4, it would be treated as Streaming-Video traffic; and if it is marked to IPP 6 or 7, it could interfere with routing or Network Control traffic.

Therefore, a two-step workaround is recommended for marking DLSw+ traffic:

Step 1   Disable native DLSw+ ToS markings with the **dlsw tos disable** command.

Step 2   Identify DLSw+ traffic either with access lists (matching the DLSw+ TCP ports 1981 to 1983 or 2065) or with the **match protocol dlsw** command.

When DLSw+ traffic is identified, it can be marked as either Transactional (AF21) or Mission-Critical Data (DSCP 25), depending on the organization's preference.

QoS Requirements of the Control Plane

Unless the network is up, QoS is irrelevant. Therefore, it is critical to provision QoS for control-plane traffic, which includes IP routing traffic and network management.

IP Routing

When addressing the QoS needs of IP routing traffic, the following guidelines are recommended:

- IP routing traffic should be marked to DSCP CS6; this is default behavior on Cisco IOS platforms.

- Interior gateway protocols usually adequately are protected with the Cisco IOS internal PAK_priority mechanism. Exterior gateway protocols, such as BGP, are recommended to have an explicit class for IP routing with a minimal bandwidth guarantee.

Cisco IOS automatically marks IP routing traffic to DSCP CS6.

By default, Cisco IOS Software (in accordance with RFC 791 and RFC 2474) marks Interior Gateway Protocol (IGP) traffic (such as Routing Information Protocol [RIP and RIPv2], Open Shortest Path First [OSPF], and Enhanced Interior Gateway Routing Protocol [EIGRP]) to DSCP CS6. However, Cisco IOS Software also has an internal mechanism for granting priority to important control datagrams as they are processed through the router. This mechanism is called PAK_priority.

As datagrams are processed though the router and down to the interfaces, they internally are encapsulated with a small packet header, referred to as the PAKTYPE structure. Within the fields of this internal header is a PAK_priority flag that indicates the relative importance of control packets to the router's internal processing systems. PAK_priority designation is a critical internal Cisco IOS Software operation and, as such, is not administratively configurable in any way.

It is important to note that although exterior gateway protocol (EGP) traffic, such as Border Gateway Protocol (BGP) traffic, is marked by default to DSCP CS6, it does not receive such PAK_priority preferential treatment and might need to be protected explicitly to maintain peering sessions.

NOTE   Additional information on PAK_priority can be found at http://www.cisco.com/warp/public/105/rtgupdates.html.

Network-Management

When addressing the QoS needs of Network-Management traffic, the following guidelines are recommended:

- Network-Management traffic should be marked to DSCP CS2.

- Network-Management applications should be protected explicitly with a minimal bandwidth guarantee.

Network-Management traffic is important in performing trend and capacity analyses and troubleshooting. Therefore, a separate minimal bandwidth queue can be provisioned for Network-Management traffic, which could include SNMP, NTP, Syslog, and NFS and other management applications.

Scavenger Class

When addressing the QoS treatment of Scavenger traffic, the following guidelines are recommended:

- Scavenger traffic should be marked to DSCP CS1.

- Scavenger traffic should be assigned the lowest configurable queuing service; for instance, in Cisco IOS, this means assigning a CBWFQ of 1 percent to Scavenger.

The Scavenger class is intended to provide deferential services, or less-than best-effort services, to certain applications. Applications assigned to this class have little or no contribution to the organizational objectives of the enterprise and are typically entertainment oriented in nature. These include peer-to-peer media-sharing applications (KaZaa, Morpheus,

Groekster, Napster, iMesh, and so on), gaming applications (Doom, Quake, Unreal Tournament, and so on), and any entertainment video applications.

Assigning Scavenger traffic to minimal bandwidth queue forces it to be squelched to virtually nothing during periods of congestion, but it allows it to be available if bandwidth is not being used for business purposes, such as might occur during off-peak hours.

The Scavenger class is a critical component to the DoS and worm mitigation strategy, discussed next.

DoS and Worm Mitigation Strategy Through Scavenger Class QoS

Worms are nothing new; they have been around in some form since the beginning of the Internet and steadily have been increasing in complexity, as shown in Figure 2-6.

Figure 2-6   *Business Security Threat Evolution*

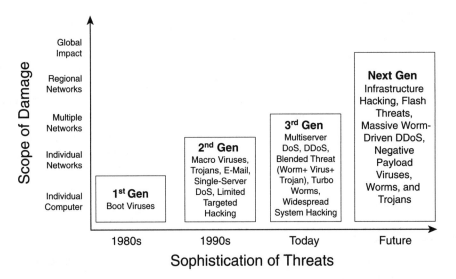

Particularly since 2002, there has been an exponential increase not only in the frequency of DoS and worm attacks, but also in their relative sophistication and scope of damage. For example, more than 994 new Win32 viruses and worms were documented in the first half of 2003, more than double the 445 documented in the first half of 2002. Some of these more recent worms are shown in Figure 2-7.

Figure 2-7   *Recent Internet Worms*

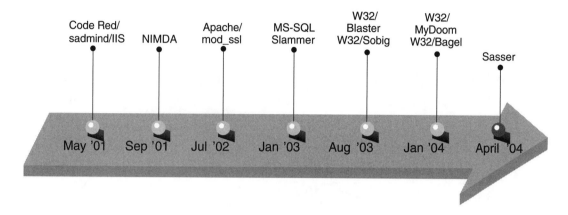

DoS or worm attacks can be categorized into two main classes:

- **Spoofing attacks**—The attacker pretends to provide a legitimate service but provides false information (if any) to the requester.

- **Flooding attacks**—The attacker exponentially generates and propagates traffic until service resources (servers or network infrastructure) are overwhelmed.

Spoofing attacks best are addressed by authentication and encryption technologies; flooding attacks, on the other hand, can be mitigated using QoS technologies.

The majority of flooding attacks target PCs and servers, which, when infected, target other PCs and servers, thus multiplying traffic flows. Network devices themselves are not usually the direct targets of attacks. But the rapidly multiplying volumes of traffic flows eventually drown the CPU and hardware resources of routers and switches in their paths, causing denial of service to legitimate traffic flows. The end result is that network devices become indirect victims of the attack. This is illustrated in Figure 2-8.

A reactive approach to mitigating such attacks is to reverse-engineer the worm and set up intrusion-detection mechanisms or ACLs to limit its propagation. However, the increased sophistication and complexity of today's worms make them harder to identify from legitimate traffic flows. This exacerbates the finite time lag between when a worm begins to propagate and when the following occurs:

- Sufficient analysis has been performed to understand how the worm operates and what its network characteristics are.

- An appropriate patch, plug, or ACL is disseminated to network devices that might be in the path of the worm. This task might be hampered by the attack itself because network devices might become unreachable for administration during the attacks.

Figure 2-8   *Impact of an Internet Worm—Direct and Collateral Damage*

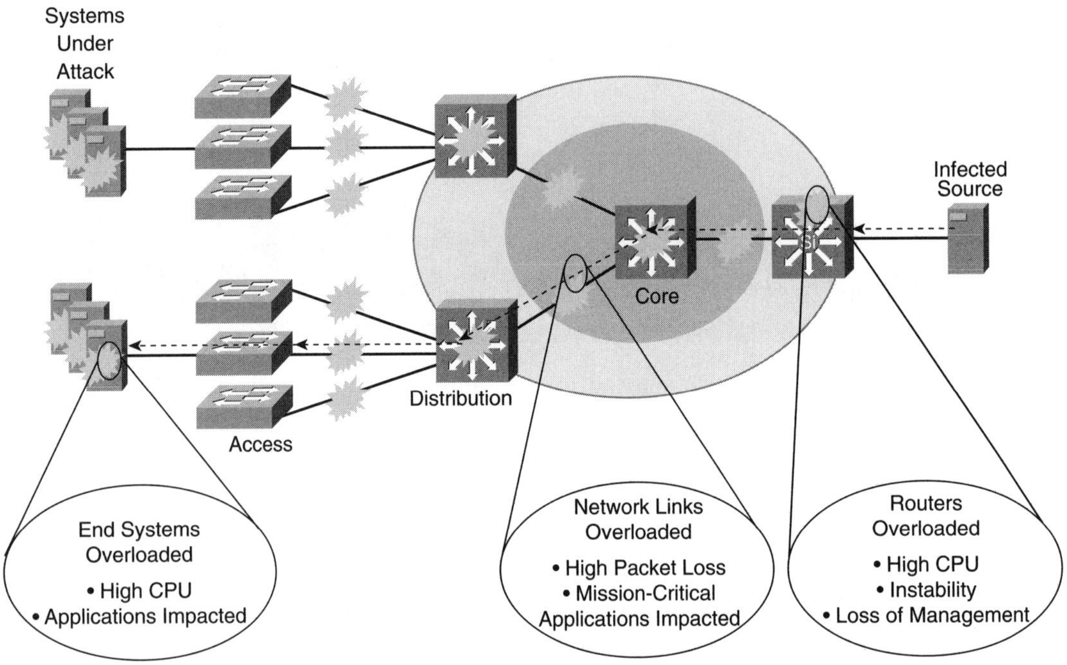

These time lags might not seem long in absolute terms, such as in minutes, but the relative window of opportunity for damage is huge. For example, in 2003, the number of hosts infected with the Slammer worm (a Sapphire worm variant) doubled every 8.5 seconds on average, infecting more than 75,000 hosts in just 11 minutes and performing scans of 55 million more hosts within the same time period.

NOTE   Interestingly, a 2002 CSI/FBI report stated that the majority of network attacks occur from within an organization, typically by disgruntled employees.

A proactive approach to mitigating DoS and worm flooding attacks within enterprise networks is to respond immediately to out-of-profile network behavior indicative of a DoS or worm attack via campus Access-Layer policers. Such policers can meter traffic rates received from endpoint devices and, when these exceed specified watermarks (at which point they no longer are considered normal flows), can mark down excess traffic to the Scavenger class marking (DSCP CS1).

In this respect, the policers would be fairly "dumb." They would not be matching specific network characteristics of specific types of attacks, but they simply would be metering traffic volumes and responding to abnormally high volumes as close to the source as possible. The simplicity of this approach negates the need for the policers to be programmed with knowledge of the specific details of how the attack is being generated or propagated. It is precisely this "dumbness" of such Access-Layer policers that allows them to maintain relevancy as worms mutate and become more complex: The policers don't care how the traffic was generated or what it looks like; all they care about is how much traffic is being put onto the wire. Therefore, they continue to police even advanced worms that continually change the tactics of how traffic is being generated.

For example, in most enterprises, it is quite abnormal (within a 95 percent statistical confidence interval) for PCs to generate sustained traffic in excess of 5 percent of their link's capacity. In the case of a Fast Ethernet switch port, this means that it would be unusual in most organizations for an end user's PC to generate more than 5 Mbps of uplink traffic on a sustained basis.

NOTE   It is important to recognize that this value (≤ 5 percent) for normal access-edge utilization by endpoints is just an example value. This value would likely vary from industry vertical to vertical, and from enterprise to enterprise.

It is important to recognize that what is being proposed is not to police all traffic to 5 Mbps and automatically drop the excess. If that were the case, there would not be much reason for deploying Fast Ethernet or Gigabit Ethernet switch ports to endpoint devices because even 10BASE-T Ethernet switch ports would have more uplink capacity than a 5 Mbps policer-enforced limit. Furthermore, such an approach supremely would penalize legitimate traffic that exceeded 5 Mbps on a Fast Ethernet switch port.

A less draconian approach is to couple Access-Layer policers with hardware and software (campus, WAN, and VPN) queuing policies, with both sets of policies provisioning for a less-than best-effort Scavenger class.

This would work by having Access-Layer policers mark down out-of-profile traffic to DSCP CS1 (Scavenger) and then have all congestion-management policies (whether in Catalyst hardware or in Cisco IOS Software) provision a less-than best-effort service for any traffic marked to DSCP CS1.

Let's examine how this might work, for both legitimate traffic exceeding the Access-Layer policer's watermark and illegitimate excess traffic (the result of a DoS or worm attack).

In the former case, imagine that the PC generates more than 5 Mbps of traffic, perhaps because of a large file transfer or backup. Because there is generally abundant capacity within the campus to carry the traffic, congestion (under normal operating conditions) is rarely, if ever, experienced. Typically, the uplinks to the distribution and core layers of the campus network are Gigabit Ethernet, which requires 1000 Mbps of traffic from the Access-Layer switch to create congestion. If the traffic was destined to the far side of a WAN or VPN link (which are rarely more than 5 Mbps in speed), dropping would occur even without the Access-Layer policer, simply because of the campus/WAN speed mismatch and resulting bottleneck. TCP's sliding-windows mechanism eventually would find an optimal speed (less than 5 Mbps) for the file transfer.

To make a long story short, Access-Layer policers that mark down out-of-profile traffic to Scavenger (CS1) would not affect legitimate traffic, aside from the obvious re-marking. No reordering or dropping would occur on such flows as a result of these policers (that would not have occurred anyway).

In the latter case, the effect of Access-Layer policers on traffic caused by DoS or worm attacks is quite different. As hosts become infected and traffic volumes multiply, congestion might be experienced even within the campus. If just 11 end-user PCs on a single switch begin spawning worm flows to their maximum Fast Ethernet link capacities, the GE uplink from the Access-Layer switch to the Distribution-Layer switch will congest and queuing or reordering will engage. At such a point, VoIP and critical data applications, and even Best-Effort applications, would gain priority over worm-generated traffic (and Scavenger traffic would be dropped the most aggressively); network devices would remain accessible for administration of patches, plugs, and ACLs required to fully neutralize the specific attack.

WAN links also would be protected: VoIP, critical data, and even best-effort flows would continue to receive priority over any traffic marked down to Scavenger/CS1. This is a huge advantage because generally WAN links are the first to be overwhelmed by DoS and worm attacks. The bottom line is that Access-Layer policers significantly mitigate network traffic generated by DoS or worm attacks.

It is important to recognize the distinction between mitigating an attack and preventing it entirely: The strategy being presented does not guarantee that no denial of service or worm attacks ever will happen, but it can reduce the risk and impact that such attacks could have on the network infrastructure.

Principles of QoS Design

The richness of the Cisco QoS toolset allows for a myriad of QoS design and deployment options. However, a few succinct design principles can help simplify strategic QoS designs and lead to an expedited, cohesive, and holistic end-to-end deployment. Some of these design principles are summarized here; others, which are LAN-, WAN- or VPN-specific, are covered in detail in their respective design chapters.

General QoS Design Principles

A good place to begin is to decide which comes first: the cart or the horse. The horse, in this context, serves to pull the cart and is the enabler for this objective. Similarly, QoS technologies are simply the enablers to organizational objectives. Therefore, the way to begin a QoS deployment is not by glossing over the QoS toolset and picking à la carte tools to deploy. In other words, do not enable QoS features simply because they exist. Instead, start from a high level and clearly define the organizational objectives.

Some questions for high-level consideration include the following:

- Is the objective to enable VoIP only?
- Is video also required? If so, what type(s) of video: interactive or streaming?
- Are some applications considered mission critical? If so, what are they?
- Does the organization want to squelch certain types of traffic? If so, what are they?

All traffic classes specified in the QoS Baseline model except one—the Locally-Defined, Mission-Critical Data application class—are determined by objective networking characteristics. These applications, a subset of the Transactional Data class, are selected for a dedicated, preferential class of service because of their significant impact on the organization's main business objectives.

This is usually a highly subjective evaluation that can excite considerable controversy and dispute. An important principle to remember when assigning applications to the Mission-Critical Data class is that as few applications as possible should be assigned to the Locally-Defined Mission-Critical class.

If too many applications are assigned to it, the Mission-Critical Data class will dampen, and possibly even negate, the value of having a separate class (from Transactional Data). For example, if 10 applications are assigned as Transactional Data (because of their interactive, foreground networking characteristics) and all 10 are determined to be classified as Mission-Critical Data, the whole point of a separate class for these applications becomes moot. However, if only one or two of the Transactional Data applications are assigned to the Mission-Critical Data class, the class will prove highly effective.

Related to this point, it is recommended always to seek executive endorsement of the QoS objectives before design and deployment. By its very nature, QoS is a system of managed unfairness and, as such, almost always creates political and organizational repercussions when implemented. To minimize the effects of such nontechnical obstacles to deployment, which could prevent the QoS implementation altogether, it is recommended to address these political and organizational issues as early as possible and to solicit executive endorsement whenever possible.

As stated previously, it is not mandated that enterprises deploy all 11 classes of the QoS Baseline model; this model is designed to be a forward-looking guide for consideration of the many classes of traffic that have unique QoS requirements. Being aware of this model can help bring about a smooth expansion of QoS policies to support additional applications as future requirements arise. However, at the time of QoS deployment, the organization needs to clearly define how many classes of traffic are required to meet the organizational objectives.

This consideration should be tempered with the consideration of how many classes of applications the networking administration team feels comfortable with deploying and supporting. Platform-specific constraints or service-provider constraints also might come into play when arriving at the number of classes of service. At this point, it also would be good to consider a migration strategy to allow the number of classes to be expanded smoothly as future needs arise, as illustrated in Figure 2-9.

Figure 2-9 *Example Strategy for Expanding the Number of Classes of Service over Time*

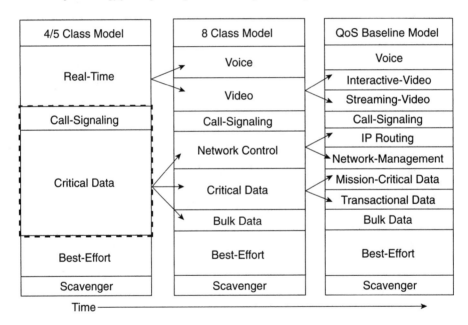

When the number of classes of service has been determined, the details of the required marking, policing, and queuing policies can be addressed. When deciding where to enable such policies, keep in mind that QoS policies always should be performed in hardware instead of software whenever a choice exists.

Cisco IOS routers perform QoS in software, which places incremental loads on the CPU (depending on the complexity and functionality of the policy). Cisco Catalyst switches, on the other hand, perform QoS in dedicated hardware ASICS and, as such, do not tax their main CPUs to administer QoS policies. This allows complex policies to be applied at line rates at even 1-Gbps or 10-Gigabit speeds.

Classification and Marking Principles

When it comes to classifying and marking traffic, an unofficial Differentiated Services design principle is to classify and mark applications as close to their sources as technically and administratively feasible. This principle promotes end-to-end Differentiated Services and per-hop behaviors (PHBs). Sometimes endpoints can be trusted to set CoS and DSCP markings correctly, but, in most cases, it is not a good idea to trust markings that users can set on their PCs (or other similar devices). This is because users easily could abuse provisioned QoS policies if permitted to mark their own traffic. For example, if DSCP EF receives priority services throughout the enterprise, a user easily could configure the PC to mark all traffic to DSCP EF right on the NIC, thus hijacking network-priority queues to service that user's non-real-time traffic. Such abuse easily could ruin the service quality of real-time applications (such as VoIP) throughout the enterprise. For this reason, the clause "as close as . . . *administratively* feasible" is included in the design principle.

Following this rule, it further is recommended to use DSCP markings whenever possible because these are end to end, more granular, and more extensible than Layer 2 markings. Layer 2 markings are lost when media changes (such as at a LAN-to-WAN or VPN edge). An additional constraint to Layer 2 marking is that there is less marking granularity; for example, 802.1Q/p CoS supports only 3 bits (values 0 through 7), as does MPLS EXP. Therefore, only (up to) eight classes of traffic can be supported at Layer 2, and interclass relative priority (such as RFC 2597 assured-forwarding class markdown) is not supported. On the other hand, Layer 3 DSCP markings allow for up to 64 classes of traffic, which is more than enough for most enterprise requirements for the foreseeable future.

Because the line between enterprises and service providers is blurring and the need for interoperability and complementary QoS markings is critical, it is recommended to follow standards-based DSCP PHB markings to ensure interoperability and future expansion. The QoS Baseline marking recommendations are standards based, making it easier for enterprises adopting these markings to interface with service provider classes of service. Network mergers are also easier to manage when standards-based DSCP markings are used, whether these mergers are the result of acquisitions, partnerships, or strategic alliances.

Policing and Markdown Principles

There is little sense in forwarding unwanted traffic only to police and drop it at a subsequent node. This is especially the case when the unwanted traffic is the result of DoS or worm attacks. The overwhelming volumes of traffic that such attacks can create readily can drive network device processors to their maximum levels, causing network outages. Therefore, it is recommended to police traffic flows as close to their sources as possible. This principle applies to legitimate flows also because DoS and worm-generated traffic might be masquerading under legitimate, well-known TCP and UDP ports, causing extreme amounts of traffic to be poured onto the network infrastructure. Such excesses should be monitored at the source and marked down appropriately.

Whenever supported, markdown should be done according to standards-based rules, such as RFC 2597 ("Assured Forwarding PHB Group"). In other words, whenever supported, traffic marked to AFx1 should be marked down to AFx2 or AFx3. For example, in the case of a single-rate policer, excess traffic originally marked AF11 should be marked down to AF12. In the case of a dual-rate policer (as defined in RFC 2698), excess traffic originally marked AF11 should be marked down to AF12, and violating traffic should be marked down further to AF13. Following such markdowns, congestion-management policies, such as DSCP-based WRED, should be configured to drop AFx3 more aggressively than AFx2, which, in turn, is dropped more aggressively than AFx1.

However, at the time of writing, Cisco Catalyst switches do not perform DSCP-based WRED, so this standards-based strategy cannot be implemented fully. As an alternative workaround, single-rate policers can be configured to mark down excess traffic to DSCP CS1 (Scavenger); dual-rate policers can be configured to mark down excess traffic to AFx2, while marking down violating traffic to DSCP CS1. Such workarounds yield an overall similar effect as the standards-based policing model. However, when DSCP-based WRED is supported on all routing and switching platforms, it would be more standards compliant to mark down assured-forwarding classes by RFC 2597 rules.

Queuing and Dropping Principles

Critical applications, such as VoIP, require service guarantees regardless of network conditions. The only way to provide service guarantees is to enable queuing at any node that has the potential for congestion—regardless of how rarely, in fact, this might occur. This principle applies not only to campus-to-WAN or VPN edges, where speed mismatches are most pronounced, but also to campus interlayer links (where oversubscription ratios create the potential for congestion). There is simply no other way to guarantee service levels than to enable queuing wherever a speed mismatch exists.

When provisioning queuing, some best-practice rules of thumb also apply. For example, as discussed previously, the Best-Effort class is the default class for all data traffic. Only if an application has been selected for preferential or deferential treatment is it removed from the default class. Because many enterprises have several hundred, if not thousands of, data applications running over their networks, adequate bandwidth must be provisioned for this class as a whole to handle the sheer volume of applications that default to it. Therefore, it is recommended that at least 25 percent of a link's bandwidth be reserved for the default Best-Effort class.

Another class of traffic that requires special consideration when provisioning queuing is the Real-Time or Strict-Priority class (which corresponds to RFC 3246, "An Expedited Forwarding Per-Hop Behavior"). The amount of bandwidth assigned to the Real-Time queuing class is variable. However, if too much traffic is assigned for strict-priority queuing, the overall effect is a dampening of QoS functionality for non-real-time applications.

The goal of convergence cannot be overemphasized: to enable voice, video, and data to coexist transparently on a single network. When real-time applications (such as Voice or Interactive-Video) dominate a link (especially a WAN/VPN link), data applications will fluctuate significantly in their response times, destroying the transparency of the "converged" network.

Cisco Technical Marketing testing has shown a significant decrease in data application response times when real-time traffic exceeds one-third of a link's bandwidth capacity. Extensive testing and customer deployments have shown that a general best queuing practice is to limit the amount of strict-priority queuing to 33 percent of a link's capacity. This strict-priority queuing rule is a conservative and safe design ratio for merging real-time applications with data applications.

Cisco IOS Software allows the abstraction (and, thus, configuration) of multiple (strict-priority) low-latency queues. In such a multiple-LLQ context, this design principle applies to the sum of all LLQs: They should be within one-third of a link's capacity.

NOTE This strict-priority queuing rule (limit to 33 percent) is simply a best-practice design recommendation; it is not a mandate. In some cases, specific business objectives cannot be met while holding to this recommendation. In such cases, enterprises must provision according to their detailed requirements and constraints. However, it is important to recognize the trade-offs involved with overprovisioning strict-priority traffic with respect to the negative performance impact on response times in non-real-time applications.

Whenever a Scavenger queuing class is enabled, it should be assigned a minimal amount of bandwidth. On some platforms, queuing distinctions between Bulk Data and Scavenger class traffic flows cannot be made because queuing assignments are determined by CoS values, and these applications share the same CoS value of 1. In such cases, the Scavenger/ Bulk Data queuing class can be assigned a bandwidth percentage of 5. If Scavenger and Bulk traffic can be assigned uniquely to different queues, the Scavenger queue should be assigned a bandwidth percentage of 1.

The Real-Time, Best-Effort, and Scavenger classes queuing best-practice principles are illustrated in Figure 12-10.

Figure 2-10 *Real-Time, Best-Effort, and Scavenger Queuing Rules*

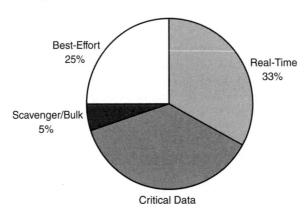

Some platforms support different queuing structures than others. To ensure consistent PHBs, configure consistent queuing policies according to platform capabilities.

For example, on a platform that supports only four queues with CoS-based admission (such as a Catalyst switch), a basic queuing policy could be as follows:

- Real-Time (≤ 33 percent)
- Critical Data
- Best-Effort (≥ 25 percent)
- Scavenger/Bulk(< 5 percent)

However, on a platform that supports a full QoS Baseline queuing model, the queuing policies can be expanded, yet in such a way that they provide consistent servicing to Real-Time, Best-Effort, and Scavenger class traffic. For example, on a platform that supports 11 queues with DSCP-based admission (such as a Cisco IOS router), an advanced queuing policy could be as follows:

- Voice (≤ 18 percent)
- Interactive-Video (≤ 15 percent)
- Internetwork Control
- Call-Signaling
- Mission-Critical Data
- Transactional Data
- Network-Management
- Streaming-Video Control

- Best-Effort (≥ 25 percent)
- Bulk Data (4 percent)
- Scavenger (1 percent)

Figure 2-11 illustrates the interrelationship between these compatible queuing models.

Figure 2-11 *Compatible 4-Class and 11-Class Queuing Models Following Real-Time, Best-Effort, and Scavenger Class Queuing Rules*

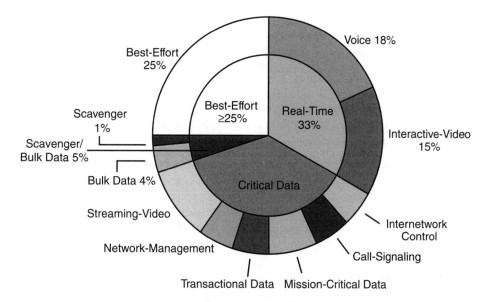

In this manner, traffic will receive compatible queuing at each node, regardless of platform capabilities—which is the overall objective of DiffServ per-hop behavior definitions.

Whenever supported, it is recommended to enable WRED (preferably DSCP-based WRED) on all TCP flows. In this manner, WRED congestion avoidance will prevent TCP global synchronization and will increase overall throughput and link efficiency. Enabling WRED on UDP flows is optional.

DoS and Worm Mitigation Principles

Whenever part of the organization's objectives is to mitigate DoS and worm attacks through Scavenger-class QoS, the following best practices apply.

First, the network administrators need to profile applications to determine what constitutes normal versus abnormal flows, within a 95 percent confidence interval. Thresholds differentiating normal and abnormal flows vary from enterprise to enterprise and from application to application. Caution must be extended not to overscrutinize traffic behavior because this could be time and resource exhaustive and easily could change from one day to the next. Remember, the presented Scavenger-class strategy will not apply a penalty to legitimate traffic flows that exceed thresholds (aside from re-marking); only sustained, abnormal streams generated simultaneously by multiple hosts (highly indicative of DoS and worm attacks) are subject to aggressive dropping, and only after legitimate traffic has been serviced.

To contain such abnormal flows, it is recommended to deploy campus Access-Edge policers to re-mark abnormal traffic to Scavenger (DSCP CS1). Additionally, whenever Catalyst 6500s with Supervisor 720s are deployed in the distribution layer, it is recommended to deploy a second line of policing defense, at the distribution layer via per-user microflow policing.

To complement these re-marking policies, it is necessary to enforce end-to-end Scavenger-class queuing policies, where flows marked as Scavenger will receive a less-than best-effort service whenever congestion occurs.

It is important to note that even when Scavenger-class QoS has been deployed end to end, this strategy only mitigates DoS and worm attacks and does not prevent them or remove them entirely. Therefore, it is critical to overlay security, firewall, intrusion detection, and identity systems, along with Cisco Guard and Cisco Security Agent solutions, on top of the QoS-enabled network infrastructure.

Deployment Principles

After the QoS designs have been finalized, it is vital that the networking team thoroughly understand the QoS features and syntax before enabling features on production networks. Such knowledge is critical for both deployment and troubleshooting QoS-related issues.

Furthermore, it is a general best practice to schedule proof-of-concept (PoC) tests to verify that the hardware and software platforms in production support the required QoS features in combination with all the other features that they currently are running. Remember, in theory, theory and practice are the same. In other words, there is no substitute for testing.

When testing has validated the designs, it is recommended to schedule network downtime to deploy QoS features. Although QoS is required end to end, it does not have to be deployed end to end at a single instance. A pilot network segment can be selected for an initial deployment, and, pending observation, the deployment can be expanded in stages to encompass the entire enterprise. A rollback strategy always is recommended, to address unexpected issues that arise from the QoS deployment.

Summary

This chapter began by reviewing the QoS requirements of voice, video, and data applications.

Voice requires 150-ms one-way, end-to-end (mouth-to-ear) delay; 30 ms of one-way jitter; and no more than 1 percent packet loss. Voice should receive strict-priority servicing, and the amount of priority bandwidth assigned for it should take into account the VoIP codec; the packetization rate; IP, UDP, and RTP headers (compressed or not); and Layer 2 overhead. Additionally, provisioning QoS for IP Telephony requires that a minimal amount of guaranteed bandwidth be allocated to Call-Signaling traffic.

Video comes in two flavors: Interactive-Video and Streaming-Video. Interactive-Video has the same service-level requirements as VoIP because embedded within the video stream is a voice call. Streaming-Video has much laxer requirements because of a high amount of buffering that has been built into the applications.

Control plane requirements, such as provisioning moderate bandwidth guarantees for IP routing protocols and network-management protocols, should not be overlooked.

Data comes all shapes and sizes but generally can be classified into four main classes: Best-Effort (the default class), Bulk Data (noninteractive background flows), Transactional/Interactive (interactive, foreground flows), and Mission-Critical Data. Mission-Critical Data applications are locally defined, meaning that each organization must determine the select few Transactional Data applications that contribute the most significantly to its overall business objectives.

A less-than best-effort Scavenger class of traffic was introduced, and a strategy for using this class for DoS and worm mitigation was presented. Specifically, flows can be monitored at the campus Access-Edge, and out-of-profile flows can be marked down to the Scavenger marking (of DSCP CS1). To complement these policers, queues providing a less-than best-effort Scavenger service during periods of congestion are deployed in the LAN, WAN, and VPN.

The chapter concluded with a set of general best-practice principles relating to QoS planning, classification, marking, policing, queuing, and deployment. These best practices include the following:

- Clearly defining the organization's business objectives to be addressed by QoS
- Selecting an appropriate number of service classes to meet these business objectives
- Soliciting executive endorsement, whenever possible, of the traffic classifications, especially when determining any mission-critical applications
- Performing QoS functions in (Catalyst switch) hardware instead of (Cisco IOS router) software, whenever possible
- Classifying traffic as close to the source as administratively feasible, preferably at Layer 3 with standards-based DSCP markings

- Policing traffic as close to the source as possible, following standards-based rules (such as RFC 2597, "Assured Forwarding Markdown"), whenever possible

- Provisioning at least one-quarter of a link to service Best-Effort traffic

- Provisioning no more than one-third of a link to service real-time and strict-priority traffic

- Provisioning a less-than best-effort Scavenger queue, which should be assigned as low of a bandwidth allocation as possible

- Understanding and thoroughly testing desired QoS features in conjunction with features already enabled on the production network

- Deploying end-to-end QoS in stages during scheduled network downtime, with a recommended rollback strategy

Further Reading

Standards:

- RFC 791, "Internet Protocol Specification": http://www.ietf.org/rfc/rfc791.

- RFC 2474, "Definition of the Differentiated Services Field (DS Field) in the IPv4 and IPv6 Headers": http://www.ietf.org/rfc/rfc2474.

- RFC 2597, "Assured Forwarding PHB Group": http://www.ietf.org/rfc/rfc2597.

- RFC 2697, "A Single Rate Three Color Marker": http://www.ietf.org/rfc/rfc2697.

- RFC 2698, "A Two Rate Three Color Marker": http://www.ietf.org/rfc/rfc2698.

- RFC 3168, "The Addition of Explicit Congestion Notification (ECN) to IP": http://www.ietf.org/rfc/rfc3168.

- RFC 3246, "An Expedited Forwarding PHB (Per-Hop Behavior)": http://www.ietf.org/rfc/rfc3246.

Cisco documentation:

- Cisco IOS QoS Configuration Guide, Cisco IOS version 12.3: http://www.cisco.com/univercd/cc/td/doc/product/software/ios123/123cgcr/qos_vcg.htm.

- Cisco IOS Configuration Guide—Configuring Data Link Switching Plus, Cisco IOS version 12.3: http://www.cisco.com/univercd/cc/td/doc/product/software/ios122/122cgcr/fibm_c/bcfpart2/bcfdlsw.htm.

- Understanding how routing updates and Layer 2 control packets are queued on an interface with a QoS service policy (PAK_priority): http://www.cisco.com/warp/public/105/rtgupdates.html.

When Layer 3 or 4 parameters are insufficient to positively identify an application, NBAR is a viable alternative solution.

NBAR is the most sophisticated classifier in the Cisco IOS tool suite. NBAR can recognize packets on a complex combination of fields and attributes. However, it is important to recognize that NBAR is merely a *classifier*, nothing more. NBAR can identify packets that belong to a certain traffic stream by performing deep-packet inspection, but it is up to the policy map to determine what should be done with these packets after they have been identified (in other words, whether they should be marked, policed, dropped, and so on).

NBAR's deep-packet classification examines the data payload of stateless protocols and identifies application layer protocols by matching them against a Protocol Description Language Module (PDLM), which is essentially an application signature. Cisco IOS software supports 98 protocols via PDLMs as of IOS 12.3. Furthermore, because PDLMs are modular, they can be added to a system without requiring a Cisco IOS upgrade.

NBAR is dependent on Cisco Express Forwarding (CEF) and performs deep-packet classification only on the first packet of a packet stream. The remainder of the packets belonging to the stream then are CEF-switched. CEF is one of the packet-forwarding mechanisms within the Cisco IOS Software; there are also fast- and process-switching forwarding paths.

NOTE   The NBAR classifier is triggered by the **match protocol** command within a class map definition. It is a more CPU-intensive classifier than classifiers that match traffic by DSCPs or ACLs.

NBAR Protocol Classification

NBAR can classify packets based on Layer 4 through Layer 7 protocols, which dynamically assign TCP/UDP ports. By looking beyond the TCP/UDP port numbers of a packet (known as *subport classification*), NBAR examines the packet payload itself and classifies packets on the payload content, such as transaction identifiers, message types, or other similar data. For example, HTTP traffic can be classified by URLs or Multipurpose Internet Mail Extension (MIME) types using regular expressions within the CLI.

NBAR also can classify Citrix Independent Computing Architecture (ICA) traffic and can perform subport classification of Citrix traffic based on Citrix published applications. Requests from Citrix ICA clients can be monitored for a published application that is destined for a Citrix ICA master browser. After receiving the client requests to the published

First-True-Match logic that policy maps employ. If the sequence of these two statements were reversed, the policy would work very differently: No traffic would ever show against the VOICE class because both voice and fax-relay traffic would be matched on DSCP EF and would be assigned to the FAX-RELAY class. All other traffic would fall into the implicit class-default class. Figure 3-2 shows the decision hierarchy for each packet examined by the policy map VOICE-AND-FAX.

Figure 3-2 *Classification Decisions by Policy Map VOICE-AND-FAX*

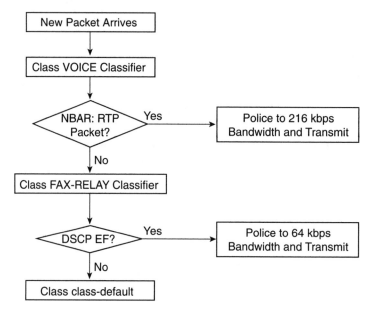

It is important to note that class map and policy map names (similar to ACL names) are case sensitive to the Cisco IOS. Thus, **class-map foo** is different from **class-map Foo**, which is different from **class-map FOO**. Therefore, it is very important that the class map names and cases match exactly to the class names called out under policy maps. In this book, such names are shown in uppercase letters to clearly distinguish them from Cisco IOS commands. This is entirely an administrative preference.

Network-Based Application Recognition

Although the majority of data applications can be identified using Layer 3 or Layer 4 criteria (such as discrete IP addresses or well-known TCP/UDP ports), some applications cannot be identified by such criteria alone. This might be because of legacy limitations, but more likely it is by deliberate design. For example, peer-to-peer media-sharing applications (such as KaZaa, Morpheus, and Napster) deliberately negotiate ports dynamically with the objective of penetrating firewalls.

marked to DSCP EF at their respective sources. Therefore, the question is how to treat these two traffic types differently because they are marked the same.

The policy map shown in Example 3-2 is unusual, although valid, in two respects:

- **Multiple priority classes**—Both voice and fax traffic must be prioritized (as covered in Chapter 5, "Congestion-Management Tools," a later chapter on queuing). Typically, both these traffic classes would be handled by a single class definition, but in this case, the desire was to control strictly the bandwidth used by each class of traffic. This required two different priority class definitions.

- **Police statements in the priority classes**—Normally, priority class traffic is not explicitly policed, as IOS has an implicit policer, which is discussed in additional detail in Chapter 5, "Congestion-Management Tools," to prevent the starvation of other queues. However, this example shows how a service-level agreement (SLA) can be strictly enforced so that different classes of traffic cannot exceed the agreed-upon bandwidth allocation.

Example 3-2 *Class Definition Sequence in Policy Map*

```
Router#show run
class-map match-all FAX-RELAY
 match ip dscp ef
class-map match-all VOICE
 match protocol rtp audio
!
policy-map VOICE-AND-FAX
 class VOICE
  priority 216
  police cir 216000
 class FAX-RELAY
  priority 64
  police cir 64000
 class class-default
  fair-queue
```

The policy map VOICE-AND-FAX provides the answer through careful ordering of the classes within it. First, all packets are checked against the class VOICE, which performs Network-Based Application Recognition (NBAR) classification to identify whether the traffic is Real-Time Protocol audio (in other words, voice). Only traffic that fails this examination is checked against the second class under the policy map (the class FAX-RELAY).

The class FAX-RELAY checks whether the packet's DSCP value is EF. Because only two types of traffic can have DSCP values of EF (voice and fax-relay) and voice has already been filtered out, any remaining traffic that matches these criteria must be fax-relay. Fax-relay traffic then is administratively assigned a slightly different treatment. The details of the treatment in this example are irrelevant. The emphasis is on how the ordering of the classes within policy maps can offer more granular classification options because of the

Modular QoS Command-Line Interface Class Maps

The principle tool for QoS classification within Cisco IOS today is *modular QoS CLI* (MQC)–based class maps. Class maps identify traffic flows using a wide array of filtering criteria, which are individually defined by **match** statements within the class map. Multiple **match** statements can be defined under a single class map. When multiple match statements are used, the class map can be specified as follows:

- **match-all**—A logical AND operand, meaning that *all* **match** statements must be true at the same time for the class map condition to be true

- **match-any**—A logical OR operand, meaning that *any* of the **match** statements can be true for the class map condition to be true

Including **match-any** or **match-all** when defining a class map is optional, but it is important to note that if neither is specified, the default behavior is **match-all**. For example, if **class-map FOO** is entered, the Cisco IOS parser actually expands this to **class-map match-all FOO** within the configuration. Example 3-1 illustrates the matching criteria available within MQC class-maps.

Example 3-1   **match-all** *as Default Cisco IOS Behavior*

```
Router(config) class-map FOO
Router(config-cmap)#match ?
  access-group        Access group
  any                 Any packets
  class-map           Class map
  cos                 IEEE 802.1Q/ISL class of service/user priority values
  destination-address Destination address
  input-interface     Select an input interface to match
  ip                  IP specific values
  mpls                Multi Protocol Label Switching specific values
  not                 Negate this match result
  protocol            Protocol
  qos-group           Qos-group
  source-address      Source address
```

Although the sequence in which class maps are defined within the configuration is unimportant, the sequence of classes within a *policy map* is important. This is because, as with access list (ACL) logic, policy maps apply the *First-True-Match rule*, meaning that the classes examine a packet until a match is found. When a match is found, the classification process finishes and no further class maps are checked. If no matches are found, the packet ends up in an implicit class default, which essentially means "everything else."

For example, consider the service policy shown in Example 3-2 that illustrates the classification of two classes of traffic: VOICE for voice traffic and FAX-RELAY for fax traffic. The sequence of **class-map FAX-RELAY** and **class-map VOICE** within the global configuration does not matter to the classification functionality; these can be entered in any order. The assumption in this example is that both voice traffic and fax-relay traffic are

Classification Tools

Classification tools examine any of the following criteria to identify a flow and assign it for preferential or deferential treatment:

- **Layer 1 (L1) parameters**—Physical interface, subinterface, PVC, or port
- **Layer 2 (L2) parameters**—MAC address, 802.1Q/p class of service (CoS) bits, VLAN identification, experimental bits (MPLS EXP), ATM cell loss priority (CLP), and Frame Relay discard eligible (DE) bits
- **Layer 3 (L3) parameters**—IP Precedence, DiffServ code point (DSCP), source/destination IP address
- **Layer 4 (L4) parameters**—TCP or User Datagram Protocol (UDP) ports
- **Layer 7 (L7) parameters**—Application signatures and uniform resource locators (URLs) in packet headers or payload

Figure 3-1 shows the progressive depth at which a frame or packet may be examined to make a classification decision. It is not shown to scale because of space limitations.

Figure 3-1 *Frame/Packet Classification Fields*

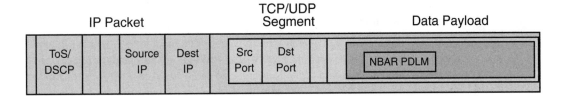

NOTE	Figure 3-1 is intended to represent only the comparisons of data-link, network, transport, and application layer QoS filtering criteria and, therefore, many fields have been omitted and the diagram is not to scale.

Only after traffic is positively identified can policies be applied to it. Therefore, best-practice design recommendations are to identify and mark traffic (with DSCP values) as close to the source of the traffic as possible, typically in the wiring closet or within the trusted devices (such as IP phones) themselves. If markings and trusts are set correctly, the intermediate hops do not have to repeat the same in-depth classification. Instead, they can administer QoS policies (such as scheduling) based on the previously set markings, which appear close to the beginning of the frame or packet.

Classification and Marking Tools

The first step in defining a Quality-of-Service (QoS) policy is to identify the traffic that is to be treated differently (either preferentially or differentially). This is accomplished through classification and marking.

Although the terms *classification* and *marking* often are used interchangeably, the terms represent distinct and different actions that work together but also can be used independently.

- *Classification* tools sort packets into different traffic types, to which different policies then can be applied. The classification of packets normally occurs at each node in the network but is not required to be done everywhere. Classification of packets can happen without marking.

- *Marking* (or re-marking) typically establishes a trust boundary on which scheduling tools later depend. The network edge where markings are accepted (or rejected) is referred to as the *trust-boundary*. Marking also can be used in other locations in the network, as necessary, and is not always used solely for purposes of classification.

As with the general terms *classification* and *marking*, there is a difference in the action that the actual tools, named classifiers and markers, take on traffic.

- **Classifiers**—Inspect one or more fields in a packet to identify the type of traffic that the packet is carrying. After being identified, the traffic is directed to the applicable policy-enforcement mechanism for that traffic type, where it receives predefined treatment (either preferential or deferential). Such treatment can include marking and re-marking, queuing, policing, shaping, or any combination of these (and other) actions.

- **Markers**—Write a field within the packet, frame, cell, or label to preserve the classification decision that was reached at the trust boundary. By marking traffic at the trust boundary edge, subsequent nodes do not have to perform the same in-depth classification and analysis to determine how to treat the packet.

This chapter includes the following topics:

- Classification and marking

- Discussion of Layer 2 and Layer 3 marking fields and how these translate to each other

- Packet marking in different technologies, such as IP, MPLS, ATM, Frame Relay, and Ethernet

- Class-based classification and marking techniques and other mechanisms to achieve these results

QoS Toolset

Part II of this book provides context for the design chapters that follow by presenting a brief overview of Cisco QoS tools. Particular emphasis is placed on tool-specific idiosyncrasies and tool-interaction caveats (many of which are not included in IOS documentation). A basic understanding and familiarity of these QoS tools is assumed.

The chapters in this part of the book are as follows:

application, the Citrix ICA master browser directs the client to the server with the most available memory. The Citrix ICA client then connects to this Citrix ICA server for the application.

A summary of protocols that NBAR can use for classification follows. Because new capabilities are added all the time, this is not an exhaustive list. Not all NBAR classification involves stateful inspection, and not all **match protocol** commands trigger NBAR.

Statefully inspected protocols include the following:

FTP	Oracle SQL*NET
Exchange	SunRPC
HTTP (URL and MIME)	TFTP
NetShow	StreamWorks
RealAudio	VDOLive
r-commands	

Static protocols include the following:

Exterior Gateway Protocol (EGP)	NNTP
Generic Routing Encapsulation (GRE)	Notes
ICMP	Network Time Protocol (NTP)
IPinIP	PCAnywhere
IPSec	POP3
EIGRP	Point-to-Point Tunneling Protocol (PPTP)
BGP	RIP
CU-SeeMe	Resource Reservation Protocol (RSVP)
DHCP/BOOTP	Secure FTP (SFTP)
Domain Name System (DNS)	SHTTP
Finger	SIMAP
Gopher	SIRC
HTTP	SLDAP
Secure HTTP (HTTP)	SNNTP
Internet Message Access Protocol (IMPA)	SMTP
Internet Relay Chat (IRC)	SNMP
Kerberos	SOCKS
Layer 2 Tunnel Protocol (L2TP)	SPOP3
LDAP	Secure Shell (SSH)
MS-PPTP	Secure Telnet (STELNET)
MS-SQLServer	Syslog
NetBIOS	Telnet
Network File System (NFS)	X Window System

Example 3-3 shows the CLI of some NBAR classification configurations.

Example 3-3 *NBAR Classification Examples*

```
Router(config)# class-map match-any ERP
Router(config-cmap)# match protocol sqlnet
Router(config-cmap)# match protocol ftp
Router(config-cmap)# match protocol telnet

Router(config)# class-map match-any AUDIO-VIDEO
Router(config-cmap)# match protocol http mime "*/audio/*"
Router(config-cmap)# match protocol http mime "*/video/*"

Router(config)# class-map match-any WEB-IMAGES
Router(config-cmap)# match protocol http url "*.gif"
Router(config-cmap)# match protocol http url "*.jpg|*.jpeg"
```

Example 3-3 defines three different class maps. The first one, the class map ERP, instructs the classifier (NBAR) to pick traffic of any of the protocols listed in the subsequent statements, which include SQLNET, FTP, or Telnet traffic. In the class map AUDIO-VIDEO, the classifier is looking for MIME traffic of particular types—audio and video, in this case. The last class map, WEB-IMAGES, is filtering out HTTP traffic for picture (GIF or JPEG) content.

In addition to classification, NBAR can perform protocol discovery using the sniffing capabilities of its classification engine. Even if NBAR is not required for QoS policy classification, its protocol-discovery mode can provide valuable information about traffic present on the network and how much bandwidth each traffic type is using. Such information can be used in bandwidth provisioning exercises or for capacity planning. An example output of NBAR's protocol-discovery mode is shown in Example 3-4.

Example 3-4 *NBAR Protocol Discovery*

```
Router#show ip nbar protocol-discovery stats byte-rate FastEthernet1/0

                        Input                Output
       Protocol      30second bit rate    30second bit rate
                          (bps)                (bps)
    --------------    -----------------    -----------------
       telnet             368000                0
       ftp                163000                0
       http               163000                0
       unknown            614000                0
       Total             1308000                0
```

NBAR RTP Payload Classification

Stateful identification of real-time audio and video traffic can differentiate and classify traffic on the basis of audio and video codec fields within the Real-Time Transport Protocol (RTP) payload of the packet. Although most voice classification is done in coarser granularity (by merely separating signaling traffic from speech path [media] traffic) and network access often is allowed or denied based on the originating port or IP address, sometimes traffic is desired to be classified by codec. One instance in which this is useful is at the trust boundary between an enterprise and a service provider network where the SLA is, for example, for G.729 and G.711 traffic only. In this instance, NBAR can be used to ensure that voice calls of other codecs are not allowed onto the network.

The same mechanisms can be used if codecs of different bandwidth needs must be filtered out, for example, to ensure that call admission control (CAC) in the network is not broken. In this case, low-bandwidth codecs such as G.729 and G.723 can be separated from G.711 traffic.

Filtering traffic by codec can be done by inspecting the payload type (PT) field within the RTP header, as defined by the following:

- RFC 1889: "RTP: A Transport Protocol for Real-Time Applications"
- RFC 1890: "RTP Profile for Audio and Video Conferences with Minimal Control"

The command to configure this is as follows:

```
match protocol rtp [audio | video | payload-type payload-string]
```

Here, the following is true:

- **audio**—Specifies matching by payload-type values 0 to 23
- **video**—Specifies matching by payload-type values 24 to 33
- **payload-type**—Specifies matching by payload-type value, for more granular matching

For example, the following command instructs NBAR to match RTP traffic with the payload types 0, 1, 4, 5, 6, 7, 8, 9, 10, 11, 12, 13, 14, 15, 16, 17, 18, or 64:

```
match protocol rtp payload-type "0, 1, 4 - 0x10, 10001b - 10010b, 64"
```

As shown in the example, the parameters to the **match protocol** statement can be given in decimal, hexadecimal (the 0x notation), or binary (the 10001b notation) numbers. Individual numbers separated by commas can be specified, and ranges of numbers can be used, as in the case of 4 – 0x10, which means a decimal value of 4 to a hexadecimal value of 10 (which equates to a decimal value of 16). Therefore, all RTP payload types between 4 and 16 are matched for this part of the statement. Similarly, the binary range 10001b to 10010b equates to 17 to 18 in decimal.

Marking Tools

The main marking tools used today are class-based marking and marking using class-based policing. Some legacy marking techniques include committed access rate (CAR) and policy-based routing (PBR). Voice gateway packet marking is another option for IP telephony applications.

Class-Based Marking

Class-based marking, introduced in Cisco IOS Software Release 12.1(2)T, is an MQC-based syntax that uses the **set** command within a policy map to mark packets, frames, cells, or labels. Class-based marking was CEF dependent in early Cisco IOS releases (just after its introduction), but this limitation was listed in subsequent releases soon afterward. If you are using one of the initial releases, **ip cef** must be enabled in the global configuration before using **set** commands.

Example 3-5   *Class-Based Marking Options*

```
Router(config)#policy-map CB-MARKING
Router(config-pmap)#class FOO
Router(config-pmap-c)#set ?
  atm-clp        Set ATM CLP bit to 1
  cos            Set IEEE 802.1Q/ISL class of service/user priority
  discard-class  Discard behavior identifier
  dscp           Set DSCP in IP(v4) and IPv6 packets
  fr-de          Set FR DE bit to 1
  ip             Set IP specific values
  mpls           Set MPLS specific values
  precedence     Set precedence in IP(v4) and IPv6 packets
  qos-group      Set QoS Group
```

It is important to remember that class-based marking occurs *after* classification of the packet (in other words, **set** happens after the match criteria). Thus, if used on an output policy, the packet marking applied can be used by the next-hop node to classify the packet but cannot be used on *this* node for classification purposes. On the other hand, if class-based marking is used on an ingress interface as an input policy, the marking applied to the packet can be used on the same device on its egress interface for classification purposes.

Another point to note for output policies is that both classification and marking can happen *after* tunnel encapsulation, depending on where the service policy is attached. Therefore, if a policy is attached to a GRE or IPSec tunnel interface, the marking is applied to the original inner packet header. In most cases, this marking automatically is copied to the tunnel header. On the other hand, if the policy is attached to the physical interface, only the tunnel header (the outer header) is marked and the inner packet header is left unchanged.

As an alternative, QoS preclassification, discussed later in this chapter in the section titled "Layer 3 Tunnel Marking Tools," can be used to ensure that classification of the packet happens on the inner packet header and not the tunnel header values.

Class-Based Policing

Policing and other rate-limiting tools (which are discussed in more detail in Chapter 4, "Policing and Shaping Tools") constitute one of the ways that packets can be marked. Instead of just marking every packet of a certain type as a particular value, a policer generally can re-mark (or even drop) packets that violate an SLA. The following command shows the syntax for a rate-limiter that transmits packets if they conform to a specified rate, re-marks packets if they exceed the rate, and drops packets if they violate the rate.

```
police cir 1000000 bc 1000 pir 1000000 be 1000 conform-action transmit
exceed-action set-clp-transmit violate-action drop
```

Class-based policing can set the IP Precedence, DSCP, MPLS EXP, Frame Relay DE, or ATM CLP of a packet based on rate-limiting measurements, as shown in Example 3-6.

Example 3-6 *Re-Marking Options for the Class-Based Policer*

```
Router(config)#policy-map CB-POLICING
Router(config-pmap)#class FOO
lab-2691(config-pmap-c)#police 8000 conform-action ?
  drop                               drop packet
  exceed-action                      action when rate is within conform and
                                     conform + exceed burst
  set-clp-transmit                   set atm clp and send it
  set-discard-class-transmit         set discard-class and send it
  set-dscp-transmit                  set dscp and send it
  set-frde-transmit                  set FR DE and send it
  set-mpls-exp-imposition-transmit   set exp at tag imposition and send it
  set-mpls-exp-topmost-transmit      set exp on topmost label and send it
  set-prec-transmit                  rewrite packet precedence and send it
  set-qos-transmit                   set qos-group and send it
  transmit                           transmit packet
```

Committed Access Rate

As with class-based policing, committed access rate (CAR) can be used to set or change packet markings. However, CAR is an older Cisco IOS policer tool that generally is not integrated with the MQC syntax and can yield undesirable results if used in conjunction with service policies. Therefore, CAR is no longer a recommended policer.

Policy-Based Routing

Policy-based routing (PBR) also is an older, non-MQC tool that can perform limited traffic marking. Although packet marking is not the major function of PBR, it can be used for writing IP Precedence for packets that match specific criteria.

Voice Gateway Packet Marking

For voice traffic originating on a Cisco voice gateway router, H.323, Media Gateway Control Protocol (MGCP), and Session Initiation Protocol (SIP) traffic can be marked by the source gateway. For a long time, only IP Precedence marking was available for VoIP dial peers, and this only for media (voice) packets. In early releases, ACLs were required to mark call-signaling packets in conjunction with class-based marking.

Cisco IOS Software Release 12.2(2)T introduced the capability to mark voice-sourced packets on the voice gateway with DSCPs, together with the capability to mark signaling packets separate from media packets and to mark voice traffic that did not use dial peers (such as MGCP). The following commands were introduced as part of the simplification of QoS. They are used for marking the voice traffic at its source, which is more efficient and easier to manage than manually marking such traffic on the nearest network edge.

H.323 and SIP use a VoIP dial peer command to mark signaling or media packets:

```
ip qos dscp [af11-af43 | cs1-cs7 | default | ef | num_0-63] [media | signaling]
```

MGCP uses a global gateway command to mark signaling or media packets:

```
mgcp ip-tos [rtp | signaling] precedence [0-7]
mgcp ip qos dscp [af11-af43 | cs1-cs7 | default | ef | num_0-63] [media | signaling]
```

Another move toward simplification in Cisco IOS Software Release 12.2(2)T was to mark voice and call signaling by default with the appropriate DSCPs. This renders explicit marking unnecessary unless markings other than the recommended values are desired.

Voice gateway packet-marking features are detailed in Table 3-1.

Table 3-1   *Voice Gateway Packet Marking Feature Summary by Cisco IOS Release*

Cisco IOS Release	Protocol	QoS Marking Tools	IP P	DSCP	Default Marking
Up to 12.1.5T and 12.2 mainline	SIP, H.323	Dial peer for media PBR, ACL, CB marking for signaling	Yes	Dial peer, PBR: No CB marking: Yes	Media: 0 Signaling: 0
12.2.2T and later	SIP, H.323	Dial peer for media and signaling marking	Yes	Yes	Media: 0 Signaling: 0
12.1.5XM and 12.2.2T and later	MGCP	**mgcp ip tos** for media and signaling	Yes	No	Media: 5 Signaling: 3
12.2.11T and later	SIP, H.323	Dial peer for media and signaling marking	Yes	Yes	Media: 5, EF Signaling: 3, AF31
12.2.11T and later	MGCP	**mgcp ip qos dscp** for media and signaling	Yes	Yes	Media: 5, EF Signaling: 3, AF31

At the same time, changes were made to the Cisco IP phones and Cisco CallManager to mark, by default, voice media and signaling packets sourced by these devices. The default markings are listed in Table 3-2.

Table 3-2   *IP Phone and Cisco CallManager Default Voice and Signaling Marking Summary*

	DSCP	IPP	802.1Q/p CoS
Media	EF	5	5
Signaling	AF31 or CS3	3	3

Layer 2 Marking Fields

Several cell, frame, or packet fields can be used to carry markings, including the following:

- **Layer 2 marking fields**—802.1Q/p CoS bits, MPLS EXP, ATM CLP, and Frame Relay DE bits
- **Layer 3 marking fields**—IP Precedence or DSCP

Because Cisco Catalyst switches perform scheduling based on Layer 2 802.1Q/p CoS markings, it is important that Ethernet frames be correctly marked in campus or branch LANs. However, Layer 2 markings (Ethernet or otherwise) are seldom of end-to-end significance. This is because Layer 2 markings are lost whenever the Layer 2 media changes (for example, from Ethernet to WAN media). In addition, care should be taken that Layer 2 markings are translated to and from Layer 3 markings to ensure consistent end-to-end QoS for the frame or packet, regardless of where it might travel in the network.

Ethernet 802.1Q/p

Ethernet frames can be marked with their relative importance at Layer 2 by setting the 802.1p User Priority bits (CoS) of the 802.1Q header, as shown in Figure 3-3.

Figure 3-3   *Ethernet Frame—802.1Q/p CoS Field*

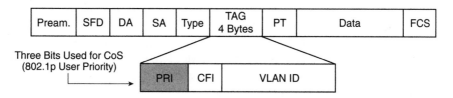

Only 3 bits are available for 802.1p marking. Therefore, only eight classes of service (0 through 7) can be marked on Layer 2 Ethernet frames. These CoS values are identical to IP Precedence values and typically are assigned according to Table 3-3.

Table 3-3 *CoS/IP Precedence Values by Application Types*

CoS Value	Application
7	Reserved
6	Reserved
5	Voice
4	Videoconferencing
3	Call signaling
2	High-priority data
1	Medium-priority data
0	Best-effort data

The possible values of the 802.1Q/p CoS bits are the same as those for IP Precedence. Because the field length is the same, IP Precedence can readily be mapped one to one into and out of 802.1Q/p CoS values. However, DSCP values (which are 6 bits) cannot be maintained at the same granularity when mapped into and out of 802.1Q/p CoS values because some information is lost in the translations.

Ethernet 802.1Q Tunnels

The Cisco Catalyst 3550 switches offer an 802.1Q tunneling feature that enables service providers to provide Layer 2 VPN tunnels by double-tagging Ethernet frames. As a tunneling technology, this encapsulates traffic from multiple VLANs of one customer with a single service provider tag. It preserves the customer VLAN tag over the service provider network so that the service provider can offer a large number of VLANs to many customers.

Because of the double-tagging of Ethernet frames in 802.1Q tunneling, the CoS value of the inner frame is not visible to QoS features in the service provider network. Because the CoS value from the inner frame currently is not copied to the outer frame when the tunnel is entered, the only form of QoS that the service provider can provide for customer traffic is QoS on the ingress port, as shown in Example 3-7 (for a Cisco 3550 switch).

Example 3-7 *Setting QoS on an Ingress Port of Cisco 3550 Switch*

```
Switchport(config)#interface fastethernet0/1
Switchport(config-if)#mls qos cos 5
! Sets 802.1Q CoS to 5 on outer frame
Switchport(config-if)#mls qos cos override
! Overrides any existing CoS value on the outer frame
```

Layer 2 protocol packets can be given high priority by using the **l2protocol-tunnel cos** global command.

Frame-Relay Discard Eligible Bit

The Frame Relay DE bit in the address field of a Frame Relay frame is used to indicate which packets are less important and, therefore, eligible to be dropped before others if congestion occurs within a Frame Relay cloud. As its name implies, the Frame Relay DE bit is a single bit that can represent only one of two settings: 0 or 1. If congestion occurs in a Frame Relay network, frames with the DE bit set at 1 are discarded before frames with the DE bit set at 0.

Traditionally, Cisco IOS routers could not control the Frame Relay DE bit. The default Frame Relay DE setting was 0, and only the Frame Relay switch on the service provider network entry point could set this bit to 1 if the CIR was violated. However, the class-based marking feature was enhanced in Cisco IOS Software Release 12.2(2)T to allow the router to control this bit; it provided the option of setting the bit to 1 before traffic exits the router, and it supported the capability to read the bit upon traffic ingress. Therefore, although the Frame Relay DE bit is a fairly crude marking option, it can be used in a Frame Relay network to indicate high-priority traffic (DE bit 0, the default value) and lower-priority traffic (DE bit 1), which can be dropped should congestion occur. The following is an example of how the Frame Relay DE bit can be set with class-based marking on traffic that previously was identified as out-of-contract.

NOTE   In older Cisco IOS releases, class-based marking is dependent on CEF. Therefore, whenever MQC **set** commands are to be used, **ip cef** already must be enabled within the configuration. In later Cisco IOS releases, this restriction has been lifted.

Example 3-8 shows how the Frame Relay DE bit can be set inside a service policy.

Example 3-8 *Setting the Frame Relay DE Bit*

```
Router#show run
policy-map SET-FR-DE
 class OUT-OF-SLA
  set fr-de
 class class-default
  fair-queue
```

ATM Cell-Loss Priority Bit

The purpose of the ATM CLP bit is exactly the same as that of the Frame Relay DE bit. It is a binary field with two values: 0 (the default), which indicates higher-priority traffic, and 1, for cells carrying lower-priority traffic that is eligible to be dropped if congestion is encountered.

Although the capability to set the CLP bit has been available in a policy map since Cisco IOS Software Release 12.1.5T with the introduction of class-based marking, it is important to note that not all ATM interface drivers allow this capability. The Cisco 7200 ATM port adapters (PAs) have long had this capability. The Cisco 2600/3600/3700 ATM interfaces implemented this capability in Cisco IOS Software Release 12.2.1(1)T, and the digital sub-scriber line (DSL) interfaces (ADSL and G.SHDSL) require Cisco IOS Software Release 12.2.8YN or later to achieve this feature. Example 3-9 shows how the ATM CLP bit can be set with class-based marking on traffic that previously was identified as out-of-contract.

Example 3-9 *Marking with ATM-CLP*

```
Router# show run
policy-map SET-ATM-CLP
 class OUT-OF-SLA
  set atm-clp
 class class-default
  fair-queue
```

MPLS Experimental Bits

MPLS is a tunneling technology that envelops an IP packet with an MPLS label that has its own field definitions for routing and QoS. More than one MPLS label can be used to envelop a packet. Typically, two labels are used in most MPLS VPN scenarios. In some scenarios, three labels are used. MPLS labels contain 3 bits for CoS marking. These bits are referred to as the MPLS EXP bits.

The possible values of the MPLS EXP bits for CoS are the same as those for 802.1Q/p CoS and IP Precedence. Because of the same length translations (3 bits to/from 6 bits) explained earlier for 802.1Q/p CoS, IP Precedence (which are 3 bits) readily can be mapped into and out of MPLS EXP values, but DSCP values (which are 6 bits) cannot be maintained at the same granularity. Figure 3-4 shows the MPLS EXP bits within an MPLS label.

As of Cisco IOS Software Release 12.1(5)T, the MPLS EXP bits can be read (**match** command within a class map) and written (**set** command within a policy map) using MQC. When a packet enters the MPLS network at the provider edge (PE) router, the IP Precedence of the packet (by default) automatically is copied to the MPLS EXP field in the MPLS header. No explicit action is typically necessary to mark MPLS EXP values, unless the values require re-marking because of administrative policies.

In theory, upon exiting the MPLS network, the original IP packet re-emerges unchanged with its IP header type of service (ToS) field intact. Again, no explicit action needs to be taken unless the value requires re-marking. While inside the MPLS network, the packet's ToS field (IP Precedence or DSCP) is irrelevant because the MPLS EXP bits are used to determine the QoS treatment of the packet within the MPLS cloud, as shown in Figure 3-5.

Figure 3-4   *MPLS EXP Bits Within an MPLS Label*

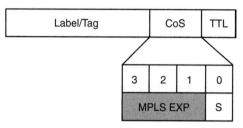

Label/Tag: 20 Bits
MPLS Experimental (CoS): 3 Bits
Bottom of Stack Indicator (S): 1 Bit
Time-to-Live (TTL): 8 bits

Figure 3-5   *Relationship of IP and MPLS Packet Marking*

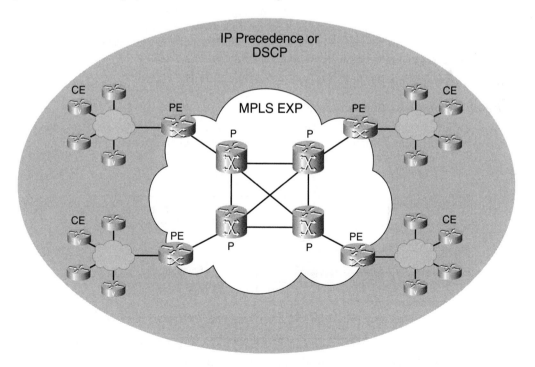

In MPLS tunneling scenarios (further discussed in Chapter 16, "IPSec VPN QoS Design"), there can be multiple MPLS headers on a packet. To accommodate marking of all or some of these headers, there are two options on the **set mpls experimental** command:

- **set mpls experimental imposition**—Sets a specific value on *all* labels that are pushed onto the packet

- **set mpls experimental topmost**—Sets a specific value *only* on the topmost MPLS label on the packet

In practice, however, some service providers currently re-mark the IP Precedence or ToS fields of packets traversing their MPLS Virtual Private Networks (VPN) to enforce SLAs. Three main tunneling modes are used for mapping Layer 3 (IP Precedence/DSCP) markings to and from MPLS EXP values: uniform mode, short-pipe mode, and pipe mode. These modes are discussed in detail in Chapter 16.

Layer 3 Marking Fields

Layer 3 packet marking with IP Precedence and DSCPs is the most widely deployed marking option because Layer 3 packet markings have end-to-end network significance and easily can be translated to the Layer 2 frame markings previously discussed.

As with Layer 2 tunneling, Layer 3 tunneling technologies pose a challenge in preserving packet markings by enveloping the packet with a new header/packet. Some technologies automatically copy the inner packet ToS field to the outer header packet, whereas others do not.

IP Type of Service and IP Precedence

The second byte in an IPv4 packet is the type of service (ToS) byte. The first 3 bits (by themselves) are referred to as the IP Precedence bits, as shown in Figure 3-6.

Figure 3-6 *IPv4 Type of Service Byte (IP Precedence Bits and DSCP)*

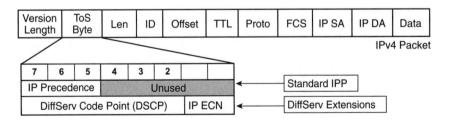

The IP Precedence bits, similar to the 802.1Q/p CoS bits and the MPLS EXP bits, allow for only eight values of marking (0 through 7). Because values 6 and 7 generally are reserved for network control traffic (such as routing) and value 0 is the default marking value, really only five remaining values can be used to differentiate non-best-effort traffic. Of these five remaining values, however, the following is true:

- IP Precedence value 5 is recommended for voice.
- IP Precedence value 4 is shared by videoconferencing and streaming video.
- IP Precedence value 3 is recommended for call signaling.

This leaves only two marking values (IP Precedence 1 and 2) available for all data application marking options. Thus, many enterprises find IP Precedence marking to be overly restrictive and favor instead the 6-bit/64-value DSCP marking model.

NOTE	In this book, IP Precedence is viewed as a legacy technology, and all Layer 3 marking recommendations are based on DSCP only (unless specific constraints exist).

Differentiated Services Code Points

As shown in Figure 3-6, DSCPs use the same 3 bits as IP Precedence and combine these with the next 3 bits of the ToS byte to provide a 6-bit field for QoS marking. Thus, DSCP values range from 0 (000000) to 63 (111111). This range provides unprecedented richness in marking granularity.

DSCP values can be expressed in numeric form or by special keyword names, called *per-hop behaviors* (PHB). Three defined classes of DSCP PHBs exist: Best-Effort (BE or DSCP 0), Assured Forwarding (AFxy), and Expedited Forwarding (EF). In addition to these three defined PHBs, Class-Selector (CSx) codepoints have been defined to be backward compatible with IP Precedence (in other words, CS1 through CS7 are identical to IP Precedence values 1 through 7). The RFCs describing these PHBs are 2547, 2597, and 3246.

RFC 2597 defines four Assured Forwarding classes, denoted by the letters AF followed by two digits. The first digit denotes the AF class and can range from 1 through 4. (Incidentally, these values correspond to the three most significant bits of the codepoint, or the IPP value that the codepoint falls under.) The second digit refers to the level of drop preference within each AF class and can range from 1 (lowest drop preference) to 3 (highest drop preference). For example, during periods of congestion (on an RFC 2597–compliant node), AF33 would be dropped more often (statistically) than AF32, which, in turn, would be dropped more often (statistically) than AF31. Figure 3-7 shows the Assured Forwarding PHB encoding scheme.

Figure 3-7 *DiffServ Assured Forwarding PHB Encoding Scheme*

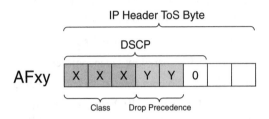

Figure 3-8 shows a summary of PHBs along with their decimal and binary equivalents.

Figure 3-8 *DiffServ PHBs with Decimal and Binary Equivalents*

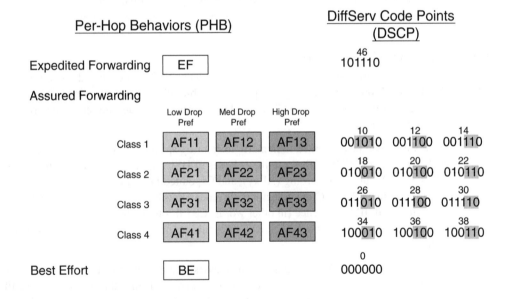

Layer 3 Tunnel Marking Tools

Cisco routers offer a variety of tunneling features, such as GRE, IPSec, and L2TP, which enable service providers to provide Layer 3 VPN tunnels by enveloping one IP packet within another. Such encapsulation masks the original header information to provide features such as privacy, encryption, and address preservation. Tunneling technologies also are used to carry non-IP protocols over an IP backbone.

A wide range of packet header layouts with tunneling technologies exist, but the primary characteristic that they have in common is that the original IP header is enveloped in an outer header packet. While in the tunnel, only the outer IP header's ToS byte is examined to determine what QoS policies should be applied to the packet. The ToS byte from the inner packet might or might not be copied automatically to the outer header packet. If it is not copied automatically, explicit commands are required to copy the ToS byte (or to set the outer header ToS byte, independent of the inner packet's ToS values).

Some example packet header layouts of GRE and IPSec packets are shown in Figure 3-9.

Figure 3-9   *L3 Tunnel Packet Layout Examples*

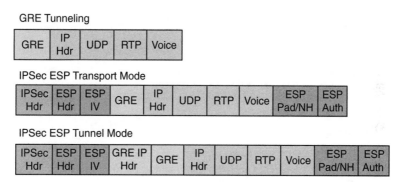

Three methods provide QoS marking for Layer 3 tunnels: QoS preclassification (QoS for VPNs feature), ToS copying/reflection, and independent header-packet marking. Each is discussed in more detail in the following sections.

QoS Preclassify

The QoS preclassify feature was introduced in Cisco IOS Software Release 12.1(5)T on Cisco 7100 and 7200 series routers and in Cisco IOS Software Release 12.2(2)T for lower-end routers. This command creates a clone of the inner packet header (strictly for internal router processing) before the packet is enveloped. Upon egress, the router compares the cloned header against any policies applied to the egress interface (because it no longer can read information from the original packet header because it is enveloped). Then the applicable policies are serviced on the packet flow, and the clone is discarded. An advantage of the QoS preclassify feature is that not only is the ToS byte of the inner header used for QoS classification purposes, but other IP/TCP/UDP header parameters such as source/destination IP addresses and source/destination ports can be used.

Strictly speaking, the QoS preclassify feature is only a classification feature. Its marking functionality is only transient, in the sense that it makes a copy of the inner packet header and its markings, but this header never is transmitted as part of the packet.

Examples of the **qos pre-classification** command for various types of tunnels are shown in Example 3-10.

Example 3-10 *QoS Preclassification Examples*

```
GRE and IPIP Tunnels
Router(config)# interface tunnel0
Router(config-if)# qos pre-classify

L2F and L2TP Tunnels:
Router(config)# interface virtual-template1
Router(config-if)# qos pre-classify

IPsec Tunnels:
Router(config)# crypto map secured-partner-X
Router(config-crypto-map)# qos pre-classify
```

ToS Reflection

QoS marking for tunnels also can be achieved by copying the ToS byte from the inner header to the outer header. This is done by default on most platforms for IPSec and GRE tunnels. For L2TP, the **l2tp tos reflect** command can be used.

Independent Header-Packet Marking

Another option is to mark the tunnel header explicitly as any other packet would be marked. This might be the least useful of the tunnel-marking methods because the characteristics for QoS treatment almost always are associated with the inner packet. Nevertheless, it is possible to mark the tunnel header independently with IP Precedence or DSCPs.

Translating Layer 2 and Layer 3 Packet Markings

The Layer 2 and Layer 3 marking fields discussed in the previous sections are summarized in Table 3-4.

It is important to remember that several technologies change packet headers or wrap one packet into another outer packet so that one packet or frame becomes the payload of the next. When this happens, packet marking is lost unless it explicitly is carried forward to the new packet (or frame) header. These repacketization changes occur when a data segment crosses a Layer 3 or Layer 2 technology boundary or when tunneling technologies are used. To preserve packet markings end to end, there is often the need to translate one type of marking to another at a network boundary (for example, LAN to WAN edge) or technology boundary (for example, the start of an encryption tunnel between two sites).

Table 3-4   *L2 and L3 Marking Options Summary*

Technology	Layer	Marking Field	Field Width (Bits)	Value Range
Ethernet	2	802.1Q/p	3	0 to 7
Frame Relay	2	DE bit	1	0 to 1
ATM	2	CLP bit	1	0 to 1
MPLS	2	EXP	3	0 to 7
IP	3	IP Precedence	3	0 to 7
IP	3	DSCP	6	0 to 63

Some examples include these:

- **VoIP over Frame Relay**—A translation from Layer 3 to Layer 2 in which a VoIP packet is enveloped within a Frame Relay frame. The Frame Relay frame header marking field (DE bit) is 0 unless it is marked explicitly.

  Recommendation: Leave the voice packet's DE bit as 0, but consider marking low-priority data packets sharing the same congestion points with DE bit 1.

- **VoIP over ATM**—A translation from Layer 3 to Layer 2 translation in which a VoIP packet is enveloped within multiple ATM cells (typically AAL5). The ATM cell header marking field (CLP) should be clear.

  Recommendation: Leave the voice packet's ATM CLP as 0, but consider marking low-priority data packets that share the same congestion points with CLP 1.

- **VoIP over Ethernet to VoIP over a WAN**—A translation from Layer 2 to Layer 3 in which VoIP on a LAN segment carries an 802.1Q/p packet header marking. When the packet hits a router and heads out over the WAN, the Layer 3 IP packet containing the voice payload might or might not be marked appropriately, depending on the configuration and capabilities of the switch, router, or IP phone.

  Recommendation: Configure that LAN switch to convert 802.1Q/p marking to DSCPs if the packet is handed off to a Layer 3 segment. If the switch is not capable of such mapping, perform the mapping from Layer 2 to Layer 3 on the router's LAN edge. A mapping from Layer 3 to Layer 2 also might be needed on remote-branch routers to restore lost CoS mappings for VoIP Ethernet frames entering the branch from the WAN.

- **VoIP over MPLS**—A translation of Layer 3 to Layer 2. As with other tunneling technologies, MPLS envelops the IP packet with another header (MPLS label). On tunnel entry, the IP packet's ToS field is mapped to the MPLS EXP bits by default.

  Recommendation: Ensure that the default mapping feature has been implemented in the Cisco IOS software release and platform; otherwise, mark the MPLS EXP field explicitly. Keep in mind that the MPLS EXP field is only 3 bits long, so IP Precedence will translate correctly, but DSCPs will lose granularity in the translation(s). Many enterprise networks do not have control over the MPLS backbone they might use. If so, work with the service provider offering the MPLS network to ensure that the network is configured correctly.

- **Tunnel technologies such as L2TP, IPSec, and GRE**—A translation of Layer 3 to Layer 3. These technologies wrap an IP packet inside another IP packet by putting a tunnel header in the front of the packet. Aside from the fact that there are bandwidth provisioning implications with such additional overhead, this masks the packet header marking of the inner packet. Note that this situation is potentially problematic only upon *entering* the tunnel because a new packet header is added to the existing packet. Upon *exiting* the tunnel, the original packet re-emerges with its marking intact, so no extra action or caution is necessary.

  Recommendation: Use the QoS preclassify feature to ensure that packet classification happens on the inner packet.

802.1Q/p to and from DSCP

Figure 3-10 shows an example of how Layer 2 (802.1Q/p CoS) markings can be translated to Layer 3 (DSCP) markings using class-based marking. In this example, CoS 5 is mapped to and from DSCP EF, and CoS 3 is mapped to and from DSCP CS3. (These are the typical values used for voice and call signaling for IP telephony.) Cisco IP phones mark voice packets to CoS 5 and DSCP EF, and call signaling packets to CoS 3 and DSCP CS3 or AF31 automatically and by default (rendering such mapping of Layer 2 to Layer 3 unnecessary, in most cases).

NOTE   Ethernet 802.1Q/p is the only Layer 2 marking technology that might require bidirectional mappings (Layer 2 to Layer 3 and Layer 3 to Layer 2). Cisco Catalyst switches (including those at remote branch locations) assign scheduling based on Layer 2 802.1p CoS markings, which are lost when the packets traverse a WAN media. All other Layer 2 marking options are applicable to the WAN/VPN transit cloud only and lose their relevance after the frame is received at the remote branch. Because of this, and because the underlying Layer 3 markings are preserved through the transit cloud, a second mapping is rarely necessary with Frame Relay DE, ATM CLP, and MPLS EXP markings.

Figure 3-10 *LAN-to-WAN Mapping of CoS and DSCP*

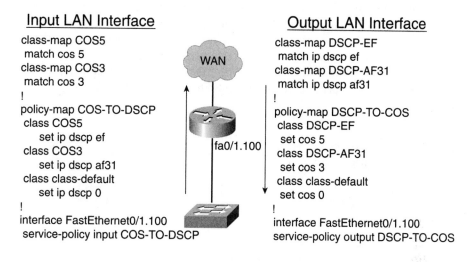

Example 3-11 shows how the policy maps in Figure 3-10 can be applied to outgoing Voice VLAN and Data VLAN FastEthernet 802.1Q subinterfaces on the router.

Example 3-11 *Applying L3-to-L2 Marking on LAN Interface*

```
Router#sh run
interface FastEthernet0/1
 no ip address
 full-duplex
 !
interface FastEthernet0/1.100
 description Voice-VLAN
 encapsulation dot1Q 100
 ip address 10.6.0.129 255.255.255.192
 service-policy input COS-TO-DSCP
 service-policy output DSCP-TO-COS
 !
interface FastEthernet0/1.500
 description DATA-VLAN
 encapsulation dot1Q 500
 ip address 10.6.0.1 255.255.255.128
 service-policy input COS-TO-DSCP
 service-policy output DSCP-TO-COS
 !
```

DSCP to Frame Relay DE Bit

Figure 3-11 shows an example of using the Frame Relay DE bit to preserve some level of priority in the Frame Relay cloud. Within this enterprise, scavenger traffic is marked to DSCP CS1. If congestion occurs within the Frame Relay cloud, such traffic should be the first to be dropped. On the router's egress interface, all frames carrying scavenger traffic are to have their Frame Relay DE bits set to 1. Furthermore, all other traffic is rate limited, and frames of traffic that exceed this limit also have their Frame Relay DE set to 1.

Figure 3-11 *Traffic Priority Marking with Frame Relay DE Bits*

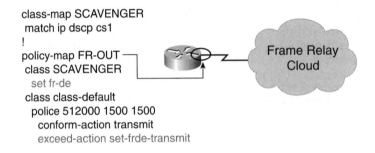

DSCP to ATM CLP Bit

Figure 3-12 shows an example of using the ATM-CLP bit to preserve some level of priority in the ATM cloud. As in the previous example, scavenger traffic is marked to DSCP CS1. If congestion occurs within the ATM cloud, such traffic should be the first to be dropped. On the router's egress interface, all frames carrying scavenger traffic are to have their ATM CLP bits set to 1. Furthermore, all other traffic is being rate limited, and cells of traffic that exceed this limit also have their ATM CLP bits set to 1.

Figure 3-12 *Traffic Priority Marking with ATM CLP Bits*

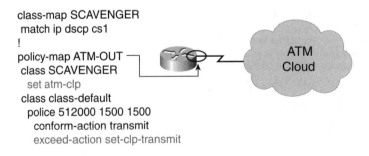

DSCP to MPLS EXP Bits

Figure 3-13 shows an example of mapping DSCPs to MPLS EXPs. This might be needed when MPLS VPN service providers offer various levels of service based on MPLS EXP markings. Currently, though, most service providers base their admission to various levels of service by examining the DSCP markings of packets offered to them from their enterprise customer edge (CE) routers. In this example, the service provider is offering three levels of service: Realtime (as admitted by MPLS EXP value 5), Business-Data (as admitted by MPLS EXP value 3), and Best Effort (everything else). The CE-to-PE link in this example is a T1 and, as such, has no serialization issues (which are discussed in greater detail later). The enterprise customer wants *both* voice and call-signaling traffic to be admitted to the service provider's Realtime class. Therefore, the customer maps both DSCP EF and DSCP AF31 to MPLS EXP 5.

By default, voice automatically would have been mapped from DSCP EF to MPLS EXP 5. However, call signaling would have been mapped to MPLS EXP 3 by default. Furthermore, the enterprise customer has transactional data marked to DSCP AF21 and bulk data marked to DSCP AF11, which, by default, would be mapped to MPLS EXP 2 and 1, respectively. The enterprise customer wants both of these to be admitted to the service provider's Business-Data class. To accomplish this, the enterprise customer manually maps DSCP AF21 and AF11 to MPLS EXP 3. Everything else is marked to MPLS EXP 0.

Figure 3-13 illustrates how and where the mapping of the DSCP to MPLS EXP value could occur, in the case of a service-provider managed CE scenario: specifically, under a Pipe Mode with Explicit Null LSP configuration (for more detail on this design option, refer to Chapter 15 "MPLS VPN QoS Design").

However, in most scenarios, enterprise customers have no control or visibility into the MPLS backbone, which typically is owned and managed by the service provider.

IP Precedence to ATM/Frame Relay PVCs (PVC Bundling)

Under some circumstances, multiple permanent virtual circuit (PVC) models might be economically attractive to enterprise customers. Such multiple-PVC models offer enterprise customers more granular levels of service across ATM or Frame Relay clouds than simple CLP or DE bit markings alone. When multiple PVCs exist, enterprises can use PVC bundles to assign relative traffic priorities over these WAN topologies.

NOTE   Although bundling is widely deployed, it is an aging and inefficient QoS technology. At the time of this writing, it supports only IP Precedence, not DSCP. Bundling is inefficient because lower-priority applications never gain access to any excess bandwidth that might exist on higher-priority PVCs. Therefore, any unused bandwidth on these PVCs is wasted.

Figure 3-13 *Traffic Priority Marking with MPLS EXP Bits*

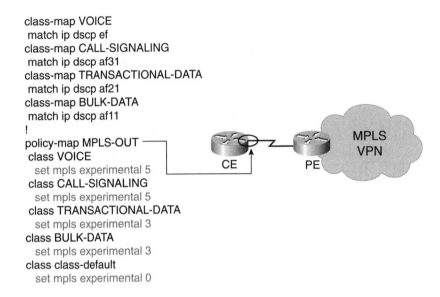

```
class-map VOICE
 match ip dscp ef
class-map CALL-SIGNALING
 match ip dscp af31
class-map TRANSACTIONAL-DATA
 match ip dscp af21
class-map BULK-DATA
 match ip dscp af11
!
policy-map MPLS-OUT
 class VOICE
   set mpls experimental 5
 class CALL-SIGNALING
   set mpls experimental 5
 class TRANSACTIONAL-DATA
   set mpls experimental 3
 class BULK-DATA
   set mpls experimental 3
 class class-default
   set mpls experimental 0
```

An example of bundling is outlined in Figure 3-14. An enterprise has purchased four separate ATM PVCs with varying levels of ATM QoS. It wants voice (IP Precedence 5) to be assigned to a dedicated variable bit rate real-time (VBR-rt) PVC, video (IP Precedence 4) and call signaling (IP Precedence 3) to be assigned to a variable bit rate non-real-time (VBR-nrt) PVC, transactional data (IP Precedence 2) and bulk data (IP Precedence 1) to be assigned to an available bit rate (ABR) PVC, and everything else to be assigned to an unspecified bit rate (UBR) PVC.

Figure 3-14 *IP Precedence to ATM PVC Bundle Example*

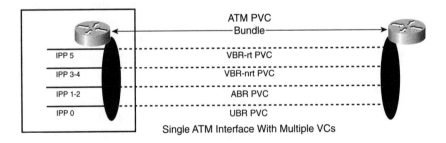

A sample ATM PVC bundling configuration that corresponds to the example is shown in Example 3-12.

IP Precedence-to-ATM VC bundling has been a Cisco IOS feature for several years. Bundling functionality for Frame Relay PVCs was introduced in Cisco IOS Software Release 12.2.1(3)T. Mapping IP Precedence markings to ATM VCs provides truer levels of service because of the ATM service class attributes that define the ATM PVCs. Frame Relay PVCs have no intrinsic service class attributes associated with them, but they do offer the capability to guarantee bandwidth to a particular class of traffic across the backbone.

Example 3-12 *Sample ATM PVC Bundling Configuration*

```
Router# show run
vc-class atm VOICE-PVC-256
  vbr-rt 256 256
  tx-ring-limit 3
  precedence 5
  no bump traffic
  protect group
!
vc-class atm VIDEO-PVC-256
  vbr-nrt 256 256
  tx-ring-limit 3
  precedence 4-3
  no bump traffic
  protect group
!
vc-class atm BUSINESS-DATA-PVC-512
  abr 512 512
  precedence 2-1
  no bump traffic
  protect group
!
vc-class atm BEST-EFFORT-PVC-512
  ubr 512
  tx-ring-limit 3
  precedence other
```

VC bundling offers QoS by separating classes of traffic over individual PVCs. Therefore, it is important to remember that other QoS tools targeted at prioritizing different types of traffic on the *same* VC, such as LLQ, do not readily apply here. Also, PVC bundles do not offer bandwidth-sharing arrangements (such as Multilink Point-to-Point Protocol [MLP] and Frame Relay multilink bundling) because they dedicate a particular PVC to a given class of traffic. If that class does not use its bandwidth allocation, it cannot be reallocated to other types of traffic. If bandwidth-sharing features are required, Multilink PPP over ATM (MLPoATM) or Multilink PPP over Frame Relay (MLPoFR) bundles must be used in conjunction with MQC-based LLQ/CBWFQ policies.

Table Map Feature

Although the **set** command can be used individually, as discussed in the previous sections, to translate a packet marking from one type to another, this might be cumbersome in the configuration if the same translation is required in many places. To ease the configuration of translating packet markings, the **table map** feature can be used. The command syntax is as follows:

```
table-map table-map-name map from from-value to to-value
[default default-action-or-value]
```

This can be used on the **set** command as shown in Example 3-13.

Example 3-13 *Configuring the Table Map Feature*

```
Router(config)#table-map table1
Router(config-tablemap)#map from 2 to 1
Router(config)#policy-map CB-marking
Router(config-pmap)#class FOO
Router(config-pmap-c)#set mpls experimental topmost qos-group table table1
```

Example 3-14 shows a number of **set** command examples using the table map feature to translate from one type of packet marking to another.

Example 3-14 *Use of the Table Map Feature*

```
set precedence cos table table-map-name
set dscp cos table table-map-name
set cos precedence table table-map-name
set cos dscp table table-map-name
set qos-group precedence table table-map-name
set qos-group dscp table table-map-name
set mpls experimental topmost qos-group table table-map-name
set mpls experimental imposition precedence table table-map-name
set mpls experimental imposition dscp table table-map-name
set qos-group mpls exp topmost table table-map-name
set precedence qos-group table table-map-name
set dscp qos-group table table-map-name
```

Summary

This chapter examined classification and marking features and tools. Classification is the action of inspecting a packet (certain fields within the packet) to determine what type of packet or traffic it is. This determination is used to guide the treatment that the packet (and other packets of the same traffic type or stream) will receive from the node and the network.

Marking is the action of changing a field within the packet header to note the determination reached by the classifier. The various ways of doing packet marking at L2 and L3 up to L7 were illustrated, and ways to translate one type of marking to another were discussed.

The treatment of the packet, which is based on the classification and marking results, includes capabilities such as policing, shaping, and queuing. Policing and shaping are discussed in Chapter 4, "Policing and Shaping Tools," and queuing is discussed in Chapter 5, "Congestion-Management Tools."

Further Reading

General

- Class-based marking: http://www.cisco.com/univercd/cc/td/doc/product/software/ios122/122cgcr/fqos_c/fqcprt1/qcfcbmrk.htm.

- Class-based policing (Cisco IOS Software Release 12.2.2T): http://www.cisco.com/univercd/cc/td/doc/product/software/ios122/122cgcr/fqos_c/fqcprt4/qcfpoli.htm.

- Frame Relay DE bit marking (Cisco IOS Software Release 12.2.2T): http://www.cisco.com/univercd/cc/td/doc/product/software/ios121/121newft/121t/121t5/cbpmark2.htm#1037921.

- Enhanced packet marking (Cisco IOS Software Release 12.2.1[3]T): http://www.cisco.com/univercd/cc/td/doc/product/software/ios122/122newft/122t/122t13/ftenpkmk.htm.

- Packet classification based on Layer 3 packet length (Cisco IOS Software Release 12.2.13T): http://www.cisco.com/univercd/cc/td/doc/product/software/ios122/122newft/122t/122t13/ftmchpkt.htm.

- Packet classification using the Frame Relay DLCI number (Cisco IOS Software Release 12.2.13T): http://www.cisco.com/univercd/cc/td/doc/product/software/ios122/122newft/122t/122t13/ftpcdlci.htm.

DiffServ

- DiffServ for end-to-end quality of service (Cisco IOS Software Release 12.1.5T): http://www.cisco.com/univercd/cc/td/doc/product/software/ios121/121newft/121t/121t5/dtdfsv.htm.

- Classifying VoIP signaling and media with DSCP for QoS (Cisco IOS Software Release 12.2.2T): http://www.cisco.com/univercd/cc/td/doc/product/software/ios122/122newft/122t/122t2/ft_dscp.htm.

- Control plane DSCP support for RSVP (Cisco IOS Software Release 12.2.2T): http://www.cisco.com/univercd/cc/td/doc/product/software/ios122/122newft/122t/122t2/dscprsvp.htm.

- Voice Gateway Packet Marking (Cisco IOS Software Release 12.2.2T): http://www.cisco.com/univercd/cc/td/doc/product/software/ios122/122newft/122t/122t2/ft_dscp.htm.

L2 Protocol Tunneling

- Catalyst 3550 IOS (Cisco IOS Software Release 12.1.14EA1) documentation: http://www.cisco.com/univercd/cc/td/doc/product/lan/c3550/12114ea1/3550scg/swtunnel.htm.

- Catalyst 3550 802.1Q Tunneling Configuration Guide: http://wwwin.cisco.com/eag/dsbu/solutions/documents/06_802.1Q%20Tunneling%20Config%20Guide.doc.

- L2TP IP ToS reflect command IOS (Cisco IOS Software Release 12.3) documentation: http://www.cisco.com/univercd/cc/td/doc/product/software/ios123/123cgcr/dial_r/dia_11g.htm#1131064.

VPN

- Quality of service for Virtual Private Networks (Cisco IOS Software Release 12.1.5T): http://www.cisco.com/univercd/cc/td/doc/product/software/ios121/121newft/121t/121t5/dtqosvpn.htm.

- Quality of service for Virtual Private Networks (Cisco IOS Software Release 12.2.2T): http://www.cisco.com/univercd/cc/td/doc/product/software/ios122/122newft/122t/122t2/ftqosvpn.htm.

NBAR

- Network-Based Application Recognition and Distributed Network-Based Application Recognition (Cisco IOS Software Release 12.1.5T): http://www.cisco.com/univercd/cc/td/doc/product/software/ios122/122newft/122t/122t8/dtnbarad.htm.

- NBAR RTP Payload Classification (Cisco IOS Software Release 12.2.8T): http://www.cisco.com/univercd/cc/td/doc/product/software/ios122/122newft/122t/122t8/dtnbarad.htm.

- Network-Based Application Recognition Protocol Discovery Management Information Base (Cisco IOS Software Release 12.2.1[5]T): http://www.cisco.com/univercd/cc/td/doc/product/software/ios122/122newft/122t/122t15/ftpdmib.htm.

MPLS

- MPLS class of service enhancements (Cisco IOS Software Release 12.1.5T): http://www.cisco.com/univercd/cc/td/doc/product/software/ios121/121newft/121t/121t5/mct1214t.htm.

- MPLS QoS multi-VC mode for PA-A3 (Cisco IOS Software Release 12.2.2T): http://www.cisco.com/univercd/cc/td/doc/product/software/ios122/122newft/122t/122t2/cos1221t.htm.

- DiffServ-aware MPLS traffic engineering (DS-TE) (Cisco IOS Software Release 12.2.4T): http://www.cisco.com/univercd/cc/td/doc/product/software/ios122/ 122newft/122t/122t4/ft_ds_te.htm.

- MPLS DiffServ-aware traffic engineering (DS-TE) over ATM (Cisco IOS Software Release 12.2.8T): http://www.cisco.com/univercd/cc/td/doc/product/software/ ios122/122newft/122t/122t8/ft_ds_te.htm.

IP—ATM/Frame Relay Bundles

- IP to ATM class of service (Cisco IOS Software Release 12.0.3T): http://www.cisco.com/univercd/cc/td/doc/product/software/ios120/120newft/ 120t/120t3/ipatmcs2.htm.

- IP to ATM CoS, per VC WFQ and CBWFQ (Cisco IOS Software Release 12.0.5T): http://www.cisco.com/univercd/cc/td/doc/product/software/ios120/120newft/120t/ 120t5/ipatm3.htm.

- IP to ATM class of service mapping for SVC bundles (Cisco IOS Software Release 12.2.4T): http://www.cisco.com/univercd/cc/td/doc/product/software/ios122/ 122newft/122t/122t4/ftsvbund.htm.

- MPLS EXP to ATM VC bundling (Cisco IOS Software Release 12.2.8T): http://www.cisco.com/univercd/cc/td/doc/product/software/ios122/122newft/122t/ 122t8/ftmpls.htm.

- Frame Relay PVC bundles with QoS support for IP and MPLS (Cisco IOS Software Release 12.2.13T): http://www.cisco.com/univercd/cc/td/doc/product/software/ ios122/122newft/122t/122t13/ft_frbnd.htm.

- MPLS EXP to Frame Relay VC bundling (Cisco IOS Software Release 12.2.13T): http://www.cisco.com/univercd/cc/td/doc/product/software/ios122/122newft/122t/ 122t13/ft_frbnd.htm.

Level 2 to Level 3 Packet-Marking Translation

- Enhanced packet marking (Cisco IOS Software Release 12.2.1[3]T): http://www.cisco.com/univercd/cc/td/doc/product/software/ios122/122newft/122t/ 122t13/ftenpkmk.htm.

This chapter includes the following topics:

- Policing, shaping, and the differences between the intent and operation of these techniques

- Policing tools such as committed access rate (CAR) and class-based policing

- Advanced policing topics, such as the single-rate and two-rate three-color policers, and hierarchical, multiaction, color-aware, and percentage-based policing

- Shaping tools such as ATM and Frame Relay traffic shaping (FRTS), generic traffic shaping (GTS), and class-based shaping

CHAPTER 4

Policing and Shaping Tools

Policers and shapers are the oldest forms of QoS mechanisms. These tools have similar objectives—namely, to identify and respond to traffic violations. Policers and shapers usually identify traffic violations in an identical manner. However, they differ in how they respond to the violations.

Policers perform instantaneous checks for traffic violations and take immediate prescribed actions when such violations occur. For example, a policer can determine whether the offered load is in excess of the defined traffic rate and then can re-mark or drop the out-of-contract traffic. Figure 4-1 shows only a dropping action taken by the policer, although other types of actions (for example, re-marking the packet or simply transmitting it) are also possible.

Shapers are traffic-smoothing tools that work in conjunction with queuing mechanisms. The objective of a shaper is to send all the traffic offered to an interface, but to smooth it out so that it never exceeds a given rate. Shapers usually are employed to meet service-level agreements (SLA) or to compensate for nonbroadcast, multiple-access idiosyncrasies. If the offered traffic momentarily exceeds the defined rate, the excess traffic is buffered and delayed until the offered traffic once again dips below the defined rate.

Figure 4-1 illustrates the difference between policing and shaping. Both mechanisms measure traffic against a given traffic rate.

Figure 4-1 *Generic Policing Versus Shaping*

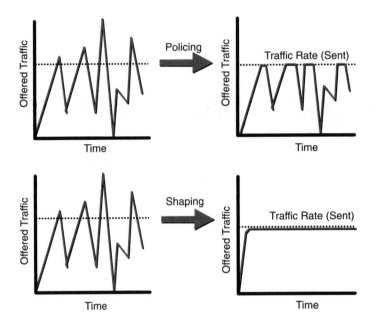

Table 4-1 compares the characteristics of policing and shaping tools.

Table 4-1 *Comparisons Between Policers and Shapers*

Policer	Shaper
Causes TCP resends as traffic is dropped	Typically delays (rather than drops) traffic; involves fewer TCP resends
Inflexible and inadaptable; makes instantaneous packet drop decisions	Can adapt to network congestion by queuing excess traffic
An ingress or egress interface tool	Typically an egress interface tool
Rate limiting without buffering	Rate limiting with buffering

Although policing and shaping tools are not employed directly to provide QoS for real-time packets (such as voice and interactive video), they do regulate and stabilize traffic flows so that service guarantees can be made for such real-time applications. Without policers and shapers, unexpected bursts in data traffic could affect the jitter and latency thresholds adversely for real-time traffic.

Also of note is that policers and shapers can work in tandem; they are not mutually exclusive tools.

Token Bucket Algorithms

Cisco IOS policers and shapers are modeled after token bucket algorithms. Essentially, *token bucket* algorithms are metering engines that keep track of how much traffic can be sent to conform to the specified traffic rates. A token permits the algorithm to send a single bit (or, in some cases, a byte) of traffic. These tokens are granted at the beginning of some time increment, typically every second, according to the specified rate referred to as the *committed information rate* (CIR). The CIR is the access bit rate contracted with a service provider or the service level to be maintained.

For example, if the CIR is set to 8000 bps, then 8000 tokens are placed in a "bucket" at the beginning of the time period. (Note that this description represents a simplified view of the algorithm and might not be strictly true in all cases, but it illustrates the general operation of the policing mechanism.) Each time a bit of traffic is offered to the policer, the bucket is checked for tokens. If there are tokens in the bucket, the traffic is passed. One token is removed from the bucket for each bit of traffic that is passed. Therefore, traffic is viewed to *conform* the rate, and the specified action for conforming traffic is taken. (Typically, the conforming traffic is transmitted.) When the bucket runs out of tokens, any additional offered traffic is viewed to *exceed* the rate, and the exceed action is taken. (The exceeding traffic typically either is re-marked or is dropped.)

NOTE   At the end of the second, there might be unused tokens. The handling of the unused tokens is a key differentiator among policers. This is discussed in the "Policers" section later in this chapter.

Because the clock rate of the interface cannot change to enforce a policy, the only way that a rate limit can be imposed on an interface is to use *time-division multiplexing* (TDM). With TDM, when a rate limit (or CIR) is imposed on an interface, the limited traffic is allocated a subsecond time slice during which it can be sent. This subsecond time slice is referred to as the *interval* (or Tc). For example, if an 8-kbps CIR is imposed on a 64-kbps link, traffic can be sent for an interval of 125 ms (64,000 bps / 8000 bits).

The entire amount of the CIR (8000 bits) could be sent at once, but then the algorithm would have to wait 875 ms before it could send any more data (to impose the rate limit). Such an interpacket delay likely would be viewed as excessive. Therefore, to smooth out the flow over each second, the CIR is divided into smaller units, referred to as the *committed burst* (Bc), which is the sustained number of bits that can be transmitted per interval. These smaller units are sent over multiple instances during a single second. Continuing with the previous example, if the Bc is set to 1000, each committed burst can take only 15.6 ms (1000 bits / 64,000 bps) to send traffic out the interface at the clock rate. The algorithm waits 109.4 ms (125 ms – 15.6 ms) and sends another 15.6 ms of data. This process is repeated a total of eight times during the second.

Therefore, the token bucket algorithm is as follows:

$$CIR = Bc / Tc$$

Cisco IOS Software does not permit the explicit definition of the interval. Instead, it takes the CIR and Bc as arguments from which the interval and the number of bursts per second are derived. For example, if the CIR is 8000 and the Bc is set to 4000, two bursts occur per second (Tc = 500 ms). If the Bc is set to 2000, four bursts occur per second (Tc = 250 ms). If the Bc is set to 1000, eight bursts occur per second (Tc = 125 ms).

The preceding example illustrates the operation of the feature from a theoretical perspective. From a practical perspective, when implementing networks, Tc should not exceed 125 ms. Shorter intervals can be configured and are necessary to limit jitter in real-time traffic, but longer intervals are not practical for most networks because the interpacket delay becomes too large.

The earliest policers all use a single-rate two-color marker/policer model with a single token bucket algorithm. In this model, traffic is identified as one of two states (colors): conforming to or exceeding the CIR. Marking and dropping actions are performed on each of these two states of traffic. This type of marker/policer is fairly crude and is illustrated in Figure 4-2.

Figure 4-2   *Single-Rate Two-Color Policer Effect on Traffic Flow (Single Token Bucket Policer)*

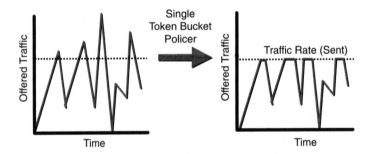

Although a policer can be deployed at ingress or egress interfaces, it often is deployed at the network edge on traffic ingress. If packets will be dropped, there is little point in spending valuable CPU cycles routing and processing these packets. However, policers also often are deployed at the traffic egress interface to control bandwidth used or are allocated to a particular class of traffic. This bandwidth decision often is not made until the packets reach the egress interface.

Policers

As mentioned before, policers determine whether each packet conforms or exceeds (or, optionally, violates) to the traffic configured policies and take the prescribed action. The action taken can include dropping or re-marking the packet. *Conforming* traffic is traffic that falls within the rate configured for the policer. *Exceeding* traffic is traffic that is above the policer rate but still within the burst parameters specified. *Violating* traffic is traffic that is above both the configured traffic rate and the burst parameters.

How traffic is separated, where it is policed, and why are important questions to keep in mind in the overall network QoS design. It is not productive, for example, to police DSCP EF (typically voice) traffic or call-signaling traffic because the incoming rates of these traffic types do not tolerate packet loss and delay. Instead, the maximum rates of these traffic types should be controlled at their origin by call admission control mechanisms (which are discussed in Chapter 9, "Call Admission Control [CAC]") so that excessive real-time traffic is not allowed onto the network.

Policers as Markers

If none of the configured actions for conform or exceed includes a drop function, the operation of the policer becomes that of a conditional marker. This is why the terms *marker* and *policer* often are used interchangeably, as they are in this chapter.

Re-marking packets with a policer should be done with care, keeping in mind the overall policies of the network. Packets typically are marked as close to the source as technically and administratively feasible (either at the source itself, if trusted, or at a network trust boundary). In these locations, the traffic typically is marked by application: voice, call signaling, video, high-priority data, and so on. This can be thought of as a *vertical separation of traffic*.

A policer, however, has no direct knowledge of applications and marks traffic (if configured to perform marking) based on the traffic rate. This can be thought of as *a horizontal separation of traffic*. A policer could have indirect knowledge of an application by virtue of the class where the policer is applied—in this configuration, the application already has been separated from other traffic into its own horizontal class. The policer itself, however, does not look at the class; it looks at only the traffic rate for the traffic flowing through it.

Committed Access Rate

CAR is the oldest policing tool offered in the Cisco IOS Software and is included in this chapter primarily for historical reasons. However, the Cisco 7300 platforms still use CAR in certain configurations. RFC-compliant policers are available in newer releases of the Cisco IOS Software, so CAR is not generally recommended for QoS deployments.

In addition to packet-drop capabilities, CAR can classify and mark packets using IPP, DSCPs, and QoS group settings. Example 4-1 illustrates how to use CAR rate limiting on applications such as web and FTP traffic, to ensure available capacity for other traffic.

Example 4-1 *CAR Policing Example*

```
Router# sh run
interface Hssi0/0/0
 description 45Mbps to Router2
 rate-limit input access-group 101 20000000 24000 32000
  conform-action set-prec-transmit 2 exceed-action set-prec-transmit 0
 rate-limit input access-group 102 10000000 24000 32000
  conform-action set-prec-transmit 2 exceed-action drop
 rate-limit input 8000000 16000 24000 conform-action set-prec-transmit 5
  exceed-action drop
 ip address 200.200.14.250 255.255.255.252

access-list 101 permit tcp any any eq www
access-list 102 permit tcp any any eq ftp
```

Access list 101 defines and matches web (WWW) traffic. The first **rate-limit** statement works on traffic matched by this access list:

```
rate-limit input access-group 101 20000000 24000 32000
  conform-action set-prec-transmit 2 exceed-action set-prec-transmit 0
```

It limits the rate of web traffic to 20 Mbps, with a normal burst size of 24,000 bytes and an excess burst size of 32,000 bytes. Traffic that conforms to the rate (less than 20 Mbps) is marked with an IP Precedence of 2; traffic that exceeds the rate is marked with an IP Precedence of 0. No traffic is dropped by this statement.

Access list 102 defines and matches FTP traffic. The second **rate-limit** statement works on traffic matched by this access list:

```
rate-limit input access-group 102 10000000 24000 32000
  conform-action set-prec-transmit 2 exceed-action drop
```

It limits the rate of FTP traffic to 10 Mbps, with a normal burst size of 24,000 bytes and an excess burst size of 32,000 bytes. Traffic that conforms to the rate (less than 10 Mbps) is marked with an IP Precedence of 2; traffic that exceeds the rate is dropped.

The third **rate-limit** statement works on remaining traffic:

```
rate-limit input 8000000 16000 24000 conform-action set-prec-transmit 5
  exceed-action drop
```

It limits this traffic to 8 Mbps, with a normal burst size of 16,000 bytes and an excess burst size of 24,000 bytes. Traffic that conforms to the rate (less than 8 Mbps) is marked with an IP Precedence of 5; traffic that exceeds the rate is dropped.

Class-Based Policing

Configuring class-based policing using the MQC syntax is an easy way to activate policing for only certain classes of traffic. With class-based policing, class definitions represent application separation, and policing is performed only on the classes configured in the policy map. This generally includes AF and BE classes in which the drop priority is increased on out-of-contract traffic (for instance, re-marking from AF21 to AF22 or AF23) or the traffic is dropped outright.

Traffic in classes that are not policed contends for bandwidth availability along with all other traffic on the interface. When no congestion exists, all traffic is transmitted. When congestion is experienced, packets can be dropped out of nonpoliced classes as well as policed classes.

Class-based policing uses class maps and policy maps. A class map identifies the traffic to be policed (or the policer can be applied to class-default to police everything). The policy map then details the CIR, Bc, and other policing parameters, including the conform and exceed actions to be taken.

Class-based policing was introduced in Cisco IOS Software Release 12.1(5)T. Enhancements were made in Cisco IOS Software Release 12.2(2)T. Class-based policing is supported in the CEF path and in the fast- and process-switching paths. The policer can be specified at the interface, subinterface, or even ATM/Frame Relay PVC levels. Class-based policing works on both unicast and multicast packets.

Class-Based Policing Benefits

Class-based policing is the currently recommended tool for policing. Its major advantages over CAR are summarized here:

- Class-based policing is compliant with DiffServ RFCs (CAR is not).

- Policing feature enhancements (such as percentage-based bandwidth specification and hierarchical policing) are made only to the class-based policing features, not to CAR.

- CAR does not exist within the MQC syntax. Therefore, its statistics cannot be tied back to the policy statistics shown by the **show policy interface** command.

- Class-based policing statistics are available in the CISCO-CLASS-BASED-QOS-MIB, offering enhanced network management and monitoring capability.

- The granularity of classification for class-based policing is far superior to that available for CAR. For example, NBAR can be used with class-based policing but not with CAR.

Single-Rate Three-Color Marker/Policer

An improvement to the single-rate two-color marker/policer algorithm is based on RFC 2697, which details the logic of a single-rate three-color marker.

The single-rate three-color marker/policer uses an algorithm with two token buckets. Any unused tokens in the first bucket are placed in a second token bucket to be used as credits later for temporary bursts that might exceed the CIR. The allowance of tokens placed in this second bucket is called the *excess burst* (Be), and this number of tokens is placed in the bucket when Bc is full. When the Bc is not full, the second bucket contains the unused tokens. The Be is the maximum number of bits that can exceed the burst size.

This two token bucket mechanism allows three possible traffic conditions to be identified (hence the term *three-color*). Traffic can be identified as follows:

- **Conform**—To the CIR
- **Exceed**—The CIR within the excess burst allowance credits
- **Violate**—Beyond both the CIR and any excess burst allowance credits

For these rate-based decisions, the following actions can be specified:

- **Conform**—Optionally re-mark and transmit
- **Exceed**—Drop or optionally re-mark and transmit
- **Violate**—Drop or optionally re-mark and transmit

Policing is used not only to drop out-of-profile packets, but also to re-mark them, thus indicating to downstream dropping mechanisms that they should be dropped ahead of the in-profile packets.

The single-rate three-color marker uses the following definitions within the RFC:

- **CIR**—Committed information rate, the policed rate
- **CBS**—Committed burst size, the maximum size of the first token bucket
- **EBS**—Excess burst size, the maximum size of the second token bucket
- **Tc**—Token count of CBS, the instantaneous number of tokens left in the CBS bucket (Do not confuse the term Tc here with the earlier use of Tc in the context of time elapsed for policing or shaping traffic intervals.)
- **Te**—Token count of EBS, the instantaneous number of tokens left in the EBS bucket.
- **B**—Byte size of offered packet

Figure 4-3 illustrates the logical flow of the single-rate three-color marker/policer (two token bucket) algorithm.

The single-rate three-color policer's tolerance of temporary bursts, shown in Figure 4-4, results in fewer TCP retransmissions and, thus, more efficient bandwidth utilization. Furthermore, it is a highly suitable tool for marking according to RFC 2597 AF classes, which have three "colors" (or drop preferences) defined per class (AFx1, AFx2, and AFx3).

Figure 4-3 *RFC 2697 Single-Rate Three-Color Policer Logic (Two Token Bucket Algorithm)*

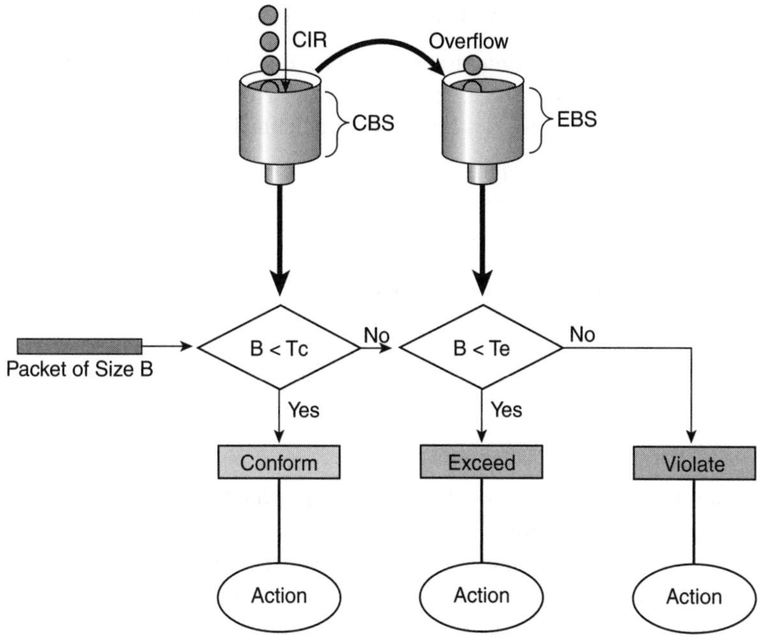

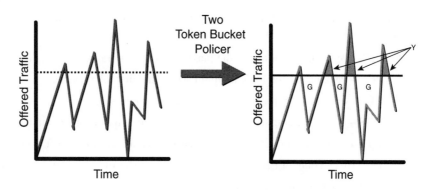

Figure 4-4 *RFC 2697 Single-Rate Three-Color Policer Effect on Traffic Flow (Two Token Bucket Policer)*

Temporary bursts (marked Y)
are permitted in excess of the CIR
only if unused token credits
(marked G) have been
accumulated.

Temporary bursts (shown shaded above the line in the graph on the right in Figure 4-4) are permitted in excess of the CIR only if unused token credits (shown shaded below the line in the graph) have been accumulated. Otherwise, this traffic is dropped.

Example 4-2 shows the configuration to police traffic in class-default to a CIR of 256 kbps, with a Bc of 8000 bytes and a Be of 8000 bytes. Note that, for this policer, the CIR is defined in bits per second, but Bc and Be are defined in bytes.

Example 4-2 *Class Default Policing Example*

```
Router# sh run
policy-map RFC2697-POLICER
 class class-default
   police cir 256000 bc 8000 be 8000
     conform-action set-dscp-transmit af31
     exceed-action  set-dscp-transmit af32
     violate-action set-dscp-transmit af33
```

Two-Rate Three-Color Marker/Policer

The single-rate three-color marker/policer was a significant improvement for policers, in that it made allowance for temporary traffic bursts (as long as the overall average transmitted rate was equal to or below the CIR). However, the variation in the number of accumulated excess burst credits could cause a degree of unpredictability in traffic flows. To improve on this, a two-rate three-color marker/policer was defined in RFC 2698. This policer addresses the peak information rate (PIR), which is unpredictable in the RFC 2697 model. Furthermore, the two-rate three-color marker/policer allows for a sustainable excess burst (negating the need to accumulate credits to accommodate temporary bursts) and allows for different actions for the traffic exceeding the different burst values.

The two-rate three-color marker/policer was introduced in Cisco IOS Software Release 12.2(4)T and uses the following parameters to meter the traffic stream:

- **PIR**—Peak information rate, the maximum rate that traffic ever is allowed
- **PBS**—Peak burst size, the maximum size of the first token bucket
- **CIR**—Committed information rate, the policed rate
- **CBS**—Committed burst size, the maximum size of the second token bucket
- **Tp**—Token count of CBS, the instantaneous number of tokens left in the PBS bucket
- **Tc**—Token count of EBS, the instantaneous number of tokens left in the CBS bucket
- **B**—Byte size of offered packet

The two-rate three-color policer also uses an algorithm with two token buckets, but the logic varies slightly. Instead of transferring unused tokens from one bucket to another, this policer has two separate buckets that are filled each second with two separate token rates. The first bucket is filled with the PIR number of tokens and the second bucket is filled with the CIR number of tokens. In this model, the Be works the same as the Bc, except for the PBS bucket (not the CBS bucket). This means that Be represents the peak limit of traffic that can be sent during a subsecond interval.

The logic varies further in that the initial check is to see whether the traffic is within the PIR. Only then is the traffic compared against the CIR. (In other words, a violate condition is checked for first, then an exceed condition, and finally a conform condition, which is the reverse of the logic of the previous model.) This logic is illustrated in Figure 4-5.

Figure 4-5   *RFC 2698 Two-Rate Three-Color Policer Logic (Two Token Bucket Algorithm)*

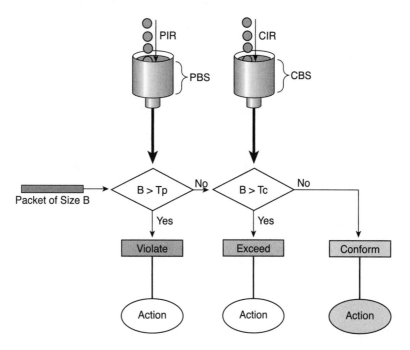

The two-rate three-color marker allows for sustainable excess bursts (and is not dependent on accumulating credits) and has a hard-top peak limit, as shown in Figure 4-6.

Figure 4-6 *RFC 2698 Two-Rate Three-Color Policer Effect on Traffic Flow (Two Token Bucket Policer)*

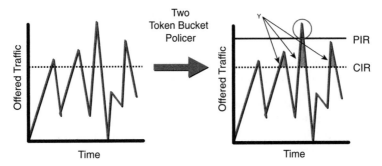

Sustained Excess Bursts (marked Y) are permitted in excess of the CIR (no accumulation of unused token credits is necessary) but only until the PIR. Traffic above the PIR (circled) is subject to the violate action.

Sustained excess bursts (shown shaded) are permitted in excess of the CIR (no accumulation of unused token credits is necessary), but only until the PIR is reached.

Example 4-3 shows the configuration to police traffic on class-default to a CIR of 8000 bps, a Bc of 1000 bytes, a Be of 2000 bytes, and a PIR of 10000 bps. Note that, for this policer, CIR and PIR are defined in bits per second, but Bc and Be are defined in bytes.

Example 4-3 *Two-Rate Three-Color Policer Example*

```
Router# sh run
policy-map RFC2698-POLICER
 class class-default
  police cir 8000 bc 1000 pir 10000 be 2000
    conform-action set-dscp-transmit af31
    exceed-action  set-dscp-transmit af32
    violate-action set-dscp-transmit af32
```

Hierarchical Policing

It is advantageous to police some applications at multiple levels. For example, it might be desirable to limit all TCP traffic to 10 Mbps, while at the same time limiting FTP traffic (which is a subset of TCP traffic) to no more than 1.5 Mbps. To achieve this nested policing requirement, hierarchical policing can be used. Two-level hierarchical policing was introduced in Cisco IOS Software Release 12.1(5)T. Later, in Release 12.2.1(3)T, three-level hierarchical policing was introduced for the 7200 and 7500 platforms.

The policer at the second level in the hierarchy acts on packets transmitted or marked by the policer at the first level. Therefore, the second level does not see any packets that the first level drops. The sum of packets that the lower-level policers see is equal to the sum of packets that the higher-level policer transmits or marks. This feature supports up to three nested levels.

Example 4-4 shows the configuration for the nested, two-level, hierarchical policing of TCP and FTP traffic.

Example 4-4 *Nested, Hierarchical Policing Example*

```
Router# sh run
policy-map FTP-POLICER
  class FTP
    police cir 1500000
      conform-action transmit
      exceed-action  drop
!
 policy-map TCP-POLICER
  class TCP
    police cir 10000000
      conform-action transmit
      exceed-action  drop
      service-policy FTP-POLICER
```

Multiaction Policing

At times, packets need to be marked at both Layer 2 and Layer 3. To accommodate such a requirement, a multiaction policer was introduced in Cisco IOS Software Release 12.2(8)T. The commands in Example 4-5 illustrate the configuration.

Example 4-5 *Multiaction Policer CLI*

```
Router(config)# policy-map MULTIACTION-POLICER
Router(config-pmap)# class class-default
(config-pmap-c)#police cir [bc] [be] ?
   conform-action action1
   conform-action action2
   conform-action action3
   conform-action action4

   exceed-action  action1
   exceed-action  action2
   exceed-action  action3
   exceed-action  action4

   violate-action action1
   violate-action action2
```

For each type of traffic, such as the conforming traffic, multiple actions can be specified. The same is true for the exceeding traffic and the violating traffic. Example 4-6 illustrates how to mark exceeding traffic with both IP Precedence 4 (at Layer 3) and the Frame Relay DE bit (at Layer 2).

Example 4-6 *Multiaction Policer Example*

```
Router# sh run
policy-map MULTIACTION-POLICER
  class class-default
   police cir 10000 pir 2000000
    conform-action transmit
    exceed-action set-prec-transmit 4
    exceed-action set-frde
    violate-action set-prec-transmit 2
    violate-action set-frde-transmit
```

Example 4-7 shows how a packet can be marked with DSCP AF31 (at Layer 3) and MPLS 3 (at Layer 2) at the same time.

Example 4-7 *Multiaction Policer Example*

```
Router# sh run
policy-map MULTIACTION-POLICER2
  class class-default
   police cir 10000
    conform-action set-dscp-transmit af31
    conform-action set-mpls-exp-topmost-transmit 3
```

Color-Aware Policing

RFC 2697 and RFC 2698 describe three-color policers, meaning that the packets can be colored to three separate values to indicate whether they conform to, exceed, or violate the policing conditions. The single-rate three-color marker and the two-rate three-color marker initially were implemented (in Cisco IOS Software Releases 12.2[2]T and 12.2[4]T, respectively) to operate in color-blind mode. This means that the policer assumes that the packet stream previously was uncolored. The RFCs also define a color-aware mode, which means that the policer assumes that some preceding entity already has colored the packet stream. At the time of this writing, the color-aware mode is available only in Cisco IOS Software Release 12.0.26S; it is not yet available in any 12.2T release.

Table 4-2 shows the two-rate policer decisions for color-blind versus color-aware modes. The number of bytes in the packet under consideration is indicated by pkt-length.

Percentage-Based Policing

Most networks contain a wide array of interfaces with different bandwidths. If absolute bandwidth rates are used in policing policies, the policy must be re-entered for each different interface size. This reduces policy modularity and makes policy management more cumbersome across the enterprise. It often is desirable to have an overall network policy in which, for example, FTP traffic is not to exceed 10 percent of the bandwidth on any interface—regardless of absolute speed. This can be achieved using percentages in the policing statements. Thus, a single policy can be reused across many interfaces in the network.

Table 4-2 *Color-Blind Versus Color-Aware Policing Modes for the Two-Rate Policer*

Color Blind	Color Aware
If (pkt-length > PIR + PBS), mark the packet as violating.	If the packet already is marked as violating OR (pkt-length > PIR + PBS), mark the packet as violating.
If (pkt-length < PIR + PBS) AND (pkt-length > CIR + CBS), mark the packet as exceeding.	If the packet already is marked as exceeding OR ((pkt-length < PIR + PBS) AND (pkt-length > CIR + CBS)), mark the packet as exceeding.
Otherwise, mark the packet as conforming.	Otherwise, mark the packet as conforming.

The command for this is as follows:

```
police cir percent xx
police cir percent xx pir percent xx
```

Only the CIR and PIR values can be specified with percent, not the burst sizes; the burst sizes are configured in units of milliseconds. If the CIR is configured in percent, the PIR also must be. When the service-policy is attached to an interface, the CIR (and PIR, if configured) is determined as a percentage of the interface bandwidth. If the interface bandwidth is changed, the CIR and PIR values and burst sizes automatically are recalculated using the new interface bandwidth value. For subinterfaces, the bandwidth of the main interface is used for the calculation. For ATM, the VC bandwidth is used; for Frame Relay, the CIR value of the PVC is used.

If the percent feature is used in a second- or third-level policy, the bandwidth of the lower-level policy statement is determined by the configuration of the higher or parent level. Table 4-3 summarizes this decision process.

Defaults

The burst parameters and actions of the policer are optional. The default conform action is to transmit the packet, and the default exceed action is to drop the packet. The default violate option is the same as the exceed action. The default burst values are 250 ms of the specified traffic rate.

Table 4-3 *CIR/PIR Policing Behavior Based on Percentages*

Configuration	Decision
CIR and PIR configured	• If the conform action is drop, the bandwidth is 0. (This is most likely not a practically useful configuration, but it is nevertheless the result of the **police** statement if this should be configured.) • If the exceed action is drop, the CIR specification is used as the bandwidth. • If the violate action is drop, the PIR specification is used as the bandwidth.
CIR configured	• If the conform action is drop, the bandwidth is 0. (This is most likely not a practically useful configuration, but it is nevertheless the result of the **police** statement if this should be configured.) • If the exceed action is drop, the CIR specification is used as the bandwidth. • If the violate action is drop, the CIR specification is used as the bandwidth.
Neither CIR nor PIR configured	• If this is a second- or third-level policy, the rate is determined by the parent class. • If this is a first level policy, the interface of the PVC bandwidth is used.

Shapers

Similar to policers, shapers meter the transmission rate of packets through a network. However, unlike policers, shapers delay (instead of drop or re-mark) packets that exceed the CIR. Such delaying smoothes out bursts in traffic flows and allows for conformance to SLAs, as shown in Figure 4-7.

Figure 4-7 *Generic Traffic Shaping Effect on Traffic Flow*

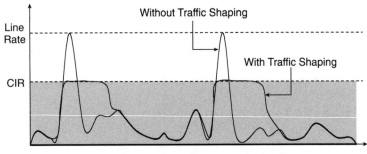

Traffic shaping limits the transmit rate of traffic
to a value (CIR) lower than the interface's line rate.

Shaping is crucial on nonbroadcast multiaccess (NBMA) topologies, such as ATM and Frame Relay, in which potential speed mismatches exist.

Figure 4-8   *NBMA Scenarios Requiring Traffic Shaping*

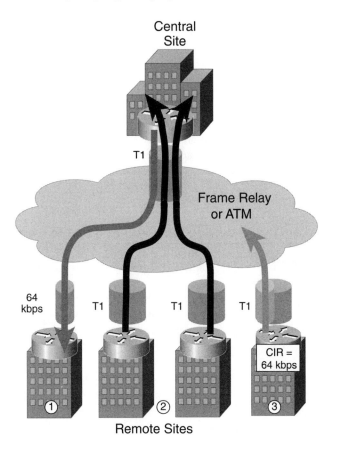

In Figure 4-8, a traffic shaper is used in the following situations:

- **A line speed mismatch**—In this case, the central site has a T1 link, but the remote site has only a 64-kbps link. Without traffic shaping, frames and cells could accumulate and drop in the carrier's cloud.

- **Remote to central site aggregate oversubscription**—In this case, if both remote sites begin transmitting at the same time, multiple remote sites (each with T1 links) begin sending at line rates back to a central site (which has only a single T1 link), thereby oversubscribing the central T1 and again causing drops within the carrier's cloud.

- **SLA enforcement** — The enterprise has contracted for a 64-kbps CIR from its carrier, and the carrier offers no service guarantees for traffic exceeding this rate. Service guarantees are critical when planning IP telephony or IP videoconferencing deployments.

Because shaping involves buffering, various scheduling techniques can be used when the shaping buffer starts filling. These scheduling techniques are discussed in more detail in Chapter 5, "Congestion-Management Tools."

Shaping Algorithms

Similar to policers, shapers use token bucket algorithms. By default, some shapers set the Bc to equal CIR/8, which yields an interval (Tc) of 125 ms. Although this interval value might be adequate for data applications, it introduces unnecessary interpacket delays for real-time networks. Consider the example shown in Figure 4-9.

Figure 4-9 *Shaping Behavior with Default Bc Values*

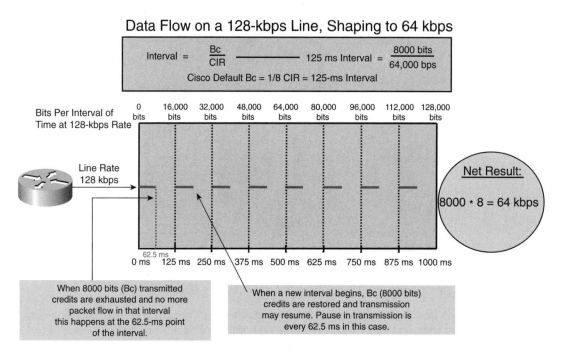

A shaper uses the CIR, Bc, and Be to smooth a traffic stream to a specified rate. It achieves the given CIR by dividing the line speed of the interface into equal-length time slots (intervals, or Tc). Then it sends a smaller portion (Bc) of the traffic during each time slot.

The time slot size is governed by the Bc parameter (Tc = Bc/CIR). In Figure 4-9, a line rate of 128 kbps is shaped to 64 kbps. For Frame Relay traffic shaping, the Bc, by default, is one eighth of the CIR (or 8 kbps). Each second is divided into eight time slots of 125 ms each, and the shaped rate of 64,000 bps is divided into eight bursts of 8000 bps each (Bc). Each burst takes 62.5 ms to transmit (at a 128-kbps line rate), so the shaper transmits information for the first 62.5 ms of each 125-ms time slot and is silent for the remaining 62.5 ms of the time slot. Over the span of a second, this achieves the average rate of CIR.

The Be value is used to determine the peak rate of sending and is calculated as follows:

Peak Rate = CIR (1+ Be / Bc)

Peak-rate shaping allows the router to burst higher than average-rate shaping. However, when peak-rate shaping is enabled, any traffic that exceeds the CIR could be dropped if the network becomes congested.

The design goal for one-way latency across a real-time network is 150 ms (per the G.114 specification for voice end-to-end delay), and the jitter target is less than 10 ms per hop. Introducing up to 125 ms of shaping delays at a single hop destroys VoIP quality. Therefore, it is recommended that shaped interfaces carrying real-time traffic be shaped to 10-ms intervals (Tc). Because the Tc cannot be administered directly by Cisco IOS commands, Bc tuning is required to affect Tc indirectly. This interval value can be achieved (remember, Tc = Bc / CIR) by setting the Bc equal to CIR/100, which results in a Tc value of 10 ms. The recommended value for Bc on an 64-kbps interface/PVC carrying real-time traffic is, therefore, 64,000 / 100, which equals 640 bits and represents 10 ms of transmission on a 64-kbps line.

Shaping on ATM and Frame Relay Networks

ATM and Frame Relay are NBMA topologies that have inherent and specific requirements for traffic shaping. Therefore, these topologies have customized shaping tools that are not available to other topologies. These custom-shaping tools include ATM traffic contracts and Frame Relay traffic shaping.

ATM Traffic Contracts

In ATM, shaping is an integral part of the PVC specification. This is because ATM achieves different QoS levels by configuring different PVC traffic contracts, such as real-time variable bit rate (VBR-RT), non-real–time variable bit rate (VBR-NRT), available bit rate (ABR), and unspecified bit rate (UBR). The ATM traffic contract shaping commands are summarized in Table 4-4.

Table 4-4 *ATM Traffic Contract PVC Parameter Configuration Commands*

Command	Purpose
Router(config-if-atm-vc)# **abr** *output-pcr output-mcr*	Configures the ABR
Router(config-if-atm-vc)# **ubr** *output-pcr*	Configures the UBR
Router(config-if-atm-vc)# **ubr+** *output-pcr output-mcr*	Configures the UBR with a minimum guaranteed rate
Router(config-if-atm-vc)# **vbr-nrt** *output-pcr output-scr output-mbs*	Configures the non-real–time VBR
Router(config-if-atm-vc)# **vbr-rt** *peak-rate average-rate burst*	Configures the real-time VBR

The *-pcr* and *-mcr* arguments are the peak cell rate and minimum cell rate, respectively. The *-scr* and *-mbs* arguments are the sustainable cell rate and maximum burst size, respectively.

The parameters specified on the ATM PVC configuration determine the shaped average or peak rates, as well as the burst parameters, as shown in Example 4-8.

Example 4-8 *ATM PVC Configuration*

```
Router# sh run
interface ATM3/0.1 point-to-point
 description OC3 Link to Site-B
 ip address 10.2.12.1 255.255.255.252
 pvc 0/12
  vbr-nrt 149760 149760
```

General Cisco IOS shaping tools, such as generic traffic shaping and class-based shaping, are not supported on ATM interfaces, including digital subscriber line (DSL).

Frame Relay Traffic Shaping

Traffic shaping is imperative for Frame Relay PVCs if QoS guarantees are required over them. The initial shaping mechanism developed for Frame Relay interfaces was Frame Relay traffic shaping (FRTS). Example 4-9 shows a sample configuration of FRTS.

Example 4-9 *Frame Relay Traffic Shaping*

```
Router# sh run
interface Serial0/1
 no ip address
 encapsulation frame-relay
 frame-relay traffic-shaping
 !
interface Serial0/1.50 point-to-point
```

Example 4-9 *Frame Relay Traffic Shaping (Continued)*

```
 description FR Link to BRANCH#50
 bandwidth 1536
 ip address 10.200.50.1 255.255.255.252
 frame-relay interface-dlci 150
  class FRTS-1536
 !
map-class frame-relay FRTS-1536
 frame-relay cir 1536000
 frame-relay bc 15360
 frame-relay be 0
 frame-relay mincir 1536000
 no frame-relay adaptive-shaping
```

In line with the previously discussed shaping recommendations, the Bc is set to CIR/100. The Be is set to 0 to prevent any excess bursting. The problem with provisioning the Be in real-time networks is that it can create buffering delays within a Frame Relay network (because the receiving side can "pull" the traffic from a circuit only at the rate of Bc, not Bc + Be). To remove the potential for buffering delays, the recommendation is to set the Be to 0.

Frame Relay also has the capability to adapt to explicit congestion notices, either in the forward direction through forward explicit congestion notifications (FECNs) or in the reverse direction through backward explicit congestion notifications (BECNs). Adaptive traffic shaping even can be triggered by other notifications, such as foresight or interface congestion (as of Cisco IOS Software Release 12.2[4]T). When adaptive shaping is enabled and congestion notifications have been received, the FRTS engine rates down the flow to the minimum CIR (minCIR), which, by default, is CIR/2. Because such congestion adaptation introduces variations in transmission rates and, thus, service levels, the recommendation is to disable adaptive shaping in networks carrying real-time traffic.

Class-Based Frame Relay Traffic Shaping

In Cisco IOS Software Release 12.2(13)T, FRTS functionality was migrated into the MQC syntax using class-based shaping commands. This is the currently recommended method for configuring traffic shaping on Frame Relay data-link connection identifiers (DLCIs). Translating Example 4-9 into the class-based FRTS syntax yields the results shown in Example 4-10.

Example 4-10 *Frame Relay Traffic Shaping Using Class-Based Syntax*

```
Router# sh run
policy-map CB-FRTS-1536
  class class-default
   shape average 1536000 15360 0
```

continues

Example 4-10 *Frame Relay Traffic Shaping Using Class-Based Syntax (Continued)*

```
!
...
!
interface Serial0/1
 no ip address
 encapsulation frame-relay
!
interface Serial0/1.50 point-to-point
 description FR Link to BRANCH#50
 bandwidth 1536
 ip address 10.200.50.1 255.255.255.252
 frame-relay interface-dlci 150
  class FRTS-1536
!
...
!
map-class frame-relay FRTS-1536
 service-policy output CB-FRTS-1536
```

The class-based FRTS configuration retains remnants of FRTS, such as the need to associate the DLCI to a Frame Relay map class and then attach the class-based FRTS policy to this map class.

Frame Relay Voice-Adaptive Traffic Shaping

Supporting voice traffic with predictable QoS on a Frame Relay PVC requires traffic shaping to be deployed on the PVC and shaped strictly to the CIR. This is because any traffic in excess of the CIR could be marked as Frame Relay DE-bit 1 and could be dropped by the Frame Relay backbone network during congestion (because it violates the SLA). Many customer edge networks, however, are designed and configured to oversubscribe the CIR because the backbone network seldom exhibits congestion and, if it does, the higher-layer protocols take care of recovering the session. Voice traffic cannot be treated in the same manner because the QoS for voice needs to be predictable and guaranteed.

The Frame Relay backbone network does not know which frames contain voice and which contain data. Therefore, if any traffic violates the CIR, the backbone switch does not know how to drop only data and not to drop voice—even if the voice traffic by itself is below the contracted SLA rate. This necessitates shaping strictly to the CIR to ensure that voice traffic is protected. Adaptive shaping (through BECNs, FECNs, and other notification mechanisms) cannot resolve this problem because by the time the shaper receives the congestion notices and reacts to them, many voice packets might already have been delayed or dropped. Therefore, to address the needs of voice traffic in a Frame Relay network, the Frame Relay voice-adaptive traffic shaping (FR-VATS) feature was introduced in Cisco IOS Software Release 12.2(15)T.

FR-VATS monitors the Frame Relay PVC. When voice activity is present, it automatically shapes to the CIR (which, in this specific case, is configured as the minCIR). However, if no voice is present, it allows the traffic to burst to the line rate (which, in this specific case, is configured as the CIR). This unique feature determines the presence of voice based on packets entering a priority class or low-latency queue (a scheduling feature that is discussed in Chapter 5). It then automatically determines whether to shape the traffic to minCIR (voice present) or not (no voice present). Similarly, FR-VATS automatically engages Frame Relay fragmentation (FRF.12) on links less than 768 kbps when voice packets are present, to prevent unnecessary serialization delays. (FRF.12 is discussed in more detail in Chapter 7, "Link-Specific Tools.")

Because FR-VATS automatically detects the presence of voice, there could be some brief quality degradation in the first couple of seconds of the first voice call made across a PVC. This occurs while the interfaces comprising the PVC reconfigure themselves to shape to the minCIR and empty out their buffers. FR-VATS is not a predictive algorithm. The change in behavior is triggered by voice packets flowing across the PVC.

The FR-VATS deactivation period is tunable and, by default, is set to 30 seconds. If tuned, this timer should be set so that the feature will not turn off frequently during normal business use (for example, between every two calls). The feature works better on PVCs that always have at least one voice call present during daytime use and relinquish shaping only at night.

Example 4-11 shows a configuration of FR-VATS.

Example 4-11 *FR-VATS Configuration*

```
Router# sh run
policy-map FR-VATS-768
 class class-default
  shape average 768600 3648 0          → sets CIR to 768 kbps and Bc to minCIR/100
  shape adaptive 364800                → sets the minCIR to 364.8kbps
  shape fr-voice-adapt deactivation 30 → enables default FR VATS deactivation timer
 !
 ...
 !
interface Serial0/1
 no ip address
 encapsulation frame-relay
 serial restart_delay 0
 frame-relay fragmentation voice-adaptive deactivation 30 → enables FR Voice
                              Adaptive Fragmentation (sub-component of FR VATS)
 !
interface Serial0/1.50 point-to-point
 description FR Link to BRANCH#50
 bandwidth 768
 ip address 10.200.50.1 255.255.255.252
 frame-relay interface-dlci 150
  class FRTS-768                        → applies the FR map-class to the DLCI
```

continues

Example 4-11 *FR-VATS Configuration (Continued)*

```
!
...
!
map-class frame-relay FRTS-768
 service-policy output FR-VATS-768
 frame-relay fragment 480          → sets fragment size for 384 kbps (minCIR) link
 !
```

Generic Traffic Shaping

Generic traffic shaping (GTS) is the oldest shaping tool in the Cisco IOS Software and is included in this chapter for historical reasons only. It was introduced in Cisco IOS Software Release 11.2 and is enabled using the **traffic-shape rate** command. This feature is not recommended for use in QoS deployments because it lacks many of the RFC-compliant features contained in the class-based shaping tools discussed in this chapter. Instead, class-based shaping should be used wherever possible. In older IOS releases for Frame Relay interfaces, FRTS should be used.

Class-Based Shaping

Class-based shaping (available within the MQC syntax) uses class maps and policy maps. A class map identifies the traffic to be shaped (or the shaper can be applied to class-default to shape everything). The policy map then details the CIR, Bc, Be, and other shaping parameters.

Class-based shaping was introduced in Cisco IOS Software Release 12.1(2)T. Conceptually, it was a migration of GTS into the MQC syntax. However, the class-based shaping code is different from GTS. This feature should not be assumed to behave in exactly the same manner as GTS.

The command to configure class-based shaping follows:

> **shape** [**average** | **peak**] [*cir*] [*burst_size* [*excess_burst_size*]]

Example 4-12 uses class-based shaping on a T1 interface to shape to 768-kbps CIR with the Bc set to the recommended value for real-time networks (CIR/100 and Be set to 0).

Example 4-12 *Class-Based Shaping on a T1 Interface*

```
Router# sh run
policy-map CBS-768
  class class-default
    shape average 768000 7680 0
```

Hierarchical Class-Based Shaping

As with hierarchical policing, sometimes shaping policies need to shape aggregate levels and provide additional QoS functions on sublevels of traffic. Hierarchical shaping was introduced in Cisco IOS Software Release 12.1(2)T.

For example, consider the case of a service provider that wants to shape a customer's aggregate traffic to 384,000 and, within that, wants to provide a bandwidth guarantee of 200 kbps for transactional data and a bandwidth guarantee of 100 kbps for bulk data. This can be achieved with a nested, or hierarchical, shaping policy, as shown in Example 4-13.

Example 4-13 *Hierarchical Class-Based Shaping*

```
Router# sh run
policy-map CUSTOMER1-SHAPING-AND-QUEUING-POLICY    parent policy
  class CUSTOMER1-TRAFFIC
    shape average 384000
    service-policy CUSTOMER1-QUEUING-POLICIES      includes the child policy
!
policy-map CUSTOMER1-QUEUING-POLICIES              child policy
  class CUSTOMER1-TRANSACTIONAL-DATA
    bandwidth 200
  class CUSTOMER1-BULK-DATA
    bandwidth 100
!
```

Percentage-Based Shaping

As with policing, shaping can be stated as a percentage of bandwidth instead of absolute bandwidth. This feature enhancement was introduced in Cisco IOS Software Release 12.2(13)T and is enabled with the following command:

```
shape [average | peak] percent xx
```

Burst sizes cannot be configured using percentages, but they can be specified in terms of milliseconds on the command. When a percentage configuration is used for average or peak shaping rates, the default burst sizes automatically are assigned and can be seen using the **show policy interface** command, as shown in Example 4-14. When the service policy is attached to an interface, the CIR value is determined from the interface bandwidth in conjunction with the configured CIR percent value.

Example 4-14 *Percent-Based Shaping*

```
Router#show policy-map interface fastEthernet 0/1 output
  FastEthernet0/1
   Service-policy output: ex-shape
    Class-map: example (match-all)
      0 packets, 0 bytes
      5 minute offered rate 0 bps, drop rate 0 bps
      Match: access-group 101
```

continues

Example 4-14 *Percent-Based Shaping (Continued)*

```
    Traffic Shaping
        Target/Average    Byte     Sustain    Excess     Interval   Increment
          Rate            Limit    bits/int   bits/int   (ms)       (bytes)
          80 (%)                   0 (ms)     0 (ms)
        80000000/80000000  500000  2000000    2000000    25         250000
    Adapt  Queue   Packets   Bytes           Packets    Bytes      Shaping
    Active Depth                             Delayed    Delayed    Active
      -       0         0         0             0          0         no
    Class-map: class-default (match-any)
      15 packets, 1225 bytes
      5 minute offered rate 0 bps, drop rate 0 bps
      Match: any
```

Distributed Traffic Shaping

On distributed platforms, such as the Cisco 7500 VIP, class-based shaping is not supported. Instead, a counterpart feature, distributed traffic shaping (DTS), is used.

Although DTS on the Cisco 7500 is very similar to class-based shaping on nondistributed platforms, there are two main differences to keep in mind. The first is that, with DTS, the CIR must be defined in multiples of 8000. The second is that the Cisco 7500 VIP requires the interval (Tc) to be defined in increments of 4 ms. Because the target interval for all platforms is 10 ms, which is not evenly divisible by 4 ms, the recommendation for Cisco 7500 VIP is to use an interval of 8 ms. The interval can be set to 8 ms by defining the burst using the following formula:

Bc = CIR / 125

Detailed examples of DTS in WAN environments are provided in Chapter 13, "WAN Aggregator QoS Design." The behavior of traffic shaping for the 7500 platforms currently is being reworked, but the previous functionality exists in Cisco IOS Software releases up to 12.3 mainline and 12.3T.

Further Reading

DiffServ Policing Standards

- RFC 2697, "A Single Rate Three Color Marker": http://www.ietf.org/rfc/rfc2697.
- RFC 2698, "A Two Rate Three Color Marker": http://www.ietf.org/rfc/rfc2698.

Policing

- Traffic policing (12.1.5T): http://www.cisco.com/univercd/cc/td/doc/product/software/ios121/121newft/121t/121t5/dtpoli.htm.

- Traffic policing enhancements (12.2.2T): http://www.cisco.com/univercd/cc/td/doc/product/software/ios122/122newft/122t/122t2/ftpoli.htm.

- Two-rate policer (12.2.4T): http://www.cisco.com/univercd/cc/td/doc/product/software/ios122/122newft/122t/122t4/ft2rtplc.htm.

- Policer enhancement—multiple actions (12.2.8T): http://www.cisco.com/univercd/cc/td/doc/product/software/ios122/122newft/122t/122t8/ftpolenh.htm.

- Percentage-based policing and shaping (12.2.13T): http://www.cisco.com/univercd/cc/td/doc/product/software/ios122/122newft/122t/122t13/ftpctpol.htm.

- Color-aware policer (12.0.26S): http://www.cisco.com/univercd/cc/td/doc/product/software/ios120/120newft/120limit/120s/120s26/12s_cap.htm.

ATM PVC Traffic Parameters

- Configuring ATM traffic parameters: http://www.cisco.com/univercd/cc/td/doc/product/software/ios122/122cgcr/fwan_c/wcfatm.htm#1001126.

Frame Relay Traffic Shaping

- Adaptive Frame Relay traffic shaping for interface congestion (12.2.4T): http://www.cisco.com/univercd/cc/td/doc/product/software/ios122/122newft/122t/122t4/ft_afrts.htm.

- MQC-based Frame Relay traffic shaping (12.2.13T): http://www.cisco.com/univercd/cc/td/doc/product/software/ios122/122newft/122t/122t13/frqosmqc.htm.

- Percentage-based policing and shaping (12.2.13T): http://www.cisco.com/univercd/cc/td/doc/product/software/ios122/122newft/122t/122t13/ftpctpol.htm.

- Frame Relay queuing and fragmentation at the interface (12.2.13T): http://www.cisco.com/univercd/cc/td/doc/product/software/ios122/122newft/122t/122t13/frfrintq.htm.

- Frame Relay voice-adaptive traffic shaping and fragmentation (12.2.15T): http://www.cisco.com/univercd/cc/td/doc/product/software/ios122/122newft/122t/122t15/ft_vats.htm.

Traffic Shaping

- Generic traffic shaping (11.2): http://www.cisco.com/univercd/cc/td/doc/product/
  software/ios112/112cg_cr/1rbook/1rsysmgt.htm#23613.

- Class-based shaping (12.1.2T): http://www.cisco.com/univercd/cc/td/doc/product/
  software/ios121/121newft/121t/121t2/clsbsshp.htm.

- Distributed traffic shaping (12.1.5T): http://www.cisco.com/univercd/cc/td/doc/
  product/software/ios121/121newft/121t/121t5/dtdts.htm.

This chapter includes the following topics:

- Scheduling and queuing
- Legacy Layer 3 mechanisms
- Currently recommended Layer 3 mechanisms
- Layer 2 queuing tools
- Tx-ring
- PAK_priority

CHAPTER 5

Congestion-Management Tools

Of all the mechanisms within the QoS toolset, congestion-management tools provide the most significant impact on application service levels. Congestion-management tools, also known as *queuing tools*, apply to interfaces that may experience congestion. This could be the case in either a WAN or a LAN environment (although LAN queuing tools are discussed in Chapter 10, "Catalyst QoS Tools") because speed mismatches can occur in either setting. Whenever packets enter a device faster than they can exit it, the potential for congestion exists and queuing tools apply.

It is important to recognize that queuing tools are activated only when congestion exists on an interface. When no congestion exists on an interface, packets are sent out over the interface as soon as they arrive. However, when congestion occurs, packets must be *buffered*, or queued, to mitigate dropping.

Packet markings at either Layer 2 or Layer 3, or the absence of a marking on a packet, influence queuing policies so that the router can reorder packets before transmission. Therefore, queuing policies are usually complementary and depend on classification and marking policies within converged networks.

This chapter examines the difference between scheduling and queuing, and the different OSI layers where queuing might occur. Legacy Layer 3 queuing algorithms are reviewed to provide context for the more recent queuing algorithms, such as Class-Based Weighted Fair Queuing (CBWFQ) and Low-Latency Queuing (LLQ), that evolved from them. LLQ and CBWFQ are examined in detail because these are the principal recommended queuing mechanisms for converged networks in which different traffic types such as voice, video, and data all share the same transmission media.

Lower-level queuing algorithms, such as Layer 2 mechanisms and the Tx-ring, also are discussed because these tools have an impact on successful end-to-end QoS design. Finally, the internal Cisco IOS mechanism for protecting routing and control packets (PAK_priority) within the router is introduced.

Understanding Scheduling and Queuing

The phrase *scheduling tools* refers to the set of features that determines how a frame, cell, or packet exits a device. Whenever packets enter a device faster than they can exit it, as is the case with interface speed mismatches (for example, Fast Ethernet traffic heading to a serial WAN interface), a point of potential congestion, or a bottleneck, occurs. Devices have buffers that allow for temporarily storing and subsequent scheduling of these backed-up packets. This process commonly is referred to as *queuing*. As these buffers (or queues) fill, packets can be reordered so that higher-priority packets exit the device sooner than lower-priority ones. Figure 5-1 shows a general example of queuing.

Figure 5-1 *Generic Queuing Example*

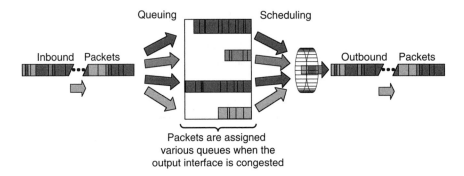

Conceptually, queuing and scheduling are complementary but intertwined processes. These terms quite often are incorrectly used interchangeably:

- *Queuing* is the logic of ordering packets in linked output buffers. It is important to recognize that queuing processes are engaged only when the interface is experiencing congestion and are deactivated shortly after the interface congestion clears.

- *Scheduling* is the process of deciding which packet to transmit next. Scheduling occurs when the interface is experiencing congestion, but also (unlike queuing) when the interface is not experiencing congestion (that is, there is still a decision, albeit a simple one, of which packet should be transmitted next, even if there is no congestion on the interface). If there is no congestion on the interface, packets are transmitted as they arrive. If the interface is experiencing congestion, queuing algorithms are engaged. However, the scheduler still has to decide which queue to service next. This decision is made using various types of scheduling logic algorithms:

  - **Strict priority**—The lower-priority queues are served only if the higher-priority queues are completely empty. This type of scheduling exhibits the potential to starve traffic in lower-priority queues.

- **Round-robin**—Queues are served in a sequence. Although they never starve traffic, round-robin schedulers exhibit the potential to cause unpredictable delay in queues that hold real-time, delay-sensitive traffic that requires a more strict priority-scheduling algorithm.
- **Weighted fair**—Packets in the queues are weighted, typically by IP precedence, so that some queues are served more frequently than others. Although this solves the downsides of both the strict priority and round-robin algorithms, it does not provide the bandwidth guarantee that real-time flows require. The resulting bandwidth per flow instantaneously varies based on the number of flows present and the weights of each of the other flows.

The buffer space (or memory) for queues is finite in capacity and acts very much like a funnel for water that is being poured into a small opening. If water continually is entering the funnel much faster than it exits, eventually the funnel begins to overflow from the top. When queuing buffers begin overflowing, packets might be dropped either as they arrive (tail drop) or selectively, before all buffers are filled. Selective dropping of packets when the queues are filling is referred to as *congestion avoidance*. Congestion-avoidance mechanisms work best with TCP-based applications because selective dropping of packets causes the TCP windowing mechanisms to throttle back and adjust the rate of flows to manageable rates.

Congestion-avoidance mechanisms are complementary to queuing algorithms and are discussed in more detail in Chapter 6, "Congestion-Avoidance Tools." The relationship between congestion-management tools (or scheduling algorithms) and congestion-avoidance tools (or selective-dropping algorithms) is as follows: With congestion management, the scheduling algorithms manage the *front* of a queue; with congestion avoidance, the mechanisms manage the *tail* of a queue.

Congestion-management and congestion-avoidance tools employed in converged networks include these:

- **Low-Latency Queuing (LLQ)**—Congestion management
- **Class-Based Weighted Fair Queuing (CBWFQ)**—Congestion management
- **Weighted Random Early Detection (WRED)**—Congestion avoidance

LLQ and CBWFQ are discussed in detail in this chapter. WRED is covered in Chapter 6.

To understand queuing, you first must understand the various levels of queuing and how queuing has evolved. A fundamental concept in Cisco IOS queuing is that queuing is performed at multiple layers of the OSI model.

Layer 3 queuing subsystems operate at the network layer and are applied to Layer 3 packets at a logical level. Because Cisco IOS Layer 3 queuing subsystems are independent of the egress interface type, they can be applied to Asynchronous Transfer Mode (ATM), Frame Relay, High-Level Data Link Control (HDLC), Point-to-Point Protocol (PPP), Multilink

Point-to-Point Protocol (MLP), or tunnel interfaces. It is important to recognize that Layer 3 queuing typically considers only the IP overhead in its bandwidth provisioning. Layer 2 overhead such as the ATM cell tax is not factored into the equation and, therefore, must be provisioned explicitly for drop-sensitive applications such as Voice over IP (VoIP).

Layer 2 queuing subsystems accommodate media-specific requirements and idiosyncrasies. For example, ATM and Frame Relay media support multiple Layer 2 logical interfaces (for example, PVCs and DLCIs) per physical interface and require special scheduling to accommodate such circuits. Layer 2 media-specific shapers, such as Frame Relay traffic shaping, also interact with queuing, in that the shapers determine the output rate of packets onto the interface and, therefore, push packets arriving too fast back into the queues. When the Layer 2 queues fill up, they, in turn, push back packets into the Layer 3 queues. Fragmentation and interleaving also are performed within Layer 2 queuing subsystems.

A final queue, usually referred to as a *transmit ring* (or Tx-ring), is located within the device driver itself. Tx-rings are media and hardware dependent and can operate quite differently on different routers, cards, and modules. The purpose of the Tx-ring is to ensure that there is always a packet ready to be placed onto the media, with the objective of driving interface utilization to 100 percent. Furthermore, the Tx-ring indicates to the queuing algorithms whether the interface is congested. (If the Tx-ring is full, the interface is congested.) When the Tx-ring limit is reached, queuing algorithms engage. Some interfaces report the length of the Tx-ring in packets. Other interfaces, such as ATM, report the length in particles. (Particle length is variable but is set to 576 bytes for most ATM port adaptors.)

It is important to note that not all three levels of queuing are always present.

Legacy Layer 3 Queuing Mechanisms

There is a long history of queuing algorithms in Cisco IOS Software, not all of which are covered in this chapter because they are not applicable to QoS deployment for converged networks. Newer queuing and scheduling algorithms are simply combinations and enhancements of older queuing algorithms. For a historical perspective and an understanding of why these mechanisms are insufficient for today's converged networks, it is helpful to review some of these legacy queuing techniques. The three basic legacy queuing types (beyond simple FIFO) are these:

- Priority queuing (PQ)
- Custom queuing (CQ)
- Weighted Fair Queuing (WFQ)

From these three basic algorithms, combinations and enhancements were developed. These newer queuing mechanisms sought to combine the best features of the basic algorithms and, at the same time, to minimize their drawbacks. These enhanced queuing algorithms include the following:

- IP RTP priority queuing (PQ-WFQ). This was a transient method and soon was superceded by low-latency queuing.
- CBWFQ
- LLQ

Table 5-1 compares the attributes of the different algorithms and their suitability to handling real-time, delay-sensitive traffic, such as voice. This traffic requires two things from a queuing/scheduling algorithm:

- An absolute bandwidth guarantee
- A delay guarantee

Priority Queuing

The oldest queuing algorithm is PQ, which consists of only four queues (high, medium, normal/default, and low). The scheduler begins by emptying the high queue and begins to service lower queues only when upper queues are completely empty. This basic algorithm proved very successful in handling real-time traffic, but it posed starvation possibilities to lower-priority traffic flows.

Custom Queuing

CQ addressed the concern of traffic starvation, common in PQ scenarios. By introducing a round-robin scheduler that was based on byte counts, not only did custom queuing prevent bandwidth starvation, but it also became the first queuing mechanism to provide *bandwidth guarantees*. Although custom queuing (which supports up to 16 distinct queues) introduced a fairness that PQ did not have, it lost the capability to provide strict priority to real-time flows.

Weighted Fair Queuing

WFQ was developed to expand on the principle of fairness that CQ broached.

The fair-queuing algorithm within WFQ simply divides the interface's bandwidth by the number of flows, ensuring an equitable distribution of bandwidth for all applications.

Table 5-1 *Queuing Algorithm Compariso*

	FIFO	PQ	CQ	WFQ	PQ-WFQ	CBWFQ	LLQ
Classification	Per interface	Per protocol, per interface	Per protocol, per interface	IP prec, RSVP, RTP Reserve, protocol, port	RTP port for PQ; IP prec for WFQ	Class-based classification	Class-based classification
Number of queues	1	4	16	Per flow	1 PQ + WFQ	Up to 256 classes	1 PQ + CBWFQ
Scheduling	FIFO	Strict priority	Round robin	Weighted fair (based on IP prec)	PQ: Strict		
WFQ: Weighted fair (based on IP prec)	Weighted fair (based on bandwidth)	PQ: Strict					
CBWFQ: Weighted fair (based on bandwidth)							
Delay guarantee	No	Yes for traffic in highest-priority queue only	No	No	Yes for PQ traffic	No	Yes for PQ traffic
Bandwidth guarantee	No	No	Yes	No	Yes for PQ traffic	Yes	Yes
Recommended for voice	No	No	No	No	No	No	Yes

By adding a fixed weight (based on the packet's IPP value) to the calculation, WFQ introduced a method for moderately skewing bandwidth allotments by favoring higher-priority flows (priority being a function of IPP marking). Although such skewing preferred certain flows over others, WFQ lost CQ's capability to provide bandwidth guarantees because bandwidth allocations continuously changed as flows were added or ended.

IP RTP Priority Queuing

IP RTP priority (PQ-WFQ) was a transient feature in the step-by-step evolution of developing QoS mechanisms for voice.

IP RTP priority queuing was introduced between WFQ and LLQ in Cisco IOS Software Release 12.0(5)T for interfaces and MLP links, and in Cisco IOS Software Release 12.0(7)T for Frame Relay. LLQ was introduced soon afterward in Cisco IOS Software Release 12.0(7)T for interfaces and MLPPP links, and in Cisco IOS Software Release 12.1(2)T for Frame Relay. Therefore, the only legitimate current uses for IP RTP priority queuing are on routers that handle voice traffic and that are running code levels between these two releases. LLQ should be used in all other cases.

Currently Recommended Layer 3 Queuing Mechanisms

Each of the previously described Layer 3 queuing tools had serious shortcomings in handling the traffic mix required by converged networks. Either they handled data fairly well or could prioritize real-time applications, such as voice. But none of these tools was capable of handling both types of traffic efficiently. Therefore, enhanced algorithms were developed to leverage the strengths of each type of legacy algorithm and, at the same time, to minimize their weaknesses.

This section provides an overview of the hybrid queuing mechanisms used today for Layer 3: CBWFQ and LLQ.

Class-Based Weighted Fair Queuing

CBWFQ, introduced in Cisco IOS Software Release 12.0(5)T, is a hybrid queuing algorithm that combines the capability to guarantee bandwidth (from CQ) with the capability to dynamically ensure fairness to other flows within a class of traffic (from WFQ).

CBWFQ enables the creation of up to 256 classes of traffic, each with its own reserved queue. Each queue is serviced based on the bandwidth assigned to each class.

A major difference between WFQ and CBWFQ is that, with WFQ, the bandwidth of the flow is calculated instantaneously; but with CBWFQ, a minimum bandwidth explicitly is defined and enforced. Additionally, CBWFQ uses Modular QoS CLI (MQC)–based class maps for classification, which provide the richest and most granular recognition criteria within the Cisco IOS QoS toolset. When class maps are combined with CBWFQ bandwidth statements, minimum-bandwidth guarantees can be provisioned for almost any application.

Example 5-1 shows two applications of CBWFQ. First, a minimum bandwidth guarantee is given to the MISSION-CRITICAL-DATA class. Second, all other traffic (which falls into class-default) is fair queued.

Example 5-1 *CBWFQ Policy for Multiple Levels of Data*

```
policy-map WAN-EDGE
  class MISSION-CRITICAL-DATA
    bandwidth percent 20 → sets the bandwidth for this class to 20%
  class class-default
    fair-queue  → sets WFQ as the queuing algorithm for unclassified traffic
```

NOTE The **percent** keyword was added in Cisco IOS Software Release 12.0(7)T, allowing bandwidth to be allocated as relative percentages of the link, or shaping rate, instead of in absolute values (in kilobits per second). The **percent** keyword increases CBWFQ policy modularity because the same policies can be applied to many interfaces, regardless of their link speeds. Additionally, the **percent** keyword makes future expansion easier to manage because the relative bandwidth allocations automatically will increase as the link speeds themselves increase.

CBWFQ is a highly efficient algorithm for data applications, but it lacks the capability to provide strict-priority servicing to real-time applications, such as voice or interactive video. This is because it provides a bandwidth guarantee but not a latency guarantee. Therefore, to service such real-time applications, a strict-priority queue was added to the CBWFQ algorithm; the resulting algorithm was named low-latency queuing.

Low-Latency Queuing

LLQ is an enhanced combination of all three legacy queuing algorithms: PQ, CQ, and WFQ. It was introduced in Cisco IOS Software Release 12.0(7)T.

LLQ is essentially CBWFQ combined with a strict PQ. Traffic assigned to the strict priority queue, using the **priority** command, is serviced up to its assigned bandwidth before all other CBWFQ queues are serviced.

NOTE	The original name for the LLQ algorithm was PQ-CBWFQ. Although this name was technically correct, it was obviously clumsy from a marketing perspective. Hence, the algorithm was renamed LLQ.

LLQ also has an implicitly defined burst parameter (added in Cisco IOS Software Release 12.1[3]T) that accommodates temporary bursts of real-time traffic. By default, LLQs are provisioned to protect bursts up to 200 ms, defined in bytes. The burst parameter becomes significant in certain interactive video scenarios (which are discussed in more detail in Chapter 13, "WAN Aggregator QoS Design").

In Example 5-2, up to one-third of the link's (or shaper's) bandwidth is assigned for strict priority treatment of voice.

Example 5-2 *LLQ for VoIP and Multiple Levels of Data*

```
policy-map WAN-EDGE
  class VOICE
    priority percent 33   → sets the LLQ bandwidth to 33%
  class CALL-SIGNALING
    bandwidth percent 2
  class MISSION-CRITICAL-DATA
    bandwidth percent 20
  class class-default
   fair-queue
```

NOTE	The **percent** keyword was added to the LLQ **priority** command in Cisco IOS Software Release 12.2(2)T.

The next sections discuss further details about LLQ, such as its operation, the implicit policing done by the queuing algorithm, bandwidth provisioning, and the lesser-known interactions between LLQ, IPSec, cRTP, and LFI, and bundling technologies such as ATM, MLP, and Frame Relay bundles.

LLQ Operation

LLQ is designed exclusively for converged networks that carry voice and interactive video. It contains two components, a PQ for the real-time sensitive traffic and a class-based complex of queues (CBWFQ). The PQ is the optimal queueing mechanism for real-time traffic, whereas CBWFQ is the best queuing algorithm for data applications. Converged networks require LLQ to be configured so that voice, interactive video, and data all are given the service levels they require.

The Layer 3 queuing subsystem for LLQ is shown on the left side of Figure 5-2. In this illustration, voice traffic is classified and placed in the PQ. When traffic is present in the PQ, it is serviced with exhaustive priority treatment up to the bandwidth maximum configured for the priority class (that is, voice is sent out first until no more voice is present or the bandwidth assigned is exceeded). The L2 subsystem is discussed later in this chapter.

Figure 5-2 *LLQ Operation Logic*

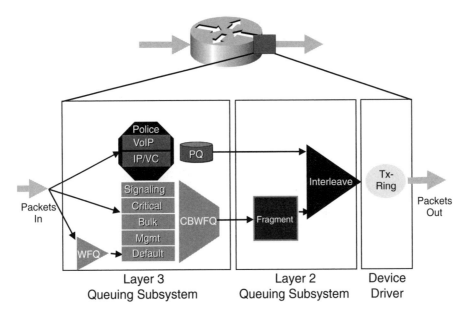

LLQ Policing

The threat posed by any strict priority-scheduling algorithm is that it could starve lower-priority traffic. To prevent this, the LLQ mechanism has a built-in policer. This policer (like the queuing algorithm itself) engages only when the interface is experiencing congestion. Therefore, it is important to provision the priority classes properly. If the total amount of priority class bandwidth provisioned is lower than the total amount of voice traffic offered to the PQ (including the Layer 2 overhead), the excess voice traffic might be dropped (by the LLQ policer). As with any other policer, LLQ's policer, when engaged, drops traffic indiscriminately and affects the quality of *all* voice calls active on the interface (not just the last one to go through). Strategies to accommodate this behavior of LLQ are discussed in more detail in Chapter 9, "Call Admission Control (CAC)." In earlier Cisco IOS Releases, the PQ of LLQ policed strictly to the bandwidth assigned, regardless of traffic present or absent in other classes. In later releases, this operation changed to police strictly only if the interface was congested—that is if other classes were underutilized, PQ traffic would be allowed to exceed its bandwidth without dropping packets.

Another benefit provided by the implicit policer within the LLQ mechanism is the capability to use TDM for the single strict-priority queue. TDM abstracts the fact that only a single strict-priority queue exists and allows for the configuration and servicing of "multiple" low-latency queues.

In Example 5-3, separate priority classes on a dual-T1 MLP link are assigned for voice and videoconferencing. Each priority class is policed (to 540 kbps for voice and 460 kbps for video). Under the hood, however, there is only a single 1-Mbps PQ (540 kbps + 460 kbps), which is time shared between these two applications by the implicit policer.

Example 5-3 *LLQ Policy for VoIP, Interactive Video, and Multiple Levels of Data*

```
policy-map WAN-EDGE
  class VOICE
    priority 540  → creates a LLQ of 540 kbps
  class INTERACTIVE-VIDEO
    priority 460  → creates a "second" LLQ of 460 kbps
  class CALL-SIGNALING
    bandwidth percent 2
  class MISSION-CRITICAL-DATA
    bandwidth percent 20
  class class-default
    fair-queue
```

Bandwidth Provisioning

Most applications default to the best-effort default class. Because enterprises have hundreds, if not thousands, of applications on their networks, it is a general best practice to provision at least 25 percent of a link's bandwidth for "class-default." This recommendation has been coded into older Cisco IOS Software releases for the lower-end platforms (Cisco 7200 and below). If present, this restriction can be overridden manually (using the **max-reserved-bandwidth** interface command).

A similar consideration must be given to the sum of all traffic assigned for all priority classes. It is important to remember the goal of convergence: to allow voice, video, and data to coexist *transparently* on a single network. If real-time applications dominate a network, as in the case of a dominantly provisioned LLQ (in which the priority classes have the lion's share of the bandwidth), data applications might fluctuate significantly in their network response times when voice/videoconference calls are made. This destroys the transparency of the converged network. User feedback consistently has reflected that most users prefer consistent (even if moderately slower) application response times over varying response times (as would occur if LLQs dominated WAN links). Cisco Technical Marketing testing has revealed a conservative rule of thumb for priority class provisioning, which is to limit the sum of all priority class traffic to no more than 33 percent of the WAN link's capacity. This *33 percent LLQ rule* has been deployed widely and successfully.

Figure 5-3 illustrates these bandwidth-provisioning recommendations—namely, that the aggregate bandwidth of all priority classes should be no more than 33 percent of the link's capacity and that all bandwidth guarantees within LLQ should be no more than 75 percent of the link capacity.

Figure 5-3   *LLQ Bandwidth Provisioning*

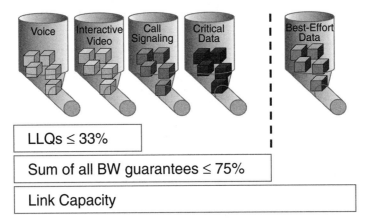

Because of the policing function within LLQ, it is important to accurately provision bandwidth required for voice calls. LLQ is a Layer 3 queuing mechanism and, as such, accounts for only Layer 3 packet bandwidth. (It does not take Layer 2 headers into account.) Furthermore, the Layer 3 bandwidth required by a voice call is determined by a number of factors. These factors include the codec used, the sampling size, and the compression techniques, such as cRTP (also known as RTP header compression). Cisco has provided a voice bandwidth calculator to determine the correct bandwidth to provision in LLQ for voice calls. The calculator is located on the web at http://tools.cisco.com/Support/VBC/jsp/Codec_Calc1.jsp.

When the percentage-remaining (**bandwidth remaining percent**) form of LLQ configuration is used, the 75 percent rule no longer applies. This is because the remaining percent statement refers to the instantaneous residual bandwidth, after the PQ (priority classes) has been serviced, on the interface. In Example 5-4, up to 33 percent of the link can be dedicated for voice traffic. After voice traffic has been serviced, however, all remaining bandwidth is divided equally between the MISSION-CRITICAL-DATA class and the default class.

Example 5-4 *LLQ Policy for VoIP and Multiple Levels of Data Using Remaining Percentage Allocations*

```
policy-map WAN-EDGE
  class VOICE
    priority percent 33
  class MISSION-CRITICAL-DATA
    bandwidth remaining percent 50
  class class-default
    bandwidth remaining percent 50
```

LLQ and IPSec

Encrypting a link that carries different classes of traffic and employs LLQ has several implications:

- Encryption happens before queuing. Therefore, classification of all traffic must be carefully considered, and inner and outer headers must be marked appropriately to ensure correct classification for egress queuing purposes.

- Encryption changes packet sizes because it adds headers to the packet and thus affects bandwidth allocation for both voice and data traffic. The effect is much more significant for voice because the packets are relatively small, making the relative overhead of the new headers far greater. Figure 5-4 illustrates how tunneling and encryption overhead can more than double the Layer 3 bandwidth required for a voice packet.

- The bottleneck within the network node that applies the encryption potentially moves from the egress interface to the encryption engine. On most routers that have encryption accelerators, the combined throughput of egress interfaces that can be supported far exceeds the throughput of the encryption engines. Therefore, encryption for traffic must be engineered carefully, especially if converged traffic is sent through an encrypted tunnel.

If encryption is used, especially on the lower-end router platforms, hardware accelerators should be used. If the egress interface throughput exceeds the throughput of the encryption engine, packets might heap up waiting to enter the crypto engine; therefore, LLQ must be applied on the IPSec engine entrance instead of the egress interface, as illustrated in Figure 5-5. This is a feature named LLQ Before Crypto that became available in Cisco IOS Software Release 12.2(13)T.

LLQ and cRTP

Traditionally, packet-compression techniques occurred at Layer 2 and, therefore, were not visible to the LLQ algorithm at Layer 3. LLQ priority class bandwidth thus requires careful provisioning to reflect the actual bandwidth required, after compression but inclusive of Layer 2 overhead.

Figure 5-4 *G.729 Voice Bandwidth with GRE and IPSec*

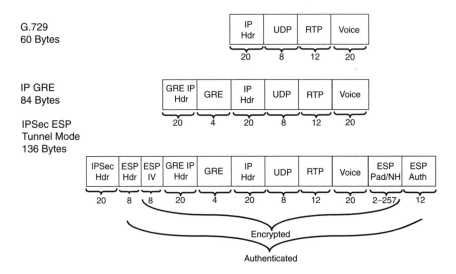

Figure 5-5 *LLQ for IPSec Encryption Engines*

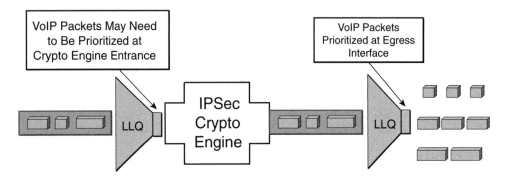

Typical Layer 2 data-compression techniques, such as FRF.9 or PPP STAC compression, tend to have only a mild effect on voice packets. This is because codec compression, such as G.729, already does very tight compression. Little or no repetitive patterns can be optimized by applying yet another generic compression technique.

At 40 bytes, the standard IP/RTP/UDP header overhead of a voice packet is quite substantial, especially when compared to the relatively small size of the payloads (20 bytes for G.729 to 160 bytes for G.711). RTP header compression (or cRTP), which is discussed in greater detail in Chapter 7, "Link-Specific Tools," can reduce the overhead requirements of voice packets from 40 bytes to between 2 and 5 bytes.

A new feature in Cisco IOS Software Release 12.2(13)T allows cRTP to be configured within the MQC syntax and performed in the CEF switch path. Class-based cRTP also improves the feedback mechanism to the LLQ policing engine.

LLQ and LFI

Link Fragmentation and Interleaving (LFI) is a QoS technique to minimize serialization delay on slow (typically less than 768-kbps) WAN links. Essentially, LFI tools chop large data packets into smaller ones and interleave these data packet fragments with voice packets. LFI techniques are discussed in more detail in Chapter 7, "Link-Specific Tools," but they have an important relationship with the LLQ mechanism that bears pointing out at this time.

As shown in Figure 5-2, packets that are assigned to the PQ inside LLQ might escape the fragmentation engine (the fragmentation engine is represented by the box labeled *fragment*). Therefore, traffic with large packet sizes (such as interactive video) should not be assigned to priority classes on slow-speed links (typically less than 768 kbps). For example, if one priority class is assigned to VoIP and another is assigned to interactive video on a 512-kbps link, whenever a 1500-byte video packet is scheduled for transmission, it will require 23 ms to serialize ($(1500 \times 8) / 512,000$). This exceeds the per-hop latency target for voice (10 ms) and nearly consumes the entire one-way jitter allowance target of 30 ms. If a second 1500-byte IP/VC packet also is scheduled for transmission, voice conversations audibly will become degraded. Therefore, voice *and* interactive video never should be assigned dual-LLQ policies on link speeds less than 768 kbps.

LLQ and ATM PVC Bundles

When different traffic types are converged on a single ATM PVC, the normal LLQ operation for any interface or PVC applies. However, when PVCs are bundled together, special considerations must be taken, and these are discussed further in this section.

ATM PVC bundles (previously discussed in Chapter 3, "Classification and Marking Tools," do not require LLQ. Remember that ATM PVC bundles use multiple PVCs to provide different classes of service over the network backbone. Each PVC is dedicated to a particular class of traffic. The very nature of LLQ is to separate different classes of traffic on the *same* egress interface (or PVC). ATM PVC bundling does just the opposite: It separates different classes of traffic onto *separate*, dedicated egress interfaces (or PVCs). For this reason, LLQ is not supported (or needed) on ATM PVC bundles.

For ATM PVC bundles, keep the following points in mind:

- LLQ is not supported.
- LFI is not supported.
- cRTP is not supported.
- No packet reordering occurs.
- All VCs must exist on a single physical interface.
- There is no bandwidth sharing. Each PVC is dedicated to traffic of a particular type, and unused bandwidth cannot be used by traffic of other classes.
- Tx-rings should be set to their default.

LLQ and MLP/Frame Relay Bundles

Other bundling techniques have different QoS characteristics: in particular, MLP and Frame Relay bundles. These tools aggregate bandwidth across multiple physical interfaces and bind them together as a larger logical interface. These tools offer additional flexibility, especially with respect to ease of expansion: They simplify management to a large degree.

Interfaces bundled in this manner have the following QoS requirements:

- LLQ is supported (and required).
- LFI is supported if the aggregate bandwidth of the bundle is still below 768 kbps. (This is likely not required because bundling most often allows bandwidths above 768 kbps so that LFI is no longer necessary.)
- cRTP is supported.
- Packet reordering occurs.
- Multiple physical interfaces are bound together.
- There is bandwidth sharing across the aggregate bandwidth of all the links in the bundle.
- Tx-rings should be set to a minimal value, such as 3.

Figure 5-6 shows this principle in an MLP bundle aggregating several ATM PVCs spread across multiple DSL interfaces. The DSL interfaces are terminated by the DSLAM equipment in the network, and the bundled PVCs are delivered on a high-speed ATM interface, such as an OC-3, at the aggregation site. In this case, LLQ is applied at the MLP bundle interface, not to the actual physical interfaces.

Figure 5-6   *MLP PVC Bundling*

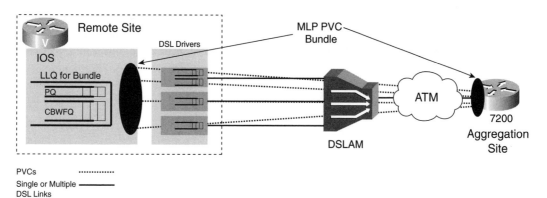

LLQ and VoFR

Voice over Frame Relay (VoFR) is an older technique of transporting voice traffic over Frame Relay networks. It existed before VoIP became implemented widely. VoFR is a pure Layer 2 method of transporting voice and, for the most part, has been replaced by VoIP in combination with LLQ.

Cisco IOS Software traditionally has prioritized VoFR packets by default into the same PQ that is used by LLQ priority classes. The bandwidth allotted to VoFR packets is assigned by the voice-bandwidth statement in the Frame Relay map class. VoFR packets are funneled into the PQ of the LLQ algorithm.

NOTE   Care must be taken to never put VoFR and VoIP traffic on the same Frame Relay DLCI on slow speed links that require fragmentation and interleaving (that is, less than or equal to 768 kbps). This is because VoFR and VoIP require different fragmentation standards (FRF.11 and FRF.12, respectively). If both VoFR and VoIP are configured on the same DLCI with fragmentation for each enabled, FRF.11 overrides FRF.12 and disables the interleaving scheme that VoIP packets require. Obviously then, the quality of VoIP will deteriorate significantly.

Layer 2 Queuing Tools

Layer 2 queuing tools are required to resolve the prioritization issues generated by multiple logical interfaces (such as Frame Relay DLCIs and ATM PVCs) as they contend for the scheduling of a single physical parent interface. These include the following:

- Frame Relay Dual-FIFO
- PVC Interface Priority Queuing (PIPQ)

Frame Relay Dual-FIFO

On the low-end router non-distributed platforms (Cisco 7200 and lower), Frame Relay employs a dual-FIFO queuing technique that automatically is invoked at the interface level when FRF.12, which is discussed in detail in Chapter 7, is configured. FRF.12 depends on Frame Relay traffic shaping (FRTS) or class-based FRTS being enabled.

In a Frame Relay environment, the Tx-ring does not directly provide back pressure to the Layer 3 queuing algorithm. Instead, when the Tx-ring is full, it provides back pressure to the shaper (FRTS or CB-FRTS), which, in turn, signals the Layer 3 queuing system (LLQ) to engage. Because the FRTS mechanism does not take into account Frame Relay headers and cyclic redundancy checks (CRCs) in its calculations, it generally is recommended that you shape to 95 percent of CIR on Frame Relay circuits up to T1/E1 speeds. This, in turn, engages the LLQ algorithm slightly earlier and improves performance for real-time traffic.

Traffic from each PQ for each DLCI is funneled into the high-priority, dual-FIFO interface queue; all traffic from the CBWFQ queues from the DLCIs is assigned to the lower-priority, dual-FIFO interface queue. Thus, the dual-FIFO Layer 2 queues ensure that the "priority" class traffic from one DLCI is not delayed by CBWFQ traffic from another DLCI. Frame Relay Layer 3 and Layer 2 queuing and shaping logic is illustrated in Figure 5-7.

PVC Interface Priority Queuing

Traffic of different importance levels sometimes is separated onto different PVCs for management or other network design reasons. In such designs, all traffic on the priority PVC should overtake all traffic on lower-priority PVCs when contending for a single egress interface. PVC interface priority queuing (PIPQ) is the Layer 2 queuing mechanism that accomplishes this reordering. It typically is found in service provider scenarios where dedicated PVCs are used to provide priority services.

PIPQ defines four queues at the interface level. Each PVC on the interface can be assigned to one of four priorities. As with all PQ techniques, the higher-priority queues have exhaustive priority over the lower-priority ones and can therefore potentially starve them. The operation of PIPQ is illustrated in Figure 5-8.

Figure 5-7   *LLQ on Frame Relay PVCs with FRTS and Dual-FIFO*

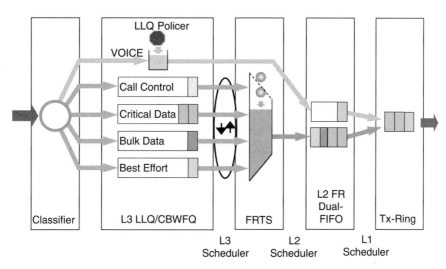

Figure 5-8   *PVC Interface Priority Queuing (PIPQ) for Frame Relay*

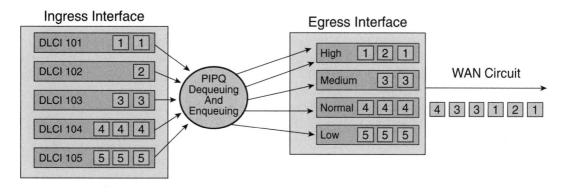

In Figure 5-8, DLCIs 101 and 102 are designated as high priority, while DLCIs 103, 104, and 105 are mapped to the medium, normal, and low queues, respectively. Traffic on DLCIs 101 and 102 will, therefore, have priority over any of the other PVCs, and DLCI 105 will be capable of sending traffic only if none of the other PVCs has a frame ready to be transmitted.

A practical application for this queuing technique is to place voice traffic on DLCI 101, a financial ticker on DLCI 102, and various levels of data traffic on the other three PVCs. Example 5-5 shows the configuration of PIPQ for DLCI 101.

Example 5-5 *Frame Relay PIPQ Example*

```
interface serial0.101
  frame-relay interface-queue priority 10 20 30 40
  frame-relay interface-dlci 101
    class HIGH-PVC

map-class frame-relay HIGH-PVC
  frame-relay interface-queue priority high
```

Tx-ring

The Tx-ring is a final FIFO queue that holds frames to be placed immediately on the physical interface. Its purpose is to ensure that a frame always will be available when the interface is ready to transmit traffic so that link utilization will be driven to 100 percent of capacity.

The placement of the Tx-ring is shown on the right of Figures 5-2 and 5-7. The size of the Tx-ring depends on the hardware, software, Layer 2 media, and queuing algorithm configured on the interface. It is a general best practice to set the Tx-ring to a value of 3 on slow-link interfaces (less than or equal to 768 kbps).

The Tx-ring is especially important on ATM links (including DSL), in which each PVC has a dedicated driver-level queue (Tx-ring) to ensure adherence to the ATM class-of-service traffic contract of the PVC. Default ATM Tx-rings are typically deep, containing 64 or more particles (typically, each particle is 576 bytes) to ensure that enough particles exist in the buffer to drive the PVC to its full bandwidth utilization. A shallow Tx-ring increases the number of interrupts and the wait states between the driver and the main CPU. Packets are downloaded from the Layer 3 queues to the driver for transmission, which is usually suboptimal at higher speeds.

On the other hand, a deep Tx-ring can impact voice quality. For example, assume that a 50-packet burst of data passes through the LLQ system and into the FIFO Tx-ring. A voice packet then arrives and is packet number 51 for transmission. The LLQ no longer has the opportunity to prioritize it over the data packets. A shallow Tx-ring pushes packets back into LLQ, where prioritization and packet reordering can be accomplished before the packets are downloaded to the driver. Once in the driver level, the packets have a very short wait time until transmission.

Thus, the tuning of the Tx-ring is a compromise between optimizing real-time packet delays and achieving maximum CPU efficiency. The higher the bandwidth of the PVC is, the deeper the Tx-ring can be set without adversely affecting voice quality. For slow links (less than or equal to 768 kbps), however, a Tx-ring of 3 is recommended to maintain voice quality.

PAK_priority

Certain traffic types, such as Layer 2 keepalives and Layer 3 routing protocol messages, are absolutely critical to maintaining network stability. Therefore, it is vital to understand how the Cisco IOS Software handles these traffic types, especially when provisioning WAN links that might experience sustained periods of congestion.

By default, Cisco IOS Software (in accordance with RFC 791 and RFC 2474) marks Interior Gateway Protocol (IGP) traffic (such as Routing Information Protocol [RIP/RIPv2], Open Shortest Path First [OSPF], and Enhanced Interior Gateway Routing Protocol [EIGRP]) to IPP6/CS6. These precedence values specify PHBs for these control packets as they pass *through the network*. However, Cisco IOS Software also has an internal mechanism for granting priority to important control datagrams as they are processed through the router. This mechanism is called *PAK_priority*.

As datagrams are processed though the router and down to the interfaces, they are *encapsulated internally* with a small packet header, referred to by an internal label. Within the fields of this label is a PAK_priority flag that indicates the relative importance of control packets to the router's internal processing systems. PAK_priority designation is a critical internal Cisco IOS Software operation and, as such, is not administratively configurable in any way.

The default internal treatment of PAK_priority datagrams varies slightly between distributed platforms and nondistributed platforms when MQC policies are bound to the outgoing interfaces.

- Distributed platforms place the PAK_priority datagrams into the class-default queue and use the PAK_priority flag to avoid dropping the packets.

- Nondistributed platforms place PAK_priority datagrams into a separate and dedicated set of queues (257–263) from the class-default, and mark them with a special weight value (1024).

As noted previously, IGPs are not only marked IPP6/CS6, but they also receive PAK_priority treatment within the routers. For routing packets that are not marked with IPP6/CS6, special bandwidth considerations should be given.

Additionally, several non-IP control packets, including the following, receive PAK_priority:

- Intermediate System-to-Intermediate System (IS-IS) routing protocol messages
- Point-to-Point Protocol (PPP) keepalives on serial and Packet over SONET (POS) interfaces
- High-Level Data Link Control (HDLC) keepalives on serial and POS interfaces
- ATM operation, administration, and maintenance (OAM) and Address Resolution Protocol (ARP) cells
- Frame Relay Local Management Interface (LMI) messages

Summary

Congestion-management tools were overviewed in this chapter, with an emphasis on the LLQ algorithm, because this is the principal recommended Cisco IOS queuing tool for converged networks.

The operation of the LLQ algorithm is important to understand because it directly impacts QoS design recommendations. Additionally, the interdependence of the QoS toolset is highlighted because congestion-management tools are shown to be complementary to classification and marking tools, policing and shaping tools, congestion-avoidance tools, and link-efficiency mechanisms.

Although most queuing policies occur at Layer 3, it is important to consider any impacts that lower levels of queuing, such as Frame Relay Dual-FIFO, Tx-ring, and PAK_priority, may have on the overall network design.

Further Reading

Layer 3 Queuing

- Configuring priority queuing: http://www.cisco.com/univercd/cc/td/doc/product/software/ios122/122cgcr/fqos_c/fqcprt2/qcfpq.htm.
- Configuring custom queuing: http://www.cisco.com/univercd/cc/td/doc/product/software/ios122/122cgcr/fqos_c/fqcprt2/qcfcq.htm.
- Configuring weighted fair queuing: http://www.cisco.com/univercd/cc/td/doc/product/software/ios122/122cgcr/fqos_c/fqcprt2/qcfwfq.htm.
- IP RTP priority (Cisco IOS Software Release 12.0.5T): http://www.cisco.com/univercd/cc/td/doc/product/software/ios120/120newft/120t/120t5/iprtp.htm.

- Class-based weighted fair queuing (Cisco IOS Software Release 12.0.5T): http://www.cisco.com/univercd/cc/td/doc/product/software/ios120/120newft/120t/120t5/cbwfq.htm.

- Low-latency queuing (Cisco IOS Software Release 12.0.7T): http://www.cisco.com/univercd/cc/td/doc/product/software/ios120/120newft/120t/120t7/pqcbwfq.htm.

- Low-latency queuing for Frame Relay (Cisco IOS Software Release 12.1.2T): http://www.cisco.com/univercd/cc/td/doc/product/software/ios121/121newft/121t/121t2/dtfrpqfq.htm.

- Configuring burst size in low-latency queuing (Cisco IOS Software release 12.1.3T): http://www.cisco.com/univercd/cc/td/doc/product/software/ios121/121newft/121t/121t3/dtcfgbst.htm.

- RSVP support for low-latency queuing (Cisco IOS Software Release 12.1.3T): http://www.cisco.com/univercd/cc/td/doc/product/software/ios121/121newft/121t/121t3/rsvp_llq.htm.

- Distributed low-latency queuing (Cisco IOS Software Release 12.1.5T): http://www.cisco.com/univercd/cc/td/doc/product/software/ios121/121newft/121t/121t5/dtllqvip.htm.

- Low-latency queuing with priority percentage support (Cisco IOS Software Release 12.2.2T): http://www.cisco.com/univercd/cc/td/doc/product/software/ios122/122newft/122t/122t2/ftllqpct.htm.

- Low-latency queuing (LLQ) for IPSec encryption engines (Cisco IOS Software Release 12.2.13T): http://www.cisco.com/univercd/cc/td/doc/product/software/ios122/122newft/122t/122t13/llqfm.htm.

Layer 2 Queuing

- Voice over Frame Relay Queuing Enhancement (Cisco IOS Software Release 12.0.5T): http://www.cisco.com/univercd/cc/td/doc/product/software/ios120/120newft/120t/120t5/vofrque.htm.

- Frame Relay IP RTP Priority (Cisco IOS Software Release 12.0.7T): http://www.cisco.com/univercd/cc/td/doc/product/software/ios120/120newft/120t/120t7/friprtp.htm.

- Frame Relay PVC interface priority queuing (Cisco IOS Software Release 12.1.1T): http://www.cisco.com/univercd/cc/td/doc/product/software/ios121/121newft/121t/121t1/dtfrpipq.htm.

- Multilink Frame Relay (FRF.16) (Cisco IOS Software release 12.2.8T): http://www.cisco.com/univercd/cc/td/doc/product/software/ios122/122newft/122t/122t8/ft_mfr.htm.

- Enhanced Voice and QoS for ADSL and G.SHDSL (Cisco IOS Software Release 12.2.13T): http://www.cisco.com/univercd/cc/td/doc/product/software/ios122/122newft/122limit/122y/122yn8/ft_ipqos.htm.

- Frame Relay queuing and fragmentation at the Interface (Cisco IOS Software Release 12.2.13T): http://www.cisco.com/univercd/cc/td/doc/product/software/ios122/122newft/122t/122t13/frfrintq.htm.

- Multiclass multilink PPP (Cisco IOS Software Release 12.2.13T): http://www.cisco.com/univercd/cc/td/doc/product/software/ios122/122newft/122t/122t13/ftmmlppp.htm.

- Frame Relay PVC interface priority queueing (Cisco IOS Software Release 12.1.1T): http://www.cisco.com/univercd/cc/td/doc/product/software/ios121/121newft/121t/121t1/dtfrpipq.htm.

Tx-ring

- Understanding and Tuning tx-ring-limit value: http://www.cisco.com/en/US/tech/tk39/tk824/technologies_tech_note09186a00800fbafc.shtml.

PAK_priority

- How routing updates and Layer 2 control packets are queued on an interface with a QoS service policy: http://www.cisco.com/warp/public/105/rtgupdates.html.

This chapter includes the following topics:

- Random Early Detection
- Weighted Random Early Detection
- DSCP-Based Weighted Random Early Detection
- Explicit congestion notification

CHAPTER **6**

Congestion-Avoidance Tools

Congestion-avoidance mechanisms, such as Weighted Random Early Detection (WRED), are complementary to (and dependent on) queuing algorithms. Queuing/scheduling algorithms manage the *front* of a queue, whereas congestion-avoidance mechanisms manage the *tail* of a queue.

Congestion-avoidance QoS tools are designed to handle TCP-based data traffic. TCP has built-in flow-control mechanisms that operate by increasing the transmission rates of traffic flows (even though bounded by buffers and window sizes) until packet loss occurs. At this point, TCP abruptly squelches the transmission rate and gradually begins to ramp the transmission rates higher again. This behavior makes a strong case against the statement "QoS isn't necessary; just throw more bandwidth at it." If left unchecked, lengthy TCP sessions (as are typical with bulk data and scavenger applications) can consume any and all available bandwidth, simply because of the nature of TCP.

When no congestion-avoidance algorithms are enabled on an interface, the interface is said to tail drop. That is, after the queuing buffers have filled, all other packets are dropped as they arrive.

In a constricted channel, such as in a WAN or a VPN, all the TCP connections eventually synchronize with each other as they compete for the channel. Without congestion-avoidance mechanisms, they all ramp up together, lose packets together, and back off together. This behavior is referred to as *global synchronization*. In effect, waves of TCP traffic flow through the network nodes, with packets overflowing the buffers at each wave peak and lulls in traffic between the waves.

Figure 6-1 illustrates TCP global synchronization behavior attributable to tail-dropping and the suboptimal effect that this behavior has on bandwidth utilization.

Figure 6-1 *TCP Global Synchronization*

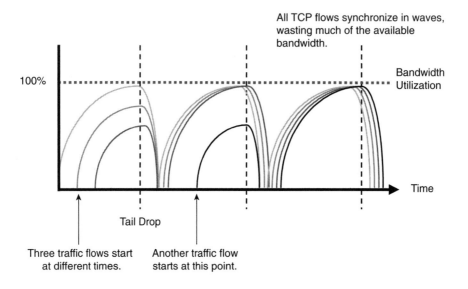

This chapter looks at several variations of the Random Early Detection QoS tool, which strives to combat this global synchronization behavior exhibited by TCP traffic. Explicit congestion notification is another tool that can be employed to improve bandwidth utilization of TCP traffic. The operation and configuration of these tools are discussed in the following sections.

Random Early Detection

Random Early Detection (RED) counters the effects of TCP global synchronization by randomly dropping packets before the queues fill to capacity. Randomly dropping packets instead of dropping them all at once, as is done in a tail drop, avoids global synchronization of TCP streams.

Instead of waiting for queuing buffers to fill before dropping packets, RED causes the router to monitor the buffer depth and perform early discards (drops) on random packets when the minimum defined queue threshold has been exceeded.

RED drops occur within the operational bounds of TCP retry timers, which slow the transmission rates of the sessions but prevent them from starting slow. Thus, RED optimizes network throughput of TCP sessions.

Because UDP does not have any retry logic, congestion-avoidance techniques such as RED (and variants) do not apply to UDP-based traffic.

The Cisco IOS Software does not support RED; it supports only Weighted RED (WRED). It is important to note that the **random-detect** Cisco IOS software CLI command enables WRED. However, if all the packets assigned to an interface or class have the same IPP or DSCP markings, the effective policy is simply RED.

Weighted Random Early Detection

WRED is an enhancement to RED that enables a degree of influence over the "randomness" of the selection of packets to be dropped. WRED factors the weight, or IPP, of the packet into the drop-selection process.

Within the WRED algorithm, a minimum threshold for a given IPP value determines the queue depth at which packets of that IPP value *begin* to be randomly dropped. The maximum threshold determines the queue depth at which *all* packets of that IPP value are dropped. These thresholds are tunable, as is the mark probability denominator, which determines how aggressively the packets of a given IPP value are dropped. (For example, a mark probability denominator value of 10 indicates that up to 1 in 10 packets of a certain precedence value will be dropped randomly—the maximum rate of 1 in 10 happens at the maximum threshold, and the drop rate is linear up to this maximum, as shown in Figure 6-2.)

By default, WRED drops packets with lower IPP values sooner than packets with higher IPP values. A simplified illustration of WRED operation is shown in Figure 6-2.

Figure 6-2   *Weighted Random Early Detection*

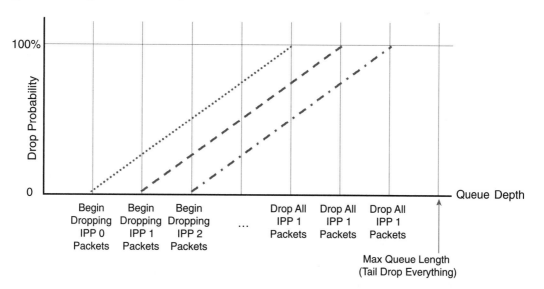

WRED can be configured as an interface command, but it is recommended that it be configured within the MQC syntax because this improves granularity, modularity, and manageability of the WRED algorithm.

As previously noted, WRED is dependent on queuing. Therefore, before WRED can be enabled on a class of traffic, a queuing option (usually either bandwidth or fair-queue) must be enabled on the class. Example 6-1 shows an example of a WRED configuration applied to the default traffic class.

Example 6-1 *WRED Policy Map*

```
class class-default
 fair-queue
 random-detect → enables WRED
```

DSCP-Based Weighted Random Early Detection

DSCP-based WRED was introduced in Cisco IOS Software Release 12.1(5)T. DSCP-based WRED configures the WRED algorithm to use the AF drop-preference values (as defined in RFC 2597) of a packet's DSCP markings to influence its drop probability as queues fill. Remember that the second digit of an AF codepoint indicates drop preference and can range from 1 (lowest drop preference) to 3 (highest drop preference). For example, if DSCP-based WRED is enabled on an interface, AF23 would be dropped more often (statistically) than AF22, which, in turn, would be dropped more often (statistically) than AF21.

Figure 6-3 illustrates a simplified (3 PHB) example of DSCP-based WRED.

Figure 6-3 *DSCP-Based WRED for AF21, AF22, and AF23*

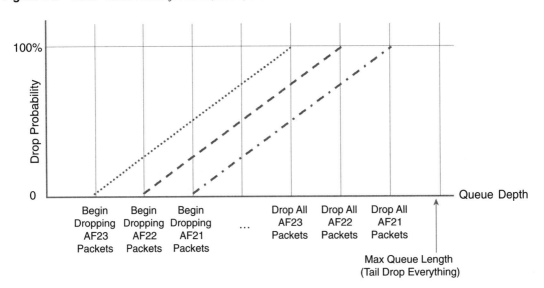

The default DSCP-based WRED configuration can be enabled using the **dscp-based** keyword of the **random-detect** command, as shown in Example 6-2.

Example 6-2 *DSCP-Based WRED Policy Map*

```
class class-default
 fair-queue
 random-detect dscp-based → enables (RFC 2597) DSCP-based WRED
```

As with WRED, DSCP-based WRED thresholds and mark probability denominators are tunable on a per-codepoint basis. In Example 6-3, the minimum threshold is set to begin dropping AF11-marked packets at 5 (that is, as soon as the queue depth reaches five packets, WRED will randomly begin dropping AF11 packets). The maximum threshold for AF11 (at which *all* AF11-marked packets will be dropped) is set to 20 packets in Example 6-3. The mark probability denominator is set to 8 (meaning that, between these two thresholds, up to 1 in 8 packets marked with AF11 will be dropped, and at the maximum threshold of 20, exactly 1 in 8 packets will be dropped—above the maximum threshold of 20, all packets marked with AF11 will be dropped).

Example 6-3 *DSCP-Based WRED Configuration Dropping AF11 packets*

```
Router(config)#policy-map DSCP-WRED
Router(config-pmap)#class class-default
Router(config-pmap-c)#random-detect dscp af11 5 20 8
```

Explicit Congestion Notification

Traditionally, the only way to inform sending hosts that there was congestion on the network so that the hosts would slow their transmission rates was to drop TCP packets.

RFC 3168, however, defined a new and more efficient way for the network to communicate congestion to sending hosts: adding explicit congestion notification (ECN) to IP. By marking the final 2 bits of the ToS byte of the IP header, devices can communicate to each other and to endpoints that they are experiencing congestion. These two bits have been defined as follows:

- **ECN-Capable Transport (ECT) bit**—This bit indicates whether the device supports ECN.

- **Congestion Experienced (CE) bit**—This bit (in conjunction with the ECT bit) indicates whether congestion was experienced en route.

Figure 6-4 shows the location of the ECN bits in the TOS byte of an IP packet header.

Figure 6-4 *IP ToS Byte ECN Bits*

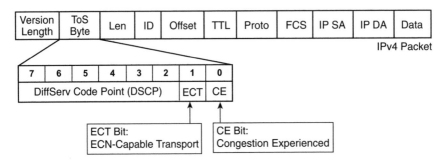

During periods of congestion, WRED (and DSCP-based WRED) drops packets when the average queue length exceeds a specific threshold value. ECN is an extension to WRED, in that ECN marks packets instead of dropping them, to communicate the existence of congestion when the average queue length exceeds a specific threshold value. Routers configured with the WRED ECN feature, introduced in Cisco IOS Software Release 12.2(8)T, use this marking as a signal that the network is congested. This way, TCP transmission rates can be controlled without dropping packets, or at least with dropping far fewer packets.

Table 6-1 lists the ECN bit combinations and their meanings.

Table 6-1 *ECN Bit Combinations*

ECT Bit	CE Bit	Combination Indicates
0	0	Not ECN-capable
0	1	Endpoints of the transport protocol are ECN-capable
1	0	Endpoints of the transport protocol are ECN-capable
1	1	Congestion experienced

The bit-setting combinations have the following meanings:

- The ECN field combination 00 indicates that a packet is not using ECN.

- The ECN field combinations 01 and 10, which are called ECT(1) and ECT(0), respectively, are set by the data sender to indicate that the endpoints of the transport protocol are ECN-capable. Routers treat these two field combinations identically. Data senders can use either or both of these combinations.

- The ECN field combination 11 indicates congestion to the endpoints. Packets arriving into a full queue of a router are dropped.

WRED ECN takes the following actions, depending on the ECN bit settings:

- If the number of packets in the queue is below the minimum threshold, packets are transmitted. This happens whether or not ECN is enabled. This treatment is identical to the treatment that a packet receives when only WRED is being used on the network.

- If the number of packets in the queue is between the minimum threshold and the maximum threshold, one of the following three scenarios can occur:
  - If the ECN field on the packet indicates that the endpoints are ECN-capable (that is, the ECT bit is set to 1 and the CE bit is set to 0, or the ECT bit is set to 0 and the CE bit is set to 1) and the WRED algorithm determines that the packet should be dropped based on the drop probability, the ECT and CE bits for the packet are changed to 1 and the packet is transmitted. This happens because ECN is enabled, and the packet gets marked instead of dropped.
  - If the ECN field on the packet indicates that neither endpoint is ECN-capable (that is, the ECT bit is set to 0 and the CE bit is set to 0), the packet can be dropped based on the WRED drop probability. This is the identical treatment that a packet receives when WRED is enabled without ECN configured on the router.
  - If the ECN field on the packet indicates that the network is experiencing congestion (that is, both the ECT bit and the CE bit are set to 1), the packet is transmitted. No further marking is required.

- If the number of packets in the queue is above the maximum threshold, all packets are dropped and the drop probability is 1. This is the identical treatment that a packet receives when WRED is enabled without ECN configured on the router, and the packet flow exceeds its maximum threshold.

WRED ECN is enabled with the **ecn** keyword on the **random-detect** command. **WRED ECN** cannot be enabled by itself and must be used in conjunction with WRED or DSCP-based WRED (as is shown in Example 6-4).

Example 6-4 *WRED-ECN Policy Map Example*

```
Router#sh run
  class class-default
   fair-queue
   random-detect dscp-based
   random-detect ecn → enables (RFC 3168) ECN-based WRED
```

Summary

Congestion-avoidance tools such as WRED variations and ECN were overviewed in this chapter.

WRED is used to drop packets randomly (based on configured parameters that control the drop probabilities) from a TCP session in the network to optimize bandwidth utilization of TCP traffic. The global synchronization problem of unguarded TCP sessions was discussed, and the chapter showed how WRED can be used to combat this behavior.

ECN is a newer congestion-avoidance tool, and its operation and configuration was discussed briefly.

Further Reading

DiffServ Standards Relating to WRED

- RFC 2597, "An Assured Forwarding PHB Group": http://www.ietf.org/rfc/rfc2597.txt.
- RFC 3168, "The Addition of Explicit Congestion Notification (ECN) to IP": http://www.ietf.org/rfc/rfc3168.txt.

Cisco IOS WRED Documentation

- MQC-based WRED (Cisco IOS Software Release 12.0.5T): http://www.cisco.com/univercd/cc/td/doc/product/software/ios120/120newft/120t/120t5/cbwfq.htm.
- DiffServ-compliant Weighted Random Early Detection (Cisco IOS Software Release 12.1.5T): http://www.cisco.com/univercd/cc/td/doc/product/software/ios121/121newft/121t/121t5/dtdswred.htm.
- Distributed class-based weighted fair queuing and distributed Weighted Random Early Detection (Cisco IOS Software Release 12.1.5T): http://www.cisco.com/univercd/cc/td/doc/product/software/ios121/121newft/121t/121t5/dtcbwred.htm.
- WRED—explicit congestion notification (Cisco IOS Software Release 12.2.8T): http://www.cisco.com/univercd/cc/td/doc/product/software/ios122/122newft/122t/122t8/ftwrdecn.htm.

This chapter discusses link-specific QoS tools needed on links of a specific type such as Frame Relay or MLP, including the following topics:

- RTP header compression
- Link Fragmentation and Interleaving

CHAPTER 7

Link-Specific Tools

Link-specific tools refer to mechanisms that are enabled in a point-to-point manner on both ends of WAN links. These tools combine Layer 2 and Layer 3 features in their functionality. This chapter covers two types of link-specific tools:

- **Header-compression techniques**—These mechanisms can reduce bandwidth requirements for both voice and data traffic.

- **Link Fragmentation and Interleaving tools**—These mechanisms minimize serialization delays common to slow-speed WAN links.

The link-specific tools frequently are categorized as QoS tools because they often are used in conjunction with other QoS techniques, as discussed in this chapter. However, both tools have application outside the realm of QoS and were developed originally as generic Cisco IOS Software features, not specifically as QoS tools. This chapter limits the discussion to how these techniques are applied to improve the QoS of the network.

The first half of this chapter looks at header-compression techniques, which are a suite of features that reduce the size of the IP packet header. For large data packets, the ratio of the header bytes to the payload bytes is usually not significant, and header compression is seldom a compelling feature. But for short voice packets, the IP (and UDP and RTP) headers can triple the size of the packet and, therefore, the bandwidth required for a voice call. These extra bytes also contribute to increased delay, so reducing the size of the header can provide significant savings. Although the focus of the following sections is on RTP header compression, these sections also examine dependencies that this feature has on related features, such as TCP header compression.

The last half of the chapter explores Link Fragmentation and Interleaving. On links of 768 kbps or higher, this technique has little to no value. However, on slow WAN links, transmitting a 1500-byte data packet can take long enough that it incurs undue delay in a voice packet that waits behind it to be transmitted. In these situations, it makes sense to divide the data packet into smaller segments so that a small voice packet can be interleaved in between the segments of a large data packet. This bounds the delay incurred on a voice packet.

Header-Compression Techniques

One of the key drivers to many VoIP deployments is the financially attractive bandwidth savings they deliver. For example, a regular TDM voice call requires a fixed allocation of 64 kbps of bandwidth, whereas a comparable quality VoIP call can be reduced to approximately 12 kbps. Two types of compression are performed on voice packets to achieve such bandwidth reductions:

- Payload compression, through codecs such as G.729

- Header compression, through features such as RTP header compression (also known as *Compressed RTP or cRTP*)

G.729 voice compression enables a 64-kbps TDM voice call to be reduced to 8 kbps—a savings of a factor of 8. The compressed speech samples are carried in VoIP using RTP packets with 20 bytes of payload per packet (by default). RTP header compression (cRTP) is a method for making RTP packet headers smaller so that VoIP bandwidth is used more efficiently. cRTP compresses the 40-byte IP/UDP/RTP header of a VoIP packet down to 2 to 5 bytes per packet. This reduces the L3 bandwidth required for a G.729 VoIP call to less than 12 kbps, as illustrated in Figure 7-1.

Figure 7-1   *RTP Header Compression (cRTP)*

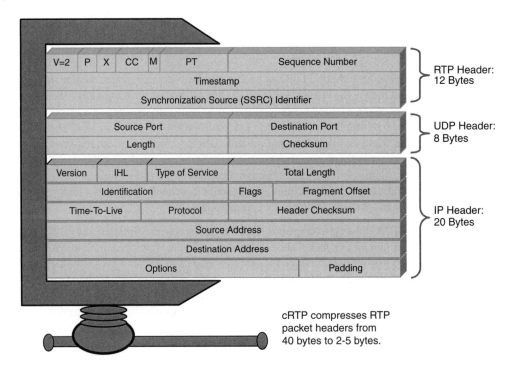

Related Standards

Header-compression techniques are described by several standards. The first header-compression scheme was developed by Van Jacobson to compress IP/TCP headers over slow-speed serial links. An improvement to this method was offered by the IP header compression (IPHC) scheme, with an RTP compression extension designed to handle any IP packet. The most recent addition to the header-compression portfolio is robust header compression (ROHC), which is a scheme designed for unreliable, high-latency mobile links, in which bandwidth is very scarce and the links are prone to error (cRTP over satellite links, a Cisco IOS 12.3[2]T feature, is based on the ROHC compression scheme).

The various IETF RFCs pertaining to header-compression techniques are listed here:

- **RFC 1144**—"Compresses TCP/IP Headers for Low-Speed Serial Links"
- **RFC 2507**—"IP Header Compression"
- **RFC 2508**—"Compressing IP/UDP/RTP Headers for Low-Speed Serial Links"
- **RFC 2509**—"IP Header Compression over PPP"
- **RFC 3095**—"Robust Header Compression (ROHC)"

This is the framework and four profiles: RTP, UDP, ESP, and uncompressed. There is also a Frame Relay standard that describes the use of cRTP on Frame Relay PVCs: "FRF.20: Frame Relay IP Header Compression Implementation Agreement." This standard describes how IP packets compressed by cRTP should be represented in the Frame Relay frame that transports them.

TCP Header Compression

As the name implies, TCP header compression (cTCP) is a method of compressing the headers of TCP/IP segments. However, header compression is much less advantageous, in terms of the percentage of bandwidth savings, on 1500-byte data packets than cRTP is on small 20-byte voice packets.

TCP header compression was more relevant in the era when home and remote office connections ranged from 9.6 to 19.2 kbps. Although such scenarios are rarely the case today, it is important to note that the RFCs state that TCP header compression must be enabled automatically whenever cRTP is enabled. This is the case with Cisco's implementations of cRTP over PPP links.

RTP Header Compression

The capability to support cRTP to gain bandwidth savings for voice streams on slow links is of paramount importance to private and public VoIP networks. Therefore, cRTP is a key QoS technique in converged networks with slow-speed edge links. Without cRTP, VoIP service on links slower than about 128 kbps becomes unpractical. Even with cRTP, care must be taken in the network design that acceptable voice quality can be maintained.

cRTP has the following QoS network design implications:

- It changes the packet header and, therefore, must be decompressed before routing can take place. This makes cRTP a hop-by-hop protocol, with decompression and recompression occurring in every routing node in which the feature is enabled.

- It changes the bandwidth required for a voice call and, therefore, affects provisioning and engineering of queuing, policing, shaping, and call admission control policies.

- It is a compression algorithm and, therefore, CPU intensive. When cRTP is enabled on a router, care must be taken so that the platform has enough CPU power to perform this task for the maximum number of calls that might traverse it, and still have enough CPU for the other data traffic and routing tasks that the CPU must perform. Proof-of-concept testing for cRTP-enabled configurations is strongly encouraged.

- The use of cRTP is dependent on the underlying Layer 2 protocol.

Because cRTP essentially suppresses the Layer 3 and higher headers, it can be used only on point-to-point Layer 2 connections or links; it *cannot* be used on broadcast media such as Ethernet and cable, where reading the packet header is critical for the destination node to recognize that it is the intended recipient of the frame. Although the RFCs describe the actual algorithms that header compression protocols use, the protocols are not as much "compression" protocols as they are "suppression" protocols. For example, cRTP works by keeping the header context (for example, the current values of all the fields in the header) in both the sender and receiver nodes' memory. Compression is based on the principle that few fields (other than sequence numbers) in the headers change in subsequent packets that belong to the same flow. cRTP simply omits the transmission of header fields that have not changed, transmitting instead a reference number or pointer so that the receiving node can index its memory to find the actual values of header fields.

During a voice conversation, cRTP does not compress all packets. When the RTP stream starts up, a few packets have full headers until the compression contexts between the sender and receiver are established. After that, all packets should be compressed. A full header in the middle of a conversation is very rare but could be triggered by events such as these:

- An event change within the flow cannot be communicated in the compressed header.

- One of the samples is too large to be encoded in the compressed header.

An error packet was received, forcing a resynchronization of contexts. It is important to remember that a few packets at the start of the flow always have full headers, and the occasional communication of some field changes also requires full packets with headers. Nonetheless, the average cRTP stream has a 2- to 5-byte header.

Compression Formats

The compression formats that cRTP uses have changed over the years. To achieve backward compatibility, these are implemented as different options on the interface command, as follows:

```
ip rtp header-compression [passive | iphc-format | ietf-format] [periodic-refresh]
```

The **passive** option means that the software waits until it receives a compressed packet before engaging header compression on outgoing RTP packets. This is a legacy command from the Serial Line IP (SLIP) protocol and is used mainly for dialer situations. PPP negotiates the use of **header-compression** regardless of whether the **passive** option is used.

NOTE The use of the **passive** keyword with PPP as the underlying L2 protocol recently has been disabled to prevent confusion.

The IPHC and IETF formats are discussed in the following sections. The **periodic-refresh** option was introduced in Cisco IOS 12.3(2)T Software as part of the robust cRTP over satellite links feature. It allows a full header to be resent periodically (configurable) to ensure that compression continues to function over high-loss links.

Cisco Proprietary Format

The original format of cRTP implementation within Cisco IOS was the Cisco proprietary version that compresses packets only recognized as RTP. RTP packets are recognized by ensuring that the destination port number is even and within the range of 16385 to 32767 (for audio streams) or 49152 to 65535 (for video streams). The original format of cRTP allows only up to 256 contexts.

IP Header Compression Format

The IP header compression (IPHC) format was the initial Cisco IOS implementation of RFC 2507 and RFC 2508. RFC 2507 specifies the format for TCP and UDP compression, and RFC 2508 specifies extensions to RFC 2507—specifically, to compress RTP packet headers. In IPHC format over PPP links, TCP and RTP compression are inseparable, as described by RFC 2509, which specifies the PPP negotiation for header compression. RFC 2509 states that on PPP, it is impossible to negotiate one type of compression (cTCP or cRTP) without the other. Thus, when enabling cRTP on a PPP interface, cTCP also automatically is enabled. RFC 2509bis (*bis* indicates a standards update to the original RFC 2509) decouples cRTP from cTCP but is not yet (fully) implemented within Cisco IOS.

However, use of class-based cRTP within the MQC construct can achieve the decoupling of cTCP and cRTP. This is discussed with additional details later in this chapter. IPHC format compresses all TCP and UDP packets. Packets that match RTP criteria are compressed using the compressed RTP format, while other packets are compressed using the compressed non-TCP format. The compressed UDP format is used to compress only RTP packets that do not fit into the compressed RTP template. These formats, and the differences between them, are discussed in RFCs 2507 and 2508, as follows:

- **Compressed TCP**—The frame contains a datagram with a compressed header with the format specified in RFC 2507 Section 6a.

- **Compressed TCP-NODELTA**—The frame contains a datagram with a compressed header with the format specified in RFC 2507 Section 6b.

- **Compressed non-TCP**—The frame contains a datagram with a compressed header with the format specified in either Section 6c or Section 6d of RFC 2507.

- **Compressed RTP-8**—The frame contains a datagram with a compressed header with the format specified in RFC 2508 Section 3.3.2, using an 8-bit context identifier.

- **Compressed RTP-16**—The frame contains a datagram with a compressed header with the format specified in RFC 2508 Section 3.3.2, using a 16-bit context identifier.

- **Compressed UDP-8**—The frame contains a datagram with a compressed header with the format specified in RFC 2508 Section 3.3.3, using an 8-bit context identifier.

- **Compressed UDP-16**—The frame contains a datagram with a compressed header with the format specified in RFC 2508 Section 3.3.3, using a 16-bit context identifier.

IETF Format

The initial Cisco IOS Software implementations of RFCs 2508 and 2509 were not in perfect compliance with the standards. IETF format, the most recently introduced option (Cisco IOS 12.3[2]T) for cRTP, attempts to address all of these incompatibilities and to match the RFCs as closely as possible. In IETF format, as with IPHC format, cTCP and cRTP are inseparable for PPP links. All TCP and UDP packets are compressed, but only packets recognized as RTP are compressed using the more efficient compressed RTP format. However, the restriction of recognizing only RTP streams on certain port ranges for compression has been removed, and cRTP uses any even port over 1024 when the **ietf-format** keyword is used.

Layer 2 Encapsulation Protocol Support

The previous sections discussed the standards and formats that govern cRTP in general. Another dependency of cRTP is on the specific L2 link and the protocol encapsulation configured for this link.

The RFCs tend to discuss only PPP links, yet cRTP is supported over point-to-point links with HDLC, PPP, Frame Relay, and ATM encapsulations. The implementations over Frame Relay and HDLC are proprietary, while those over PPP are standards compliant with the RFCs discussed previously. cRTP on ATM is supported only via PPP or MLP over ATM (PPPoA or MLPoATM, respectively).

As mentioned earlier, cRTP cannot be supported on broadcast Layer 2 media such as Ethernet or cable. cRTP works only on point-to-point connections in which there is a single possible destination for the packet.

The following sections provide additional details about the implementation of cRTP on each of the link encapsulation types where it is supported.

HDLC

cRTP is implemented over HDLC links in its proprietary version; HDLC itself is a Cisco-proprietary protocol. Cisco format compression is the default, yet IPHC format also is supported within the CLI. Because the cRTP implementation over HDLC is proprietary, cTCP and cRTP can be controlled independently (for instance, the implementation does not have to conform to RFC 2509).On HDLC links, header compression is configured on the interface using these commands:

```
ip tcp header-compression [passive | iphc-format | ietf-format]
ip rtp header-compression [passive | iphc-format | ietf-format]
ip tcp compression-connections [3-256]
ip rtp compression-connections [3-1000]
```

The first two commands turn on cTCP and cRTP, respectively, as discussed earlier. The **compression-connections** commands state the maximum number of cTCP or cRTP sessions that are possible over this link. It is important for this number to match on both sides of the link, and it should be configured carefully because this governs the amount of memory set aside to keep the session contexts to compress/decompress the headers. The defaults and supported ranges have changed over time, so check the Cisco IOS documentation for the software release that you are running for the correct values.

PPP

The default cRTP format for PPP is IPHC format. PPP negotiates the use of header compression regardless of whether the **passive** option is used (additionally, the use of **passive** with PPP recently has been disabled, to prevent confusion). For IPHC format and IETF format, turning on either cTCP or cRTP automatically also enables the other type.

On PPP links, header compression is configured at the interface using the same commands as given previously for HDLC.

ATM

cRTP is not supported over native ATM because no standard describes such an implementation. However, a new feature in Cisco IOS 12.2(2)T introduced cRTP over ATM through PPP over ATM (PPPoATM) and MLP over ATM (MLPoATM). The initial feature release applied to general ATM interfaces; DSL interface support for this feature followed in Release 12.3(2)T. cRTP over ATM is configured through PPP using a virtual template. Virtual templates frequently are used with PPP and MLP configurations. They provide a way to specify a template configuration only once and then apply that template to multiple links, virtual circuits, or interfaces. This simplifies the maintenance of the configuration if there are many links with similar characteristics.

Any of the configurations given in Example 7-1 can be used for cRTP over ATM links.

Example 7-1   *cRTP Configuration for ATM Links*

```
Router#sh run
interface ATM6/1.1 point-to-point
 pvc 0/50
   encapsulation aal5mux ppp Virtual-Template1
or
interface ATM6/1.1 point-to-point
 pvc 0/50
   encapsulation aal5snap
   protocol ppp Virtual-Template1
or
interface ATM6/1.1 point-to-point
 pvc 0/50
   encapsulation aal5ciscoppp Virtual-Template1
Coupled with:
!
interface Virtual-Template1
 bandwidth 768
 ip address 10.200.60.1 255.255.255.252
 ip rtp header-compression [passive | iphc-format | ietf-format] [periodic-refresh]
```

The cRTP configuration (the highlighted text in the example) is the general cRTP command discussed in an earlier section. Here is it specified within the template Virtual-Template1, which is, in turn, applied to the ATM PVCs in the example.

Frame Relay

cRTP has been supported on Frame Relay links since the mid-1990s because this encapsulation is used so frequently on slow-speed access links to remote offices. The use of cRTP on Frame Relay has only more recently been standardized as FRF.20 (June 2001).

The implementation of cRTP on Cisco Frame Relay PVCs is currently still proprietary and will remain so until Cisco implements FRF.20. The current implementation is very close to the FRF.20 standard but is not exactly the same. cRTP is not supported on IETF PVCs because this support will require FRF.20 compliance. The fact that this is currently a proprietary implementation also means that cTCP and cRTP can be controlled independently.

cRTP on PPP over Frame Relay (PPPoFR) and MLP over Frame Relay (MLPoFR) are standards compliant; this is the same as with the PPP implementations discussed earlier in this chapter. Therefore, cRTP on PPPoFR is supported on both Cisco and IETF PVCs. If a standards-compliant implementation of cRTP on Frame Relay is required for a network design, this form of cRTP should be used.

Although there are many ways to configure cRTP on Frame Relay links, the most common method is shown in Example 7-2.

Example 7-2   *Common cRTP Configuration*

```
Router#sh run
interface Serial 2/0
        encapsulation frame-relay
!
    interface Serial 2/0.100 point-to-point
        encapsulation frame-relay
        ip address 192.168.0.1 255.255.255.0
        frame-relay interface-dlci 100
        frame-relay ip rtp header-compression
```

The format of the cRTP command is different for Frame Relay than the commands discussed previously. The options on this command include only the **passive** and **periodic-refresh** parameters. As discussed earlier, the IETF format of cRTP does not apply to Frame Relay links.

Frame Relay and ATM Service Interworking

If Frame Relay-to-ATM interworking (FRF.5 or FRF.8) is used in a network and cRTP is required as well, PPP must be used over the entire link (for example, PPPoATM to PPPoFR, or MLPoATM to MLPoFR). cRTP is supported over such interworked links as of Cisco IOS Software Release 12.2(2)T.

Summary of cRTP Formats and Protocol Encapsulations

Table 7-1 summarizes the different formats of cTCP and cRTP that can be used with different Layer 2 link encapsulations. The table also gives important performance information in the Switching Path columns. As mentioned earlier, cRTP is CPU intensive; if it is process-switched, it is significantly more so. cRTP was implemented in the fast and CEF switching paths several years ago, but for older releases of Cisco IOS Software, it is important to check that this is not process-switched before turning on the feature. If it is process-switched, upgrade to a Cisco IOS release in which cRTP is supported in the fast or CEF paths.

Table 7-1 *cRTP Format and Encapsulation Options*

Encapsulation	Compression Formats				Switching Path			
	TCP Original	RTP Original	IPHC Format	IETF Format	Process	Fast	CEF	dCEF
HDLC	Yes	Yes	Yes	12.3.2T	Yes	Yes	Yes	12.1.5T
PPP	Yes		Yes	12.3.2T	Yes	Yes	Yes	12.1.5T
MLPPP	Yes		Yes	12.3.2T	Yes	Yes	Yes	12.1.5T
Frame Relay	Yes	Yes			Yes	Yes	Yes	12.1.5T
PPPoFR	Yes		Yes	12.3.2T	Yes	Yes	Yes	12.2.2T
MLPoFR	Yes		Yes	12.3.2T	Yes	Yes	Yes	12.2.2T
PPPoATM	Yes		Yes	12.3.2T	Yes	Yes	Yes	12.2.2T
MLPoATM	Yes		Yes	12.3.2T	Yes	Yes	Yes	12.2.2T

Class-Based Header Compression

In Cisco IOS Software Release 12.2(13)T, cRTP was made available within the MQC syntax, allowing it to be configured on a per-class basis. Class-based cRTP thus improves the granularity of what traffic is to be compressed, which is a feature often needed to work around the RFC 2509's requirement that cTCP and cRTP must be negotiated together for PPP links. Furthermore, class-based cRTP includes cRTP statistics for outbound packets within the output of the **show policy-map interface** command, thus improving its manageability. Sample output for this command is shown in Example 7-3. For compression statistics on inbound packets, the **show ip rtp header-compression** command can be used.

Example 7-3 *cRTP Statistics*

```
Router#show policy-map interface Serial 4/1
Serial4/1
Service-policy output:p1
   Class-map:class-default (match-any)
      1005 packets, 64320 bytes
      30 second offered rate 16000 bps, drop rate 0 bps
      Match:any
      compress:
          header ip rtp
          UDP/RTP Compression:
          Sent:1000 total, 999 compressed,
                41957 bytes saved, 17983 bytes sent
                3.33 efficiency improvement factor
                99% hit ratio, five minute miss rate 0 misses/sec, 0 max
                 rate 5000 bps
```

On RFC-compliant software, if cRTP is activated on a certain class of traffic within a service policy, both cTCP and cRTP are applied for the class of traffic (based on the standards discussed previously in this chapter). However, because TCP and RTP traffic are separated out into different classes by the classification criteria, usually no TCP traffic is present in the class where cRTP is enabled. Conversely, there is typically no RTP traffic in a TCP traffic class. Therefore, cRTP effectively can be decoupled from cTCP within the MQC syntax structure. Such decoupling of the automatic enabling of cTCP whenever cRTP is activated often is desired for these reasons:

- Header-compression ratios on TCP traffic are small, resulting in nominal bandwidth savings.

- Compression algorithms are CPU intensive and should be enabled carefully to provide the greatest bandwidth returns for the increased CPU cost (for example, on VoIP, not data).

Data traffic is not real-time sensitive, and header compression does not provide significant savings on packets with large payloads. Therefore, cTCP provides negligible packet-transmission performance improvements. The match criteria within the class maps determine what traffic is given to the compressor. Decompression, on the other hand, is not controlled by class maps; cRTP decompresses all packets that arrive compressed from the other side of the link.

The default mode for cRTP inside an MQC class is IPHC format for all encapsulations that support it, including ATM, PPP, and HDLC. For Frame Relay links, in which IPHC format is unavailable, the original (Cisco proprietary) format is used as the default. Example 7-4 shows a cRTP configuration inside an MQC class.

Example 7-4 *MQC-Based cRTP Configuration*

```
Router#sh run
policy-map CB-CRTP
 class VOIP
   compression header ip rtp
   priority 200
 class class-default
   fair-queue
```

In a similar manner, **compression header ip tcp** can be used for a data traffic class.

The interface configuration for enabling header compression is mutually exclusive with class-based cRTP. The IPHC format and **passive** options are autoconfigured based on the interface encapsulation and do not appear as being configurable, as shown in Example 7-5. The number of concurrent connections also is autoconfigured and calculated based on the sum of the bandwidths allocated to the classes that have header compression configured (one connection per 4 kbps of bandwidth available). This must be the same on both ends of the link.

Example 7-5 *Class-Based cRTP Configuration*

```
Router(config-pmap-c)#compression header ip ?
  rtp   configure rtp header compression
  tcp   configure tcp header compression
```

Advanced Topics on cRTP

Several other Cisco IOS features should be considered in conjunction with cRTP when designing converged networks. These are discussed in the following sections.

Tunnels

Although cRTP is an action that works on Layer 3 headers and up, it can be viewed as a Layer 2 function because it is applied to the packet just before it exits the egress interface. Therefore, when tunnel configurations (for example, GRE, MPLS, and IPSec) are used, cRTP ceases to work. (The feature can be configured, but the packets no longer are compressed.) This is because cRTP sees the packet just before it is transmitted on the egress interface, after the tunnel IP headers have been applied. The cRTP compressor no longer can recognize the encapsulated packet as an RTP packet and, thus, does not compress it.

RSVP

RSVP is a Layer 3 bandwidth-reservation protocol and generally acts on the Layer 3 packet size and bandwidth requirements. Therefore, if cRTP is used on a specific voice stream and RSVP is used to provide the call admission control for that same stream, an *over-reservation* of bandwidth will be made for the call because, until recently, RSVP did not take the bandwidth savings afforded by cRTP into account in its reservations.

As of Cisco IOS Software Release 12.2(15)T, a feedback mechanism between cRTP and RSVP has been implemented so that RSVP is cognizant of cRTP and adjusts its reservations appropriately.

RSVP and call admission control technologies are covered in Chapter 8, "Bandwidth Reservation," and Chapter 9, "Call Admission Control (CAC)."

LLQ, Policing, and Shaping

LLQ, class-based shaping, and class-based (*egress*) policing all take header compression into account as of Cisco IOS Software Release 12.2(2)T. This means that class bandwidth can be configured based on compressed packets. However, keep in mind that decompression occurs on ingress, before any of the input QoS features are activated. Therefore, any *ingress* policing policies are applied against uncompressed packets; bandwidth policing limits should be factored accordingly.

Hardware Compression

cRTP is supported only on Cisco PVCs, not on IETF PVCs (unless PPPoFR/MLPoFR is used). Until Cisco IOS Software Release 12.1(5)T, Frame Relay hardware compression (FRF.9) was supported on only IETF PVCs, making it difficult to use the optimal compression for all traffic, which is FRF.9 STAC (STAC is the name of the company that first wrote the algorithm) for data traffic and cRTP for voice. As of 12.1(5)T, FRF.9 hardware compression also is allowed on Cisco PVCs. Under such a configuration, voice traffic bypasses the STAC compressor and is compressed by a combination of cRTP and the codec, providing better compression ratios for voice traffic than STAC compression would.

Performance

Compression techniques, such as cRTP, minimize bandwidth requirements and are highly useful on slow-speed links. Because of the additional CPU loads these compression techniques require, they need to be used with caution, especially on WAN aggregation routers that attach to many remote sites.

In Cisco IOS 12.0, 12.0T, and 12.1 Software, cRTP was process-switched, which rendered it practically unusable for real networks. In several Cisco IOS releases, between 12.0(7)T and 12.1(2)T, cRTP was implemented in the fast and Cisco Express Forwarding (CEF) paths, which dramatically improved its scalability. Nonetheless, cRTP remains one of the most CPU-intensive QoS features and should be enabled with a careful eye on CPU levels, especially on large-scale WAN aggregation routers.

Performance is affected positively by the support of class-based cRTP because the traffic that is compressed now can be filtered more granularly than before. Furthermore, with class-based cRTP, cTCP use can be avoided, further improving processing efficiency.

When the CPU of the node-compressing RTP traffic runs at reasonable levels (for instance, the target ≤70 percent), cRTP does not impact delay or voice quality in any adverse manner.

Link Fragmentation and Interleaving

A problem with slow-speed WAN circuits, with respect to voice, is that large data packets take an excessively long time to be transmitted onto the wire. This delay is referred to as *serialization delay*, and it easily can cause a VoIP packet to exceed its delay or jitter tolerance. Two main tools can be used to mitigate serialization delay on slow links: Multilink PPP Link-Fragmentation and Interleaving (MLP LFI) and Frame Relay Fragmentation and Interleaving (FRF.12).

In the context of link-efficiency mechanisms, slow-speed links are defined as WAN links with clock speeds of 768 kbps or less. To offset link-specific delays, larger data packets can be fragmented and smaller voice packets can be interleaved with the fragments, as shown in Figure 7-2. This helps reduce the variation in delay caused by a periodic data packet that arrives at the egress interface just before a voice packet does and, therefore, has started transmission already, causing the voice packets to have to wait until the interface becomes free before being transmitted itself. Sophisticated queuing techniques such as LLQ do not help for this problem because this is the result of serialization delay or the elapsed time that it takes to transmit a packet on the interface. Any subsequent packet must wait for the interface to become free before starting its own transmission.

Figure 7-2 *LFI Operation on Slow-Speed Links*

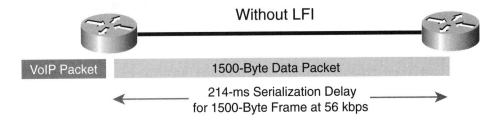

Without LFI

| VoIP Packet | 1500-Byte Data Packet |

214-ms Serialization Delay
for 1500-Byte Frame at 56 kbps

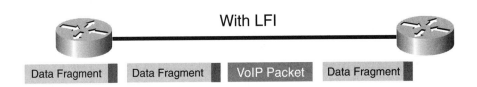

With LFI

| Data Fragment | Data Fragment | VoIP Packet | Data Fragment |

LFI tools work at Layer 2 and operate on packets that already have exited the Layer 3 queuing subsystem (LLQ/CBWFQ). As mentioned in Chapter 5, "Congestion-Management Tools," on PPP links, only packets that are *not* assigned to the PQ of LLQ are fragmented. This presents an important constraint when provisioning for voice and interactive video on slow-speed links: Because large video packets assigned to the PQ of the LLQ algorithm are not fragmented and easily could destroy voice quality, it is not recommended to provision both voice and interactive video through LLQs on slow-speed links (for instance, those less than 768 kbps).

Table 7-2 shows the serialization delays of various packet sizes on different link speeds.

Although maximum transmission unit (MTU) size constraints theoretically can be used to achieve the same purpose as LFI, this is seldom practical because MTU size settings affect Layer 3 packets and are therefore visible to the end systems. Many end-user server and desktop applications do not handle MTU size changes elegantly, and even if they do, it is impractical to change the MTU size on all the servers and user applications in the network.

Table 7-2 *Serialization Delay by Packet Size and Link Speed*

	1 Byte	64 Bytes	128 Bytes	256 Bytes	512 Bytes	1024 Bytes	1500 Bytes
56 kbps	143 μs	9 ms	18 ms	36 ms	72 ms	144 ms	214 ms
64 kbps	125 μs	8 ms	16 ms	32 ms	64 ms	128 ms	187 ms
128 kbps	62.5 μs	4 ms	8 ms	16 ms	32 ms	64 ms	93 ms
256 kbps	31 μs	2 ms	4 ms	8 ms	16 ms	32 ms	46 ms
512 kbps	15.5 μs	1 ms	2 ms	4 ms	8 ms	16 ms	23 ms
768 kbps	10 μs	640 μs	1.28 ms	2.56 ms	5.1 ms	10.2 ms	15 ms
1536 kbps	5 μs	320 μs	640 μs	1.28 ms	2.56 ms	5.12 ms	7.5 ms

Layer 2 LFI mechanisms are transparent to the Layer 3 IP applications, performing LFI within the network infrastructure only where necessary. Layer 3 packets are reassembled at the Layer 2 media edges (requiring LFI), and end systems see normal 1500-byte IP packets.

Fragment Sizes

As a general guideline, a per-hop serialization delay target within the enterprise is smaller than or equal to 10 ms. Within an SP context, this target might be even tighter.

The following formula can be used to determine the maximum fragment size (in bytes) for a given jitter target and link speed:

Fragment Size = (Maximum Allowed Jitter in milliseconds [typically 10 ms]) * (Link Speed in kbps) /8

Alternatively, Table 7-3 shows the recommended fragment sizes to achieve a 10-ms maximum serialization delay for different speed links.

The 768-kbps value to determine when LFI tools are required on a link is derived from the preceding formula. However, all resulting fragment sizes that are larger than the MTU of Ethernet (1500 bytes) are shaded in Table 7-3, indicating that no explicit LFI tool is needed to achieve the 10-ms serialization delay target in the given scenario.

Multilink PPP LFI

Multilink PPP Link Fragmentation and Interleaving (MLP LFI) is a very flexible LFI scheme that can be applied over a single leased line or multiple leased lines, MLP Bundles, ISDN, Frame Relay circuits (through MLPoFR), ATM PVCs (through MLPoATM), and ATM-to-Frame Relay Service Interworking (through MLPoFR to MLPoATM SIW).

Table 7-3 *Maximum Fragment Sizes for 10-ms Serialization Delays*

		Real-Time Packet Interval
		10 ms
Link or Virtual Circuit Speed	56 kbps	70 bytes
	64 kbps	80 bytes
	128 kbps	160 bytes
	256 kbps	320 bytes
	512 kbps	640 bytes
	768 kbps	960 bytes
	1536 kbps	1920 bytes[*]

[*]   Enabling LFI is superfluous whenever the resulting fragment sizes exceed the MTU of Ethernet (1500 bytes).

When configuring MLP LFI, the only parameter needed is the maximum serialization delay in milliseconds, which is recommended to be set to 10 ms. The software automatically calculates the fragment sizes. A sample MLP LFI configuration is shown in Example 7-6.

Example 7-6 *MLP LFI Configuration*

```
Router#sh run
interface Multilink1
 description 768kbps Leased-Line to RBR-3745-Left
 ip address 10.1.112.1 255.255.255.252
 ppp multilink
 ppp multilink fragment delay 10
 ppp multilink interleave
 ppp multilink group 1
!
...
!
interface Serial1/0
 bandwidth 786
 no ip address
 encapsulation ppp
 load-interval 30
 ppp multilink
 ppp multilink group 1
!
```

Multiclass Multilink PPP

A limitation of the original implementation of MLP was that only fragments would receive an *MLP header* (packets that were smaller than the fragment size would be encapsulated in a *PPP header*). Because PPP had no sequencing or reordering capabilities, this presented reordering limitations when cRTP (which depends on compressed packets arriving in order) was used in conjunction with MLP bundles over multiple lines, including ISDN. This issue was fixed in Cisco IOS Software Release 12.2(13)T with the introduction of the Multiclass Multilink PPP feature (MCMP). MCMP encapsulates both fragments and smaller packets with (sequenced) MLP headers and reassembles all packets in order before decompression. An example MCMP configuration for an ISDN interface is shown in Example 7-7.

Example 7-7 *MCMP Configuration for an ISDN Interface*

```
Router#sh run
interface BRI0/0
 encapsulation ppp
 dialer pool-member 1
 !
interface Dialer1
 encapsulation ppp
 dialer pool 1
 dialer remote-name routerB-dialer1
 dialer-group 1
 dialer string 12345678
 ppp multilink
 ppp multilink fragment-delay 10
 ppp multilink interleave
 ppp multilink links minimum 2
 ppp multilink multiclass
```

The **ppp multilink fragment-delay 10** command instructs the Cisco IOS Software to fragment so that no more than 10-ms delay results. The software calculates the appropriate fragment size (in bytes) automatically. It is important to add the **ppp multilink interleave** statement as well. Although this is a separate command, doing fragmentation without turning on interleaving has no QoS benefit. Both features must be turned on to achieve the desired operation.

Frame-Relay Fragmentation

Frame-Relay fragmentation, which is defined as FRF.12 for VoIP, operates in a manner very similar to that of MLP LFI. One important exception, however, is that the configuration of FRF.12 requires the maximum fragment size to be calculated beforehand and supplied as a parameter to the command.

The following sections discuss several topics that are important to keep in mind when configuring fragmentation:

- Which PVCs to fragment
- Which configuration governs that rate that should be used to determine fragment size
- The differences between FRF.11 and FRF.12 fragmentation

Which PVCs to Fragment

The purpose of LFI is to break up data frames that share the same transmission interface as voice packets. If a PVC carries only voice traffic, there is no benefit to turning on either queuing or LFI. However, if other PVCs that share the same physical egress interface carry data traffic, these PVCs should be fragmented. This is because traffic from all the PVCs comes together at the physical interface level, and data traffic from one PVC could interfere with the delay of a voice packet from another PVC. Also, as discussed in Chapter 5, enabling FRF.12 automatically engages the L2 Dual-FIFO Frame Relay interface queuing subsystem on the low-end router platforms.

Enabling FRF.12 on a Frame Relay PVC requires the configuration of a map class that is bound to the DLCI. A sample is shown in Example 7-8.

Example 7-8 *FRF.12 LFI Configuration*

```
Router# sh run
interface Serial2/0
 no ip address
 encapsulation frame-relay
!
interface Serial2/0.12 point-to-point
 ip address 10.1.121.1 255.255.255.252
 description 768kbps FR Circuit to RBR-3745-Left
 frame-relay interface-dlci 102
  class FR-MAP-CLASS-768
!
...
!
map-class frame-relay FR-MAP-CLASS-768
 frame-relay fragment 960
```

Unlike the fragmentation command for PPP that was discussed in an earlier section, the **frame-relay** command expects a byte count as the argument, given as 960 bytes in Example 7-8. Therefore, it is up to the system administrator to calculate the appropriate fragment length to achieve a delay that does not exceed 10 ms. Use the information given in Table 7-3 for this calculation. Also, on Frame Relay links, the **frame-relay fragment** command automatically enables both fragmentation and interleaving; no separate command for interleaving is necessary.

In older Cisco IOS releases, fragmentation must be turned on explicitly for each individual PVC, so it is up to the systems administrator to ensure that all PVCs that share the interface are fragmented (when necessary, as dictated by the speed of the PVC). In Cisco IOS Software Release 12.2(13)T, a more convenient feature was introduced that allows CLI at the Frame Relay interface level to automatically fragment all PVCs on that interface. A configuration of physical interface-level fragmentation is shown in Example 7-9.

Example 7-9   *Interface-Level Fragmentation*

```
Router#sh run
interface serial 0/0
   encapsulate frame-relay
   frame-relay fragment 960
```

NOTE   For ATM, only the PVC that carries combined voice and data traffic on the same VC needs to be fragmented. ATM inherently interleaves cells from different PVCs, regardless of what payload they contain.

The Rate That Governs Fragmentation

Although link speed is used as the shorthand term for determining the threshold for LFI, the shaping rate (CIR) of a Frame Relay PVC, *not* the physical port speed, really determines the fragmentation requirement. For example, a 64-kbps PVC on a physical T1 link requires large data packets be fragmented to 80 bytes to meet the 10-ms delay target. This is because the shaper, not the clock rate of the physical interface, determines how long a packet will be held up in the queues before transmission can occur on the egress interface.

FRF.11.1 and FRF.12 Fragmentation

For networks that are migrating from VoFR to VoIP, it must be kept in mind that Frame Relay LFI actually is covered by two different standards:

- FRF.11.1 Annex-C (VoFR)
- FRF.12 (VoIP)

A common misconception holds that FRF.12 fragmentation is used to support Voice over Frame Relay (VoFR), and there is a general unawareness that FRF.11 also specifies a fragmentation scheme. This causes some misunderstandings about fragmentation for VoFR and

VoIPoFR regarding when and how these two voice technologies can be used in the same network:

- **FRF.11 and FRF.12 can run on the same PVC**—This is not true. PVC runs either FRF.11 or FRF.12, never both. They are mutually exclusive.

    — If the PVC is configured for VoFR, it uses FRF.11. If fragmentation is turned on for this PVC, it uses FRF.11 Annex-C (or the Cisco derivative of this) for the fragmentation headers.

    — If the PVC is not configured for VoFR, it uses FRF.3.1 data encapsulation. If fragmentation is turned on for this PVC, it uses FRF.12 for the fragmentation headers. Because VoIP is a Layer 3 technology, which is transparent to Layer 2 Frame Relay, PVCs carrying VoIP use FRF.12 fragmentation.

- **FRF.12 is used for VoFR**—This is partly true. FRF.12 predominantly is used for VoIP. FRF.12 in a VoFR configuration is used only to fragment data PVCs that share an interface with a VoFR PVC. FRF.12 never is used on a VoFR PVC itself.

The fragmentation scheme/standard being used does not matter from a CLI point of view. In all cases, the map class command **frame-relay fragment *xxx*** is used. The software automatically uses the appropriate fragment header type, based on how the DLCI is configured. However, the fragmentation scheme/standard being used does matter to the voice network design:

- **vofr** PVCs will not interwork with **vofr cisco** PVCs.

- VoIP and VoFR cannot be supported on the same PVC if the speed is such that fragmentation is required. (VoFR will be fine, but VoIP voice quality will be impaired because VoIP packets cannot be interleaved between fragments of large data packets.)

- VoIP and VoFR can be supported on different PVCs on the same interface when fragmentation is required.

FRF.12 (VoIP) fragments voice packets if the fragmentation size is set smaller than the voice packet size; FRF.11 Annex-C (VoFR) does not fragment voice, no matter what fragmentation size is configured.

LFI for Frame Relay/ATM Service Interworking

Frame Relay and ATM networks can be interworked in two ways:

- FRF.5: network interworking

- FRF.8: service interworking

Essentially, FRF.5 is a tunneling protocol, encapsulating an intact Frame Relay frame into ATM cells and producing an unchanged Frame Relay frame again on the far side of the network. FRF.8, on the other hand, is a true conversion of the payload of the Frame Relay frame into the payload of an ATM cell, and it delivers ATM on the far side of the network.

Although FRF.5 is not widely used, it can support FRF.12 because the Frame Relay frame never is changed or disturbed; it merely is encapsulated or tunneled across ATM.

With FRF.8 interworking, a much more common method in backbone networks, FRF.12 cannot be used because there is no means of converting that to an equivalent ATM scheme. The only way that LFI can be supported end-to-end on Frame Relay/ATM networks using FRF.8 is to use MLPoFR and MLPoATM and to use MLP LFI over both segments of the network.

FRF.8 service interworking is a Frame Relay Forum standard for connecting Frame Relay networks with ATM networks. Service interworking provides a standards-based solution for service providers, enterprises, and end users. In service interworking translation mode, Frame Relay PVCs are mapped to ATM PVCs without the need for symmetric topologies; the paths can terminate on the ATM side. FRF.8 supports two modes of operation of the interworking function for upper-layer user protocol encapsulation:

- **Translation mode**—Maps between ATM and Frame Relay encapsulation. It also supports the interworking of routed or bridged protocols.

- **Transparent mode**—Does not map encapsulations, but sends them unaltered. This mode is used when translation is impractical because encapsulation methods do not conform to the supported standards for service interworking.

MLP for LFI on ATM and Frame Relay service interworking networks is supported for transparent-mode VCs and translational-mode VCs that support PPP translation (FRF 8.1).

To make MLPoFR and MLPoATM interworking possible, the interworking switch must be configured in transparent mode, and the end routers must be capable of recognizing both MLPoFR and MLPoATM headers. This is enabled with the **frame-relay interface-dlci dlci ppp** and **protocol ppp** commands for Frame Relay and ATM, respectively.

When a frame is sent from the Frame Relay side of a connection from ATM to Frame Relay service interworking, the following should happen to make interworking possible:

- The sending router encapsulates a packet in the MLPoFR header.

- In transparent mode, the carrier switch strips off the 2-byte Frame Relay DLCI field and sends the rest of the packet to its ATM interface.

- The receiving router examines the header of the received packet. If the first 2 bytes of the received packet are 0x03cf, it treats it as a legal MLPoATM packet and sends it to the MLP layer for further processing.

When an ATM cell is sent from the ATM side of an ATM to the Frame Relay service interworking connection, the following should happen to make interworking possible:

- The sending router encapsulates a packet in the MLPoATM header.

- In transparent mode, the carrier switch prepends the 2-byte Frame Relay DLCI field to the received packet and sends the packet to its Frame Relay interface.

- The receiving router examines the header of the received packet. If the first 4 bytes after the 2-byte DLCI field of the received packet are 0xfefe03cf, it treats it as a legal MLPoFR packet and sends it to the MLP layer for further processing.

A new standard for ATM to Frame Relay service interworking, FRF.8.1, supports MLP over ATM and Frame Relay service interworking, but it can be years before all switches are updated to the new standard.

IPSec Prefragmentation

A feature called prefragmentation for IPSec VPNs was introduced in Cisco IOS Software Release 12.2(13)T. This often mistakenly is thought to be an LFI feature, but, strictly speaking, it is not. It does not do LFI, as discussed in this chapter, and its purpose is not to contain delay of high-priority packets held up behind lower-priority packets on slow-speed links.

The prefragmentation for IPSec VPNs feature breaks up data packets into two segments. This is done because a 1500-byte IP packet exceeds the 1500-byte MTU size of the network when IPSec headers are added onto it, and packets exceeding the MTU size typically are dropped. This can be fixed by setting the application MTU size to 1400 bytes (or less). However, as explained earlier, changing MTU sizes in a network is cumbersome, at best, and generally difficult to manage. Therefore, this feature was developed to automatically segment IPSec frames of more than 1500 bytes into two so that MTU sizes do not need to be adjusted on the end-host applications to be usable over an IPSec VPN.

As mentioned before, this feature is not to be considered a QoS mechanism for serialization reduction and tuning purposes. A similar feature for cable/DSL links (typically a voice VPN), called adjusted maximum segment size, can be turned on with the command **ip tcp adjust-mss**. It is recommended that this be configured to 542 on both the outside and inside interfaces of a cable or DSL device.

Summary

This chapter covered the link-specific tools header compression (cRTP) and Link Fragmentation and Interleaving (LFI). The former typically is used to contain bandwidth use on low-speed links, while the latter is used to segment large data packets so that a small voice packet does not have to wait excessively long for the interface to free up.

The different standards governing header compression were discussed, along with the dependencies among the various mechanisms and the commands to turn on the feature for different types of link encapsulations.

The last half of the chapter discussed LFI mechanisms for Frame Relay, PPP, and ATM links. It also covered how to apply LFI for networks in which both Frame Relay and ATM exist and how translations between the two are done by a carrier network.

Further Reading

General

- Configuring broadband access: PPP and routed bridge encapsulation configuring PPP over ATM: http://www.cisco.com/univercd/cc/td/doc/product/software/ios122/122cgcr/fwan_c/wcfppp.htm.

- Enhanced voice and QoS for ADSL and G.SHDSL (12.3.2T): http://www.cisco.com/univercd/cc/td/doc/product/software/ios123/123newft/123t/123t_2/gtevqos.htm.

IETF Standards

- RFC 1141, "Incremental Updating of the Internet Checksum": http://wwwin-eng.cisco.com/RFC/RFC/rfc1141.txt.

- RFC 1624, "Computation of the Internet Checksum via Incremental Update": http://wwwin-eng.cisco.com/RFC/RFC/rfc1624.txt.

- RFC 1144, "Compressing TCP/IP Headers for Low-Speed Serial Links": http://wwwin-eng.cisco.com/RFC/RFC/rfc1144.txt.

- RFC 2507, "IP Header Compression": http://wwwin-eng.cisco.com/RFC/RFC/rfc2507.txt.

- RFC 2508, "Compressing IP/UDP/RTP Headers for Low-Speed Serial Links": http://wwwin-eng.cisco.com/RFC/RFC/rfc2508.txt.

- RFC 1889, "RTP: A Transport Protocol for Real-Time Applications": http://wwwin-eng.cisco.com/RFC/RFC/rfc1889.txt.

- RFC 2509, "IP Header Compression over PPP": http://wwwin-eng.cisco.com/RFC/RFC/rfc2509.txt.

- RFC 3095, "Robust Header Compression (ROHC): Framework and Four Profiles: RTP, UDP, ESP, and Uncompressed": http://wwwin-eng.cisco.com/RFC/RFC/rfc3095.txt.

Frame Relay Forum Standards

- Frame Relay/ATM PVC Network Interworking Implementation Agreement FRF.5: http://www.frforum.com/5000/Approved/FRF.5/frf.5.pdf.

- Frame Relay/ATM PVC Service Interworking Implementation Agreement, FRF.8.1: http://www.frforum.com/5000/Approved/FRF.8/FRF.8.1.pdf.

- Data Compression over Frame Relay Implementation Agreement, FRF.9: http://www.frforum.com/5000/Approved/FRF.9/frf9.pdf.

- Voice over Frame Relay Implementation Agreement, FRF.11: http://www.frforum.com/5000/Approved/FRF.11/frf_11.1.pdf.

- Frame Relay Fragmentation Implementation Agreement FRF.12: http://www.frforum.com/5000/Approved/FRF.12/frf12.pdf.

- Frame Relay IP Header Compression Implementation Agreement, FRF.20: http://www.frforum.com/5000/Approved/FRF.20/FRF.20.pdf.

Header Compression

- Express RTP and TCP header compression (Cisco IOS Software Release 12.0.7T): http://www.cisco.com/univercd/cc/td/doc/product/software/ios120/120newft/120t/120t7/rtpfast.htm.

- Frame Relay header compression compatibility enhancements (Cisco IOS Software Release 12.1.2T): http://www.cisco.com/univercd/cc/td/doc/product/software/ios121/121newft/121t/121t2/dtfrhccc.htm.

- Distributed Compressed Real-Time Transport Protocol (Cisco IOS Software Release 12.1.5T): http://www.cisco.com/univercd/cc/td/doc/product/software/ios121/121newft/121t/121t5/dtdcrtp.htm.

- IP RTP **coalesce** command (Cisco IOS Software Release 12.2.11T): http://www.cisco.com/univercd/cc/td/doc/product/software/ios122/122newft/122t/122t11/ftiprtpc.htm.

- Class-based RTP and TCP header compression (Cisco IOS Software Release 12.2.13T): http://www.cisco.com/univercd/cc/td/doc/product/software/ios122/122newft/122t/122t13/fthdrcmp.htm.

- RSVP support for RTP header compression (Cisco IOS Software Release 12.2.15T): http://www.cisco.com/univercd/cc/td/doc/product/software/ios122/122newft/122t/122t15/ftrsvpcf.htm.

- RTP header compression over satellite links (Cisco IOS Software Release 12.3.2T): http://www.cisco.com/univercd/cc/td/doc/product/software/ios123/123newft/123t/123t_2/ftcrtprf.htm.

Link Fragmentation and Interleaving

- MLP interleaving and queuing for real-time traffic (Cisco IOS Software Release 12.0): http://www.cisco.com/univercd/cc/td/doc/product/software/ios120/12cgcr/dial_c/dcppp.htm#4550.

- FRF.12 (Cisco IOS Software Release 12.0.4T): http://www.cisco.com/univercd/cc/td/doc/product/software/ios120/120newft/120t/120t4/120tvofr/index.htm.

- FRF.12 support on switched Frame Relay PVCs (Cisco IOS Software Release 12.1.2T): http://www.cisco.com/univercd/cc/td/doc/product/software/ios121/121newft/121t/121t2/dtfragsw.htm.

- Link Fragmentation and Interleaving for Frame Relay and ATM virtual circuits (Cisco IOS Software Release 12.1.5T): http://www.cisco.com/univercd/cc/td/doc/product/software/ios121/121newft/121t/121t5/dtlfifra.htm.

- Frame Relay fragmentation with hardware compression (Cisco IOS Software Release 12.1.5T): http://www.cisco.com/univercd/cc/td/doc/product/software/ios121/121newft/121t/121t5/dtfrfwhc.htm.

- Versatile interface processor-based distributed FRF.12 (Cisco IOS Software Release 12.1.5T): http://www.cisco.com/univercd/cc/td/doc/product/software/ios121/121newft/121t/121t5/dtvofrv.htm.

- Distributed Link Fragmentation and Interleaving for Frame Relay and ATM interfaces (Cisco IOS Software Release 12.2.4T): http://www.cisco.com/univercd/cc/td/doc/product/software/ios122/122newft/122t/122t4/ftdlfi.htm.

- Distributed Link Fragmentation and Interleaving over leased lines (Cisco IOS Software Release 12.2.8T): http://www.cisco.com/univercd/cc/td/doc/product/software/ios122/122newft/122t/122t8/ftdlfi2.htm.

- Frame Relay queuing and fragmentation at the interface (Cisco IOS Software Release 12.2.13T): http://www.cisco.com/univercd/cc/td/doc/product/software/ios122/122newft/122t/122t13/frfrintq.htm.

- Prefragmentation for IPSec VPNs (Cisco IOS Software Release 12.2.13T): http://www.cisco.com/univercd/cc/td/doc/product/software/ios122/122newft/122t/122t13/ftprefrg.htm.

- Multiclass Multilink PPP (Cisco IOS Software Release 12.2.13T): http://www.cisco.com/univercd/cc/td/doc/product/software/ios122/122newft/122t/122t13/ftmmlppp.htm.

This chapter includes the following topics:

- RSVP as a call admission control mechanism
- RSVP and LLQ
- RSVP and MPLS traffic engineering
- Scalability
- RSVP-DiffServ integration
- Endpoints and proxies

CHAPTER **8**

Bandwidth Reservation

The QoS tools discussed so far in this book, including marking, queuing, policing, and shaping mechanisms, primarily have been DiffServ tools. DiffServ mechanisms provide bandwidth *guarantees* (at various level of rigidity), but none of them provides bandwidth *reservations*. *Guaranteed* implies that the bandwidth will be there when needed, but it is not set aside (or reserved) for a specific application or flow. *Reserved*, on the other hand, implies that a flow of packets can be recognized and that a certain amount of bandwidth has been agreed to be set aside for that flow.

Introduced in Cisco IOS Software Release 11.2, roughly coinciding with the date of many of the relevant RFCs (summarized for reference at the end of this chapter), RSVP is one of the oldest Cisco IOS QoS tools. The development and implementation of RSVP precede the era of converged voice and data networks, yet the purpose of RSVP was always in line with these later trends: to provide predictable latency and bandwidth guarantees for time-sensitive applications. RFC 2205 defines RSVP as follows:

[RSVP is] a resource reservation setup protocol designed for an integrated services Internet [RFC 1633]. The RSVP protocol is used by a host to request specific qualities of service from the network for particular application data streams or flows. RSVP is also used by routers to deliver quality-of-service (QoS) requests to all nodes along the path(s) of the flows and to establish and maintain state to provide the requested service. RSVP requests will generally result in resources being reserved in each node along the data path.

RSVP differs from other QoS tools in the following ways:

- It is a signaling protocol.
- It reserves resources (bandwidth).
- A full implementation requires all nodes in the network to do the following:
  - Understand the RSVP protocol
  - Implement a way to reserve resources on that node

RSVP Overview

RSVP is a per-flow protocol that requests a bandwidth reservation from every node in the path of the flow. In its simplest form, RSVP is a unidirectional protocol, so if a bidirectional reservation is required for a flow, both endpoints must initiate a request for a reservation.

Basic RSVP protocol operation is shown in Figure 8-1 and its configuration in Example 8-1. The endpoints, or other network devices on behalf of the endpoints, send unicast signaling messages to establish the reservation: An RSVP PATH message travels outbound request-ing the reservation, and an RSVP RESV is returned confirming (or not) that the reservation was established. The flow can be signaled by an end station (such as Endpoint B in Figure 8-1) or by a router (such as that on behalf of Endpoint A, which is not capable of RSVP signaling). Every RSVP-enabled router in the path of the flow sees the PATH and RESV messages and allocates the appropriate queue space for the given flow.

Figure 8-1 *Basic RSVP Protocol Operation*

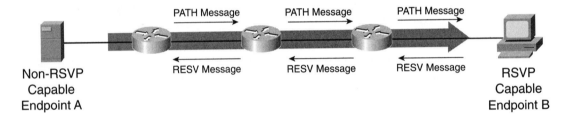

In summary, the following is true of RSVP:

- It is a protocol to signal QoS information to make a reservation of bandwidth.
- It can make resource reservations for both unicast and multicast applications.
- It is receiver oriented. (In other words, the receiver of a data flow initiates and maintains the resource reservation used for that flow.)
- It maintains state in routers and hosts.
- It is not a routing protocol, but it depends on routing protocols to determine the path of the flow.
- It supports both IPv4 and IPv6.

Example 8-1 *RSVP Configuration*

```
Router(config)#interface serial 0/1
Router(config-if)#ip rsvp bandwidth 1008 84
```

RSVP Service Types

The RSVP protocol defines two distinct service types: controlled load and guaranteed load. Each is discussed in more detail in the following sections.

Controlled Load

The controlled load service is described by RFC 2211. It provides the flow with soft QoS (not mathematically bounded, which means that there is no quantitative measure that says the QoS provided is within, as in a 50-ms delay—instead, it provides an approximate or qualitative guarantee, which means that the QoS provided is at least as good as the packet would have gotten otherwise), approximating the service that the same flow would receive from an unloaded network. The controlled load service uses admission control to ensure that the service is received even when the network element is overloaded. The controlled load service includes no quantitative guarantees, and it can be thought of as simple priority service with admission control. It allows applications to have low delay and high throughput even during times of congestion. For example, adaptive real-time applications, such as playback of a recorded conference, can use this kind of service.

To ensure that these conditions are met, clients requesting controlled load service provide the network nodes with an estimation of the data traffic they will generate, which is described in the traffic specification (or TSpec). The TSpec is one of the parameters in the RSVP request, as covered in Chapter 1, "Introduction to QoS."

Guaranteed Load

The guaranteed load service is described in RFC 2212. It provides the flow with firm bounds (mathematically provable, which means that explicit, measurable bounds on the QoS provided to the packet are specified) on end-to-end delays by guaranteeing bandwidth. Achieving a bounded delay requires that every node in the path supports guaranteed service or adequately mimics guaranteed service. Guaranteed service allows applications to reserve bandwidth to meet their requirements. Guaranteed service is invoked by specifying the traffic (TSpec) and the desired service (RSpec) to the network.

Admission Control

In addition to providing bandwidth reservation to guarantee QoS for a flow, RSVP serves another purpose of prime importance to real-time flows: call admission control (CAC). DiffServ tools are highly capable of protecting voice from data (or video from data), but they fall completely short at protecting voice from voice (or interactive video from interactive video). For example, if only enough bandwidth is set aside in LLQ for two VoIP calls, and a third call goes through, the quality of all three calls will deteriorate if only DiffServ tools are used (without any CAC). However, if a bandwidth reservation is requested before a flow is admitted onto the network, the originating node has the option to redirect or reject the flow if the reservation fails (because of insufficient bandwidth availability). To voice and interactive video traffic, the CAC functionality of RSVP is arguably more critical than the bandwidth reservation functionality (which could be engineered with DiffServ). CAC through RSVP is discussed in more depth in Chapter 9, "Call Admission Control (CAC)."

RSVP and LLQ

RSVP provides admission control. However, to implement the bandwidth and delay guarantees that RSVP provides for voice traffic, RSVP must work together with LLQ.

The RSVP support for the LLQ feature (introduced in Cisco IOS Software Release 12.1[3]T) allows RSVP to classify voice flows and queue them into the priority queue (PQ) within the LLQ system while simultaneously providing reservations for non-voice flows through CBWFQ. The logical flow of this feature is illustrated in Figure 8-2.

Figure 8-2 *RSVP and LLQ Logic*

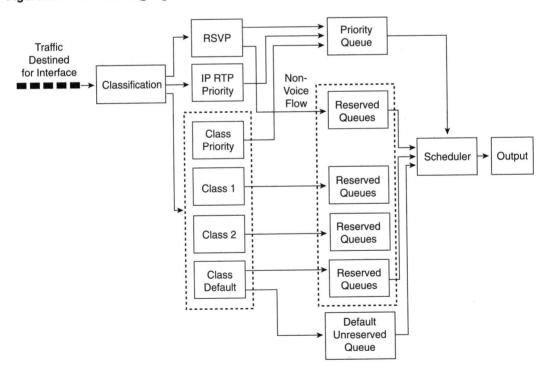

In addition to having RSVP enabled on relevant interfaces, this feature requires that traffic directed to the PQ of LLQ be identified. A built-in voice-like profile can be selected as an option; in that case, any voice traffic generated by Cisco IOS devices automatically is assigned to the LLQ. Additionally, this option directs voice traffic from RSVP-enabled applications, such as Microsoft NetMeeting, to be assigned to the PQ within LLQ. *Voice-like* traffic means that the traffic flows adhere to certain given arrival rate and packet size parameters that are derived from real voice flows.

To select the built-in voice-like profile for RSVP to classify traffic into the PQ of LLQ, use the following command:

```
Router(config)#ip rsvp pq-profile voice-like
```

MPLS Traffic Engineering

The first major deployment of RSVP technology came with Multiprotocol Label Switching (MPLS) traffic engineering (TE). MPLS traffic engineering automatically establishes and maintains label-switched paths (LSPs) across the backbone by using RSVP to establish and guarantee "tunnels" of predictable bandwidth. RSVP operates at each LSP hop and is used to signal and maintain LSPs based on the MPLS TE calculated path. MPLS TE uses principles from RFC 2205 (basic RSVP) and RFC 3209 (TE extensions for RSVP) to accomplish this objective. RSVP used for MPLS TE is illustrated in Figure 8-3. In this figure, the PATH message requests, for example, 40 Mbps of bandwidth along the path. The RESV message establishes the bandwidth at each hop and provides the label to use.

Figure 8-3   *MPLS TE PATH Setup with RSVP*

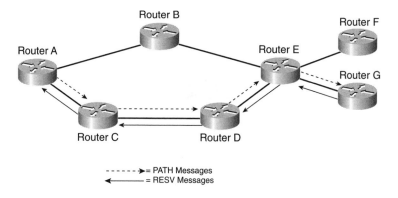

Scalability

Discussions about RSVP often are speckled by comments about scalability. Scalability concerns around RSVP argue that it does not scale well because it keeps per-flow state in every node, and because the PATH/RESV and refresh messages travel per flow between every two nodes involved in the path to keep the entire path open and functioning correctly. For this reason, various scalability enhancements have been introduced into the Cisco IOS Software, including the following:

- **Control plane priority**—Ensures that the RSVP control messages are not dropped or unduly delayed, which would cause additional messaging to tear down the path and re-establish it
- **Refresh reduction**—Summarizes the refresh information for all flows on an interface in a single message instead of sending individual messages per flow

RSVP-DiffServ Integration

RSVP-DiffServ integration provides a translation between RSVP and DiffServ technologies that is intended to leverage the strengths of each model. RSVP is used for bandwidth reservation at the edge of the network (where there are fewer flows and the most bandwidth constraints), but DiffServ is used over the backbone network so that the backbone routers do not have to keep per-flow states. This topology is shown in Figure 8-4.

Figure 8-4 *RSVP-DiffServ Integration*

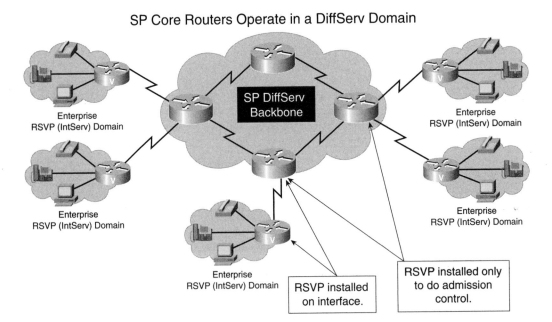

Endpoints and Proxies

Although RSVP as a specification is intended for use along the entire path between the sender and the receiver, this requires the implementation of RSVP in *all* endpoints. Most devices and applications do not comply with this requirement. Additionally, most endpoints are connected to LANs in which bandwidth is usually plentiful and bandwidth bottlenecks do not occur; only if the flow traverses the WAN edge router or ISP uplink is congested typically encountered in the path of the flow.

Summary

This chapter covered RSVP as one of the key IntServ mechanisms in a QoS toolset that is largely DiffServ oriented. RSVP provides a per-flow specification of QoS through various parameters and serves as both a call admission control mechanism (allowing or denying a flow access to the network) and a bandwidth-reservation mechanism. This chapter focused primarily on the bandwidth reservation aspect of RSVP.

The interactions between RSVP and other QoS tools such as LLQ were discussed, along with scalability and RSVP-DiffServ integration in networks that are not exclusively IntServ nor exclusively DiffServ, but that instead use some of the concepts of both worlds. Additionally, for device endpoints that are not capable of RSVP, proxies were discussed to show how networks with RSVP can be built even for these devices.

Chapter 9 explores RSVP's call admission control capabilities further.

Further Reading

Standards

- RFC 2205, "Resource Reservation Protocol (RSVP) Version 1 Functional Specification": http://www.ietf.org/rfc/rfc2205.txt.
- RFC 2206, "RSVP Management Information Base Using SMIv2": http://www.ietf.org/rfc/rfc2206.txt.
- RFC 2207, "RSVP Extensions for IPSec Data Flows": http://www.ietf.org/rfc/rfc2207.txt.
- RFC 2208, "Resource ReSerVation Protocol (RSVP) Version 1 Applicability Statement: Some Guidelines on Deployment": http://www.ietf.org/rfc/rfc2208.txt.
- RFC 2209, "Resource ReSerVation Protocol (RSVP) Version 1 Message Processing Rules": http://www.ietf.org/rfc/rfc2209.txt.

- RFC 2210, "The Use of RSVP with IETF Integrated Services": http://www.ietf.org/rfc/rfc2210.txt.

- RFC 2211, "Specification of the Controlled-Load Network Element Service": http://www.ietf.org/rfc/rfc2211.txt.

- RFC 2212, "Specification of Guaranteed Quality of Service": http://www.ietf.org/rfc/rfc2212.txt.

- RFC 2747, "RSVP Cryptographic Authentication": http://www.ietf.org/rfc/rfc2747.txt.

- RFC 2961, "RSVP Refresh Overhead Reduction Extensions": http://www.ietf.org/rfc/rfc2961.txt.

- RFC 2998, "A Framework for Integrated Services Operation over DiffServ Networks": http://www.ietf.org/rfc/rfc2998.txt.

- RFC 3175, "Aggregation of RSVP for IPv4 and IPv6 Reservations": http://www.ietf.org/rfc/rfc3175.txt.

- RFC 3209, "RSVP-TE: Extensions to RSVP for LSP Tunnels": http://www.ietf.org/rfc/rfc3209.txt.

Cisco IOS Documentation

- General:
  http://www.cisco.com/univercd/cc/td/doc/product/software/ios123/123cgcr/qos_r/qos_i1g.htm#1100504.

- RSVP support for low-latency queuing (Cisco IOS Software Release 12.1.3T):
  http://www.cisco.com/univercd/cc/td/doc/product/software/ios121/121newft/121t/121t3/rsvp_llq.htm.

- Multimedia Conference Manager with Voice Gateway Image with RSVP to ATM SVC Mapping (Cisco IOS Software Release 12.1.5T): http://www.cisco.com/univercd/cc/td/doc/product/software/ios121/121newft/121t/121t5/dt_mcm5t.htm.

- RSVP support for Frame Relay (Cisco IOS Software Release 12.1.5T):
  http://www.cisco.com/univercd/cc/td/doc/product/software/ios121/121newft/121t/121t5/rsvp_fr.htm.

- VoIP call admission control using RSVP (Cisco IOS Software Release 12.1.5T):
  http://www.cisco.com/univercd/cc/td/doc/product/software/ios121/121newft/121t/121t5/dt4trsvp.htm.

- RSVP scalability enhancements (Cisco IOS Software Release 12.2.2T):
  http://www.cisco.com/univercd/cc/td/doc/product/software/ios122/122newft/122t/122t2/rsvpscal.htm.

- RSVP support for ATM/PVCs (Cisco IOS Software Release 12.2.2T): http://www.cisco.com/univercd/cc/td/doc/product/software/ios122/122newft/122t/122t2/rsvp_atm.htm.

- MPLS DiffServ-aware Traffic Engineering (DS-TE) over ATM (Cisco IOS Software Release 12.2.8T): http://www.cisco.com/univercd/cc/td/doc/product/software/ios122/122newft/122t/122t8/ft_ds_te.htm.

- RSVP refresh reduction and reliable messaging (Cisco IOS Software Release 12.2.13T): http://www.cisco.com/univercd/cc/td/doc/product/software/ios122/122newft/122t/122t13/ftrsvpre.htm.

- RSVP local policy support (Cisco IOS Software Release 12.2.13T): http://www.cisco.com/univercd/cc/td/doc/product/software/ios122/122newft/122t/122t13/ftrsvplp.htm.

- RSVP support for RTP header compression, phase 1 (Cisco IOS Software Release 12.2.15T): http://www.cisco.com/univercd/cc/td/doc/product/software/ios122/122newft/122t/122t15/ftrsvpcf.htm.

- RSVP message authentication (Cisco IOS Software Release 12.2.15T): http://www.cisco.com/univercd/cc/td/doc/product/software/ios122/122newft/122t/122t15/ftrsvpma.htm.

This chapter discusses the Call Admission Control (CAC) QoS capabilities, and includes the following topics:

- Definition of CAC
- Resource Reservations Protocol (RSVP)
- Cisco CallManager CAC techniques
- H.323 gatekeeper CAC tools
- Cisco IOS CAC tools other than RSVP

Call Admission Control (CAC)

Call admission control (CAC) mechanisms are critical to ensuring overall quality for all traffic types that traverse converged networks, particularly for protecting voice from other voice traffic, and interactive video from other interactive video traffic.

All the QoS mechanisms discussed so far have dealt with how to treat traffic already admitted to the network. CAC is the first toolset that addresses how to keep traffic off the network (admission) when there are not enough resources to carry the packets. CAC usually does not apply to data traffic because packets simply can be dropped or delayed when the network becomes congested or oversubscribed. Real-time traffic can be neither dropped nor delayed while preserving voice or video quality at the same time. Therefore, this kind of traffic should be admitted to the network only if it can be carried in a manner that will provide the required quality.

CAC is an extensive topic in its own right and encroaches upon other areas beyond the scope of this book, such as call-routing algorithms (dialing plans) and call priority and preemption capabilities, which typically involve more end-user knowledge than the infrastructure of the network has. A call agent or call server typically makes these types of decisions. On the other hand, the network infrastructure is the only part of the network that has the knowledge of exact resource availability, such as link status, bandwidth availability, and traffic congestion points, so the infrastructure is the right place for the basic CAC (admit or deny) decisions. When a call is not admitted, the call agent or call server can make alternative routing decisions—in other words, the call can be redirected to the PSTN.

The scope of the CAC discussion in this chapter is to provide an overview of the basic CAC mechanisms and to underscore their importance in QoS design for converged networks. This chapter examines the three most common methods—RSVP, CallManager locations, and H.323 gatekeeper CAC—and provides a brief overview of other Cisco IOS–based techniques that can be used for aspects of CAC.

CAC Overview

As discussed in Chapter 5, "Congestion-Management Tools," and Chapter 6, "Congestion-Avoidance Tools," data applications are controlled by resolving congestion in the network instead of applying admission policies. If data applications encounter congestion, packets typically are dropped. Protocols such as TCP have inherent detection, recovery, and retransmission logic, which ensures that the session is recovered for the end user. Congestion-management policies cannot be applied to real-time applications, such as voice and video-conferencing, and still maintain predictable quality. When the packets that belong to these applications are admitted onto the network, they cannot be dropped. Traditional TDM applications such as voice, modem, fax, and video calls assume that bandwidth is available and do not recover from lost information. Because information arrival is so time sensitive, there is no point in building error-detection and recovery mechanisms, such as retransmission logic, into these real-time protocols. If the packet cannot be delivered within a small window of time, it might as well never arrive. "Better late than never" does not apply to real-time flows.

CAC Defined

By definition, network bandwidth is finite, and points of congestion do occur. Both real-time and non-real-time traffic types encounter this congestion. If packets cannot be dropped to resolve congestion, packet flows that cause congestion should not be allowed onto the network. This makes the case for the deployment of CAC tools—these are, in essence, the congestion-avoidance mechanisms for real-time applications. After it is admitted, a real-time flow such as a voice call must be carried; if there aren't sufficient bandwidth resources to carry the flow within the delay and loss bounds of the application, the flow must be rejected or redirected before it is admitted into the network.

Another way to look at CAC is that most of the QoS tools discussed thus far in this book strive to protect voice traffic from data traffic. CAC tools protect voice traffic from other voice traffic (and interactive video from interactive video). For example, if there is sufficient bandwidth provisioned through LLQ to carry only two calls across a link, admitting a third call will cause packet drops and will impair the voice quality of all three calls in progress. Such scenarios necessitate the use of CAC to ensure that no more real-time flows are admitted into the network beyond what the QoS engineering of the nodes allows. This is illustrated in Figure 9-1.

Formally defined, CAC is a deterministic decision before call establishment on whether the network resources are available to provide the required QoS to the new call. CAC features allow VoIP systems to make an informed decision before admitting a new call, based on the condition of the network. If the call is not admitted, the call can be given the reorder (or overflow) tone or a recorded announcement can inform the caller that the network is too busy to complete the call attempt. The caller must try again later, or the call can be redirected to another VoIP route, or the call can be redirected through the PSTN.

Figure 9-1   *Protecting Voice from Voice*

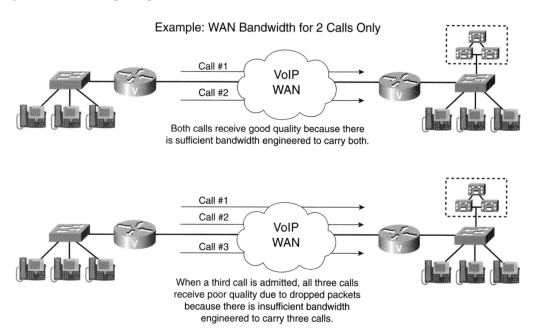

Example: WAN Bandwidth for 2 Calls Only

Call #1

Call #2

VoIP WAN

Both calls receive good quality because there is sufficient bandwidth engineered to carry both.

Call #1

Call #2

Call #3

VoIP WAN

When a third call is admitted, all three calls receive poor quality due to dropped packets because there is insufficient bandwidth engineered to carry three calls.

CAC Tool Categories

Three broad categories of CAC tools exist:

- **Local**—The node makes an admission decision based on local information or conditions at the node.
- **Measurement-based**—A decision on admitting a new flow is reached based on a combination of configuration information and reported information of other entities (such as calls, sessions, flows, bandwidth, memory use, and time slots).
- **Reservation-based**—Reservation of resources is performed before admitting the new flow.

Each of these categories of tools is discussed in the following sections.

Local CAC Tools

Local CAC mechanisms perform a voice gateway router function and typically function at the outgoing gateway. The CAC decision is based on nodal information such as the state of the outgoing LAN/WAN link that the voice call would traverse if it were allowed to proceed. Clearly, if the local packet network link is down, there is no point in executing complex decision logic based on the state of the rest of the network (because that network is unreachable). Other local mechanisms include configuration items to disallow more than a fixed number of calls. If the network designer already knows that no more than five calls will fit across the outgoing WAN link's LLQ configuration because of bandwidth limitations, it would be an obvious choice to configure the local gateway node to not allow more than five simultaneous calls. The following Cisco IOS features or network design techniques fall in the local CAC mechanisms category:

- Physical DS0 limitation
- Max-connections
- Voice-bandwidth
- Trunk conditioning
- Local voice busyout (LVBO)

Measurement-Based CAC Tools

Measurement-based CAC techniques look ahead into the packet network to gauge the state of the network to determine whether to allow a new call. This usually implies sending probes to the destination IP address (which could be the terminating gateway or endpoint, or another device in between). The probe returns some measured information on the conditions that it found while traversing the network to the outgoing (sending) gateway or endpoint. Typically, loss and delay characteristics are the interesting elements of information for voice CAC decisions. The outgoing device then uses this information in combination with configured information to decide whether the network conditions exceed a given or configured threshold. The following Cisco IOS features or network design techniques fall in the measurement-based CAC mechanisms category, and both use Service Assurance Agent (SAA) probes:

- Advanced voice busyout (AVBO)
- PSTN fallback

Resource-Based CAC Tools

Two types of resource-based mechanisms exist: those that *calculate* needed or available resources, and those that *reserve* resources for the call. Resources of interest include link bandwidth, DSP availability and DS0 time slots on the connecting TDM trunks to a voice gateway, CPU power, and memory. Several of these resources could be constrained at any nodes or multiple nodes that the call traverses to its destination. The following features or network design techniques fall in this category:

- Gatekeeper resource activity indicator (RAI)
- Gatekeeper zone bandwidth
- Cisco CallManager Locations CAC
- RSVP

CallManager Locations CAC

Most of the features mentioned in the previous section are Cisco IOS features and pertain to employing CAC when Cisco IOS voice gateway routers connect traditional telephony equipment into an IP network. Much of the voice traffic in VoIP networks, however, originates from IP phones, not from gateways, and none of these features (other than potentially RSVP) applies to traffic from these devices.

Therefore, Cisco CallManager has additional CAC features to cover the management of IP phone network deployments. These features are not mutually exclusive. Although CallManager Locations CAC is deployed in the overall network to manage VoIP bandwidth availability for both IP phones and voice gateways, a feature such as local or advanced voice busyout can be deployed at the same time on the voice gateway to push back calls into the PBX or reroute though the PSTN if IP network conditions do not allow their entry into the VoIP network.

CallManager Locations CAC is used in a centralized deployment model (centralized Call-Manager managing phones in both central and remote locations) and is based on the premise that bandwidth is constrained between locations or sites in the network. Therefore, only a certain number of calls, regardless of their origination on an IP phone or gateway, can be allowed into or out of a site at any one time, as shown in Figure 9-2. The premise of this tool includes an assumption that the bandwidth *within* a location is unlimited and that constraints exist only *between* different locations.

Looking at the configuration given in Figure 9-2, Location 2 has WAN bandwidth of 128 kbps available for voice traffic. This does not indicate the total bandwidth into that site, but just the bandwidth available for voice, as configured into the CallManager at Location 1. It can represent 50 percent of the total bandwidth into the site and should be correlated to the amount of bandwidth set aside in the LLQ priority class for Location 2.

Figure 9-2 *CallManager Locations CAC*

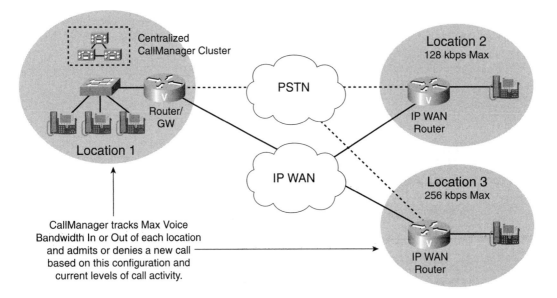

The term *correlated* is used instead of *matched* because CallManager takes into account only the uncompressed Layer 3 bandwidth of a call into its call-counting CAC algorithm. On the other hand, LLQ, as discussed in Chapter 5, also must account for various other factors, such as cRTP, that affect the bandwidth required for a voice call and must make provision for the call-signaling bandwidth.

The CallManager Locations CAC feature works in conjunction with CallManager regions (a feature that controls codec selection between devices that want to communicate), so bandwidth-constrained links between sites typically are configured to use the G.729 codec and a counting mechanism within CallManager limits the number of calls into or out of each site. IP phones and voice gateways are associated with both a region (for codec selection) and a location (for CAC purposes) in the CallManager configuration. For every call set up, CallManager looks at the source and destination locations of the call and makes a CAC decision to allow or deny the new call, based on how many calls are already active between the same two locations and the codecs involved in the calls. Calls confined within a location are not subject to CAC; as determined by the regions feature, these calls typically use the G.711 codec.

Examining the example configuration in Figure 9-2 once more, Location 2 has 128 kbps of bandwidth available for voice. If the CallManager regions feature is configured so that any call into or out of Location 2 uses the G.729 codec, 24 kbps of bandwidth are required per call, and CallManager's locations CAC algorithm will allow a maximum of 5 (128 / 24) simultaneous calls to Location 2.

CallManager Locations CAC is a heavily deployed feature and is essential for a centralized deployment in which some IP phones or gateways are separated from each other by WAN segments of limited bandwidth. CallManager locations should be configured so that calls between sites do not oversubscribe the bandwidth allocated to the VoIP LLQ in the WAN routers. CallManager Locations CAC is a simple call-counting mechanism and is unaware of the topology or state of the network connections. It allows a configured amount of bandwidth (for example, 200 kbps) between two sites. For every call, it subtracts a fixed amount based on the codec selected by the regions feature. Thus, locations CAC works well only for hub-and-spoke topologies. It is also unaware of L2 protocol overheads (it calculates purely L3 bandwidth required) and bandwidth-altering features, such as cRTP and tunneling technologies such as GRE and IPSec.

Gatekeeper CAC

Gatekeepers (GK) often are used to arbitrate bandwidth in both CallManager and traditional toll-bypass networks. As with CallManager Locations CAC, gatekeepers employ a call-counting mechanism (based on codec per call) between sites (zones), track bandwidth at an L3 level, and are also unaware of the network topology. Thus, gatekeeper call admission control (GK CAC) generally solves the same problem as CallManager Locations CAC and suffers from the same drawbacks. GK CAC is applicable to a wider set of devices than CallManager Locations CAC, though: GK CAC can be used to arbitrate bandwidth between any two devices that register with the GK, whereas CallManager Locations CAC can be used only between IP phones and voice gateways within CallManager's management area. GK CAC in CallManager networks is used primarily in distributed deployment models to provide CAC on the intercluster trunks or the connections between the CallManager clusters, as shown in Figure 9-3.

GK CAC also often is deployed in videoconferencing networks to arbitrate bandwidth among video endpoints, gateways, and MCUs. Unlike CallManager Locations CAC, the bandwidth subtracted per call is not fixed based purely on the codec (CallManager Locations CAC handles only G.729 and G.711 calls); instead, the bandwidth needed for the call is requested from the GK as part of the H.225 admissions request traveling from the endpoint or gateway to the GK.

Figure 9-3 *Gatekeeper CAC in CallManager Networks*

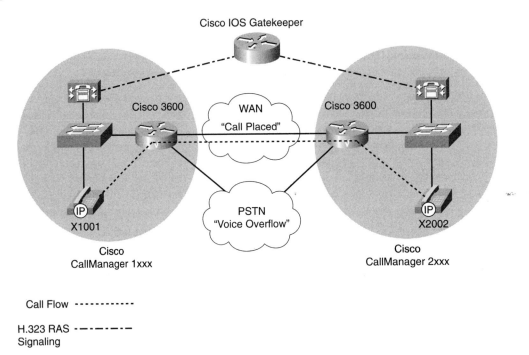

RSVP

RSVP's use in providing QoS for real-time flows has a checkered past in the industry, in the IETF, and in Cisco IOS implementation. However, RSVP is looking increasingly promising as the *only* technology that can provide true real-time communications CAC for complex network topologies and varying traffic patterns. Factors that have contributed to RSVP's spotty deployment to provide QoS for real-time traffic include the following (most of which have been resolved):

- **State-machine synchronization**— RSVP provides benefit to voice calls only if its state machine and that of the call setup flow are synchronized to provide an RSVP reservation for the call before the destination party's phone rings. This is referred to as *prering CAC*. This synchronization is now in place for H.323 as of Cisco IOS Software Release 12.1.5T, and for SIP and MGCP as of Cisco IOS Software Release 12.2.8T. The synchronized call setup logic for H.323 is shown in Figure 9-4.

Figure 9-4 *H.323: RSVP Synchronized Call Setup*

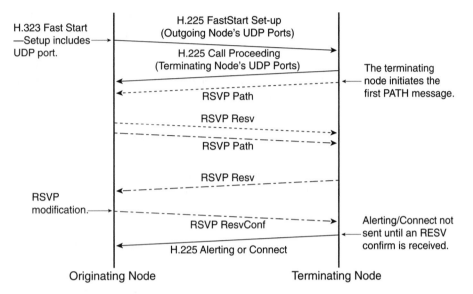

The flow shown in Figure 9-4 depicts only the RSVP messages between the two communicating endpoints. As discussed in Chapter 8, "Bandwidth Reservation," the RSVP messages actually travel between each two nodes in the network connecting two endpoints together; each node makes a decision on whether to make or deny the requested reservation. The flow in Figure 9-4 shows only the end result of the RSVP messages having traversed all the nodes between the two endpoints.

- **Scalability**—These concerns have been addressed with the scalability improvement and RSVP-DiffServ Integration features discussed in the previous chapter.

- **Interoperability with other QoS features**—Various improvements have been made to RSVP in recent Cisco IOS releases, including control plane prioritization in Release 12.2.2T and feedback with cRTP in Release 12.2.15T, to ensure that an accurate amount of bandwidth is reserved and that RSVP works seamlessly with the other QoS tools.

- **Security**—To guard against rogue applications initiating reservations, either for calls that should not be allowed onto the network or for denial-of-service purposes, RSVP was enhanced in Cisco IOS Release 12.2.15T. It now does authentication checks on RSVP messaging to ensure that messages requesting bandwidth are sourced by legitimate endpoints or nodes and that the requests are for legitimate purposes.

- **Lack of endpoint implementation**—The only remaining factor that keeps RSVP from wide deployment for CAC purposes is its lack of support on IP phones, Call-Manager, and other voice applications (for example, Unity voicemail) platforms. However, at the time of writing, development has already begun on RSVP proxy solutions in Cisco IOS that will initiate and broker RSVP reservation across bandwidth-constrained segments of the network on behalf of endpoints such as IP phones. These Cisco IOS developments also are targeted to address scalability concerns so that RSVP reservations are made only for segments of the network in which they are necessary and do not burden the entire network and every call with a reservation.

RSVP addresses many of the shortcomings of the other more narrowly focused CAC mechanisms:

- **Only reservations mechanism**—The other CAC techniques are call-counting techniques that cannot guarantee bandwidth. RSVP is the only reservations mechanism.

- **Network topology awareness**—RSVP is the only CAC technology that can negotiate a path through any network topology and still guarantee bandwidth on every leg that the call follows, wherever the routing protocols might point to that path. The other CAC mechanisms assume simpler hub-and-spoke topologies without alternate routing capabilities or redundant links or paths— they can protect only a virtual "leg" between two sites or locations and cannot take into account that some backbone network segments contain aggregations of calls from several sites. With these mechanisms, it is still possible to oversubscribe a segment, even if all sites are within their individual CAC allocations.

- **Network state awareness**—If multiple links are bound together with technologies such as MLP bundling, RSVP can react to link failures within the bundle and, therefore, compensate for temporary loss of bandwidth availability in the affected network segment. The call-counting CAC mechanisms allow bandwidth oversubscription when failures in the network cause less bandwidth than statically configured to be available for a period of time.

- **Accommodation of bandwidth changes**—In Cisco IOS Software Release 12.2.2T and later, RSVP dynamically can adjust the bandwidth allocated to a session or flow if a higher-layer application requests it.

- **Free mix of different bandwidth requests**—GK CAC and RSVP can do appropriate CAC for mixes of voice and video calls, each potentially of a varying bandwidth size. The counting mechanisms, such as CallManager Locations CAC and GK CAC, discussed earlier, fall short of protecting network segments that aggregate calls from various sites. The complexity of bandwidth arbitration in mixed voice and video networks requires CAC beyond the capabilities of static call counting—only RSVP truly can protect these environments.

Example of VoIP CAC Through RSVP

The VoIP call admission control using RSVP feature (Cisco IOS Software Release 12.1[5]T) synchronizes RSVP signaling with H.323 Version 2 signaling to ensure that the bandwidth reservation is established in both directions before a call moves to the alerting phase (ringing). This ensures that the called party's phone rings only after the resources for the call have been reserved. Using RSVP-based admission control, VoIP applications can reserve network bandwidth and react appropriately if bandwidth reservation fails.

Synchronized RSVP is attempted for an IP call when the requested QoS for the associated dial peer is set to controlled-load or guaranteed-delay, as long as RSVP has been enabled for the interface by using the **ip rsvp bandwidth** command. If the requested QoS level is set to the default of best effort or RSVP is not enabled, bandwidth reservation is not attempted. Before Cisco IOS Software Release 12.1(5)T, VoIP gateways used H.323 Version 1 (slow connect) procedures when initiating calls that require bandwidth reservation. The VoIP CAC through RSVP feature (which is enabled by default) allows gateways to use H.323 Version 2 (fast connect) for all calls, including those that require RSVP. To enable backward compatibility, commands are available to force the originating gateway to initiate calls using slow connect procedures.

If RSVP reservation is attempted but fails, the acceptable QoS for the dial peer determines the outcome of the call. When the acceptable QoS is configured for best effort, the call setup proceeds, but without any bandwidth reservation in place. When the acceptable QoS on either gateway is configured for other than best effort and the RSVP reservation fails, the call is released. The requested QoS and acceptable QoS are configured through Cisco IOS Software by using the **req-qos** and **acc-qos** dial-peer configuration commands, respectively.

Table 9-1 summarizes the results of nine call-setup scenarios using fast connect, based on the QoS levels configured in the VoIP dial peers at the originating and terminating gateways. This table does not include cases in which the requested QoS is best effort and the acceptable QoS is other than best effort because those configurations are considered invalid. The following convention is used in the Requested QoS and Acceptable QoS columns to indicate the configuration for the scenario:

- CL: Controlled load
- GD: Guaranteed delay
- BE: Best effort

The following example, illustrated in Figure 9-5, shows how calls can be made in either direction between Gateway A and Gateway B, which are connected to POTS phones, with phone numbers 711 and 712, respectively. The requested QoS indicates that RSVP setup must complete before the destination phone rings. The acceptable QoS indicates that the call is released if the RSVP setup fails or does not complete within the allotted time. Example 9-1 gives the configuration for Gateway A; Example 9-2 gives the configuration for Gateway B.

Table 9-1 *Call Results Based on Configured QoS Levels*

	Originating Gateway		Terminating Gateway		
	Requested QoS	Acceptable QoS	Requested QoS	Acceptable QoS	Results
1	CL or GD	CL or GD	CL or GD	CL or GD	Call proceeds only if both RSVP reservations succeed.
2	CL or GD	CL or GD	CL or GD	BE	Call proceeds only if both RSVP reservations succeed.
3	CL or GD	CL or GD	BE		Call is released.
4	CL or GD	BE	CL or GD	CL or GD	Call proceeds only if both RSVP reservations succeed.
5	CL or GD	BE	CL or GD	BE	Call proceeds regardless of RSVP results. If RSVP reservation fails, call receives best-effort service.
6	CL or GD	BE	BE	BE	Call proceeds with best-effort service.
7	BE	BE	CL or GD	CL or GD	Call is released.
8	BE	BE	CL or GD	BE	Call proceeds with best-effort service.
9	BE	BE	BE	BE	Call proceeds with best-effort service.

Figure 9-5 *RSVP CAC Synchronization Example*

Example 9-1 *Gateway A Configuration*

```
Router# sh run
call rsvp-sync
call rsvp-sync resv-timer 15
!
interface Ethernet0/0
 ip address 10.10.107.107 10.255.255.255
 service-policy VOIP-LLQ
 ip rsvp bandwidth 1000 1000
!
voice-port 3/0/0
!
dial-peer voice 712 voip
 destination-pattern 712
 session target ipv4:10.10.107.108
 req-qos controlled-load
 acc-qos controlled-load
!
dial-peer voice 711 pots
 destination-pattern 711
 port 3/0/0
```

Example 9-2 *Gateway B Configuration*

```
Router# sh run
call rsvp-sync
call rsvp-sync resv-timer 15
!
interface Ethernet0/0
 ip address 10.10.107.108 10.255.255.255
 service-policy VOIP-LLQ
 ip rsvp bandwidth 1000 1000
!
voice-port 2/0/0
!
dial-peer voice 711 voip
 destination-pattern 711
 session target ipv4:10.10.107.107
 req-qos controlled-load
 acc-qos controlled-load
!
dial-peer voice 712 pots
 destination-pattern 712
 port 2/0/0
```

Summary

This chapter gave a brief overview of call admission control (CAC) techniques, the QoS tools designed to keep excess real-time traffic off the network when there isn't bandwidth to carry it. Packets cannot be dropped summarily (as is done with data traffic) to manage congestion in the network, so an informed admission decision must be made before allowing a real-time (typically voice or video) call onto the network.

CAC is a broad subject, and only a high-level overview was discussed here, with particular emphasis on the most common CAC techniques, including Cisco CallManager Locations CAC, gatekeeper CAC, and RSVP. RSVP is not deployed widely for CAC in networks today; however, as support for it increases in more endpoints, this is likely to become the more prevalent form of CAC over time because it solves many of the shortcomings of the other techniques discussed in this chapter.

Further Reading

General

- Davidson, Jonathan, et al. *Deploying Cisco Voice over IP Solutions.* Indianapolis: Cisco Press, 2001.

- VoIP call admission control: http://www.cisco.com/en/US/tech/tk652/tk701/technologies_white_paper09186a00800da467.shtml.

- CallManager call admission control: http://www.cisco.com/en/US/products/sw/voicesw/ps556/products_administration_guide_chapter09186a00800c4cab.html.

- RFC 2543, "SIP: Session Initiation Protocol": http://www.ietf.org/rfc/rfc2543.txt.

Cisco IOS Documentation

- Local voice busyout (Cisco IOS Software Release 12.0.3T): http://www.cisco.com/univercd/cc/td/doc/product/software/ios120/120newft/120t/120t3/busyfm.htm.

- Busyout monitor on Cisco 2600 and 3600 series routers (Cisco IOS Software Release 12.0.7T): http://www.cisco.com/univercd/cc/td/doc/product/software/ios120/120newft/120t/120t7/busy_t7.htm.

- Voice busyout enhancements (Cisco IOS Software Release 12.1.2T): http://www.cisco.com/univercd/cc/td/doc/product/software/ios121/121newft/121t/121t2/dt_boenh.htm.

- Advanced voice busyout (Cisco IOS Software Release 12.1.3T): http://www.cisco.com/univercd/cc/td/doc/product/software/ios121/121newft/121t/121t3/dt_avbo.htm.

- PSTN fallback (Cisco IOS Software Release 12.1.3T): http://www.cisco.com/ univercd/cc/td/doc/product/software/ios121/121newft/121t/121t3/dtpstnfb.htm.

- 7200/7500 (Cisco IOS Software Release 12.2.4T): http://www.cisco.com/univercd/ cc/td/doc/product/software/ios122/122newft/122t/122t4/ftpstn4t.htm.

- RSVP support for low-latency queuing (Cisco IOS Software Release 12.1.3T): http://www.cisco.com/univercd/cc/td/doc/product/software/ios121/121newft/ 121t/121t3/rsvp_llq.htm.

- RSVP support for Frame Relay (Cisco IOS Software Release 12.1.5T): http://www.cisco.com/univercd/cc/td/doc/product/software/ios121/121newft/ 121t/121t5/rsvp_fr.htm.

- VoIP call admission control using RSVP (Cisco IOS Software Release 12.1.5T): http://www.cisco.com/univercd/cc/td/doc/product/software/ios121/121newft/121t/ 121t5/dt4trsvp.htm.

- Control plane DSCP support for RSVP (Cisco IOS Software Release 12.2.2T): http://www.cisco.com/univercd/cc/td/doc/product/software/ios122/122newft/122t/ 122t2/dscprsvp.htm.

- Advanced voice busyout (Cisco IOS Software Release 12.2.4T): http://www.cisco.com/univercd/cc/td/doc/product/software/ios122/122newft/ 122limit/122x/122xa/122xa_2/ft_cacbo.htm.

- Call admission control for H.323 VoIP gateways (Cisco IOS Software Release 12.2.4T): http://www.cisco.com/univercd/cc/td/doc/product/software/ios122/122newft/ 122limit/122x/122xa/122xa_2/ft_pfavb.htm.

- Call admission control for H.323 VoIP gateways (Cisco IOS Software Release 12.2.8T): http://www.cisco.com/univercd/cc/td/doc/product/software/ios122/122newft/122t/ 122t8/ft_cac7x.htm.

- SIP gateway support of RSVP and TEL URL (Cisco IOS Software Release 12.2.8T): http://www.cisco.com/univercd/cc/td/doc/product/software/ios122/122newft/ 122limit/122x/122xb/122xb_2/vvfresrv.htm.

- MGCP VoIP call admission control (Cisco IOS Software Release 12.2.8T): http://www.cisco.com/univercd/cc/td/doc/product/software/ios122/122newft/122t/ 122t8/ft_04mac.htm.

- Call admission control for H.323 VoIP gateways (Cisco IOS Software Release 12.2.11T): http://www.cisco.com/univercd/cc/td/doc/product/software/ios122/122newft/122t/ 122t11/ftcac58.htm.

- Enhanced features for local and advanced voice busyout (Cisco IOS Software Release 12.2.13T): http://www.cisco.com/univercd/cc/td/doc/product/software/ ios122/122newft/122t/122t13/ft_lavbo.htm.

- RSVP support for RTP header compression, phase 1 (Cisco IOS Software Release 12.2.15T): http://www.cisco.com/univercd/cc/td/doc/product/software/ios122/122newft/122t/122t15/ftrsvpcf.htm.

- Measurement-based call admission control for SIP (Cisco IOS Software Release 12.2.15T): http://www.cisco.com/univercd/cc/td/doc/product/software/ios122/122newft/122t/122t15/ftcacsip.htm.

This chapter discusses the following Catalyst QoS tools:

- Classification and marking tools
- Mapping tools
- Policing and markdown tools
- Queuing tools

These tools are considered on a platform-specific basis on the following families of switches:

- Catalyst 2950
- Catalyst 2970
- Catalyst 3550
- Catalyst 3560
- Catalyst 3750
- Catalyst 4550 (Supervisors II+ through V)
- Catalyst 6500 (Supervisor 2 and Supervisor 720)

CHAPTER 10

Catalyst QoS Tools

Most of the QoS tools discussed to this point were covered in the context of Cisco IOS Software features. As such, these features entail a CPU tax when they are implemented, and some tools require more CPU cycles than others. The CPU overhead required increases with the line rates of the media to which the policies are applied.

In a LAN switching environment, QoS policies still are required. (The fallacy of why simply "throwing more bandwidth at it" won't solve campus QoS issues is discussed in more detail in this chapter's section discussing campus QoS design.) Implementing such policies in software at Fast Ethernet, Gigabit Ethernet, and 10-GE speeds would just about melt any Cisco box. Therefore, Cisco has ported QoS logic from Cisco IOS Software to hardware ASICs to provision QoS policies at line rates within campus environments.

The porting of QoS from software to hardware has many advantages from a design perspective, but it also has some caveats (which are discussed later). Some of these design advantages include the following:

- Classification and marking can be offloaded from routers and moved as close to the source hosts as administratively possible. This not only extends the DiffServ domain, but it also enables routers to use their CPU cycles more effectively and efficiently.

- Trust boundaries can be defined and enforced.

- Policing can be performed right at the source. This includes both RFC 2597 AF markdown policing (such as marking down out-of-contract AF11 traffic to AF12, or even AF13) or simply policing to drop unwanted traffic.

- Increased policing options, such as per-port/per-VLAN policing and microflow policing.

- Real-time applications, such as voice, can be guaranteed within campus environments because of preferential/priority hardware queuing.

- Congestion can be avoided within the campus, using WRED or similar tools.

The main caveat that arises from the porting of software QoS to hardware is that QoS features become hardware specific—that is, they can vary from platform to platform, and even from line card to line card. This increases the complexity of configuring and managing campus QoS because many idiosyncrasies need to be kept in mind for each platform or line card. This caveat further is exacerbated by the fact that some platforms require CatOS, others require Cisco IOS, and still others (such as the Catalyst 6500) can be configured using either. To address this issue, common syntaxes, such as the MQC from Cisco IOS, and command macros, such as AutoQoS, are continuing to be developed to make QoS more consistent and easier to deploy across Catalyst platforms.

This chapter first looks at generic QoS models across the Catalyst platform families and then examines the most currently relevant Catalyst platforms.

Generic Catalyst QoS Models

Platform idiosyncrasies aside for a moment, most Catalyst platforms follow the high-level generic QoS model shown in Figure 10-1.

Figure 10-1 *Generic Catalyst QoS Model*

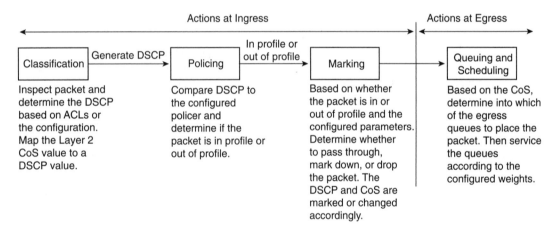

The generic Catalyst QoS functions of classification and marking, policing and marking, and scheduling (congestion management and congestion avoidance) are examined in the following sections.

Classification, Marking, and Mapping

On most Catalyst platforms (other than the Catalyst 2950), QoS is disabled by default and must be enabled globally before any function, including classification, occurs.

During QoS processing in Catalyst switches, all packets are represented with an *Internal DSCP* value. This applies even to non-IP packets because non-IP packets have their Internal DSCP generated by their CoS values (coupled with the CoS-to-DSCP mapping table settings) or are assigned the default Internal DSCP value of 0. This Internal DSCP value is derived from, among other criteria, the *trust state* of the port. The trust states can be set to the following:

- **Trust DSCP**—The Internal DSCP is set according to the received DSCP values.

- **Trust IP Precedence**—The Internal DSCP is set based on the received IP Precedence values, through a default or modified IPP-to-DSCP mapping.

- **Trust CoS**—The Internal DSCP is set based on the received CoS values, through a default or modified CoS-to-DSCP mapping.

- **Untrusted**—The received CoS is set or reset to the default value (typically 0), and the Internal DSCP value is set through a default or modified CoS-to-DSCP mapping (which, likewise, typically results in an Internal DSCP marking of 0).

Trust boundaries also can be extended to devices such as IP phones so that the switch will trust the markings that the IP phone has set. IP phones mark Voice traffic to CoS 5 and DSCP EF, and Call-Signaling traffic to CoS 3 and DSCP AF31 (or CS3 on newer software releases).

Modifiable CoS-to-DSCP maps provide network administrators granularity in these mappings. For example, by default, the 3 CoS bits are used as the three most significant bits within the DSCP (CoS 5 maps to DSCP 40, which is CS5 and not EF). But when a third-party IPT device doesn't mark Voice traffic with CoS *and* DSCP (as Cisco IP phones do), the administrator can chose to modify this mapping table to correctly map voice from CoS 5 to DSCP 46 (EF) right at the access switch.

In addition to CoS-to-DSCP maps and IPP-to-DSCP maps, DSCP values themselves can be mapped to alternate DSCP values, using DSCP mutation maps. Such DSCP-to-DSCP mutation maps are useful on the borders of two different DiffServ domains.

Classification also can be performed explicitly using access control lists (ACLs), which are comprised of access control entries (ACEs). Two main ACL types exist: IP and MAC. IP ACLs usually can use Layer 3 (source or destination addresses) or Layer 4 (TCP/UDP ports/ranges) for classification purposes. The hardware processes each ACE of an ACL for a "first-true-match" rule. Therefore, it is recommended to order the ACEs to have the most common matches closer to the top of the ACL to optimize processing.

Figure 10-2 shows a generic Catalyst classification model. Some platforms, such as the Catalyst 6500, expand on this model, but the main logic remains the same.

Figure 10-2 *Generic Catalyst Classification, Marking, and Mapping Model*

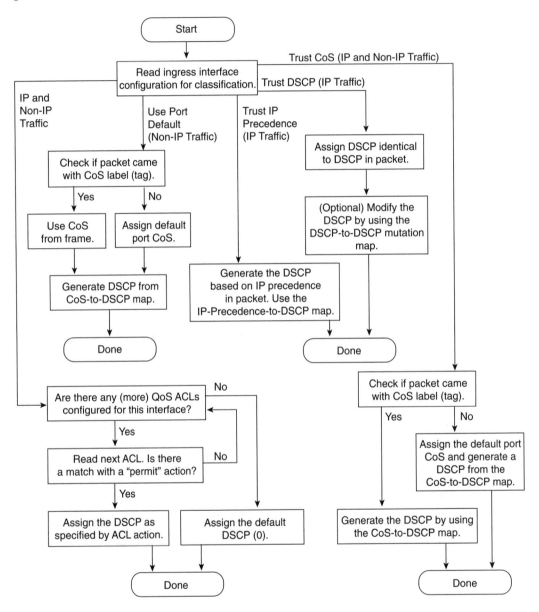

Policing and Markdown

Three types of policing are supported on Catalyst platforms:

- **Individual policing**—Applies bandwidth constraint to each interface
- **Aggregate policing**—Applies a bandwidth limit constraint among all interfaces
- **Microflow policing (Catalyst 6500 only)**—Applies a bandwidth limit constraint to each flow

As in Cisco IOS, Catalyst policers are based on token-bucket algorithms to determine in-profile and out-of-profile traffic. Out-of-profile traffic can be either dropped or marked down. Traffic that is out-of-profile and marked down has both the DSCP and Internal DSCP marked down to the new value. Figure 10-3 shows a generic Catalyst policing model.

Figure 10-3 *Generic Catalyst Policing and Markdown Model*

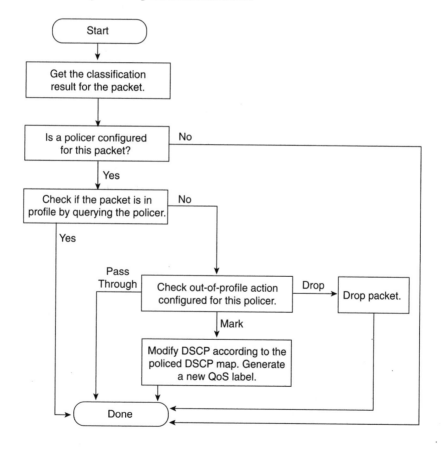

Queuing and Dropping

So far, Catalyst QoS might seem remarkably similar to Cisco IOS QoS. However, when it comes to queuing, the approaches differ to the point that confusion often sets in.

In Catalyst QoS, congestion management (queuing) is performed through a set number of queues, and congestion avoidance (selective dropping) is performed through a set number of thresholds per queue. In its most basic form, the number of queues (Q) and thresholds (T) can be expressed as xQyT. Consider a basic example using two queues with two thresholds each (2Q2T).

In this Catalyst queuing model, the buffer space for queuing for each line card's port is allocated among two separate queues: Eighty percent of the buffer space (by default) is assigned to the first queue, and the remaining 20 percent is assigned to the second queue. This buffer allocation is depicted in Figure 10-4.

Figure 10-4 *Basic Catalyst Queuing: 2Q2T Example—Buffer Allocation*

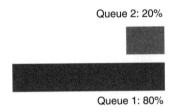

Queue 2: 20%

Queue 1: 80%

Then two thresholds are defined in each queue. By default, these thresholds are at 80 percent of the queue's depth and 100 percent of the queue's depth (the tail). These thresholds are shown in Figure 10-5.

Figure 10-5 *Basic Catalyst Queuing: 2Q2T Example—Default Thresholds*

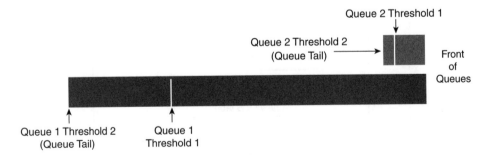

On all Catalyst platforms, CoS-to-transmit queue mappings are used to assign packets to transmit queues (although on some platforms, certain versions of software allow the option to configure DSCP-to-transmit queue mappings). Continuing this basic example, CoS values 0 through 4 are assigned to the first queue, while CoS values 5 through 7 are assigned to the second queue. This is shown in Figure 10-6.

Figure 10-6 *Basic Catalyst Queuing: 2Q2T Example—CoS-to-Queue Mappings*

Additionally, congestion management is overlaid to the queuing model so that each CoS value (or DSCP value, if the platform/software supports it) can be restricted to a certain threshold. For example, CoS values 0 and 1 can be restricted to the first-queue first-threshold (1Q1T). If the queue fills past this threshold, all packets with a CoS value of 0 and 1 will be dropped. Thus, the remainder of the first queue (1Q2T) is reserved exclusively to hold only packets with CoS values of 2, 3, and 4. Similarly, CoS values of 6 and 7 are restricted to the second queue's first threshold (2Q1T), while the remainder of the second queue (2Q2T) is explicitly reserved for CoS 5. This is shown in Figure 10-7.

Figure 10-7 *Basic Catalyst Queuing: 2Q2T Example—CoS-to-Threshold Mappings*

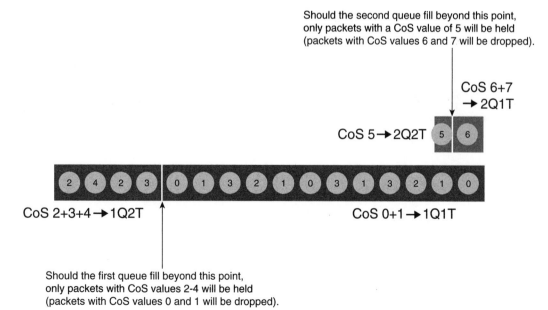

Now that CoS values have been mapped to both queues and thresholds, the scheduling (in the event of congestion) is performed on this model by a weighted round-robin algorithm. Such an algorithm favors servicing the second queue (higher CoS values) over servicing the lower queue. Usually these servicing weights (and the queue sizes) can be overridden from their default values.

In this manner, preferential service can be offered to voice and network control packets. Yet, no strict priority servicing is provided to voice, as with Cisco IOS LLQ. An improvement on the $xQyT$ Catalyst queuing model is the $1PxQyT$ model, in which a (typically single) strict-priority queue is added to the model.

As mentioned previously, queues 1 and 2 are serviced by a WRR scheduler, but if any activity is detected in the priority queue, the WRR scheduler is interrupted, the strict-priority traffic is serviced exhaustively, and the WRR scheduler resumes servicing queues 1 and 2.

An example 1P2Q2T model, complete with CoS-to-queue and threshold mappings, is shown in Figure 10-8. In this example, the first queue is allocated 70 percent of the buffer space, the second is allocated 15 percent, and the strict priority also is allocated 15 percent, by default.

Figure 10-8 *Basic Catalyst Queuing: 1P2Q2T Example*

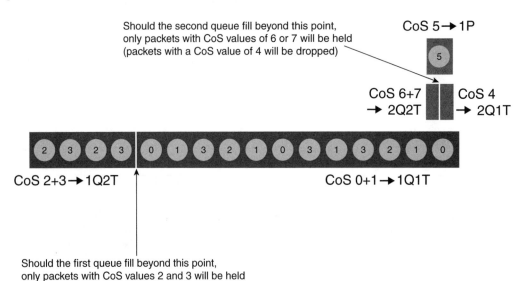

All (new) Catalyst platforms and line cards have some variations of either the $xQyT$ hardware queuing model or (more likely) the newer $1PxQyT$ hardware queuing model.

With the generic Catalyst QoS models have been laid out, it is time to examine some platform-specific applications (and idiosyncrasies) of these models. Only the current-generation switches (at the time of writing), including the Catalyst 2950, 3550, 3560, 3750, 4500 (Supervisors II+ through V), and the Catalyst 6500 Supervisor 2 and Supervisor 720 are discussed here.

NOTE   This chapter provides an overview of Catalyst QoS tools only to lay a context for the design chapters to follow. As such, some platforms have been omitted from the scope of discussion. For a comprehensive discussion of QoS features on switches not included in this list, such as the Catalyst 2900XL, 3500XL, 4000-CatOS, and 5000 series switches, refer to Cisco documentation at http://www.cisco.com/univercd/home/home.htm or to the Cisco Press book *Cisco Catalyst QoS: Quality of Service in Campus Networks*, by Mike Flannagan, Richard Froom, and Kevin Turek.

NOTE   Not every QoS feature that these platforms support is discussed in this chapter; the text is concerned only with the features that are most relevant to Chapter 12, "Campus QoS Design." All feature discussions in this chapter are based on hardware/software feature sets available at the time of writing. Refer to Cisco Catalyst documentation for the latest updates on these platforms and features.

Catalyst 2950

The Catalyst 2950, shown in Figure 10-9, supports only Layer 2 forwarding, making it a good candidate for a low-end access switch. The main difference between the Catalyst 2950 and the Catalyst 3550 is that the 3550 supports Layer 3 forwarding (IP routing) and thus can function as a distribution layer switch. Other than that, the platforms are remarkably similar. Both use the same Cisco IOS code base and have a virtually identical QoS feature set (with the 3500 boasting a few additional QoS features).

Figure 10-9 *Cisco Catalyst 2950 Series*

Two Cisco IOS software images are supported on the 2950: the Standard Image (SI) and the Enhanced Image (EI). The full 2950 QoS feature set (including classification, policing, and marking; mapping, queuing, and scheduling; and AutoQoS) is available as part of the Enhanced Image. Therefore, it is recommended to use the EI on the 2950 within a QoS-enabled campus design. For the remainder of this discussion, it is assumed that the Catalyst 2950 is running an Enhanced Image.

Catalyst 2950 Classification, Marking, and Mapping

Two methods of classification are available on the 2950: on a physical interface basis (no support exists for VLAN-based classification) and on an MQC/ACL basis.

By default, physical interfaces are untrusted, but they can be configured to trust CoS or to trust DSCP. At the time of writing, the 2950 does not support the full DSCP range; it supports only the following values: 0, 8, 10, 16, 18, 24, 26, 32, 34, 40, 46, 48, and 56.

Trust boundaries can be extended to IP phones that are connected to the interface. The switch uses Cisco Discovery Protocol (CDP) to detect the presence of IP phones.

NOTE   In the future, digital certificates will be exchanged between the switch and the IP phone to verify that an IP phone indeed is connected to the switch and is not a hacker spoofing CDP.

In Example 10-1, trust is set for CoS, and the trust boundary has been extended to any connected IP phones. The **range** keyword is used to configure multiple interfaces at once.

Example 10-1 *Configuring Trust and Trust Extensions on a Catalyst 2950*

```
CAT2950(config)#interface range FastEthernet 0/12 - 24
CAT2950(config-if-range)#mls qos trust cos
CAT2950(config-if-range)#mls qos trust device cisco-phone
```

MQC-based class maps and policy maps also can be used with ACLs to mark traffic on ingress on the 2950. ACLs supported are standard IP ACLs, extended IP ACLs, and Layer 2 MAC ACLs.

In Example 10-2, an access list identifies UDP traffic sourced from an IP/TV server (10.200.200.200). A class map references this ACL and applies a marking policy to traffic that matches this criterion, marking these flows to DSCP CS4 (32.)

Example 10-2 *Configuring MQC/ACL Classification on the Catalyst 2950*

```
CAT2950(config)#access-list 100 permit udp 10.200.200.200 255.255.255.255 any
CAT2950(config)#class-map IPTV
CAT2950(config-cmap)#match access-group 100
CAT2950(config-cmap)#exit
CAT2950(config)#policy-map MARK-IPTV-DSCP-CS4
CAT2950(config-pmap)#class IPTV
CAT2950(config-pmap-c)#set ip dscp 32
CAT2950(config-pmap-c)#interface FastEthernet 0/1
CAT2950(config-if)#service-policy input MARK-IPTV-DSCP-CS4
```

The default CoS-to-DSCP map for the Catalyst 2950 is shown in Table 10-1. This default CoS-to-DSCP mapping is actually the same across all Catalyst platforms: The CoS bits are combined with three trailing zeros (in binary) to form the default DSCP value (in decimal, the equivalent conversion is achieved by multiplying the CoS value by 8).

Table 10-1   *Cisco Catalyst Platforms Default CoS-to-DSCP Map*

CoS Value	0	1	2	3	4	5	6	7
DSCP Value	0	8	16	24	32	40	48	56

The default DSCP-to-CoS mapping table for the 2950 is shown in Table 10-2. Notice that not all DSCP values are included or supported on the Catalyst 2950.

Table 10-2   *Catalyst 2950 Default DSCP-to-CoS Map*

DSCP Values	0	8, 10	16, 18	24, 26	32, 34	40, 46	48	56
CoS Values	0	1	2	3	4	5	6	7

These mapping values can be modified away from the default settings. As shown in Example 10-3, CoS 5 is mapped to DSCP 46 (EF), and DSCP CS1 (8) is mapped to CoS 0. In the first map (CoS to DSCP), eight separate values must be supplied (in order) that are to correspond to the CoS values of 0 through 7. Notice that the sixth value (corresponding to CoS 5) is modified away from the default (40) and explicitly is set to 46 (DSCP EF). With the second mapping, up to 13 DSCP values (separated by spaces) can be mapped to a CoS value, which follows the **to** keyword.

Example 10-3   *Configuring Mapping Modifications on the Catalyst 2950*

```
CAT2950(config)#mls qos map cos-dscp 0 8 16 24 32 46 48 56
CAT2950(config)#mls qos map dscp-cos 8 to 0
```

Catalyst 2950 Policing and Markdown

Policing can be applied only on ingress on the Catalyst 2950. The Catalyst 2950 supports only individual policing. Only 60 policers are supported on Gigabit Ethernet ports, only 6 policers are supported on Fast Ethernet ports on the 2950, and granularity for average burst is limited to 8-Mbps increments for Gigabit Ethernet ports and 1-Mbps increments for Fast Ethernet ports.

In Example 10-4, all traffic offered to an interface range (Fast Ethernet 0/2 through 0/4) is policed to 25 Mbps, beyond which it is dropped.

Example 10-4   *Configuring Individual Policing on the Catalyst 2950*

```
CAT2950(config)#access-list 1 permit any
CAT2950(config)#class-map ANY
CAT2950(config-cmap)#match access-group 1
CAT2950(config-cmap)#exit
CAT2950(config)#policy-map POLICE-TO-25MBS
CAT2950(config-pmap)#class ANY
CAT2950(config-pmap-c)#police 25000000 16384 exceed-action drop
CAT2950(config)#interface range FastEthernet 0/2 - 4
CAT2950(config-if-range)#service-policy input POLICE-TO-25MBS
```

Catalyst 2950 Queuing

The Catalyst 2950 supports four egress queues but no drop thresholds (besides the tail of the queue). These queues can be configured to schedule using one of two algorithms: weighted round-robin (WRR) scheduling (4Q1T) or strict-priority scheduling (1P3Q1T). The default scheduling algorithm is strict priority.

Scheduling weights per queue are set by the **wrr-queue bandwidth** *weight1 weight2 weight3 weight4* command, with weights 1 through 4 representing the weights for each queue, respectively. The approximate bandwidth allocation per queue is the queue's weight divided by the sum of all weights. When the weight for queue 4 (weight4) is set to 0, the scheduler is operating in strict-priority fashion, with queue4 enabled as the expedite queue.

In Example 10-5, the scheduler is operating in strict-priority mode, with queue 4 as the expedite queue (configured by setting *weight4* to equal 0). The remaining bandwidth is divided among queue 1 (25 percent), queue 2 (20 percent), and queue 3 (55 percent). These percentages are derived from the weight of the queue divided by the sum of all weights (5 / [5 + 4 + 11]) and (4 / [5 + 4 + 11]) and (11 / [5 + 4 + 11]), respectively.

Example 10-5 *Configuring the Expedite Queue and WRR Priority on the Catalyst 2950*

```
CAT2950(config)#wrr-queue bandwidth 5 4 11 0
```

Finally, CoS values must be assigned to the desired queues. By default, CoS 0 and 1 are assigned to queue 1, CoS 2 and 3 are assigned to queue 2, CoS 4 and 5 are assigned to queue 3, and CoS 6 and 7 are assigned to queue 4. Usually, however, it is desirable to send only CoS 5 (voice) to the expedite queue (queue 4), reassigning CoS 6 and 7 to queue 3. This modification of the CoS-to-queue mapping can be made with the **wrr-queue cos-map** command, as shown in Example 10-6.

Example 10-6 *Configuring CoS-to-Queue Mapping on the Catalyst 2950*

```
CAT2950(config)#wrr-queue cos-map 4 5      ! Assigns CoS 5 to queue 4
CAT2950(config)#wrr-queue cos-map 3 6 7    ! Reassigns CoS 6 and 7 to queue 3
```

Catalyst 3550

The Catalyst 3550, shown in Figure 10-10, is found in both the access layer and the distribution layer as it supports IP routing. Many of the 3550's QoS features and syntax are identical to the 2950, but a few idiosyncrasies and extra features are unique to the 3550.

Figure 10-10 *Cisco Catalyst 3550 Series*

For example, by default, QoS is disabled on the 3550 and must be enabled manually for any classification or queuing to occur. Furthermore, enabling QoS on the 3550 on some versions of software requires disabling IEEE 802.3X flow control on all interfaces, as shown in Example 10-7.

Example 10-7 *Enabling QoS Globally on a Catalyst 3550*

```
CAT3550(config)#interface range FastEthernet 0/1 - 24
CAT3550(config-if-range)#flowcontrol receive off      ! Disables flowcontrol
CAT3550(config-if-range)#flowcontrol send off         ! Disables flowcontrol
CAT3550(config-if-range)#exit
CAT3550(config)#mls qos                               ! Enables QoS globally
```

When flow control has been disabled on all interfaces and QoS has been enabled globally, all other QoS features become available.

Features and syntax that are identical to the 2950 are not repeated in the following sections; only features and syntax that are unique to the 3550 are detailed in the following examples.

Catalyst 3550 Classification, Marking, and Mapping

Classification on a per-port level and a per-port, per-VLAN basis is supported on the Catalyst 3550. Classification also can be performed through port trust states or through MQC and ACLs. As with the 2950, supported ACL types are IP standard, IP extended, or a MAC ACL.

Similar to the 2950, the 3550 can trust CoS or DSCP and also limits trust to select devices, as a Cisco IP phone does. Furthermore, the 3550 supports the capability to trust IP Precedence, which might be required when interfacing with third-party IP Telephony devices. Example 10-8 shows how to enable IP Precedence trust on a 3550.

Example 10-8 *Configuring IP Precedence Trust on a Catalyst 3550*

```
CAT3550(config)#interface range FastEthernet 0/1 - 24
CAT3550(config-if-range)#mls qos trust ip-precedence
```

Classification through MQC and ACLs is identical to that for the 2950.

The default CoS-to-DSCP map on the 3550 is the same as on all Catalyst platforms (previously shown in Table 10-1). The default DSCP-to-CoS maps, shown in Table 10-3, are slightly different on the 3550 than the 2950 because the full DSCP range is supported on the 3550.

Table 10-3   *Catalyst 3500 Default DSCP-to-CoS Map*

DSCP Value	0 to 7	8 to 15	16 to 23	24 to 31	32 to 39	40 to 47	48 to 55	56 to 63
CoS Value	0	1	2	3	4	5	6	7

Additionally, the 3550 supports an IP Precedence-to-DSCP map, which is essentially identical to the CoS-to-DSCP map, with the exception that CoS values are replaced with IP Precedence values.

Mapping modifications can be configured identically to those on the 2950.

A new type of mapping, DSCP-to-DSCP mapping, can be configured on a Catalyst 3550. These maps, known as DSCP mutation maps, join autonomous DiffServ domains. Although all maps except DSCP mutation maps are defined globally, DSCP mutation maps are applied on a per-interface basis (specifically, on the interface that serves as the border between DiffServ domains). Actually, more than one DSCP mutation map can be defined when more than two autonomous DiffServ domains are being joined on a single 3550.

In Example 10-11, PHBs AF21, AF22, and AF23 from one DiffServ domain are mapped to AF11, AF12, and AF13 in the adjoining DiffServ domain. The interface joining these DiffServ domains is Gigabit 0/3.

Figure 10-11   *DSCP Mutation Application Example*

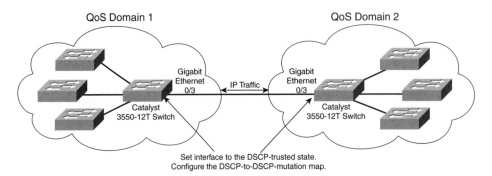

The configuration required for such mapping on the border 3550 in DiffServ domain 1 is shown in Example 10-9.

Example 10-9 *Configuring DSCP Mutation on a Catalyst 3550*

```
CAT3550(config)#mls qos map dscp-mutation DIFFSERV1-TO-DIFFSERV2 18 to 10
CAT3550(config)#mls qos map dscp-mutation DIFFSERV1-TO-DIFFSERV2 20 to 12
CAT3550(config)#mls qos map dscp-mutation DIFFSERV1-TO-DIFFSERV2 22 to 14
CAT3550(config)#int gig 0/3
CAT3550(config-if)#mls qos trust dscp
CAT3550(config-if)#mls qos dscp-mutation DIFFSERV1-TO-DIFFSERV2
```

A complementary policy would be required on the border switch for the second DiffServ domain to map in the reverse direction.

Catalyst 3550 Policing and Markdown

The 3550 supports not only ingress policing, but also egress policing on its interfaces. Furthermore, policers can be defined as individual policers or as aggregate policers. Aggregate policers are applied not to discrete flows, but cumulatively to all matched traffic flows. The aggregate rates for such a policer are defined globally.

The 3550 supports 128 policers on Gigabit Ethernet ports and 8 policers on Fast Ethernet ports. Only one policer can be applied to a packet per direction, and only eight policers can be defined on an egress port.

Configuring an individual policer is slightly different on a 3550 than on a 2950. This is because a policed-DSCP map is required to determine the value down to which an out-of-profile DSCP value is to be marked.

In Example 10-10, individual Bulk Data traffic flows (marked on a data center server connected to Fast Ethernet 0/12) in excess of 10 Mbps are marked down from AF11 (DSCP 10) to AF12 (DSCP 12).

Example 10-10 *Configuring an Individual Policer on a Catalyst 3550*

```
CAT3550(config)#mls qos map policed-dscp 10 to 12
CAT3550(config)#class-map match-any BULK
CAT3550(config-cmap)#match ip dscp af11
CAT3550(config)#policy-map BULK-MARKDOWN
CAT3550(config-pmap)#class BULK
CAT3550(config-pmap-c)#police 10000000 8000 exceed-action policed-dscp-transmit
CAT3550(config-pmap-c)#interface fa 0/12
CAT3550(config-if)#service-policy input BULK-MARKDOWN
```

The Catalyst 3550 is the only switch (at the time of writing) to support per-port/per-VLAN policing (in the ingress direction). Per-port/per-VLAN policing requires an additional class map to be defined with a **match-all** clause and two **match** statements: one for the VLAN to be matched and the other for the class map to apply. For example, if the preceding Bulk Data policing policy is to be applied only on VLAN 10, the per-port/per-VLAN policy would look like Example 10-11.

Example 10-11 *Configuring a Per-Port, Per-VLAN Individual Policer on a Catalyst 3550*

```
CAT3550(config)#mls qos map policed-dscp 10 to 12
CAT3550(config)#class-map match-any BULK
CAT3550(config-cmap)#match ip dscp af11
CAT3550(config-cmap)#class-map match-all VLAN10-BULK
CAT3550(config-cmap)#match vlan 10
CAT3550(config-cmap)#match class-map BULK
CAT3550(config-cmap)#policy-map VLAN10-BULK-MARKDOWN
CAT3550(config-pmap)#class VLAN10-BULK
CAT3550(config-pmap-c)#police 10000000 8000 exceed-action policed-dscp-transmit
CAT3550(config-pmap-c)#interface fa 0/12
CAT3550(config-if)#service-policy input VLAN10-BULK-MARKDOWN
```

In addition to individual policers, an aggregate policer can be applied to an access-to-distribution uplink on egress to mark down cumulatively out-of-profile traffic. Building on the previous example, all Bulk Data traffic in excess of 100 Mbps (regardless of how many flows are involved) is marked down to AF12 on the Gigabit 0/2 uplink. The policed-DSCP map does not need to be redefined, but it can be leveraged by both individual and aggregate policers, as shown in Example 10-12.

Example 10-12 *Configuring an Aggregate Policer on a Catalyst 3550*

```
CAT3550(config-if)#mls qos aggregate-policer BULK-MARKDOWN-AGG 1000000000 8000
  exceed-action policed-dscp-transmit
CAT3550(config)#policy-map BULK-MARKDOWN-AGG
CAT3550(config-pmap)#class BULK
```

continues

Example 10-12 *Configuring an Aggregate Policer on a Catalyst 3550 (Continued)*

```
CAT3550(config-pmap-c)#police aggregate BULK-MARKDOWN-AGG
CAT3550(config-pmap-c)#int gig 0/2
CAT3550(config-if)#service-policy output BULK-MARKDOWN-AGG
```

Catalyst 3550 Queuing and Dropping

The 3550 has four egress queues, one of which (queue 4) can be configured as a strict-priority queue that (unlike the 2950) is not enabled by default but that needs to be enabled on a per-interface basis with the **priority-queue out** command. An example of enabling the strict-priority queue on a Gigabit Ethernet uplink is shown in Example 10-13.

Example 10-13 *Configuring a Strict-Priority Queue on a Catalyst 3550*

```
CAT3550(config)#int gig 0/1
CAT3550(config-if)#priority-queue out
```

As with the 2950, weights can be configured to allocate bandwidth to each queue by the weighted round-robin scheduler. The syntax is identical to that of the 2950, except that if a strict-priority queue has been enabled on an interface, the value for *weight4* simply is ignored.

NOTE Queue limits also can be tuned away from defaults using the **wrr-queue queue-limit** command. The default queue limits are such that each queue is assigned 25 percent of the available buffer space.

It should be noted that when the queue limits are modified, the queue temporarily is shut down during the hardware reconfiguration, and the switch may drop newly arrived packets destined to the queue.

CoS values are assigned to their respective queues using the **wrr-queue cos-map** command. A difference between the Catalyst 3550 and the 2950 is that the CoS-to-queue maps are defined on a per-interface basis on the 3550 (not globally, as on a Catalyst 2950).

By default, CoS 0 and 1 are assigned to queue 1, CoS 2 and 3 are assigned to queue 2, CoS 4 and 5 are assigned to queue 3, and CoS 6 and 7 are assigned to queue 4. Usually, it is desirable to send only CoS 5 (voice) to the expedite queue (queue 4) and to reassign CoS 6 and 7 to queue 3. This modification of the CoS-to-queue mapping can be made with the **wrr-queue cos-map** interface command on the 3550, as shown in Example 10-14.

A QoS feature that the 3550 enjoys that the 2950 does not is the capability to support configurable drop thresholds per queue on Gigabit Ethernet ports. Therefore, Catalyst 3550

Example 10-14 *Configuring CoS-to-Queue Mapping on the Catalyst 3550*

```
CAT3550(config)#int gig 0/1
CAT3550(config-if)#wrr-queue cos-map 4 5     ! Assigns CoS 5 to queue 4
CAT3550(config-if)#wrr-queue cos-map 3 6 7   ! Reassigns CoS 6 and 7 to queue 3
```

Gigabit Ethernet ports can be configured to operate in a 4Q2T or 1P3Q2T manner, while Catalyst 3550 Fast Ethernet ports can be configured to operate in a 4Q1T or 1P3Q1T manner.

These drop thresholds can be configured in one of two ways: tail drop or WRED.

Tail drop is the default congestion-avoidance technique on Gigabit-capable Ethernet ports. With tail drop, packets are queued until the thresholds are exceeded. Specifically, all packets with DSCPs assigned to the first threshold are dropped until the threshold no longer is exceeded. However, packets assigned to the second threshold continue to be queued and sent as long as the second threshold is not exceeded.

You can modify the two tail-drop threshold percentages assigned to the four egress queues by using the **wrr-queue threshold** interface configuration command. Each threshold value is a percentage of the total number of allocated queue descriptors for the queue. The default threshold is 100 percent for thresholds 1 and 2.

Alternately, you can enable WRED and configure the two threshold percentages assigned to the four egress queues on a Gigabit-capable Ethernet port by using the **wrr-queue random-detect max-threshold** interface configuration command. Each threshold percentage represents where WRED starts to randomly drop packets. After a threshold is exceeded, WRED randomly begins to drop packets assigned to this threshold. As the queue limit is approached, WRED continues to drop more packets. When the queue limit is reached, WRED drops all packets assigned to the threshold. By default, WRED is disabled.

If you use WRED thresholds, you cannot use tail drop, and vice versa. If WRED is disabled, tail drop automatically is enabled with the previous configuration.

You modify the DSCP-to-threshold map to determine which DSCPs are mapped to which threshold ID by using the **wrr-queue dscp-map** interface configuration command. By default, all DSCPs are mapped to threshold 1; when this threshold is exceeded, all the packets randomly are dropped.

In Example 10-15, WRED is enabled on the three remaining queues (because queue 4 previously was enabled as the expedite/strict-priority queue). The first threshold for each remaining queue is set to 40 percent, and the second threshold is set to 100 percent (the tail of the queue). DSCP values of AF12, AF22, AF32, and AF42 (12, 20, 28, and 36, respectively) are mapped to the first thresholds. All other relevant DSCPs have been mapped to the second threshold. Because the command allows only eight DSCP values to be mapped to a threshold per command, a second entry is needed to map values DSCP values CS6 (48) and CS7 (56) to the second threshold.

Example 10-15   *Configuring WRED Thresholds and DSCP-to-Threshold Maps on a Catalyst 3550 Gigabit Ethernet Interface*

```
CAT3550(config)#int gig 0/1
CAT3550(config-if)#wrr-queue random-detect max-threshold 1 40 100
CAT3550(config-if)#wrr-queue random-detect max-threshold 2 40 100
CAT3550(config-if)#wrr-queue random-detect max-threshold 3 40 100
CAT3550(config-if)#wrr-queue dscp-map 1 12 20 28 36
CAT3550(config-if)#wrr-queue dscp-map 2 8 10 16 18 24 26 32 34
CAT3550(config-if)#wrr-queue dscp-map 2 48 56
```

Catalyst 2970, 3650, and 3750

The Cisco Catalyst 2970 series switches are entry-level Gigabit Ethernet switches that deliver wire-speed intelligent services for small and medium businesses and enterprise branch offices.

The Catalyst 2970 is available with Enhanced Image (EI) Cisco IOS Software, which supports a rich QoS features set. Additionally, the 2970 supports identity-based network services, enhancing the security of converged voice, video, and data networks, as in VoIP.

The Cisco Catalyst 3560 series switches is a line of fixed configuration, enterprise-class, IEEE 802.3af, and Cisco prestandard Power over Ethernet (PoE) switches. The Catalyst 3560 fits well in small enterprise wiring closets or branch office environments that are using their LAN infrastructure for the deployment of IP phones, wireless access points, video surveillance, building management systems, and remote video kiosks. While the Catalyst 3560 supports IP Routing, it is better suited to the access layer (when L3 is deployed to the wiring closet) than the distribution layer because its inline power capabilities are rarely required at the distribution layer.

The Cisco Catalyst 3750 series switches represent the next step in the evolution of desktop switches and feature Cisco StackWise technology. Cisco StackWise technology unites up to nine individual Cisco Catalyst 3750 switches into a single logical unit, using special stack-interconnect cables and stacking software (the stack interconnect is 32 Gbps). The stack behaves as a single switching unit that is managed by a master switch elected from one of the member switches. The master switch automatically creates and updates all the switching and optional routing tables. A working stack can accept new members or delete old ones without service interruption. Thus equipped, the Catalyst 3750 is optimized for high-density Gigabit Ethernet deployments and is suitable for access and distribution layer deployments, or even small-network core-layer requirements.

The Catalyst 3560 and 3750 series switches are available in the Standard Multilayer Software Image (SMI) or the Enhanced Multilayer Software Image (EMI). The SMI feature set includes all supported QoS tools and basic static and RIP routing functionality. The EMI provides a richer set of enterprise-class features, including advanced hardware-based IP unicast and multicast routing.

From a QoS perspective, the Catalyst 2970, 3560, and 3750 are identical and are considered together in this discussion. The Catalyst 2970 and 3750 switches are shown in Figure 10-12.

Figure 10-12 *Cisco Catalyst 2970 and 3750 Series Switches*

By default, QoS is disabled on the 2970/3560/3750 platforms and must be enabled explicitly with the global **mls qos** command.

Catalyst 2970/3560/3750 Classification, Marking, and Mapping

The Catalyst 2970/3560/3750 share many common QoS features and syntax with the Catalyst 3550. Wherever feature functionality and syntax are identical to those of the 3550, details and configuration examples are not repeated in this section.

Trust states and MQC/ACL classification and marking on the Catalyst 2970/3560/3750 are identical in function and syntax to the 3550.

All Catalyst 2970/3560/3750 default CoS-to-DSCP, IP Precedence-to-DSCP, and DSCP-to-CoS maps are identical to those for the 3550, as are mapping functions and syntax (including DSCP mutation).

Catalyst 2970/3560/3750 Policing and Markdown

Policing and markdown functionality and syntax on the 2970/3560/3750 are identical to those of the 3550, with the exception that the 2970/3560/3750 currently do not support per-Port/per-VLAN policing.

The 2970/3560/3750 support 64 policers per interface. However, whereas the configurable limit on the number of policers per interface is 64, the maximum number of policers per port ASIC is 256. This limit present the options in the following list.

- On a 24-port 10/100 + 2 Small Form-Factor Pluggable (SFP) modules chassis, there is one port ASIC. This means that that the 256 policers must be shared among 26 ports, with any 1 port having a maximum of 64 policers. However, if you configure four ports with 64 policers each, there will be no more policers left for any other ports on the chassis.

- On a 48-port 10/100 + 4 SFP chassis, there are two port ASICs. This means that you have two "sets" of 24 10/100 + 2 SFP ports internal to the switch. Each "set" of ports supports a total of 256 policers. So, once again, the maximum policers on a port is 64, but the maximum for each ASIC is 256.

These considerations should be kept in mind when designing for policing needs using the Catalyst 2970/3560/3750 switch.

Catalyst 2970/3560/3750 Queuing and Dropping

Up to this point in the discussion, the Catalyst 2970, 3560 and 3750 series switches have been shown to be remarkably identical to the Catalyst 3550 in terms of QoS features, functionality, and syntax. However, the platforms differ significantly when it comes to queuing.

The first major difference in queuing between the platforms is that the 2970/3560/3750 support ingress scheduling. However, ingress scheduling rarely is required because it provides benefits only if the (combined) input rates from any ports exceed the switching fabric rate of the switch. This is extremely rare in most campus environments.

The Catalyst 2970/3560/3750 also supports four egress queues, one of which can be configured as an expedite/priority queue through the **priority-queue out** interface command. Incidentally, on the Catalyst 2970/3560/3750, queue 1, not queue 4 (as on the 3550 and 2950) is used as an expedite queue (when configured).

Nonpriority queues are serviced through a shaped round-robin (SRR) algorithm that can be configured to operate in one of two modes: shaped or sharing.

Actually, both the ingress and egress queues are serviced by SRR, which determines the rate at which packets are sent. On the ingress queues, SRR sends packets to the stack ring. On the egress queues, SRR sends packets to the egress interface. For ingress queues, sharing is the default mode and is the only mode supported.

In shaped mode, the egress queues are guaranteed a percentage of the bandwidth and are rate limited to that amount. Shaped traffic does not use more than the allocated bandwidth even if the link is idle. Shaping provides a more even flow of traffic over time and reduces the peaks and valleys of bursty traffic. With shaping, the absolute value of each weight is used to compute the bandwidth available for the queues.

In shared mode, the queues share the bandwidth among them according to the configured weights. The bandwidth is guaranteed at this level but is not limited to it. For example, if a queue is empty and no longer requires a share of the link, the remaining queues can expand into the unused bandwidth and can share it among them. With sharing, the ratio of the weights determines the frequency of dequeuing; the absolute values are meaningless.

Additionally, both the ingress and egress queues use an enhanced version of the tail-drop congestion-avoidance mechanism called weighted tail drop (WTD). As a frame is enqueued to a particular queue, WTD uses the frame's assigned CoS value or DSCP value to assign it to different thresholds. If the threshold is exceeded for that CoS or DSCP value, the switch drops the frame. Each queue supports (up to) three WTD thresholds: Two are configurable (explicit WTD thresholds), and the third is nonconfigurable (implicit WTD threshold) and is preset to the queue-full state (100 percent).

Thus, Catalyst 2970/3560/3750 switches can be configured to operate in 4Q3T mode or 1P3Q3T mode. The Catalyst 2970/3560/3750 also supports two queue sets, meaning that different interfaces can be configured to operate in different queuing manners. For example, some interfaces might be configured to operate in 4Q3T, and others might be configured to operate in 1P3Q3T, depending on which queue set ID (qset-id) they are assigned to.

The allocated memory assigned to each queue can be modified (from the default 25 percent per queue) by using the **mls qos queue-set output** *qset-id* **buffers** *allocation1 ... allocation4* global configuration command. The sum of all the allocated buffers represents the reserved pool, and the remaining buffers are part of the common pool.

The Catalyst 2970/3560/3750 switches use a buffer-allocation scheme to reserve a minimum number of buffers for each egress queue, to prevent any queue or port from consuming all the buffers and depriving other queues, and to determine whether to grant buffer space to a requesting queue. The switch determines whether the target queue has not consumed more buffers than its reserved amount (under limit), whether it has consumed all of its maximum buffers (over limit), or whether the common pool is empty (no free buffers) or not empty (free buffers). If the queue is not over limit, the switch can allocate buffer space from the reserved pool or from the common pool (if it is not empty). If there are no free buffers in the common pool, or if the queue is over limit, the switch drops the frame.

You guarantee the availability of buffers, set drop thresholds, and configure the maximum memory allocation for a queue set by using the following global configuration command:

```
mls qos queue-set output qset-id threshold queue-id drop-threshold1
   drop-threshold2 reserved-threshold maximum-threshold
```

Each threshold value is a percentage of the queue's allocated memory.

In Example 10-16, queue set 1 has buffers allotted among queues 1 through 4 by the percentages 35, 30, 25, and 10. If 400 buffers are available, this would translate to an allocation of 140, 120, 100, and 40 buffers to queues 1 through 4, respectively. Also, WTD thresholds on queues 2 through 4 have been set to 40 percent of the buffer depth and 100 percent of the buffer depths. Each queue has its buffer allocation fully reserved (100 percent) and has its maximum memory threshold also set to 100 percent. Additionally, each queue has its reserved threshold (an amount of memory to be guaranteed or reserved for the queue—the range is 1 to 100 percent) set to 100 percent. Furthermore, each queue has its maximum threshold (which enables a queue in the full condition to obtain more buffers than are reserved for it and is the maximum memory that the queue can have before the packets are dropped—the range is 1 to 400 percent) set to 100 percent.

Finally, Fast Ethernet 0/1 on the switch that has been designated as stack member 2 is assigned to queue set 1, and queue 1 (of queue set 1) is defined as an expedite/priority queue.

Example 10-16 *Configuring Per-Queue Buffer Allocations and Thresholds on a Catalyst 2970/3560/3750*

```
CAT3750(config)#mls qos queue-set output 1 buffers 35 30 25 10
CAT3750(config)#mls qos queue-set output 1 threshold 2 40 100 100 100
CAT3750(config)#int fa 2/0/1
CAT3750(config-if)#queue-set 1
CAT3750(config-if)#priority-queue out
```

Similar to WRR, SRR allows the weights assigned to each queue to be modified. The ratio of these weights determines the frequency by which the SRR scheduler sends packets out from each queue. Shaping weights smooth or rate limit bursty or domineering flows. The inverse ratio (1/weight) determines the shaping bandwidth for each queue. For example, if a queue is to be limited to 10 percent, the shaping weight for that queue is set to 10. A shaping weight of 0 means that the queue is operating in sharing mode. Shaped mode overrides shared mode.

In shared mode, the queues share the bandwidth among them according to the configured weights. The bandwidth is guaranteed at this level but is not limited to it. For example, if a queue empties and does not require a share of the link, the remaining queues can expand into the unused bandwidth and share it among them. With sharing, the ratio of the weights determines the frequency of dequeuing; the absolute values are meaningless.

If an expedite queue has been configured, this strict-priority designation overrides any SRR weights for queue 1.

In Example 10-17, the queues are assigned 35 percent, 30 percent, 25 percent, and 10 percent shared bandwidth allocations. But, in actuality, queue 1's bandwidth allocation is ignored because it is configured as a strict-priority queue. Queues 2 and 3 are operating in shared mode (because their shaped weight is set to 0). Queue 4 is operating in shaped mode (shaped weight overrides shared weight) and is limited to no more than 10 percent of the bandwidth, regardless of whether more is available.

Example 10-17 *Configuring SRR Shaping and Sharing Weights on a Catalyst 2970/3560/3750*

```
CAT3750(config)#int gig 1/0/4
CAT3750(config-if)#srr-queue bandwidth share 35 30 25 10
CAT3750(config-if)#srr queue bandwidth shape 0 0 0 10
CAT3750(config-if)#queue-set 1
CAT3750(config-if)#priority-queue out
```

Finally, the Catalyst 2970/3560/3750 switches allow packets to be assigned to queues either by CoS values or by DSCP values, using CoS-to-queue/threshold maps or DSCP-to-queue/threshold maps.

In Example 10-18, DSCP EF (46) is assigned to queue 1 (the expedite queue). DSCP CS7 (56) and CS6 (48) are assigned to queue 2 threshold 2, and DSCP AF31 (26) and DSCP CS3 are assigned to queue 2 threshold 1. DSCP 0 is assigned to queue 3. Bulk (DSCP AF11 — 10) is assigned to queue 4 threshold 2, while Scavenger (DSCP CS1 — 8) traffic is assigned to queue 4 threshold 1.

Example 10-18 *Assigning DSCP Values to Queues/Thresholds on a Catalyst 2970/3560/3750*

```
CAT3750(config)#mls qos srr-queue output dscp-map queue 1 threshold 1 46
CAT3750(config)#mls qos srr-queue output dscp-map queue 2 threshold 2 48 56
CAT3750(config)#mls qos srr-queue output dscp-map queue 2 threshold 1 24 26
CAT3750(config)#mls qos srr-queue output dscp-map queue 3 threshold 2 0
CAT3750(config)#mls qos srr-queue output dscp-map queue 4 threshold 2 10
CAT3750(config)#mls qos srr-queue output dscp-map queue 4 threshold 1 8
```

Catalyst 4500

The Cisco Catalyst 4500, shown in Figure 10-13, finds its niche between desktop switches and the flagship Catalyst 6500. As such, it can be found in the access layer, the distribution layer, and even the core layer in midsize networks. Service providers also utilize the Catalyst 4500 because of its support of metro Ethernet options combined with its resiliency/failover options.

Figure 10-13 *Cisco Catalyst 4500 Series*

QoS support for the Catalyst 4000 Supervisor I and II cards (running CatOS) was quite limited and, as such, is omitted from this discussion. However, the Catalyst 4500 Supervisors II+ through V (running Cisco IOS) boast a much richer QoS toolset and are examined further.

Many of the QoS commands on the 4500 are similar to those on the switches previously discussed, with the exception of omitting the **mls** keyword at the beginning of the statement.

For example, by default, QoS is disabled on the 4500 and must be enabled with the global command **qos** (whereas, on previously discussed platforms, this command would have been **mls qos**). When QoS is disabled, the port interface trust states default to Trust DSCP. When QoS is enabled, this trust state changes to Untrusted, and (with no other QoS parameters explicitly defined) all egress traffic is marked to CoS 0 and DSCP 0. Incidentally, QoS can be disabled on a per-interface basis using the interface command **no qos** (see Example 10-19).

Example 10-19 *Enabling QoS on a Catalyst 4500*

```
CAT4500(config)#qos
```

QoS policies can be applied to individual ports or to VLANs. MQC policies can be applied to VLANs by attaching the **service-policy** statement to the VLAN interface and configuring all ports belonging to the VLAN to use VLAN-based QoS (using the **qos vlan-based** interface command). If the interface is configured to use VLAN-based QoS, the traffic received or sent through the interface is classified, policed, and marked according to the policy map attached to the VLAN (configured on the VLAN interface) to which the packet belongs. If no policy map is attached to the VLAN to which the packet belongs, the policy map attached to the interface is used. Furthermore, VLAN-based policies supercede any policies configured on individual ports if the port has been assigned to operate in VLAN-based QoS mode.

Catalyst 4500 Classification, Marking, and Mapping

The Catalyst 4500 can be configured to trust CoS or DSCP. Additionally, it can be configured to selectively trust a device, such as an IP phone (through CDP detection). Configuring trusts is very similar to previously discussed syntaxes, but without the **mls** keyword. Refer to Example 10-20.

Example 10-20 *Enabling QoS on a Catalyst 4500*

```
CAT4500(config)#interface range fa 2/1 - 48
CAT4500(config-if-range)#qos trust cos
CAT4500(config-if-range)#qos trust device cisco-phone
```

The configuration of MQC/ACL–based classification is the same as in previously discussed examples. However, if the **set** command is used in a policy map for marking, IP routing (disabled by default) must be enabled on the 4500. At a minimum, this requires enabling IP routing and setting a default route to a next-hop device capable of forwarding.

CoS-to-DSCP maps are the same as on all Catalyst switches (shown in Table 10-1). DSCP-to-CoS maps are identical to the Cisco 3550 and 3750 DSCP-to-CoS maps (shown in Table 10-3) because the 4500 also supports the full DSCP range of values (0 to 63).

As always, these mapping values can be modified away from the default settings. The syntax is again similar, without the **mls** keyword.

As shown in Example 10-21, CoS 5 is mapped to DSCP 46 (EF), and DSCP CS1 (8) is mapped to CoS 0. In the first map (CoS-to-DSCP), eight separate values must be supplied (in order) that are to correspond to the CoS values of 0 through 7. Notice that the sixth value (corresponding to CoS 5) is modified away from the default (40) and explicitly is set to 46 (DSCP EF). With the second mapping, up to eight DSCP values (separated by spaces) can be mapped to a CoS value, which follows the **to** keyword.

Example 10-21   *Configuring Mapping Modifications on the Catalyst 4500*

```
CAT4500(config)#qos map cos-dscp 0 8 16 24 32 46 48 56
CAT4500(config)#qos map dscp-cos 8 to 0
```

DSCP mutation currently is not supported on the Catalyst 4500.

Catalyst 4500 Policing and Markdown

The Catalyst 4500 supports individual and aggregate policers, as well as port-based and VLAN-based policing, in both the ingress and egress directions.

The switch limits the number of input policers and output policers to 1024 each. But in actuality, because the software reserves four input policers and four output policers for null processing, this leaves 1020 policers available for input policing and 1020 policers available for output processing.

The Catalyst 4500 has a handy syntax for defining bit rates: It uses the prefixes **k** for kilo, **m** for mega, and **g** for giga. Instead of getting lost in zeros, a value such as 1,250,000,000 bps can be expressed as 1.25 Gbps. This syntax alternative can reduce configuration errors introduced by typos.

In Example 10-22, individual Bulk Data traffic flows (marked on a data center server connected to Fast Ethernet 2/12) in excess of 10 Mbps are marked down from AF11 (10) to AF12 (12).

Example 10-22 *Configuring an Individual Policer on a Catalyst 4500*

```
CAT4500(config)#qos map dscp policed 10 to dscp 12
CAT4500(config)#class-map match-any BULK
CAT4500(config-cmap)# match ip dscp af11
CAT4500(config-cmap)#policy-map BULK-MARKDOWN
CAT4500(config-pmap)# class BULK
CAT4500(config-pmap-c)#police 10 mbps 8000 conform-action transmit
exceed-action policed-dscp-transmit
CAT4500(config-pmap-c)#int fa 2/12
CAT4500(config-if)#service-policy input BULK-MARKDOWN
```

In addition to individual policers, an aggregate policer can be applied to a Catalyst 4500 access-to-distribution uplink to mark down cumulatively out-of-profile traffic.

Building on the previous example, all Bulk Data traffic in excess of 100 Mbps (regardless of how many flows are involved) is marked down to AF12 on the Gigabit 1/1 uplink. The policed-DSCP map does not need to be redefined, but both individual and aggregate policers can leverage it. Refer to Figure 10-23.

Example 10-23 *Configuring an Aggregate Policer on a Catalyst 4500*

```
CAT4500(config)#qos aggregate-policer BULK-MARKDOWN 100 mbps
     8000 conform transmit exceed-action policed-dscp-transmit
CAT4500(config)#policy-map BULK-MARKDOWN-AGG
CAT4500(config-pmap)#class BULK
CAT4500(config-pmap-c)# police aggregate BULK-MARKDOWN-AGG
CAT4500(config-pmap-c)#int gig 1/1
CAT4500(config-if)# service-policy output BULK-MARKDOWN-AGG
```

Catalyst 4500 Queuing and Dropping

The Catalyst 4500 supports four egress queues, one of which can be configured as a priority queue. No thresholds (other than the tail of the queue) are configurable (at the time of writing), allowing the 4500 to be configured through a 4Q1T or 1P3Q1T model.

On the Catalyst 4500, Gigabit Ethernet interfaces employ a queue size of 1920 packets, and Fast Ethernet interfaces use a queue size of 240 packets.

Only queue 3 can be configured as a priority queue.

By default, nonpriority queues are scheduled in a round-robin manner and share bandwidth equally among them. However, bandwidth allocations can be configured explicitly on the following ports:

- Uplink ports on supervisor engines
- Ports on the WS-X4306-GB line card
- The two 1000BASE-X ports on the WS-X4232-GB-RJ line card

- The first two ports on the WS-X4418-GB line card
- The two 1000BASE-X ports on the WS-X4412-2GB-TX line card

Minimum bandwidth allocations can be defined in absolute kbps (again, the **k**, **m**, and **g** prefixes can be used to define the rate in bits per second). Alternatively, minimum bandwidth allocations also can be expressed as percentages.

Complementarily, each transmit queue can be configured to transmit a maximum rate using the **shape** command. This command enables you to specify the maximum rate of traffic that the queue services. Any traffic that exceeds the configured shape rate is queued and transmitted at the configured rate. If the burst of traffic exceeds the size of the queue, packets are dropped to maintain transmission at the configured shape rate. As with the bandwidth command, the shaped rate can be expressed in absolute bits per second (the **k**, **m**, and **g** prefixes can be used to define the rate in bits per second) or as a percentage.

In Example 10-24, queue 3 is assigned to be a strict-priority queue. Queue 1 is assigned 30 percent of the available bandwidth (after the priority queue has been fully serviced), and queue 2 is assigned 25 percent. Queue 4 is assigned to be shaped to 10 percent.

Example 10-24 *Configuring a Priority Queue and Bandwidth Allocations on a Catalyst 4500*

```
CAT4500(config)#int gig 1/1
CAT4500(config-if)#tx-queue 1
CAT4500(config-if-tx-queue)#bandwidth percent 30
CAT4500(config-if-tx-queue)#tx-queue 2
CAT4500(config-if-tx-queue)#bandwidth percent 25
CAT4500(config-if-range)#tx-queue 3
CAT4500(config-if-tx-queue)#priority high
CAT4500(config-if-tx-queue)#tx-queue 4
CAT4500(config-if-tx-queue)#shape percent 10
```

The Catalyst 4500 supports DSCP-to-queue maps, with the default DSCP-to-queue assignment shown in Table 10-4.

Table 10-4 *Catalyst 4500 Default DSCP-to-Queue Maps*

DSCP Value	Transmit Queue
DSCP 0-15	Queue 1
DSCP 16-31	Queue 2
DSCP 32-47	Queue 3
DSCP 48-63	Queue 4

These assignments can be modified with the **qos map dscp** dscp **to tx-queue** queue command. Up to eight DSCP values (separated by spaces) can be assigned to a queue in a single command.

Continuing from Example 1-24, queue 1 carries Mission-Critical traffic, such as Network-Control (CS7/56), Routing (CS6/48), Call-Signaling (AF31/26), Transactional Data (AF21/18), and Network-Management (CS2/16). Voice (EF/46) is mapped to priority queue 3. Queue 2 is assigned as a Best-Effort queue (DSCP 0). Less-than-best-effort traffic, such as Bulk Data (AF11/AF12, which are DSCP 10 and 12, respectively) and Scavenger (CS1/8) traffic, is assigned to queue 4.

Example 10-25 *Configuring DSCP-to-Queue Assignments on a Catalyst 4500*

```
CAT4500(config)#qos map dscp 56 48 26 18 16 to tx-queue 1
CAT4500(config)#qos map dscp 0 to tx-queue 2
CAT4500(config)#qos map dscp 46 to tx-queue 3
CAT4500(config)#qos map dscp 8 10 12 to tx-queue 4
```

As previously noted, the Catalyst 4500 does not (yet) support drop thresholds, but it does support a congestion-avoidance feature called dynamic buffer limiting (DBL).

DBL tracks the queue length for each traffic flow in the switch. When the queue length of a flow exceeds its limit, DBL drops packets or sets the explicit congestion notification (ECN) bits in the packet headers. ECN bits, based on RFC 3168, were covered in Chapter 6, "Congestion-Avoidance Tools."

DBL classifies flows in two categories, adaptive and aggressive. Adaptive flows reduce the rate of packet transmission after it receives congestion notification. Aggressive flows do not take corrective action in response to congestion notification.

Queue length is measured by the number of packets. The number of packets in the queue determines the amount of buffer space that a flow is given. When a flow has a high queue length, the computed value is lowered. This enables new incoming flows to receive buffer space in the queue. This allows all flows to get a proportional share of packets through the queue.

DBL, with ECN notification, can be enabled globally using the command in Example 10-26.

Example 10-26 *Configuring DBL with ECN on a Catalyst 4500*

```
CAT4500(config)#qos dbl exceed-action ecn
```

Catalyst 6500

The Catalyst 6500, shown in Figure 10-14, is indisputably Cisco's main switch and, as such, boasts the richest feature sets, not only in QoS, but in all services, such as high availability, multicast, security, and management. It is the preferred switch in large enterprise environments at all layers: access, distribution, and core. Additionally, the Catalyst 6500 is very prevalent in service provider environments. In the context of our discussions, "Catalyst 6500" is used to refer to Catalyst 6500s with Supervisor 2 (PFC2) and Catalyst 6500s with Supervisor 720 (PFC3) because these are the current versions of supervisor hardware at the time of writing.

Figure 10-14   *Cisco Catalyst 6500 Series*

Hardware QoS on the Catalyst 6500 is performed principally within the Policy Feature Card (PFC), which is now in its third generation (with each successive generation of PFC having progressively richer QoS features—refer to Cisco Catalyst 6500 documentation for complete details).

The PFC is responsible for classification, marking, mapping, and policing. Individual line cards perform the queuing and dropping functions. Thus, multiple combinations of queues and thresholds (varying by line card) can exist for 6500 switches.

On the Catalyst 6500, PFC QoS can be configured in one of two ways:

- **Hybrid mode**—This mode uses the Catalyst Operating System (CatOS) to configure the Supervisor and PFC. The Layer 3 forwarding engine (the Multilayer Switch Feature Card, or MSFC) then is configured using Cisco IOS. The term *hybrid* is used to convey that two operating systems (and two independent consoles) are used to manage the Catalyst 6500.

- **Native mode**—This mode uses a single image of Cisco IOS to configure the Supervisor + PFC, along with the MSFC. Only a single console is required to manage the Catalyst 6500.

NOTE   For the QoS features discussed in this chapter, both the CatOS and Cisco IOS commands are shown in the examples.

In both cases, QoS is disabled by default and needs to be globally enabled, as shown in Example 10-27.

Example 10-27 *Enabling QoS Globally on the Catalyst 6500 (CatOS and Cisco IOS)*

```
CAT6500-CATOS> (enable) set qos enable
QoS is enabled.



CAT6500-CATOS> (enable)
```
```
CAT6500-IOS(config)#mls qos
CAT6500-IOS(config)#
```

QoS policies on the 6500 can be applied at the individual port level or on a per-VLAN basis (but, by default, all ports are configured for port-based QoS). This implies that all classification policies, and marking and policing, configured for the port are applicable only to the port to which they are applied. Conversely, VLAN-based QoS enables the administrator to apply a uniform policy to all ports configured for a specific VLAN. VLAN-based QoS might be preferred in certain situations, such as when voice VLANs have been deployed for IP Telephony environments. To alter the port policy from the default port-based QoS setting to VLAN-based QoS, use the commands shown in Example 10-28.

Example 10-28 *Configuring VLAN-Based QoS on the Catalyst 6500 (CatOS and Cisco IOS)*

```
CAT6500-CATOS> (enable) set port qos 3/1 vlan-based
Qos interface is set to vlan-based for ports 3/1
CAT6500-CATOS> (enable)
```
```
CAT6500-IOS(config)#interface FastEthernet3/1
CAT6500-IOS(config-if)#mls qos vlan-based
```

When VLAN-based QoS has been enabled, service-policy statements are attached to the VLAN interfaces, which then apply to all ports assigned to the VLAN.

Catalyst 6500 Classification, Marking, and Mapping

All Catalyst 6500 line cards support the trusting of CoS markings. However, not all of them support DSCP trust or IP Precedence trust (refer to Cisco Catalyst 6500 documentation for complete details).

By default, when QoS is enabled globally on the 6500, the trust state of all ingress ports is untrusted. In Example 10-29, the default trust state is changed from Untrusted to Trust CoS.

Example 10-29 *Configuring Trust on the Catalyst 6500 (CatOS and Cisco IOS)*

```
CAT6500-CATOS> (enable) set port qos 3/1 trust trust-cos
Port  3/1 qos set to trust-cos
CAT6500-CATOS> (enable)

CAT6500-IOS(config)#interface FastEthernet3/1
CAT6500-IOS(config-if)#mls qos trust cos
CAT6500-IOS(config-if)#
```

NOTE   Under some circumstances, the administrator must perform additional configuration steps beyond what is noted in the preceding commands. For example, the WS-X6224/6248 and WS-X6324/6348 line cards have hardware restrictions that prevent them from passing CoS values to the switching engine. Although the line cards recognize the arriving CoS and use that value for input scheduling, when the frame header is passed to the switching engine for forwarding, the CoS value for the frame is not preserved and is rewritten to 0. Therefore, it is necessary to configure additional commands, as shown in Example 10-30.

Example 10-30 *Alternate Trust Configuration on the Catalyst 6500 (CatOS)*

```
CAT6500-CATOS> (enable) set port qos 3/1 trust trust-cos
Trust type trust-cos not supported on this port.
Receive thresholds are enabled on port 3/1.
Port  3/1 qos set to untrusted.
CAT6500-CATOS> (enable) set qos acl ip TRUSTCOS trust-cos any
Warning: ACL trust-cos should only be used with ports that are also
configured with port trust=trust-cos.
TRUSTCOS editbuffer modified. Use 'commit' command to apply changes.
CAT6500-CATOS> (enable) commit qos acl TRUSTCOS
QoS ACL 'TRUSTCOS' successfully committed.
CAT6500-CATOS> (enable) set qos acl map TRUSTCOS 3/1
ACL TRUSTCOS is successfully mapped to port 3/1.
The old ACL mapping is replaced by the new one.
CAT6500-CATOS> (enable)
```

The PFC also can be configured to identify and mark flows to specific DSCP values by either Layer 3 or Layer 4 parameters, and defined in access lists. This is shown in Example 10-31, in which TCP traffic within the destination port range of 9000 to 9005 is marked as Transactional Data (DSCP AF21 or 18).

Example 10-31 *ACL-Based Classification and Marking on the Catalyst 6500 (CatOS and Cisco IOS)*

```
CAT6500-CATOS> (enable) set qos acl ip TRANSACTIONAL-DATA dscp 18
tcp any any range 9000 9005
TRANSACTIONAL-DATA editbuffer modified. Use 'commit' command to apply changes.
CAT6500-CATOS> (enable) commit qos acl TRANSACTIONAL-DATA
QoS ACL 'TRANSACTIONAL-DATA' successfully committed.
CAT6500-CATOS> (enable) set qos acl map TRANSACTIONAL-DATA 3/1
ACL TRANSACTIONAL-DATA is successfully mapped to port 3/1.
The old ACL mapping is replaced by the new one.
CAT6500-CATOS> (enable)
```

```
CAT6500-IOS(config)#access-list 100 permit tcp any any range 9000 9005
CAT6500-IOS(config)#class-map TRANSACTIONAL-DATA
CAT6500-IOS(config-cmap)#match access-group 100
CAT6500-IOS(config-cmap)#policy-map ACCESS-MARKING
CAT6500-IOS(config-pmap)#class TRANSACTIONAL-DATA
CAT6500-IOS(config-pmap-c)#set dscp af21
CAT6500-IOS(config-pmap-c)#interface FastEthernet 3/1
CAT6500-IOS(config-if)#service-policy input ACCESS-MARKING
```

The default CoS-to-DSCP maps, IP Precedence-to-DSCP maps, and DSCP-to-CoS maps are the same as have been discussed on previous switches (except for the Catalyst 2950, which does not support the full DSCP range at the time of writing).

CoS-to-DSCP maps can be overwritten from the defaults using the syntaxes shown. In both cases, eight DSCP values must be supplied that correspond to CoS values 0 through 7, respectively. In Example 10-32, CoS 5 is mapped to DSCP EF (46), CoS 4 is mapped to DSCP AF41 (34), and CoS 3 is mapped to DSCP AF31 (26).

Example 10-32 *CoS-to-DSCP Mapping Modification on the Catalyst 6500 (CatOS and Cisco IOS)*

```
CAT6500-CATOS> (enable) set qos cos-dscp 0 8 16 26 34 46 48 56
QoS cos-dscp-map set successfully.
CAT6500-CATOS> (enable)
```

```
CAT6500-IOS(config)#mls qos map cos-dscp 0 8 16 26 34 46 48 56
CAT6500-IOS(config)#
```

IP Precedence-to-DSCP maps use identical syntax, except that the **cos** keyword is replaced with **ipprec** (CatOS) and **ip-prec** (Cisco IOS).

Default DSCP-to-CoS modifications can be configured, as shown in Example 10-33. In this example, DSCP values CS1 (8) through DSCP 15 are remapped to CoS 0.

Example 10-33 *DSCP-to-CoS Mapping Modification on the Catalyst 6500 (CatOS and Cisco IOS)*

```
CAT6500-CATOS> (enable) set qos dscp-cos-map 8-15:0
QoS dscp-cos-map set successfully.
CAT6500-CATOS> (enable)

CAT6500-IOS(config)#mls qos map dscp-cos 8 9 10 11 12 13 14 15 to 0
CAT6500-IOS(config)#
```

DSCP-to-DSCP maps, or DSCP mutation maps, also can be configured explicitly on the Catalyst 6500, but DSCP mutation currently is in native IOS mode only. Up to 15 DSCP mutation maps can be configured on the Catalyst 6500. The commands to configure DSCP mutation maps on the 6500 are identical to those used in the examples of DSCP mutation previously discussed in this chapter.

Catalyst 6500 Policing and Markdown

The Catalyst 6500 supports two main types of policers: microflow and aggregate. Both microflow and aggregate policers can be configured on a per-port or per-VLAN basis. The Catalyst 6500 supports 63 microflow and 1023 aggregate policers.

Microflow policers differ from individual policers (which limit traffic on a per-interface basis), in that they limit traffic on a per-flow basis. A flow is defined by a socket (source/destination address pairing combined with an identical Layer 4 protocol and the source/destination port pairing). However, microflow policers can be configured to use only the source or only the destination addresses for policing purposes.

NOTE   By default, microflow policers affect only traffic routed by the MSFC. To enable microflow policing of bridged traffic, either the CatOS **set qos bridged-microflow-policing enable** global command or the Cisco IOS **mls qos bridged** interface command must be used.

The commands to configure microflow policing on the Catalyst 6500 are shown in Example 10-34, where no single flow is permitted to exceed 1 Mbps. In CatOS, this requires a microflow policer to be defined and referenced by an ACL. The ACL, in turn, is committed and mapped to the interface. In Cisco IOS, an MQC policy is defined with the **police flow** keywords and is attached to an interface. Notice in Example 10-34 that policing rates might be adjusted marginally because of hardware granularity restrictions.

Aggregate policers can be defined on a per-interface basis. Alternatively, you can define named aggregate policers that can be applied to multiple interfaces.

Example 10-34 *Configuring Microflow Policing on the Catalyst 6500 (CatOS and Cisco IOS)*

```
CAT6500-CATOS> (enable) set qos policer microflow ONE-MEG-FLOWS
  rate 1000 burst 8 drop
QoS policer for microflow ONE-MEG-FLOWS created successfully.
Rate is set to 992 and burst is set to 8 in hardware due to hardware granularity.
CAT6500-CATOS> (enable) set qos acl ip ONE-MEG-FLOW-ACL dscp 0
  microflow ONE-MEG-FLOWS ip any any
ONE-MEG-FLOW-ACL editbuffer modified. Use 'commit' command to apply changes.
CAT6500-CATOS> (enable) commit qos acl ONE-MEG-FLOW-ACL
QoS ACL 'ONE-MEG-FLOW-ACL' successfully committed.
CAT6500-CATOS> (enable) set qos acl map ONE-MEG-FLOW-ACL 3/1
ACL ONE-MEG-FLOW-ACL is successfully mapped to port 3/1.
CAT6500-CATOS> (enable)

CAT6500-IOS(config)#access-list 1 permit any
CAT6500-IOS(config)#class-map ANY
CAT6500-IOS(config-cmap)#match access-group 1
CAT6500-IOS(config-cmap)#policy-map MICROFLOW
CAT6500-IOS(config-pmap)#class ANY
CAT6500-IOS(config-pmap-c)#police flow 1000000 8000 conform transmit
  exceed-action drop
CAT6500-IOS(config-pmap-c)#interface FastEthernet 3/1
CAT6500-IOS(config-if)#service-policy input MICROFLOW
```

Furthermore, aggregate policers on the PFC2 or PFC3 support the added functionality of dual-rate policing, as defined in RFC 2698 and overviewed in Chapter 4, "Policing and Shaping Tools," under the "Two-Rate Three-Color Marker" section. Dual-rate policers require defining not only a CIR, but also a PIR. However, the out-of-profile PIR action (violate) cannot be less severe than the out-of-profile CIR action (exceed). For instance, if the exceed action is to mark down, the violate action cannot be to transmit.

In Example 10-35, FTP traffic is transmitted with DSCP AF11 (DSCP 10) if it is less than 1 Mbps. Any FTP traffic over 1 Mbps but less than 2 Mbps is marked down to AF12 (DSCP 12). Any FTP traffic in excess of 2 Mbps is marked down further to AF13 (DSCP 14). The aggregate policing policy is applied to VLAN 10 as a whole.

Example 10-35 *Configuring Dual-Rate Aggregate Policers on the Catalyst 6500 (CatOS and Cisco IOS)*

```
CAT6500-CATOS> (enable) set qos policed-dscp-map normal 10:12
CAT6500-CATOS> (enable) set qos policed-dscp-map excess 10:14
CAT6500-CATOS> (enable) set qos policer aggregate FTP-POLICER
  rate 1000 policed-dscp erate 2000 policed-dscp burst 8 eburst 8
QoS policer for aggregate FTP-POLICER created successfully.
Rate is set to 992 and erate is set 1984 and burst is set to 8
and eburst is set to 8 in hardware due to hardware granularity.
CAT6500-CATOS> (enable) set qos acl ip FTP-ACL dscp 10 aggregate FTP-POLICER
  tcp any any eq ftp
FTP-ACL editbuffer modified. Use 'commit' command to apply changes.
```

Example 10-35 *Configuring Dual-Rate Aggregate Policers on the Catalyst 6500 (CatOS and Cisco IOS) (Continued)*

```
CAT6500-CATOS> (enable) set qos acl ip FTP-ACL dscp 10 aggregate FTP-POLICER
tcp any any eq ftp-data
FTP-ACL editbuffer modified. Use 'commit' command to apply changes.
CAT6500-CATOS> (enable) commit qos acl FTP-ACL
QoS ACL 'FTP-ACL' successfully committed.
CAT6500-CATOS> (enable) set qos acl map FTP-ACL 10
ACL FTP-ACL is successfully mapped to vlan 10.
CAT6500-CATOS> (enable)

CAT6500-IOS(config)#mls qos map policed-dscp normal-burst 10 to 12
CAT6500-IOS(config)#mls qos map policed-dscp max-burst 10 to 14
CAT6500-IOS(config)#mls qos aggregate-policer FTP-AGG-POLICER 1000000 pir 2000000
        conform-action set-dscp-transmit 10 exceed-action policed-dscp-transmit
        violate-action policed-dscp-transmit
CAT6500-IOS(config)#access-list 100 permit tcp any any eq ftp
CAT6500-IOS(config)#access-list 100 permit tcp any any eq ftp-data
CAT6500-IOS(config)#class-map FTP
CAT6500-IOS(config-cmap)#match access-group 100
CAT6500-IOS(config-cmap)#policy-map FTP-MQC-POLICER
CAT6500-IOS(config-pmap)#class FTP
CAT6500-IOS(config-pmap-c)#police aggregate FTP-AGG-POLICER
CAT6500-IOS(config-pmap-c)#interface vlan 10
CAT6500-IOS(config-if)#service-policy input FTP-MQC-POLICER
```

Microflow and aggregate policers are not mutually exclusive. For example, you could create a microflow policer with a bandwidth limit suitable for individuals in a group, and you could create a named aggregate policer with bandwidth limits suitable for the group as a whole. You could include both policers in policy map classes that match the group's traffic. The combination would affect individual flows separately and the group aggregately.

Catalyst 6500 Queuing and Dropping

As mentioned, queuing and threshold support on Catalyst 6500 varies from line card to line card. To check the queuing structure of the line card or port in question, use the commands in Example 10-36.

Example 10-36 *Queue Structure Verification on the Catalyst 6500 (CatOS and Cisco IOS)*

```
CAT6500-CATOS> (enable) show port capabilities 1/1
Model                   WS-X6K-SUP1A-2GE
Port                    1/1
Type                    1000BaseSX
Speed                   1000
```

continues

Example 10-36 *Queue Structure Verification on the Catalyst 6500 (CatOS and Cisco IOS) (Continued)*

```
Duplex                   full
Trunk encap type         802.1Q,ISL
Trunk mode               on,off,desirable,auto,nonegotiate
Channel                  yes
Broadcast suppression    percentage(0-100)
Flow control             receive-(off,on,desired),send-(off,on,desired)
Security                 yes
Dot1x                    yes
Membership               static,dynamic
Fast start               yes
QOS scheduling           rx-(1p1q4t),tx-(1p2q2t)
```

```
CAT6500-CATOS> (enable)
CAT6500-IOS#show queueing interface gig 1/1
Interface GigabitEthernet1/1 queueing strategy:  Weighted Round-Robin
  Port QoS is enabled
  Trust state: trust DSCP
  Extend trust state: not trusted [COS = 0]
  Default COS is 0
    Queueing Mode In Tx direction: mode-cos
    Transmit queues [type = 1p2q2t]:
...
CAT6500-IOS#
```

The commands display some of the following queue structures:

- **2q2t** indicates two standard queues, each with two configurable tail-drop thresholds.
- **1p2q1t** indicates the following:
  - One strict-priority queue
  - Two standard queues, each with one WRED-drop threshold
  - One nonconfigurable (100 percent) tail-drop threshold
- **1p2q2t** indicates the following:
  - One strict-priority queue
  - Two standard queues, each with two configurable WRED-drop thresholds
- **1p3q1t** indicates the following:
  - One strict-priority queue
  - Three standard queues, each with one threshold configurable as either WRED drop or tail drop
  - One nonconfigurable (100 percent) tail-drop threshold

- **1p3q8t** indicates the following:
  - One strict-priority queue
  - Three standard queues, each with eight thresholds, with each threshold configurable as either WRED drop or tail drop
- **1p7q8t** indicates the following:
  - One strict-priority queue
  - Seven standard queues, each with eight thresholds, with each threshold configurable as either WRED drop or tail drop

For port types with a strict-priority queue, the switch services traffic in the strict-priority transmit queue before servicing the standard queues. When the switch is servicing a standard queue, after transmitting a packet, it checks for traffic in the strict-priority queue. If the switch detects traffic in the strict-priority queue, it suspends its service of the standard queue and completes service of all traffic in the strict-priority queue before returning to the standard queue.

Catalyst 6500 PFC QoS schedules traffic through the transmit queues based on Layer 2 CoS values. In the default configuration, PFC QoS assigns all traffic with CoS 5 to the strict-priority queue (if present); PFC QoS assigns all other traffic to standard queues. In the absence of a strict-priority queue, PFC QoS assigns all traffic to the standard queues.

NOTE   The default queue sizes, thresholds definitions, and bandwidth allocation ratios are usually adequate for most cases. In the rare event that these need to be tuned, experienced administrators should refer to Cisco Catalyst 6500 documentation for default values for threshold percentages, queue sizes, and bandwidth-allocation ratios for each queuing structure.

Keep these points in mind when configuring CoS to queue/threshold assignments and parameters:

- Number 1 is the lowest-priority standard queue.
- Higher-numbered queues are higher-priority standard queues.

When you configure multiple-threshold standard queues, note the following:

- The first percentage that you enter sets the lowest-priority threshold.
- The second percentage that you enter sets the next highest-priority threshold.
- The last percentage that you enter sets the highest-priority threshold.
- The percentages range from 1 to 100. A value of 10 indicates a threshold when the buffer is 10 percent full.
- Always set highest-numbered threshold to 100 percent.

When configuring the WRED-drop thresholds, note the following:

- Each WRED-drop threshold has a low-WRED and a high-WRED value.

- Low-WRED and high-WRED values are a percentage of the queue capacity (the range is from 1 to 100).

- The low-WRED value is the traffic level under which no traffic is dropped. The low-WRED value must be lower than the high-WRED value.

- The high-WRED value is the traffic level above which all traffic is dropped.

- Traffic in the queue between the low- and high-WRED values has an increasing chance of being dropped as the queue fills.

In the 1P2Q2T model shown in Example 10-37, Scavenger traffic (CoS 1) is mapped to the first standard queue, first threshold; Best-Effort traffic (CoS 0) is mapped to the first queue, second threshold; Transactional Data, Network-Management traffic (CoS 2), and Video (CoS 4) are mapped to the second queue, first threshold; Call-Signaling and Network-Control traffic (CoS values 3, 6, and 7) are mapped to the second queue, second threshold. Voice (CoS 5) is mapped to the priority queue.

Example 10-37 *Configuring CoS-to-Queue/Threshold Assignments on the Catalyst 6500 (CatOS and Cisco IOS)*

```
CAT6500-CATOS> (enable) set qos map 1p2q2t tx 1 1 cos 1
QoS tx priority queue and threshold mapped to cos successfully.
CAT6500-CATOS> (enable) set qos map 1p2q2t tx 1 2 cos 0
QoS tx priority queue and threshold mapped to cos successfully.
CAT6500-CATOS> (enable) set qos map 1p2q2t tx 2 1 cos 2,4
QoS tx priority queue and threshold mapped to cos successfully.
CAT6500-CATOS> (enable) set qos map 1p2q2t tx 2 2 cos 3,6,7
QoS tx priority queue and threshold mapped to cos successfully.
CAT6500-CATOS> (enable) set qos map 1p2q2t tx 3 1 cos 5
QoS tx priority queue and threshold mapped to cos successfully.
CAT6500-CATOS> (enable)

CAT6500-IOS(config)# interface GigabitEthernet2/1
CAT6500-IOS(config-if)#wrr-queue cos-map 1 1 1
  cos-map configured on:  Gi2/1 Gi2/2 Gi2/3 Gi2/4 Gi2/5 Gi2/6 Gi2/7 Gi2/8
CAT6500-IOS(config-if)#wrr-queue cos-map 1 2 0
  cos-map configured on:  Gi2/1 Gi2/2 Gi2/3 Gi2/4 Gi2/5 Gi2/6 Gi2/7 Gi2/8
CAT6500-IOS(config-if)#wrr-queue cos-map 2 1 2 4
  cos-map configured on:  Gi2/1 Gi2/2 Gi2/3 Gi2/4 Gi2/5 Gi2/6 Gi2/7 Gi2/8
CAT6500-IOS(config-if)#wrr-queue cos-map 2 2 3 6 7
  cos-map configured on:  Gi2/1 Gi2/2 Gi2/3 Gi2/4 Gi2/5 Gi2/6 Gi2/7 Gi2/8
CAT6500-IOS(config-if)#priority-queue cos-map 1 5
  cos-map configured on:  Gi2/1 Gi2/2 Gi2/3 Gi2/4 Gi2/5 Gi2/6 Gi2/7 Gi2/8
CAT6500-IOS(config-if)#
```

| NOTE | Notice that although the number of the priority queue in CatOS will be 3 (or higher), in Cisco IOS, the priority queue number when using the **priority-queue cos-map** interface command is always 1. |

It cannot be stressed enough that this chapter is by no means a thorough discussion on Catalyst QoS; it is merely an overview to provide adequate context for the design chapters to follow. For a complete discussion of Catalyst QoS, refer to Cisco Catalyst QoS documentation and also the Cisco Press book *Cisco Catalyst QoS: Quality of Service in Campus Networks*, by Michael Flannagan, Richard Froom, and Kevin Turek.

Summary

For QoS features to be available at line rates in campus environments, they have to be done in hardware. Porting QoS features to hardware presents many advantages, such as the capability to mark and police at the traffic sources, and the enforcement of trust boundaries and queuing at (momentarily) congested uplinks and downlinks. However, porting QoS functionality into hardware also presents an undesired caveat from a configuration and management perspective: As hardware varies, QoS also does in functionality and configuration, leading to significant complexity in managing campus QoS. To address this caveat, tools such as MQC and AutoQoS are continuing to be developed to simplify campus QoS.

This chapter examined basic Catalyst QoS models, which, for the most part, can be broken down into three main areas:

- **Classification, marking, and mapping**—These operations are responsible for generating the Internal DSCP value by which all subsequent QoS functions will be referenced. These values may be generated by the configured trust states (**untrusted**, **trust-cos**, **trust-ipprec**, or **trust-dscp**), explicit marking policies, or mapping functions.

- **Policing and markdown**—These functions monitor traffic flows as to whether they are in profile or out of profile. Markdown actions can be assigned to out-of-profile traffic (alternatively, out-of-profile traffic can be dropped). Catalyst platforms support individual, aggregate, or microflow (6500 only) policers.

- **Queuing and dropping**—Hardware queuing models, such as xQyT or xPyQzT models, were examined from both congestion-management and congestion-avoidance functionality perspectives.

Having laid a framework for a generic Catalyst QoS model, the model was applied to each of the main Catalyst platforms (at the time of writing), including the Catalyst 2950, 2970, 3550, 3560, 3750, 4500, and 6500. Configuration syntax and idiosyncrasies were addressed to lay a basic context for the design discussions to follow.

Table 10-5 shows a summary of the QoS features supported by Catalyst platforms.

Table 10-5 *Summary of QoS Features Supported by Catalyst Platforms*

Platform/ Feature	Catalyst 2950	Catalyst 3550	Catalyst 2970/3560/ 3750	Catalyst 4500	Catalyst 6500
QoS on by default?	Yes	No	No	No	No
Default trust (with QoS enabled)	Untrusted	Untrusted	Untrusted	Untrusted	Untrusted
Port-based QoS	Yes	Yes	Yes	Yes	Yes
VLAN-based QoS	No	Yes	No	Yes	Yes
Full DSCP-CoS maps	No	Yes	Yes	Yes	Yes
DSCP mutation	No	Yes	Yes	No	Yes
Ingress policing	Yes	Yes	Yes	Yes	Yes
Egress policing	No	Yes	Yes	Yes	Yes
Aggregate policing	No	Yes	Yes	Yes	Yes
Dual-rate policing	No	No	No	No	Yes
Microflow policing	No	No	No	No	Yes
Per-user microflow policing	No	No	No	No	PFC3 only
Policers per port	6 per 10/100 ports; 60 per GE ports	8 per 10/100 ports; 128 per GE ports	64 per port; 256 per-port ASIC	1020 per port	1023 per port
Minimum policing rate/ granularity	1 Mbps	8 kbps	8 kbps	32 kbps	32 kbps

Table 10-5 *Summary of QoS Features Supported by Catalyst Platforms (Continued)*

Platform/ Feature	Catalyst 2950	Catalyst 3550	Catalyst 2970/3560/ 3750	Catalyst 4500	Catalyst 6500
Queuing structures	4Q1T or 1P3Q1T	10/100 ports: 4Q1T or 1P3Q1T GE ports: 4Q2T or 1P3Q2T	4Q3T or 1P3Q3T	4Q1T or 1P3Q1T	(Line-card dependent) 2Q2T 1P2Q1T 1P2Q2T 1P3Q1T 1P3Q8T 1P7Q8T
Priority queue	Q4	Q4	Q1	Q3	(Line-card dependent) 2Q2T: None 1P2Q1T: Q3 1P2Q2T: Q3 1P3Q1T: Q4 1P3Q8T: Q4 1P7Q8T: Q8
WTD	No	No	Yes	No	No
WRED	No	Yes	No	No	(Line-card dependent) 2Q2T: No 1P2Q1T: Yes 1P2Q2T: Yes 1P3Q1T: Yes 1P3Q8T: Yes 1P7Q8T: Yes
DBL	No	No	No	Yes	No
AutoQoS	Yes	Yes	Yes	Yes	CatOS: Yes Cisco IOS: No

NOTE   "Catalyst 4500" refers to Catalyst 4500 with Sup3-5 running Cisco IOS; "Catalyst 6500" refers to Catalyst 6500 with PFC2 (Supervisor 2) or PFC3 (Supervisor 720) running either CatOS or Cisco IOS. All values were current at the time of writing; check the Cisco platform documentation for the latest information at http://www.cisco.com/univercd/home/home.htm.

Further Reading

Books:

- Flannagan, Micheal, Richard Froom, and Kevin Turek. *Cisco Catalyst QoS: Quality of Service in Campus Networks*. Indianapolis: Cisco Press, 2003.

Cisco Catalyst documentation:

- Configuring QoS on the Catalyst 2950 (Cisco IOS Release 12.1[19]EA1): http://www.cisco.com/univercd/cc/td/doc/product/lan/cat2950/12119ea1/2950scg/swqos.htm.

- Configuring QoS on the Catalyst 3550 (Cisco IOS Release 12.1[19]EA1): http://www.cisco.com/univercd/cc/td/doc/product/lan/c3550/12119ea1/3550scg/swqos.htm.

- Configuring QoS on the Catalyst 3560 (Cisco IOS Release 12.2[20]SE): http://www.cisco.com/univercd/cc/td/doc/product/lan/cat3560/12220se/3560scg/swqos.htm.

- Configuring QoS on the Catalyst 3750 (Cisco IOS Release 12.1[19]EA1): http://www.cisco.com/univercd/cc/td/doc/product/lan/cat3750/12119ea1/3750scg/swqos.htm.

- Configuring QoS on the Catalyst 4500 (Cisco IOS Release 12.1[20]EW) http://www.cisco.com/univercd/cc/td/doc/product/lan/cat4000/12_1_20/config/qos.htm.

- Configuring QoS on the Catalyst 6500 (Cisco IOS Release 12.2[17a]SX1): http://www.cisco.com/univercd/cc/td/doc/product/lan/cat6000/122sx/swcg/qos.htm.

- Configuring QoS on the Catalyst 6500 (Cisco CatOS Release 8.2): http://www.cisco.com/univercd/cc/td/doc/product/lan/cat6000/sw_8_2/confg_gd/qos.htm.

This chapter discusses wireless LAN QoS tools, including the following:

- IEEE 802.11 Distributed Coordination Function (DCF)
- IEEE 802.11 Enhanced Distributed Coordination Function (EDCF)
- IEEE 802.11 QoS basic service set (QBSS)
- IEEE 802.1D classes of service

CHAPTER 11

WLAN QoS Tools

In the past, WLANs mainly were used to transport low-bandwidth data-application traffic. Today, with the expansion of WLANs into enterprises, small businesses, mobile "hotspots," and home environments, WLANs are used to transport high-bandwidth data applications in conjunction with time-sensitive multimedia applications. These evolving requirements have led to the necessity for wireless QoS tools.

However, unique challenges are presented with the use of radio waves as a transmission medium. For example, radio waves are a shared, half-duplex medium that might not always be fully controlled (because signals are subject to interference).

Several vendors support proprietary wireless QoS schemes for voice applications. However, a unified approach to wireless QoS would speed up the rate of wireless QoS adoption and would provide QoS support for time-sensitive applications in multivendor wireless environments. The IEEE 802.11e working group within the IEEE 802.11 standards committee is defining a wireless QoS standard that was finalized in mid-2004. Other groups, including the WiFi Alliance, are also drafting standards for wireless QoS.

Cisco Aironet products support QoS based on the IEEE 802.11e draft standard specifications as of November 2002. Cisco IOS Software Release 12.2(4)JA for the Cisco Aironet 1100 Series and Cisco Aironet VxWorks Release 12.00T for Cisco Aironet 1200, 350, and 340 Series products support IEEE 802.11e Enhanced Distributed Coordination Function (EDCF)–based wireless QoS.

An example deployment of wireless QoS within a Cisco Aironet environment is shown in Figure 11-1.

Figure 11-1 *Cisco Wireless QoS Deployment Example*

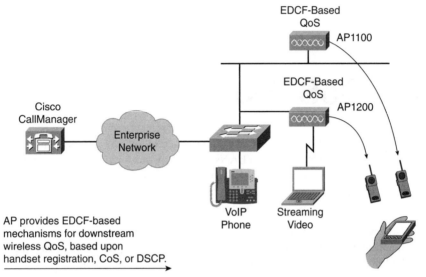

QoS for Wireless LANs Versus QoS on Wired LANs

The QoS implementation for wireless LANs differs from QoS implementations on other (wired) Cisco devices. With QoS enabled, wireless access points (APs) perform the following QoS functions:

- They prioritize packets based on DSCP value, client type (such as a wireless phone), or the priority value in the 802.1q or 802.1p tag; however, they do not classify packets.

- They support mapping by assigning IP DSCP, Precedence, or Protocol values to Layer 2 CoS values; they do not construct internal DSCP values.

- They support EDCF (which is discussed in more detail in the section titled "IEEE 802.11e EDCF"), such as queuing on the (downstream) radio egress port only.

- They support only FIFO queuing on the (upstream) Ethernet egress port.

- They support only 802.1Q/P tagged packets. Access points do not support ISL.

- They support only the MQC **policy-map set cos** action.

- They prioritize the traffic from voice clients (such as Symbol phones) over traffic from other clients when the QoS Element for Wireless Phones (which is discussed later in this chapter in the section titled "QoS Basic Service Set Information Element") feature is enabled.

- They support Spectralink phones using the **class-map IP protocol** clause with the protocol value set to 119.

Just as in other media, you might not notice the effects of QoS on a lightly loaded wireless LAN (WLAN). The benefits of QoS become more obvious as the load on the wireless LAN increases, keeping the latency, jitter, and loss for selected traffic types within an acceptable range.

QoS on the wireless LAN focuses on downstream prioritization from the access point.

Upstream Versus Downstream QoS

Communication streams in a WLAN environment are over either Ethernet or radio media. Furthermore, the flows occur in either the *upstream* or *downstream* direction, as shown in Figure 11-2.

Figure 11-2 *Ethernet/Radio Upstream/Downstream Flows*

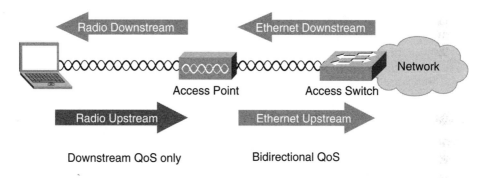

Ethernet downstream refers to traffic leaving the switch/router traveling to the access point (AP). QoS may be applied at this point to prioritize and rate-limit traffic to the AP.

Radio downstream QoS refers to the traffic leaving the AP and traveling to the WLAN clients. Radio downstream QoS is the primary focus of this chapter.

Radio upstream QoS refers to traffic leaving the WLAN clients and traveling to the AP. No vendor support is currently available for radio upstream QoS features for WLAN clients. This support is specified in the 802.11e draft but has not yet been implemented. By providing downstream prioritization from the AP, upstream client traffic is treated as best effort. A client must compete with other clients for (upstream) transmission and also must compete with best-effort (downstream) transmission from the AP because of the half-duplex nature of WLAN radio. Under certain load conditions, a client can experience upstream congestion, and the performance of QoS sensitive applications might be unacceptable, despite the downstream QoS features on the AP.

Ethernet upstream refers to traffic leaving the AP traveling to the switch. The AP classifies traffic from the AP to the upstream network according to the traffic classification. However, only FIFO queuing is supported (which is adequate for almost all cases) at this point.

IEEE 802.11 DCF

Data frames in 802.11 are sent using the Distributed Coordination Function (DCF). The DCF is composed of two main components:

- Interframe spaces (IFS)
- Random backoffs/contention windows (CW)

DCF is used in 802.11 networks to manage access to the RF medium. A baseline understanding of DCF is necessary to provide context in understanding and deploying 802.11e-based Enhanced Distributed Coordination Function (EDCF).

Interframe Spaces

Interframe Spaces, shown in Figure 11-3, allow 802.11 to control which traffic gets first access to the channel when carrier sense declares the channel to be free.

Figure 11-3 *IEEE 802.11 DCF Interframe Spaces*

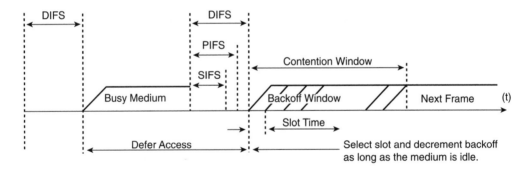

802.11 currently defines three interframe spaces:

- Short interframe spaces (SIFS), which are 10 μ long
- Point interframe spaces (PIFS), which are 30 μ long (SIFS + 1 [20 μ] slot time = 30 μ)
- Distributed interframe spaces (DIFS), which are 50 μ long (SIFS + 2 [20 μ] slot times = 50 μ)

SIFS

Important frames (such as acknowledgments) await the SIFS before transmitting. There is no random backoff when using the SIFS because frames using the SIFS are used when multiple stations would not be trying to send frames at the same time. The SIFS provide a short and deterministic delay for packets that must go through as soon as possible. SIFS are not available for use by data frames; only 802.11 management and control frames use SIFS.

PIFS

An optional portion of the 802.11 standard defines priority mechanisms for traffic via PIFS. No random backoff mechanisms are associated with PIFS because it relies solely on a polling mechanism to control which station may transmit. The option has not been adopted widely because of the associated overhead and lack of flexibility in its application.

DIFS

Data frames must wait out the DIFS before beginning the random backoff procedure, which is part of the DCF. This longer wait ensures that traffic using SIFS or PIFS timing always gets an opportunity to send before any traffic using the DIFS attempts to send. (In other words, management or priority traffic always gets to send before generic data.)

Random Backoffs/Contention Windows

When a data frame using DCF (shown in Figure 11-4) is ready to be sent, the sending station goes through the following steps:

1 A random backoff number between 0 and a minimum contention window (CWmin) is generated.

2 The station waits until the channel is free for a DIFS interval.

3 If the channel is still free, the random backoff number is decremented once for every slot time (20 μ) that the channel remains free.

4 If the channel becomes busy (for example, if another station gets to 0 before your station), the decrementing of the random backoff number stops and steps 2 through 4 are repeated.

5 If the channel remains free until the random backoff number reaches 0, the frame may be sent.

Figure 11-4 shows a simplified example of how the DCF process works. (In this simplified DCF example, no acknowledgments are shown and no fragmentation occurs.)

Figure 11-4 *IEEE 802.11 DCF Transmission Example*

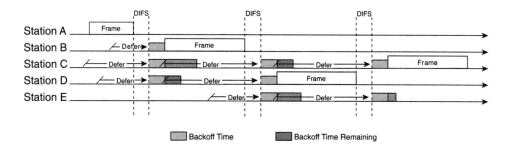

The DCF steps illustrated in Figure 11-4 work as follows:

1 Station A successfully sends a frame, and three other stations also want to send frames but must defer to Station A's traffic.

2 When Station A completes transmission, all the stations must still defer to the DIFS. When the DIFS is complete, stations that want to send a frame can begin decrementing their backoff counters (decrementing by one for every slot time that passes). If their backoff counters reach 0 and the wire is available, they may send their frame.

3 Station B's backoff counter reaches 0 before Stations C and D, so Station B begins transmitting its frame.

4 When Stations C and D detect that Station B is transmitting, they must stop decrementing their backoff counters and again defer until the frame is transmitted and a DIFS has passed.

5 During the time that Station B is transmitting a frame, Station E gets a frame to transmit, but because Station B is sending a frame, Station E must defer in the same manner as Stations C and D.

6 When Station B completes transmission and the DIFS has passed, stations with frames to send begin decrementing their backoff counters again. In this case, Station D's backoff counter reaches 0 first, and the station begins transmission of its frame.

7 The process continues as traffic arrives on different stations.

CWmin, CWmax, and Retries

DCF uses a contention window (CW) to control the size of the random backoff. The contention window is defined by two parameters:

- CWmin
- CWmax

The random number used in the random backoff is initially a number between 0 and CWmin. If the initial random backoff expires without successfully sending the frame, the station or AP increments the retry counter and doubles the value of the random backoff window size. This doubling in size continues until the size equals CWmax. The retries continue until the maximum retries or Time-To-Live (TTL) is reached. This process of doubling the backoff window often is referred to as a binary exponential backoff; it is illustrated in Figure 11-5.

Figure 11-5 *IEEE 802.11 Random Backoff Ranges with Retries*

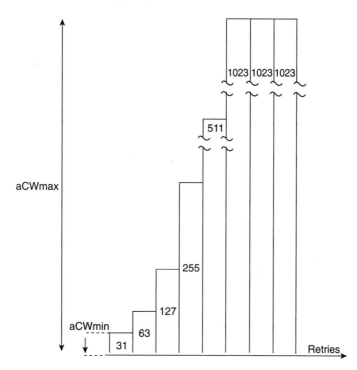

IEEE 802.11e EDCF

The current IEEE 802.11e draft describes an Enhanced Distributed Coordination Function (EDCF). EDCF is an enhancement of DCF, previously described. The main enhancement is the adjustment of variable CWmin and CWmax random backoff values based upon traffic classification. This feature is supported in current Cisco Aironet software.

Figure 11-6 shows the principle behind different CWmin values per traffic classification. All traffic waits the same DIFS, but the CWmin value used to generate the random backoff number depends upon the traffic classification. High-priority traffic has a smaller CWmin value, granting it a shorter random backoff value, whereas best-effort traffic has a larger CWmin value that (on average) generates a longer random backoff value.

Figure 11-6 *IEEE 802.11e EDCF Random Backoff by Traffic Classification*

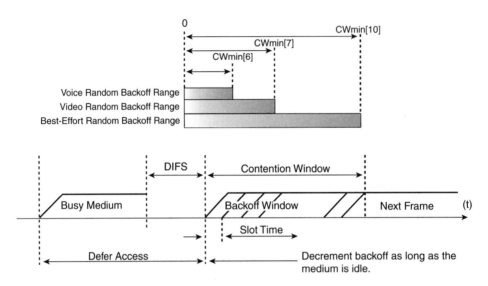

Figure 11-7 illustrates how different CWmin values (by traffic class) impact traffic priority over the WLAN.

Figure 11-7 *IEEE 802.11e EDCF Operation Example*

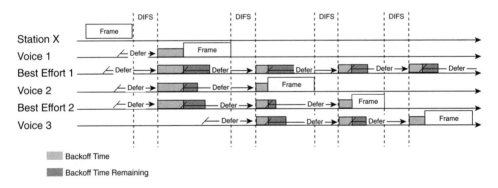

The process illustrated in Figure 11-7 follows this sequence:

   1 While Station X is transmitting its frame, three other stations determine that they also must send frames. Each station defers (because a frame already was being transmitted), and each station generates a random backoff number.

2 Stations Voice 1 and Voice 2 have the traffic classification of voice, so they use an initial CWmin of 3 and, therefore, generate short random backoff values. Best Effort 1 and Best Effort 2 generate longer random backoff times because their CWmin value is 31.

3 Voice 1 has the shortest random backoff time and, therefore, starts transmitting first. When Voice 1 starts transmitting, all other stations defer. While Voice 1 station is transmitting, station Voice 3 finds that it, too, needs to send a frame and generates a random backoff number. However, station Voice 3 defers transmission because of station Voice 1's transmission.

4 When station Voice 1 finishes transmitting, all stations await the DIFS and then begin decrementing their random backoff counters again.

5 Station Voice 2 completes decrementing its random backoff counter first and begins transmission. All other stations defer.

6 When Station Voice 2 has finished transmitting, all stations wait the DIFS and then begin decrementing their random backoff counters again.

7 Best Effort 2 completes decrementing its random backoff counter first and begins transmission. All other stations defer. This happens even though there is a voice station waiting to transmit. This shows that best-effort traffic is not starved by voice traffic because the process of random backoff decrementing eventually brings the best-effort backoff value down to similar values as initially generated by high-priority traffic. Additionally, the random process occasionally generates a small random backoff number for best-effort traffic.

8 When Best Effort 2 finishes transmitting, all stations await the DIFS and then begin decrementing their random backoff counters again.

9 Station Voice 3 completes decrementing its random backoff counter first and begins transmission. All other stations defer.

10 The process continues as other traffic enters the system.

The overall impact of the different CWmin and CWmax values is statistical in nature. It is sometimes simpler to compare two examples and show the impact of these different values in the average times that should be generated by the random backoff counters.

If Voice and Best Effort are compared, these traffic categories have default defined CWmin values of 2 and 5, and CWmax values of 8 and 10, respectively. Each class of traffic can have a different fixed slot time, which specifies the fixed slot backoff interval (0 to 20). The default values for these parameters for each traffic class are shown in Table 11-1.

From Table 11-1, you can see that that if two stations were contending to transmit voice and best-effort data at the same time, the station transmitting voice would back off to a random value between 3 and 4 (Voice CWmin and CWmax), while the station transmitting date would back off to a value between 5 and 10 (Best Effort CWmin and CWmax). Therefore, the voice frame would be transmitted before the data frame.

Table 11-1 *Cisco Access Points IEEE 802.11e EDCF CWmin, CWmax, and Fixed Slot Time Default Values (Cisco IOS 12.2[15]JA)*

Class of Service	CWmin (Min Contention Window)	CWmax (Max Contention Window)	Fixed Slot Time
Best Effort	5	10	6
Background	5	10	2
Video < 100 ms Latency	4	5	1
Voice < 100 ms Latency	3	4	1

NOTE   Within EDCF, voice statistically is transmitted before best-effort data. However, voice might not be serviced ahead of data in every case because of the random element of the algorithm. Thus, although EDCF does provide a mechanism for preferentially servicing voice, it is important to note that this is not a strict-priority mechanism.

The average maximum random backoff value gives an indication of how quickly and how large the random backoff counters can grow in the event of a retransmission. Traffic classes with the smallest average maximum values behave the most aggressively.

No matter how many times it has retried, voice's random backoff delay should not, on average, be above that of the minimum delay of best-effort traffic. This means that the average worst-case backoff delay for voice traffic would be the same as the average best case for best-effort traffic.

NOTE   In this EDCF operation example, all WLAN clients are treated equally for upstream transmission (from the WLAN clients to the AP).

QoS Basic Service Set Information Element

The WLAN infrastructure devices (such as APs) advertise QoS parameters. WLAN clients with QoS requirements use these advertised QoS parameters to determine the best AP with which to associate.

Cisco Aironet software supports the QoS basic service set (QBSS), which is based on IEEE 802.11e draft version 3.3.

Figure 11-8 shows the QBSS information element (IE) advertised by a Cisco AP. The Channel Utilization field indicates the portion of available bandwidth currently used to transport data within the WLAN. The Frame Loss Rate field indicates the portion of transmitted frames that requires retransmission or is discarded as undeliverable.

Figure 11-8 *IEEE 802.11e Draft Version 3.3: QBSS IE Implementation*

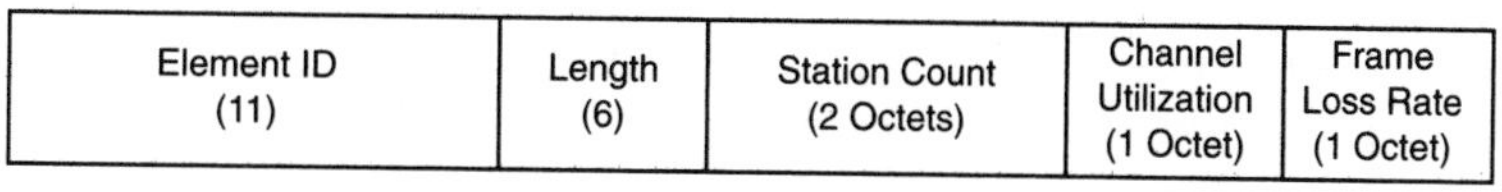

Element ID (11)	Length (6)	Station Count (2 Octets)	Channel Utilization (1 Octet)	Frame Loss Rate (1 Octet)

Enabling IEEE 802.11 QBSS adds information to the access point beacons and probe responses. This information helps some 802.11 phones make intelligent choices about the access point with which they should associate. Some phones do not associate with an access point without this additional information. The QBSS can be enabled through the Cisco IOS CLI (as shown in Example 11-1) or by the web GUI (as shown in Figure 11-11).

Example 11-1 *Enabling IEEE 802.11E QBSS Through Cisco IOS CLI on a Cisco Aironet 1100 AP*

```
AP1100(config)#dot11 phone
```

IEEE 802.1D Classes of Service

IEEE 802.11e classes of service borrow the classes originally defined in IEEE 802.1D, as illustrated in Table 11-2.

Table 11-2 *IEEE 802.1D Classes of Service*

user_priority	Abbreviation	Traffic Type
1	BK	Background
2	—	Spare
0 (default)	BE	Best effort
3	EE	Excellent effort
4	CL	Controlled load
5	VI	"Video," < 100 ms latency and jitter
6	VO	"Voice," < 10 ms latency and jitter
7	NC	Network control

Compatibility issues are presented with the use of these 802.1D classes of service with respect to Cisco defaults.

For example, Cisco telephony devices, such as IP phones, follow the IETF recommendations (RFC 3268) of marking real-time traffic (voice) to DSCP EF. The simplest mapping from (6-bit) DSCP values to (3-bit) IP Precedence, CoS, or even MPLS EXP values is to use the three most significant bits of the DSCP for the IP Precedence/CoS/MPLS EXP values. This would map DSCP EF to CoS 5, which is what Cisco devices do. However, according to the (aging) IEEE 802.1D standard, voice should be mapped to CoS 6. To compensate for this seeming inconsistency between standards, Cisco Aironet software (by default when QoS is enabled) maps IEEE 802.1Q/p CoS 5 to IEEE 802.11e CoS 6 so that voice traffic is given highest priority over the WLAN.

QoS Operation on Cisco APs

When you enable QoS, the access point queues packets based on the Layer 2 class of service value for each packet. The access point applies QoS policies in this order:

- **Packets already classified.** When the access point receives packets from a QoS-enabled switch or router that already has classified the packets with nonzero 802.1Q/P user_priority values, the access point uses that classification and does not apply other QoS policy rules to the packets. An existing classification takes precedence over all other policies on the access point.

NOTE   Even if you have not configured a QoS policy, the access point always honors tagged 802.1P packets that it receives over the radio interface.

- **QoS Element for Wireless Phones setting.** If you enable the QoS Element for Wireless Phones setting, traffic from voice clients takes priority over other traffic, regardless of other policy settings. The QoS Element for Wireless Phones setting takes precedence over other policies, second only to previously assigned packet classifications.

- **Policies you create on the access point.** QoS policies that you create and apply to VLANs or to the access point interfaces are third in precedence after previously classified packets and the QoS Element for Wireless Phones setting.

- **Default classification for all packets on VLAN.** If you set a default classification for all packets on a VLAN, that policy is fourth in the precedence list.

Configuring QoS on Cisco APs

QoS is disabled by default; however, the radio interface always honors tagged 802.1P packets even when you haven't configured a QoS policy. QoS can be configured through either the Cisco IOS (MQC) CLI or the web-interface configuration utility provided by the AP software.

The Cisco IOS MQC CLI provides a very familiar syntax for QoS configuration on Cisco APs. In Example 11-2, DSCP EF is mapped to IEEE 802.1D CoS 6 (the IEEE definition for voice CoS) and is applied to the IEEE 802.11B radio interface (because this mapping already is enabled by default, this part of the policy is actually moot and is provided for syntax example purposes only).

Furthermore, the CWmin and CWmax values for the Best Effort and Background classes have been tuned (away from the defaults shown in Table 11-1) to assign Background traffic a significantly less-than best-effort service (compatible to the Scavenger service). Specifically, Best-Effort (Traffic Class 0) is set with a CWmin of 5 and a CWmax of 8, and Background traffic (Traffic Class 1) is set to a CWmin of 9 and a CWmax of 10.

Example 11-2 *Configuring QoS on a Cisco Aironet 1100 AP*

```
AP1100(config)#class-map match-all VOICE
AP1100(config-cmap)#  match ip dscp ef     ! Matches voice by DSCP EF
AP1100(config-cmap)#policy-map AP-DOWNSTREAM
AP1100(config-pmap)#  class VOICE
AP1100(config-pmap-c)#  set cos 6          ! Sets IEEE 802.11e CoS for voice
AP1100(config-pmap-c)#interface Dot11Radio0
AP1100(config-if)# traffic-class best-effort cw-min 5 cw-max 8 fixed-slot 2
AP1100(config-if)# traffic-class background cw-min 9 cw-max 10 fixed-slot 6
AP1100(config-if)# service-policy output AP-DOWNSTREAM
```

Alternatively, QoS for APs can be configured from the web GUI. From the home page, choose **Services > QoS** to bring up the main QoS configuration screen, shown in Figure 11-9.

Figure 11-9 *Cisco Aironet Software Web-Based Configurator: QoS Main Screen*

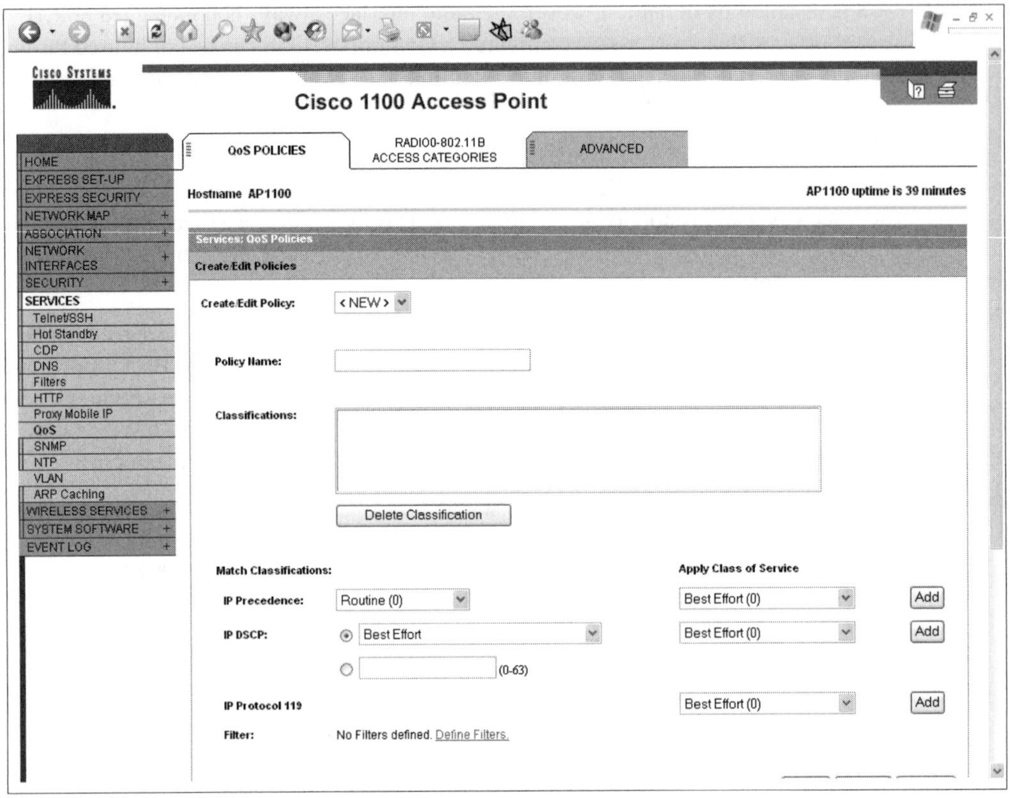

CWmin and CWmax values for each of the four queues can be adjusted from the 802.11B Access Categories tab (see Figure 11-10).

Advanced options, such as enabling the QBSS information element and disabling the default AVVID priority mapping (of 802.1Q/p CoS 5 to IEEE 802.11e CoS 6), can be selected from the Advanced screen, shown in Figure 11-11.

Figure 11-10 *Cisco Aironet Software Web-Based Configurator: 802.11B Access Categories Screen*

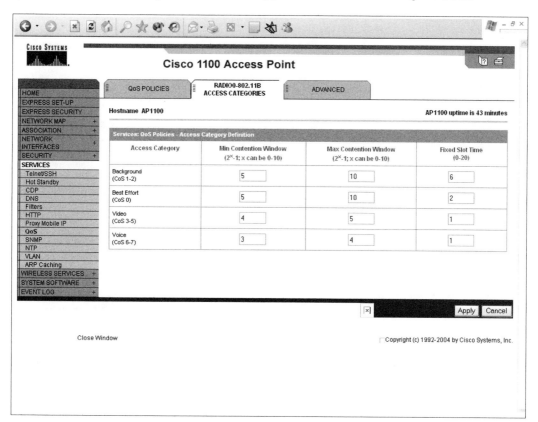

NOTE   The option for mapping IEEE 802.1Q/p Ethernet packets marked with CoS 5 to IEEE 802.11e CoS 6 (shown in the Advanced screen) is enabled by default. This enables simpler integration with existing AVVID networks already using 802.1Q/p CoS 5 to identify voice traffic. This option also can be disabled (if necessary) through the Cisco IOS CLI with the **no dot11 priority-map avvid** command.

Figure 11-11 *Cisco Aironet Software Web-Based Configurator: QoS Advanced Screen*

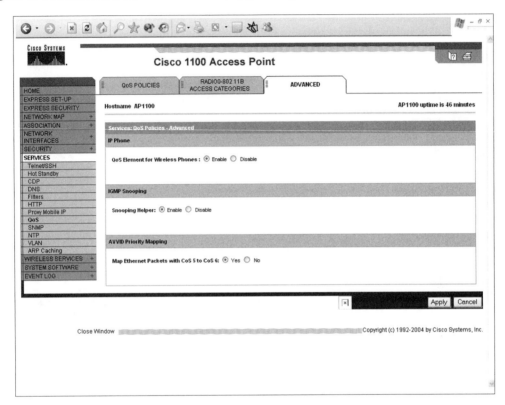

Summary

As WLANs continue to proliferate into enterprises, into small/medium businesses, into mobile hotspots, and even within home networks, their use is expanding rapidly to carry multiservice traffic, including time-sensitive/interactive applications such as wireless VoIP and video.

To ensure that the WLAN does not become the weakest link in an end-to-end QoS chain, standards bodies such as the IEEE 802.11e working group are formalizing specifications to deliver granular service levels across WLAN media.

This chapter overviewed IEEE 802.11 DCF operation, including the function of interframe spaces and contention windows. Building on this review, IEEE 802.11e EDCF was introduced; it allows for contention window variance for different traffic classes. EDCF operation was examined to demonstrate how contention window variance translates into relative traffic class priorities on the WLAN. The IEEE 802.1e QBSS information element also was covered in brief.

Cisco AP software QoS operation and configuration was introduced, including the Cisco IOS MQC CLI for AP QoS and the web-based GUI screens required to set wireless access-point QoS.

Further Reading

- IEEE 802.11 working group: http://www.ieee802.org/11/.
- IEEE 802.11e status: http://grouper.ieee.org/groups/802/11/Reports/tge_update.htm.
- IEEE 802.11e WLAN QoS: http://www.eecs.umich.edu/~shchoi/My_Papers_Published/Conferences/02-EW.pdf.
- IEEE 802.11e contention-based channel access (EDCF) performance evaluation: http://path.berkeley.edu/dsrc/reading/03-ICC-EDCF.pdf.
- Configuring QoS for WLANs: Cisco IOS Software 12.2.15JA documentation: http://www.cisco.com/univercd/cc/td/doc/product/wireless/airo1100/accsspts/i12215ja/i12215sc/s15qos.htm.

LAN QoS Design

Part III of this book provides an in-depth discussion of QoS considerations and designs for the access, distribution, and core layers of an enterprise campus network. Detailed QoS designs for the Cisco Catalyst 2950, 2970, 3550, 3560, 3750, 4500, and 6500 switch platforms are presented.

The chapter in this part of the book is as follows:

Chapter 12   Campus QoS Design

This chapter discusses QoS considerations and design principles for the access, distribution, and core layers of an enterprise campus network. These include access edge models for trusted, untrusted, and conditionally trusted endpoints, along with queuing models that vary on a per-platform or per-line card basis.

Detailed QoS designs for the following Catalyst switch platforms are presented:

- Catalyst 2950
- Catalyst 2970
- Catalyst 3550
- Catalyst 3560
- Catalyst 3750
- Catalyst 4500 (Supervisors II+ through V)
- Catalyst 6500 (Supervisor 2/PFC2 and Supervisor 720/PFC3)

Campus QoS Design

The case for QoS in WANs and VPNs is, for the most part, self evident simply because of the low-bandwidth links involved compared to the high-bandwidth requirements of most applications. However, in Gigabit and Ten Gigabit campus LAN environments, bandwidth is so plentiful that sometimes the need for QoS is overlooked or outright challenged.

This is often the case when network administrators equate QoS with queuing only. But, as has been shown, the QoS toolset extends considerably beyond just queuing tools. In addition to queuing, classification, marking, and policing are all important QoS functions that are performed optimally within the campus network, particularly at the access-layer ingress edge (access edge).

Three important QoS design principles come into play to make the case for deploying campus QoS policies.

The first is that applications should be classified and marked as close to their sources as technically and administratively feasible. This principle promotes end-to-end Differentiated Services and Per-Hop Behaviors.

Sometimes endpoints can be trusted to set CoS and DSCP markings correctly, but, in most cases it is not a good idea to trust markings that users can set on their PCs (or other similar devices). This is because users easily could abuse provisioned QoS policies if permitted to mark their own traffic. For example, if DSCP EF received priority services throughout the enterprise, a user could configure his PC to mark *all* his traffic to DSCP EF right on the NIC, thus hijacking network priority queues to service non-real-time traffic. Such abuse could ruin the service quality of Real-Time applications (such as VoIP) throughout the enterprise. For this reason, the clause "as close as . . . administratively feasible" is included in the design principle.

A second important QoS design principle relating to access-edge QoS design is that unwanted traffic flows should be policed as close to their sources as possible. There is little sense in forwarding unwanted traffic only to police and drop it at a subsequent node. This is especially the case when the unwanted traffic is the result of DoS or worm attacks. The overwhelming volumes of traffic that such attacks create can readily drive network device processors to their maximum levels, causing network outages.

The third important design principle is that QoS always should be performed in hardware rather than software when a choice exists. Cisco IOS routers perform QoS in software, which places additional taxes on the CPU (depending on the complexity and functionality of the policy). Cisco Catalyst switches, on the other hand, perform QoS in dedicated hardware ASICS and, as such, do not tax their main CPUs to administer QoS policies. Therefore, complex QoS policies can be applied at Gigabit and Ten Gigabit Ethernet line speeds in these switches.

For these reasons, QoS policies, such as classification and marking policies to establish and enforce trust boundaries, as well as policers to protect against undesired flows, should be enabled at the access edge of the LAN. However, the need for queuing in the campus should not be dismissed.

Some studies have shown that 95 percent of the time, campus access-layer links are utilized at less than 5 percent of their capacity. Such underutilization permits campus networks to be designed to accommodate oversubscription among access, distribution, and core layers. Oversubscription allows for uplinks to be utilized more efficiently and, more important, reduces the overall cost to build the campus network. Some typical values for campus oversubscription are 20:1 for the access-to-distribution layers and 4:1 for the distribution-to-core layers, as shown in Figure 12-1.

Figure 12-1 *Typical Campus Oversubscription Ratios*

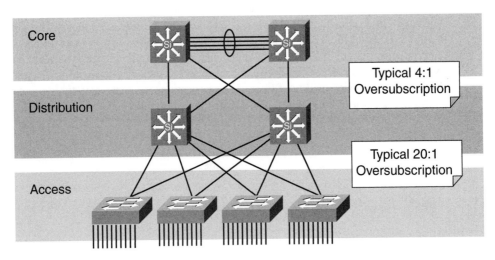

Under normal operating conditions, it is quite rare for campus networks to experience congestion and, thus, have a need for queuing. When congestion does occur, it is usually momentary and not sustained, as at a WAN edge.

Nonetheless, critical applications, such as VoIP, require service guarantees regardless of network conditions. The only way to provide service guarantees is to enable queuing at any node that has the *potential* for congestion—regardless of how rarely this actually might occur. Because of the oversubscription ratios just discussed, the potential for congestion exists in campus uplinks. Furthermore, the potential for congestion also exists in campus downlinks because of mismatches (such as Gigabit Ethernet–to–Fast Ethernet links). In both cases, the only way to ensure service guarantees in the event of congestion is to enable queuing at these points.

So far, this discussion for enabling queuing within the campus has revolved around network requirements under normal operating conditions. However, probably the strongest case for enabling QoS within the campus is to consider what happens under abnormal network conditions, such as a DoS or worm attack. During such conditions, network traffic increases exponentially until links are utilized fully. Without QoS, applications are drowned out by the worm-generated traffic, causing DoS through unavailability. On the other hand, when QoS policies are enabled within the campus (as detailed later in this chapter), VoIP, critical applications, and even Best-Effort traffic is protected and serviced if a worm attack occurs, thus maintaining the network's availability.

In such worst-case scenarios, the intrinsic interdependencies of network QoS, high-availability, and security are clearly manifest.

So where is QoS required in the campus?

Access switches require the following QoS policies:

- Appropriate (endpoint-dependent) trust policies
- Classification and marking policies
- Policing and markdown policies
- Queuing policies

Distribution and core switches require the following:

- DSCP-trust policies
- Queuing policies
- Optionally, per-user microflow policing policies (on distribution-layer Catalyst 6500s with Supervisor 720s only)

Figure 12-2 summarizes these recommendations.

Figure 12-2 *Where QoS Is Required Within the Campus*

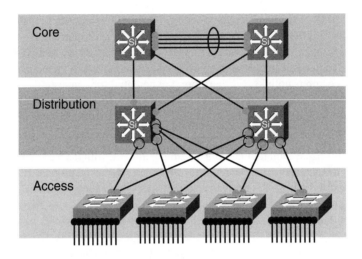

- Access Edges: Trust, Classification, Marking, Policing, and Queuing Policies
- Interswitch Links: DSCP-Trust and Queuing Policies
- Optional (C6500-PFC3 Only): Per-User Microflow Policing on Uplinks from Access Layer

Some important considerations to keep in mind when defining campus QoS designs follow:

- DoS/worm-mitigation strategies
- Call-signaling TCP/UDP ports in use
- Access-edge trust models
- WAN aggregator and branch router connections

Each of these concerns is discussed in the following sections.

DoS/Worm-Mitigation Strategies

A proactive approach to mitigating DoS/worm flooding attacks within campus environments is to respond immediately to out-of-profile network behavior that indicates a DoS or worm attack using access-layer policers. Such policers could meter traffic rates received from endpoint devices, and when these exceed specified watermarks (at which point they no longer are considered normal flows), these policers could mark down excess traffic.

In this respect, the policers would be fairly "dumb." They would not be matching specific network characteristics of specific types of attacks, but they simply would be metering traffic volumes and responding to abnormally high volumes as close to the source as possible. The simplicity of this approach negates the need for the policers to be programmed with knowledge of the specific details of how the attack is being generated or propagated.

It is precisely this "dumbness" of such access-layer policers that enables them to maintain relevancy as worms mutate and become more complex: The policers don't care how the traffic was generated, what it looks like, or what port it is being served on—all they care about is how much traffic is being put onto the wire. Therefore, they continue to police even advanced worms that continually change the tactics of how traffic is being generated.

For example, in most enterprises, it is abnormal (within a 95-percent statistical confidence interval) for PCs to generate sustained traffic in excess of 5 percent of their link's capacity. In the case of a Fast Ethernet switch port, this would mean that it would be unusual in most organizations for an end user's PC to generate more than 5 Mbps of uplink traffic on a sustained basis.

NOTE   It is important to recognize that this value (≤ 5 percent) for normal access-edge utilization by endpoints is just an example value. This value likely varies from industry vertical to vertical, and from enterprise to enterprise. To keep things simple, this 5-percent value is being used in the examples presented in this design chapter.

It is important to recognize that what is being proposed is not policing all traffic to 5 Mbps and automatically dropping the excess. If that was the case, there would not be much reason to deploy Fast Ethernet or Gigabit Ethernet switch ports to endpoint devices because even 10BASE-T Ethernet switch ports would have more uplink capacity than a 5 Mbps policer-enforced limit. Furthermore, such an approach supremely would penalize legitimate traffic that did exceed 5 Mbps on an FE switch port.

A less draconian approach is to couple access-layer policers with hardware and software (campus, WAN, VPN) queuing polices, with both sets of policies provisioning for a less-than best-effort Scavenger class.

This could work by having access-layer policers mark down out-of-profile traffic to DSCP CS1 (Scavenger) and then have all congestion-management policies (whether in Catalyst hardware or in Cisco IOS Software) provision a less-than best-effort service for any traffic marked to CS1 during periods of congestion.

Scavenger-Class QoS Operation

This section examines how the Scavenger-class QoS strategy for DoS/worm mitigation might work, both for legitimate traffic that exceeds the access-layer policer's watermark and also in the case of illegitimate excess traffic (the result of a DoS or worm attack).

In the former case, imagine that the PC generates more than 5 Mbps of traffic—perhaps because of a large file transfer or backup. Within the campus, there is generally abundant capacity to carry the traffic, so congestion (under normal operating conditions) is rarely, if ever, experienced. This is usually the case because the uplinks to the distribution and core layers of the campus network are typically Gigabit Ethernet and would require (at least) 1000 Mbps of traffic from the access-layer switch to experience congestion.

If the traffic were destined for the far side of a WAN or VPN link (these are rarely greater than 5 Mbps in speed), dropping would occur even without the access-layer policer simply because of bottlenecks resulting from the campus/WAN speed mismatch. TCP's sliding windows mechanism eventually would find an optimal speed (less than 5 Mbps) for the file transfer.

To summarize, access-layer policers that mark down out-of-profile traffic to Scavenger (CS1) would not affect legitimate traffic, aside from the obvious re-marking. No reordering or dropping would occur on such flows as a result of these policers (that would not have occurred anyway).

In the latter case, the effect of access-layer policers on traffic caused by DoS or worm attacks is quite different. As hosts become infected and traffic volumes multiply, congestion might be experienced even within the campus. If just 11 end-user PCs on a single switch begin spawning worm flows to their maximum Fast Ethernet link capacities, a GE uplink from the access-layer switch to the distribution-layer switch will become congested, and queuing and reordering will engage. At such a point, VoIP and critical data applications— and even Best-Effort applications—would gain priority over worm-generated traffic (because this Scavenger-marked traffic would be dropped the most aggressively); network devices would remain accessible for the administration of patches, plugs, and ACLs required to fully neutralize the specific attack.

WAN links also would be protected: VoIP, Critical Data, and even Best-Effort flows would continue to receive priority over any traffic marked down to Scavenger/CS1. This is a huge advantage because generally WAN links are the first to be overwhelmed by DoS/worm attacks.

The bottom line is that access-layer policers significantly will mitigate network traffic generated by DoS or worm attacks.

It is important to recognize the distinction between mitigating an attack and preventing it entirely: The strategy being presented will not guarantee that no DoS or worm attacks ever will happen; it only reduces the risk and impact that such attacks could have on the campus network infrastructure and then, by extension, the WAN and VPN network infrastructure.

Call-Signaling TCP/UDP Ports in Use

In this design chapter, to keep the examples relatively simple, only Skinny Call Control Protocol (SCCP) ports (TCP ports 2000–2002) are used to identify call-signaling protocols.

However, SCCP is by no means the only call-signaling protocol used in IP Telephony environments. Table 12-1 shows many of the TCP/UDP ports used in a Cisco CallManager environment.

All relevant call-signaling ports that are required for a given IPT environment are recommended to be included in the access lists that identify call-signaling protocols. Furthermore, firewalls protecting CallManagers should enable additional ports to provide the supplementary services that CallManagers provide or require.

Table 12-1 *Example TDP/UDP Ports Used in a Cisco CallManager Environment*

Protocol	Remote Source Port	CallManager Destination Port	CallManager Source Port	Remote Device Destination Port	Remote Devices	Notes
DTC			TCP 135		CallManagers in the same cluster	
SSH		TCP 22			Secure Shell client	
Telnet		TCP 23			Telnet client	
DNS		UDP 53			DNS servers	
DHCP	UDP 68	UDP 67			DHCP server	
DHCP			UDP 68	UDP 67	DHCP client	
TFTP		UDP 69				Dynamic ports used after initial connect
HTTP		TCP 80			Administrator/user web browsers	CCMAdmin and CCMUser pages
OSI (DAP, DSP, DISP)		TCP or UDP 120			DCD Directory	
NTP		UDP 123				
WINS		UDP 137 to 139			WINS Server	Windows Internet Name Service
SNMP		UDP 161				
SNMP Trap				UDP 162		
LDAP		TCP 389		TCP 389	Directory Services	When integrated with Corporate Directory
HTTPS/SSL		TCP 443				
SMB		TCP 445		TCP 445	CallManagers in the same cluster	
Syslog		TCP 514		UDP 514	Syslog service	

Table 12-1 *Example TDP/UDP Ports Used in a Cisco CallManager Environment (Continued)*

Protocol	Remote Source Port	CallManager Destination Port	CallManager Source Port	Remote Device Destination Port	Remote Devices	Notes
RMI		TCP 1099 to 1129			RMI Service Attendant Console	
MS SQL		TCP 1433		TCP 1433	CallManagers in the same cluster	
H.323 RAS				TCP 1719	Gatekeeper RAS	CallManager earlier than 3.3, Cisco Conference Connection
H.323 RAS			TCP 1024 to 4999	TCP 1719	Gatekeeper RAS	CallManager 3.3
H.323, H.225		TCP 1720		TCP 1720	H.323 gateways, anonymous device Cisco Conference Connection, non-Gatekeeper-controlled H.323 trunk	
H.323, H.225/ICT		TCP 1024 to 4999			CallManager Gatekeeper-controlled H.323 trunks	CallManager 3.3
H.323, H.245		TCP 1024 to 4999	TCP 1024 to 4999		CallManager H.323 gateways, anonymous device, H.323 trunks	

continues

Table 12-1 *Example TDP/UDP Ports Used in a Cisco CallManager Environment (Continued)*

Protocol	Remote Source Port	CallManager Destination Port	CallManager Source Port	Remote Device Destination Port	Remote Devices	Notes
H.323, H.245		TCP 11000 to 11999			Cisco IOS H.323 gateways, Cisco Conference Connection	
SCCP		TCP 2000			Skinny Clients (IP phones)	
Skinny Gateway (Analog)		TCP 2001			Analog Skinny Gateway	
Skinny Gateway (Digital)		TCP 2002			Digital Skinny Gateway	
MGCP Control		UDP 2427			MGCP Gateway Control	
MGCP Backhaul		TCP 2428			MGCP Gateways Backhaul	
RTS Serv			2500			
Cisco Extended Service		TCP 2551			Active/backup determination	
Cisco Extended Service		TCP 2552			DB change notification	
RIS Data Collector		TCP 2555			Inter-RIS communication	
RIS Data Collector		TCP 2556			Used by clients (IIS) to communicate with RIS	

Table 12-1 *Example TDP/UDP Ports Used in a Cisco CallManager Environment (Continued)*

Protocol	Remote Source Port	CallManager Destination Port	CallManager Source Port	Remote Device Destination Port	Remote Devices	Notes
CTI/QBE		TCP 2748			TAPI/JTAPI applications	Connects with CTI Manager; used by IVR, CCC, PA, Cisco SoftPhone, CRS, ICD, IPCC, IPMA, Attendant Console, and any other application that utilizes the TAPI or JTAPI plug-in; TSP
IPMA Service		TCP 2912			IPMA Assistant Console	
Media Streaming Application		UDP 3001			Change notification	
SCCP		TCP 3224			Media resources	Conference bridges, Xcoders
MS Terminal Services		TCP 3389			Windows Terminal Services	
Entercept HID Agent				TCP 5000	Host Intrusion Detection Console	
CallManager SIP		TCP/UDP 5060		TCP 5060	SIP Trunk default port	Can use TCP 1024 to 65,535
VNC HTTP Helper		TCP 580x				Remote control

continues

Table 12-1 *Example TDP/UDP Ports Used in a Cisco CallManager Environment (Continued)*

Protocol	Remote Source Port	CallManager Destination Port	CallManager Source Port	Remote Device Destination Port	Remote Devices	Notes
VNC Display		TCP 690x			Virtual Network Computer Display	Remote control
CallManager Change Notification		TCP 7727			CallManager change notification, Cisco database layer monitor, Cisco TFTP, Cisco IP media streaming, Cisco TCD, Cisco MOH	Real-time change notification
IPMA Service		TCP 8001			IP Manager Assistant	Change notification
ICCS		TCP 8002		TCP 8002	CallManagers in the same cluster	Intracluster communication
CTIM		TCP 8003				
Cisco Tomcat		TCP 8007			Web requests	
Cisco Tomcat		TCP 8009			Web requests	
Cisco Tomcat		TCP 8111			IIS, web requests to IPMA worker thread	
Cisco Tomcat		TCP 8222			IIS, web requests to EM application worker thread	
Cisco Tomcat		TCP 8333			IIS, web requests to WebDialer application worker thread	

Table 12-1 *Example TDP/UDP Ports Used in a Cisco CallManager Environment (Continued)*

Protocol	Remote Source Port	CallManager Destination Port	CallManager Source Port	Remote Device Destination Port	Remote Devices	Notes
DC Directory		TCP 8404			Embedded Directory Services	Used for Directory services, application authentication/ configuration, SoftPhone directory, user directory
Cisco Tomcat		TCP 8444			IIS, web requests to EM service worker thread	
Cisco Tomcat		TCP 8555			IIS, web requests to Apache SOAP worker thread	
Cisco Tomcat		TCP 8998			Web requests	
Cisco Tomcat		TCP 9007			IIS, web requests to CAR worker thread	
RTP	UDP 16384 to 32767			UDP 16384 to 32767	Voice media	IP IVR media, CCC IVR media, Cisco SoftPhone, Media Streaming Application
Cisco SNMP Trap Agent		UDP 61441			Cisco Alarm Interface	Receives some SNMP alarm in XML format

Access-Edge Trust Models

A primary function of access-edge policies is to establish and enforce trust boundaries. A trust boundary is the point within the network where markings (such as CoS or DSCP) begin to be accepted. Previously set markings are overridden (as required) at the trust boundary.

The design objective relating to trust boundaries is to enforce these as close to the endpoints as technically and administratively possible. This is illustrated in Figure 12-3.

Figure 12-3 *Establishing Trust Boundaries*

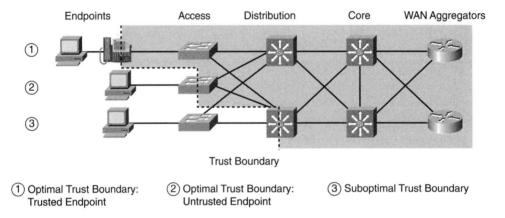

① Optimal Trust Boundary: Trusted Endpoint   ② Optimal Trust Boundary: Untrusted Endpoint   ③ Suboptimal Trust Boundary

The definition of the trust boundary depends on the capabilities of the endpoints that are being connected to the access edge of the LAN. Three main categories of endpoints exist, as they relate to trust boundaries:

- Trusted endpoints
- Untrusted endpoints
- Conditionally trusted endpoints

Each of these categories of endpoints is discussed in detail in the following sections.

Trusted Endpoint Models

Trusted endpoints have the capabilities and intelligence to mark application traffic to the appropriate CoS and DSCP values. Trusted endpoints also possess the capability to re-mark traffic that previously was marked by an untrusted device. For the most part, trusted endpoints are not mobile devices—the switch port that they are plugged into generally does not change.

NOTE   IP phones, which often change switch ports as users move, more appropriately are included in the category of conditionally trusted endpoints.

Examples of trusted endpoints include these:

- **Analog gateways**—These devices are deployed to connect analog devices (such as fax machines, modems, TDD/TTYs, and analog phones) to the VoIP network so that the analog signals can be packetized and transmitted over the IP network. Examples of analog gateways include these:

  - The NM-1V and NM2-V network modules, which support either High-Density or Low-Density Voice/Fax Interface Cards or VICs

  - The Cisco Communication Media Module (CMM) line card

  - The Catalyst 6500 Analog Interface Module (WS-X6624-FXS)

  - The Cisco VG224 and VG248 Cisco IOS–based voice gateways

  - The Cisco ATA 186/188 Analog Telephony Adaptors

- **IP conferencing stations**—These devices are designed for meeting-room VoIP conferencing. Essentially, they are specialized IP phones with 360° microphones and advanced speakerphones. Examples of such devices include the Cisco 7935 and 7936.

- **Videoconferencing gateways and systems**—These devices transmit interactive video across the IP network. Examples of such devices capable of setting DSCP markings include the Cisco IP/VC 3511, 3521, 3526, and 3540 videoconferencing gateways and systems.

- **Video surveillance units**—These (third-party) devices are used for security and remote-monitoring purposes over an IP (as opposed to a closed-circuit) network. These might support DSCP marking, in which case they can be considered trusted endpoints.

- **Servers**—Certain servers, within the data center or otherwise, might be capable of correctly marking their traffic on their NICs. In such cases, the network administrator can choose to trust such markings. However, enforcing such a trust boundary requires cooperation between network administrators and system or server administrators, an alliance that is often fragile, at best, and usually involves considerable finger pointing. Additionally, network administrators should bear in mind that the majority of DoS/ worm attacks target servers. Infected servers not only might spew profuse amounts of traffic onto the network, but, in such cases, they might do so with trusted markings. There's no hard-and-fast rule that will apply to every situation. Some administrators prefer to trust certain servers, like Cisco CallManagers, due to the large number of ports that may be in use to provide services (refer to Table 12-1) rather than administer complex access lists. In either case, consider the tradeoffs involved when deciding whether or not to trust a server.

- **Wireless access points**—Some wireless APs have the capability to mark or re-mark 802.1p CoS or DSCP values and, therefore, qualify as trusted endpoints. Examples include Cisco Aironet 350, 1100, and 1200 series APs.

- **Wireless IP phones**—Mobile wireless IP phones can mark DSCP values for VoIP and Call Signaling and pass these on to the wireless AP they are associated with. Examples include the Cisco 7920G wireless IP phone.

When trusted endpoints are connected to a switch port, typically all that is required is enabling the following interface command: **mls qos trust dscp**.

Optionally, if the traffic rate of the trusted application is known, the network administrator could apply an access-layer policer to protect against out-of-profile rates, in case the trusted endpoint somehow is compromised. For example, consider the case of an IP videoconferencing station that transmits 384 kbps of video (not including Layers 2 through 4 overhead) and correctly marks this traffic to DSCP AF41. An access-edge ingress policer could be applied to the switch port that this IP/VC station is connected to and could be configured to trust up to 500 kbps (allowing for Layers 2 through 4 overhead and policer granularity) of Interactive-Video traffic (marked AF41); excess traffic could be marked to CS1. Such a policy would prevent network abuse if another device was inserted into the path (perhaps through a hub) or if the trusted endpoint itself became compromised.

Untrusted Endpoint Models

As previously mentioned, trusting end users and their PCs is generally a bad idea because newer operating systems such as Windows XP and Linux make it relatively easy to set CoS or DSCP markings on PC NICs. Such markings can be set deliberately or even inadvertently. In either case, improperly set QoS markings could affect the service levels of multiple users within the enterprise and make troubleshooting a nightmare. Also, marking application traffic on server NICs has disadvantages (discussed in the previous section) that might make it preferable to treat these as untrusted devices.

Although client PCs and data center servers are related and complimentary, they also have unique considerations that affect their classification and marking policies, so they are examined individually next.

Untrusted PC with SoftPhone Model

It generally is recommended not to trust end-user PC traffic. However, some PCs might be running applications that critically require QoS treatment. A classic example is a PC running Cisco IP SoftPhone. In such a case, the critical application would need to be identified through access lists and marked or re-marked at the access edge. Re-marking can be done with either the MLS QoS **set ip dscp** command or with a policer.

NOTE   In this context, SoftPhone can be used to refer to any PC-based IP telephony application.

A policer is recommended in this case because limits on the amount of traffic being marked could be imposed (again, to prevent abuse). SoftPhones can use regular G.711 codecs (in which case, 128 kbps is adequate), or they can be configured to use a G.722 (wide codec, in which case 320 kbps is required). The tighter the policer is, the better (provided that adequate bandwidth has been allocated for the application's requirements).

Additionally, the UDP ports used by SoftPhone can be defined explicitly within the application (instead of simply picking random ports within the UDP range of 16,383 to 32,767). This is recommended, because this would allow for a more granular access list to match legitimate SoftPhone traffic, thereby tightening the overall security of the policy.

Figure 12-4 illustrates the logic of such an access-edge policer marking SoftPhone traffic from an untrusted PC endpoint.

Figure 12-4 *Untrusted Endpoint Policing: PC with SoftPhone Example*

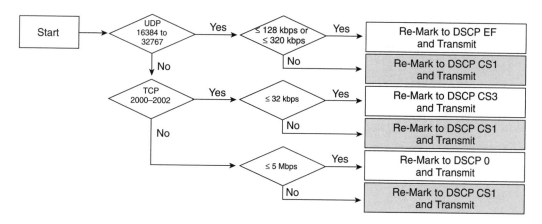

The syntax for implementing such a policer might vary slightly from platform to platform, as is detailed in the coming platform-specific sections.

Untrusted Server Model

As with PCs, servers are subject to attack and infection by worms and viruses and also should be policed for the amounts of traffic they admit onto the network. Granted, the values are much greater than with PC endpoints, and it is up to network administrators to profile traffic patterns from servers to baseline what is normal and abnormal behavior.

As an example, assume that a single server is running multiple applications—in this case, SAP (TCP ports 3200 to 3203 and also 3600), Lotus Notes (TCP port 1352), and IMAP (TCP ports 143 and 220). SAP is considered a Mission-Critical application and (until Call Signaling marking on IP Telephony equipment fully migrates from DSCP AF31 to CS3) should be marked to DSCP 25. Lotus Notes is classed as a Transactional Data application and should be marked to DSCP AF21; IMAP is considered a Bulk Data application and should be marked to DSCP AF11.

Application baselining has shown that, 95 percent of the time, the traffic rates for SAP, Lotus Notes, and IMAP are less than 15 Mbps, 35 Mbps, and 50 Mbps, respectively. No other traffic should emanate from the server; to ensure this, a final policer to catch any other type traffic is included. Remember, if legitimate traffic temporarily exceeds these values, no dropping or reordering of packets will occur. However, if this server becomes infected and begins sending sustained traffic in excess of these normal rates, the excess would be subject to aggressive dropping in the event of link congestion. Figure 12-5 shows the logic of such a policer.

Figure 12-5 *Untrusted Endpoint Policing: Multiapplication Server Example*

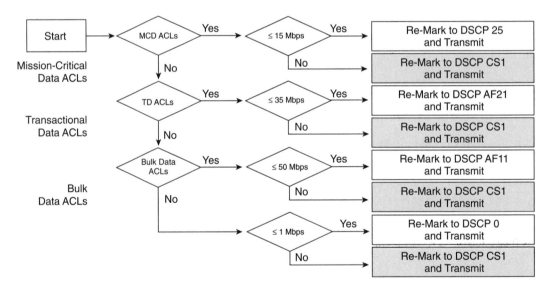

One of the critical concerns in deploying QoS designs for untrusted servers is to remember that the applications usually are identified by source ports, not destination ports (as is the case with client-to-server access lists).

Thus, the access lists for server-to-client traffic becomes this:

```
permit [ tcp | udp ] any [ eq | range ] any
```

instead of the access list for client-to-server traffic:

```
permit [ tcp | udp ] any any [ eq | range ]
```

This is a subtle but critical difference.

Conditionally Trusted Endpoint(s) Models

One of the main business advantages of IP Telephony is the simplicity and related cost savings of user adds, moves, and changes. To move, all a user has to do is pick up the IP phone; plug it into the new location. To move, all a user has to do is pick up the IP phone, plug it into the new location, and carry on business as usual. If the infrastructure supports inline power, it is literally a matter of unplugging a single RJ-45 cable and plugging it in at the new location.

IP phones are trusted devices; PCs are not. This presents a problem when it comes to provisioning trust in a mobile environment. Consider the following example: Port A is configured to trust the endpoint connected to it, which initially is an IP phone. Port B is configured not to trust the endpoint connected to it, which initially is a PC. As the result of a move, these endpoints end up plugged into the opposite ports. This breaks the VoIP quality of calls made from the IP phone (now plugged into untrusted Port B) and opens the network for unintentional or deliberate abuse of provisioned QoS by the PC (now plugged into the trusted Port A).

One solution is to place a call to the networking help desk when the move is scheduled so that the switch ports can be reconfigured to trust or untrust the endpoints, as required. However, this approach would dampen the mobility business advantage of IP Telephony because manual network administration then would be required to complete the move.

Another solution is to have an intelligent exchange of information between the switch and the devices plugged into the ports. If the switch discovers a device that is "trustworthy," it can extend trust to it dynamically; if not, it will not extend that trust.

Cisco IP phones use the latter solution. In the current Cisco implementation, the intelligent exchange of information is performed through the Cisco Discovery Protocol (CDP). Figure 12-6 shows a conditional trust-boundary extension granted to an IP phone that has passed a CDP exchange.

Figure 12-6 *Conditionally Trusted Endpoint: IP Phone Trust Boundary Extension and Operation*

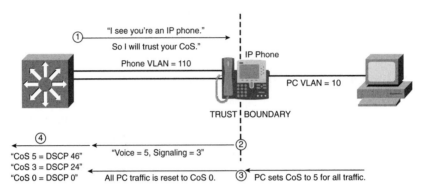

① Switch and phone exchange CDP; trust boundary is extended to IP phone.

② Phone sets CoS to 5 for VoIP and to 3 for Call-Signaling traffic.

③ Phone rewrites CoS from PC Port to 0.

④ Switch trusts CoS from phone and maps CoS ⟶ DSCP for output queuing.

CDP is a lightweight, proprietary protocol engineered to perform neighbor discovery. It never was intended as a security or authentication protocol. Therefore, to improve the security of conditional trust extension, the next generation of Cisco IP Telephony products will incorporate the use of advanced protocols, such as 802.1*x* and Extensible Authentication Protocols (EAP), combined with digital certificates, to perform authentication.

- **Cisco 7902G**—The 7902G is an entry-level IP phone that addresses the voice-communication needs of areas where only a minimal amount of features is required, such as lobbies, hallways, and break rooms. These phones probably would not be moved. The 7902G has only a single 10BASE-T Ethernet port on the back of the phone; therefore, there is no hardware support to connect a PC to it.

- **Cisco 7905G**—The 7905G is a basic IP phone that addresses the voice-communication needs of a cubicle worker who conducts low to medium telephone traffic. The Cisco 7905G has only a single 10BASE-T Ethernet port on the back of the phone; therefore, there is no hardware support to connect a PC to it.

- **Cisco 7910G and 7910G+SW**—The 7910G and 7910G+SW IP phones address the voice-communication needs associated with a reception area, lab, manufacturing floor, or employee with a minimal amount of telephone traffic. The only difference between the Cisco 7910G and the Cisco 7910G+SW is that the former has a single 10BASE-T Ethernet port (therefore, there is no hardware support to connect a PC to it), and the latter has two 10/100BASE-T Ethernet ports, which allow a PC to be connected to the IP phone.

- **Cisco 7912G**—The 7912G is a basic IP phone that addresses the voice-communication needs of a cubicle worker who conducts low to medium telephone traffic. The 7912G supports inline power and an integrated 10/100 Ethernet switch for connecting a PC. The switch used in the 7912G has the capability to mark CoS and DSCP of Voice and Call Signaling traffic that originates from the IP phone, but the Cisco 7912G does not have the capability to re-mark CoS values of PC-generated traffic.

- **Cisco 7940G**—The 7940G IP phone is suited best for an employee in a basic office cubicle environment—a transaction-type worker, for example—who conducts a medium amount of business by telephone. The 7940G supports inline power and has an integrated 10/100 Ethernet switch for connecting a PC.

- **Cisco 7960G**—The 7960G is designed to meet the communication needs of a profes-sional worker in an enclosed office environment—an employee who experiences a high amount of phone traffic in the course of a business day. The 7960G supports inline power and has an integrated 10/100 Ethernet switch for connecting a PC.

- **Cisco 7970G**—The 7970G not only addresses the needs of the executive or major decision maker, but also brings network data and applications to users without PCs. This IP phone includes a backlit, high-resolution color touch-screen display. Cur-rently, Cisco 7970G is the only Cisco IP phone that supports both Cisco prestandard Power over Ethernet (PoE) and the IEEE 802.3af PoE. The 7970G has an integrated 10/100 Ethernet switch for connecting a PC.

All these IP phones have the capability to mark 802.1Q/p CoS values for both VoIP and Call Signaling (default values are 5 and 3, respectively). Furthermore, they have the capability to mark DSCP values for both VoIP and Call Signaling (current defaults are EF and AF31, respectively; future software releases will change these values to EF and CS3, respectively).

IP phone models 7902G, 7905G, and 7910G lack the hardware to connecting a PC behind the IP phone. All other IP phone models from the preceding list (except the 7912G) have the hardware support to connect a PC behind the IP phone and also support 802.1Q/p CoS re-marking of tagged packets that originate from such PCs.

The 10/100 Ethernet switch built into the 7912G does not have the support to re-mark CoS values that might have been set by a PC, as illustrated in Figure 12-7. This re-marking limitation represents a potential security hole for enterprises deploying these IP phones. However, this hole can be plugged, for the most part, with access-edge policers, as will be detailed in this chapter. It is important to note that if 7912G IP phones are deployed to users that move locations, *all* user switch ports within the enterprise should have access-edge policers set on them to ensure mobility and security if a 7912G user moves the phones to another port.

Figure 12-7 *Conditionally Trusted Endpoint: 7912G IP Phone Trust Boundary Extension and Operation*

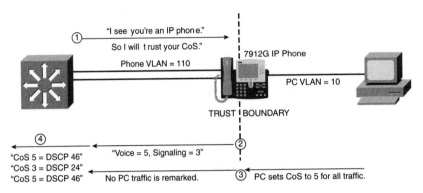

1. Switch and phone exchange CDP; trust boundary is extended to IP phone.
2. Phone sets CoS to 5 for VoIP and to 3 for Call-Signaling traffic.
3. Cisco 7912G IP phone does not rewrite CoS from PC port to 0.
4. Switch trusts CoS from phone and maps CoS ⟶ DSCP for output queuing.

Conditionally Trusted IP Phone + PC: Basic Model

In this model, trust (of CoS markings) is extended to CDP-verified IP phones. An additional layer of protection can be offered by access-edge policers. As stated previously, the tighter the policers are, the better, provided that adequate bandwidth is permitted for legitimate applications. The most granular policing can be achieved by the use of per-port or per-VLAN policers.

NOTE   At the time of this writing, only the Catalyst 3550 family supports per-port and per-VLAN policing as a feature. Other platforms already have committed to supporting this feature in the near future. For platforms that do not yet support this feature, equivalent logic can be achieved by including subnet information within the access lists being referenced by the class maps. Such examples are provided later in this chapter.

For example, the peak amounts of legitimate traffic originating from the voice VLAN (VVLAN) are as follows:

- 128 kbps for Voice traffic (marked CoS 5/DSCP EF—this is 320 kbps, in the case of G.722 codecs)

- 32 kbps for Call-Signaling traffic (marked CoS 3/DSCP AF31 or CS3)
- 32 kbps of Best-Effort services traffic (marked CoS 0)

No other traffic should originate from the VVLAN, so the policer could be configured to re-mark anything else from the VVLAN (because such traffic would be considered illegitimate and indicative of an attack).

These policers then could be combined with a policer to meter traffic from the data VLAN (DVLAN), marking down traffic in excess of 5 percent (5 Mbps for FE ports) to Scavenger/CS1.

Figure 12-8 illustrates the logic of these policers.

Figure 12-8 *Conditionally Trusted Endpoint Policing: IP Phone + PC (Basic Model)*

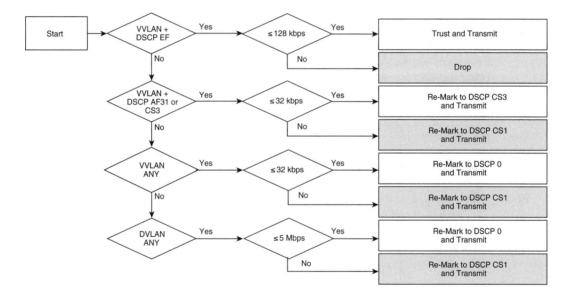

Conditionally Trusted IP Phone + PC: Advanced Model

Building on the previous model, additional marking and policing can be added for PC-based videoconferencing and multiple levels of data applications.

Desktop videoconferencing applications use the same UDP port range, by default, as does SoftPhone. If the UDP ports that the desktop videoconferencing application uses can be defined explicitly within the application, as with SoftPhone, two policers can be used: one for IP/VC and another for SoftPhone. Otherwise, a single policer covering the UDP port range of 16,384 to 32,767 is required. This policer would be provisioned for the worst-case scenario of legitimate traffic. In this case, this would be the videoconferencing application's requirement of 500 kbps (for a 384-kbps desktop IP/VC application), as compared to SoftPhone's requirement of 128 kbps (or 320 kbps for G.722 codecs).

Additional data VLAN policers can be added to meter Mission-Critical, Transactional, and Bulk Data flows. Each of these classes can be policed on ingress to the switch port to an in-profile amount, such as 5 percent each.

NOTE   Because Mission-Critical and Transactional Data applications are interactive foreground applications that require user input, it is highly unlikely that both of these types of applications will be generating 5 Mbps each simultaneously from a client PC. However, in the rare case that they are, these flows are policed further by any per-user microflow policing policies that are deployed on distribution-layer Catalyst 6500 Supervisor 720s (PFC3s), as detailed later in this chapter.

Another factor to keep in mind is that certain Catalyst platforms allow only up to eight policers per Fast Ethernet port. Therefore, the model presented here is made to conform to this constraint, to make it more generic and modular. For this reason, a separate policer has not been defined for Call-Signaling traffic from SoftPhone, but an access list to identify such traffic could be included within the Mission-Critical Data access lists, which is detailed in the configuration examples presented later in this chapter.

Figure 12-9 illustrates the logic of these advanced policers.

Figure 12-9 *Conditionally Trusted Endpoint Policing: IP Phone + PC (Advanced Model)*

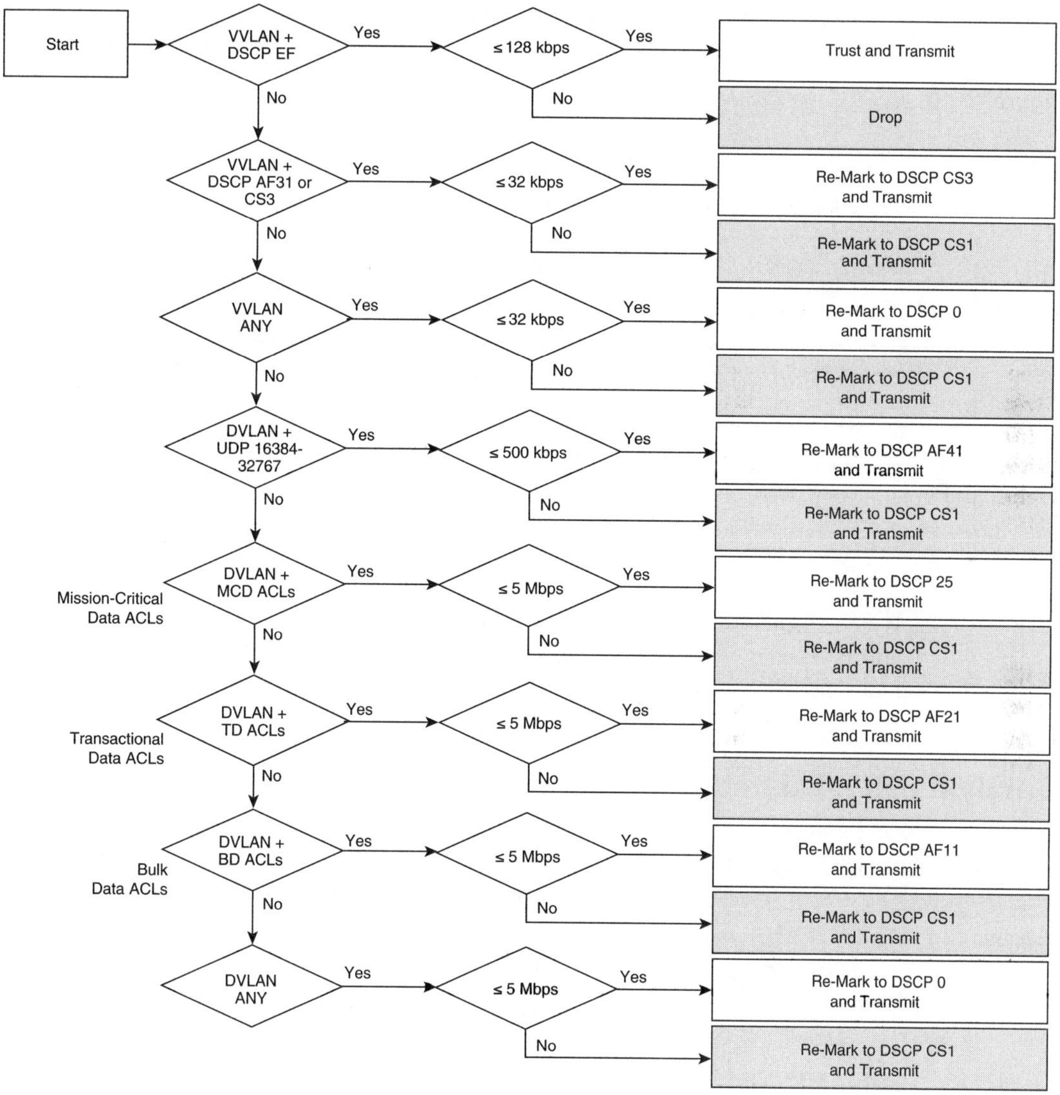

Catalyst 2950 QoS Considerations and Design

The Catalyst 2950 does not support Layer 3 forwarding and, as such, is applicable only as a (low-end) access-layer switch. Figure 12-10 shows the QoS design options for a Catalyst 2950.

Figure 12-10 *Access-Layer Catalyst 2950 QoS Design*

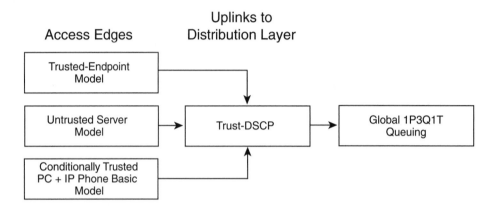

It is recommended to use the Enhanced Image (EI) versions of Cisco IOS Software on these platforms because these offer additional QoS features, such as MQC/ACL classification options, policing and markdown functions, mapping tables, and AutoQoS.

Catalyst 2950: Trusted Endpoint Model

Configuring a Catalyst 2950 campus to trust an endpoint is fairly straightforward, as shown in Example 12-1. The trusted endpoint should be assigned either the voice VLAN (VVLAN) or the data VLAN (DVLAN) with the appropriate switch port commands.

Example 12-1 *Catalyst 2950: Trusted Endpoint Example*

```
CAT2950(config)#interface FastEthernet0/1
CAT2950(config-if)#mls qos trust dscp
```

Catalyst MLS QoS verification command:

- **show mls qos interface**

Catalyst MLS QoS Verification Command: **show mls qos interface**

The **show mls qos interface** verification command reports the configured trust state and the current operating trust mode of a switch port interface.

In Example 12-2, the command verifies that interface FastEthernet 0/1 correctly is trusting the DSCP values of the endpoint to which it is connected.

Example 12-2 **show mls qos interface** *Verification of a Switch Port Connected to a Trusted Endpoint*

```
CAT2950#show mls qos interface FastEthernet0/1
FastEthernet0/1
trust state: trust dscp       ! Configured trust state is to trust DSCP
trust mode: trust dscp        ! Current operating mode is to trust DSCP
COS override: dis
default COS: 0
pass-through: none
trust device: none
CAT2950#
```

Catalyst 2950: Untrusted PC with SoftPhone Model

The Catalyst 2950 does not support the **range** keyword within an ACL when the ACL is being referenced by an MQC class map. Therefore, a policy to mark UDP flows in the port range of 16,384 through 32,767 cannot be configured on the Catalyst 2950.

A possible workaround to this limitation is to preset the port(s) to be used by SoftPhone within the application itself. In such a case, these ports would have to be matched discretely by ACL entries on the Catalyst 2950. Furthermore, each port being used for Call-Signaling also would require a discrete ACL entry.

However, even when all these ports are buttoned down and discrete ACLs are configured on the Catalyst 2950 to match them, another limitation of the switch comes into play. Specifically, the Catalyst 2950 can support policing in only 1-Mbps increments on Fast Ethernet ports. Such lax policing leaves a fairly large hole to allow unauthorized traffic that is mimicking Voice or Call-Signaling to be admitted onto the network.

Because of these limitations, it is not recommended to use a Catalyst 2950 to support an untrusted PC running SoftPhone.

Catalyst 2950: Untrusted Server Model

For the most part, the Catalyst 2950 can support the Untrusted Multiapplication Server model, illustrated in Figure 12-5. Only the final element of the logical model—namely, the policing of all other traffic to 1 Mbps (re-marking traffic in excess of this limit to CS1)—is not supported on the Catalyst 2950.

These main platform-specific caveats should be kept in mind when deploying this model on the Catalyst 2950:

- Nonstandard DSCP values are not supported; therefore, Mission-Critical Data traffic cannot be marked to DSCP 25 on Catalyst 2950s (a temporary recommendation during the interim of the Cisco Call-Signaling marking migration from AF31 to CS3). Such application traffic alternatively can be marked to the more general class of Transactional Data (AF21), of which it is a subset.

- The **mls qos cos override interface** command must be used to ensure that untrusted CoS values explicitly are set to 0 (default).

- The **range** keyword cannot be used in the ACLs being referenced by the class maps; server ports should be defined explicitly with a separate access control entry (ACE) per TCP/UDP port.

- User-defined masks must be consistent for all ACLs being referenced by class maps. (If filtering is being done against TCP/UDP ports, all ACEs should be set to filter by TCP/UDP ports instead of some ACEs filtering by ports and others by subnet or host addresses.)

- System-defined masks (such as **permit ip any any**) cannot be used in conjunction with user-defined masks (such as **permit tcp any any eq 3200**) within the same policy map. Therefore, if some traffic is being matched against TCP/UDP ports, a final ACL cannot be used to match all other traffic through a **permit ip any any** statement.

- The Catalyst 2950 IOS implementation of MQC's class-default currently does not function compatibly with mainline Cisco IOS. The QoS features and actions defined within class-default should be applied to all other traffic that is not matched explicitly by a class map, but testing has shown that this is not the case.

NOTE   These limitations are based on testing performed using Catalyst 2950 IOS 12.1(19)EA1 versions a through c and 12.1(20)EA1. Additional information on these caveats can be found at

http://www.cisco.com/univercd/cc/td/doc/product/lan/cat2950/12119ea1/2950scg/swacl.htm

and

http://www.cisco.com/univercd/cc/td/doc/product/lan/cat2950/12119ea1/2950scg/swqos.htm.

Example 12-3 details the Catalyst 2950 configuration to support the Untrusted Multiapplication Server model (illustrated in Figure 12-5).

Example 12-3 *Catalyst 2950: Untrusted Multiapplication Server Example*

```
CAT2950(config)#class-map SAP
CAT2950(config-cmap)# match access-group name SAP
CAT2950(config-cmap)#class-map LOTUS
CAT2950(config-cmap)# match access-group name LOTUS
CAT2950(config-cmap)#class-map IMAP
CAT2950(config-cmap)# match access-group name IMAP
CAT2950(config-cmap)#exit
CAT2950(config)#
CAT2950(config)#policy-map UNTRUSTED-SERVER
CAT2950(config-pmap)# class SAP
CAT2950(config-pmap-c)# set ip dscp 18      ! DSCP 25 is not supported
CAT2950(config-pmap-c)# police 15000000 8192 exceed-action dscp 8
        ! Out-of-profile Mission-Critical is marked down to Scavenger (CS1)
CAT2950(config-pmap-c)# class LOTUS
CAT2950(config-pmap-c)#  set ip dscp 18      ! Transactional Data is marked AF21
CAT2950(config-pmap-c)#  police 35000000 8192 exceed-action dscp 8
        ! Out-of-profile Transactional Data is marked down to Scavenger (CS1)
CAT2950(config-pmap-c)# class IMAP
CAT2950(config-pmap-c)#  set ip dscp 10      ! Bulk Data is marked AF11
CAT2950(config-pmap-c)#  police 50000000 8192 exceed-action dscp 8
        ! Out-of-profile Bulk Data is marked down to Scavenger (CS1)
CAT2950(config-pmap-c)# exit
CAT2950(config-pmap)# exit
CAT2950(config)#
CAT2950(config)#interface FastEthernet0/1
CAT2950(config-if)# mls qos cos override      ! Untrusted CoS is remarked to 0
CAT2950(config-if)# service-policy input UNTRUSTED-SERVER
CAT2950(config-if)#exit
CAT2950(config)#
CAT2950(config)#ip access-list extended SAP
CAT2950(config-ext-nacl)# permit tcp any eq 3200 any
CAT2950(config-ext-nacl)# permit tcp any eq 3201 any
CAT2950(config-ext-nacl)# permit tcp any eq 3202 any
CAT2950(config-ext-nacl)# permit tcp any eq 3203 any
CAT2950(config-ext-nacl)# permit tcp any eq 3600 any
CAT2950(config-ext-nacl)#
CAT2950(config-ext-nacl)#ip access-list extended LOTUS
CAT2950(config-ext-nacl)# permit tcp any eq 1352 any
CAT2950(config-ext-nacl)#
CAT2950(config-ext-nacl)#ip access-list extended IMAP
CAT2950(config-ext-nacl)# permit tcp any eq 143 any
CAT2950(config-ext-nacl)# permit tcp any eq 220 any
CAT2950(config-ext-nacl)#end
CAT2950#
```

Catalyst MLS QoS verification commands:

- **show mls qos interface**
- **show mls qos interface policers**
- **show class-map**
- **show policy-map**
- **show mls masks qos**

Catalyst MLS QoS Verification Command: **show mls qos interface policers**

The **show mls qos interface policers** verification command reports all configured policers attached to the specified interface.

In Example 12-4, the policers defined for Mission-Critical, Transactional, and Bulk Data that are applied to Fast Ethernet 0/1 are confirmed.

Example 12-4 **show mls qos interface policers** *Verification of a Switch Port Connected to an Untrusted Multiapplication Server*

```
CAT2950#show mls qos interface FastEthernet0/1 policers
FastEthernet0/1
policymap=UNTRUSTED-SERVER
type=Single rate=15000000, burst=8192        ! Mission-Critical Data Policer
type=Single rate=35000000, burst=8192        ! Transactional Data Policer
type=Single rate=50000000, burst=8192        ! Bulk Data Policer
CAT2950#
```

Catalyst MLS QoS Verification Commands: **show class-map** and **show policy-map**

The **show class-map** and **show policy-map** verification commands report the class map and policy maps that have been configured globally (regardless of whether they've been applied to an interface).

In Example 12-5, the class maps for SAP, LOTUS, and IMAP are displayed, as is the policy map UNTRUSTED-SERVER that is referencing these.

Example 12-5 **show class-map** *and* **show policy-map** *Verification of a Switch Connected to an Untrusted Multiapplication Server*

```
CAT2950#show class-map
 Class Map match-all SAP (id 1)
   Match access-group name SAP
 Class Map match-all LOTUS (id 2)
   Match access-group name LOTUS
 Class Map match-all IMAP (id 3)
   Match access-group name IMAP
 Class Map match-any class-default (id 0)
   Match any
```

Example 12-5 show class-map *and* show policy-map *Verification of a Switch Connected to an Untrusted Multiapplication Server (Continued)*

```
CAT2950#show policy-map
 Policy Map UNTRUSTED-SERVER
  class  SAP
   set ip dscp 18
   police 15000000 8192 exceed-action dscp 8
  class  LOTUS
   set ip dscp 18
   police 35000000 8192 exceed-action dscp 8
  class  IMAP
   set ip dscp 10
   police 50000000 8192 exceed-action dscp 8
CAT2950#
```

Catalyst MLS QoS Verification Command: **show mls masks qos**

The **show mls masks qos** verification command is helpful in keeping track of the number of user-defined or system-defined masks that are being applied by ACEs that are referenced by MQC class maps.

In Example 12-6, the ACEs being referenced by QoS policies are using IP protocol masks, including (TCP/UDP) source ports.

Example 12-6 show mls masks qos *Verification of a Switch Connected to an Untrusted Multiapplication Server*

```
CAT2950#show mls masks qos
Mask1
    Type : qos
    Fields : ip-proto, src-port
    Policymap : UNTRUSTED-SERVER
        Interfaces : Fa0/1
CAT2950#
```

Catalyst 2950: Conditionally Trusted IP Phone + PC: Basic Model

When configuring an access switch to trust or conditionally trust CoS, the default mapping for CoS 5 should be adjusted to point to DSCP EF (46) instead of DSCP CS5 (40). This modification is shown in Example 12-7.

Example 12-7 *Catalyst 2950: CoS-to-DSCP Marking Modification for Voice*

```
CAT2950(config)#mls qos map cos-dscp 0 8 16 24 32 46 48 56   ! Maps CoS 5 to EF
CAT2950(config)#
```

NOTE   Adjusting the default CoS-to-DSCP mapping for Call Signaling (which formerly was mapped from CoS 3 to DSCP AF31/26) no longer is required. This is because the default mapping of CoS 3 points to DSCP CS3 (24), which is the Call-Signaling marking that all Cisco IP Telephony devices markings will migrate to.

Catalyst MLS QoS verification commands:

- **show mls qos map**
- **show mls qos map cos-dscp**
- **show mls qos map dscp-cos**

Catalyst MLS QoS Verification Command: **show mls qos map [cos-dscp | dscp-cos]**

The **show mls qos map** verification command returns the DSCP-to-CoS and CoS-to-DSCP mappings. These mappings can be either the default mappings or manually configured overrides.

In Example 12-8, the default mapping for CoS 5 (DSCP CS5) has been modified to point to DSCP EF instead.

Example 12-8   **show mls qos map** *Verification for a Catalyst 2950 Switch*

```
CAT2950#show mls qos map
  Dscp-cos map:
     dscp:   0   8 10 16 18 24 26 32 34 40 46 48 56
     --------------------------------------------------
      cos:   0   1   1   2   2   3   3   4   4   5   5   6   7

  Cos-dscp map:
      cos:   0   1   2   3   4   5   6   7
     --------------------------------------------------
     dscp:   0   8  16  24  32  46  48  56        ! CoS 5 is now mapped to DSCP EF
CAT2950#
```

The Catalyst 2950's hardware policers lack the granularity to implement the Conditionally Trusted IP Phone + PC: Basic model, illustrated in Figure 12-8. However, they can implement a simplified version of this model, shown in Figure 12-11.

It should be kept in mind that the coarse granularity of the Catalyst 2950's policers (which are configured in 1 Mbps minimum increments on Fast Ethernet interfaces) potentially could allow up to 1 Mbps of traffic mimicking legitimate voice traffic per conditionally trusted switch port.

Figure 12-11 *Catalyst 2950: Conditionally Trusted Endpoint Policing: IP Phone + PC (Basic Model)*

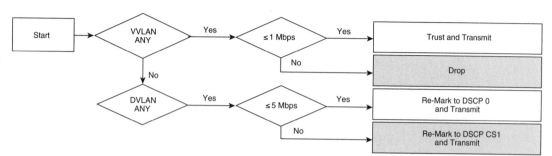

Example 12-9 shows the configuration for configuring a switch port to conditionally trust an IP phone that has a PC connected to it.

Example 12-9 *Catalyst 2950: Conditionally Trusted IP Phone + PC: Basic Model Example*

```
CAT2950(config)#mls qos map cos-dscp 0 8 16 24 32 46 48 56  ! Maps CoS 5 to EF
CAT2950(config)#
CAT2950(config)#class-map VVLAN-ANY
CAT2950(config-cmap)# match access-group name VVLAN-ANY
CAT2950(config-cmap)#class-map DVLAN-ANY
CAT2950(config-cmap)# match access-group name DVLAN-ANY
CAT2950(config-cmap)#exit
CAT2950(config)#
CAT2950(config)#policy-map IPPHONE+PC
CAT2950(config-pmap)#  class VVLAN-ANY
CAT2950(config-pmap-c)#    police 1000000 8192 exceed-action drop
        ! Out-of-profile traffic from the VVLAN is dropped
CAT2950(config-pmap-c)#  class DVLAN-ANY
CAT2950(config-pmap-c)#    set ip dscp 0
        ! Optional remarking in case trust is compromised
CAT2950(config-pmap-c)#    police 5000000 8192 exceed-action dscp 8
        ! Out-of-profile data traffic is marked down to Scavenger
CAT2950(config-pmap-c)#exit
CAT2950(config-pmap)#exit
CAT2950(config)#
CAT2950(config)#
CAT2950(config)#interface FastEthernet0/1
CAT2950(config-if)# switchport access vlan 10! DVLAN
CAT2950(config-if)# switchport voice vlan 110! VVLAN
CAT2950(config-if)# mls qos trust device cisco-phone ! Conditional trust
CAT2950(config-if)# mls qos trust cos               ! Trust CoS from IP Phone
CAT2950(config-if)# service-policy input IPPHONE+PC ! Policing policy
CAT2950(config-if)#exit
CAT2950(config)#
CAT2950(config)#ip access-list standard VVLAN-ANY
```

continues

Example 12-9 *Catalyst 2950: Conditionally Trusted IP Phone + PC: Basic Model Example (Continued)*

```
CAT2950(config-std-nacl)# permit 10.1.110.0 0.0.0.255      ! VVLAN subnet
CAT2950(config-std-nacl)#
CAT2950(config-std-nacl)#ip access-list standard DVLAN-ANY
CAT2950(config-std-nacl)# permit 10.1.10.0 0.0.0.255       ! DVLAN subnet
CAT2950(config-std-nacl)#end
CAT2950#
```

Catalyst MLS QoS verification commands:

- **show mls qos interface**
- **show mls qos interface policers**
- **show mls qos map**
- **show class-map**
- **show policy-map**
- **show mls masks qos**

Catalyst 2950: Conditionally Trusted IP Phone + PC: Advanced Model

Because of the previously discussed caveats and limitations of the Catalyst 2950 (including the maximum number of policers supported per FE interface, the overly coarse policer granularity, the incapability to mix user-defined masks with system-defined masks, and other constraints), the Conditionally Trusted IP Phone + PC: Advanced model, shown in Figure 12-9, cannot be supported on this platform.

Catalyst 2950: Queuing

The Catalyst 2950 can be configured to operate in a 4Q1T mode or in a 1P3Q1T mode (with queue 4 being configured as a strict-priority queue); the 1P3Q1T mode is recommended for converged networks.

The strict-priority queue is enabled by configuring the fourth queue's weight parameter, as defined in the **wrr-queue bandwidth** command, to be 0 (as shown in Example 12-10).

The remaining bandwidth is allocated to the other queues according to their defined weights. To allocate remaining bandwidths of 5 percent, 25 percent, and 70 percent to queues 1, 2, and 3, weights of 5, 25, and 70 can be assigned to these queues, respectively. The logic of these bandwidth allocations recommendations is discussed in more detail momentarily.

Example 12-11 **show wrr-queue bandwidth** *Verification for a Catalyst 2950 Switch*

```
CAT2950#show wrr-queue bandwidth
WRR Queue  :   1   2   3   4
Bandwidth  :   5  25  70   0      ! Q1 gets 5%, Q2 gets 25%,
CAT2950#
```

Example 12-12 shows the CoS-to-queue mapping configuration f

Example 12-12 *Catalyst 2950 CoS-to-Queue Mapping Example*

```
CAT2950(config)#wrr-queue cos-map 1 1       ! Scavenger/
CAT2950(config)#wrr-queue cos-map 2 0       ! Best Effor
CAT2950(config)#wrr-queue cos-map 3 2 3 4 6 7   ! CoS 2,3,4,
CAT2950(config)#wrr-queue cos-map 4 5       ! VoIP is as
CAT2950(config)#
```

Catalyst MLS QoS verification command:

- **show wrr-queue cos-map**

Catalyst MLS QoS Verification Command: **show wrr-queue cos-r**

The **show wrr-queue cos-map** verification command displays the CoS value has been assigned.

In Example 12-13, CoS 0 (Best-Effort) is assigned to Q2 and CoS assigned to Q1. CoS values 2, 3, 4, 6, and 7 have all been assigned has been assigned to the priority queue, Q4.

Example 12-13 **show wrr-queue cos-map** *Verification for a Catalyst 2950 Switch*

```
CAT2950#show wrr-queue cos-map
CoS Value      :  0  1  2  3  4  5  6  7
Priority Queue :  2  1  3  3  3  4  3  3
CAT2950#
```

Catalyst 3550 QoS Considerations and Des

The Catalyst 3550 supports IP routing and, thus, can be found in eit distribution layer of the campus.

As for QoS, the Catalyst 3550 supports a richer feature set than the Ca an advanced policing feature that is ideal for out-of-profile policing, per-VLAN policing. The access-layer design options and distributio mendations for a Catalyst 3550 are shown in Figures 12-13 and 12-1

NOTE   The absolute values assigned to these queue weights are meaningless, as these weights are entirely relative. Therefore, these weights can be reduced by dividing each weight by the lowest common denominator (in this case, 5) to arrive at queue weights of 1, 5, and 14 for queues 1, 2, and 3, respectively.

Reduction is strictly optional and makes no difference to the servicing of the queues. Many network administrators tend to prefer defining bandwidth allocation ratios as percentages, so bandwidth weight ratios are not reduced in this design chapter.

So far, campus QoS designs have been presented for the first half of the DoS/worm-mitigation strategy discussed at the beginning of this chapter—namely, designs for access-layer policers to mark down out-of-profile traffic to the Scavenger class PHB of CS1.

The second vital component of this strategy is to map Scavenger class traffic into a less-than best-effort queuing structure, ensuring that all other traffic will be serviced ahead of it in the event of congestion.

The Catalyst 2950, like most Catalyst platforms, supports the mapping of CoS values into queues. The CoS value that corresponds to Scavenger (DSCP CS1) is CoS 1; this CoS value is shared with Bulk Data (DSCP AF11). Therefore, a small amount of bandwidth (5 percent) is allocated to the less-than-best-effort queue: Q1. Q1 thus services legitimate Bulk Data traffic but constrains out-of-profile Scavenger traffic—which could be the result of a DoS/worm attack—to a small amount (less than 5 percent), in the event of congestion.

The next queue, Q2, then is assigned to service Best-Effort traffic. A previously discussed design principle regarding Best-Effort bandwidth allocation is to allocate approximately 25 percent of a link's bandwidth to service Best-Effort traffic. In this manner, the sheer volume of traffic that defaults to Best-Effort continues to get adequate bandwidth, both in the event of momentary campus congestion (because of bursts in the amount of legitimate traffic) and even in the case of a DoS/worm attack.

Preferential applications, such as Transactional Data, Mission-Critical Data, Call-Signaling, Network and Internetwork Control and Management, and both Interactive- and Streaming-Video, are serviced by Q3. Q3 is allocated 70 percent of the remaining bandwidth (after the PQ has serviced its Voice traffic).

Figure 12-12 illustrates the recommended 1P3Q1T queuing model for the Catalyst 2950, along with CoS-to-queue assignments.

Figure 12-12 *Catalyst 2950 1P3Q1T Queuing Model*

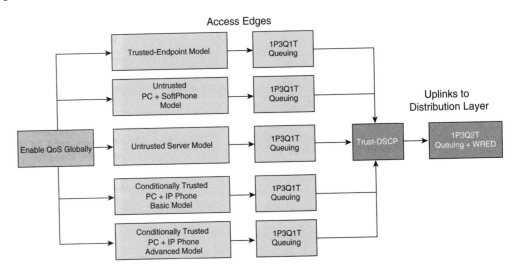

The configuration of the priority queue (Q4) and the bandwidth alloc[...] remaining queues (Q1, Q2, and Q3) are shown in Example 12-10.

Example 12-10 *Catalyst 2950 Scheduling Configuration: 1P3Q1T Example*

```
CAT2950(config)#wrr-queue bandwidth 5 25 70 0   ! Q1-5%, Q2-25%,
CAT2950(config)#
```

Catalyst MLS QoS verification command:

- **show wrr-queue bandwidth**

Catalyst MLS QoS Verification Command: **show wrr-queue bandwi[...]**

The **show wrr-queue bandwidth** verification command displays the [...] been assigned to the queues. If the command returns a value of 0 for the [...] queue, this indicates that the scheduler is operating in 1P3Q1T mode, [...] strict-priority queue.

In Example 12-11, the scheduler has been configured for 1P3Q1T queuin[...] of the remaining bandwidth (after the priority queue has been fully se[...] percent, and Q3 gets 70 percent.

Figure 12-13 *Access-Layer Catalyst 3550 QoS Design*

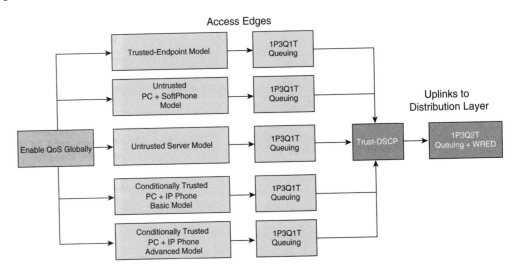

Figure 12-14 *Distribution-Layer Catalyst 3550 QoS Design*

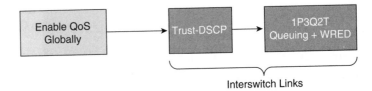

An important point to remember about the Catalyst 3550 is that QoS is disabled by default and must be enabled globally for configured policies to become effective. While QoS is disabled, all frames and packets are passed through the switch unaltered (which is equivalent to a trust CoS and trust DSCP state on all ports). When QoS is enabled globally, however, all DSCP and CoS values (by default) are set to 0 (which is equivalent to an untrusted state on all ports). Example 12-14 shows how to verify whether QoS has been enabled not and also how it can be enabled globally.

Example 12-14 *Enabling QoS Globally on the Catalyst 3550*

```
CAT3550#show mls qos
QoS is disabled              ! By default QoS is disabled
CAT3550#
```

Example 12-14 *Enabling QoS Globally on the Catalyst 3550 (Continued)*

```
CAT3550#configure terminal
Enter configuration commands, one per line.  End with CNTL/Z.
CAT3550(config)#mls qos        ! Enables QoS globally for the Cat3550
CAT3550(config)#exit
CAT3550#

CAT3550#show mls qos
QoS is enabled                 ! Verifies that QoS is enabled globally
CAT3550#
```

NOTE   Depending on the software version, enabling QoS in the Catalyst 3550 might require IEEE 802.3*x* flow control to be disabled on all interfaces (if it is enabled). Flow control can be disabled on an interface or interface range by using the interface configuration commands **flowcontrol receive off** and **flowcontrol send off**. Check the Catalyst 3550 IOS documentation (QoS chapter) to verify whether this is a requirement for the version of software in use.

Catalyst 3550: Trusted Endpoint Model

Configuring a Catalyst 3550 switch port to trust an endpoint is identical to configuring a Catalyst 2950 (provided that QoS has been enabled globally on the Catalyst 3550). It is shown in Example 12-15.

Example 12-15 *Catalyst 3550: Trusted Endpoint Example*

```
CAT3550(config)#interface FastEthernet0/1
CAT3550(config-if)#mls qos trust dscp
```

Catalyst MLS QoS verification commands:

- **show mls qos**
- **show mls qos interface**

Catalyst 3550: Untrusted PC with SoftPhone Model

Unlike the Catalyst 2950, the Catalyst 3550 has all the necessary QoS features to support and enforce the Untrusted PC with SoftPhone model, as illustrated in Figure 12-4. Example 12-16 shows the Catalyst 3550 configuration for this access edge model.

Example 12-16 *Catalyst 3550: Untrusted PC with SoftPhone Example*

```
CAT3550(config)#mls qos map policed-dscp  0 24 46 to 8
        ! Excess traffic marked 0 or CS3 or EF will be remarked to CS1
CAT3550(config)#
CAT3550(config)#class-map match-all SOFTPHONE-VOICE
```

continues

Example 12-16 *Catalyst 3550: Untrusted PC with SoftPhone Example (Continued)*

```
CAT3550(config-cmap)#  match access-group name SOFTPHONE-VOICE
CAT3550(config-cmap)#class-map match-all SOFTPHONE-SIGNALING
CAT3550(config-cmap)#  match access-group name SOFTPHONE-SIGNALING
CAT3550(config-cmap)#exit
CAT3550(config)#
CAT3550(config)#policy-map SOFTPHONE-PC
CAT3550(config-pmap)#class SOFTPHONE-VOICE
CAT3550(config-pmap-c)# set ip dscp 46         ! Softphone VoIP is marked to DSCP EF
CAT3550(config-pmap-c)# police 128000 8000 exceed-action policed-dscp-transmit
         ! Out-of-profile SoftPhone voice traffic is marked down to Scavenger (CS1)
CAT3550(config-pmap-c)#class SOFTPHONE-SIGNALING
CAT3550(config-pmap-c)# set ip dscp 24         ! Signaling is marked to DSCP CS3
CAT3550(config-pmap-c)# police 32000 8000 exceed-action policed-dscp-transmit
        ! Out-of-profile Signaling traffic is marked down to Scavenger (CS1)
CAT3550(config-pmap-c)#class class-default
CAT3550(config-pmap-c)# set ip dscp 0
CAT3550(config-pmap-c)# police 5000000 8000 exceed-action policed-dscp-transmit
        ! Out-of-profile data traffic is marked down to Scavenger (CS1)
CAT3550(config-pmap-c)# exit
CAT3550(config-pmap)#exit
CAT3550(config)#
CAT3550(config)#interface FastEthernet0/1
CAT3550(config-if)# service-policy input SOFTPHONE-PC  ! Applies policy to int
CAT3550(config-if)#exit
CAT3550(config)#
CAT3550(config)#ip access-list extended SOFTPHONE-VOICE
CAT3550(config-ext-nacl)# permit udp any any range 16384 32767 ! VoIP ports
CAT3550(config-ext-nacl)#
CAT3550(config-ext-nacl)#ip access-list extended SOFTPHONE-SIGNALING
CAT3550(config-ext-nacl)# permit tcp any any range 2000 2002   ! SCCP ports
CAT3550(config-ext-nacl)#end
CAT3550#
```

Catalyst MLS QoS verification commands:

- **show mls qos**
- **show mls qos map**
- **show mls qos interface**
- **show mls qos interface policers**
- **show mls qos statistics**
- **show class-map**
- **show policy-map**
- **show policy interface**

Catalyst MLS QoS Verification Command: **show mls qos interface statistics**

The **show mls qos interface statistics** verification command reports dynamic counters for a given policy, including how many packets were classified and policed by the policy.

In Example 12-17, untrusted packets from the PC are classified and policed according to the limits shown in Figure 12-4 for the Untrusted PC with SoftPhone access-edge endpoint policing model.

Example 12-17   **show mls qos interface statistics** *Verification of a Catalyst 3550 Switch Port Connected to an Untrusted PC with SoftPhone*

```
CAT3550#show mls qos interface FastEthernet0/1 statistics
FastEthernet0/1
Ingress
  dscp: incoming   no_change   classified policed     dropped (in bytes)
Others: 1275410698 31426318    1243984380 1674978822 0
Egress
  dscp: incoming   no_change   classified policed     dropped (in bytes)
Others: 7271494       n/a         n/a      0          0
CAT3550#
```

Catalyst MLS QoS Verification Command: **show policy interface**

The **show policy interface** verification command displays the policy maps (and related classes) that are attached to a given interface.

In Example 12-18, a summary of the untrusted PC with SoftPhone policing policy is shown as applied to FastEthernet0/1.

Example 12-18   **show policy interface** *Verification of a Catalyst 3550 Switch Port Connected to an Untrusted PC with SoftPhone*

```
CAT3550#show policy interface FastEthernet0/1
 FastEthernet0/1
  service-policy input: SOFTPHONE-PC
    class-map: SOFTPHONE-VOICE (match-all)
      0 packets, 0 bytes
      5 minute offered rate 0 bps, drop rate 0 bps
      match: access-group name SOFTPHONE-VOICEqm_police_inform_feature:
CLASS_SHOW
    class-map: SOFTPHONE-SIGNALING (match-all)
      0 packets, 0 bytes
      5 minute offered rate 0 bps, drop rate 0 bps
      match: access-group name SOFTPHONE-SIGNALINGqm_police_inform_feature:
CLASS_SHOW
    class-map: class-default (match-any)
      0 packets, 0 bytes
      5 minute offered rate 0 bps, drop rate 0 bps
      match: any
        0 packets, 0 bytes
        5 minute rate 0 bpsqm_police_inform_feature: CLASS_SHOW
CAT3550#
```

NOTE	At the time of this writing, the counters reported by the **show policy interface** command on the Catalyst 3550 are not being incremented, as is the case with the mainline Cisco IOS version of this command. This has been reported as a bug. In other words, all counters currently are frozen at zero; however, when this bug is fixed, they should increment dynamically. Catalyst 3550 IOS versions tested and affected with this bug include 12.1(19)EA1 a through c and 12.1(20)EA1.

Catalyst 3550: Untrusted Server Model

The Catalyst 3550 fully supports the Untrusted Multiapplication Server model, depicted in Figure 12-5. Example 12-19 shows the configuration for this model.

Example 12-19 *Catalyst 3550: Untrusted Multiapplication Server Example*

```
CAT3550(config)#mls qos map policed-dscp  0 10 18 25 to 8
 ! Excess traffic marked 0 or AF11 or AF21 or DSCP 25 will be remarked to CS1
CAT3550(config)#
CAT3550(config)#class-map SAP
CAT3550(config-cmap)# match access-group name SAP
CAT3550(config-cmap)#class-map LOTUS
CAT3550(config-cmap)# match access-group name LOTUS
CAT3550(config-cmap)#class-map IMAP
CAT3550(config-cmap)# match access-group name IMAP
CAT3550(config-cmap)#exit
CAT3550(config)#
CAT3550(config)#policy-map UNTRUSTED-SERVER
CAT3550(config-pmap)#class SAP
CAT3550(config-pmap-c)# set ip dscp 25       ! SAP is marked as Mission-Critical
CAT3550(config-pmap-c)# police 15000000 8000 exceed-action policed-dscp-transmit
        ! Out-of-profile SAP is marked down to Scavenger (CS1)
CAT3550(config-pmap-c)#class LOTUS
CAT3550(config-pmap-c)# set ip dscp 18       ! Lotus is marked as Transactional
CAT3550(config-pmap-c)# police 35000000 8000 exceed-action policed-dscp-transmit
        ! Out-of-profile LOTUS is marked down to Scavenger (CS1)
CAT3550(config-pmap-c)#class IMAP
CAT3550(config-pmap-c)# set ip dscp 10       ! IMAP is marked as Bulk Data
CAT3550(config-pmap-c)# police 50000000 8000 exceed-action policed-dscp-transmit
        ! Out-of-profile IMAP is marked down to Scavenger (CS1)
CAT3550(config-pmap-c)#class class-default
CAT3550(config-pmap-c)# set ip dscp 0
CAT3550(config-pmap-c)# police 1000000 8000 exceed-action policed-dscp-transmit
        ! Excess data traffic is marked to Scavenger (CS1)
CAT3550(config-pmap-c)# exit
CAT3550(config-pmap)#exit
CAT3550(config)#
CAT3550(config)#interface FastEthernet0/1
CAT3550(config-if)# service-policy input UNTRUSTED-SERVER
CAT3550(config-if)#exit
CAT3550(config)#
```

Example 12-19 *Catalyst 3550: Untrusted Multiapplication Server Example (Continued)*

```
CAT3550(config)#ip access-list extended SAP
CAT3550(config-ext-nacl)# permit tcp any range 3200 3203 any
CAT3550(config-ext-nacl)# permit tcp any eq 3600 any
CAT3550(config-ext-nacl)#
CAT3550(config-ext-nacl)#ip access-list extended LOTUS
CAT3550(config-ext-nacl)#permit tcp any eq 1352 any
CAT3550(config-ext-nacl)#
CAT3550(config-ext-nacl)#ip access-list extended IMAP
CAT3550(config-ext-nacl)#permit tcp any eq 143 any
CAT3550(config-ext-nacl)#permit tcp any eq 220 any
CAT3550(config-ext-nacl)#end
CAT3550#
```

Catalyst MLS QoS verification commands:

- **show mls qos**
- **show mls qos map**
- **show mls qos interface**
- **show mls qos interface policers**
- **show mls qos statistics**
- **show class-map**
- **show policy-map**
- **show policy interface**

Catalyst 3550: Conditionally Trusted IP Phone + PC: Basic Model

The Catalyst 3550's support of per-port and per-VLAN policing gives it a distinct advantage over other platforms when provisioning a (basic or advanced) Conditionally Trusted Endpoint model. This is because per-port/per-VLAN policies can be provisioned without having to enter subnet-specific information for each switch. This makes such policies more modular and portable.

In Example 12-20, VLAN 10 is the DVLAN and VLAN 110 is the VVLAN.

Example 12-20 *Catalyst 3550: Conditionally Trusted IP Phone + PC: Basic Model Example*

```
CAT3550(config)#mls qos map cos-dscp 0 8 16 24 32 46 48 56
       ! Modifies CoS-to-DSCP mapping to map CoS 5 to DSCP EF
CAT3550(config)#mls qos map policed-dscp 0 24 to 8
       ! Excess DVLAN & VVLAN traffic will be remarked to Scavenger (CS1)
CAT3550(config)#
CAT3550(config)#
CAT3550(config)#class-map match-all VOICE
```

continues

Example 12-20 *Catalyst 3550: Conditionally Trusted IP Phone + PC: Basic Model Example (Continued)*

```
CAT3550(config-cmap)# match ip dscp 46       ! DSCP EF (voice)
CAT3550(config-cmap)#class-map match-any CALL-SIGNALING  ! Need 'match-any' here
CAT3550(config-cmap)# match ip dscp 26       ! DSCP AF31 (old Call-Signaling)
CAT3550(config-cmap)# match ip dscp 24       ! DSCP CS3 (new Call-Signaling)
CAT3550(config-cmap)#
CAT3550(config-cmap)#class-map match-all VVLAN-VOICE
CAT3550(config-cmap)# match vlan  110        ! VLAN 110 is VVLAN
CAT3550(config-cmap)# match class-map VOICE  ! Matches VVLAN DSCP EF
CAT3550(config-cmap)#
CAT3550(config-cmap)#class-map match-all VVLAN-CALL-SIGNALING
CAT3550(config-cmap)# match vlan  110        ! VLAN 110 is VVLAN
CAT3550(config-cmap)# match class-map CALL-SIGNALING !Matches VVLAN AF31/CS3
CAT3550(config-cmap)#
CAT3550(config-cmap)#class-map match-all ANY
CAT3550(config-cmap)# match access-group name ANY  ! Workaround ACL
CAT3550(config-cmap)#
CAT3550(config-cmap)#class-map match-all VVLAN-ANY
CAT3550(config-cmap)# match vlan  110        ! VLAN 110 is VVLAN
CAT3550(config-cmap)# match class-map ANY    ! Matches any other VVLAN traffic
CAT3550(config-cmap)#
CAT3550(config-cmap)#class-map match-all DVLAN-ANY
CAT3550(config-cmap)# match vlan  10         ! VLAN 10 is DVLAN
CAT3550(config-cmap)# match class-map ANY    ! Matches all DVLAN traffic
CAT3550(config-cmap)#
CAT3550(config-cmap)#policy-map IPPHONE+PC-BASIC
CAT3550(config-pmap)#class VVLAN-VOICE
CAT3550(config-pmap-c)# set ip dscp 46       ! DSCP EF (Voice)
CAT3550(config-pmap-c)# police 128000 8000 exceed-action drop
          ! Only one voice call is permitted per switchport VVLAN
CAT3550(config-pmap-c)#class VVLAN-CALL-SIGNALING
CAT3550(config-pmap-c)# set ip dscp 24       ! DSCP CS3 (Call-Signaling)
CAT3550(config-pmap-c)# police 32000 8000 exceed-action policed-dscp-transmit
          ! Out-of-profile Call-Signaling is marked down to Scavenger (CS1)
CAT3550(config-pmap-c)#class VVLAN-ANY
CAT3550(config-pmap-c)# set ip dscp 0
CAT3550(config-pmap-c)# police 32000 8000 exceed-action policed-dscp-transmit
          ! Unauthorized VVLAN traffic is marked down to Scavenger (CS1)
CAT3550(config-pmap-c)#class DVLAN-ANY
CAT3550(config-pmap-c)# set ip dscp 0
CAT3550(config-pmap-c)# police 5000000 8000 exceed-action policed-dscp-transmit
          ! Out-of-profile data traffic is marked down to Scavenger (CS1)
CAT3550(config-pmap-c)# exit
CAT3550(config-pmap)#exit
CAT3550(config)#
CAT3550(config)#interface FastEthernet0/1
CAT3550(config-if)# switchport access vlan 10             ! DVLAN
CAT3550(config-if)# switchport voice vlan 110             ! VVLAN
CAT3550(config-if)# mls qos trust device cisco-phone      ! Conditional Trust
CAT3550(config-if)# service-policy input IPPHONE+PC-BASIC ! Attaches policy
CAT3550(config-if)#exit
CAT3550(config)#
```

Example 12-20 *Catalyst 3550: Conditionally Trusted IP Phone + PC: Basic Model Example (Continued)*

```
CAT3550(config)#
CAT3550(config)#ip access-list standard ANY    ! Workaround ACL
CAT3550(config-std-nacl)# permit any
CAT3550(config-std-nacl)#end
CAT3550#
```

Catalyst MLS QoS verification commands:

- **show mls qos**
- **show mls qos map**
- **show mls qos interface**
- **show mls qos interface policers**
- **show mls qos statistics**
- **show class-map**
- **show policy-map**
- **show policy interface**

NOTE   Although Catalyst 3550 IOS syntax supports the **match any** criteria within a class map (which the parser allows to be configured in conjunction with a per-VLAN policy), testing with the Catalyst 3500 IOS versions listed previously has shown that there is a bug with this function because it does not match any other traffic on a per-VLAN basis. Therefore, an explicit access list named ANY has been used in Example 12-20 as a workaround to this issue. Once this issue has been resolved, it is simpler to use the **match-any** keyword within the class-maps (rather than the workaround ACL).

Catalyst 3550: Conditionally Trusted IP Phone + PC: Advanced Model

The Conditionally Trusted IP Phone + PC: Advanced model builds on the basic model by including policers for PC-based videoconferencing (and PC SoftPhone), Mission-Critical, Transactional, and Bulk Data applications. This model is depicted in Figure 12-9. The Catalyst 3550 can support eight policers per 10/100 Ethernet port and can support this advanced model.

Example 12-21 shows the Catalyst 3550 configuration for the Conditionally Trusted IP Phone + PC: Advanced model. In this example, the same server-to-client applications are used as in the untrusted multiapplication server example. However, notice that the source and destination ports are reversed for the client-to-server direction of traffic flow. Also, because of the limit of the number of policers per Fast Ethernet port (eight), there is no explicit policer for SoftPhone Call-Signaling traffic; to work around this limitation, SoftPhone Call-Signaling traffic is included in the Mission-Critical Data applications access list.

Example 12-21 *Catalyst 3550: Conditionally Trusted IP Phone + PC: Advanced Model Example*

```
CAT3550(config)#mls qos map cos-dscp 0 8 16 24 32 46 48 56
        ! Modifies CoS-to-DSCP mapping to map CoS 5 to DSCP EF
CAT3550(config)#mls qos map policed-dscp 0 10 18 24 25 34 to 8
        ! Excess DVLAN traffic marked 0, AF11, AF21, CS3, DSCP 25,
        ! and AF41 will be remarked to Scavenger (CS1)
CAT3550(config)#
CAT3550(config)#class-map match-all VOICE
CAT3550(config-cmap)# match ip dscp 46       ! DSCP EF (voice)
CAT3550(config-cmap)#class-map match-any CALL-SIGNALING ! Need 'match-any' here
CAT3550(config-cmap)# match ip dscp 26       ! DSCP AF31 (old Call-Signaling)
CAT3550(config-cmap)# match ip dscp 24       ! DSCP CS3 (new Call-Signaling)
CAT3550(config-cmap)#class-map match-all PC-VIDEO
CAT3550(config-cmap)# match access-group name PC-VIDEO
CAT3550(config-cmap)#class-map match-all MISSION-CRITICAL-DATA
CAT3550(config-cmap)# match access-group name MISSION-CRITICAL-DATA
CAT3550(config-cmap)#class-map match-all TRANSACTIONAL-DATA
CAT3550(config-cmap)# match access-group name TRANSACTIONAL-DATA
CAT3550(config-cmap)#class-map match-all BULK-DATA
CAT3550(config-cmap)# match access-group name BULK-DATA
CAT3550(config-cmap)#class-map match-all ANY
CAT3550(config-cmap)# match access-group name ANY  ! Workaround ACL
CAT3550(config-cmap)#
CAT3550(config-cmap)#class-map match-all VVLAN-VOICE
CAT3550(config-cmap)# match vlan 110          ! VLAN 110 is VVLAN
CAT3550(config-cmap)# match class-map VOICE ! Matches VVLAN DSCP EF
CAT3550(config-cmap)#class-map match-all VVLAN-CALL-SIGNALING
CAT3550(config-cmap)# match vlan 110          ! VLAN 110 is VVLAN
CAT3550(config-cmap)# match class-map CALL-SIGNALING ! Matches VVLAN AF31/CS3
CAT3550(config-cmap)#class-map match-all VVLAN-ANY
CAT3550(config-cmap)# match vlan 110          ! VLAN 110 is VVLAN
CAT3550(config-cmap)# match class-map ANY    ! Matches any other VVLAN traffic
CAT3550(config-cmap)#
CAT3550(config-cmap)#
CAT3550(config-cmap)#class-map match-all DVLAN-PC-VIDEO
CAT3550(config-cmap)# match vlan 10           ! VLAN 10 is DVLAN
CAT3550(config-cmap)# match class-map PC-VIDEO ! Matches PC-Video class-map
CAT3550(config-cmap)#
CAT3550(config-cmap)#class-map match-all DVLAN-MISSION-CRITICAL-DATA
CAT3550(config-cmap)# match vlan 10           ! VLAN 10 is DVLAN
CAT3550(config-cmap)# ! Matches MCD class-map
CAT3550(config-cmap)#
CAT3550(config-cmap)#class-map match-all DVLAN-TRANSACTIONAL-DATA
CAT3550(config-cmap)# match vlan 10           ! VLAN 10 is DVLAN
CAT3550(config-cmap)# match class-map TRANSACTIONAL-DATA ! Matches TD class-map
CAT3550(config-cmap)#
CAT3550(config-cmap)#class-map match-all DVLAN-BULK-DATA
CAT3550(config-cmap)# match vlan 10           ! VLAN 10 is DVLAN
CAT3550(config-cmap)# ! Matches Bulk Data class-map
```

Example 12-21 *Catalyst 3550: Conditionally Trusted IP Phone + PC: Advanced Model Example (Continued)*

```
CAT3550(config-cmap)#
CAT3550(config-cmap)#class-map match-all DVLAN-ANY
CAT3550(config-cmap)#  match vlan 10           ! VLAN 10 is DVLAN
CAT3550(config-cmap)#  match class-map ANY     ! Matches all other DVLAN traffic
CAT3550(config-cmap)#
CAT3550(config-cmap)#
CAT3550(config-cmap)#policy-map IPPHONE+PC-ADVANCED
CAT3550(config-pmap)#  class VVLAN-VOICE
CAT3550(config-pmap-c)#  set ip dscp 46         ! DSCP EF (Voice)
CAT3550(config-pmap-c)#  police 128000 8000 exceed-action drop
         ! Only one voice call is permitted per switchport VVLAN
CAT3550(config-pmap-c)#class VVLAN-CALL-SIGNALING
CAT3550(config-pmap-c)#  set ip dscp 24         ! DSCP CS3 (Call-Signaling)
CAT3550(config-pmap-c)#  police 32000 8000 exceed-action policed-dscp-transmit
         ! Out-of-profile Call-Signaling is marked down to Scavenger (CS1)
CAT3550(config-pmap-c)#class VVLAN-ANY
CAT3550(config-pmap-c)#  set ip dscp 0
CAT3550(config-pmap-c)#  police 32000 8000 exceed-action policed-dscp-transmit
         ! Unauthorized VVLAN traffic is marked down to Scavenger (CS1)
CAT3550(config-pmap-c)#class DVLAN-PC-VIDEO
CAT3550(config-pmap-c)#  set ip dscp 34         ! DSCP AF41 (Interactive-Video)
CAT3550(config-pmap-c)#  police 500000 8000 exceed-action policed-dscp-transmit
         ! Only one IP/VC stream will be permitted per switchport
CAT3550(config-pmap-c)#class DVLAN-MISSION-CRITICAL-DATA
CAT3550(config-pmap-c)#  set ip dscp 25         ! Interim Mission-Critical Data
CAT3550(config-pmap-c)#  police 5000000 8000 exceed-action policed-dscp-transmit
         ! Out-of-profile Mission-Critical Data is marked down to Scavenger (CS1)
CAT3550(config-pmap-c)#class DVLAN-TRANSACTIONAL-DATA
CAT3550(config-pmap-c)#  set ip dscp 18         ! DSCP AF21 (Transactional Data)
CAT3550(config-pmap-c)#  police 5000000 8000 exceed-action policed-dscp-transmit
         ! Out-of-profile Transactional Data is marked down to Scavenger (CS1)
CAT3550(config-pmap-c)#class DVLAN-BULK-DATA
CAT3550(config-pmap-c)#  set ip dscp 10         ! DSCP AF11 (Bulk Data)
CAT3550(config-pmap-c)#  police 5000000 8000 exceed-action policed-dscp-transmit
         ! Out-of-profile Bulk Data is marked down to Scavenger (CS1)
CAT3550(config-pmap-c)#class DVLAN-ANY
CAT3550(config-pmap-c)#  set ip dscp 0
CAT3550(config-pmap-c)#  police 5000000 8000 exceed-action policed-dscp-transmit
         ! Out-of-profile data traffic is marked down to Scavenger (CS1)
CAT3550(config-pmap-c)#  exit
CAT3550(config-pmap)#exit
CAT3550(config)#
CAT3550(config)#interface FastEthernet0/1
CAT3550(config-if)#  switchport access vlan 10                ! DVLAN
CAT3550(config-if)#  switchport voice vlan 110                ! VVLAN
CAT3550(config-if)#  mls qos trust device cisco-phone         ! Conditional Trust
CAT3550(config-if)#  service-policy input IPPHONE+PC-ADVANCED! Attaches policy
CAT3550(config-if)#exit
CAT3550(config)#
CAT3550(config)#ip access-list standard ANY   ! Workaround ACL
```

continues

Example 12-21 *Catalyst 3550: Conditionally Trusted IP Phone + PC: Advanced Model Example (Continued)*

```
CAT3550(config-std-nacl)# permit any
CAT3550(config-std-nacl)#
CAT3550(config-std-nacl)#ip access-list extended PC-VIDEO        ! IP/VC or SoftPhone
CAT3550(config-ext-nacl)# permit udp any any range 16384 32767
CAT3550(config-ext-nacl)#
CAT3550(config-ext-nacl)#ip access-list extended MISSION-CRITICAL-DATA
CAT3550(config-ext-nacl)# permit tcp any any range 3200 3203    ! SAP
CAT3550(config-ext-nacl)# permit tcp any any eq 3600            ! SAP
CAT3550(config-ext-nacl)# permit tcp any any range 2000 2002    ! SoftPhone SCCP
CAT3550(config-ext-nacl)#
CAT3550(config-ext-nacl)#ip access-list extended TRANSACTIONAL-DATA
CAT3550(config-ext-nacl)# permit tcp any any eq 1352           ! Lotus
CAT3550(config-ext-nacl)#
CAT3550(config-ext-nacl)#ip access-list extended BULK-DATA
CAT3550(config-ext-nacl)# permit tcp any any eq 143            ! IMAP
CAT3550(config-ext-nacl)# permit tcp any any eq 220            ! IMAP
CAT3550(config-ext-nacl)#end
CAT3550#
```

Catalyst MLS QoS verification commands:

- **show mls qos**
- **show mls qos map**
- **show mls qos interface**
- **show mls qos interface policers**
- **show mls qos statistics**
- **show class-map**
- **show policy-map**
- **show policy interface**

Catalyst 3550: Queuing and Dropping

Like the Catalyst 2950, the Catalyst 3550 supports a 1P3Q1T queuing model for all ports. Gigabit Ethernet ports have the additional option of being configured as 1P3Q2T, with either tail-drop or WRED thresholds. However, unlike the Catalyst 2950, the Catalyst 3550 queuing parameters are set on a per-interface basis, not globally. Nonetheless, uniform queuing policies can be deployed expeditiously using the **interface range** configuration command.

The strict-priority queue is enabled on a per-interface basis on the Catalyst 3550 with the **priority-queue out** interface command. Bandwidth is allocated among the remaining queues using the **wrr-queue bandwidth** command. A twist with the Catalyst 3550 is that queue 4's WRR weight is set to 1 (indicating that it does not participate in the WRR scheduler because it is configured as a strict-priority queue) instead of 0 (as is the case on the Catalyst 2950). Recommended remaining bandwidth allocations (after the PQ has been serviced fully) are 5 percent for the Scavenger queue (Q1), 25 percent for the Best-Effort queue (Q2), and 70 percent for the preferential application queue (Q3).

Following this, CoS 1 (Scavenger/Bulk Data) would be assigned to Q1; CoS 0 (Best-Effort) would be assigned to Q2; CoS values 2 (Transactional Data and Network-Management), 3 (Call-Signaling and Mission-Critical Data), 4 (Interactive- and Streaming-Video), 6 (Internetwork Control), and 7 (Network Control/Spanning-Tree) would be assigned to Q3; and CoS 5 (voice) would be assigned to the strict-priority Q4. These assignments and allocations are illustrated in Figure 12-15 (the thresholds shown in Q1 and Q3 are discussed shortly).

Figure 12-15 *Catalyst 3550 1P3Q2T Queuing Model*

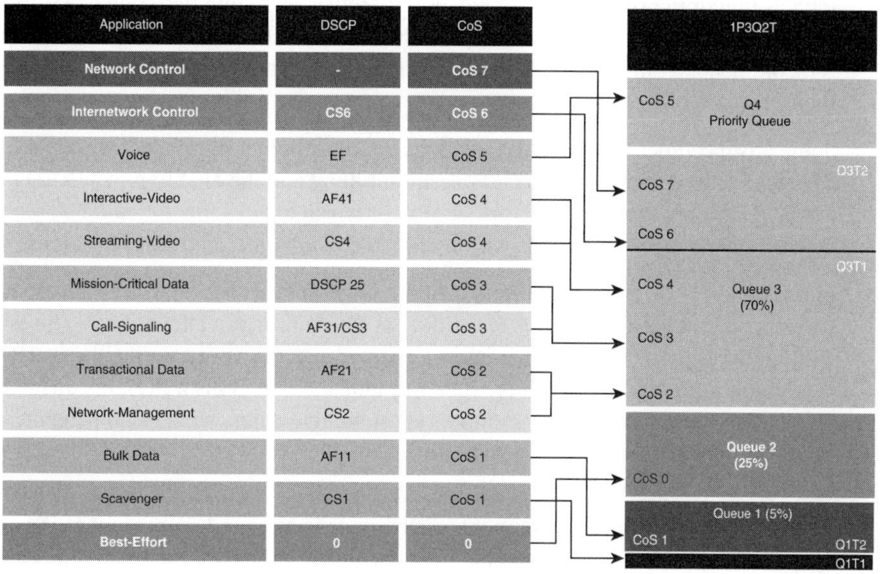

Example 12-22 shows the interface-mode configuration commands to configure this 1P3Q1T queuing model, for either Fast Ethernet or Gigabit Ethernet Catalyst 3550 interfaces.

Example 12-22 *Catalyst 3550 Fast Ethernet and Gigabit Ethernet Interface Queuing Configuration: 1P3Q1T Example*

```
CAT3550(config)#interface range FastEthernet0/1 - 48
CAT3550(config-if)# wrr-queue bandwidth 5 25 70 1   ! Q1-5% Q2-25% Q3-70% Q4=PQ
CAT3550(config-if)# wrr-queue cos-map 1 1      ! Assigns Scavenger to Q1
CAT3550(config-if)# wrr-queue cos-map 2 0      ! Assigns Best Effort to Q2
CAT3550(config-if)# wrr-queue cos-map 3 2 3 4 6 7 ! Assigns CoS 2,3,4,6,7 to Q3
CAT3550(config-if)# wrr-queue cos-map 4 5      ! Assigns VoIP to Q4 (PQ)
CAT3550(config-if)# priority-queue out         ! Enables Q4 as PQ
CAT3550(config-if)#end
CAT3550#
```

Catalyst MLS QoS verification command:

- **show mls qos interface queueing**

The Catalyst 3550 offers some advanced "nerd-knob" queuing options on 10/100 interfaces, such as tuning minimum reserve thresholds. However, testing has shown that such tuning makes a highly negligible difference, at best. Therefore, tuning minimum reserve thresholds is recommended only for advanced network administrators or when using automated tools, such as AutoQoS.

Some advanced nerd knobs also exist for Gigabit Ethernet interfaces. A couple of these advanced tuning options include queue-limit tuning and the enabling of WRED thresholds for 1P3Q2T operation. In the event of DoS or worm attacks, the Gigabit Ethernet uplinks may become congested, so it is worthwhile to examine these advanced options.

In Example 12-23, the queue limits for both Gigabit Ethernet interfaces are tuned to correspond to the WRR weights of the queues (the bandwidth allocations). This is achieved with the **wrr-queue queue-limit** interface command. However, unlike the WRR weight bandwidth ratio for Q4 (which is set to 1 to indicate that Q4 is a PQ), the queue limit for Q4 needs to be set explicitly to a more representative value, such as 30 percent.

NOTE   The default queue limits are such that each queue is assigned 25 percent of the available buffer space. It should be noted that when the queue limits are modified, the queue temporarily is shut down during the hardware reconfiguration, and the switch might drop newly arrived packets destined to the queue. Thus, it is advisable not to tune the queue limits on Catalyst 3550 switches already in production networks unless downtime has been scheduled.

Additionally, WRED is enabled on each (nonpriority) queue. This allows for the preferential treatment of Bulk Data (DSCP AF11) over Scavenger (CS1) within Q1, as well as the preferential treatment of internetworking or networking protocols (DSCP CS6 and CS7, respectively) over all other applications assigned to Q3. Even though Q2 has only Best-Effort traffic assigned to it, enabling WRED on this queue increases the efficiency of TCP applications within this queue during periods of congestion.

A low WRED threshold, such as 40 percent, can be set for Q1 to aggressively drop Scavenger traffic to preferentially service Bulk Data. The WRED thresholds for Q2 and Q3 can be set to higher levels, such as 80 percent.

By default, all DSCP values are mapped to the first WRED threshold of whichever queue their CoS values are assigned to. Therefore, only DSCP values that are to be mapped to the second WRED thresholds (of their respective queues) need to be configured manually. In this case, Bulk Data (DSCP AF11/10), Internetwork Control (DSCP CS6/48), and Network Control (DSCP CS7/56) all need to be mapped explicitly to the second WRED threshold using the **wrr-queue dscp-map** interface configuration command.

NOTE	Network Control traffic in the campus primarily refers to Spanning Tree Protocol (STP) traffic, such as bridge protocol data units (BPDUs). Although these Layer 2 Ethernet frames are marked CoS 7, they (obviously) do not have any capabilities to carry Layer 3 DSCP markings. Thus, it might seem moot to map DSCP CS7 (56) to a higher WRED threshold. However, it should be kept in mind that Catalyst switches generate internal DSCP values for all frames (regardless of whether they are carrying IP). These internal DSCP values are used for QoS decisions, such as WRED, in this case. Therefore, because STP BPDU frames (marked CoS 7) generate an internal DSCP value of 56, mapping DSCP 56 to the second threshold of Q3 provides preferential treatment for these important Layer 2 frames.

Example 12-23 shows the configuration for these tuning options, which are available only on Gigabit Ethernet interfaces on the Catalyst 3550.

Example 12-23 *Catalyst 3550 Gigabit Ethernet Interface Queuing and Dropping Configuration: 1P3Q2T Example*

```
CAT3550(config)#interface range GigabitEthernet 0/1 - 2
CAT3550(config-if-range)# wrr-queue bandwidth 5 25 70 1
     ! Q1 gets 5% BW, Q2 gets 25% BW, Q3 gets 70% BW, Q4 is the PQ
CAT3550(config-if-range)# wrr-queue queue-limit 5 25 40 30
     ! Tunes buffers to 5% for Q1, 25% for Q2, 40% for Q3 and 30% for Q4
CAT3550(config-if-range)# wrr-queue random-detect max-threshold 1 40 100
     ! Sets Q1 WRED threshold 1 to 40% and threshold 2 to 100%
CAT3550(config-if-range)# wrr-queue random-detect max-threshold 2 80 100
     ! Sets Q2 WRED threshold 1 to 80% and threshold 2 to 100%
CAT3550(config-if-range)# wrr-queue random-detect max-threshold 3 80 100
     ! Sets Q3 WRED threshold 1 to 80% and threshold 2 to 100%
CAT3550(config-if-range)# wrr-queue cos-map 1 1                ! Assigns Scavenger to Q1
```

continues

Example 12-23 *Catalyst 3550 Gigabit Ethernet Interface Queuing and Dropping Configuration: 1P3Q2T Example (Continued)*

```
CAT3550(config-if-range)# wrr-queue cos-map 2 0           ! Assigns Best Effort to Q2
CAT3550(config-if-range)# wrr-queue cos-map 3 2 3 4 6 7
            ! Assigns CoS 2,3,4,6,7 to Q3
CAT3550(config-if-range)# wrr-queue cos-map 4 5           ! Assigns VoIP to Q4 (PQ)
CAT3550(config-if-range)# wrr-queue dscp-map 2 10 48 56
            ! Maps Bulk Data (10), Routing (48) and Spanning Tree (Internal DSCP 56)
            ! to WRED threshold 2 of their respective queues - all other DSCP values
            ! are mapped (by default) to WRED threshold 1 of their respective queues
CAT3550(config-if-range)# priority-queue out             ! Enables Q4 as PQ
CAT3550(config-if-range)#end
CAT3550#
```

Catalyst MLS QoS verification commands:

- **show mls qos interface queueing**
- **show mls qos interface buffers**

Catalyst MLS QoS Verification Command: **show mls qos interface buffers**

The **show mls qos interface buffers** verification command displays the queue sizes (as per-queue buffer allocation percentages of the total buffer space). Also, the command displays whether WRED has been enabled on a queue and, if so, displays the first and second thresholds (as percentages of the queue's depth).

In Example 12-24, the queue limits are set to 5 percent, 25 percent, 40 percent, and 30 percent of the total queuing buffer space for queues 1 through 4 (respectively). Additionally, WRED is enabled on queues 1 through 3 (but not Q4 because it is the priority queue). The first WRED threshold is set to 5 percent on Q1 and is set to 80 percent on queues 2 and 3.

Example 12-24 **show mls qos interface buffers** *Verification for a Catalyst 3550 Switch*

```
CAT3550#show mls qos interface GigabitEthernet0/1 buffers
GigabitEthernet0/1
Notify Q depth:
qid-size
 1 - 5        ! Q1 queue-limit is set to 5% of total buffer space
 2 - 25       ! Q2 queue-limit is set to 25% of total buffer space
 3 - 40       ! Q3 queue-limit is set to 40% of total buffer space
 4 - 30       ! Q4 queue-limit is set to 30% of total buffer space
qid WRED thresh1 thresh2
1    ena  40     100   ! WRED is enabled on Q1 - first threshold is set to 40%
2    ena  80     100   ! WRED is enabled on Q2 - first threshold is set to 80%
3    ena  80     100   ! WRED is enabled on Q3 - first threshold is set to 80%
4    dis  100    100   ! WRED is disabled on Q4 (as it is the PQ)
CAT3550#
```

Catalyst MLS QoS Verification Command: **show mls qos interface queueing**

The **show mls qos interface queueing** verification command displays the CoS-to-queuing mappings that have been configured, in addition to the bandwidth allocations per queue. On Gigabit Ethernet interfaces with WRED enabled, the output also includes the DSCP-to-WRED threshold mappings. This information is displayed in a table form, with the first digit of the decimal DSCP value along the y-axis (in rows) and the second digit of the decimal DSCP value along the x-axis (in columns).

In Example 12-25, the output verifies that the egress expedite queue (priority queue, Q4) is enabled. Also, the WRR bandwidth weights show that, of the remaining bandwidth, Q1 is allocated 5 percent, Q2 is allocated 25 percent, and Q3 is allocated 70 percent.

Additionally, the DSCP-to-WRED table verifies that Bulk Data (AF11/10), Internetwork Control (DSCP CS6/48), and Network Control (DSCP CS7/56) each is mapped to the second WRED threshold (T2) of its respective queue (as determined by the CoS-to-queue mappings).

Finally, the CoS-to-queue map shows that CoS 0 (Best-Effort) is assigned to Q2; CoS 1 (Scavenger) has been assigned to Q1; CoS values 2, 3, 4, 6, and 7 have been assigned to Q3; and CoS 5 (Voice) has been assigned to the priority queue, Q4.

Example 12-25 **show mls qos interface queueing** *Verification for a Catalyst 3550 Switch*

```
CAT3550#show mls qos interface GigabitEthernet0/1 queueing
GigabitEthernet0/1
Egress expedite queue: ena              ! Q4 is enabled as a PQ

wrr bandwidth weights:
qid-weights
 1 - 5                                  ! Q1 is allocated 5%
 2 - 25                                 ! Q2 is allocated 25%
 3 - 70                                 ! Q3 is allocated 70&
 4 - 1     when expedite queue is disabled

Dscp-threshold map:
      d1 :  d2 0  1  2  3  4  5  6  7  8  9
      ------------------------------------------
       0 :     01 01 01 01 01 01 01 01 01 01
       1 :     02 01 01 01 01 01 01 01 01 01   ! DSCP 10 is mapped to WRED T2
       2 :     01 01 01 01 01 01 01 01 01 01
       3 :     01 01 01 01 01 01 01 01 01 01
       4 :     01 01 01 01 01 01 01 01 02 01   ! DSCP 48 is mapped to WRED T2
       5 :     01 01 01 01 01 01 02 01 01 01   ! DSCP 56 is mapped to WRED T2
       6 :     01 01 01 01

Cos-queue map:
cos-qid
 0 - 2            ! Best-Effort is assigned to Q2
 1 - 1            ! Scavenger and Bulk are assigned to Q1
 2 - 3            ! Transactional Data and Network Management are assigned to Q3
```

continues

Example 12-25 **show mls qos interface queueing** *Verification for a Catalyst 3550 Switch (Continued)*

```
3 - 3      ! Mission-Critical Data and Call-Signaling are assigned to Q3
4 - 3      ! Interactive- and Streaming-Video are assigned to Q3
5 - 4      ! Voice is assigned to the priority queue: Q4
6 - 3      ! Internetwork Control (Routing) is assigned to Q3
7 - 3      ! Network Control (Spanning Tree) is assigned to Q3
CAT3550#
```

Catalyst 2970/3560/3750 QoS Considerations and Design

The Catalyst 2970 does not support Layer 3 routing and, as such, is restricted to the role of an access-layer switch. The 3560 does support Layer 3 routing as well as inline power—a feature that is rarely, if ever, required at the distribution layer—and so will only be considered in an access-layer context. The Catalyst 3750 also supports Layer 3 routing and may be found in either the access layer or the distribution layer.

Figure 12-16 shows the QoS design options for access-layer Catalyst 2970s, 3560s, or 3750s, and Figure 12-17 shows the QoS design recommendations for a distribution-layer Catalyst 3750.

Figure 12-16 *Access-Layer Catalyst 2950/3560/3750 QoS Design*

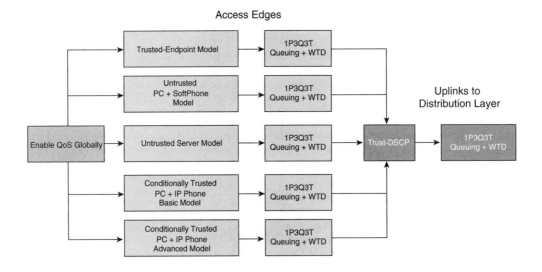

Figure 12-17 *Distribution-Layer Catalyst 3750 QoS Design*

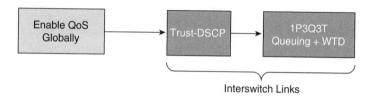

Because (as pointed out in Chapter 10, "Catalyst QoS Tools") the QoS features and configuration syntax are identical for the Catalyst 2970, 3560, and 3750, from a QoS design recommendation perspective they can be discussed as a single switch.

As with the Catalyst 3550, QoS is disabled globally by default on the Catalyst 2970/3560/ 3750. While QoS is disabled, all frames and packets are passed through the switch unaltered (which is equivalent to a trust CoS and trust DSCP state on all ports). When QoS is enabled globally, however, all DSCP and CoS values (by default) are set to 0 (which is equivalent to an untrusted state on all ports).

QoS must be enabled globally for configured policies to become effective. Example 12-26 shows how to verify whether QoS has been enabled and also how it can be enabled globally.

Example 12-26 *Enabling QoS Globally on the Catalyst 2970/3560/3750*

```
CAT2970#show mls qos
QoS is disabled
CAT2970#

CAT2970#configure terminal
Enter configuration commands, one per line.  End with CNTL/Z.
CAT2970(config)#mls qos
CAT2970(config)#end
CAT2970#

CAT2970#show mls qos
QoS is enabled
CAT2970#
```

Catalyst 2970/3560/3750: Trusted Endpoint Model

The Trusted Endpoint model configuration for the Catalyst 2970/3560/3750 is identical to the configuration of the switches previously discussed (namely, the Catalyst 2950 and 3550); it is shown in Example 12-27.

Example 12-27 *Catalyst 2970/3560/3750: Trusted Endpoint Example*

```
CAT2970(config)#interface GigabitEthernet0/1
CAT2970(config-if)#mls qos trust dscp
```

Catalyst MLS QoS verification commands:

- **show mls qos**
- **show mls qos interface**

Catalyst 2970/3560/3750: Untrusted PC with SoftPhone Model

The Untrusted PC with SoftPhone model configuration for the Catalyst 2970/3560/3750 is identical to the Catalyst 3550's for the same access edge model and is shown in Example 12-28.

Example 12-28 *Catalyst 2970/3560/3750: Untrusted PC with SoftPhone Example*

```
CAT2970(config)#mls qos map policed-dscp  0 24 46 to 8
          ! Excess traffic marked 0 or CS3 or EF will be remarked to CS1
CAT2970(config)#
CAT2970(config)#class-map match-all SOFTPHONE-VOICE
CAT2970(config-cmap)#  match access-group name SOFTPHONE-VOICE
CAT2970(config-cmap)#class-map match-all SOFTPHONE-SIGNALING
CAT2970(config-cmap)#  match access-group name SOFTPHONE-SIGNALING
CAT2970(config-cmap)#exit
CAT2970(config)#
CAT2970(config)#policy-map SOFTPHONE-PC
CAT2970(config-pmap)#class SOFTPHONE-VOICE
CAT2970(config-pmap-c)# set ip dscp 46      ! Softphone VoIP is marked to DSCP EF
CAT2970(config-pmap-c)# police 128000 8000 exceed-action policed-dscp-transmit
          ! Out-of-profile SoftPhone voice traffic is marked down to Scavenger (CS1)
CAT2970(config-pmap-c)#class SOFTPHONE-SIGNALING
CAT2970(config-pmap-c)# set ip dscp 24      ! Signaling is marked to DSCP CS3
CAT2970(config-pmap-c)# police 32000 8000 exceed-action policed-dscp-transmit
          ! Out-of-profile Signaling traffic is marked down to Scavenger (CS1)
CAT2970(config-pmap-c)#class class-default
CAT2970(config-pmap-c)# set ip dscp 0
CAT2970(config-pmap-c)# police 5000000 8000 exceed-action policed-dscp-transmit
          ! Out-of-profile data traffic is marked down to Scavenger (CS1)
CAT2970(config-pmap-c)# exit
CAT2970(config-pmap)#exit
CAT2970(config)#
CAT2970(config)#interface GigabitEthernet0/1
CAT2970(config-if)# service-policy input SOFTPHONE-PC  ! Applies policy to int
CAT2970(config-if)#exit
CAT2970(config)#
CAT2970(config)#ip access-list extended SOFTPHONE-VOICE
CAT2970(config-ext-nacl)# permit udp any any range 16384 32767 ! VoIP ports
CAT2970(config-ext-nacl)#
CAT2970(config-ext-nacl)#ip access-list extended SOFTPHONE-SIGNALING
CAT2970(config-ext-nacl)# permit tcp any any range 2000 2002   ! SCCP ports
CAT2970(config-ext-nacl)#end
CAT2970#
```

Catalyst MLS QoS verification commands:

- **show mls qos**
- **show mls qos map**
- **show mls qos interface**
- **show mls qos interface policers**
- **show class-map**
- **show policy-map**
- **show policy interface**

Catalyst 2970/3560/3750: Untrusted Server Model

The Untrusted Multiapplication Server model configuration for the Catalyst 2970/3560/3750 is identical to the configuration of the Catalyst 3550 and is shown in Example 12-29.

Example 12-29 *Catalyst 2970/3560/3750: Untrusted Multiapplication Server Example*

```
CAT2970(config)#mls qos map policed-dscp  0 10 18 25 to 8
  ! Excess traffic marked 0 or AF11 or AF21 or DSCP 25 will be remarked to CS1
CAT2970(config)#
CAT2970(config)#class-map SAP
CAT2970(config-cmap)# match access-group name SAP
CAT2970(config-cmap)#class-map LOTUS
CAT2970(config-cmap)# match access-group name LOTUS
CAT2970(config-cmap)#class-map IMAP
CAT2970(config-cmap)# match access-group name IMAP
CAT2970(config-cmap)#exit
CAT2970(config)#
CAT2970(config)#policy-map UNTRUSTED-SERVER
CAT2970(config-pmap)#class SAP
CAT2970(config-pmap-c)# set ip dscp 25      ! SAP is marked as Mission-Critical
CAT2970(config-pmap-c)# police 15000000 8000 exceed-action policed-dscp-transmit
     ! Out-of-profile SAP is marked down to Scavenger (CS1)
CAT2970(config-pmap-c)#class LOTUS
CAT2970(config-pmap-c)# set ip dscp 18      ! Lotus is marked as Transactional
CAT2970(config-pmap-c)# police 35000000 8000 exceed-action policed-dscp-transmit
     ! Out-of-profile LOTUS is marked down to Scavenger (CS1)
CAT2970(config-pmap-c)#class IMAP
CAT2970(config-pmap-c)# set ip dscp 10      ! IMAP is marked as Bulk Data
CAT2970(config-pmap-c)# police 50000000 8000 exceed-action policed-dscp-transmit
     ! Out-of-profile IMAP is marked down to Scavenger (CS1)
CAT2970(config-pmap-c)#class class-default
CAT2970(config-pmap-c)# set ip dscp 0
CAT2970(config-pmap-c)# police 1000000 8000 exceed-action policed-dscp-transmit
     ! Out-of-profile excess data traffic is marked down to Scavenger (CS1)
CAT2970(config-pmap-c)# exit
CAT2970(config-pmap)#exit
```

continues

Example 12-29 *Catalyst 2970/3560/3750: Untrusted Multiapplication Server Example (Continued)*

```
CAT2970(config)#
CAT2970(config)#interface GigabitEthernet0/1
CAT2970(config-if)# service-policy input UNTRUSTED-SERVER
CAT2970(config-if)#exit
CAT2970(config)#
CAT2970(config)#ip access-list extended SAP
CAT2970(config-ext-nacl)# permit tcp any range 3200 3203 any
CAT2970(config-ext-nacl)# permit tcp any eq 3600 any
CAT2970(config-ext-nacl)#
CAT2970(config-ext-nacl)#ip access-list extended LOTUS
CAT2970(config-ext-nacl)# permit tcp any eq 1352 any
CAT2970(config-ext-nacl)#
CAT2970(config-ext-nacl)#ip access-list extended IMAP
CAT2970(config-ext-nacl)# permit tcp any eq 143 any
CAT2970(config-ext-nacl)# permit tcp any eq 220 any
CAT2970(config-ext-nacl)#end
CAT2970#
```

Catalyst MLS QoS verification commands:

- **show mls qos**
- **show mls qos map**
- **show mls qos interface**
- **show mls qos interface policers**
- **show class-map**
- **show policy-map**
- **show policy interface**

Catalyst 2970/3560/3750: Conditionally Trusted IP Phone + PC: Basic Model

The Catalyst 2970/3560/3750 does not support per-port and per-VLAN policing at the time of this writing. Therefore, access lists are required to match Voice and Call-Signaling traffic sourced from the VVLAN. These ACLs require the administrator to specify the VVLAN subnet information. Example 12-30 shows the configuration for a Conditionally Trusted IP Phone + PC: Basic model for a Catalyst 2970/3560/3750.

Example 12-30 *Catalyst 2970/3560/3750: Conditionally Trusted IP Phone + PC: Basic Model Example*

```
CAT2970(config)#mls qos map cos-dscp 0 8 16 24 32 46 48 56
       ! Modifies CoS-to-DSCP mapping to map CoS 5 to DSCP EF
CAT2970(config)#mls qos map policed-dscp 0 24 to 8
       ! Excess VVLAN & DVLAN traffic will be remarked to Scavenger (CS1)
CAT2970(config)#
CAT2970(config)#
```

Example 12-30 *Catalyst 2970/3560/3750: Conditionally Trusted IP Phone + PC: Basic Model Example*

```
CAT2970(config)#class-map match-all VVLAN-VOICE
CAT2970(config-cmap)#  match access-group name VVLAN-VOICE
CAT2970(config-cmap)#
CAT2970(config-cmap)#class-map match-all VVLAN-CALL-SIGNALING
CAT2970(config-cmap)#  match access-group name VVLAN-CALL-SIGNALING
CAT2970(config-cmap)#
CAT2970(config-cmap)#class-map match-all VVLAN-ANY
CAT2970(config-cmap)#  match access-group name VVLAN-ANY
CAT2970(config-cmap)#
CAT2970(config-cmap)#
CAT2970(config-cmap)#policy-map IPPHONE+PC-BASIC
CAT2970(config-pmap)#class VVLAN-VOICE
CAT2970(config-pmap-c)# set ip dscp 46      ! DSCP EF (Voice)
CAT2970(config-pmap-c)# police 128000 8000 exceed-action drop
      ! Only one voice call is permitted per switchport VVLAN
CAT2970(config-pmap-c)#class VVLAN-CALL-SIGNALING
CAT2970(config-pmap-c)# set ip dscp 24      ! DSCP CS3 (Call-Signaling)
CAT2970(config-pmap-c)# police 32000 8000 exceed-action policed-dscp-transmit
      ! Out-of-profile Call-Signaling is marked down to Scavenger (CS1)
CAT2970(config-pmap-c)#class VVLAN-ANY
CAT2970(config-pmap-c)# set ip dscp 0
CAT2970(config-pmap-c)# police 32000 8000 exceed-action policed-dscp-transmit
       ! Unauthorized VVLAN traffic is marked down to Scavenger (CS1)
CAT2970(config-pmap-c)#class class-default
CAT2970(config-pmap-c)# set ip dscp 0
CAT2970(config-pmap-c)# police 5000000 8000 exceed-action policed-dscp-transmit
       ! Out-of-profile data traffic is marked down to Scavenger (CS1)
CAT2970(config-pmap-c)# exit
CAT2970(config-pmap)#exit
CAT2970(config)#
CAT2970(config)#
CAT2970(config)#interface GigabitEthernet0/1
CAT2970(config-if)# switchport access vlan 10          ! DVLAN
CAT2970(config-if)# switchport voice vlan 110           ! VVLAN
CAT2970(config-if)# mls qos trust device cisco-phone    ! Conditional Trust
CAT2970(config-if)# service-policy input IPPHONE+PC-BASIC  ! Attaches policy
CAT2970(config-if)#exit
CAT2970(config)#
CAT2970(config)#
CAT2970(config)#ip access-list extended VVLAN-VOICE
CAT2970(config-ext-nacl)#permit udp 10.1.110.0 0.0.0.255
       any range 16384 32767 dscp ef
       ! Voice is matched by VVLAN subnet and DSCP EF
CAT2970(config-ext-nacl)#exit
CAT2970(config)#
CAT2970(config)#ip access-list extended VVLAN-CALL-SIGNALING
CAT2970(config-ext-nacl)#permit tcp 10.1.110.0 0.0.0.255
       any range 2000 2002 dscp af31
       ! Call-Signaling is matched by VVLAN subnet and DSCP AF31
```

continues

Example 12-30 *Catalyst 2970/3560/3750: Conditionally Trusted IP Phone + PC: Basic Model Example*

```
CAT2970(config-ext-nacl)#permit tcp 10.1.110.0 0.0.0.255
     any range 2000 2002 dscp cs3
     ! Call-Signaling is matched by VVLAN subnet and DSCP CS3
CAT2970(config-ext-nacl)#exit
CAT2970(config)#
CAT2970(config)#ip access-list extended VVLAN-ANY
CAT2970(config-ext-nacl)# permit ip 10.1.110.0 0.0.0.255 any
     ! Matches all other traffic sourced from the VVLAN subnet
CAT2970(config-ext-nacl)#end
CAT2970#
```

Catalyst MLS QoS verification commands:

- **show mls qos**
- **show mls qos map**
- **show mls qos interface**
- **show mls qos interface policers**
- **show class-map**
- **show policy-map**
- **show policy interface**

Catalyst 2970/3560/3750: Conditionally Trusted IP Phone + PC: Advanced Model

Building on the previous model, PC applications, such as Interactive-Video, Mission-Critical Data, Transactional Data, and Bulk Data, are identified by access lists. Example 12-31 shows the configuration for the Conditionally Trusted IP Phone + PC Advanced model for the Catalyst 2970/3560/3750.

Example 12-31 *Catalyst 2970/3560/3750: Conditionally Trusted IP Phone + PC: Basic Model Example*

```
CAT2970(config)#mls qos map cos-dscp 0 8 16 24 32 46 48 56
     ! Modifies CoS-to-DSCP mapping to map CoS 5 to DSCP EF
CAT2970(config)#mls qos map policed-dscp 0 10 18 24 25 34 to 8
     ! Excess DVLAN traffic marked 0, AF11, AF21, CS3, DSCP 25
     ! and AF41 will be remarked to Scavenger (CS1)
CAT2970(config)#
CAT2970(config)#
CAT2970(config)#class-map match-all VVLAN-VOICE
CAT2970(config-cmap)#  match access-group name VVLAN-VOICE
CAT2970(config-cmap)#
CAT2970(config-cmap)#class-map match-all VVLAN-CALL-SIGNALING
CAT2970(config-cmap)#  match access-group name VVLAN-CALL-SIGNALING
CAT2970(config-cmap)#
CAT2970(config-cmap)#class-map match-all VVLAN-ANY
```

Example 12-31 *Catalyst 2970/3560/3750: Conditionally Trusted IP Phone + PC: Basic Model Example*

```
CAT2970(config-cmap)#  match access-group name VVLAN-ANY
CAT2970(config-cmap)#
CAT2970(config-cmap)#class-map match-all DVLAN-PC-VIDEO
CAT2970(config-cmap)# match access-group name DVLAN-PC-VIDEO
CAT2970(config-cmap)#
CAT2970(config-cmap)#class-map match-all DVLAN-MISSION-CRITICAL-DATA
CAT2970(config-cmap)# match access-group name DVLAN-MISSION-CRITICAL-DATA
CAT2970(config-cmap)#
CAT2970(config-cmap)#class-map match-all DVLAN-TRANSACTIONAL-DATA
CAT2970(config-cmap)# match access-group name DVLAN-TRANSACTIONAL-DATA
CAT2970(config-cmap)#
CAT2970(config-cmap)#class-map match-all DVLAN-BULK-DATA
CAT2970(config-cmap)# match access-group name DVLAN-BULK-DATA
CAT2970(config-cmap)#exit
CAT2970(config)#
CAT2970(config)#policy-map IPPHONE+PC-ADVANCED
CAT2970(config-pmap)#class VVLAN-VOICE
CAT2970(config-pmap-c)# set ip dscp 46      ! DSCP EF (Voice)
CAT2970(config-pmap-c)# police 128000 8000 exceed-action drop
       ! Only one voice call is permitted per switchport VVLAN
CAT2970(config-pmap-c)#class VVLAN-CALL-SIGNALING
CAT2970(config-pmap-c)# set ip dscp 24      ! DSCP CS3 (Call-Signaling)
CAT2970(config-pmap-c)# police 32000 8000 exceed-action policed-dscp-transmit
       ! Out-of-profile Call-Signaling is marked down to Scavenger (CS1)
CAT2970(config-pmap-c)#class VVLAN-ANY
CAT2970(config-pmap-c)# set ip dscp 0
CAT2970(config-pmap-c)# police 32000 8000 exceed-action policed-dscp-transmit
       ! Unauthorized VVLAN traffic is marked down to Scavenger (CS1)
CAT2970(config-pmap-c)#class DVLAN-PC-VIDEO
CAT2970(config-pmap-c)# set ip dscp 34      ! DSCP AF41 (Interactive-Video)
CAT2970(config-pmap-c)# police 496000 8000 exceed-action policed-dscp-transmit
       ! Only one IP/VC stream will be permitted per switchport
CAT2970(config-pmap-c)#class DVLAN-MISSION-CRITICAL-DATA
CAT2970(config-pmap-c)# set ip dscp 25      ! Interim Mission-Critical Data
CAT2970(config-pmap-c)# police 5000000 8000 exceed-action policed-dscp-transmit
       ! Out-of-profile Mission-Critical Data is marked down to Scavenger (CS1)
CAT2970(config-pmap-c)#class DVLAN-TRANSACTIONAL-DATA
CAT2970(config-pmap-c)# set ip dscp 18      ! DSCP AF21 (Transactional Data)
CAT2970(config-pmap-c)# police 5000000 8000 exceed-action policed-dscp-transmit
       ! Out-of-profile Transactional Data is marked down to Scavenger (CS1)
CAT2970(config-pmap-c)#class DVLAN-BULK-DATA
CAT2970(config-pmap-c)# set ip dscp 10      ! DSCP AF11 (Bulk Data)
CAT2970(config-pmap-c)# police 5000000 8000 exceed-action policed-dscp-transmit
       ! Out-of-profile Bulk Data is marked down to Scavenger (CS1)
CAT2970(config-pmap-c)#class class-default
CAT2970(config-pmap-c)# set ip dscp 0
CAT2970(config-pmap-c)# police 5000000 8000 exceed-action policed-dscp-transmit
       ! Out-of-profile data traffic is marked down to Scavenger (CS1)
CAT2970(config-pmap-c)# exit
CAT2970(config-pmap)#exit
```

continues

Example 12-31 *Catalyst 2970/3560/3750: Conditionally Trusted IP Phone + PC: Basic Model Example*

```
CAT2970(config)#
CAT2970(config)#interface GigabitEthernet0/1
CAT2970(config-if)# switchport access vlan 10                ! DVLAN
CAT2970(config-if)# switchport voice vlan 110                ! VVLAN
CAT2970(config-if)# mls qos trust device cisco-phone         ! Conditional Trust
CAT2970(config-if)# service-policy input IPPHONE+PC-ADVANCED ! Attaches Policy
CAT2970(config-if)#exit
CAT2970(config)#
CAT2970(config)#
CAT2970(config)#ip access-list extended VVLAN-VOICE
CAT2970(config-ext-nacl)#permit udp 10.1.110.0 0.0.0.255
       any range 16384 32767 dscp ef
             ! Voice is matched by VVLAN subnet and DSCP EF
CAT2970(config-ext-nacl)#exit
CAT2970(config)#
CAT2970(config)#ip access-list extended VVLAN-CALL-SIGNALING
CAT2970(config-ext-nacl)#permit tcp 10.1.110.0 0.0.0.255
       any range 2000 2002 dscp af31
CAT2970(config-ext-nacl)#permit tcp 10.1.110.0 0.0.0.255
       any range 2000 2002 dscp cs3
              ! Call-Signaling is matched by VVLAN subnet and DSCP AF31 or CS3
CAT2970(config-ext-nacl)#exit
CAT2970(config)#
CAT2970(config)#ip access-list extended VVLAN-ANY
CAT2970(config-ext-nacl)# permit ip 10.1.110.0 0.0.0.255 any
        ! Matches all other traffic sourced from the VVLAN subnet
CAT2970(config-ext-nacl)#
CAT2970(config-ext-nacl)#ip access-list extended DVLAN-PC-VIDEO
CAT2970(config-ext-nacl)# permit udp any any range 16384 32767    ! IP/VC
CAT2970(config-ext-nacl)#
CAT2970(config-ext-nacl)#ip access-list extended DVLAN-MISSION-CRITICAL-DATA
CAT2970(config-ext-nacl)# permit tcp any any range 3200 3203    · ! SAP
CAT2970(config-ext-nacl)# permit tcp any any eq 3600             ! SAP
CAT2970(config-ext-nacl)# permit tcp any any range 2000 2002     ! SCCP
CAT2970(config-ext-nacl)#
CAT2970(config-ext-nacl)#ip access-list extended DVLAN-TRANSACTIONAL-DATA
CAT2970(config-ext-nacl)# permit tcp any any eq 1352             ! Lotus
CAT2970(config-ext-nacl)#
CAT2970(config-ext-nacl)#ip access-list extended DVLAN-BULK-DATA
CAT2970(config-ext-nacl)# permit tcp any any eq 143              ! IMAP
CAT2970(config-ext-nacl)# permit tcp any any eq 220              ! IMAP
CAT2970(config-ext-nacl)#end
CAT2970#
```

Catalyst MLS QoS verification commands:

- **show mls qos**
- **show mls qos map**
- **show mls qos interface**

- **show mls qos interface policers**
- **show class-map**
- **show policy-map**
- **show policy interface**

Catalyst 2970/3560/3750: Queuing and Dropping

For the most part, the Catalyst 2970/3560/3750 is relatively compatible in QoS features and syntax with the Catalyst 3550, except with respect to per-port/per-VLAN policing and queuing/dropping.

The Catalyst 2970/3560/3750 supports four egress queues, which can be configured on a per-interface basis to operate in either 4Q3T or 1P3Q3T modes. Additionally, the Catalyst 2970/3560/3750 supports two queue sets, allowing certain interfaces to be configured in one manner and others to be configured in a different manner. For example, some interfaces can be assigned to queue set (qset) 1 operating in 4Q3T mode, while others can be assigned to queue set 2 operating in 1P3Q3T mode.

However, unlike the Catalyst 2950 and 3550, the Catalyst 2970/3560/3750 has queue 1 (not queue 4) as the optional priority queue. In a converged campus environment, it is recommended to enable the priority queue using the **priority-queue out** interface command.

NOTE   The Catalyst 2970/3560/3750 also supports two configurable ingress queues (normal and expedite). Ingress scheduling, however, is rarely, if ever, required because it becomes enabled only if the combined input rates from any switch port exceeds the switch fabric's capacity. Such cases are extremely difficult to achieve, even in controlled lab environments. In the extreme case that such a scenario should develop in a production environment, the default settings of the ingress queues are acceptable for maintaining VoIP quality and network availability.

The three remaining egress queues on the Catalyst 2970/3560/3750 are scheduled by a *shaped round-robin* (SRR) algorithm, which can be configured to operate in shaped mode or in shared mode. In shaped mode, assigned bandwidth is limited to the defined amount; in shared mode, any unused bandwidth is shared among other classes (as needed).

Shaped or shared bandwidth weights can be assigned to a queue using the **srr-queue bandwidth shape** and **srr-queue bandwidth share** interface commands. Shaped-mode weights override shared-mode weights. Also, if shaped weights are set to 0, the queue is operating in shared mode.

To make the queuing structure consistent with examples provided for previously discussed platforms, queues 2 through 4 should be set to operate in shared mode (which is the default mode of operation on queues 2 through 4). The ratio of the shared weights determines the relative bandwidth allocations (the absolute values are meaningless). Because the PQ of the Catalyst 2970/3560/3750 is Q1 (not Q4, as in the Catalyst 3550), the entire queuing model can be flipped upside down, with Q2 representing the critical data queue, Q3 representing the Best-Effort queue, and Q1 representing the Scavenger queue. Therefore, shared weights of 70, 25, and 5 percent can be assigned to queues 2, 3, and 4, respectively.

NOTE	Although the Catalyst 2970/3560/3750 supports the tweaking of queue buffers, testing has shown that this can interfere with ingress policing policies (on Catalyst IOS versions 12.2[19]EA1a–d and 12.2[18]SE for the Catalyst 2970). Furthermore, adjusting the default thresholds on the Catalyst 3750 sometimes causes similar interference with ingress policing policies (on Catalyst IOS versions 12.2[19]EA1a–d and 12.2[18]SE for the Catalyst 3750).

Additionally, the Catalyst 2970/3560/3750 supports three weighted tail drop (WTD) thresholds per queue. Two of these thresholds are configurable (explicit); the third is nonconfigurable (implicit) because it is set to the queue-full state (100 percent). These thresholds can be defined with the **mls qos queue-set output qset-id threshold** global command. The only queues that these thresholds need to define (away from defaults) are queues 2 and 4. In queue 2, it is recommended to set the first threshold to 70 percent and the second to 80 percent, which leaves the third (implicit) threshold set at 100 percent (the tail of the queue). In queue 4, it is recommended to set the first threshold to 40 percent, leaving the default values for both the second and third thresholds at 100 percent.

After the queues and thresholds have been defined, traffic can be assigned to queues and thresholds by either CoS values or DSCP values, using the **mls qos srr-queue output cos-map queue** and **mls qos srr-queue output dscp-map queue** global commands, respectively. Although DSCP-to-queue/threshold maps override CoS-to-queue/threshold maps, these mappings should be as consistent as possible, to ensure predictable behavior and simplify troubleshooting.

That being said, CoS 0/DSCP 0 (Best-Effort traffic) should be mapped to queue 3 threshold 3 (the tail of the queue) because no other traffic is to be assigned to queue 3.

CoS 1 (Scavenger and Bulk Data) should be mapped to queue 4 threshold 3. Scavenger traffic can then be contained further by a DSCP-to-queue/threshold mapping assigning DSCP CS1 to queue 4 threshold 1 (previously set at 40 percent); Bulk Data using DSCP values AF11, AF12, or AF13 (decimal values 10, 12, and 14, respectively) can use the remainder of the queue. Bulk Data can use either threshold 2 or threshold 3 as its WTD limit (both of which are set to 100 percent).

CoS 2 and DSCP CS2, AF21, AF22, and AF23 (decimal values 16, 18, 20, and 22, respectively) can be assigned to queue 2 threshold 1 (previously set at 70 percent). This limits Network-Management and Transactional Data to a subset of queue 2. The temporary marking value for Mission-Critical Data traffic, DSCP 25, also should be assigned to queue 2 threshold 1.

CoS 3, along with DSCP CS3 and AF31 (decimal values 24 and 26, respectively) can be assigned to queue 2 threshold 2 (previously set to 80 percent). This allows for preferential treatment of Call-Signaling traffic within queue 2.

CoS 4 and DSCP CS4, AF41, AF42, and AF43 (decimal values 32, 34, 36, and 38, respectively) can be assigned to queue 2 threshold 1. In this manner, video (both interactive and streaming) will not drown out Call-Signaling or Network and Internetwork Control traffic within queue 2.

CoS 5 and DSCP EF (decimal value 46) should be assigned to queue 1 threshold 3 because Voice is the only traffic to be assigned to the strict-priority queue.

CoS 6 and DSCP CS6 (decimal value 48), and CoS 7 and DSCP CS7 (decimal value 56) should be assigned to queue 2 threshold 3. In this manner, there will always be some room available in queue 2 to service Network and Internetwork Control traffic.

Figure 12-18 illustrates these recommended Catalyst 2970/3560/3750 assignments from CoS/DSCP to queues/thresholds.

Figure 12-18 *Catalyst 2970/3550 1P3Q3T Queuing Model*

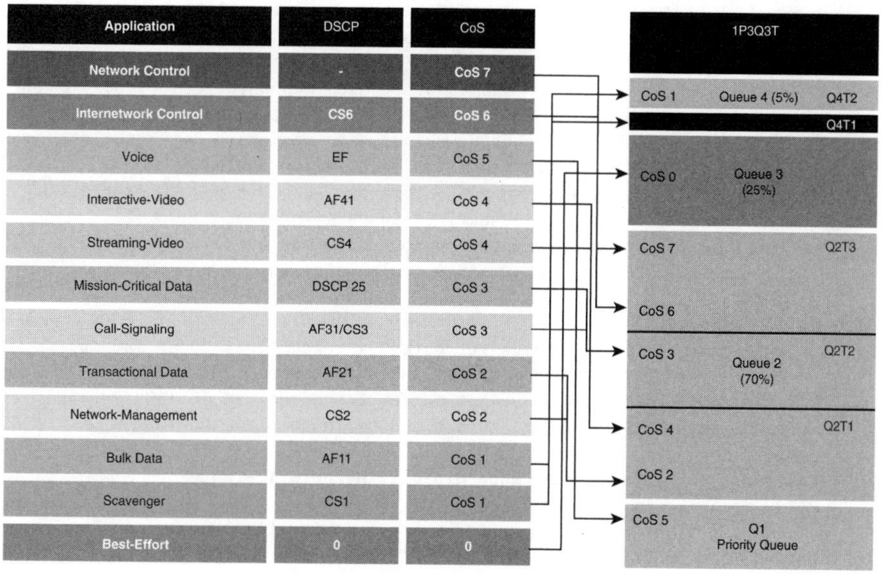

Example 12-32 shows the Catalyst 2970/3560/3750 queuing and dropping configuration recommendations.

Example 12-32 *Catalyst 2970/3560/3750: Queuing and Dropping Example*

```
CAT2970(config)#mls qos srr-queue output cos-map queue 1 threshold 3  5
        ! Maps CoS 5 to Queue 1 Threshold 3 (Voice gets all of Queue 1)
CAT2970(config)#mls qos srr-queue output cos-map queue 2 threshold 1  2 4
        ! Maps CoS 2 and CoS 4 to Queue 2 Threshold 1
CAT2970(config)#mls qos srr-queue output cos-map queue 2 threshold 2  3
        ! Maps CoS 3 to Queue 2 Threshold 2
CAT2970(config)#mls qos srr-queue output cos-map queue 2 threshold 3  6 7
        ! Maps CoS 6 and CoS 7 to Queue 2 Threshold 3
CAT2970(config)#mls qos srr-queue output cos-map queue 3 threshold 3  0
        ! Maps CoS 0 to Queue 3 Threshold 3 (Best Efforts gets all of Q3)
CAT2970(config)#mls qos srr-queue output cos-map queue 4 threshold 3  1
        ! Maps CoS1 to Queue 4 Threshold 3 (Scavenger/Bulk gets all of Q4)
CAT2970(config)#
CAT2970(config)#
CAT2970(config)#mls qos srr-queue output dscp-map queue 1 threshold 3  46
        ! Maps DSCP EF (Voice) to Queue 1 Threshold 3
CAT2970(config)#mls qos srr-queue output dscp-map queue 2 threshold 1  16
        ! Maps DSCP CS2 (Network Management) to Queue 2 Threshold 1
CAT2970(config)#mls qos srr-queue output dscp-map queue 2 threshold 1  18 20 22
        ! Maps DSCP AF21, AF22, AF23 (Transactional Data) to Queue 2 Threshold 1
CAT2970(config)#mls qos srr-queue output dscp-map queue 2 threshold 1  25
        ! Maps DSCP 25 (Mission-Critical Data) to Queue 2 Threshold 1
CAT2970(config)#mls qos srr-queue output dscp-map queue 2 threshold 1  32
        ! Maps DSCP CS4 (Streaming Video) to Queue 2 Threshold 1
CAT2970(config)#mls qos srr-queue output dscp-map queue 2 threshold 1  34 36 38
        ! Maps DSCP AF41, AF42, AF43 (Interactive-Video) to Queue 2 Threshold 1
CAT2970(config)#mls qos srr-queue output dscp-map queue 2 threshold 2  24 26
        ! Maps DSCP CS3 and DSCP AF31 (Call-Signaling) to Queue 2 Threshold 2
CAT2970(config)#mls qos srr-queue output dscp-map queue 2 threshold 3  48 56
        ! Maps DSCP CS6 and CS7 (Network/Internetwork) to Queue 2 Threshold 3
CAT2970(config)#mls qos srr-queue output dscp-map queue 3 threshold 3  0
        ! Maps DSCP 0 (Best Effort) to Queue 3 Threshold 3
CAT2970(config)#mls qos srr-queue output dscp-map queue 4 threshold 1  8
        ! Maps DSCP CS1 (Scavenger) to Queue 4 Threshold 1
CAT2970(config)#mls qos srr-queue output dscp-map queue 4 threshold 3  10 12 14
        ! Maps DSCP AF11, AF12, AF13 (Bulk Data) to Queue 4 Threshold 3
CAT2970(config)#
CAT2970(config)#
CAT2970(config)#mls qos queue-set output 1 threshold 2 70 80 100 100
        ! Sets Q2 Threshold 1 to 70% and Q2 Threshold 2 to 80%
CAT2970(config)#mls qos queue-set output 1 threshold 4 40 100 100 100
        ! Sets Q4 Threshold 1 to 40% and Q4 Threshold 2 to 100%
CAT2970(config)#
CAT2970(config)#interface range GigabitEthernet0/1 - 28
CAT2970(config-if-range)# queue-set 1
        ! Assigns interface to Queue-Set 1 (default)
CAT2970(config-if-range)# srr-queue bandwidth share 1 70 25 5
        ! Q2 gets 70% of remaining BW; Q3 gets 25% and Q4 gets 5%
```

Example 12-32 *Catalyst 2970/3560/3750: Queuing and Dropping Example (Continued)*

```
CAT2970(config-if-range)# srr-queue bandwidth shape 30 0 0 0
      ! Q1 is limited to 30% of the total available BW
CAT2970(config-if-range)# priority-queue out
      ! Q1 is enabled as a PQ
CAT2970(config-if-range)#end
CAT2970#
```

Catalyst MLS QoS verification commands:

- **show mls qos interface buffers**
- **show mls qos interface queueing**
- **show mls qos queue-set**
- **show mls qos maps cos-output-q**
- **show mls qos maps dscp-output-q**

Catalyst MLS QoS Verification Command: **show mls qos queue-set**

The **show mls qos queue-set** verification command returns the configured buffer allocations and defined thresholds for each queue set.

In Example 12-33, each queue has a default buffer allocation of 25 percent. Additionally, all WTD thresholds are set to 100 percent (the tail of the queue), except for queue 2 threshold 1 (set to 70 percent), queue 2 threshold 2 (set to 80 percent), and queue 4 threshold 1 (set to 40 percent).

Example 12-33 show mls qos queue-set *Verification for a Catalyst 2970/3560/3750 Switch*

```
CAT2970#show mls qos queue-set 1
Queueset: 1
Queue      :      1      2      3      4
---------------------------------------------
buffers    :     25     25     25     25
threshold1:     100     70    100     40
threshold2:     100     80    100    100
reserved   :      50    100     50    100
maximum    :     400    100    400    100
CAT2970#
```

Catalyst MLS QoS Verification Command: **show mls qos maps cos-output-q**

The **show mls qos maps cos-output-q** verification command truncates the **show mls qos maps** output to report only the CoS-to-queue/threshold mappings for egress queues.

In Example 12-34, CoS 0 is mapped to Q3T3, CoS 1 is mapped to Q4T3, CoS 2 is mapped to Q2T1, CoS 3 is mapped to Q2T2, CoS 4 is mapped to Q2T1, CoS 5 is mapped to Q1T3 (the PQ), and CoS 6 and CoS 7 are mapped to Q2T3.

Example 12-34 show mls qos maps cos-output-q *Verification for a Catalyst 2970/3560/3750 Switch*

```
CAT2970#show mls qos maps cos-output-q
  Cos-outputq-threshold map:
              cos:  0   1   2   3   4   5   6   7
              ------------------------------------
  queue-threshold: 3-3 4-3 2-1 2-2 2-1 1-3 2-3 2-3
CAT2970#
```

Catalyst MLS QoS Verification Command: **show mls qos maps dscp-output-q**

The **show mls qos maps dscp-output-q** verification command truncates the **show mls qos maps** output to report only the DSCP-to-queue/threshold mappings for egress queues. The output is shown in tabular form, with the first digit of the decimal DSCP value in rows and the second digit in columns.

In Example 12-35, only standard DSCP PHBs are being mapped away from the default settings (with the exception of the temporary marking of DSCP 25 for Mission-Critical Data). The other nonstandard values can be mapped to reflect the CoS-to-queue mappings, but, for example simplicity, this has not been done in this case.

Specifically, DSCP 0 is mapped to Q3T3; DSCP CS1 (8) is mapped to Q4T1; DSCP AF11, AF12, and AF13 (10, 12, 14) are mapped to Q4T3; DSCP CS2 (16) is mapped to Q2T1, as are DSCP AF21, AF22, and AF23 (18, 20, 22); DSCP CS3 (24) and AF31 (26) are mapped to Q2T2; DSCP CS4 (32) is mapped to Q2T1, as are DSCP AF41, AF42, and AF43 (34, 36, 38); DSCP EF (46) is mapped to Q1T3 (the PQ); and DSCP CS6 (48) and CS7 (56) are mapped to Q2T3. The nonstandard DSCP 25 is mapped to Q2T1.

Example 12-35 show mls qos maps dscp-output-q *Verification for a Catalyst 2970/3560/3750 Switch*

```
CAT2970#show mls qos maps dscp-output-q
  Dscp-outputq-threshold map:
    d1 :d2    0     1     2     3     4     5     6     7     8     9
    ---------------------------------------------------------------------
     0 :    03-03 02-01 02-01 02-01 02-01 02-01 02-01 02-01 04-01 02-01
     1 :    04-03 02-01 04-03 02-01 04-03 02-01 02-01 03-01 02-01 03-01
     2 :    02-01 03-01 02-01 03-01 02-02 02-01 02-02 03-01 03-01 03-01
     3 :    03-01 03-01 02-01 04-01 02-01 04-01 02-01 04-01 02-01 04-01
     4 :    01-01 01-01 01-01 01-01 01-01 01-01 01-03 01-01 02-03 04-01
     5 :    04-01 04-01 04-01 04-01 04-01 04-01 02-03 04-01 04-01 04-01
     6 :    04-01 04-01 04-01 04-01
CAT2970#
```

Catalyst 4500-SupII+/III/IV/V QoS Considerations and Design

The Catalyst 4500 with Supervisors II+ through V can be found at either the access layer or the distribution layer of the campus. Furthermore, because of their high performance, they also can be found at the core layer of some campus networks.

Figure 12-19 shows the QoS design options for access-layer Catalyst 4500 design; Figure 12-20 shows the distribution- and core-layer recommendations.

Figure 12-19 *Access-Layer Catalyst 4500 QoS Design*

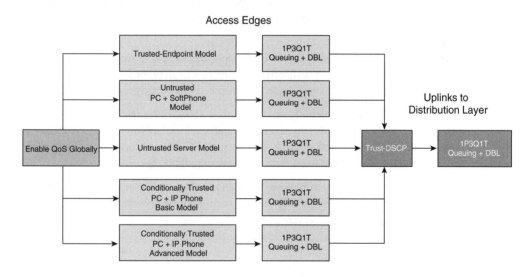

Figure 12-20 *Distribution- and Core-Layer Catalyst 4500 QoS Design*

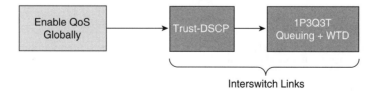

NOTE   To narrow the scope of this discussion to the most current and relevant versions of the
Catalyst 4500 switch family, only the only the Catalyst 4500 with Supervisors II+ through
V is examined is examined in this design chapter. For discussions about older versions of
Catalyst 4000/4500s, refer to the Cisco Press book *Cisco Catalyst QoS: Quality of Service
in Campus Networks*, by Mike Flannagan, Richard Froom, and Kevin Turek.

Much of the Catalyst MLS QoS syntax is supported on the Catalyst 4500; however, the **mls**
prefix keyword usually is omitted from the configuration commands. For example, as with
the Catalyst 3550 and 2970/3560/3750, QoS is disabled globally on the Catalyst 4500, by
default. However, the command to enable QoS globally on a Catalyst 4500 is simply **qos**,
not **mls qos**.

The verification commands are issued in the same manner: with the **mls** keyword omitted.
Generally, **show mls qos [...]** verification commands from other Catalyst platforms are
translated to **show qos [...]** verification commands on the Catalyst 4500 platforms.

Although QoS is disabled globally on the Catalyst 4500, all frames and packets are passed
through the switch unaltered (which is equivalent to a trust CoS and trust DSCP state on all
ports). When QoS is enabled globally, however, all DSCP and CoS values (by default) are
set to 0 (which is equivalent to an untrusted state on all ports).

Example 12-36 shows the verification command to check whether QoS has been globally
enabled on the Catalyst 4500, along with the configuration command to do so.

Example 12-36 *Enabling QoS Globally on the Catalyst 4500*

```
CAT4500#show qos
QoS is disabled globally
IP header DSCP rewrite is enabled
CAT4500#

CAT4500#configure terminal
Enter configuration commands, one per line.  End with CNTL/Z.
CAT4500(config)#qos
CAT4500(config)#end
CAT4500#

CAT4500#show qos
QoS is enabled globally
IP header DSCP rewrite is enabled
CAT4500#
```

Catalyst 4500: Trusted Endpoint Model

To enable a given Catalyst 4500 interface to trust the DSCP markings of an endpoint, the **qos trust dscp** interface command is used, as shown in Example 12-37.

Example 12-37 *Catalyst 4500: Trusted Endpoint Example*

```
CAT4500(config)#interface FastEthernet2/1
CAT4500(config-if)# qos trust dscp
CAT4500(config-if)#end
CAT4500#
```

Catalyst 4500 QoS verification commands:

- **show qos**
- **show qos interface**

NOTE   Because most Catalyst 4500 verification commands are reasonably similar to the MLS QoS verification commands previously discussed (albeit without the **mls** keyword), to minimize redundancy, the MLS QoS verification commands that already have been detailed are not repeated in this section.

Catalyst 4500: Untrusted PC with SoftPhone Model

The Untrusted PC with SoftPhone access edge model for Catalyst 4500s, shown in Example 12-38, is similar to the examples given for previously discussed platforms. A few distinctions exist, such as the absence of the **mls** keyword in defining the policed-DSCP map (along with some slight syntax variation for this command) and the (optional) use of **kbps** and **mbps** (denoting kilobits and megabits, respectively) within the policing statements.

Example 12-38 *Catalyst 4500: Untrusted PC with SoftPhone Model Example*

```
CAT4500-SUP4(config)#qos map dscp policed 0 24 46 to dscp 8
     ! Excess traffic marked 0 or CS3 or EF will be remarked to CS1
CAT4500-SUP4(config)#
CAT4500-SUP4(config)#class-map match-all SOFTPHONE-SIGNALING
CAT4500-SUP4(config-cmap)# match access-group name SOFTPHONE-SIGNALING
CAT4500-SUP4(config-cmap)#class-map match-all SOFTPHONE-VOICE
CAT4500-SUP4(config-cmap)# match access-group name SOFTPHONE-VOICE
CAT4500-SUP4(config-cmap)#exit
CAT4500-SUP4(config)#
CAT4500-SUP4(config)#policy-map SOFTPHONE-PC
CAT4500-SUP4(config-pmap)# class SOFTPHONE-VOICE
```

continues

Example 12-38 *Catalyst 4500: Untrusted PC with SoftPhone Model Example (Continued)*

```
CAT4500-SUP4(config-pmap-c)# set ip dscp ef
    ! Softphone VoIP is marked to DSCP EF
CAT4500-SUP4(config-pmap-c)# police 128 kbps 8000 byte exceed-action
       policed-dscp-transmit
    ! Out-of-profile SoftPhone voice traffic is marked down to Scavenger (CS1)
CAT4500-SUP4(config-pmap-c)#class SOFTPHONE-SIGNALING
CAT4500-SUP4(config-pmap-c)# set ip dscp cs3
    ! SoftPhone Call-Signaling is marked to DSCP CS3
CAT4500-SUP4(config-pmap-c)# police 32 kbps 8000 byte exceed-action
       policed-dscp-transmit
    ! Out-of-profile Signaling traffic is marked down to Scavenger (CS1)
CAT4500-SUP4(config-pmap-c)#class class-default
CAT4500-SUP4(config-pmap-c)# set ip dscp default
CAT4500-SUP4(config-pmap-c)# police 5 mbps 8000 byte exceed-action
       policed-dscp-transmit
    ! Out-of-profile data traffic is marked down to Scavenger (CS1)
CAT4500-SUP4(config-pmap-c)#exit
CAT4500-SUP4(config)#
CAT4500-SUP4(config)#interface FastEthernet2/1
CAT4500-SUP4(config-if)# service-policy input SOFTPHONE-PC      ! Applies policy
CAT4500-SUP4(config-if)#exit
CAT4500-SUP4(config)#
CAT4500-SUP4(config)#ip access-list extended SOFTPHONE-VOICE
CAT4500-SUP4(config-ext-nacl)# permit udp any any range 16384 32767     ! VoIP
CAT4500-SUP4(config-ext-nacl)#
CAT4500-SUP4(config-ext-nacl)#ip access-list extended SOFTPHONE-SIGNALING
CAT4500-SUP4(config-ext-nacl)# permit tcp any any range 2000 2002       ! SCCP
CAT4500-SUP4(config-ext-nacl)#end
CAT4500-SUP4#
```

Catalyst 4500 QoS verification commands:

- **show qos**
- **show qos maps**
- **show qos interface**
- **show class-map**
- **show policy-map**
- **show policy interface**

Catalyst 4500: Untrusted Server Model

Example 12-39 shows the Catalyst 4500 Untrusted Multiapplication Server model. The main changes for the Catalyst 4500 for this model are the syntax defining the policed-DSCP map and the policer definitions (using the abbreviation **mbps** for megabits per second).

Example 12-39 *Catalyst 4500: Untrusted Multiapplication Server Model Example*

```
CAT4500-SUP4(config)#qos map dscp policed 0 10 18 25 to dscp 8
        ! Excess traffic marked 0 or AF11 or AF21 or DSCP 25 will be remarked to CS1
CAT4500-SUP4(config)#
CAT4500-SUP4(config)#class-map SAP
CAT4500-SUP4(config-cmap)# match access-group name SAP
CAT4500-SUP4(config-cmap)#
CAT4500-SUP4(config-cmap)#class-map LOTUS
CAT4500-SUP4(config-cmap)# match access-group name LOTUS
CAT4500-SUP4(config-cmap)#
CAT4500-SUP4(config-cmap)#class-map IMAP
CAT4500-SUP4(config-cmap)# match access-group name IMAP
CAT4500-SUP4(config-cmap)#exit
CAT4500-SUP4(config)#
CAT4500-SUP4(config)#policy-map UNTRUSTED-SERVER
CAT4500-SUP4(config-pmap)#class SAP
CAT4500-SUP4(config-pmap-c)# set ip dscp 25
        ! SAP is marked as Mission-Critical (DSCP 25)
CAT4500-SUP4(config-pmap-c)#  police 15 mbps 8000 byte exceed-action
        policed-dscp-transmit
        ! Out-of-profile SAP is marked down to Scavenger (CS1)
CAT4500-SUP4(config-pmap-c)#class LOTUS
CAT4500-SUP4(config-pmap-c)# set ip dscp 18
        ! Lotus is marked as Transactional Data (DSCP AF21)
CAT4500-SUP4(config-pmap-c)#  police 35 mbps 8000 byte exceed-action
        policed-dscp-transmit
        ! Out-of-profile LOTUS is marked down to Scavenger (CS1)
CAT4500-SUP4(config-pmap-c)#class IMAP
CAT4500-SUP4(config-pmap-c)# set ip dscp 10
        ! IMAP is marked as Bulk Data (DSCP AF11)
CAT4500-SUP4(config-pmap-c)#  police 50 mbps 8000 byte exceed-action
        policed-dscp-transmit
        ! Out-of-profile IMAP is marked down to Scavenger (CS1)
CAT4500-SUP4(config-pmap-c)#class class-default
CAT4500-SUP4(config-pmap-c)# set ip dscp 0
CAT4500-SUP4(config-pmap-c)#  police 1 mbps 8000 byte exceed-action
        policed-dscp-transmit
        ! Out-of-profile excess data traffic is marked down to Scavenger (CS1)
CAT4500-SUP4(config-pmap-c)# exit
CAT4500-SUP4(config-pmap)#exit
CAT4500-SUP4(config)#
CAT4500-SUP4(config)#
CAT4500-SUP4(config)#interface FastEthernet2/1
CAT4500-SUP4(config-if)# service-policy input UNTRUSTED-SERVER
CAT4500-SUP4(config-if)#exit
CAT4500-SUP4(config)#
CAT4500-SUP4(config)#
CAT4500-SUP4(config)#ip access-list extended SAP
CAT4500-SUP4(config-ext-nacl)# permit tcp any range 3200 3203 any
CAT4500-SUP4(config-ext-nacl)# permit tcp any eq 3600 any
CAT4500-SUP4(config-ext-nacl)#
```

continues

Example 12-39 *Catalyst 4500: Untrusted Multiapplication Server Model Example (Continued)*

```
CAT4500-SUP4(config-ext-nacl)#ip access-list extended LOTUS
CAT4500-SUP4(config-ext-nacl)# permit tcp any eq 1352 any
CAT4500-SUP4(config-ext-nacl)#
CAT4500-SUP4(config-ext-nacl)#ip access-list extended IMAP
CAT4500-SUP4(config-ext-nacl)# permit tcp any eq 143 any
CAT4500-SUP4(config-ext-nacl)# permit tcp any eq 220 any
CAT4500-SUP4(config-ext-nacl)#end
CAT4500-SUP4#
```

Catalyst 4500 QoS verification commands:

- **show qos**
- **show qos maps**
- **show qos interface**
- **show class-map**
- **show policy-map**
- **show policy interface**

Catalyst 4500: Conditionally Trusted IP Phone + PC: Basic Model

At the time of this writing, the Catalyst 4500 does not support per-port/per-VLAN policing. Therefore, access lists that include the VVLAN subnet are required to achieve granular policing of the VVLAN and DVLAN subnets, as shown in Example 12-40.

Example 12-40 *Catalyst 4500: Conditionally Trusted IP Phone + PC: Basic Model Example*

```
CAT4500-SUP4(config)#qos map cos 5 to dscp 46
     ! Modifies CoS-to-DSCP mapping to map CoS 5 to DSCP EF
CAT4500-SUP4(config)#qos map dscp policed 0 24 to dscp 8
     ! Excess DVLAN & VVLAN traffic will be marked down to Scavenger (CS1)
CAT4500-SUP4(config)#
CAT4500-SUP4(config)#
CAT4500-SUP4(config)#class-map match-all VVLAN-VOICE
CAT4500-SUP4(config-cmap)# match access-group name VVLAN-VOICE
CAT4500-SUP4(config-cmap)#
CAT4500-SUP4(config-cmap)#class-map match-all VVLAN-CALL-SIGNALING
CAT4500-SUP4(config-cmap)# match access-group name VVLAN-CALL-SIGNALING
CAT4500-SUP4(config-cmap)#
CAT4500-SUP4(config-cmap)#class-map match-all VVLAN-ANY
CAT4500-SUP4(config-cmap)# match access-group name VVLAN-ANY
CAT4500-SUP4(config-cmap)#
CAT4500-SUP4(config-cmap)#
CAT4500-SUP4(config-cmap)#policy-map IPPHONE+PC-BASIC
CAT4500-SUP4(config-pmap)#class VVLAN-VOICE
CAT4500-SUP4(config-pmap-c)# set ip dscp 46          ! DSCP EF (Voice)
CAT4500-SUP4(config-pmap-c)# police 128 kbps 8000 byte exceed-action drop
     ! Only one voice call is permitted per switchport VVLAN
```

Example 12-40 *Catalyst 4500: Conditionally Trusted IP Phone + PC: Basic Model Example (Continued)*

```
CAT4500-SUP4(config-pmap-c)#class VVLAN-CALL-SIGNALING
CAT4500-SUP4(config-pmap-c)# set ip dscp 24          ! DSCP CS3 (Call-Signaling)
CAT4500-SUP4(config-pmap-c)# police 32 kbps 8000 byte exceed-action
        policed-dscp-transmit
    ! Out-of-profile Call-Signaling is marked down to Scavenger (CS1)
CAT4500-SUP4(config-pmap-c)#class VVLAN-ANY
CAT4500-SUP4(config-pmap-c)# set ip dscp 0
CAT4500-SUP4(config-pmap-c)# police 32 kbps 8000 byte exceed-action
        policed-dscp-transmit
    ! Unauthorized VVLAN traffic is marked down to Scavenger (CS1)
CAT4500-SUP4(config-pmap-c)#class class-default
CAT4500-SUP4(config-pmap-c)# set ip dscp 0
CAT4500-SUP4(config-pmap-c)# police 5 mbps 8000 byte exceed-action
        policed-dscp-transmit
    ! Out-of-profile data traffic is marked down to Scavenger (CS1)
CAT4500-SUP4(config-pmap-c)# exit
CAT4500-SUP4(config-pmap)#exit
CAT4500-SUP4(config)#
CAT4500-SUP4(config)#
CAT4500-SUP4(config)#interface FastEthernet2/1
CAT4500-SUP4(config-if)# switchport access vlan 10          ! DVLAN
CAT4500-SUP4(config-if)# switchport voice vlan 110           ! VVLAN
CAT4500-SUP4(config-if)# qos trust device cisco-phone        ! Conditional Trust
CAT4500-SUP4(config-if)# service-policy input IPPHONE+PC-BASIC   ! MQC Policy
CAT4500-SUP4(config-if)#exit
CAT4500-SUP4(config)#
CAT4500-SUP4(config)#
CAT4500-SUP4(config)#ip access-list extended VVLAN-VOICE
CAT4500-SUP4(config-ext-nacl)# permit udp 10.1.110.0 0.0.0.255 any
        range 16384 32767
    ! Voice is matched by VVLAN subnet and UDP port-range
CAT4500-SUP4(config-ext-nacl)#exit
CAT4500-SUP4(config)#
CAT4500-SUP4(config)#ip access-list extended VVLAN-CALL-SIGNALING
CAT4500-SUP4(config-ext-nacl)# permit tcp 10.1.110.0 0.0.0.255 any
        range 2000 2002
    ! Call-Signaling is matched by VVLAN subnet and TCP port-range
CAT4500-SUP4(config-ext-nacl)#exit
CAT4500-SUP4(config)#
CAT4500-SUP4(config)#ip access-list extended VVLAN-ANY
CAT4500-SUP4(config-ext-nacl)# permit ip 10.1.110.0 0.0.0.255 any
    ! Matches all other traffic sourced from the VVLAN subnet
CAT4500-SUP4(config-ext-nacl)#end
CAT4500-SUP4#
```

Catalyst 4500 QoS verification commands:

- **show qos**
- **show qos maps**
- **show qos interface**

- **show class-map**
- **show policy-map**
- **show policy interface**

Catalyst 4500: Conditionally Trusted IP Phone + PC: Advanced Model

Building on the previous model, PC applications such as Interactive-Video, Mission-Critical Data, Transactional Data, and Bulk Data are identified by access lists. Example 12-41 shows the configuration for the Conditionally Trusted IP Phone + PC: Advanced model for the Catalyst 4500.

Example 12-41 *Catalyst 4500: Conditionally Trusted IP Phone + PC: Advanced Model Example*

```
CAT4500-SUP4(config)#qos map cos 5 to dscp 46
     ! Modifies CoS-to-DSCP mapping to map CoS 5 to DSCP EF
CAT4500-SUP4(config)#qos map dscp policed 0 10 18 24 25 34 to dscp 8
     ! Excess DVLAN traffic marked 0, AF11, AF21, CS3, DSCP 25
     ! and AF41 will be remarked to Scavenger (CS1)
CAT4500-SUP4(config)#
CAT4500-SUP4(config)#
CAT4500-SUP4(config)#class-map match-all VVLAN-VOICE
CAT4500-SUP4(config-cmap)#  match access-group name VVLAN-VOICE
CAT4500-SUP4(config-cmap)#
CAT4500-SUP4(config-cmap)#class-map match-all VVLAN-CALL-SIGNALING
CAT4500-SUP4(config-cmap)#  match access-group name VVLAN-CALL-SIGNALING
CAT4500-SUP4(config-cmap)#
CAT4500-SUP4(config-cmap)#class-map match-all VVLAN-ANY
CAT4500-SUP4(config-cmap)#  match access-group name VVLAN-ANY
CAT4500-SUP4(config-cmap)#
CAT4500-SUP4(config-cmap)#class-map match-all DVLAN-PC-VIDEO
CAT4500-SUP4(config-cmap)# match access-group name DVLAN-PC-VIDEO
CAT4500-SUP4(config-cmap)#
CAT4500-SUP4(config-cmap)#class-map match-all DVLAN-MISSION-CRITICAL-DATA
CAT4500-SUP4(config-cmap)# match access-group name DVLAN-MISSION-CRITICAL-DATA
CAT4500-SUP4(config-cmap)#
CAT4500-SUP4(config-cmap)#class-map match-all DVLAN-TRANSACTIONAL-DATA
CAT4500-SUP4(config-cmap)# match access-group name DVLAN-TRANSACTIONAL-DATA
CAT4500-SUP4(config-cmap)#
CAT4500-SUP4(config-cmap)#class-map match-all DVLAN-BULK-DATA
CAT4500-SUP4(config-cmap)# match access-group name DVLAN-BULK-DATA
CAT4500-SUP4(config-cmap)#exit
CAT4500-SUP4(config)#
CAT4500-SUP4(config)#policy-map IPPHONE+PC-ADVANCED
CAT4500-SUP4(config-pmap)#class VVLAN-VOICE
CAT4500-SUP4(config-pmap-c)# set ip dscp 46           ! DSCP EF (Voice)
CAT4500-SUP4(config-pmap-c)# police 128 kbps 8000 byte exceed-action drop
     ! Only one voice call is permitted per switchport VVLAN
CAT4500-SUP4(config-pmap-c)#class VVLAN-CALL-SIGNALING
CAT4500-SUP4(config-pmap-c)# set ip dscp 24           ! DSCP CS3 (Call-Signaling)
```

Example 12-41 *Catalyst 4500: Conditionally Trusted IP Phone + PC: Advanced Model Example (Continued)*

```
CAT4500-SUP4(config-pmap-c)# police 32 kbps 8000 byte exceed-action
      policed-dscp-transmit
      ! Out-of-profile Call-Signaling is marked down to Scavenger (CS1)
CAT4500-SUP4(config-pmap-c)#class VVLAN-ANY
CAT4500-SUP4(config-pmap-c)# set ip dscp 0
CAT4500-SUP4(config-pmap-c)# police 32 kbps 8000 byte exceed-action
      policed-dscp-transmit
      ! Unauthorized VVLAN traffic is marked down to Scavenger (CS1)
CAT4500-SUP4(config-pmap-c)#class DVLAN-PC-VIDEO
CAT4500-SUP4(config-pmap-c)# set ip dscp 34       ! DSCP AF41 (Int-Video)
CAT4500-SUP4(config-pmap-c)# police 500 kbps 8000 byte exceed-action
      policed-dscp-transmit
      ! Only one IP/VC stream will be permitted per switchport
CAT4500-SUP4(config-pmap-c)#class DVLAN-MISSION-CRITICAL-DATA
CAT4500-SUP4(config-pmap-c)# set ip dscp 25       ! Interim Mission-Critical
CAT4500-SUP4(config-pmap-c)# police 5 mbps 8000 byte exceed-action
      policed-dscp-transmit
      ! Out-of-profile Mission-Critical Data is marked down to Scavenger (CS1)
CAT4500-SUP4(config-pmap-c)#class DVLAN-TRANSACTIONAL-DATA
CAT4500-SUP4(config-pmap-c)# set ip dscp 18       ! DSCP AF21
CAT4500-SUP4(config-pmap-c)# police 5 mbps 8000 byte exceed-action
      policed-dscp-transmit
      ! Out-of-profile Transactional Data is marked down to Scavenger (CS1)
CAT4500-SUP4(config-pmap-c)#class DVLAN-BULK-DATA
CAT4500-SUP4(config-pmap-c)# set ip dscp 10       ! DSCP AF11
CAT4500-SUP4(config-pmap-c)# police 5 mbps 8000 byte exceed-action
      policed-dscp-transmit
      ! Out-of-profile Bulk Data is marked down to Scavenger (CS1)
CAT4500-SUP4(config-pmap-c)#class class-default
CAT4500-SUP4(config-pmap-c)# set ip dscp 0
CAT4500-SUP4(config-pmap-c)# police 5 mbps 8000 byte exceed-action
      policed-dscp-transmit
      ! Out-of-profile data traffic is marked down to Scavenger (CS1)
CAT4500-SUP4(config-pmap-c)#exit
CAT4500-SUP4(config-pmap)#exit
CAT4500-SUP4(config)#
CAT4500-SUP4(config)#
CAT4500-SUP4(config)#interface FastEthernet2/1
CAT4500-SUP4(config-if)# switchport access vlan 10        ! DVLAN
CAT4500-SUP4(config-if)# switchport voice vlan 110        ! VVLAN
CAT4500-SUP4(config-if)# qos trust device cisco-phone     ! Conditional Trust
CAT4500-SUP4(config-if)# service-policy input IPPHONE+PC-ADVANCED   ! MQC Policy
CAT4500-SUP4(config-if)#exit
CAT4500-SUP4(config)#
CAT4500-SUP4(config)#ip access-list extended VVLAN-VOICE
CAT4500-SUP4(config-ext-nacl)# permit udp 10.1.110.0 0.0.0.255 any
      range 16384 32767
      ! Voice is matched by VVLAN subnet and UDP port-range
CAT4500-SUP4(config-ext-nacl)#
CAT4500-SUP4(config-ext-nacl)#ip access-list extended VVLAN-CALL-SIGNALING
```

continues

Example 12-41 *Catalyst 4500: Conditionally Trusted IP Phone + PC: Advanced Model Example (Continued)*

```
CAT4500-SUP4(config-ext-nacl)# permit tcp 10.1.110.0 0.0.0.255 any
      range 2000 2002
      ! Call-Signaling is matched by VVLAN subnet and TCP port-range
CAT4500-SUP4(config-ext-nacl)#
CAT4500-SUP4(config-ext-nacl)#ip access-list extended VVLAN-ANY
CAT4500-SUP4(config-ext-nacl)# permit ip 10.1.110.0 0.0.0.255 any    ! VVLAN ANY
CAT4500-SUP4(config-ext-nacl)#
CAT4500-SUP4(config-ext-nacl)#ip access-list extended DVLAN-PC-VIDEO
CAT4500-SUP4(config-ext-nacl)# permit udp any any range 16384 32767 ! IP/VC
CAT4500-SUP4(config-ext-nacl)#
CAT4500-SUP4(config-ext-nacl)#ip access-list extended DVLAN-MISSION-CRITICAL-DATA
CAT4500-SUP4(config-ext-nacl)# permit tcp any any range 3200 3203   ! SAP
CAT4500-SUP4(config-ext-nacl)# permit tcp any any eq 3600           ! SAP
CAT4500-SUP4(config-ext-nacl)# permit tcp any any range 2000 2002   ! SCCP
CAT4500-SUP4(config-ext-nacl)#
CAT4500-SUP4(config-ext-nacl)#ip access-list extended DVLAN-TRANSACTIONAL-DATA
CAT4500-SUP4(config-ext-nacl)# permit tcp any any eq 1352           ! Lotus
CAT4500-SUP4(config-ext-nacl)#
CAT4500-SUP4(config-ext-nacl)#ip access-list extended DVLAN-BULK-DATA
CAT4500-SUP4(config-ext-nacl)# permit tcp any any eq 143            ! IMAP
CAT4500-SUP4(config-ext-nacl)# permit tcp any any eq 220            ! IMAP
CAT4500-SUP4(config-ext-nacl)#end
CAT4500-SUP4#
```

Catalyst 4500 QoS verification commands:

- **show qos**
- **show qos maps**
- **show qos interface**
- **show class-map**
- **show policy-map**
- **show policy interface**

Catalyst 4500: Queuing

The Catalyst 4500 supports four egress queues for scheduling, which can be configured in either 4Q1T or 1P3Q1T modes. The strict-priority queue on the Catalyst 4500 is transmit queue 3.

Although tail-drop or WRED thresholds are not supported on the Catalyst 4500, it does support one of the most advanced congestion-avoidance mechanisms in the Catalyst family. This congestion-avoidance feature is performed by dynamic buffer limiting (DBL). DBL tracks the queue length for each traffic flow in the switch and, when the queue length of a flow exceeds its limit, drops packets or sets the (RFC 3168) explicit congestion notification (ECN) bits in the IP packet headers. Of course, setting ECN bits is of value only if the end-point applications also support ECN (as discussed in Chapter 6, "Congestion-Avoidance Tools").

DBL can be enabled globally with the **qos dbl** global command or on a per-class basis within a policy map with the **dbl** policy command. A default DBL policy can be applied to all transmit queues, as shown in the upcoming Example 12-42.

By default, all queues are scheduled in a round-robin manner. The third transmit queue can be designated as an optional strict-priority queue. This can be enabled as a **via the tx-queue 3** interface command, followed by the **priority high interface transmit-queue** subcommand. This queue can be defined to be shaped to a peak limit, such as 30 percent, to allow bandwidth to be available to nonvoice applications. This would be valuable if a trust boundary has been compromised and a DoS or worm attack is saturating voice queues.

Bandwidth allocations also can be assigned to queues (for certain interfaces) using the **tx-queue** interface command, followed by the **bandwidth** subcommand. Bandwidth allocations to queues can be assigned only on the following interface types:

- Uplink ports on supervisor engines
- Ports on the WS-X4306-GB line card
- The two 1000BASE-X ports on the WS-X4232-GB-RJ line card
- The first two ports on the WS-X4418-GB line card
- The two 1000BASE-X ports on the WS-X4412-2GB-TX line card

The Catalyst 4500 does not support CoS-to-queue mappings; it supports only DSCP-to-queue mappings. These can be defined with the **qos map dscp to tx-queue** global command.

Given these features and the objective to make queuing as consistent across platforms as possible, it is recommended to enable DBL globally on the Catalyst 4500 and to enable Q3 as the strict-priority queue on all interfaces (so that the switch will operate in 1P3Q1T mode). This queue can be shaped to 30 percent of the link's capacity. Furthermore, Q1 can be used as the Scavenger/Bulk Data queue, Q2 can be used as the Best-Effort queue, and Q4 can be used as the preferential queue.

On interfaces that support bandwidth allocation, 5 percent can be assigned to Q1, 25 percent can be assigned to Q2, and 40 percent can be assigned to Q3. Unlike bandwidth weights that are used on other platforms, these bandwidth allocations are defined in absolute bits per second or as relative percentages of the link's bandwidth. In either case, they should not total in excess of the link's bandwidth limit (1 Gbps, or 100 percent), including the priority-bandwidth allocation for Q3.

By default, the DSCP-to-queue assignments are as follows:

- DSCP 0 to 15: queue 1
- DSCP 16 to 31: queue 2

- DSCP 32 to 47: queue 3
- DSCP 48 to 63: queue 4

The recommended DSCP-to-queue assignments for the Catalyst 4500 are as follows:

- DSCP 0 should be assigned to Q2.
- DSCP CS1 (Scavenger) and DSCP AF11, AF12, and AF13 (Bulk Data) should be assigned to Q1.
- DSCP CS2 (Network-Management) and AF21, AF22, and AF23 (Transactional Data) should be assigned to Q4.
- DSCP CS3 and AF31 (Call-Signaling) should be assigned to Q4.
- DSCP 25 (temporary marking for Mission-Critical Data) should be assigned to Q4.
- DSCP CS4 (Streaming-Video) and AF41, AF42, and AF43 (Interactive-Video) should be assigned to Q4.
- DSCP EF (Voice) should be assigned to Q3 (the strict-priority queue).
- DSCP CS6 (Internetwork Control) and CS7 (Network Control/STP) should be assigned to Q4.

Figure 12-21 illustrates the queuing recommendations for the Catalyst 4500 (Supervisors II+ through V).

Figure 12-21 *Catalyst 4500-SupII+/III/IV/V 1P3Q1T Queuing Model*

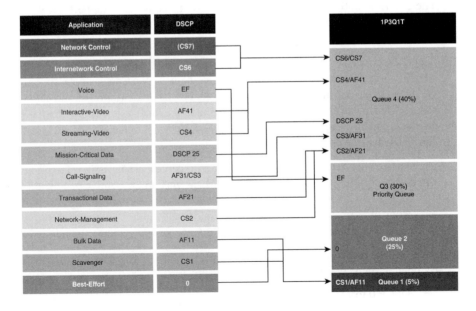

Example 12-42 shows the configurations for enabling queuing on the Catalyst 4500 per these recommendations. Two separate examples are given: one for a Fast Ethernet interface that doesn't support bandwidth allocations, and another for a Gigabit Ethernet interface that does. Some of the DSCP-to-queue mappings shown are not required (because they overlap with the default settings), but they are shown nonetheless to complete the logic of the example.

Example 12-42 *Catalyst 4500: Queuing and Dropping Examples*

```
CAT4500-SUP4(config)#qos dbl
       ! Globally enables DBL
CAT4500-SUP4(config)#qos dbl exceed-action ecn
        ! Optional: Enables DBL to mark RFC 3168 ECN bits in the IP ToS Byte
CAT4500-SUP4(config)#
CAT4500-SUP4(config)#qos map dscp 0 to tx-queue 2
        ! Maps DSCP 0 (Best Effort) to Q2
CAT4500-SUP4(config)#qos map dscp 8 10 12 14 to tx-queue 1
        ! Maps DSCP CS1 (Scavenger) and AF11/AF12/AF13 (Bulk) to Q1
CAT4500-SUP4(config)#qos map dscp 16 18 20 22 to tx-queue 4
        ! Maps DSCP CS2 (Net-Mgmt) and AF21/AF22/AF23 (Transactional) to Q4
CAT4500-SUP4(config)#qos map dscp 24 25 26 to tx-queue 4
        ! Maps DSCP CS3 and AF31 (Call-Signaling) and DSCP 25 (MC Data) to Q4
CAT4500-SUP4(config)#qos map dscp 32 34 36 38 to tx-queue 4
        ! Maps DSCP CS4 (Str-Video) and AF41/AF42/AF43 (Int-Video) to Q4
CAT4500-SUP4(config)#qos map dscp 46 to tx-queue 3
        ! Maps DSCP EF (VoIP) to Q3 (PQ)
CAT4500-SUP4(config)#qos map dscp 48 56 to tx-queue 4
        ! Maps DSCP CS6 (Internetwork) and CS7 (Network) Control to Q4
CAT4500-SUP4(config)#
CAT4500-SUP4(config)#policy-map DBL
CAT4500-SUP4(config-pmap)#class class-default
CAT4500-SUP4(config-pmap-c)# dbl    ! Enables DBL on all traffic flows
CAT4500-SUP4(config-pmap-c)# exit
CAT4500-SUP4(config-pmap)#exit
CAT4500-SUP4(config)#
CAT4500-SUP4(config)#interface range FastEthernet2/1 - 48
CAT4500-SUP4(config-if-range)# service-policy output DBL     ! Applies DBL policy
CAT4500-SUP4(config-if-range)# tx-queue 3
CAT4500-SUP4(config-if-tx-queue)# priority high             ! Enables Q3 as PQ
CAT4500-SUP4(config-if-tx-queue)# shape percent 30          ! Shapes PQ to 30%
CAT4500-SUP4(config-if-tx-queue)# exit
CAT4500-SUP4(config-if-range)#exit
CAT4500-SUP4(config)#
CAT4500-SUP4(config)#interface range GigabitEthernet1/1 - 2
CAT4500-SUP4(config-if-range)# service-policy output DBL     ! Applies DBL policy
CAT4500-SUP4(config-if-range)# tx-queue 1
CAT4500-SUP4(config-if-tx-queue)# bandwidth percent 5       ! Q1 gets 5%
CAT4500-SUP4(config-if-tx-queue)# tx-queue 2
CAT4500-SUP4(config-if-tx-queue)# bandwidth percent 25      ! Q2 gets 25%
CAT4500-SUP4(config-if-tx-queue)# tx-queue 3
CAT4500-SUP4(config-if-tx-queue)# priority high            ! Enables Q3 as PQ
CAT4500-SUP4(config-if-tx-queue)# bandwidth percent 30     ! PQ gets 30%
CAT4500-SUP4(config-if-tx-queue)# shape percent 30         ! Shapes PQ to 30%
```

continues

Example 12-42 *Catalyst 4500: Queuing and Dropping Examples (Continued)*

```
CAT4500-SUP4(config-if-tx-queue)# tx-queue 4
CAT4500-SUP4(config-if-tx-queue)# bandwidth percent 40        ! Q4 gets 40%
CAT4500-SUP4(config-if-tx-queue)#end
CAT4500-SUP4#
```

Catalyst 4500 QoS verification commands:

- **show qos dbl**
- **show qos maps dscp tx-queue**
- **show qos interface**

Catalyst 4500 QoS Verification Command: **show qos dbl**

The Catalyst 4500 **show qos dbl** verification command returns whether DBL has been enabled, along with some of the operating parameters that have been defined for its operation. These parameters include allowing DBL to set RFC 3168 ECN bits in IP headers, as shown in Example 12-43.

Example 12-43 **show qos dbl** *Verification for a Catalyst 4500 Switch*

```
CAT4500-SUP4#show qos dbl
QOS is enabled globally
DBL is enabled globally
DBL flow includes vlan
DBL flow includes layer4-ports
DBL uses ecn to indicate congestion
DBL exceed-action probability: 15%
DBL max credits: 15
DBL aggressive credit limit: 10
DBL aggressive buffer limit: 2 packets
CAT4500-SUP4#
```

Catalyst 4500 QoS Verification Command: **show qos maps dscp tx-queue**

The Catalyst 4500 **show qos maps dscp tx-queue** verification command truncates the **show qos maps** output to report only the DSCP-to-queue mappings for egress queues. The output is shown in tabular form, with the first digit of the decimal DSCP value in rows and the second digit in columns.

In Example 12-44, only DSCP 0 is mapped to Q2; DSCP CS1 (8) and AF11, AF12, and AF13 (10, 12, and 14) are mapped to Q1; DSCP CS2 (16) and AF22, AF22, and AF23 (18, 20, and 22) are mapped to Q4; DSCP CS3 (24) and AF31 (26) are mapped to Q4, as is the nonstandard DSCP 25; DSCP CS4 (32) and AF41, AF42, and AF43 (34, 36, and 38) are mapped to Q4, as are DSCP CS6 (48) and CS7 (56); and DSCP EF (46) is mapped to Q3.

Example 12-44 **show qos maps dscp tx-queue** *Verification for a Catalyst 4500 Switch*

```
CAT4500-SUP4#show qos maps dscp tx-queue
DSCP-TxQueue Mapping Table (dscp = d1d2)
d1 : d2  0  1  2  3  4  5  6  7  8  9
----------------------------------------
0 :     02 01 01 01 01 01 01 01 01 01    ! DSCP 0 => Q2; DSCP CS1 => Q1
1 :     01 01 01 01 01 01 04 02 04 02    ! DSCP AF11/AF12/AF13 => Q1
                                          ! DSCP CS2 and AF21 => Q4
2 :     04 02 04 02 04 04 04 02 02 02    ! DSCP AF22/AF23 => Q4
                                          ! DSCP CS3, 25 and AF31 => Q4
3 :     02 02 04 03 04 03 04 03 04 03    ! DSCP CS4 and AF41/AF42/AF43 => Q4
4 :     03 03 03 03 03 03 03 03 04 04    ! DSCP EF => Q3; DSCP CS6 => Q4
5 :     04 04 04 04 04 04 04 04 04 04    ! DSCP CS7 => Q4
6 :     04 04 04 04
CAT4500-SUP4#
```

Catalyst 4500 QoS Verification Command: **show qos interface**

The Catalyst 4500 **show qos interface** verification command displays the global state of QoS (enabled or not), the trust state of an interface, and any queuing or shaping parameters that have been defined for the interface.

In Example 12-45, the **show qos interface** command is being applied on an access-edge Fast Ethernet interface that has been configured to conditionally trust Cisco IP phones. Furthermore, the output reports that Q3 has been enabled as the priority queue on this interface and is shaped to 30 Mbps (30 percent). Bandwidth cannot be assigned for nonpriority queues on this interface, as is indicated by the "N/A" entries under the bandwidth column.

In Example 12-45, the **show qos interface** command is being applied to a Gigabit Ethernet uplink interface that has been configured to trust-DSCP. As before, Q3 has been enabled as the priority queue and has been shaped to 30 percent, which now translates to 300 Mbps. Bandwidth is assignable on this interface; therefore, Q1 is allocated 50 Mbps (5 percent), Q2 is allocated 250 Mbps (25 percent), Q3 is allocated 300 Mbps (30 percent), and Q4 is allocated 400 Mbps (40 percent).

Example 12-45 **show qos interface** *Verification for a Catalyst 4500 Switch*

```
CAT4500-SUP4#show qos interface FastEthernet2/1
QoS is enabled globally
Port QoS is enabled
Administrative Port Trust State: 'cos'
Operational Port Trust State: 'cos'
Trust device: cisco-phone
Default DSCP: 0 Default CoS: 0
Appliance trust: none
Tx-Queue   Bandwidth    ShapeRate    Priority   QueueSize
           (bps)        (bps)                   (packets)
   1       N/A          disabled     N/A        240
   2       N/A          disabled     N/A        240
```

continues

Example 12-45 **show qos interface** *Verification for a Catalyst 4500 Switch (Continued)*

```
    3        N/A     30000000    high        240
    4        N/A     disabled    N/A         240
CAT4500-SUP4#

CAT4500-SUP4#show qos interface GigabitEthernet1/1
QoS is enabled globally
Port QoS is enabled
Administrative Port Trust State: 'dscp'
Operational Port Trust State: 'dscp'
Trust device: none
Default DSCP: 0 Default CoS: 0
Appliance trust: none
Tx-Queue  Bandwidth   ShapeRate   Priority   QueueSize
          (bps)       (bps)                  (packets)
    1     50000000    disabled    N/A        1920
    2     250000000   disabled    N/A        1920
    3     300000000   300000000   high       1920
    4     700000000   disabled    N/A        1920
CAT4500-SUP4#
```

Catalyst 6500 QoS Considerations and Design

The Catalyst 6500 is the undisputed flagship of the Cisco family of LAN switches: It is the most powerful and flexible Cisco switching platform. As such, it can be found in all three layers of a campus network (access, distribution, and core).

NOTE   The Cisco 7600 router is identical in hardware QoS features and configuration to Catalyst 6500s running Cisco IOS. However, the Cisco 7600 is better suited to a MAN or MPLS VPN environment than a campus context, which is the scope of this chapter. Therefore, although much of this chapter is applicable to the Cisco 7600, this discussion centers on Catalyst 6500 QoS.

When configured as an access-layer switch, the preferred software for the Supervisor is CatOS; when configured as a distribution- or core-layer switch, the preferred software is Cisco IOS. Figure 12-22 summarizes the QoS design recommendations for a Catalyst 6500 switch at the access layer; Figure 12-23 shows the corresponding recommendations for Catalyst 6500s deployed in the distribution or core layers.

Figure 12-22 *Access-Layer (CatOS) Catalyst 6500 QoS Design*

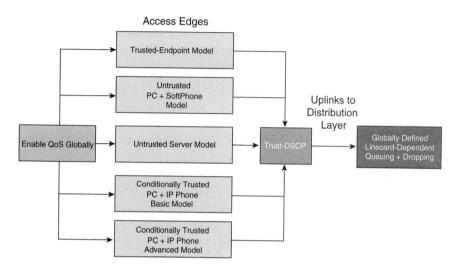

Figure 12-23 *Distribution- or Core-Layer (Cisco IOS) Catalyst 6500 QoS Design*

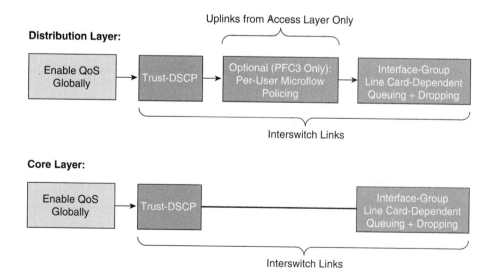

NOTE	To narrow the scope of the discussion to the most current and relevant versions of the Catalyst 6500 switch family, only the Catalyst 6500 with Supervisor 2 (PFC2) and Supervisor 720 (PFC3) is examined in this design chapter. For discussions on older versions of Catalyst 6000/6500s (such as Supervisor 1, 1a with or without a PFC), refer to the Cisco Press book *Cisco Catalyst QoS: Quality of Service in Campus Networks*, by Mike Flannagan, Richard Froom, and Kevin Turek.

QoS is disabled globally by default on Catalyst 6500s running either CatOS or Cisco IOS. When QoS is disabled globally, all frames and packets that are passed through the switch remain unaltered (which is equivalent to a trust CoS and trust DSCP state on all ports). When QoS is enabled globally, however, all DSCP and CoS values are (by default) set to 0 (which is equivalent to an untrusted state on all ports).

The commands to globally enable and verify QoS on a Catalyst 6500 are shown in Example 12-46 for CatOS and Example 12-47 for Cisco IOS.

Example 12-46 *Enabling QoS Globally on a Catalyst 6500: CatOS*

```
CAT6500-PFC2-CATOS> (enable) set qos enable
QoS is enabled.
CAT6500-PFC2-CATOS> (enable)

CAT6500-PFC2-CATOS> (enable) show qos status
QoS is enabled on this switch.
CAT6500-PFC2-CATOS> (enable)
```

Example 12-47 *Enabling QoS Globally on a Catalyst 6500: Cisco IOS*

```
CAT6500-PFC2-IOS(config)#mls qos
CAT6500-PFC2-IOS(config)#end
CAT6500-PFC2-IOS#

CAT6500-PFC2-IOS#show mls qos
 QoS is enabled globally
 Microflow policing is enabled globally
Vlan or Portchannel(Multi-Earl) policies supported: Yes
 ----- Module [2] -----
 QoS global counters:
   Total packets: 65
   IP shortcut packets: 0
   Packets dropped by policing: 0
   IP packets with TOS changed by policing: 0
   IP packets with COS changed by policing: 0
   Non-IP packets with COS changed by policing: 0
CAT6500-PFC2-IOS#
```

Catalyst 6500: CatOS Defaults and Recommendations

CatOS specifies a number of default QoS settings per port that do not appear in the normal configuration output. However, it is beneficial to be aware of what these defaults are and what they do, so as not to override them by mistake.

For example, CatOS allows the QoS policy source to be defined by the local configuration or by the Common Open Policy Source (COPS) protocol, referring to a COPS policy-decision point (PDP) Server. COPS is a QoS administration protocol that is both dynamic and scalable, but, unfortunately, it never gained mainstream acceptance. It is recommended to leave the switch's default policy source as local (except, of course, in the extremely rare occurrence that COPS actually is deployed on the network).

Additionally, QoS policies can be applied to VLANs or to ports. There was never any significant advantage of using one base over the other, but AutoQoS tools favor port-based QoS because it is marginally simpler to configure. Port-based QoS is the default per-port setting, and all examples in this chapter are configured using port-based QoS.

All ports (after QoS has been enabled globally) are set to an untrusted state, by default. The port CoS setting that all packets are tagged with is 0, by default. Also by default, the trust extension state is set to untrusted, and the extended-CoS is correspondingly set to 0; this indicates that any connected IP phones should re-mark PC traffic to 0 on their ASICs.

It is recommended to leave all these port QoS settings at their defaults, with the exception of trust—depending on the access edge model to be applied, as discussed in the following section.

Catalyst 6500: Trusted Endpoint Model

For most Catalyst 6500 switch ports, setting the trust state to trust DSCP is a relatively straightforward command (in either CatOS or Cisco IOS).

In Example 12-48, DSCP-trust is configured on a port in CatOS; in Example 12-51, DSCP-trust is configured on a port/interface in Cisco IOS.

Example 12-48 *Catalyst 6500 CatOS: Trusted Endpoint Example*

```
CAT6500-PFC2-CATOS> (enable) set port qos 3/1 trust trust-dscp
Port  3/1 qos set to trust-dscp.
CAT6500-PFC2-CATOS> (enable)
```

Catalyst 6500 CatOS QoS verification commands:

- **show qos status**
- **show port qos**

Catalyst 6500 CatOS QoS Verification Command: **show port qos**

The Catalyst 6500 CatOS **show port qos** verification command returns the configured and runtime QoS states of a port. These might differ because certain commands need to be committed (programmed into hardware) before they become effective.

In Example 12-49, the switch has QoS globally enabled, and the source of QoS policy decisions is the local configuration instead of a Common Open Policy Source policy-decision point (COPS PDP).

Furthermore, the output shows that the port is configured for port-based QoS (by default) and has been set to trust DSCP from connected endpoints. No trust extension has been configured because this is not a conditionally trusted endpoint model.

The output includes the line card's queuing capabilities—1P3Q1T (Transmit) and 1P1Q0T (Receive)—along with any ACLs that might be mapped to the port. However, no ACLs have been mapped to this port in this particular example.

Example 12-49 **show port qos** *Verification for a Catalyst 6500-CatOS Switch*

```
CAT6500-PFC2-CATOS> (enable) show port qos 3/1
QoS is enabled for the switch.
QoS policy source for the switch set to local.
Port  Interface Type Interface Type Policy Source Policy Source
      config         runtime        config        runtime
----- -------------- -------------- ------------- -------------
 3/1     port-based     port-based     COPS          local
Port  TxPort Type RxPort Type Trust Type    Trust Type    Def CoS Def CoS
                              config        runtime       config  runtime
----- ----------- ----------- ------------- ------------- ------- -------
 3/1        1p3q1t      1p1q0t   trust-dscp    trust-dscp       0       0
Port  Ext-Trust Ext-Cos Trust-Device
----- --------- ------- ------------
 3/1  untrusted       0         none
(*)Runtime trust type set to untrusted.
Config:
Port  ACL name                         Type
----- -------------------------------- ----
No ACL is mapped to port 3/1.
Runtime:
Port  ACL name                         Type
----- -------------------------------- ----
No ACL is mapped to port 3/1.
CAT6500-PFC2-CATOS> (enable)
```

On non–Gigabit Ethernet line cards that use 2Q2T transmit queuing and 1Q4T receive queuing, a hardware limitation prevents the proper functioning of port-based trust (which affects trust-cos, trust-ipprec, and trust-dscp). The **show port qos** command can be used to determine whether the line card is a 2Q2T-Tx/1Q4T-Rx line card. These cards also are listed in Table 12-2.

On such line cards, a workaround ACL can be used to achieve trust functionality for trust-cos, trust-ipprec, and trust-dscp. Example 12-50 shows the workaround ACL for trust-DSCP functionality on such line cards.

Example 12-50 *Trust-DSCP Workaround ACL for Catalyst 6500 2Q2T-TX/1Q4T-Rx Non-Gigabit Line Cards*

```
CAT6500-PFC2-CATOS> (enable) set qos acl ip TRUST-DSCP trust-dscp any
TRUST-DSCP editbuffer modified. Use 'commit' command to apply changes.
CAT6500-PFC2-CATOS> (enable) commit qos acl TRUST-DSCP
QoS ACL 'TRUST-DSCP' successfully committed.
CAT6500-PFC2-CATOS> (enable)
CAT6500-PFC2-CATOS> (enable) set qos acl map TRUST-DSCP 4/1
```

NOTE   To apply the QoS ACL that you have defined (previously), the ACL must be committed to hardware. The process of committing copies the ACL from a temporary editing buffer to the PFC hardware. When it is resident in the PFC memory, the policy defined in the QoS ACL can be applied to all traffic that matches the ACEs. For ease of configuration, most administrators issue a **commit all** command. However, you can commit a specific ACL (by name) to be sent from the editing buffer to PFC memory, as shown in Example 12-50.

In Example 12-51, DSCP-trust is configured on a port/interface in Cisco IOS.

Example 12-51 *Catalyst 6500 Cisco IOS: Trusted Endpoint Example*

```
CAT6500-PFC2-IOS(config)#interface FastEthernet3/1
CAT6500-PFC2-IOS(config-if)#mls qos trust dscp
```

Catalyst MLS QoS verification commands:

- **show mls qos**
- **show mls qos interface**

NOTE   The ACL trust workaround to the 2Q2T line card (non–Gigabit Ethernet interfaces) limitation of not supporting trust applies only in the access layer or the campus (where CatOS is the recommended software for the Catalyst 6500). In the distribution and core layers, where Cisco IOS is the preferred software, all interfaces are recommended to be Gigabit Ethernet or higher. Therefore, a Cisco IOS workaround solution for this limitation of 10/100 2Q2T ports is not warranted.

Catalyst 6500: Untrusted PC with SoftPhone Model

The radical difference in syntax between CatOS and Cisco IOS becomes increasingly apparent as more complex access edge models are presented.

In the Untrusted PC with SoftPhone model, shown in Example 12-52, per-application aggregate policers are defined—one each for SoftPhone VoIP traffic, SoftPhone Call-Signaling traffic, and PC data traffic. Then an ACL (titled SOFTPHONE-PC) with multiple ACEs is defined, with each ACE referencing its associated aggregate policer. When complete, the ACL is committed to PFC memory and then mapped to the desired switch port(s). Switch responses to the commands have been omitted to simplify the example.

Example 12-52 *Catalyst 6500 CatOS: Untrusted PC with SoftPhone Model Example*

```
CAT6500-PFC2-CATOS> (enable) set qos policed-dscp-map 0,24,46:8
    ! Excess traffic marked DSCP 0 or CS3 or EF will be remarked to CS1
CAT6500-PFC2-CATOS> (enable)
CAT6500-PFC2-CATOS> (enable) set qos policer aggregate SOFTPHONE-VOICE
    rate 128 burst 8 policed-dscp
    ! Defines the policer for SoftPhone VoIP traffic
CAT6500-PFC2-CATOS> (enable) set qos policer aggregate SOFTPHONE-SIGNALING
    rate 32 burst 8 policed-dscp
    ! Defines the policer for SoftPhone Call-Signaling traffic
CAT6500-PFC2-CATOS> (enable) set qos policer aggregate PC-DATA
    rate 5000 burst 8 policed-dscp
    ! Defines the policer for PC Data traffic
CAT6500-PFC2-CATOS> (enable)
CAT6500-PFC2-CATOS> (enable) set qos acl ip SOFTPHONE-PC dscp 46
    aggregate SOFTPHONE-VOICE udp any any range 16384 32767
    ! Binds ACL to policer and marks in-profile SoftPhone VoIP to DSCP EF
CAT6500-PFC2-CATOS> (enable) set qos acl ip SOFTPHONE-PC dscp 24
    aggregate SOFTPHONE-SIGNALING tcp any any range 2000 2002
    ! Binds ACL to policer marks in-profile Call-Signaling to DSCP CS3
CAT6500-PFC2-CATOS> (enable) set qos acl ip SOFTPHONE-PC dscp 0
    aggregate PC-DATA any
    ! Binds ACL to policer and marks in-profile PC Data traffic to DSCP 0
CAT6500-PFC2-CATOS> (enable)
CAT6500-PFC2-CATOS> (enable) commit qos acl SOFTPHONE-PC
    ! Commits ACL to PFC memory
CAT6500-PFC2-CATOS> (enable) set port qos 3/1 trust untrusted
    ! Sets the port trust state to untrusted
CAT6500-PFC2-CATOS> (enable) set qos acl map SOFTPHONE-PC 3/1
    ! Attaches ACL to switch port
CAT6500-PFC2-CATOS> (enable)
```

Catalyst 6500 CatOS QoS verification commands:

- **show qos status**
- **show qos maps**
- **show port qos**

- **show qos acl**
- **show qos policer**
- **show qos statistics**

Catalyst 6500 CatOS QoS Verification Command: **show qos maps**

The Catalyst 6500 CatOS **show qos maps** verification command is fairly similar to the **show mls qos maps** MLS QoS verification command. It returns the configured CoS-DSCP, IPPrec-DSCP, DSCP-CoS, and Normal-Rate and Excess-Rate Policed-DSCP maps. The command can return configured maps (which might or might not be committed to the PFC) or runtime maps.

In the (truncated) runtime example shown in Example 12-53, all maps are at their default states, with the exception of the Normal-Rate Policed-DSCP map, which has DSCP 0, CS3 (24), and EF (46) mapped for out-of-profile markdown to DSCP CS1 (8).

Example 12-53 **show qos maps** *Verification for a Catalyst 6500-CatOS Switch*

```
CAT6500-PFC2-CATOS> (enable) show qos maps runtime
CoS - DSCP map:
CoS   DSCP
---   ----
  0    0
  1    8
  2   16
  3   24
  4   32
  5   40
  6   48
  7   56


IP-Precedence - DSCP map:
IP-Prec   DSCP
-------   ----
      0    0
      1    8
      2   16
      3   24
      4   32
      5   40
      6   48
      7   56

DSCP - CoS map:
DSCP                                    CoS
------------------------------------    ---
                              0-7   0
                              8-15  1
                              16-23 2
```

continues

Example 12-53 show qos maps *Verification for a Catalyst 6500-CatOS Switch (Continued)*

```
                            24-31  3
                            32-39  4
                            40-47  5
                            48-55  6
                            56-63  7

DSCP - Policed DSCP map normal-rate:
DSCP                                    Policed DSCP
--------------------------------        ------------
                             1  1
                             2  2
                             3  3
                             4  4
                             5  5
                             6  6
                             7  7
                    0,8,24,46  8
                             9  9
                            10  10
<output truncated>
                            63  63
DSCP - Policed DSCP map excess-rate:
DSCP                                    Policed DSCP
--------------------------------        ------------
                             0  0
                             1  1
                             2  2
                             3  3
                             4  4
                             5  5
<output truncated>
                            63  63
CAT6500-PFC2-CATOS> (enable)
```

Catalyst 6500 CatOS QoS Verification Command: **show qos acl**

The Catalyst 6500 CatOS **show qos acl** verification command returns information about ACLs and ACEs that have been configured for QoS purposes. ACL information can be displayed for configuration ACLs or runtime ACLs.

Example 12-54 displays three variations of the **show qos acl** command.

The first one displays the QoS ACLs that are still in the edit buffer and indicates whether the ACLs have been committed to PFC memory. In this example, the ACL SOFTPHONE-PC has been committed to the PFC.

The second example displays runtime ACE-level information for a given ACL (or all ACLs, if the keyword **all** is used instead of the ACL name). Each ACE's DSCP markings, associated aggregate policer, and filtering criteria are displayed.

The third example displays the VLANs and ports that the ACL has been applied to. In this specific example, port 3/1 has the SOFTPHONE-PC ACL applied to it.

Example 12-54 **show qos acl** *Verification for a Catalyst 6500-CatOS Switch*

```
CAT6500-PFC2-CATOS> (enable) show qos acl editbuffer
ACL                                 Type Status
----------------------------------  ---- ----------
SOFTPHONE-PC                        IP   Committed
CAT6500-PFC2-CATOS> (enable)


CAT6500-PFC2-CATOS> (enable) show qos acl info runtime SOFTPHONE-PC
set qos acl IP SOFTPHONE-PC
---------------------------------------------
1. dscp 46 aggregate SOFTPHONE-VOICE udp any any range 16384 32767
2. dscp 24 aggregate SOFTPHONE-SIGNALING tcp any any range 2000 2002
3. dscp 0 aggregate PC-DATA any
CAT6500-PFC2-CATOS> (enable)


CAT6500-PFC2-CATOS> (enable) show qos acl map runtime SOFTPHONE-PC
QoS ACL mappings on input side:
ACL name                            Type Vlans
----------------------------------  ---- --------------------------------
SOFTPHONE-PC                        IP
ACL name                            Type Ports
----------------------------------  ---- --------------------------------
SOFTPHONE-PC                        IP 3/1
CAT6500-PFC2-CATOS> (enable)
```

Catalyst 6500 CatOS QoS Verification Command: **show qos policer**

The Catalyst 6500 CatOS **show qos policer** verification command displays the normal and excess rates and burst for policers.

In Example 12-55, three aggregate policers have been defined: SOFTPHONE-VOICE, SOFTPHONE-SIGNALING, and PC-DATA, with normal rates of 128 kbps, 32 kbps, and 5 Mbps, respectively. Each of these policers marks down excess traffic according to the policed-DSCP normal rate and are attached to the ACL SOFTPHONE-PC.

Example 12-55 **show qos policer** *Verification for a Catalyst 6500-CatOS Switch*

```
CAT6500-PFC2-CATOS> (enable) show qos policer runtime all
Warning: Runtime information may differ from user configured setting due to
hardware granularity.
QoS microflow policers:
QoS aggregate policers:
Aggregate name        Avg. rate (kbps) Burst size (kb) Normal action
--------------------  ---------------- --------------- -------------
```

continues

Example 12-55 show qos policer *Verification for a Catalyst 6500-CatOS Switch (Continued)*

```
SOFTPHONE-VOICE                        128            8   policed-dscp
                        Excess rate (kbps) Excess burst size (kb) Excess action
                        ------------------ ---------------------- -------------
                            31457280                   31744  policed-dscp
                            ACL attached
                            ------------------------------------------
                            SOFTPHONE-PC
Aggregate name          Avg. rate (kbps) Burst size (kb) Normal action
--------------------    ---------------- --------------- -------------
SOFTPHONE-SIGNALING                     32             8   policed-dscp
                        Excess rate (kbps) Excess burst size (kb) Excess action
                        ------------------ ---------------------- -------------
                            31457280                   31744  policed-dscp
                            ACL attached
                            ------------------------------------------
                            SOFTPHONE-PC
Aggregate name          Avg. rate (kbps) Burst size (kb) Normal action
--------------------    ---------------- --------------- -------------
PC-DATA                               4864             8   policed-dscp
                        Excess rate (kbps) Excess burst size (kb) Excess action
                        ------------------ ---------------------- -------------
                            31457280                   31744  policed-dscp
                            ACL attached
                            ------------------------------------------
                            SOFTPHONE-PC
CAT6500-PFC2-CATOS> (enable)
```

Catalyst 6500 CatOS QoS Verification Command: **show qos statistics**

The Catalyst 6500 CatOS **show qos statistics** verification command displays various dynamic statistics regarding the QoS policies.

In the three parts of Example 12-56, the first variation of the command **show qos statistics** *mod | port* returns queuing statistics for the port. Specifically, it reports any drops because of queue buffer overfill and breaks down these drops by queues or thresholds, depending on the queuing structure of the module. In this first part of the example, no drops have occurred because of queuing buffer overfills.

In the second part of Example 12-56, aggregate policing statistics are displayed through the **show qos statistics aggregate-policer** variation of the command. The number of packets that conform to or exceed a given policer is reported. In this part of the example, the command reports that no packets have exceeded the SOFTPHONE-VOIP or SOFTPHONE-SIGNALING policers, but a few have exceeded the PC-DATA policer.

Finally, in the third part of Example 12-56, the number of packets that have been dropped because of policing or have been re-marked at Layer 3 or Layer 2 is reported with the **show qos statistics l3stats** command. In this final part of the example, the command reports that no packets have been dropped because of policing, but thousands of packets have had their L3 and L2 markings modified by the configured policy.

Example 12-56 **show qos statistics** *Verification for a Catalyst 6500-CatOS Switch*

```
CAT6500-PFC2-CATOS> (enable) show qos statistics 3/1
Tx port type of port 3/1 : 1p3q1t
WRED and tail drops are accumulated in one counter per queue.
Q #  Packets dropped
---  ----------------------------------------------
1    0 pkts
2    0 pkts
3    0 pkts
4    0 pkts
Rx port type of port 3/1 : 1p1q0t
For untrusted ports all the packets are sent to the same queue,
Rx thresholds are disabled, tail drops are reported instead.
Q #  Threshold #:Packets dropped
---  ----------------------------------------------
1    0:0 pkts
2    0:0 pkts
CAT6500-PFC2-CATOS> (enable)


CAT6500-PFC2-CATOS> (enable) show qos statistics aggregate-policer
QoS aggregate-policer statistics:
Aggregate policer              Allowed packet Packets exceed
                               count          excess rate
-------------------------------- --------------- ---------------
SOFTPHONE-VOICE                      27536               0
SOFTPHONE-SIGNALING                    224               0
PC-DATA                             470069             645
CAT6500-PFC2-CATOS> (enable)


CAT6500-PFC2-CATOS> (enable) show qos statistics l3stats
Packets dropped due to policing:        0
IP packets with ToS changed:       169286
IP packets with CoS changed:        83507
Non-IP packets with CoS changed:        0
CAT6500-PFC2-CATOS> (enable)
```

Catalyst 6500: Untrusted Server Model

Additional flexibility is offered to the Untrusted Server model with the Catalyst 6500 PFC2/PFC3's support of dual-rate policing (as described in RFC 2698, "A Two Rate Three Color Marker," and as illustrated in Figure 4-5).

Using a dual-rate policer, three colors are used to indicate the following:

- Conforming traffic (within the normal rate)
- Excess traffic (exceeding the normal rate but less than the excess rate)
- Violating traffic (exceeding both the normal and excess rates)

The dual-rate policer is intended to complement the RFC 2597 assured-forwarding groups DiffServ marking scheme. To illustrate this, consider Transactional Data traffic, which is marked to AF Class 2. Conforming Transactional Data should be marked to AF21, excess Transactional Data traffic should be marked down to AF22, and violating Transactional Data traffic should be marked down further to AF23.

Such a markdown scheme is intended to be complemented further by DSCP-based WRED congestion avoidance. In this manner, if congestion occurs, AF23 is dropped more aggressively than AF22, which, in turn, is dropped more aggressively than AF21.

However, because Catalyst 6500 queuing and congestion avoidance are determined primarily by CoS markings, the standards-based DSCP model cannot be followed completely at this time on this platform. (Because AF21, AF22, and AF23 all share CoS 3, this does not allow for granular subclass QoS.) Therefore, Scavenger class markings for violating traffic could be used to achieve a similar overall effect, while maintaining consistency with QoS designs previously presented for other Catalyst platforms.

Under such a modified Untrusted Multiapplication Server model, excess Transactional Data traffic can be marked down to AF22 and violating Transactional Data traffic can be marked down to DSCP CS1 (Scavenger). Similarly, excess Bulk Data traffic can be marked down to AF12 and violating Bulk Data traffic can be marked down to DSCP CS1 (Scavenger). This modified model is shown in Figure 12-24.

Figure 12-24 *Catalyst 6500 PFC2/PFC3 Untrusted Endpoint Dual-Rate Policing: Multiapplication Server Example*

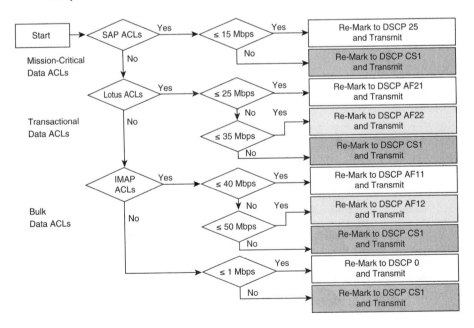

Example 12-57 shows the configuration for a Catalyst 6500 CatOS untrusted endpoint dual-rate policing of a multiapplication server.

Example 12-57 *Catalyst 6500 CatOS: Untrusted Multiapplication Server Example (Dual-Rate Policing)*

```
CAT6500-PFC2-CATOS> (enable) set qos policed-dscp-map normal-rate 0,25:8
       ! Excess SAP and Data traffic is marked down to DSCP CS1 (Scavenger)
CAT6500-PFC2-CATOS> (enable) set qos policed-dscp-map normal-rate 18:20
       ! Excess Transactional Data traffic is marked down from DSCP AF21 to AF22
CAT6500-PFC2-CATOS> (enable) set qos policed-dscp-map excess-rate 18:8
       ! Violating Transactional Data traffic is marked down to CS1
CAT6500-PFC2-CATOS> (enable) set qos policed-dscp-map normal-rate 10:12
       ! Excess Bulk Data traffic is marked down from DSCP AF11 to AF12
CAT6500-PFC2-CATOS> (enable) set qos policed-dscp-map excess-rate 10:8
       ! Violating Bulk Data traffic is marked down to CS1
CAT6500-PFC2-CATOS> (enable)
CAT6500-PFC2-CATOS> (enable) set qos policer aggregate SAP
       rate 15000 burst 8 policed-dscp
       ! Defines the policer for Mission-Critical Data (SAP) traffic
CAT6500-PFC2-CATOS> (enable) set qos policer aggregate LOTUS
       rate 25000 policed-dscp erate 35000 policed-dscp burst 8
       ! Defines the dual-rate policer for Transactional Data (Lotus) traffic
CAT6500-PFC2-CATOS> (enable) set qos policer aggregate IMAP
       rate 40000 policed-dscp erate 50000 policed-dscp burst 8
       ! Defines the dual-rate policer for Bulk Data (IMAP) traffic
CAT6500-PFC2-CATOS> (enable) set qos policer aggregate DATA
       rate 1000 burst 8 policed-dscp
       ! Defines the policer for other data traffic
CAT6500-PFC2-CATOS> (enable)
CAT6500-PFC2-CATOS> (enable) set qos acl ip UNTRUSTED-SERVER dscp 25
       aggregate SAP tcp any range 3200 3203 any
       ! Binds ACL to policer and marks in-profile SAP to DSCP 25
CAT6500-PFC2-CATOS> (enable) set qos acl ip UNTRUSTED-SERVER dscp 25
       aggregate SAP tcp any eq 3600 any
       ! Binds ACL to policer and marks in-profile SAP to DSCP 25
CAT6500-PFC2-CATOS> (enable)
CAT6500-PFC2-CATOS> (enable) set qos acl ip UNTRUSTED-SERVER dscp 18
       aggregate LOTUS tcp any eq 1352 any
       ! Binds ACL to dual-rate policer and marks in-profile Lotus to DSCP AF21
CAT6500-PFC2-CATOS> (enable)
CAT6500-PFC2-CATOS> (enable) set qos acl ip UNTRUSTED-SERVER dscp 10
       aggregate IMAP tcp any eq 143 any
       ! Binds ACL to dual-rate policer and marks in-profile IMAP to DSCP AF11
CAT6500-PFC2-CATOS> (enable) set qos acl ip UNTRUSTED-SERVER dscp 10
       aggregate IMAP tcp any eq 220 any
       ! Binds ACL to dual-rate policer and marks in-profile IMAP to DSCP AF11
CAT6500-PFC2-CATOS> (enable)
CAT6500-PFC2-CATOS> (enable) set qos acl ip UNTRUSTED-SERVER dscp 0
       aggregate DATA any
CAT6500-PFC2-CATOS> (enable)
CAT6500-PFC2-CATOS> (enable)
```

continues

Example 12-57 *Catalyst 6500 CatOS: Untrusted Multiapplication Server Example (Dual-Rate Policing) (Continued)*

```
CAT6500-PFC2-CATOS> (enable) commit qos acl UNTRUSTED-SERVER
CAT6500-PFC2-CATOS> (enable)
CAT6500-PFC2-CATOS> (enable) set port qos 3/1 trust untrusted
        ! Sets the port trust state to untrusted
CAT6500-PFC2-CATOS> (enable) set qos acl map UNTRUSTED-SERVER 3/1
CAT6500-PFC2-CATOS> (enable)
```

Catalyst 6500 CatOS QoS verification commands:

- **show qos status**
- **show qos maps**
- **show port qos**
- **show qos acl**
- **show qos policer**
- **show qos statistics**

Catalyst 6500: Conditionally Trusted IP Phone + PC: Basic Model

In the Conditionally Trusted IP Phone + PC model for the Catalyst 6500 (CatOS), four aggregate policers are defined, one each for Voice from the VVLAN, Call Signaling from the VVLAN, all other traffic from the VVLAN, and all PC data traffic. Conditional trust is extended to the IP phones using the **trust-device** command, as shown in Example 12-58.

Example 12-58 *Catalyst 6500 CatOS: Conditionally Trusted IP Phone + PC: Basic Model Example*

```
CAT6500-PFC2-CATOS> (enable) set qos cos-dscp-map 0 8 16 24 32 46 48 56
        ! Modifies default CoS-DSCP mapping so that CoS 5 is mapped to DSCP EF
CAT6500-PFC2-CATOS> (enable) set qos policed-dscp-map 0,24:8
        ! Excess traffic marked DSCP 0 or CS3 is remarked to CS1
CAT6500-PFC2-CATOS> (enable)
CAT6500-PFC2-CATOS> (enable) set qos policer aggregate VVLAN-VOICE
        rate 128 burst 8 drop
        ! Defines the policer for IP Phone VoIP traffic
CAT6500-PFC2-CATOS> (enable) set qos policer aggregate VVLAN-SIGNALING
        rate 32 burst 8 policed-dscp
        ! Defines the policer for IP Phone Call-Signaling traffic
CAT6500-PFC2-CATOS> (enable) set qos policer aggregate VVLAN-ANY
        rate 32 burst 8 policed-dscp
        ! Defines the policer for any other traffic sourced from the VVLAN
CAT6500-PFC2-CATOS> (enable) set qos policer aggregate PC-DATA
        rate 5000 burst 8 policed-dscp
        ! Defines the policer for PC Data traffic
CAT6500-PFC2-CATOS> (enable)
CAT6500-PFC2-CATOS> (enable) set qos acl ip IPPHONE-PC-BASIC dscp 46
        aggregate VVLAN-VOICE udp 10.1.110.0 0.0.0.255 any range 16384 32767
        ! Binds ACL to policer and marks in-profile VVLAN VoIP to DSCP EF
```

Example 12-58 *Catalyst 6500 CatOS: Conditionally Trusted IP Phone + PC: Basic Model Example (Continued)*

```
CAT6500-PFC2-CATOS> (enable) set qos acl ip IPPHONE-PC-BASIC dscp 24
        aggregate VVLAN-SIGNALING udp 10.1.110.0 0.0.0.255 any range 2000 2002
        ! Binds ACL to policer marks in-profile VVLAN Call-Signaling to DSCP CS3
CAT6500-PFC2-CATOS> (enable) set qos acl ip IPPHONE-PC-BASIC dscp 0
        aggregate VVLAN-ANY 10.1.110.0 0.0.0.255
        ! Binds ACL to policer and marks all other VVLAN traffic to DSCP 0
CAT6500-PFC2-CATOS> (enable) set qos acl ip IPPHONE-PC-BASIC dscp 0
        aggregate PC-DATA any
        ! Binds ACL to policer and marks in-profile PC Data traffic to DSCP 0
CAT6500-PFC2-CATOS> (enable)
CAT6500-PFC2-CATOS> (enable) commit qos acl IPPHONE-PC-BASIC
        ! Commits ACL to PFC memory
CAT6500-PFC2-CATOS> (enable)
CAT6500-PFC2-CATOS> (enable) set port qos 3/1 trust-device ciscoipphone
        ! Conditional trust (for Cisco IP Phones only)
CAT6500-PFC2-CATOS> (enable) set qos acl map IPPHONE-PC-BASIC 3/1
        ! Attaches ACL to switch port
CAT6500-PFC2-CATOS> (enable)
```

Catalyst 6500 CatOS QoS verification commands:

- **show qos status**
- **show qos maps**
- **show port qos**
- **show qos acl**
- **show qos policer**
- **show qos statistics**

NOTE As previously mentioned, on non–Gigabit Ethernet line cards that use 2Q2T transmit queuing and 1Q4T receive queuing, a hardware limitation prevents the proper functioning of port-based trust (which affects trust-cos, trust-ipprec, and trust-dscp). On such line cards, a workaround ACL can be used to achieve trust functionality. For such an example, see the section "Catalyst 6500 CatOS QoS Verification Command: **show port qos**" (see Example 12-50), earlier in this chapter.

Catalyst 6500: Conditionally Trusted IP Phone + PC: Advanced Model

The Catalyst 6500 Conditionally Trusted IP Phone: Advanced model leverages the dual-rate policing capabilities of the PFC2/PFC3. In Example 12-59, the dual-rate policing feature is applied to client-to-server flows to complement the Untrusted Server model.

Dual-rate policing, in this context, allows for graduated markdown of Interactive-Video (from PCs), Transactional Data, and Bulk Data. Specifically, in this example, Interactive-

Video is marked down to AF42 if it is in excess of 300 kbps but less than 500 kbps; if it is greater than 500 kbps, it is marked down to Scavenger (CS1). Similarly, Transactional Data and Bulk Data are marked down to AF22 and AF12 (respectively) if they are in excess of 3 Mbps but less than 5 Mbps; if they are in excess of 5 Mbps, they are both marked down to Scavenger (CS1). All other policers are consistent with the single-rate policer model.

The Catalyst 6500 PFC2/PFC3 Conditionally Trusted Endpoint Dual-Rate Policing: IP Phone + PC Advanced model is illustrated in Figure 12-25.

Figure 12-25 *Catalyst 6500 PFC2/PFC3 Conditionally Trusted Endpoint Dual-Rate Policing: IP Phone + PC (Advanced Model) Example*

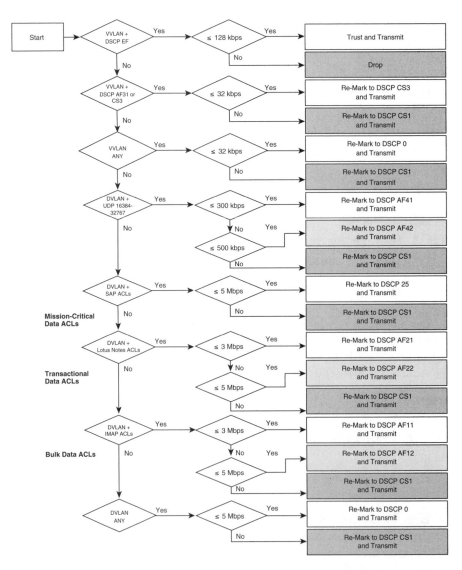

NOTE   The discrete traffic watermarks at which graduated markdown should occur are at the network administrator's discretion and vary among enterprises and applications.

Example 12-59 shows a configuration for a Catalyst 6500 CatOS Conditionally Trusted IP Phone + PC: Advanced model.

Example 12-59 *Catalyst 6500 CatOS: Conditionally Trusted IP Phone + PC: Advanced Model Example*

```
CAT6500-PFC2-CATOS> (enable) set qos cos-dscp-map 0 8 16 24 32 46 48 56
             ! Modifies default CoS-DSCP mapping so that CoS 5 is mapped to DSCP EF
CAT6500-PFC2-CATOS> (enable) set qos policed-dscp-map normal-rate 0,24,25:8
             ! Excess Data, Call-Signaling and MC-Data traffic is marked down to CS1
CAT6500-PFC2-CATOS> (enable) set qos policed-dscp-map normal-rate 10:12
             ! Excess Bulk traffic is marked down from DSCP AF11 to AF12
CAT6500-PFC2-CATOS> (enable) set qos policed-dscp-map excess-rate 10:8
             ! Violating Bulk traffic is marked down to DSCP CS1
CAT6500-PFC2-CATOS> (enable) set qos policed-dscp-map normal-rate 18:20
             ! Excess Transactional Data traffic is marked down from AF21 to AF22
CAT6500-PFC2-CATOS> (enable) set qos policed-dscp-map excess-rate 18:8
             ! Violating Transactional Data traffic is marked down to DSCP CS1
CAT6500-PFC2-CATOS> (enable) set qos policed-dscp-map normal-rate 34:36
             ! Excess Interactive-Video traffic is marked down from AF41 to AF42
CAT6500-PFC2-CATOS> (enable) set qos policed-dscp-map excess-rate 34:8
             ! Violating Interactive-Video traffic is marked down to DSCP CS1
CAT6500-PFC2-CATOS> (enable)
CAT6500-PFC2-CATOS> (enable)
CAT6500-PFC2-CATOS> (enable) set qos policer aggregate VVLAN-VOICE
         rate 128 burst 8 drop
             ! Defines the policer for IP Phone VoIP traffic
CAT6500-PFC2-CATOS> (enable) set qos policer aggregate VVLAN-SIGNALING
         rate 32 burst 8 policed-dscp
             ! Defines the policer for IP Phone Call-Signaling traffic
CAT6500-PFC2-CATOS> (enable) set qos policer aggregate VVLAN-ANY
         rate 32 burst 8 policed-dscp
             ! Defines the policer for any other traffic sourced from the VVLAN
CAT6500-PFC2-CATOS> (enable) set qos policer aggregate PC-VIDEO
         rate 300  policed-dscp erate 500 policed-dscp burst 8
             ! Defines the Dual-Rate policer for Interactive-Video
CAT6500-PFC2-CATOS> (enable) set qos policer aggregate MISSION-CRITICAL
         rate 5000 burst 8 policed-dscp
             ! Defines the policer for Mission-Critical Data
CAT6500-PFC2-CATOS> (enable) set qos policer aggregate TRANSACTIONAL
         rate 3000 policed-dscp erate 5000 policed-dscp burst 8
             ! Defines the Dual-Rate policer for Transactional Data
CAT6500-PFC2-CATOS> (enable) set qos policer aggregate BULK
         rate 3000 policed-dscp erate 5000 policed-dscp burst 8
             ! Defines the Dual-Rate policer for Bulk Data
```

continues

Example 12-59 *Catalyst 6500 CatOS: Conditionally Trusted IP Phone + PC: Advanced Model Example (Continued)*

```
CAT6500-PFC2-CATOS> (enable) set qos policer aggregate PC-DATA
        rate 5000 burst 8 policed-dscp
        ! Defines the policer for all other PC Data traffic
CAT6500-PFC2-CATOS> (enable)
CAT6500-PFC2-CATOS> (enable)
CAT6500-PFC2-CATOS> (enable) set qos acl ip IPPHONE-PC-ADVANCED dscp 46
        aggregate VVLAN-VOICE udp 10.1.110.0 0.0.0.255 any range 16384 32767
        ! Binds ACL to policer and marks in-profile VVLAN VoIP to DSCP EF
CAT6500-PFC2-CATOS> (enable) set qos acl ip IPPHONE-PC-ADVANCED dscp 24
        aggregate VVLAN-SIGNALING tcp 10.1.110.0 0.0.0.255 any range 2000 2002
        ! Binds ACL to policer marks in-profile VVLAN Call-Signaling to DSCP CS3
CAT6500-PFC2-CATOS> (enable) set qos acl ip IPPHONE-PC-ADVANCED dscp 0
        aggregate VVLAN-ANY 10.1.110.0 0.0.0.255
        ! Binds ACL to policer and marks all other VVLAN traffic to DSCP 0
CAT6500-PFC2-CATOS> (enable) set qos acl ip IPPHONE-PC-ADVANCED dscp 34
        aggregate PC-VIDEO udp any any range 16384 32767
        ! Binds ACL to Dual-Rate policer and marks in-profile PC Video to AF41
CAT6500-PFC2-CATOS> (enable) set qos acl ip IPPHONE-PC-ADVANCED dscp 25
        aggregate MISSION-CRITICAL tcp any any range 3200 3203
        ! Binds ACL to policer and marks in-profile SAP to DSCP 25
CAT6500-PFC2-CATOS> (enable) set qos acl ip IPPHONE-PC-ADVANCED dscp 25
        aggregate MISSION-CRITICAL tcp any any eq 3600
        ! Binds ACL to policer and marks in-profile SAP to DSCP 25
CAT6500-PFC2-CATOS> (enable)
CAT6500-PFC2-CATOS> (enable) set qos acl ip IPPHONE-PC-ADVANCED dscp 18
        aggregate TRANSACTIONAL tcp any any eq 1352
        ! Binds ACL to Dual-Rate policer and marks in-profile Lotus to AF21
CAT6500-PFC2-CATOS> (enable)
CAT6500-PFC2-CATOS> (enable) set qos acl ip IPPHONE-PC-ADVANCED dscp 10
        aggregate BULK tcp any any eq 143
        ! Binds ACL to Dual-Rate policer and marks in-profile IMAP to AF11
CAT6500-PFC2-CATOS> (enable) set qos acl ip IPPHONE-PC-ADVANCED dscp 10
        aggregate BULK tcp any any eq 220
        ! Binds ACL to Dual-Rate policer and marks in-profile IMAP to AF11
CAT6500-PFC2-CATOS> (enable) set qos acl ip IPPHONE-PC-ADVANCED dscp 0
        aggregate PC-DATA any
        ! Binds ACL to policer and marks other in-profile PC data to DSCP 0
CAT6500-PFC2-CATOS> (enable)
CAT6500-PFC2-CATOS> (enable)
CAT6500-PFC2-CATOS> (enable) commit qos acl IPPHONE-PC-ADVANCED
        ! Commits ACL to PFC memory
CAT6500-PFC2-CATOS> (enable) set port qos 3/1 trust-device ciscoipphone
        ! Conditional trust (for Cisco IP Phones only)
CAT6500-PFC2-CATOS> (enable) set qos acl map IPPHONE-PC-ADVANCED 3/1
        ! Attaches ACL to switch port
CAT6500-PFC2-CATOS> (enable)
```

Catalyst 6500 CatOS QoS verification commands:

- **show qos status**
- **show qos maps**
- **show port qos**
- **show qos acl**
- **show qos policer**
- **show qos statistics**

NOTE   As previously mentioned, on non–Gigabit Ethernet line cards that use 2Q2T transmit queuing and 1Q4T receive queuing, a hardware limitation prevents the proper functioning of port-based trust (which affects trust-cos, trust-ipprec, and trust-dscp). On such line cards, a workaround ACL can be used to achieve trust functionality. For such an example, see the section "Catalyst 6500 CatOS QoS Verification Command: **show port qos**" (see Example 12-50), earlier in this chapter.

Catalyst 6500: Queuing and Dropping

Although the Catalyst 6500 PFC performs classification, marking, mapping, and policing functions, all queuing and dropping policies are administered by the Catalyst 6500 line cards. This inevitably leads to per-line card hardware-specific capabilities and syntax when it comes to configuring queuing and dropping.

As previously discussed in relation to other platforms that support ingress queuing, receive queues are extremely difficult to congest, even in controlled lab environments. This is especially so if access-edge policies, as detailed in this chapter, are used on all access-layer switches.

Ingress congestion implies that the combined ingress rates of traffic exceed the switch's processing capability and, thus, packets would need to be queued simply to gain access to the switching fabric. On newer platforms, such as the Catalyst 6500 Supervisor 720, this means that a combined ingress rate of more than 720 Gbps would have to be sent to the switch, which is extremely unlikely.

To obviate such an extreme event, the Catalyst 6500 schedules ingress traffic through the receive queues based on CoS values. In the default configuration, the scheduler assigns all traffic with CoS 5 to the strict-priority queue (if present); in the absence of a strict-priority queue, the scheduler assigns all traffic to the standard queues. All other traffic is assigned to the standard queue(s) (with higher CoS values being assigned preference over lower CoS values, wherever supported). Additionally, if a port is configured to trust CoS, the ingress scheduler implements CoS value-based receive-queue drop thresholds, to avoid congestion in received traffic. Thus, even if the extremely unlikely event of ingress congestion occurs, the default settings for the Catalyst 6500 line card receive queues are more than adequate to protect VoIP and Network-Control traffic.

Therefore, the focus of this section is on Catalyst 6500 egress/transmit queuing design recommendations. At the time of writing, there are six main transmit queuing/dropping options for Catalyst 6500 line cards:

- **2Q2T**—Indicates two standard queues, each with two configurable tail-drop thresholds.

- **1P2Q1T**—Indicates one strict-priority queue and two standard queues, each with one configurable WRED drop threshold. (However, each standard queue also has one nonconfigurable tail-drop threshold.)

- **1P2Q2T**—Indicates one strict-priority queue and two standard queues, each with two configurable WRED drop thresholds.

- **1P3Q1T**—Indicates one strict-priority queue and three standard queues, each with one configurable WRED drop threshold. (However, each standard queue also has one nonconfigurable tail-drop threshold.)

- **1P3Q8T**—Indicates one strict-priority queue and three standard queues, each with eight configurable WRED drop thresholds. (However, each standard queue also has one nonconfigurable tail-drop threshold.)

- **1P7Q8T**—Indicates one strict-priority queue and seven standard queues, each with eight configurable WRED drop thresholds. (On 1p7q8t ports, each standard queue also has one nonconfigurable tail-drop threshold.)

Almost all Catalyst 6500 line cards support a strict-priority queue, and, when supported, the switch services traffic in the strict-priority transmit queue before servicing the standard queues. When the switch is servicing a standard queue, after transmitting a packet, it checks for traffic in the strict-priority queue. If the switch detects traffic in the strict-priority queue, it suspends its service of the standard queue and completes service of all traffic in the strict-priority queue before returning to the standard queue.

Additionally, Catalyst 6500 line cards implement CoS value-based transmit-queue drop thresholds to avoid congestion in transmitted traffic. WRED thresholds also can be defined on certain line cards, where the CoS value of the packet (not the IP Precedence value, although they likely will match) determines the WRED weight. WRED parameters include a lower and upper threshold: The low WRED threshold is the queue level where (assigned) traffic begins to be dropped selectively, and the high WRED threshold is the queue level above which all (assigned) traffic is dropped. Furthermore, packets in the queue between the low and high WRED thresholds have an increasing chance of being dropped as the queue fills.

The transmit queuing and dropping capabilities can be returned with the following commands.

CatOS:

- **show port capabilities**
- **show port qos**
- **show qos info**

Cisco IOS:

- **show queueing interface**

Table 12-2 includes the Catalyst 6500 line cards that were available at the time of this writing, along with their respective queuing and dropping structures.

Table 12-2   *Catalyst 6500 Line Card Queuing Structures*

C2 (xCEF720) Modules	Description	ReceiveQueue Structure	Transmit Queue Structure	Buffer Size
WS-X6704-10GE	Catalyst 6500 4-port 10 Gigabit Ethernet module	1Q8T (8Q8T with DFC3a)	1P7Q8T	16 MB per port
WS-X6724-SFP	Catalyst 6500 24-port Gigabit Ethernet SFP module	1Q8T (2Q8T with DFC3a)	1P3Q8T	1 MB per port
WS-X6748-GE-TX	Catalyst 6500 48-port 10/100/1000 RJ-45 module	1Q8T (2Q8T with DFC3a)	1P3Q8T	1 MB per port
WS-X6748-SFP	Catalyst 6500 48-port Gigabit Ethernet SFP module	1Q8T (2Q8T with DFC3a)	1P3Q8T	1 MB per port
Classic/CEF256 Ethernet Modules	**Description**	**ReceiveQueue Structure**	**Transmit Queue Structure**	**Buffer Size**
WS-X6024-10FL-MT	Catalyst 6000 24-port 10BASE-FL MT-RJ module	1Q4T	2Q2T	64 KB per port
WS-X6148-RJ21	Catalyst 6500 48-port 10/100 RJ-21 module (upgradeable to Voice)	1Q4T	2Q2T	128 KB per port
WS-X6148-RJ21V	Catalyst 6500 48-port 10/100 Inline Power RJ-21 module	1Q4T	2Q2T	128 KB per port
WS-X6148-RJ45	Catalyst 6500 48-port 10/100; RJ-45 module (upgradeable to Voice)	1Q4T	2Q2T	128 KB per port

continues

Table 12-2 *Catalyst 6500 Line Card Queuing Structures (Continued)*

Classic/CEF256 Ethernet Modules	Description	ReceiveQueue Structure	Transmit Queue Structure	Buffer Size
WS-X6148-RJ45V	Catalyst 6500 48-port 10/100 Inline Power RJ-45 module	1Q4T	2Q2T	128 KB per port
WS-X6148-GE-TX	Catalyst 6500 48-port 10/100/1000 RJ-45 module	1Q2T	1P2Q2T	1 MB per 8 ports
WS-X6148V-GE-TX	Catalyst 6500 48-port 10/100/1000 Inline Power RJ-45 module	1Q2T	1P2Q2T	1 MB per 8 ports
WS-X6316-GE-TX	Catalyst 6000 16-port 1000TX Gigabit Ethernet RJ-45 module	1P1Q4T	1P2Q2T	512 KB per port
WS-X6324-100FX-MM	Catalyst 6000 24-port 100FX MT-RJ MMF module (with Enhanced QoS)	1Q4T	2Q2T	128 KB per port
WS-X6324-100FX-SM	Catalyst 6000 24-port 100FX MT-RJ SMF module (with Enhanced QoS)	1Q4T	2Q2T	128 KB per port
WS-X6348-RJ-21	Catalyst 6000 48-port 10/100 RJ-21 module	1Q4T	2Q2T	128 KB per port
WS-X6348-RJ21V	Catalyst 6000 48-port 10/100 Inline Power RJ-21 module	1Q4T	2Q2T	128 KB per port
WS-X6348-RJ-45	Catalyst 6500 48-port 10/100 RJ-45 module (upgradeable to Voice)	1Q4T	2Q2T	128 KB per port
WS-X6348-RJ45V	Catalyst 6500 48-port 10/100 Inline Power RJ-45 module	1Q4T	2Q2T	128 KB per port
WS-X6408A-GBIC	Catalyst 6000 8-port Gigabit Ethernet module (with Enhanced QoS; requires GBICs)	1P1Q4T	1P2Q2T	512 KB per port

Table 12-2   *Catalyst 6500 Line Card Queuing Structures (Continued)*

Classic/CEF256 Ethernet Modules	Description	ReceiveQueue Structure	Transmit Queue Structure	Buffer Size
WS-X6416-GBIC	Catalyst 6000 16-port Gigabit Ethernet module (requires GBICs)	1P1Q4T	1P2Q2T	512 KB per port
WS-X6416-GE-MT	Catalyst 6000 16-port Gigabit Ethernet MT-RJ module	1P1Q4T	1P2Q2T	512 KB per port
WS-X6501-10GEX4	1-port 10 Gigabit Ethernet module	1P1Q8T	1P2Q1T	64 MB per port
WS-X6502-10GE	Catalyst 6500 10 Gigabit Ethernet Base module (requires OIM)	1P1Q8T	1P2Q1T	64 MB per port
WS-X6516A-GBIC	Catalyst 6500 16-port Gigabit Ethernet module (fabric enabled; requires GBICs)	1P1Q4T	1P2Q2T	1 MB per port
WS-X6516-GBIC	Catalyst 6500 16-port Gigabit Ethernet module (fabric enabled; requires GBICs)	1P1Q4T	1P2Q2T	512 KB per port
WS-X6516-GE-TX	Catalyst 6500 16-port Gigabit Ethernet Copper module; (crossbar enabled)	1P1Q4T	1P2Q2T	512 KB per port
WS-X6524-100FX-MM	Catalyst 6500 24-port 100FX MT-RJ module (fabric enabled)	1P1Q0T	1P3Q1T	1 MB per port
WS-X6548-RJ-21	Catalyst 6500 48-port 10/100 RJ-21 module (fabric enabled)	1P1Q0T	1P3Q1T	1 MB per port
WS-X6548-RJ-45	Catalyst 6500 48-port 10/100 RJ-45 module (crossbar enabled)	1P1Q0T	1P3Q1T	1 MB per port
WS-X6548V-GE-TX	Catalyst 6500 48-port 10/100/1000 Inline Power RJ-45 module (fabric enabled)	1Q2T	1P2Q2T	1 MB per 8 ports

continues

Table 12-2 *Catalyst 6500 Line Card Queuing Structures (Continued)*

Classic/CEF256 Ethernet Modules	Description	ReceiveQueue Structure	Transmit Queue Structure	Buffer Size
WS-X6548-GE-TX	Catalyst 6500 48-port 10/100/1000 RJ-45 module (fabric enabled)	1Q2T	1P2Q2T	1 MB per 8 ports
WS-X6816-GBIC	Catalyst 6500 16-port Gigabit Ethernet module (fabric enabled; requires GBICs)	1P1Q4T	1P2Q2T	512 KB per port

Design recommendations for each of these six main Catalyst 6500 queuing structures follow.

Catalyst 6500: 2Q2T Queuing and Dropping

Line cards that support only 2Q2T queuing models have no provision for priority queuing. Nonetheless, tuning the weighted round-robin (WRR) weights and the queue sizes can help offset this limitation.

For example, if Q1 is to service Scavenger/Bulk Data (CoS 1) and Best-Effort (CoS 0) traffic, assigning 30 percent of the buffer space to the first queue is adequate; the remaining 70 percent can be assigned to Q2.

The WRR weights can be set to the same ratio of 30:70 for servicing Q1:Q2.

Because the 2Q2T model supports configurable tail-drop thresholds, these can be tuned to provide an additional layer of QoS granularity. For example, the first queue's first threshold can be set at 40 percent, to prevent Scavenger/Bulk Data traffic from dominating Q1. Similarly, the second queue's first threshold can be set to 80 percent, to always allow some room in the queue for VoIP. The second threshold of each queue always should be set to the tail of the queue (100 percent).

After the queues and thresholds have been defined as such, CoS 1 (Scavenger/Bulk Data) can be assigned to Q1T1; CoS 0 (Best Effort) can be assigned to Q1T2; CoS 2 (Network-Management and Transactional Data), CoS 3 (Call-Signaling and Mission-Critical Data), CoS 4 (Interactive- and Streaming-Video), and CoS 6 and 7 (Internetwork and Network Control) can be assigned to Q21T; and CoS 5 (VoIP) can be assigned to Q2T2.

Figure 12-26 illustrates these 2Q2T queuing recommendations.

Figure 12-26 *Catalyst 6500 2Q2T Queuing Model*

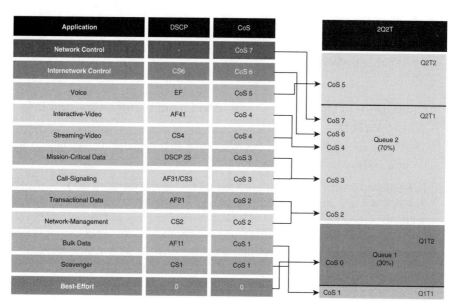

Example 12-60 shows the Catalyst 6500 CatOS configurations to configure 2Q2T queuing recommendations.

Example 12-60 *Catalyst 6500 CatOS: 2Q2T Queuing Example*

```
CAT6500-PFC2-CATOS> (enable) set qos txq-ratio 2q2t 30 70
        ! Sets the buffer allocations to 30% for Q1 and 70% for Q2
CAT6500-PFC2-CATOS> (enable) set qos wrr 2q2t 30 70
        ! Sets the WRR weights for 30:70 (Q1:Q2) bandwidth servicing
CAT6500-PFC2-CATOS> (enable)
CAT6500-PFC2-CATOS> (enable) set qos drop-threshold 2q2t tx queue 1 40 100
        ! Sets Q1T1 to 40% to limit Scavenger/Bulk from dominating Q1
CAT6500-PFC2-CATOS> (enable) set qos drop-threshold 2q2t tx queue 2 80 100
        ! Sets Q2T1 to 80% to always have room in Q2 for VoIP
CAT6500-PFC2-CATOS> (enable)
CAT6500-PFC2-CATOS> (enable) set qos map 2q2t tx 1 1 cos 1
        ! Assigns Scavenger/Bulk to Q1T1
CAT6500-PFC2-CATOS> (enable) set qos map 2q2t tx 1 2 cos 0
        ! Assigns Best Effort to Q1T2
CAT6500-PFC2-CATOS> (enable) set qos map 2q2t tx 2 1 cos 2,3,4,6,7
        ! Assigns CoS 2,3,4,6 and 7 to Q2T1
CAT6500-PFC2-CATOS> (enable) set qos map 2q2t tx 2 2 cos 5
        ! Assigns VoIP to Q2T2
CAT6500-PFC2-CATOS> (enable)
```

Catalyst 6500 CatOS QoS verification commands:

* **show qos info config 2q2t tx**
* **show qos info runtime**
* **show qos statistics**

Catalyst 6500 CatOS QoS Verification Command: **show qos info config 2q2t tx**

The Catalyst 6500 CatOS **show qos info config 2q2t tx** verification command displays the queuing and dropping parameters for 2Q2T line cards.

In Example 12-61, CoS 1 is assigned to Q1T1; CoS 0 is assigned to Q1T2; CoS values 2, 3, 4, 6, and 7 are assigned to Q2T1; and CoS 5 is assigned to Q2T2. The first thresholds are set to 40 percent and 80 percent of their respective queues, and the second thresholds are set to the tail of the queue. The size ratio has been allocated 30 percent for Q1 and 70 percent for Q2, and the WRR weights are set to 30:70 to service Q1 and Q2, respectively.

Example 12-61 **show qos info config 2q2t tx** *Verification for a Catalyst 6500-CatOS Switch*

```
CAT6500-PFC2-CATOS> (enable) show qos info config 2q2t tx
QoS setting in NVRAM for 2q2t transmit:
QoS is enabled
Queue and Threshold Mapping for 2q2t (tx):
Queue Threshold CoS
----- --------- ----------------
1      1         1
1      2         0
2      1         2 3 4 6 7
2      2         5
Tx drop thresholds:
Queue #  Thresholds - percentage
-------  ------------------------------------
1        40% 100%
2        80% 100%
Tx WRED thresholds:
WRED feature is not supported for this port type.
Tx queue size ratio:
Queue #  Sizes - percentage
-------  ------------------------------------
1        30%
2        70%
Tx WRR Configuration of ports with 2q2t:
Queue #  Ratios
-------  ------------------------------------
1        30
2        70
CAT6500-PFC2-CATOS> (enable)
```

Catalyst 6500 CatOS QoS Verification Command: **show qos info runtime**

The Catalyst 6500 CatOS **show qos info runtime** verification command reports similar information as the **show qos info** config command, but it displays the runtime information (committed to the PFC and line card) instead of only the configured information.

In Example 12-62, CoS 1 is assigned to Q1T1; CoS 0 is assigned to Q1T2; CoS values 2, 3, 4, 6, and 7 are assigned to Q2T1; and CoS 5 is assigned to Q2T2. The first thresholds are set to 40 percent and 80 percent of their respective queues, and the second thresholds are set to the tail of the queue. The size ratio has been allocated 30 percent for Q1 and 70 percent for Q2, and the WRR weights are set to 30:70 to service Q1 and Q2, respectively.

Example 12-62 *show qos info runtime Verification for a Catalyst 6500-CatOS Switch*

```
CAT6500-PFC3-CATOS> (enable) show qos info runtime 3/1
Run time setting of QoS:
QoS is enabled
Policy Source of port 3/1: Local
Tx port type of port 3/1 : 2q2t
Rx port type of port 3/1 : 1q4t
Interface type: port-based
ACL attached:
The qos trust type is set to untrusted.
Default CoS = 0
Queue and Threshold Mapping for 2q2t (tx):
Queue Threshold CoS
----- --------- ----------------
1     1         1
1     2         0
2     1         2 3 4 6 7
2     2         5
Queue and Threshold Mapping for 1q4t (rx):
All packets are mapped to a single queue.
Rx drop thresholds:
Rx drop thresholds are disabled.
Tx drop thresholds:
Queue #  Thresholds - percentage (* abs values)
-------  ---------------------------------------
1        40% (6144 bytes) 100% (15360 bytes)
2        80% (28672 bytes) 100% (35840 bytes)
Rx WRED thresholds:
Rx WRED feature is not supported for this port type.
Tx WRED thresholds:
WRED feature is not supported for this port type.
Tx queue size ratio:
Queue #  Sizes - percentage (* abs values)
-------  ---------------------------------------
1        30% (17408 bytes)
2        70% (37888 bytes)
Rx queue size ratio:
Rx queue size-ratio feature is not supported for this port type.
Tx WRR Configuration of ports with speed 10Mbps:
```

continues

Example 12-62 show qos info runtime *Verification for a Catalyst 6500-CatOS Switch (Continued)*

```
Queue #  Ratios (* abs values)
-------  -------------------------------------
1         30 (7648 bytes)
2         70 (17840 bytes)
(*) Runtime information may differ from user configured setting due to hardware
granularity.
CAT6500-PFC3-CATOS> (enable)
```

Example 12-63 shows the Catalyst 6500 IOS configurations to configure 2Q2T queuing recommendations.

Example 12-63 *Catalyst 6500 IOS: 2Q2T Queuing Example*

```
CAT6500-PFC3-IOS(config)# interface range FastEthernet6/1 - 48
CAT6500-PFC3-IOS(config-if)# wrr-queue queue-limit 30 70
     ! Sets the buffer allocations to 30% for Q1 and 70% for Q2
CAT6500-PFC3-IOS(config-if)# wrr-queue bandwidth 30 70
     ! Sets the WRR weights for 30:70 (Q1:Q2) bandwidth servicing
CAT6500-PFC3-IOS(config-if)#
CAT6500-PFC3-IOS(config-if)# wrr-queue threshold 1 40 100
     ! Sets Q1T1 to 40% to limit Scavenger/Bulk from dominating Q1
CAT6500-PFC3-IOS(config-if)# wrr-queue threshold 2 80 100
     ! Sets Q2T1 to 80% to always have room in Q2 for VoIP
CAT6500-PFC3-IOS(config-if)#
CAT6500-PFC3-IOS(config-if)# wrr-queue cos-map 1 1 1
     ! Assigns Scavenger/Bulk to Q1T1
CAT6500-PFC3-IOS(config-if)# wrr-queue cos-map 1 2 0
     ! Assigns Best Effort to Q1T2
CAT6500-PFC3-IOS(config-if)# wrr-queue cos-map 2 1 2 3 4 6 7
     ! Assigns CoS 2,3,4,6 and 7 to Q2T1
CAT6500-PFC3-IOS(config-if)# wrr-queue cos-map 2 2 5
     ! Assigns VoIP to Q2T2
CAT6500-PFC3-IOS(config-if)#end
CAT6500-PFC3-IOS#
```

Catalyst 6500 MLS QoS verification command:

* **show queueing interface**

Catalyst 6500 IOS QoS Verification Command: **show queueing interface**

The Catalyst 6500 IOS **show queueing interface** verification command displays the queuing parameters for a given interface (according to the line card's capabilities).

In Example 12-64, the line card has 2Q2T transmit queuing. The WRR scheduling weights are set to 30:70 to service Q1 and Q2, respectively. The transmit queue size ratios have been allocated 30 percent for Q1 and 70 percent for Q2. The first queue's tail-drop thresholds are set to 40 percent and 100 percent, while the second queue's tail-drop thresholds are set to

80 percent and 100 percent. CoS 1 is assigned to Q1T1; CoS 0 is assigned to Q1T2; CoS values 2, 3, 4, 6, and 7 are assigned to Q2T1; and CoS 5 is assigned to Q2T2.

Example 12-64 **show queueing interface** *Verification for a Catalyst 6500 IOS Switch*

```
CAT6500-PFC3-IOS#show queueing interface FastEthernet6/1
Interface FastEthernet6/1 queueing strategy:  Weighted Round-Robin
  Port QoS is enabled
  Port is untrusted
  Extend trust state: not trusted [COS = 0]
  Default COS is 0
    Queueing Mode In Tx direction: mode-cos
    Transmit queues [type = 2q2t]:
    Queue Id    Scheduling  Num of thresholds
    -----------------------------------------
       1           WRR low          2
       2           WRR high         2
    WRR bandwidth ratios:    30[queue 1]  70[queue 2]
    queue-limit ratios:      30[queue 1]  70[queue 2]
    queue tail-drop-thresholds
    --------------------------
    1    40[1] 100[2]
    2    80[1] 100[2]
    queue thresh cos-map
    ---------------------------------------
    1    1    1
    1    2    0
    2    1    2 3 4 6 7
    2    2    5
    <output truncated>
CAT6500-PFC3-IOS#
```

Catalyst 6500: 1P2Q1T Queuing and Dropping

The 1P2Q1T queuing model builds on the previous 2Q2T model, bringing with it the advantages of strict-priority queuing (for VoIP) and a tunable WRED (not tail drop) threshold per queue.

The term *1P2Q1T* is a bit of a misnomer in the CatOS version of this queuing structure because, in CatOS, there are actually two thresholds per queue: the tunable WRED threshold and the nonconfigurable tail-of-the-queue (100 percent) tail-drop threshold.

Under such a model, buffer space can be allocated as follows: 30 percent for Scavenger/Bulk Data plus Best-Effort queue (Q1), 40 percent for Q2, and 30 percent for the PQ (Q3).

The WRR weights for Q1 and Q2 (for dividing the remaining bandwidth, after the priority queue has been serviced fully) can be set to 30:70, respectively, for Q1:Q2.

Under the 1P2Q1T model, each queue's WRED threshold is defined with a lower and upper limit. For example, the WRED threshold 40:80 indicates that packets assigned to this

WRED threshold will begin being randomly dropped when the queue fills to 40 percent and that these packets will be tail-dropped if the queue fills beyond 80 percent.

Furthermore, in CatOS within the 1P2Q1T queuing structure, each CoS value can be assigned to a queue and a WRED threshold or just to a queue. When assigned to a queue (only), the CoS value will be limited only by the tail of the queue. (In other words, it is assigned to the queue with a tail drop threshold of 100 percent.)

Thus (in CatOS), the tunable WRED threshold for Q1 can be set to 40:80, meaning that Scavenger/Bulk Data will be WRED-dropped if Q1 fills to 40 percent and will be tail-dropped if Q1 fills past 80 percent of capacity. This prevents Scavenger/Bulk Data from drowning out Best-Effort traffic in Q1. The WRED threshold for Q2 can be set to 70:80 to provide congestion avoidance for all applications assigned to it and to ensure that there will always be room in the queue to service Network and Internetwork Control traffic.

Therefore, when the queues and thresholds have been defined as such, CoS 1 (Scavenger/Bulk Data) can be assigned to Q1T1; CoS 0 (Best-Effort) can be assigned to Q1 only (tail); CoS 2 (Network-Management and Transactional Data), CoS 3 (Call-Signaling and Mission-Critical Data) and CoS 4 (Interactive- and Streaming-Video) can be assigned to Q2T1; CoS 6 and 7 (Internetwork and Network Control) can be assigned to Q2 only (tail); and CoS 5 (VoIP) can be assigned to Q3 (the PQ).

Figure 12-27 illustrates these 1P2Q1T queuing recommendations.

Figure 12-27 *Catalyst 6500 1P2Q1T Queuing Model (CatOS Supports 1P2Q2T)*

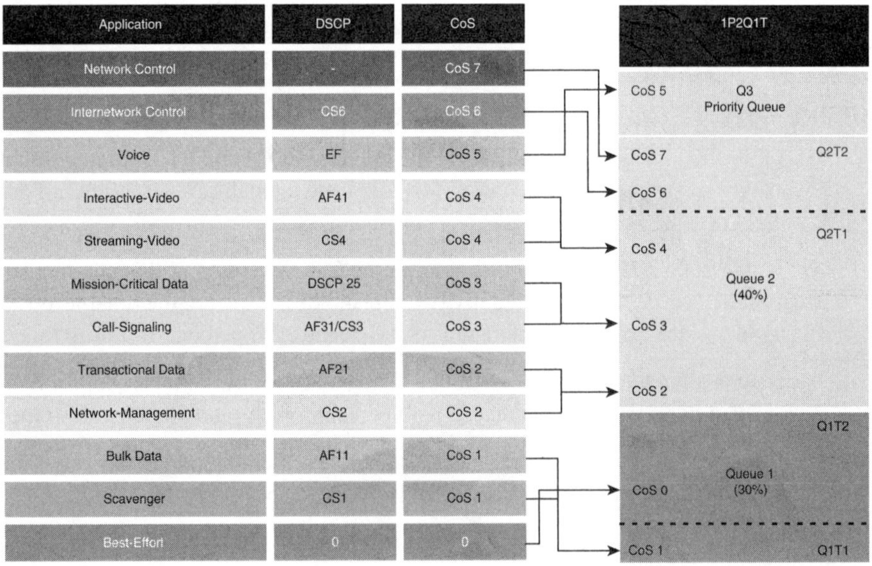

Example 12-65 shows the Catalyst 6500 CatOS configurations to configure 1P2Q1T queuing recommendations.

Example 12-65 *Catalyst 6500 CatOS: 1P2Q1T (Technically, 1P2Q2T) Queuing Example*

```
CAT6500-PFC2-CATOS> (enable) set qos txq-ratio 1p2q1t 30 40 30
        ! Sets the buffer allocations to 30% for Q1, 40% for Q2, 30% for Q3 (PQ)
CAT6500-PFC2-CATOS> (enable) set qos wrr 1p2q1t 30 70
        ! Sets the WRR weights for 30:70 (Q1:Q2) bandwidth servicing
CAT6500-PFC2-CATOS> (enable)
CAT6500-PFC2-CATOS> (enable) set qos wred 1p2q1t tx queue 1 40:80
        ! Sets Q1 WRED Threshold to 40:80 to limit Scavenger/Bulk from dominating Q1
CAT6500-PFC2-CATOS> (enable) set qos wred 1p2q1t tx queue 2 70:80
        ! Sets Q2 WRED Threshold to 70:80 to force room for Network Control traffic
CAT6500-PFC2-CATOS> (enable)
CAT6500-PFC2-CATOS> (enable) set qos map 1p2q1t tx 1 1 cos 1
        ! Assigns Scavenger/Bulk to Q1 WRED Threshold
CAT6500-PFC2-CATOS> (enable) set qos map 1p2q1t tx 1 cos 0
        ! Assigns Best Effort to Q1 tail (100%) threshold
CAT6500-PFC2-CATOS> (enable) set qos map 1p2q1t tx 2 1 cos 2,3,4
        ! Assigns CoS 2,3,4 to Q2 WRED Threshold
CAT6500-PFC2-CATOS> (enable) set qos map 1p2q1t tx 2 cos 6,7
        ! Assigns Network/Internetwork Control to Q2 tail (100%) threshold
CAT6500-PFC2-CATOS> (enable) set qos map 1p2q1t tx 3 cos 5
        ! Assigns VoIP to PQ (Q3)
CAT6500-PFC2-CATOS> (enable)
```

Catalyst 6500 CatOS QoS verification commands:

- **show qos info config 1p2q1t tx**
- **show qos info runtime**
- **show qos statistics**

NOTE   The Catalyst 6500 CatOS **show qos info** verification commands are reasonably similar for each queuing structure and, as such, are not detailed for each queuing model example.

In Cisco IOS, for any 1PxQyT queuing structure, setting the size of the priority queue is not supported. The only exception to this rule is the 1P2Q2T structure, in which the priority queue (Q3) indirectly is set to equal Q2's size. Therefore, in all examples of Catalyst 6500 IOS queuing structure configurations that follow that follow—except for the 1P2Q2T example—only the sizes of the standard queues are being set.

Furthermore, specific to the 1P2Q1T queuing structure, CoS values cannot be mapped to
the tail of the queue, as in CatOS. CoS values can be mapped only to the single WRED
threshold for each queue. Therefore, the 1P2Q1T queuing and dropping recommendation
requires some slight alterations for Cisco IOS. These include changing Q1T1's WRED
threshold to 80:100 and, likewise, changing Q2T1's WRED threshold to 80:100.

The syntax logic for setting WRED thresholds in Cisco IOS is different than in CatOS. In
CatOS, minimum and maximum WRED thresholds are set on the same line; in Cisco IOS,
minimum and maximum WRED thresholds are set on different lines.

After these WRED thresholds have been altered, CoS 1 (Scavenger/Bulk Data) and CoS 0
(Best-Effort) can be assigned to Q1T1; CoS 2 (Network-Management and Transactional
Data), CoS 3 (Call-Signaling and Mission-Critical Data), CoS 4 (Interactive- and Streaming-
Video), and CoS 6 and 7 (Internetwork and Network Control) can be assigned to Q2T1; and
CoS 5 (VoIP) can be assigned to Q3 (the PQ).

Example 12-66 shows the Catalyst 6500 IOS configurations to configure 1P2Q1T queuing
recommendations.

Example 12-66 *Catalyst 6500 IOS: 1P2Q1T Queuing Example*

```
CAT6500-PFC3-IOS(config)#interface TenGigabitEthernet1/1
CAT6500-PFC3-IOS(config-if)# wrr-queue queue-limit 30 40
      ! Sets the buffer allocations to 30% for Q1 and 40% for Q2
CAT6500-PFC3-IOS(config-if)# wrr-queue bandwidth 30 70
      ! Sets the WRR weights for 30:70 (Q1:Q2) bandwidth servicing
CAT6500-PFC3-IOS(config-if)#
CAT6500-PFC3-IOS(config-if)# wrr-queue random-detect min-threshold 1 80
      ! Sets Min WRED Threshold for Q1T1 to 80%
CAT6500-PFC3-IOS(config-if)# wrr-queue random-detect max-threshold 1 100
      ! Sets Max WRED Threshold for Q1T1 to 100%
CAT6500-PFC3-IOS(config-if)# wrr-queue random-detect min-threshold 2 80
      ! Sets Min WRED Threshold for Q2T1 to 80%
CAT6500-PFC3-IOS(config-if)# wrr-queue random-detect max-threshold 2 100
      ! Sets Max WRED Threshold for Q2T1 to 100%
CAT6500-PFC3-IOS(config-if)#
CAT6500-PFC3-IOS(config-if)# wrr-queue cos-map 1 1 1 0
      ! Assigns Scavenger/Bulk and Best Effort to Q1 WRED Threshold 1
CAT6500-PFC3-IOS(config-if)# wrr-queue cos-map 2 1 2 3 4 6 7
      ! Assigns CoS 2,3,4,6 and 7 to Q2 WRED Threshold 1
CAT6500-PFC3-IOS(config-if)# priority-queue cos-map 1 5
      ! Assigns VoIP to PQ (Q3)
CAT6500-PFC3-IOS(config-if)#end
CAT6500-PFC3-IOS(config-if)#
```

Catalyst 6500 MLS QoS verification command:

- **show queueing interface**

Catalyst 6500: 1P2Q2T Queuing and Dropping

The 1P2Q2T queuing model is essentially identical to the 1P2Q1T model, except that it supports two configurable WRED thresholds per queue.

Under a 1P2Q2T model, buffer space can be allocated as follows: 40 percent for Q1 (the Scavenger/Bulk Data + Best-Effort queue), 30 percent for Q2 (the preferential queue), and 30 percent for the Q3 (the priority queue).

The WRR weights for Q1 and Q2 (for dividing the remaining bandwidth, after the priority queue has been serviced fully) remain at 30:70, respectively, for Q1:Q2.

Under the 1P2Q2T model, each WRED threshold is defined with a lower and upper limit. Therefore, the first WRED threshold for Q1 can be set to 40:80, so that Scavenger/Bulk Data traffic can be WRED-dropped if Q1 hits 40 percent and can be tail-dropped if Q1 exceeds 80 percent of its capacity (this prevents Scavenger/Bulk Data from drowning out Best-Effort traffic in Q1). The second WRED threshold for Q1 can be set to 80:100 to provide congestion avoidance for Best-Effort traffic.

Similarly, the first WRED threshold of Q2 can be set to 70:80, and the second can be set to 80:100. In this manner, congestion avoidance will be provided for all traffic types in Q2, and there will always be room in the queue to service Network and Internetwork Control traffic.

Therefore, after the queues have been defined as mentioned previously, CoS 1 (Scavenger/ Bulk Data) can be assigned to Q1T1; CoS 0 (Best-Effort) can be assigned to Q1T2; CoS 2 (Network-Management and Transactional Data), CoS 3 (Call-Signaling and Mission-Critical Data), and CoS 4 (Interactive- and Streaming-Video) can be assigned to Q2T1; CoS 6 and 7 (Internetwork and Network Control) can be assigned to Q2T2; and CoS 5 (VoIP) can be assigned to Q3T1 (the PQ).

Figure 12-28 illustrates these 1P2Q2T queuing recommendations.

Figure 12-28 *Catalyst 6500 1P2Q2T Queuing Model*

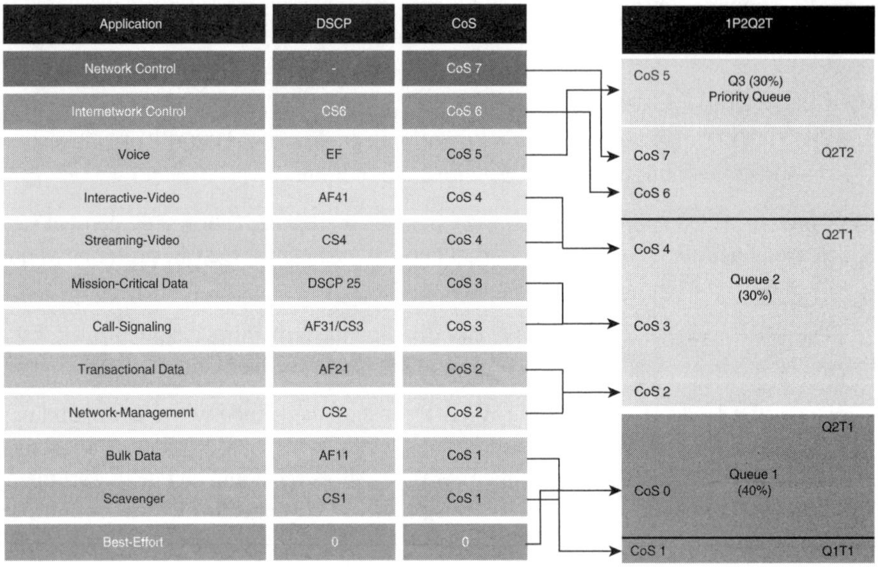

Example 12-67 shows the Catalyst 6500 CatOS configurations to configure 1P2Q1T queuing recommendations.

Example 12-67 *Catalyst 6500 CatOS: 1P2Q2T Queuing Example*

```
CAT6500-PFC2-CATOS> (enable) set qos txq-ratio 1p2q2t 40 30 30
       ! Sets the buffer allocations to 40% for Q1, 30% for Q2, 30% for Q3 (PQ)
CAT6500-PFC2-CATOS> (enable) set qos wrr 1p2q2t 30 70
       ! Sets the WRR weights for 30:70 (Q1:Q2) bandwidth servicing
CAT6500-PFC2-CATOS> (enable)
CAT6500-PFC2-CATOS> (enable) set qos wred 1p2q2t tx queue 1 40:80 80:100
       ! Sets Q1 WRED T1 to 40:80 to limit Scavenger/Bulk from dominating Q1
       ! Sets Q1 WRED T2 to 80:100 to provide congestion-avoidance for Best Effort
CAT6500-PFC2-CATOS> (enable) set qos wred 1p2q2t tx queue 2 70:80 80:100
       ! Sets Q2 WRED T1 to 70:80 to provide congestion-avoidance
       ! Sets Q2 WRED T2 to 80:100 to force room for Network Control traffic
CAT6500-PFC2-CATOS> (enable)
CAT6500-PFC2-CATOS> (enable) set qos map 1p2q2t tx 1 1 cos 1
       ! Assigns Scavenger/Bulk to Q1 WRED Threshold 1
CAT6500-PFC2-CATOS> (enable) set qos map 1p2q2t tx 1 2 cos 0
       ! Assigns Best Effort to Q1 WRED Threshold 2
CAT6500-PFC2-CATOS> (enable) set qos map 1p2q2t tx 2 1 cos 2,3,4
       ! Assigns CoS 2,3,4 to Q2 WRED Threshold 1
CAT6500-PFC2-CATOS> (enable) set qos map 1p2q2t tx 2 2 cos 6,7
       ! Assigns Network/Internetwork Control to Q2 WRED Threshold 2
```

Example 12-67 *Catalyst 6500 CatOS: 1P2Q2T Queuing Example (Continued)*

```
CAT6500-PFC2-CATOS> (enable) set qos map 1p2q2t tx 3 1 cos 5
        ! Assigns VoIP to PQ
CAT6500-PFC2-CATOS> (enable)
```

Catalyst 6500 CatOS QoS verification commands:

- **show qos info config 1p2q2t tx**
- **show qos info runtime**
- **show qos statistics**

Example 12-68 shows the compatible Catalyst 6500 IOS configurations to configure 1P2Q1T queuing recommendations. Notice that the buffer allocation for the PQ (Q3) is not configurable but, by default (for the 1P2Q2T queuing structure only), is set to equal the size defined for Q2. Therefore, Q1 is set to 40 percent and Q2 is set to 30 percent, which indirectly sets Q3 to match at 30 percent.

Example 12-68 shows the Catalyst 6500 IOS configurations to configure 1P2Q2T queuing recommendations.

Example 12-68 *Catalyst 6500 IOS: 1P2Q2T Queuing Example*

```
CAT6500-PFC3-IOS(config)#interface range GigabitEthernet4/1 - 8
CAT6500-PFC3(config-if-range)# wrr-queue queue-limit 40 30
        ! Sets the buffer allocations to 40% for Q1 and 30% for Q2
        ! Indirectly sets PQ (Q3) size to equal Q2 (which is set to 30%)
CAT6500-PFC3(config-if-range)# wrr-queue bandwidth 30 70
        ! Sets the WRR weights for 30:70 (Q1:Q2) bandwidth servicing
CAT6500-PFC3(config-if-range)#
CAT6500-PFC3(config-if-range)# wrr-queue random-detect min-threshold 1 40 80
        ! Sets Min WRED Thresholds for Q1T1 and Q1T2 to 40 and 80, respectively
CAT6500-PFC3(config-if-range)# wrr-queue random-detect max-threshold 1 80 100
        ! Sets Max WRED Thresholds for Q1T1 and Q1T2 to 80 and 100, respectively
CAT6500-PFC3(config-if-range)#
CAT6500-PFC3(config-if-range)# wrr-queue random-detect min-threshold 2 70 80
        ! Sets Min WRED Thresholds for Q2T1 and Q2T2 to 70 and 80, respectively
CAT6500-PFC3(config-if-range)# wrr-queue random-detect max-threshold 2 80 100
        ! Sets Max WRED Thresholds for Q2T1 and Q2T2 to 80 and 100, respectively
CAT6500-PFC3(config-if-range)#
CAT6500-PFC3(config-if-range)# wrr-queue cos-map 1 1 1
        ! Assigns Scavenger/Bulk to Q1 WRED Threshold 1
CAT6500-PFC3(config-if-range)# wrr-queue cos-map 1 2 0
        ! Assigns Best Effort to Q1 WRED Threshold 2
CAT6500-PFC3(config-if-range)# wrr-queue cos-map 2 1 2 3 4
        ! Assigns CoS 2,3,4 to Q2 WRED Threshold 1
CAT6500-PFC3(config-if-range)# wrr-queue cos-map 2 2 6 7
        ! Assigns Network/Internetwork Control to Q2 WRED Threshold 2
```

continues

Example 12-68 *Catalyst 6500 IOS: 1P2Q2T Queuing Example (Continued)*

```
CAT6500-PFC3(config-if-range)#
CAT6500-PFC3(config-if-range)# priority-queue cos-map 1 5
       ! Assigns VoIP to PQ
CAT6500-PFC3(config-if-range)#end
CAT6500-PFC3-IOS#
```

Catalyst 6500 MLS QoS verification command:

- **show queueing interface**

Catalyst 6500: 1P3Q1T Queuing and Dropping

The 1P3Q1T queuing structure is identical to the 1P2Q1T structure, except that an additional standard queue has been added to it and that it does not support tuning the transmit size ratios. Under this model, Q4 is the strict-priority queue.

The WRR weights for the standard queues (Q1, Q2, Q3), for dividing the remaining bandwidth after the priority queue has been serviced serviced, can be set to 5:25:70, respectively, for Q1:Q2:Q3.

In CatOS, within the 1P3T1T queuing structure, each CoS value can be assigned to a queue and a WRED threshold or just to a queue. When assigned to a queue (only), the CoS value is limited only by the tail of the queue (in other words, it is assigned to the queue with a tail drop threshold of 100 percent). Therefore, CatOS essentially supports 1P3Q2T for this type of line card.

Thus, the tunable WRED threshold for Q1 can be set to 80:100 to provide congestion avoidance for Scavenger/Bulk Data traffic. The WRED threshold for Q2 similarly can be set to 80:100 to provide congestion avoidance on all Best-Effort flows. The WRED threshold for Q3 can be set to 70:80, to provide congestion avoidance for all applications assigned to it and to ensure that there will always be room in the Q3 to service Network and Internetwork Control traffic.

Therefore, when the queues and thresholds have been defined as such, CoS 1 (Scavenger/Bulk Data) can be assigned to Q1T1; CoS 0 (Best-Effort) can be assigned to Q2T1; CoS 2 (Network-Management and Transactional Data), CoS 3 (Call-Signaling and Mission-Critical Data), and CoS 4 (Interactive- and Streaming-Video) can be assigned to Q3T1; CoS 6 and 7 (Internetwork and Network Control) can be assigned to Q3 (tail); and CoS 5 (VoIP) can be assigned to Q4 (the PQ).

Figure 12-29 illustrates these 1P3Q1T queuing recommendations.

Figure 12-29 *Catalyst 6500 1P3Q1T Queuing Model (CatOS Supports 1P3Q2T)*

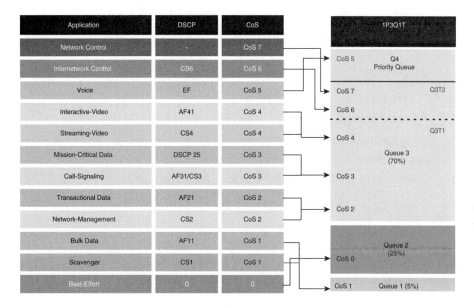

Example 12-69 shows the Catalyst 6500 CatOS configurations to configure 1P3Q1T queuing recommendations.

Example 12-69 *Catalyst 6500 CatOS: 1P3Q1T (Technically, 1P3Q2T) Queuing Example*

```
CAT6500-PFC2-CATOS> (enable) set qos wrr 1p3q1t 5 25 70
        ! Sets the WRR weights for 5:25:70 (Q1:Q2:Q3) bandwidth servicing
CAT6500-PFC2-CATOS> (enable)
CAT6500-PFC2-CATOS> (enable) set qos wred 1p3q1t tx queue 1 80:100
        ! Sets Q1 WRED T1 to 80:100 to provide congestion-avoidance for Scavenger
CAT6500-PFC2-CATOS> (enable) set qos wred 1p3q1t tx queue 2 80:100
        ! Sets Q2 WRED T1 to 80:100 to provide congestion-avoidance for Best Effort
CAT6500-PFC2-CATOS> (enable) set qos wred 1p3q1t tx queue 3 70:80
        ! Sets Q3 WRED T1 to 70:80 to provide congestion-avoidance for CoS 2,3,4
        ! and to force room (via tail-drop) for Network Control traffic
CAT6500-PFC2-CATOS> (enable)
CAT6500-PFC2-CATOS> (enable) set qos map 1p3q1t tx 1 1 cos 1
        ! Assigns Scavenger/Bulk to Q1 WRED Threshold 1 (80:100)
CAT6500-PFC2-CATOS> (enable) set qos map 1p3q1t tx 2 1 cos 0
        ! Assigns Best Effort to Q2 WRED Threshold 1 (80:100)
CAT6500-PFC2-CATOS> (enable) set qos map 1p3q1t tx 3 1 cos 2,3,4
        ! Assigns CoS 2,3,4 to Q3 WRED Threshold 1 (70:80)
CAT6500-PFC2-CATOS> (enable) set qos map 1p3q1t tx 3 cos 6,7
        ! Assigns Network/Internetwork Control to Q3 Tail (100%)
```

continues

Example 12-69 *Catalyst 6500 CatOS: 1P3Q1T (Technically, 1P3Q2T) Queuing Example (Continued)*

```
CAT6500-PFC2-CATOS> (enable) set qos map 1p3q1t tx 4 cos 5
        ! Assigns VoIP to PQ (Q4)
CAT6500-PFC2-CATOS> (enable)
```

Catalyst 6500 CatOS QoS verification commands:

- **show qos info config 1p3q1t tx**
- **show qos info runtime**
- **show qos statistics**

In Cisco IOS, the 1P3Q1T, 1P3Q8T, and 1P7Q8T queuing structures can be configured to use tail drop or WRED. By default, WRED is disabled. Therefore, it is good practice to always explicitly enable WRED on a queue before setting WRED thresholds for these queuing structures.

Additionally, in Cisco IOS, the 1P3Q1T queuing structure does not support mapping CoS values to the tail of the queue (only to the single WRED threshold). Therefore, the queuing recommendation requires slight alterations for Cisco IOS: changing all three WRED thresholds to 80:100 and mapping CoS values 2, 3, 4, 6, and 7 to Q3T1.

Example 12-70 shows the Catalyst 6500 IOS configurations to configure 1P3Q1T queuing recommendations.

Example 12-70 *Catalyst 6500 IOS: 1P3Q1T Queuing Example*

```
CAT6500-PFC3-IOS(config)# interface range FastEthernet3/1 - 48
CAT6500-PFC3-IOS(config-if)# wrr-queue bandwidth 5 25 70
        ! Sets the WRR weights for 5:25:70 (Q1:Q2:Q3) bandwidth servicing
CAT6500-PFC3-IOS(config-if)#
CAT6500-PFC3-IOS(config-if)#
CAT6500-PFC3(config-if-range)# wrr-queue random-detect 1
        ! Enables WRED on Q1
CAT6500-PFC3(config-if-range)# wrr-queue random-detect 2
        ! Enables WRED on Q2
CAT6500-PFC3(config-if-range)# wrr-queue random-detect 3
        ! Enables WRED on Q3
CAT6500-PFC3-IOS(config-if)#
CAT6500-PFC3-IOS(config-if)# wrr-queue random-detect min-threshold 1 80
        ! Sets Min WRED Threshold for Q1T1 to 80%
CAT6500-PFC3-IOS(config-if)# wrr-queue random-detect max-threshold 1 100
        ! Sets Max WRED Threshold for Q1T1 to 100%
CAT6500-PFC3-IOS(config-if)#
CAT6500-PFC3-IOS(config-if)# wrr-queue random-detect min-threshold 2 80
        ! Sets Min WRED Threshold for Q2T1 to 80%
CAT6500-PFC3-IOS(config-if)# wrr-queue random-detect max-threshold 2 100
        ! Sets Max WRED Threshold for Q2T1 to 100%
CAT6500-PFC3-IOS(config-if)#
CAT6500-PFC3-IOS(config-if)# wrr-queue random-detect min-threshold 3 80
        ! Sets Min WRED Threshold for Q3T1 to 80%
```

Example 12-70 *Catalyst 6500 IOS: 1P3Q1T Queuing Example (Continued)*

```
CAT6500-PFC3-IOS(config-if)# wrr-queue random-detect max-threshold 3 100
        ! Sets Max WRED Threshold for Q3T1 to 100%
CAT6500-PFC3-IOS(config-if)#
CAT6500-PFC3-IOS(config-if)# wrr-queue cos-map 1 1 1
        ! Assigns Scavenger/Bulk to Q1 WRED Threshold 1 (80:100)
CAT6500-PFC3-IOS(config-if)# wrr-queue cos-map 2 1 0
        ! Assigns Best Effort to Q2 WRED Threshold 1 (80:100)
CAT6500-PFC3-IOS(config-if)# wrr-queue cos-map 3 1 2 3 4 6 7
        ! Assigns CoS 2,3,4,6 and 7 to Q3 WRED Threshold 1 (80:100)
CAT6500-PFC3-IOS(config-if)# priority-queue cos-map 1 5
        ! Assigns VoIP to PQ (Q4)
CAT6500-PFC3-IOS(config-if)#end
CAT6500-PFC3-IOS#
```

Catalyst 6500 MLS QoS verification command:

- **show queueing interface**

Catalyst 6500: 1P3Q8T Queuing and Dropping

The 1P3Q8T queuing structure is identical to the 1P3Q1T structure, except it has eight tunable WRED thresholds per queue (instead of one) and it also supports tuning the transmit size ratios. Under this model, Q4 is the strict-priority queue.

Under a 1P3Q8T model, buffer space can be allocated as follows: 5 percent for the Scavenger/Bulk Data queue (Q1), 25 percent for the Best-Effort queue (Q2), 40 percent for the preferential queue (Q3), and 30 percent for the strict-priority queue (Q4).

The WRR weights for the standard queues (Q1, Q2, Q3), for dividing the remaining bandwidth after the priority queue has been serviced fully, can be set to 5:25:70, respectively, for Q1:Q2:Q3.

The tunable WRED threshold for Q1 can be set to 80:100 to provide congestion avoidance to Scavenger/Bulk Data traffic. The WRED threshold for Q2 similarly can be set to 80:100 to provide congestion avoidance on all Best-Effort flows.

The 1P3Q8T queuing structure's support for up to eight WRED thresholds per queue allows for additional QoS granularity for the applications sharing Q3. Because only five discrete CoS values are sharing this queue, only five of eight thresholds need to be defined for subqueue QoS. For example, Q3T1 could be set to 50:60, Q3T2 could be set to 60:70, Q3T3 could be set to 70:80, Q3T4 could be set to 80:90, and Q3T5 could be set to 90:100.

Therefore, when the queues and thresholds have been defined as such, CoS 1 (Scavenger/Bulk Data) can be assigned to Q1T1; CoS 0 (Best-Effort) can be assigned to Q2T1; CoS 4 (Interactive- and Streaming-Video) can be assigned to Q3T1; CoS 2 (Network-Management and Transactional Data) can be assigned to Q3T2; CoS 3 (Call-Signaling and Mission-Critical

Data) can be assigned to Q3T3; CoS 6 (Internetwork Control) can be assigned to Q3T4; CoS 7 (Internetwork and Network Control) can be assigned to Q3T5; and CoS 5 (VoIP) can be assigned to Q4 (the PQ).

Figure 12-30 illustrates these 1P3Q8T queuing recommendations.

Figure 12-30 *Catalyst 6500 1P3Q8T Queuing Model*

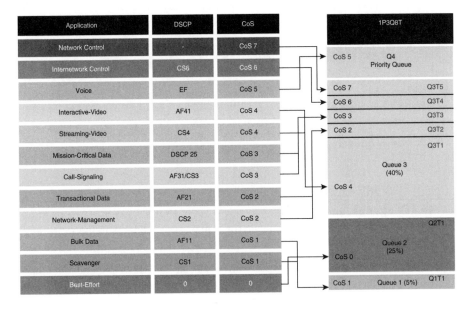

Example 12-71 shows the Catalyst 6500 (PFC3) CatOS configurations to configure 1P3Q8T queuing recommendations.

Example 12-71 *Catalyst 6500 (PFC3) CatOS: 1P3Q8T Queuing Example*

```
CAT6500-PFC3-CATOS> (enable) set qos txq-ratio 1p3q8t 5 25 40 30
         ! Allocates 5% for Q1, 25% for Q2, 40% for Q3 and 30% for Q4 (PQ)
CAT6500-PFC3-CATOS> (enable) set qos wrr 1p3q8t 5 25 70
         ! Sets the WRR weights for 5:25:70 (Q1:Q2:Q3) bandwidth servicing
CAT6500-PFC3-CATOS> (enable)
CAT6500-PFC3-CATOS> (enable) set qos wred 1p3q8t tx queue 1 80:100 100:100
         100:100 100:100 100:100 100:100 100:100 100:100
         ! Sets Q1 WRED T1 to 80:100 and all other Q1 WRED Thresholds to 100:100
CAT6500-PFC3-CATOS> (enable) set qos wred 1p3q8t tx queue 2 80:100 100:100
         100:100 100:100 100:100 100:100 100:100 100:100
         ! Sets Q2 WRED T1 to 80:100 and all other Q2 WRED Thresholds to 100:100
CAT6500-PFC3-CATOS> (enable) set qos wred 1p3q8t tx queue 3 50:60 60:70 70:80
         80:90 90:100 100:100 100:100 100:100
         ! Sets Q3 WRED T1 to 50:60, Q3T2 to 60:70, Q3T3 to 70:80,
```

Example 12-71 *Catalyst 6500 (PFC3) CatOS: 1P3Q8T Queuing Example (Continued)*

```
            ! Q3T4 to 80:90, Q3T5 to 90:100
            ! and the other two Q3 WRED Thresholds to 100:100
CAT6500-PFC3-CATOS> (enable)
CAT6500-PFC3-CATOS> (enable) set qos map 1p3q8t tx 1 1 cos 1
            ! Assigns Scavenger/Bulk to Q1 WRED Threshold 1
CAT6500-PFC3-CATOS> (enable) set qos map 1p3q8t tx 2 1 cos 0
            ! Assigns Best Effort to Q2 WRED Threshold 1
CAT6500-PFC3-CATOS> (enable) set qos map 1p3q8t tx 3 1 cos 4
            ! Assigns Video to Q3 WRED Threshold 1
CAT6500-PFC3-CATOS> (enable) set qos map 1p3q8t tx 3 2 cos 2
            ! Assigns Net-Mgmt and Transactional Data to Q3 WRED T2
CAT6500-PFC3-CATOS> (enable) set qos map 1p3q8t tx 3 3 cos 3
            ! Assigns Call-Signaling and Mission-Critical Data to Q3 WRED T3
CAT6500-PFC3-CATOS> (enable) set qos map 1p3q8t tx 3 4 cos 6
            ! Assigns Internetwork-Control (IP Routing) to Q3 WRED T4
CAT6500-PFC3-CATOS> (enable) set qos map 1p3q8t tx 3 5 cos 7
            ! Assigns Network-Control (Spanning Tree) to Q3 WRED T5
CAT6500-PFC3-CATOS> (enable) set qos map 1p3q8t tx 4 cos 5
            ! Assigns VoIP to the PQ (Q4)
CAT6500-PFC3-CATOS> (enable)
```

Catalyst 6500 (PFC3) CatOS QoS verification commands:

- **show qos info config 1p3q8t tx**
- **show qos info runtime**
- **show qos statistics**

Example 12-72 shows the Catalyst 6500 (PFC3) IOS configurations to configure 1P3Q8T queuing recommendations.

Example 12-72 *Catalyst 6500 IOS: 1P3Q8T Queuing Example*

```
CAT6500-PFC3-IOS(config)# interface range GigabitEthernet1/1 - 48
CAT6500-PFC3-IOS(config-if)# wrr-queue queue-limit 5 25 40
        ! Allocates 5% for Q1, 25% for Q2 and 40% for Q3
CAT6500-PFC3-IOS(config-if)# wrr-queue bandwidth 5 25 70
        ! Sets the WRR weights for 5:25:70 (Q1:Q2:Q3) bandwidth servicing
CAT6500-PFC3-IOS(config-if)#
CAT6500-PFC3(config-if-range)# wrr-queue random-detect 1
        ! Enables WRED on Q1
CAT6500-PFC3(config-if-range)# wrr-queue random-detect 2
        ! Enables WRED on Q2
CAT6500-PFC3(config-if-range)# wrr-queue random-detect 3
        ! Enables WRED on Q3
CAT6500-PFC3-IOS(config-if)#
CAT6500-PFC3-IOS(config-if)# wrr-queue random-detect min-threshold 1 80
        100 100 100 100 100 100 100
        ! Sets Min WRED Threshold for Q1T1 to 80% and all others to 100%
```

continues

Example 12-72 *Catalyst 6500 IOS: 1P3Q8T Queuing Example (Continued)*

```
CAT6500-PFC3-IOS(config-if)# wrr-queue random-detect max-threshold 1 100
    100 100 100 100 100 100 100
    ! Sets Max WRED Threshold for Q1T1 to 100% and all others to 100%
CAT6500-PFC3-IOS(config-if)#
CAT6500-PFC3-IOS(config-if)# wrr-queue random-detect min-threshold 2 80
    100 100 100 100 100 100 100
    ! Sets Min WRED Threshold for Q2T1 to 80% and all others to 100%
CAT6500-PFC3-IOS(config-if)# wrr-queue random-detect max-threshold 2 100
    100 100 100 100 100 100 100
    ! Sets Max WRED Threshold for Q2T1 to 100% and all others to 100%
CAT6500-PFC3-IOS(config-if)#
CAT6500-PFC3-IOS(config-if)# wrr-queue random-detect min-threshold 3 50
    60 70 80 90 100 100 100
    ! Sets Min WRED Threshold for Q3T1 to 50%, Q3T2 to 60%, Q3T3 to 70%
    ! Q3T4 to 80%, Q3T5 to 90% and all others to 100%
CAT6500-PFC3-IOS(config-if)# wrr-queue random-detect max-threshold 3 60
    70 80 90 100 100 100 100
    ! Sets Max WRED Threshold for Q3T1 to 60%, Q3T2 to 70%, Q3T3 to 80%
    ! Q3T4 to 90%, Q3T5 to 100% and all others to 100%
CAT6500-PFC3-IOS(config-if)#
CAT6500-PFC3-IOS(config-if)# wrr-queue cos-map 1 1 1
    ! Assigns Scavenger/Bulk to Q1 WRED Threshold 1
CAT6500-PFC3-IOS(config-if)# wrr-queue cos-map 2 1 0
    ! Assigns Best Effort to Q2 WRED Threshold 1
CAT6500-PFC3-IOS(config-if)# wrr-queue cos-map 3 1 4
    ! Assigns Video to Q3 WRED Threshold 1
CAT6500-PFC3-IOS(config-if)# wrr-queue cos-map 3 2 2
    ! Assigns Net-Mgmt and Transactional Data to Q3 WRED T2
CAT6500-PFC3-IOS(config-if)# wrr-queue cos-map 3 3 3
    ! Assigns Call-Signaling and Mission-Critical Data to Q3 WRED T3
CAT6500-PFC3-IOS(config-if)# wrr-queue cos-map 3 4 6
    ! Assigns Internetwork-Control (IP Routing) to Q3 WRED T4
CAT6500-PFC3-IOS(config-if)# wrr-queue cos-map 3 5 7
    ! Assigns Network-Control (Spanning Tree) to Q3 WRED T5
CAT6500-PFC3-IOS(config-if)# priority-queue cos-map 1 5
    ! Assigns VoIP to the PQ (Q4)
CAT6500-PFC3-IOS(config-if)#end
CAT6500-PFC3-IOS#
```

Catalyst 6500 MLS QoS verification command:

- **show queueing interface**

Catalyst 6500: 1P7Q8T Queuing and Dropping

The 1P7Q8T queuing structure adds four standard queues to the 1P3Q8T structure and moves the PQ from Q4 to Q8. Otherwise, it is identical.

Under a 1P7Q8T model, buffer space can be allocated as follows: 5 percent for the Scavenger/Bulk Data queue (Q1), 25 percent for the Best-Effort queue (Q2), 10 percent for the Video queue (Q3), 10 percent for the Network-Management/Transactional Data queue (Q4), 10 percent for the Call-Signaling/Mission-Critical Data queue (Q5), 5 percent for the Internetwork Control queue (Q6), 5 percent for the Network Control queue (Q7), and 30 percent for the PQ (Q8).

The WRR weights for the standard queues (Q1 through Q7), for dividing the remaining bandwidth, after the priority queue has been serviced fully, can be set to 5:25:20:20:20:5:5, respectively, for Q1 through Q7.

Because eight queues are available, each CoS value can be assigned to its own exclusive queue. WRED can be enabled on each queue to provide it with congestion avoidance, by setting the first WRED threshold of each queue to 80:100. All other WRED thresholds can remain at 100:100.

Therefore, when the queues and thresholds have been defined as mentioned previously, CoS 1 (Scavenger/Bulk Data) can be assigned to Q1T1; CoS 0 (Best-Effort) can be assigned to Q2T1; CoS 4 (Interactive- and Streaming-Video) can be assigned to Q3T1; CoS 2 (Network-Management and Transactional Data) can be assigned to Q4T1; CoS 3 (Call-Signaling and Mission-Critical Data) can be assigned to Q5T1; CoS 6 (Internetwork Control) can be assigned to Q6T1; CoS 7 (Internetwork and Network Control) can be assigned to Q7T1; and CoS 5 (VoIP) can be assigned to Q8 (the PQ).

Figure 12-31 illustrates these 1P7Q8T queuing recommendations.

Figure 12-31 *Catalyst 6500 1P7Q8T Queuing Model*

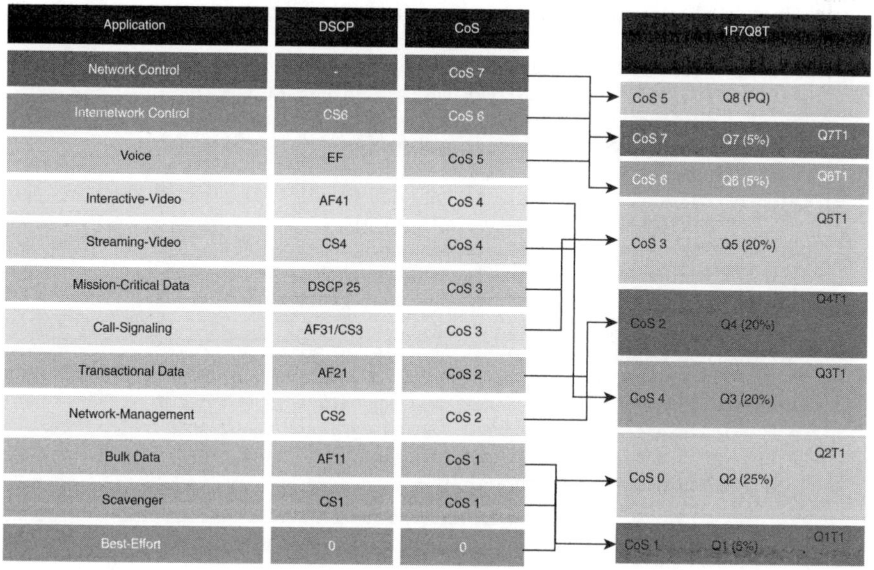

Example 12-73 shows the Catalyst 6500 (PFC3) CatOS configurations to configure 1P7Q8T queuing recommendations.

Example 12-73 *Catalyst 6500 (PFC3) CatOS: 1P7Q8T Queuing Example*

```
CAT6500-PFC3-CATOS> (enable) set qos txq-ratio 1p7q8t 5 25 10 10 10 5 5 30
        ! Allocates 5% to Q1, 25% to Q2, 10% to Q3, 10% to Q4,
        ! Allocates 10% to Q5, 5% to Q6, 5% to Q7 and 30% to the PQ (Q8)
CAT6500-PFC3-CATOS> (enable) set qos wrr 1p7q8t 5 25 20 20 20 5 5
        ! Sets the WRR weights for 5:25:20:20:20:5:5 (Q1 through Q7)
CAT6500-PFC3-CATOS> (enable)
CAT6500-PFC3-CATOS> (enable)
CAT6500-PFC3-CATOS> (enable) set qos wred 1p7q8t tx queue 1 80:100 100:100
        100:100 100:100 100:100 100:100 100:100 100:100
        ! Sets Q1 WRED T1 to 80:100 and all other Q1 WRED Thresholds to 100:100
CAT6500-PFC3-CATOS> (enable) set qos wred 1p7q8t tx queue 2 80:100 100:100
        100:100 100:100 100:100 100:100 100:100 100:100
        ! Sets Q2 WRED T1 to 80:100 and all other Q2 WRED Thresholds to 100:100
CAT6500-PFC3-CATOS> (enable) set qos wred 1p7q8t tx queue 3 80:100 100:100
        100:100 100:100 100:100 100:100 100:100 100:100
        ! Sets Q3 WRED T1 to 80:100 and all other Q3 WRED Thresholds to 100:100
CAT6500-PFC3-CATOS> (enable) set qos wred 1p7q8t tx queue 4 80:100 100:100
        100:100 100:100 100:100 100:100 100:100 100:100
        ! Sets Q4 WRED T1 to 80:100 and all other Q4 WRED Thresholds to 100:100
CAT6500-PFC3-CATOS> (enable) set qos wred 1p7q8t tx queue 5 80:100 100:100
        100:100 100:100 100:100 100:100 100:100 100:100
        ! Sets Q5 WRED T1 to 80:100 and all other Q5 WRED Thresholds to 100:100
CAT6500-PFC3-CATOS> (enable) set qos wred 1p7q8t tx queue 6 80:100 100:100
        100:100 100:100 100:100 100:100 100:100 100:100
        ! Sets Q6 WRED T1 to 80:100 and all other Q6 WRED Thresholds to 100:100
CAT6500-PFC3-CATOS> (enable) set qos wred 1p7q8t tx queue 7 80:100 100:100
        100:100 100:100 100:100 100:100 100:100 100:100
        ! Sets Q7 WRED T1 to 80:100 and all other Q7 WRED Thresholds to 100:100
CAT6500-PFC3-CATOS> (enable)
CAT6500-PFC3-CATOS> (enable)
CAT6500-PFC3-CATOS> (enable) set qos map 1p7q8t tx 1 1 cos 1
        ! Assigns Scavenger/Bulk to Q1 WRED Threshold 1
CAT6500-PFC3-CATOS> (enable) set qos map 1p7q8t tx 2 1 cos 0
        ! Assigns Best Effort to Q2 WRED Threshold 1
CAT6500-PFC3-CATOS> (enable) set qos map 1p7q8t tx 3 1 cos 4
        ! Assigns Video to Q3 WRED Threshold 1
CAT6500-PFC3-CATOS> (enable) set qos map 1p7q8t tx 4 1 cos 2
        ! Assigns Net-Mgmt and Transactional Data to Q4 WRED T1
CAT6500-PFC3-CATOS> (enable) set qos map 1p7q8t tx 5 1 cos 3
        ! Assigns Call-Signaling and Mission-Critical Data to Q5 WRED T1
CAT6500-PFC3-CATOS> (enable) set qos map 1p7q8t tx 6 1 cos 6
        ! Assigns Internetwork-Control (IP Routing) to Q6 WRED T1
CAT6500-PFC3-CATOS> (enable) set qos map 1p7q8t tx 7 1 cos 7
        ! Assigns Network-Control (Spanning Tree) to Q7 WRED T1
CAT6500-PFC3-CATOS> (enable) set qos map 1p7q8t tx 8 cos 5
        ! Assigns VoIP to the PQ (Q4)
CAT6500-PFC3-CATOS> (enable)
```

Catalyst 6500 (PFC3) CatOS QoS verification commands:

- **show qos info config 1p7q8t tx**
- **show qos info runtime**
- **show qos statistics**

Example 12-74 shows the Catalyst 6500 (PFC3) IOS configurations to configure 1P7Q8T queuing recommendations.

Example 12-74 *Catalyst 6500 (PFC3) IOS: 1P7Q8T Queuing Example*

```
CAT6500-PFC3-IOS(config)#interface range TenGigabitEthernet4/1 - 4
CAT6500-PFC3(config-if-range)# wrr-queue queue-limit 5 25 10 10 10 5 5
        ! Allocates 5% to Q1, 25% to Q2, 10% to Q3, 10% to Q4,
        ! Allocates 10% to Q5, 5% to Q6 and 5% to Q7
CAT6500-PFC3(config-if-range)# wrr-queue bandwidth 5 25 20 20 20 5 5
        ! Sets the WRR weights for 5:25:20:20:20:5:5 (Q1 through Q7)
CAT6500-PFC3(config-if-range)#
CAT6500-PFC3(config-if-range)#
CAT6500-PFC3(config-if-range)# wrr-queue random-detect 1
        ! Enables WRED on Q1
CAT6500-PFC3(config-if-range)# wrr-queue random-detect 2
        ! Enables WRED on Q2
CAT6500-PFC3(config-if-range)# wrr-queue random-detect 3
        ! Enables WRED on Q3
CAT6500-PFC3(config-if-range)# wrr-queue random-detect 4
        ! Enables WRED on Q4
CAT6500-PFC3(config-if-range)# wrr-queue random-detect 5
        ! Enables WRED on Q5
CAT6500-PFC3(config-if-range)# wrr-queue random-detect 6
        ! Enables WRED on Q6
CAT6500-PFC3(config-if-range)# wrr-queue random-detect 7
        ! Enables WRED on Q7
CAT6500-PFC3(config-if-range)#
CAT6500-PFC3(config-if-range)#
CAT6500-PFC3(config-if-range)# wrr-queue random-detect min-threshold 1 80
        100 100 100 100 100 100 100
        ! Sets Min WRED Threshold for Q1T1 to 80% and all others to 100%
CAT6500-PFC3(config-if-range)# wrr-queue random-detect max-threshold 1 100
        100 100 100 100 100 100 100
        ! Sets Max WRED Threshold for Q1T1 to 100% and all others to 100%
CAT6500-PFC3(config-if-range)#
CAT6500-PFC3(config-if-range)# wrr-queue random-detect min-threshold 2 80
        100 100 100 100 100 100 100
        ! Sets Min WRED Threshold for Q2T1 to 80% and all others to 100%
CAT6500-PFC3(config-if-range)# wrr-queue random-detect max-threshold 2 100
        100 100 100 100 100 100 100
        ! Sets Max WRED Threshold for Q2T1 to 100% and all others to 100%
CAT6500-PFC3(config-if-range)#
CAT6500-PFC3(config-if-range)# wrr-queue random-detect min-threshold 3 80
        100 100 100 100 100 100 100
        ! Sets Min WRED Threshold for Q3T1 to 80% and all others to 100%
```

continues

Example 12-74 *Catalyst 6500 (PFC3) IOS: 1P7Q8T Queuing Example (Continued)*

```
CAT6500-PFC3(config-if-range)# wrr-queue random-detect max-threshold 3 100
    100 100 100 100 100 100
        ! Sets Max WRED Threshold for Q3T1 to 100% and all others to 100%
CAT6500-PFC3(config-if-range)#
CAT6500-PFC3(config-if-range)# wrr-queue random-detect min-threshold 4 80
    100 100 100 100 100 100 100
        ! Sets Min WRED Threshold for Q4T1 to 80% and all others to 100%
CAT6500-PFC3(config-if-range)# wrr-queue random-detect max-threshold 4 100
    100 100 100 100 100 100 100
        ! Sets Max WRED Threshold for Q4T1 to 100% and all others to 100%
CAT6500-PFC3(config-if-range)#
CAT6500-PFC3(config-if-range)# wrr-queue random-detect min-threshold 5 80
    100 100 100 100 100 100 100
        ! Sets Min WRED Threshold for Q5T1 to 80% and all others to 100%
CAT6500-PFC3(config-if-range)# wrr-queue random-detect max-threshold 5 100
    100 100 100 100 100 100
        ! Sets Max WRED Threshold for Q5T1 to 100% and all others to 100%
CAT6500-PFC3(config-if-range)#
CAT6500-PFC3(config-if-range)# wrr-queue random-detect min-threshold 6 80
    100 100 100 100 100 100 100
        ! Sets Min WRED Threshold for Q6T1 to 80% and all others to 100%
CAT6500-PFC3(config-if-range)# wrr-queue random-detect max-threshold 6 100
    100 100 100 100 100 100 100
        ! Sets Max WRED Threshold for Q6T1 to 100% and all others to 100%
CAT6500-PFC3(config-if-range)#
CAT6500-PFC3(config-if-range)# wrr-queue random-detect min-threshold 7 80
    100 100 100 100 100 100 100
        ! Sets Min WRED Threshold for Q7T1 to 80% and all others to 100%
CAT6500-PFC3(config-if-range)# wrr-queue random-detect max-threshold 7 100
    100 100 100 100 100
        ! Sets Max WRED Threshold for Q7T1 to 100% and all others to 100%
CAT6500-PFC3(config-if-range)#
CAT6500-PFC3(config-if-range)#
CAT6500-PFC3(config-if-range)# wrr-queue cos-map 1 1 1
        ! Assigns Scavenger/Bulk to Q1 WRED Threshold 1
CAT6500-PFC3(config-if-range)# wrr-queue cos-map 2 1 0
        ! Assigns Best Effort to Q2 WRED Threshold 1
CAT6500-PFC3(config-if-range)# wrr-queue cos-map 3 1 4
        ! Assigns Video to Q3 WRED Threshold 1
CAT6500-PFC3(config-if-range)# wrr-queue cos-map 4 1 2
        ! Assigns Net-Mgmt and Transactional Data to Q4 WRED T1
CAT6500-PFC3(config-if-range)# wrr-queue cos-map 5 1 3
        ! Assigns Call-Signaling and Mission-Critical Data to Q5 WRED T1
CAT6500-PFC3(config-if-range)# wrr-queue cos-map 6 1 6
        ! Assigns Internetwork-Control (IP Routing) to Q6 WRED T1
CAT6500-PFC3(config-if-range)# wrr-queue cos-map 7 1 7
        ! Assigns Network-Control (Spanning Tree) to Q7 WRED T1
CAT6500-PFC3(config-if-range)# priority-queue cos-map 1 5
        ! Assigns VoIP to the PQ (Q4)
CAT6500-PFC3(config-if-range)#end
CAT6500-PFC3-IOS#
```

Catalyst 6500 MLS QoS verification command:

- **show queueing interface**

Catalyst 6500: PFC3 Distribution-Layer (Cisco IOS) Per-User Microflow Policing

In general, superior defense strategies have multiple lines of defense. In the context of the campus designs discussed in this chapter, there is a main line of defense against DoS/worm attack traffic at the access-layer edges. This line of defense can be bolstered at the distribution layer whenever Catalyst 6500 Sup720s (PFC3s) are deployed there. This can be done by leveraging the PFC3 feature of per-user microflow policing.

In Example 12-75, traffic has been assumed to be correctly classified. This might or might not be a valid assumption. If it is suspected to be invalid, ACLs should be used to identify the flows (instead of using DSCP markings). In either case, various flow types can be filtered as they arrive at the distribution layer to see if they conform to the normal limits that have been set for the enterprise. Each flow is examined by source IP address; if a source is transmitting out of profile, the excess traffic can be dropped or marked down. In this manner, spurious flows can be contained, even if access-layer switches (such as the Catalyst 2950, discussed earlier in this chapter) do not support granular policing or if policing has been misconfigured on an access-layer switch.

In this manner, the distribution-layer Catalyst 6500 PFC3 can catch any DoS/worm attack flows that might have slipped through the access-layer net.

Example 12-75 *Catalyst 6500 (PFC3) IOS—Distribution-Layer Per-User Microflow Policing Example*

```
CAT6500-PFC3-IOS(config)#mls qos map policed-dscp normal 0 24 26 34 36 to 8
       ! Excess traffic marked 0,CS3,AF31,AF41 or AF42 will be remarked to CS1
CAT6500-PFC3-IOS(config)#
CAT6500-PFC3-IOS(config)#class-map match-all VOIP
CAT6500-PFC3-IOS(config-cmap)#  match ip dscp ef
CAT6500-PFC3-IOS(config-cmap)#class-map match-all INTERACTIVE-VIDEO
CAT6500-PFC3-IOS(config-cmap)#  match ip dscp af41 af42
CAT6500-PFC3-IOS(config-cmap)#class-map match-all CALL-SIGNALING
CAT6500-PFC3-IOS(config-cmap)#  match ip dscp cs3 af31
CAT6500-PFC3-IOS(config-cmap)#class-map match-all BEST-EFFORT
CAT6500-PFC3-IOS(config-cmap)#  match ip dscp 0
CAT6500-PFC3-IOS(config-cmap)#
CAT6500-PFC3-IOS(config-cmap)#
CAT6500-PFC3-IOS(config-cmap)#pconform-action transmit exceed-action
CAT6500-PFC3-IOS(config-pmap)#  class VOIP
CAT6500-PFC3-I(config-pmap-c)# police flow mask src-only 128000 8000
       conform-action transmit exceed-action drop
       ! No source can send more than 128k worth of DSCP EF traffic
CAT6500-PFC3-I(config-pmap-c)#  class INTERACTIVE-VIDEO
```

continues

Example 12-75 *Catalyst 6500 (PFC3) IOS—Distribution-Layer Per-User Microflow Policing Example (Continued)*

```
CAT6500-PFC3-I(config-pmap-c)# police flow mask src-only 500000 8000
    conform-action transmit exceed-action policed-dscp-transmit
    ! Excess IP/VC traffic from any source is marked down to CS1
CAT6500-PFC3-I(config-pmap-c)#  class CALL-SIGNALING
CAT6500-PFC3-I(config-pmap-c)# police flow mask src-only 32000 8000
    conform-action transmit exceed-action policed-dscp-transmit
    ! Excess Call-Signaling traffic from any source is marked down to CS1
CAT6500-PFC3-I(config-pmap-c)#  class BEST-EFFORT
CAT6500-PFC3-I(config-pmap-c)# police flow mask src-only 5000000 8000
    conform-action transmit exceed-action policed-dscp-transmit
    ! Excess PC Data traffic from any source is marked down to CS1
CAT6500-PFC3-I(config-pmap-c)#  exit
CAT6500-PFC3-IOS(config-pmap)#exit
CAT6500-PFC3-IOS(config)#
CAT6500-PFC3-IOS(config)#
CAT6500-PFC3-IOS(config)#interface range GigabitEthernet4/1 - 4
CAT6500-PFC3(config-if-range)# mls qos trust dscp
CAT6500-PFC3(config-if-range)# service-policy input PER-USER-POLICING
    ! Attaches Per-User Microflow policing policy to Uplinks from Access
CAT6500-PFC3(config-if-range)#end
CAT6500-PFC3-IOS#
```

Catalyst 6500 MLS QoS verification commands:

- **show mls qos**
- **show class-map**
- **show policy-map**
- **show policy interface**

WAN Aggregator/Branch Router Handoff Considerations

A final consideration in campus Qos design is the campus-to-WAN (or VPN) handoff. In the case of a branch, this equates to a handoff from the branch switch to the branch router.

In either case, a major speed mismatch is impending because Gigabit Ethernet/Fast Ethernet campus networks are connecting to WAN links that might be only a few megabits (if that).

Granted, the WAN aggregation routers and branch routers have advanced QoS mechanisms to prioritize traffic on their links, but it is critical to keep in mind that Cisco router QoS is performed in Cisco IOS software, while Catalyst switch QoS is performed in ASIC hardware.

Therefore, the optimal distribution of QoS operations is to have as many QoS actions performed on the Catalyst switches as possible, saving the WAN/branch router valuable CPU cycles. This is an especially critical consideration when deploying DoS/worm-mitigation designs.

For example, some enterprises have deployed advanced QoS policies on their branch switches and routers, only to have DoS/worm attacks originate from within the branch. Remember, queuing will not engage on a switch unless its links are congested—and even if it does, if the branch switch hands off 100 Mbps of (correctly queued) traffic to a branch router, it more than likely will bring it down.

Thus, the following design principles for the campus-to-WAN handoff can help mitigate these types of scenarios.

First, resist the urge to use a Gigabit Ethernet connection to the WAN aggregation router, even if the router supports GE.

It is extremely unlikely that the WAN aggregator will be serving anywhere close to a (combined) WAN circuit rate of 1 Gbps. Therefore, use one (or more) Fast Ethernet connection on the distribution-layer Catalyst switch to connect to the WAG so that not only is the aggregate traffic sent to the WAG limited (in 100 Mbps increments), but (because congestion points now are pulled back into the Catalyst switch, thus forcing queuing to engage on the FE switch port) the traffic also will be queued correctly within these limits (of 100 Mbps increments).

For example, a WAN aggregation router is supporting two DS3 WAN connections (totaling 90 Mbps of WAN circuit capacity). In this case, the distribution-layer switch port connecting to the WAG should be Fast Ethernet. Then, if more than 100 Mbps of traffic attempts to traverse the WAN, the Catalyst switch will engage queuing on the switch port and aggressively drop flows according to the defined application hierarchies. Only 100 Mbps of correctly queued traffic will ever be handed off to the WAG.

In the case of a WAN aggregation router supporting over 100 Mbps of WAN circuits, as in the case of a WAG running one or more OC-3 ports (at 155 Mbps each), multiple Fast Ethernet connections can be used to connect to the WAG from the distribution-layer switch to achieve the same net effect.

The point is to bring back, as much as possible, the choke point into Catalyst hardware and engage hardware queuing there instead of overwhelming the software-based policing and queuing policies within the WAN aggregation router.

Second, if the combined WAN circuit rate is significantly below 100 Mbps, enable egress shaping on the Catalyst switches (when supported).

If there is no hope of engaging queuing on the Catalyst switch because the combined WAN circuit rates are far below those of Fast Ethernet (the minimum port speed of Catalyst switches), enable shaping on platforms that support this feature. Such platforms include the Catalyst 2970, 3560, 3750, and 4500.

In this manner, the Catalyst switch can hold back traffic and selectively drop (according to defined policies) from flows that otherwise would flood the WAN/branch router.

For example, if a branch router is using two ATM-IMA T1 links (3 Mbps combined throughput) to connect the branch to the WAN, the branch switch could be configured to shape all WAN-destined traffic to 3 Mbps or could be configured to shape on a per-application basis to smaller increments.

Refer to the queuing/dropping sections of these platforms in this chapter and Cisco IOS documentation for additional guidance on enabling shaping.

Finally, if the combined WAN circuit rate is significantly below 100 Mbps and the Catalyst switch does not support shaping, enable egress policing (when supported).

If the Catalyst switch does not support shaping, egress policing is the next-best alternative for this scenario.

For example, the Catalyst 3550 does not support shaping, but it does support up to eight policers on all egress ports. Thus, it could still protect its branch router from being overwhelmed by policing on egress. Egress policing can be done on an aggregate level or on a per-application basis.

Again, the objective is to discard, as intelligently as possible, traffic that will be dropped inevitably anyway (by the WAN/branch router), but, whenever possible, to perform the dropping within Catalyst hardware (instead of Cisco IOS Software).

Egress policers are configured in the same manner as ingress policers, but the direction specified in the **service-policy** interface-configuration statement will be **out**, not **in**.

NOTE   The only Catalyst switch discussed in this chapter that did not support either shaping or egress policing is the Catalyst 2950. Unfortunately, there is no way that the Catalyst 2950 can offload QoS from the branch router. If such functionality is required, a hardware upgrade is advisable.

Case Study: Campus QoS Design

ABC, Inc., is a young, innovative company seeking to gain competitive advantage in its industry vertical by strategic use of information technologies. As such, expectations from its network infrastructure are considerable. These expectations include strict-priority servicing of VoIP applications, and provisioning for high-quality videoconferencing and for discrete/granular service levels for multiple classes of data applications. Furthermore, ABC, Inc., expects to minimize network downtime from DoS and worm attacks by building self-defending networks that leverage intelligent network services, such as quality of service, intrusion detection, encryption, authentication, and other security technologies.

ABC, Inc., follows the Cisco recommended campus hierarchy of access, distribution, and core layers and has deployed a mix of Catalyst switching platforms at these layers. These switches include Catalyst 3550s and 3750s (at the access layer), 6500-Sup2s (within the data center), 4500-Sup4s (within the distribution layer), and 6500-Sup720s (within the distribution and core layers). Also, ABC, Inc., is connecting to Cisco 7200-NPE-G1 WAN aggregation routers that are providing WAN services at OC-3 speeds. Figure 12-32 shows the campus network topology.

Figure 12-32 *Case Study: Campus Network with QoS Policies to Protect Voice, Video, and Data While Mitigating DoS/Worm Attacks*

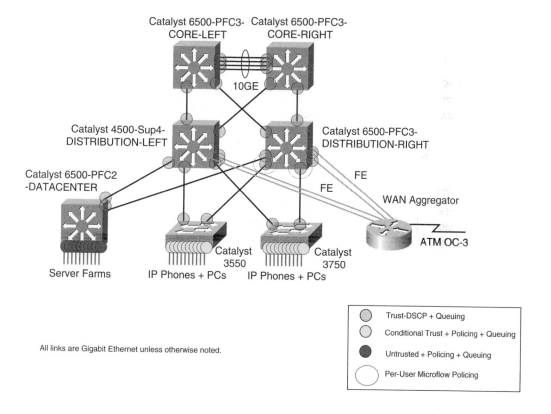

At this early phase in the network deployment, ABC, Inc., has basic networking configured and wants to overlay QoS functionality. Following this phase, it will enable additional security technologies.

ABC, Inc., has chosen to implement an Untrusted Server model within the data center because it wants to administer QoS markings and policies on the network infrastructure instead of on the application servers (which, at times, have been infected with viruses). The Mission-Critical Data application is SAP, served off TCP ports 3200 to 3203 and 3600; the Transactional Data application is Lotus Notes, served off TCP port 1352; and the Bulk Data application is IMAP for E-mail, served off TCP ports 143 and 220. The company has dedicated servers for these applications, but these servers sometimes are moved. Instead of requiring the networking team to be notified for every server move, a blanket set of policies will be deployed for these main applications on every data center switch port to correctly mark and police these flows.

ABC, Inc., has deployed Cisco IP phones and is encouraging employees to make effective use of videoconferencing applications to keep travel budgets low while maintaining productivity. Additionally, because the company has been hit hard with nearly a dozen worm attacks within the past year, it has chosen to implement a Scavenger-class markdown/queuing strategy throughout the network to mitigate the effects of such flooding attacks. Finally, because ABC, Inc., prefers data applications to receive QoS in both server-to-client and client-to-server directions, it has chosen to deploy the Conditionally Trusted Endpoint: IP Phone + PC Advanced model on all end-user access-layer switches. On the Catalyst 3550, this model is being deployed through per-port/per-VLAN policers; on the Catalyst 3750, it is being deployed by access lists that include voice VLAN subnet information.

All distribution-layer and core-layer links have been configured to trust DSCP markings. Additionally, all distribution-layer Catalyst 6500-Sup720s (with PFC3s) are configured to perform per-user microflow policing as a second line of defense against spurious flows from (non-data center access-layer switches). Queuing structures are dependant on platform and line card capabilities, as detailed in the configurations.

Finally, ABC, Inc., has a series of Cisco 7200-NPE-G1 WAN aggregation routers to provide WAN services. These WAN routers have ATM OC-3 (155-Mbps) links to their carrier and home multiple ATM PVCs to their remote sites. Although these NPE-G1 routers have Gigabit Ethernet interfaces, ABC, Inc., has chosen to connect to them using two Fast Ethernet interfaces from the campus distribution-layer switches. In this manner, the amount of traffic sent to WAN aggregators is limited to 200 Mbps, while intelligent queuing is performed—according to the enterprise-wide application hierarchy—within these physical 200-Mbps limits.

The QoS designs for the ABC campus network span six switches, but because one core switch is a mirror image of the other, only five configurations are detailed in the following example. These include the QoS configurations for the Catalyst 6500 PFC2 data center switch (see Example 12-76), the Catalyst 3550 access-layer switch (see Example 12-77), the Catalyst 3750 access-layer switch (see Example 12-78), the left Catalyst 4500-Sup4 distribution-layer switch (see Example 12-79), the right Catalyst 6500-PFC3 distribution-layer switch (see Example 12-80), and the left Catalyst 6500-PFC3 core-layer switch (see Example 12-81), of which the right Catalyst 6500-PFC3 core-layer switch is a mirror image.

Example 12-76 shows the QoS configuration for the Catalyst 6500 PFC2 data center switch.

Example 12-76 *Catalyst 6500-PFC2 (CatOS): Data Center Access Switch for Untrusted Servers (Advanced Dual-Rate Policing Model): Case Study Example*

```
!
#system
set system name  C6500-PFC2-CATOS-DATACENTER
!
#!
#vtp
set vtp domain ABC-INC
set vtp mode transparent vlan
...
set vlan 1,200
...
!
#qos
set qos enable
       ! 1P2Q2T Global Definitions (for WS-X6K-S2U-MSFC2 GE Uplinks)
set qos map 1p2q2t tx 1 2 cos 0        ! Assigns Best Effort to Q1T2
set qos map 1p2q2t tx 2 1 cos 2        ! Assigns Net-Mgmt/Trans-Data to Q2T1
set qos map 1p2q2t tx 2 1 cos 3        ! Assigns Call-Sig/MC-Data to Q2T1
set qos map 1p2q2t tx 2 2 cos 6        ! Assigns Routing to Q2T2
                                       ! All other CoS-Queue mapping remain default
set qos wrr 1p2q2t 30 70               ! Sets WRR weights to 30:70 for Q1:Q2
set qos txq-ratio 1p2q2t 30 40 30      ! Sets sizes 30%,40%,30% for Q1,Q2,Q3/PQ
set qos wred 1p2q2t tx queue 1 40:80 80:100     ! Sets WRED Thresholds for Q1
set qos wred 1p2q2t tx queue 2 70:80 80:100     ! Sets WRED Thresholds for Q2
        ! 1P3Q1T Global Definitions (for WS-X6548-RJ-45 FE switch ports)
set qos map 1p3q1t tx 2 1 cos 0        ! Assigns Best Effort to Q2T1
set qos map 1p3q1t tx 3 1 cos 2        ! Assigns Net-Mgmt/Trans-Data to Q3T1
set qos map 1p3q1t tx 3 1 cos 3        ! Assigns Call-Sig/MC-Data to Q3T1
set qos map 1p3q1t tx 3 1 cos 4        ! Assigns Video to Q3T1
set qos map 1p3q1t tx 3 cos 6          ! Assigns IP Routing to Q3 (tail)
set qos map 1p3q1t tx 3 cos 7          ! Assigns STP to Q3 (tail)
                                       ! All other CoS-Queue mapping remain default
set qos wrr 1p3q1t 5 25 70             ! Sets WRR weights to 5:25:70 for Q1:Q2:Q3
set qos wred 1p3q1t tx queue 1 80:100 ! Sets WRED Thresholds for Q1 (80% to 100%)
set qos wred 1p3q1t tx queue 2 80:100 ! Sets WRED Thresholds for Q2 (80% to 100%)
set qos wred 1p3q1t tx queue 3 70:80  ! Sets WRED Thresholds for Q3 (70% to 80%)
set qos policed-dscp-map 1:1
set qos policed-dscp-map 2:2
set qos policed-dscp-map 3:3
set qos policed-dscp-map 4:4
set qos policed-dscp-map 5:5
set qos policed-dscp-map 6:6
set qos policed-dscp-map 7:7
set qos policed-dscp-map 0,8,25:8      ! Normal markdown of 0 and 25 set to CS1
set qos policed-dscp-map 9:9
set qos policed-dscp-map 11:11
set qos policed-dscp-map 10,12:12      ! Normal markdown of AF11 set to AF12
set qos policed-dscp-map 13:13
set qos policed-dscp-map 14:14
```

continues

Example 12-76 *Catalyst 6500-PFC2 (CatOS): Data Center Access Switch for Untrusted Servers (Advanced Dual-Rate Policing Model): Case Study Example (Continued)*

```
set qos policed-dscp-map 15:15
set qos policed-dscp-map 16:16
set qos policed-dscp-map 17:17
set qos policed-dscp-map 19:19
set qos policed-dscp-map 18,20:20      ! Normal markdown of AF21 set to AF22
set qos policed-dscp-map 21:21
…
<remaining policed-dscp-map (normal rate) DSCP values are mapped to themselves>
…
set qos policed-dscp-map excess-rate 0:0
set qos policed-dscp-map excess-rate 1:1
set qos policed-dscp-map excess-rate 2:2
set qos policed-dscp-map excess-rate 3:3
set qos policed-dscp-map excess-rate 4:4
set qos policed-dscp-map excess-rate 5:5
set qos policed-dscp-map excess-rate 6:6
set qos policed-dscp-map excess-rate 7:7
set qos policed-dscp-map excess-rate 8,10,18:8
        ! Excess markdown of AF11 and AF12 set to CS1
set qos policed-dscp-map excess-rate 9:9
…
<remaining policed-dscp-map (excess rate) DSCP values are mapped to themselves>
…
set qos policer aggregate SAP rate 15000 policed-dscp erate 32000000
        policed-dscp burst 8 eburst 32000
        ! SAP traffic is (single-rate) policed to 15 Mbps
set qos policer aggregate LOTUS rate 25000 policed-dscp erate 35000
        policed-dscp burst 8 eburst 8000
        ! Lotus traffic is (dual-rate) policed to 25 Mbps and 35 Mbps
set qos policer aggregate IMAP rate 40000 policed-dscp erate 50000
        policed-dscp burst 8 eburst 8000
        ! IMAP traffic is (dual-rate) policed to 40 Mbps and 50 Mbps
set qos policer aggregate DATA rate 1000 policed-dscp erate 32000000
        policed-dscp burst 8 eburst 32000
        ! All other data is (single-rate) policed to 1 Mbps
clear qos acl all
#UNTRUSTED-SERVER
set qos acl ip UNTRUSTED-SERVER dscp 25 aggregate SAP tcp any range 3200 3203 any
set qos acl ip UNTRUSTED-SERVER dscp 25 aggregate SAP tcp any eq 3600 any
        ! Identifies SAP traffic by TCP source ports 3200-3203 and 3600
set qos acl ip UNTRUSTED-SERVER dscp 18 aggregate LOTUS tcp any eq 1352 any
        ! Identifies Lotus traffic by TCP source port 1352
set qos acl ip UNTRUSTED-SERVER dscp 10 aggregate IMAP tcp any any  eq 143
set qos acl ip UNTRUSTED-SERVER dscp 10 aggregate IMAP tcp any any  eq 220
        ! Identifies IMAP traffic by TCP source port 143 and 220
set qos acl ip UNTRUSTED-SERVER dscp 0 aggregate DATA ip any any
        ! ACL to catch all other IP traffic
#
commit qos acl all                          ! Commits all ACLs to PFC
!
# default port status is enable
```

Example 12-76 *Catalyst 6500-PFC2 (CatOS): Data Center Access Switch for Untrusted Servers (Advanced Dual-Rate Policing Model): Case Study Example (Continued)*

```
!
!
#module 1 : 2-port 1000BaseX Supervisor
clear trunk 1/1  1-199,201-1005,1025-4094
set trunk 1/1  on dot1q 200                    ! Trunks Data Center VLAN
clear trunk 1/2  1-199,201-1005,1025-4094
set trunk 1/2  on dot1q 200                    ! Trunks Data Center VLAN
commit qos set port qos 1/1-2 trust            ! Uplink ports Trust DSCP
!
#module 3 : 48-port 10/100BaseTX Ethernet
set vlan 200  3/1-48                           ! Data Center VLAN
set qos acl map UNTRUSTED-SERVER 3/1-48        ! ACL attached to all access-ports
!
```

Example 12-77 shows the QoS configuration for the (left) Catalyst 3550 access-layer switch.

Example 12-77 *Catalyst 3550 Access Switch for IP Phones + PCs (Advanced Model): Case Study Example*

```
!
hostname CAT3550-ACCESS-LEFT
!
vtp domain ABC-INC
vtp mode transparent
mls qos map policed-dscp  0 10 18 24 25 34 to 8
        ! Excess DVLAN traffic marked 0, AF11, AF21, CS3, DSCP 25 and AF41
        ! will be remarked to Scavenger (CS1)
mls qos map cos-dscp 0 8 16 24 32 46 48 56
        ! Modifies CoS-to-DSCP mapping to map CoS 5 to DSCP EF
mls qos                                        ! Enables QoS Globally
!
class-map match-all VOICE
  match ip dscp 46                             ! DSCP EF (voice)
class-map match-all VVLAN-VOICE
  match vlan  110                              ! VLAN 110 is VVLAN
  match class-map VOICE                        ! Matches VVLAN DSCP EF
!
class-map match-any CALL-SIGNALING             ! Need 'match-any' here
  match ip dscp 26                             ! DSCP AF31 (old Call-Signaling)
  match ip dscp 24                             ! DSCP CS3 (new Call-Signaling)
class-map match-all VVLAN-CALL-SIGNALING
  match vlan  110                              ! VLAN 110 is VVLAN
  match class-map CALL-SIGNALING               ! Matches VVLAN AF31/CS3
!
class-map match-all ANY
  match access-group name ANY                  ! Workaround ACL
```

continues

Example 12-77 *Catalyst 3550 Access Switch for IP Phones + PCs (Advanced Model): Case Study Example (Continued)*

```
class-map match-all VVLAN-ANY
  match vlan 10                        ! VLAN 110 is VVLAN
  match class-map ANY                  ! Matches any other VVLAN traffic
!
class-map match-all PC-VIDEO
  match access-group name PC-VIDEO
class-map match-all DVLAN-PC-VIDEO
  match vlan 10                        ! VLAN 10 is DVLAN
  match class-map PC-VIDEO             ! Matches PC IP/VC or SoftPhone
!
class-map match-all MISSION-CRITICAL-DATA
  match access-group name MISSION-CRITICAL-DATA
class-map match-all DVLAN-MISSION-CRITICAL-DATA
  match vlan 10                        ! VLAN 10 is DVLAN
  match class-map MISSION-CRITICAL-DATA  ! Matches DVLAN MC-Data
!
class-map match-all TRANSACTIONAL-DATA
  match access-group name TRANSACTIONAL-DATA
class-map match-all DVLAN-TRANSACTIONAL-DATA
  match vlan 10                        ! VLAN 10 is DVLAN
  match class-map TRANSACTIONAL-DATA   ! Matches DVLAN Transactional
!
class-map match-all BULK-DATA
  match access-group name BULK-DATA
class-map match-all DVLAN-BULK-DATA
  match vlan 10                        ! VLAN 10 is DVLAN
  match class-map BULK-DATA            ! Matches DVLAN Bulk Data
!
class-map match-all DVLAN-ANY
  match vlan 10                        ! VLAN 10 is DVLAN
  match class-map ANY                  ! Matches all other DVLAN traffic
!
!
policy-map IPPHONE+PC-ADVANCED
  class VVLAN-VOICE
    set ip dscp 46                     ! DSCP EF (Voice)
    police 128000 8000 exceed-action drop
      ! Only one voice call is permitted per switchport VVLAN
  class VVLAN-CALL-SIGNALING
    set ip dscp 24                     ! DSCP CS3 (Call-Signaling)
    police 32000 8000 exceed-action policed-dscp-transmit
      ! Out-of-profile Call-Signaling is marked down to Scavenger (CS1)
  class VVLAN-ANY
    set ip dscp 0
    police 32000 8000 exceed-action policed-dscp-transmit
      ! Unauthorized VVLAN traffic is marked down to Scavenger (CS1)
  class DVLAN-PC-VIDEO
    set ip dscp 34                     ! DSCP AF41 (Interactive-Video)
    police 496000 8000 exceed-action policed-dscp-transmit
      ! Only one IP/VC stream will be permitted per switchport
  class DVLAN-MISSION-CRITICAL-DATA
```

Example 12-77 *Catalyst 3550 Access Switch for IP Phones + PCs (Advanced Model): Case Study*
Example (Continued)

```
      set ip dscp 25                               ! Interim Mission-Critical Data
      police 5000000 8000 exceed-action policed-dscp-transmit
            ! Out-of-profile Mission-Critical Data is marked down to Scavenger (CS1)
    class DVLAN-TRANSACTIONAL-DATA
      set ip dscp 18                               ! DSCP AF21 (Transactional Data)
      police 5000000 8000 exceed-action policed-dscp-transmit
            ! Out-of-profile Transactional Data is marked down to Scavenger (CS1)
    class DVLAN-BULK-DATA
      set ip dscp 10                               ! DSCP AF11 (Bulk Data)
      police 5000000 8000 exceed-action policed-dscp-transmit
            ! Out-of-profile Bulk Data is marked down to Scavenger (CS1)
    class DVLAN-ANY
      set ip dscp 0
      police 5000000 8000 exceed-action policed-dscp-transmit
            ! Out-of-profile data traffic is marked down to Scavenger (CS1)
  !
  …
  !
  interface FastEthernet0/1
   description ACCESS-EDGE IP PHONE + PC ADVANCED MODEL
   switchport access vlan 10                       ! DVLAN
   switchport mode dynamic desirable
   switchport voice vlan 110                        ! VVLAN
   no ip address
   mls qos trust device cisco-phone                ! Conditional Trust
   service-policy input IPPHONE+PC-ADVANCED         ! Attaches policy
   wrr-queue bandwidth 5 25 70 1
          ! Q1 gets 5% BW, Q2 gets 25% BW, Q3 gets 70% BW, Q4 is the PQ
   wrr-queue cos-map 1 1                            ! Scavenger/Bulk is assigned to Q1
   wrr-queue cos-map 2 0                            ! Best Effort is assigned to Q2
   wrr-queue cos-map 3 2 3 4 6 7                    ! CoS 2,3,4,6,7 are assigned to Q3
   wrr-queue cos-map 4 5                            ! Voice is assigned to Q4 (PQ)
   priority-queue out                               ! Enables Q4 as PQ
   spanning-tree portfast
  !
  <repeated for all FE switchports>
  !
  !
  interface GigabitEthernet0/1
   description L2 UPLINK TO DISTRIBUTION CAT4500-SUP4-LEFT
   switchport trunk encapsulation dot1q
   switchport trunk allowed vlan 10,110             ! Trunks DVLAN + VVLAN
   switchport mode trunk
   no ip address
   mls qos trust dscp                               ! Trusts DSCP
   wrr-queue bandwidth 5 25 70 1
          ! Q1 gets 5% BW, Q2 gets 25% BW, Q3 gets 70% BW, Q4 is the PQ
   wrr-queue queue-limit 5 25 40 30
          ! Tunes buffers to 5% for Q1, 25% for Q2, 40% for Q3 and 30% for Q4
```

continues

Example 12-77 *Catalyst 3550 Access Switch for IP Phones + PCs (Advanced Model): Case Study Example (Continued)*

```
wrr-queue random-detect max-threshold 1 40 100
        ! Sets Q1 WRED threshold 1 to 40% and threshold 2 to 100%
wrr-queue random-detect max-threshold 2 80 100
        ! Sets Q2 WRED threshold 1 to 80% and threshold 2 to 100%
wrr-queue random-detect max-threshold 3 80 100
        ! Sets Q3 WRED threshold 1 to 80% and threshold 2 to 100%
wrr-queue cos-map 1 1                        ! Scavenger/Bulk is assigned to Q1
wrr-queue cos-map 2 0                        ! Best Effort is assigned to Q2
wrr-queue cos-map 3 2 3 4 6 7               ! CoS 2,3,4,6,7 are assigned to Q3
wrr-queue cos-map 4 5                        ! Voice is assigned to Q4 (PQ)
wrr-queue dscp-map 2 10 48 56
        ! Maps Bulk Data (10), Routing (48) and Spanning Tree (Internal DSCP 56)
        ! to WRED threshold 2 of their respective queues - all other DSCP values
        ! are mapped (by default) to WRED threshold 1 of their respective queues
 priority-queue out                          ! Enables Q4 as PQ
!
<repeated for GigabitEthernet0/2 Uplink to Distribution Cat4500-Sup4-Left>
!
...
!
ip access-list standard ANY
 permit any
!
 ip access-list extended PC-VIDEO
 permit udp any any range 16384 32767        ! IP/VC or SoftPhone
 !
ip access-list extended MISSION-CRITICAL-DATA
 permit tcp any any range 3200 3202          ! SAP
 permit tcp any any eq 3600                  ! SAP
 permit tcp any any range 2000 2002          ! Softphone SCCP
 !
ip access-list extended TRANSACTIONAL-DATA
 permit tcp any any eq 1352                  ! Lotus
 !
ip access-list extended BULK-DATA
 permit tcp any any eq 143                   ! IMAP
 permit tcp any any eq 220                   ! IMAP
 !
```

Example 12-78 shows the QoS configuration for the (right) Catalyst 3750 access-layer switch.

Example 12-78 *Catalyst 3750 Access Switch for IP Phones + PCs (Advanced Model): Case Study Example*

```
 !
hostname CAT3750-ACCESS-RIGHT
 !
 ...
 !
```

Example 12-78 *Catalyst 3750 Access Switch for IP Phones + PCs (Advanced Model): Case Study Example (Continued)*

```
vtp domain ABC-INC
vtp mode transparent
mls qos map policed-dscp 0 10 18 24 25 34 to 8
        ! Excess DVLAN traffic marked 0, AF11, AF21, CS3, DSCP 25 and AF41
        ! will be remarked to Scavenger (CS1)
mls qos map cos-dscp 0 8 16 24 32 46 48 56
        ! Modifies CoS-to-DSCP mapping to map CoS 5 to DSCP EF
!
mls qos srr-queue output cos-map queue 3 threshold 3  0
        ! Maps CoS 5 to Queue 1 Threshold 3 (Voice gets all of Queue 1)
mls qos srr-queue output cos-map queue 2 threshold 1  2 4
        ! Maps CoS 2 and CoS 4 to Queue 2 Threshold 1
mls qos srr-queue output cos-map queue 2 threshold 2  3
        ! Maps CoS 3 to Queue 2 Threshold 2
mls qos srr-queue output cos-map queue 2 threshold 3  6 7
        ! Maps CoS 6 and CoS 7 to Queue 2 Threshold 3
mls qos srr-queue output cos-map queue 3 threshold 3  0
        ! Maps CoS 0 to Queue 3 Threshold 3 (Best Efforts gets all of Q3)
mls qos srr-queue output cos-map queue 4 threshold 3  1
        ! Maps CoS 1 to Queue 4 Threshold 3 (Scavenger/Bulk gets all of Q4)
!
mls qos srr-queue output dscp-map queue 1 threshold 3  46
        ! Maps DSCP EF (Voice) to Queue 1 Threshold 3
mls qos srr-queue output dscp-map queue 2 threshold 1  16 18 20 22 25 32 34 36
        ! Maps DSCP CS2 (Net-Mgmt/Transactional) to Queue 2 Threshold 1
        ! Maps DSCP AF21, AF22, AF23 (Transactional Data) to Queue 2 Threshold 1
        ! Maps DSCP 25 (Mission-Critical Data) to Queue 2 Threshold 1
        ! Maps DSCP CS4 (Streaming Video) to Queue 2 Threshold 1
        ! Maps DSCP AF41, AF42 (Interactive-Video) to Queue 2 Threshold 1
mls qos srr-queue output dscp-map queue 2 threshold 1  38
        ! Maps DSCP AF43 (Interactive-Video) to Queue 2 Threshold 1
mls qos srr-queue output dscp-map queue 2 threshold 2  24 26
        ! Maps DSCP CS3 and DSCP AF31 (Call-Signaling) to Queue 2 Threshold 2
mls qos srr-queue output dscp-map queue 2 threshold 3  48 56
        ! Maps DSCP CS6 and CS7 (Network/Internetwork) to Queue 2 Threshold 3
mls qos srr-queue output dscp-map queue 3 threshold 3  0
        ! Maps DSCP 0 (Best Effort) to Queue 3 Threshold 3
mls qos srr-queue output dscp-map queue 4 threshold 1  8
        ! Maps DSCP CS1 (Scavenger) to Queue 4 Threshold 1
mls qos srr-queue output dscp-map queue 4 threshold 3  10 12 14
        ! Maps DSCP AF11, AF12, AF13 (Bulk Data) to Queue 4 Threshold 3
!
mls qos queue-set output 1 threshold 2 70 80 100 100
        ! Sets Q2 Threshold 1 to 70% and Q2 Threshold 2 to 80%
mls qos queue-set output 1 threshold 4 40 100 100 100
        ! Sets Q4 Threshold 1 to 40% and Q4 Threshold 2 to 100%
mls qos                                         ! Enables QoS Globally
!
```

continues

Example 12-78 *Catalyst 3750 Access Switch for IP Phones + PCs (Advanced Model): Case Study Example (Continued)*

```
class-map match-all VVLAN-VOICE
  match access-group name VVLAN-VOICE
class-map match-all VVLAN-CALL-SIGNALING
  match access-group name VVLAN-CALL-SIGNALING
class-map match-all VVLAN-ANY
  match access-group name VVLAN-ANY
!
class-map match-all DVLAN-PC-VIDEO
  match access-group name DVLAN-PC-VIDEO
class-map match-all DVLAN-MISSION-CRITICAL-DATA
  match access-group name DVLAN-MISSION-CRITICAL-DATA
class-map match-all DVLAN-TRANSACTIONAL-DATA
  match access-group name DVLAN-TRANSACTIONAL-DATA
class-map match-all DVLAN-BULK-DATA
  match access-group name DVLAN-BULK-DATA
!
policy-map IPPHONE+PC-ADVANCED
  class VVLAN-VOICE
    set ip dscp 46                          ! DSCP EF (Voice)
    police 128000 8000 exceed-action drop
      ! Only one voice call is permitted per switchport VVLAN
  class VVLAN-CALL-SIGNALING
    set ip dscp 24                          ! DSCP CS3 (Call-Signaling)
    police 32000 8000 exceed-action policed-dscp-transmit
      ! Out-of-profile Call-Signaling is marked down to Scavenger (CS1)
  class VVLAN-ANY
    set ip dscp 0
    police 32000 8000 exceed-action policed-dscp-transmit
      ! Unauthorized VVLAN traffic is marked down to Scavenger (CS1)
  class DVLAN-PC-VIDEO
    set ip dscp 34                          ! DSCP AF41 (Interactive-Video)
    police 496000 8000 exceed-action policed-dscp-transmit
      ! Only one IP/VC stream will be permitted per switchport
  class DVLAN-MISSION-CRITICAL-DATA
    set ip dscp 25                          ! Interim Mission-Critical Data
    police 5000000 8000 exceed-action policed-dscp-transmit
      ! Out-of-profile Mission-Critical Data is marked down to Scavenger (CS1)
  class DVLAN-TRANSACTIONAL-DATA
    set ip dscp 18                          ! DSCP AF21 (Transactional Data)
    police 5000000 8000 exceed-action policed-dscp-transmit
      ! Out-of-profile Transactional Data is marked down to Scavenger (CS1)
  class DVLAN-BULK-DATA
    set ip dscp 10                          ! DSCP AF11 (Bulk Data)
    police 5000000 8000 exceed-action policed-dscp-transmit
      ! Out-of-profile Bulk Data is marked down to Scavenger (CS1)
  class class-default
    set ip dscp 0
    police 5000000 8000 exceed-action policed-dscp-transmit
      ! Out-of-profile data traffic is marked down to Scavenger (CS1)
!
...
```

Example 12-78 *Catalyst 3750 Access Switch for IP Phones + PCs (Advanced Model): Case Study Example (Continued)*

```
 !
 interface FastEthernet1/0/1
  description ACCESS-EDGE IP PHONE + PC ADVANCED MODEL
  switchport access vlan 20               ! DVLAN
  switchport voice vlan 120               ! VVLAN
  no ip address
  srr-queue bandwidth share 1 70 25 5
        ! Q1 is PQ; Q2 gets 70% of remaining BW; Q3 gets 25% and Q4 gets 5%
  srr-queue bandwidth shape  30  0  0  0   ! Q1 is limited to 30%
  priority-queue out                      ! Q1 is enabled as a PQ
  mls qos trust device cisco-phone        ! Conditional Trust
  service-policy input IPPHONE+PC-ADVANCED  ! Attaches policy to interface
  no mdix auto
  spanning-tree portfast
 !
 <repeated for all FE switchports>
 !
 interface GigabitEthernet1/0/1
  description L2 UPLINK TO DISTRIBUTION CAT4500-SUP4-LEFT
  switchport trunk encapsulation dot1q
  switchport trunk allowed vlan 20,120    ! Trunks DVLAN and VVLAN
  switchport mode trunk
  no ip address
  srr-queue bandwidth share 1 70 25 5
        ! Q1 is PQ; Q2 gets 70% of remaining BW; Q3 gets 25% and Q4 gets 5%
  srr-queue bandwidth shape  30  0  0  0   ! Q1 is shaped to 30%
  priority-queue out                      ! Q1 is enabled as a PQ
  mls qos trust dscp                      ! Trusts DSCP
 !
 <repeated for GigabitEthernet1/0/2 Uplink to Distribution Cat4500-Sup4>
 !
 ...
 !
 ip access-list extended VVLAN-VOICE
  permit udp 10.1.110.0 0.0.0.255 any range 16384 32767 dscp ef
        ! Voice is matched by VVLAN subnet and DSCP EF
 !
 ip access-list extended VVLAN-CALL-SIGNALING
  permit tcp 10.1.120.0 0.0.0.255 any range 2000 2002 dscp af31
  permit tcp 10.1.120.0 0.0.0.255 any range 2000 2002 dscp cs3
        ! Call-Signaling is matched by VVLAN subnet and DSCP AF31 or CS3
 !
 ip access-list extended VVLAN-ANY
  permit ip 10.1.120.0 0.0.0.255 any
        ! Matches all other traffic sourced from the VVLAN subnet
 !
 ip access-list extended DVLAN-PC-VIDEO
  permit udp any any range 16384 32767              ! DVLAN IP/VC
 !
```

continues

Example 12-78 *Catalyst 3750 Access Switch for IP Phones + PCs (Advanced Model): Case Study Example (Continued)*

```
ip access-list extended DVLAN-MISSION-CRITICAL-DATA
 permit tcp any any range 3200 3202           ! SAP
 permit tcp any any eq 3600                   ! SAP
 permit tcp any any range 2000 2002           ! SoftPhone SCCP
 !
ip access-list extended DVLAN-TRANSACTIONAL-DATA
 permit tcp any any eq 1352                   ! IMAP
 !
ip access-list extended DVLAN-BULK-DATA
 permit tcp any any eq 143                    ! IMAP
 permit tcp any any eq 220                    ! IMAP
 !
```

Example 12-79 shows the QoS configuration for the (left) Catalyst 4500-Sup4 distribution-layer switch.

Example 12-79 *Catalyst 4500-Sup4 Distribution Switch Case Study Example*

```
!
hostname C4500-SUP4-DIST-LEFT
!
qos dbl exceed-action ecn            ! Optional: Enables DBL to mark IP ECN bits
qos dbl                              ! Globally enables DBL
qos map dscp 0 to tx-queue 2         ! Maps Best Effort to Queue 2
qos map dscp 16 18 20 22 24 25 26 32 to tx-queue 4
         ! Maps DSCP CS2 (Net-Mgmt) and AF21/AF22/AF23 (Transactional) to Q4
         ! Maps DSCP CS3 and AF31 (Call-Signaling) and DSCP 25 (MC Data) to Q4
         ! Maps DSCP CS4 (Str-Video) to Q4
qos map dscp 34 36 38 to tx-queue 4
         ! Maps DSCP AF41/AF42/AF43 (Int-Video) to Q4
         ! All other DSCP-to-Queue Mappings are remain at default
qos      ! Enables QoS Globally
!
vtp domain ABC-INC
vtp mode transparent
!
...
!
policy-map DBL
  class class-default
    dbl                              ! Enables DBL on all traffic flows
!
!
interface GigabitEthernet1/1
  description L3 UPLINK TO CORE 6500-PFC3-LEFT
  no switchport
  ip address 10.1.230.2 255.255.255.252
  service-policy output DBL          ! Applies DBL policy
  qos trust dscp                     ! Trusts DSCP
```

Example 12-79 *Catalyst 4500-Sup4 Distribution Switch Case Study Example (Continued)*

```
 tx-queue 1
   bandwidth percent 5            ! Q1 gets 5%
 tx-queue 2
   bandwidth percent 25           ! Q2 gets 25%
 tx-queue 3
   bandwidth percent 30           ! Enables Q3 as PQ
   priority high                  ! PQ gets 30%
   shape percent 30               ! Shapes PQ to 30%
 tx-queue 4
   bandwidth percent 40           ! Q4 gets 40%
 !
 <repeated for GigabitEthernet1/2 Uplink to Core 6500-PFC3-Right>
 !
 …
 !
 interface FastEthernet2/1
  description L3 FASTETHERNET LINK TO WAG 7200-NPEG1
  no switchport
  ip address 10.1.220.1 255.255.255.252
  service-policy output DBL        ! Applies DBL policy
  qos trust dscp                   ! Trusts DSCP
  tx-queue 3
    priority high                  ! PQ gets 30%
    shape percent 30               ! Shapes PQ to 30%
 !
 <repeated for FastEthernet2/2 Link to WAN Aggregator>
 !
 …
 !
 interface GigabitEthernet3/1
  description L2 DOWNLINK TO DATA CENTER 6500-PFC2
  switchport trunk encapsulation dot1q
  switchport trunk allowed vlan 200     ! Trunks Data Center VLAN
  switchport mode trunk
  service-policy output DBL              ! Applies DBL policy
  qos trust dscp                        ! Trusts DSCP
  tx-queue 1
    bandwidth percent 5                 ! Q1 gets 5%
  tx-queue 2
    bandwidth percent 25                ! Q2 gets 25%
  tx-queue 3
    bandwidth percent 30                ! Enables Q3 as PQ
    priority high                       ! PQ gets 30%
    shape percent 30                    ! Shapes PQ to 30%
  tx-queue 4
    bandwidth percent 40                ! Q4 gets 40%
 !
 <repeated for GigabitEthernet3/2 Downlink to Access-Layer Cat3550>
 <repeated for GigabitEthernet3/3 Downlink to Access-Layer Cat3750>
 !
```

Example 12-80 shows the QoS configuration for the (right) Catalyst 6500-PFC3 distribution-layer switch.

Example 12-80 *Catalyst 6500-PFC3 IOS Distribution Switch (with Per-User Microflow Policing): Case Study Example*

```
!
hostname CAT6500-PFC3-IOS-DIST-RIGHT
!
...
!
mls qos map policed-dscp normal-burst 0 24 26 34 36 to 8
            ! Excess traffic marked 0,CS3,AF31,AF41 or AF42 will be remarked to CS1
mls qos ! Enables QoS Globally
!
...
!
class-map match-all VOIP
  match ip dscp ef
class-map match-all INTERACTIVE-VIDEO
  match ip dscp af41  af42
class-map match-all CALL-SIGNALING
  match ip dscp cs3  af31
class-map match-all BEST-EFFORT
  match ip dscp default
!
!
policy-map PER-USER-POLICING
  class VOIP
      police flow mask src-only 128000 8000
        conform-action transmit exceed-action drop
        ! No source can send more than 128k worth of Voice traffic
  class INTERACTIVE-VIDEO
      police flow mask src-only 496000 8000
        conform-action transmit exceed-action policed-dscp-transmit
          ! Excess IP/VC traffic from any source is marked down to CS1
  class CALL-SIGNALING
      police flow mask src-only 32000 8000
        conform-action transmit exceed-action policed-dscp-transmit
          ! Excess Call-Signaling from any source is marked down to CS1
  class BEST-EFFORT
      police flow mask src-only 5000000 8000
        conform-action transmit exceed-action policed-dscp-transmit
          ! Excess PC Data traffic from any source is marked down to CS1
!
...
!
interface GigabitEthernet1/1        ! WS-X6408A-GBIC (1P2Q2T)
 description L3 UPLINK TO CORE 6500-PFC3-LEFT
 ip address 10.1.230.6 255.255.255.252
 wrr-queue bandwidth 30 70
          ! Sets the WRR weights for 30:70 (Q1:Q2) bandwidth servicing
 wrr-queue queue-limit 40 30
          ! Sets the buffer allocations to 40% for Q1 and 30% for Q2
```

Example 12-80 *Catalyst 6500-PFC3 IOS Distribution Switch (with Per-User Microflow Policing): Case Study Example (Continued)*

```
                    ! Indirectly sets PQ (Q3) size to equal Q2 (which is set to 30%)
 wrr-queue random-detect min-threshold 1 40 40
                    ! Sets Min WRED Thresholds for Q1T1 and Q1T2 to 40 and 80, respectively
 wrr-queue random-detect min-threshold 2 70 80
                    ! Sets Min WRED Thresholds for Q2T1 and Q2T2 to 70 and 80, respectively
 wrr-queue random-detect max-threshold 1 80 100
                    ! Sets Max WRED Thresholds for Q1T1 and Q1T2 to 80 and 100, respectively
 wrr-queue random-detect max-threshold 2 80 100
                    ! Sets Max WRED Thresholds for Q2T1 and Q2T2 to 80 and 100, respectively
 wrr-queue cos-map 1 1 1              ! Maps Scavenger/Bulk to Q1 WRED T1
 wrr-queue cos-map 1 2 0              ! Maps Best Effort to Q1 WRED T2
 wrr-queue cos-map 2 1 2 3 4          ! Maps CoS 2,3,4 to Q2 WRED T1
 wrr-queue cos-map 2 2 6 7            ! Maps CoS 6 and 7 to Q2 WRED T2
 mls qos trust dscp                   ! Trusts DSCP
 !
 <repeated for GigabitEthernet1/2 Uplink to Core 6500-PFC3-Right>
 !
 …
 !
 interface FastEthernet2/1            ! WS-X6548-RJ-45 (1P3Q1T)
  description L3 FASTETHERNET LINK TO WAG 7200-NPEG1
  ip address 10.1.220.10 255.255.255.252
 wrr-queue bandwidth 5 25 70
                    ! Sets the WRR weights for 5:25:70 (Q1:Q2:Q3) bandwidth servicing
 wrr-queue random-detect min-threshold 1 80
                    ! Sets the Min WRED Threshold for Q1T1 to 80%
 wrr-queue random-detect min-threshold 2 80
                    ! Sets Min WRED Threshold for Q2T1 to 80%
 wrr-queue random-detect min-threshold 3 80
                    ! Sets Min WRED Threshold for Q3T1 to 80%
                    ! All other WRED Thresholds are left at default (100%)
 wrr-queue cos-map 1 1 1              ! Maps Scavenger/Bulk to Q1 WRED T1
 wrr-queue cos-map 2 1 0              ! Maps Best Effort to Q1 WRED T1
 wrr-wrr-queue cos-map 3 1 2 3 4      ! Maps CoS 2,3,4,6 and 7 to Q3 WRED T1
 mls qos trust dscp                   ! Trusts DSCP
 !
 <repeated for FastEthernet2/2 Link to WAN Aggregator>
 !
 …
 !
 interface GigabitEthernet3/2         ! WS-X6408A-GBIC (1P2Q2T)
  description L2 DOWNLINK TO ACCESS-LAYER C3550 - LEFT
  no ip address
 wrr-queue bandwidth 30 70
                    ! Sets the WRR weights for 30:70 (Q1:Q2) bandwidth servicing
 wrr-queue queue-limit 40 30
                    ! Sets the buffer allocations to 40% for Q1 and 30% for Q2
                    ! Indirectly sets PQ (Q3) size to equal Q2 (which is set to 30%)
```

continues

Example 12-80 *Catalyst 6500-PFC3 IOS Distribution Switch (with Per-User Microflow Policing): Case Study Example (Continued)*

```
wrr-queue random-detect min-threshold 1 40 80
        ! Sets Min WRED Thresholds for Q1T1 and Q1T2 to 40 and 80, respectively
wrr-queue random-detect min-threshold 2 70 80
        ! Sets Min WRED Thresholds for Q2T1 and Q2T2 to 70 and 80, respectively
wrr-queue random-detect max-threshold 1 80 100
        ! Sets Max WRED Thresholds for Q1T1 and Q1T2 to 80 and 100, respectively
wrr-queue random-detect max-threshold 2 80 100
        ! Sets Max WRED Thresholds for Q2T1 and Q2T2 to 80 and 100, respectively
wrr-queue cos-map 1 1 1         ,  ! Maps Scavenger/Bulk to Q1 WRED T1
wrr-queue cos-map 1 2 0            ! Maps Best Effort to Q1 WRED T2
wrr-queue cos-map 2 1 2 3 4        ! Maps CoS 2,3,4 to Q2 WRED T1
wrr-queue cos-map 2 2 6 7          ! Maps CoS 6 and 7 to Q2 WRED T2
mls qos trust dscp                 ! Trusts DSCP
switchport
switchport trunk encapsulation dot1q
switchport trunk allowed vlan 10,110      ! Trunks DVLAN and VVLAN
switchport mode trunk
service-policy input PER-USER-POLICING    ! Attaches Per-User Policer
!
<repeated for GigabitEthernet3/3 Downlink to Access-Layer Cat3750>
<repeated for GigabitEthernet3/1 Downlink to Data Center C6500-PFC2>
<except no "service-policy input PER-USER-POLICING" for Data Center Downlink>
!
```

Example 12-81 shows the QoS configuration for the left Catalyst 6500-PFC3 core-layer switch, of which the right Catalyst 6500-PFC3 core-layer switch is a mirror image.

Example 12-81 *Catalyst 6500-PFC3 IOS Core Switch: Case Study Example*

```
!
hostname CAT6500-PFC3-IOS-CORE-LEFT
!
mls qos       ! Enables QoS Globally
!
...
!
interface Port-channel1
 description 40GE CORE BACKBONE
 ip address 10.1.240.1 255.255.255.252
 mls qos trust dscp
!
...
!
interface TenGigabitEthernet1/1    ! WS-X6704-10GE (1P7Q8T)
 no ip address
 wrr-queue bandwidth 5 25 20 20 20 5 5
        ! Sets the WRR weights for 5:25:20:20:20:5:5 (Q1 through Q7)
 wrr-queue queue-limit 5 25 10 10 10 5 5
        ! Allocates 5% to Q1, 25% to Q2, 10% to Q3, 10% to Q4,
        ! Allocates 10% to Q5, 5% to Q6 and 5% to Q7
```

Example 12-81 *Catalyst 6500-PFC3 IOS Core Switch: Case Study Example (Continued)*

```
wrr-queue random-detect min-threshold 1 80 100 100 100 100 100 100 100
       ! Sets Min WRED Threshold for Q1T1 to 80% and all others to 100%
wrr-queue random-detect min-threshold 2 1 100 100 100 100 100 100 100
       ! Sets Min WRED Threshold for Q2T1 to 80% and all others to 100%
wrr-queue random-detect min-threshold 3 80 100 100 100 100 100 100 100
       ! Sets Min WRED Threshold for Q3T1 to 80% and all others to 100%
wrr-queue random-detect min-threshold 4 80 100 100 100 100 100 100 100
       ! Sets Min WRED Threshold for Q4T1 to 80% and all others to 100%
wrr-queue random-detect min-threshold 5 80 100 100 100 100 100 100 100
       ! Sets Min WRED Threshold for Q5T1 to 80% and all others to 100%
wrr-queue random-detect min-threshold 6 80 100 100 100 100 100 100 100
       ! Sets Min WRED Threshold for Q6T1 to 80% and all others to 100%
wrr-queue random-detect min-threshold 7 80 100 100 100 100 100 100 100
       ! Sets Min WRED Threshold for Q7T1 to 80% and all others to 100%
wrr-queue random-detect max-threshold 1 100 100 100 100 100 100 100 100
       ! Sets Max WRED Threshold for Q1T1 to 100% and all others to 100%
wrr-queue random-detect max-threshold 2 100 100 100 100 100 100 100 100
       ! Sets Max WRED Threshold for Q2T1 to 100% and all others to 100%
       ! All other WRED Thresholds remain at their default values (100%)
wrr-queue random-detect 4            ! Enables WRED on Q4
wrr-queue random-detect 5            ! Enables WRED on Q5
wrr-queue random-detect 6            ! Enables WRED on Q6
wrr-queue random-detect 7            ! Enables WRED on Q7
wrr-queue cos-map 1 1 1              ! Maps Scavenger/Bulk to Q1
wrr-queue cos-map 2 1 0              ! Maps Best Effort to Q2
wrr-queue cos-map 3 1 4              ! Maps Video to Q3
wrr-queue cos-map 4 1 2              ! Maps Net-Mgmt/Transactional to Q4
wrr-queue cos-map 5 1 3              ! Maps Call-Signaling/MC-Data to Q5
wrr-queue cos-map 6 1 6              ! Maps IP Routing to Q6
wrr-queue cos-map 7 1 7              ! Maps STP to Q7
mls qos trust dscp                   ! Trusts DSCP
 channel-group 1 mode on
!
<repeated three more times on interfaces TenGigabitEthernet1/2-4>
!
...
!
interface GigabitEthernet2/1         ! WS-X6408A-GBIC (1P2Q2T)
 description L3 DOWNLINK TO DISTRIBUTION 4500-SUP4-LEFT
 ip address 10.1.230.1 255.255.255.252
wrr-queue bandwidth 30 70
       ! Sets the WRR weights for 30:70 (Q1:Q2) bandwidth servicing
wrr-queue queue-limit 40 30
       ! Sets the buffer allocations to 40% for Q1 and 30% for Q2
       ! Indirectly sets PQ (Q3) size to equal Q2 (which is set to 30%)
wrr-queue random-detect min-threshold 1 40 80
       ! Sets Min WRED Thresholds for Q1T1 and Q1T2 to 40 and 80, respectively
wrr-queue random-detect min-threshold 2 70 80
       ! Sets Min WRED Thresholds for Q2T1 and Q2T2 to 70 and 80, respectively
```

continues

Example 12-81 *Catalyst 6500-PFC3 IOS Core Switch: Case Study Example (Continued)*

```
wrr-queue random-detect max-threshold 1 80 100
        ! Sets Max WRED Thresholds for Q1T1 and Q1T2 to 80 and 100, respectively
wrr-queue random-detect max-threshold 2 80 100
        ! Sets Max WRED Thresholds for Q2T1 and Q2T2 to 80 and 100, respectively
wrr-queue cos-map 1 1 1           ! Maps Scavenger/Bulk to Q1 WRED T1
wrr-queue cos-map 1 2 0           ! Maps Best Effort to Q1 WRED T2
wrr-queue cos-map 2 1 2 3 4       ! Maps CoS 2,3,4 to Q2 WRED T1
wrr-queue cos-map 2 2 6 7         ! Maps CoS 6 and 7 to Q2 WRED T2
mls qos trust dscp                ! Trusts DSCP
!
<repeated for GigabitEthernet2/2 Downlink to Distribution 6500-PFC3-Right>
!
```

Summary

This chapter began with establishing the case for campus QoS by way of three main QoS design principles: The first is that applications should be classified and marked as close to their sources as technically and administratively feasible. The second is that unwanted traffic flows should be policed as close to their sources as possible. The third is that QoS always should be performed in hardware, instead of software, whenever a choice exists. Furthermore, it was emphasized that the only way to provide service guarantees is to enable queuing at any node that has the potential for congestion, including campus uplinks and downlinks.

A proactive approach to mitigating DoS/worm flooding attacks within campus environments was overviewed. This approach focuses on access-edge policers that meter traffic rates received from endpoint devices; when these exceed specified watermarks (at which point they no longer are considered normal flows), these policers mark down excess traffic to Scavenger (DSCP CS1). These policers are coupled with queuing policies throughout the enterprise that provision for a less-than best-effort Scavenger class on all links. In this manner, legitimate traffic bursts are not affected, but DoS/worm-generated traffic significantly is mitigated.

Common endpoints were overviewed and classified into three main groups: trusted endpoints, untrusted endpoints, and conditionally trusted endpoints. Untrusted endpoints were subdivided into two smaller models: untrusted PCs and untrusted servers. Similarly, conditionally trusted endpoints were subdivided into two models: basic and advanced.

Following these access-edge model definitions, platform-specific recommendations were given on to how to implement these access-edge models on Cisco Catalyst 2950, 2970, 3550, 3560, 3750, 4500, and 6500 series switches. Platform-specific limitations, caveats, and nerd knobs were highlighted to tailor each model to each platform's unique feature sets. All configurations were presented in config mode to continually highlight what platform was being discussed. Furthermore, many relevant verification commands were discussed in detail (in context) to illustrate how and when these can be used effectively when deploying QoS within the campus.

Recommendations also were given on how to configure queuing on a per-platform, per-line-card basis. These recommendations included configuring 1P3Q1T queuing on the Catalyst 2950, configuring 1P3Q2T queuing on the Catalyst 3550, configuring 1P3Q3T queuing on the Catalyst 2970/3560/3750, and configuring 1P3Q1T queuing (+ DBL) on the Catalyst 4500. For the Catalyst 6500, line card–specific queuing structures were examined in detail, including CatOS and Cisco IOS configurations for configuring 2Q2T, 1P2Q1T, 1P2Q2T, 1P3Q1T, 1P3Q8T, and 1P7Q8T queuing.

Following this, the Catalyst 6500 PFC3's per-user microflow policing feature was discussed in the context of how it can be leveraged to provide a second line of policing defense at the distribution layer.

Finally, campus-to-WAN/VPN handoff considerations were examined. It was recommended that you first resist the urge to use a Gigabit Ethernet connection to the WAN aggregation router, even if the router supports GE. Second, if the combined WAN circuit rate is significantly below 100 Mbps, enable egress shaping on the Catalyst switches (when supported). Third, if the combined WAN circuit rate is significantly below 100 Mbps and the Catalyst switch does not support shaping, enable egress policing (when supported).

The design chapter concluded with a case study of a fictitious enterprise, to illustrate how these various platform-specific recommendations can be brought together in an end-to-end campus QoS design for protecting voice, video, and critical data applications while mitigating DoS/worm attacks.

Further Reading

Standards:

- RFC 2474, "Definition of the Differentiated Services Field (DS Field) in the IPv4 and IPv6 Headers": http://www.ietf.org/rfc/rfc2474.
- RFC 2597, "Assured Forwarding PHB Group": http://www.ietf.org/rfc/rfc2597.
- RFC 2697, "A Single Rate Three Color Marker": http://www.ietf.org/rfc/rfc2697.
- RFC 2698, "A Two Rate Three Color Marker": http://www.ietf.org/rfc/rfc2698.
- RFC 3168, "The Addition of Explicit Congestion Notification (ECN) to IP": http://www.ietf.org/rfc/rfc3168.
- RFC 3246, "An Expedited Forwarding PHB (Per-Hop Behavior)": http://www.ietf.org/rfc/rfc3246.

Books:

- Flannagan, Michael, Richard Froom, and Kevin Turek. *Cisco Catalyst QoS: Quality of Service in Campus Networks*. Indianapolis: Cisco Press, 2003.

Cisco Catalyst documentation:

- Configuring QoS on the Catalyst 2950 (Cisco IOS Release 12.1[19]EA1):
  http://www.cisco.com/univercd/cc/td/doc/product/lan/cat2950/12119ea1/
  2950scg/swqos.htm.

- Configuring QoS on the Catalyst 3550 (Cisco IOS Release 12.1[19]EA1):
  http://www.cisco.com/univercd/cc/td/doc/product/lan/c3550/12119ea1/
  3550scg/swqos.htm.

- Configuring QoS on the Catalyst 2970 (Cisco IOS Release 12.2[18]SE):
  http://www.cisco.com/univercd/cc/td/doc/product/lan/cat2970/12218se/
  2970scg/swqos.htm.

- Configuring QoS on the Catalyst 2970 (Cisco IOS Release 12.2[18]SE):
  http://www.cisco.com/univercd/cc/td/doc/product/lan/cat3750/12218se/
  3750scg/swqos.htm.

- Configuring QoS on the Catalyst 4500 (Cisco IOS Release 12.2[18]EW):
  http://www.cisco.com/univercd/cc/td/doc/product/lan/cat4000/12_2_18/
  config/qos.htm.

- Configuring QoS on the Catalyst 6500 (Cisco CatOS Release 8.2):
  http://www.cisco.com/univercd/cc/td/doc/product/lan/cat6000/sw_8_2/
  confg_gd/qos.htm.

- Configuring Automatic QoS on the Catalyst 6500 (Cisco CatOS Release 8.2):
  http://www.cisco.com/univercd/cc/td/doc/product/lan/cat6000/sw_8_2/
  confg_gd/autoqos.htm.

- Configuring QoS on the Catalyst 6500 (Cisco IOS Release 12.2[17]SX):
  http://www.cisco.com/univercd/cc/td/doc/product/lan/cat6000/122sx/
  swcg/qos.htm.

WAN QoS Design

Part IV of this book provides an in-depth discussion of private-WAN QoS design. QoS considerations and detailed designs are presented for WAN aggregation routers connecting campus networks to various WAN media, such as leased-lines, Frame Relay, ATM and ATM-to-Frame Relay Service-Interworking. Additionally, QoS considerations and designs unique to branch routers are examined, which include using Network-Based Application Recognition (NBAR) for known-worm policing. While primarily addressing private-WAN QoS design, many of these recommendations are also applicable to VPN QoS designs (discussed in Part V) where traditional private-WAN media is used for VPN access.

The chapters in this part of the book are as follows:

Chapter 13   WAN Aggregator QoS Design

Chapter 14   Branch Router QoS Design

This chapter discusses WAN QoS considerations and designs, including the following:

- Slow-speed (≤ 768 kbps) WAN link design
- Medium-speed (768 kbps to T1/E1 speed) WAN link design
- High-speed (> T1/E1 speed) WAN link design

Additionally, these designs are applied to specific Layer 2 WAN media, including the following:

- Leased lines
- Frame Relay
- ATM
- ATM-to-Frame Relay Service Interworking
- ISDN

CHAPTER 13

WAN Aggregator QoS Design

A fundamental principle of economics states that the more scarce a resource is the more efficiently it should be managed. In an enterprise network infrastructure, bandwidth is the prime resource and also is the scarcest (and, likewise, most expensive) over the WAN. Therefore, the case for efficient bandwidth optimization using QoS technologies is strongest over the WAN, especially for enterprises that are converging their voice, video, and data networks.

The design principles described in this chapter apply primarily to Layer 2 WANs, such as leased lines, Frame Relay, and ATM (including ATM-to-Frame Relay Service Interworking). However, many service providers use these Layer 2 WAN technologies to access Layer 3 VPN services. Therefore, many of the design principles and examples presented in this chapter also apply to such VPN access scenarios.

This chapter provides design guidance for enabling QoS over the WAN. It is important to note that the recommendations in this chapter are not autonomous. They are critically dependent on the recommendations discussed in Chapter 12, "Campus QoS Design."

Where Is QoS Needed over the WAN?

Within typical WAN environments, routers play one of two roles: a WAN aggregator or a branch router. In some very complex WAN models, enterprises might have distributed WAN aggregators to cover regional branches, but the role of such middle-tier routers is not significantly different from that of a WAN aggregator located at a campus edge. This chapter focuses on WAN edge recommendations—primarily for WAN aggregator routers, but these correspondingly apply to the WAN edge designs of branch routers. QoS policies required on WAN edges are shown in Figure 13-1.

Figure 13-1 *Where Is QoS Needed over the WAN?*

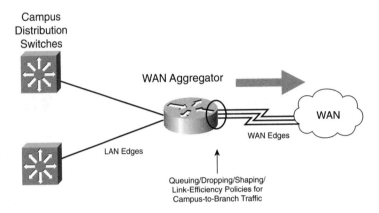

Chapter 14, "Branch Router QoS Design," discusses additional QoS considerations and designs unique to branch routers.

WAN Edge QoS Design Considerations

QoS policies required on WAN aggregators include queuing, shaping, selective dropping, and link-efficiency policies in the outbound direction of the WAN link. Traffic is assumed to be correctly classified and marked (at Layer 3) before WAN aggregator ingress. Remember, Layer 3 markings (preferably DSCP) are media independent and traverse the WAN media, whereas Layer 2 CoS is lost when the media switches from Ethernet to WAN media.

Several factors must be kept in mind when designing and deploying QoS polices on WAN edges. Some of these considerations were introduced in earlier chapters. They are re-emphasized here to underscore their importance to the context of the WAN QoS designs that follow.

Software QoS

Unlike LAN (Catalyst) queuing, which is done in hardware, WAN edge QoS is performed within Cisco IOS Software. If the WAN aggregator is homing several hundred remote branches, the collective CPU required to administer complex QoS policies might be more than some older devices can provide.

The main point to keep in mind is that QoS entails a marginal CPU load. WAN topologies and QoS policies should be designed to limit the average CPU utilization of the WAN aggregator to 75 percent (or lower) because this leaves cycles available to respond efficiently to routing updates.

Bandwidth Provisioning for Best-Effort Traffic

As discussed previously, the Best-Effort class is the default class for all data traffic. Only if an application has been selected for preferential or deferential treatment is it removed from the default class. Because many enterprises have several hundreds, if not thousands, of data applications running over their networks, adequate bandwidth must be provisioned for this class as a whole to handle the sheer volume of applications that default to it. It is recommended that at least 25 percent of a WAN link's bandwidth be reserved for the default Best-Effort class.

Bandwidth Provisioning for Real-Time Traffic

Not only does the Best-Effort class of traffic require special bandwidth-provisioning consideration, but the Real-Time class does as well. The amount of bandwidth assigned to the Real-Time class is variable; however, if too much traffic is assigned to Real-Time (strict-priority/low-latency) queuing, the overall effect is a dampening of QoS functionality for data applications.

The goal of convergence cannot be overemphasized: to enable voice, video, and data to coexist *transparently* on a single network. When real-time applications (such as voice or interactive-video) dominate a WAN link, data applications fluctuate significantly in their response times, destroying the transparency of the "converged" network.

Cisco Technical Marketing testing has shown a significant decrease in data application response times when Real-Time traffic exceeds one-third of a link's bandwidth capacity. Cisco IOS Software allows the abstraction (and, thus, configuration) of multiple LLQs. Extensive testing and production-network customer deployments have shown that limiting the sum of all LLQs to 33 percent is a conservative and safe design ratio for merging real-time applications with data applications.

Furthermore, it should be kept in mind that if VoIP traffic is set to dominate a link via low-latency queuing (which is essentially strict-priority FIFO queuing), VoIP actually could negatively impact other VoIP traffic because of extensive FIFO queuing. This easily could result in excessive serialization delays ($\geq$ 10 ms per hop) on even medium-speed links (T1/E1 links) where serialization delays ordinarily would not even be a consideration. (Serialization delays are discussed in more detail in the next section.) Such excessive serialization delays from VoIP LLQ overprovisioning would increase VoIP jitter and, thus, decrease overall call quality.

NOTE	The 33-percent limit for the sum of all LLQs is simply a best-practice design recommendation; it is not a mandate. In some cases, specific business objectives cannot be met while holding to this recommendation. In such cases, enterprises must provision according to their detailed requirements and constraints. However, it is important to recognize the trade-offs involved with overprovisioning LLQ traffic in respect to the negative performance impact on data application response times.

Serialization

Serialization delay refers to the finite amount of time it takes to clock a frame onto the physical media. Within the campus, this time is so infinitesimal that it is completely immaterial. Over the WAN, however, lower link speeds can cause sufficient serialization delay to adversely affect real-time streams, such as Voice or Interactive-Video.

Serialization delays are variable because they depend not only on the line rate of the link speed, but also on the size of the packet being serialized. Variable (network) delay also is known as jitter. Because the end-to-end one-way jitter target has been set as 30 ms, the typical per-hop serialization delay target is 10 ms (which allows for up to three intermediate hops per direction of VoIP traffic flow). This 10 ms per-hop target leads to the recommendation that a link fragmentation and interleaving (LFI) tool (either MLP LFI or FRF.12) be enabled on links with speeds at or below 768 kbps (this is because the serialization delay of a maximum-size Ethernet packet—1500 bytes—takes more than 10 ms to serialize at 768 kbps and below). Naturally, LFI tools need to be enabled on both ends of the link.

When deploying LFI tools, it is recommended that the LFI tools be enabled during a scheduled downtime. Assuming that the network administrator is within the enterprise's campus, it is recommended that LFI be enabled on the branch router first (which is on the far end of the WAN link) because this generally takes the WAN link down. Then the administrator can enable LFI on the WAN aggregator (the near end of the WAN link), and the link will come back up. Otherwise, if the administrator enables LFI on the WAN aggregator first, the link will go down, along with any in-band management access to the branch router. In such a case, the administrator would need to remove LFI from the WAN aggregator (bringing the link back up), enable LFI on the branch router, and then re-enable LFI on the WAN aggregator.

Additionally, as pointed out in Chapter 5, "Congestion-Management Tools," because traffic assigned to the LLQ escapes fragmentation, it is recommended that Interactive-Video not be deployed on slow-speed links; the large Interactive-Video packets (such as 1500-byte full-motion I-Frames) could cause serialization delays for smaller Interactive-Video packets. Interactive-Video traffic patterns and network requirements are overviewed in Chapter 2, "QoS Design Overview."

IP RTP Header Compression

Compressing IP, UDP, and RTP headers (cRTP) for VoIP calls can result in significant bandwidth gains over WAN links. However, it is important to realize that cRTP is one of the most CPU-intensive features within the Cisco IOS Software QoS toolset. Therefore, it is recommended that cRTP be used primarily on slow-speed ($\leq$ 768 kbps) links with a careful eye on CPU levels (especially for WAN aggregators that home a large number of remote branches).

Tx-ring Tuning

Newer versions of Cisco IOS Software automatically size the final interface output buffer (Tx-ring) to optimal lengths for Real-Time applications, such as Voice or Video. On some older versions of Cisco IOS Software, Tx-rings might need to be reduced on slow-speed links to avoid excessive serialization delay.

To determine the value of the Tx-ring on an interface, use the variation of the **show controllers** command shown in Example 13-1.

Example 13-1 *Displaying the Tx-ring Value with the **show controllers** Command*

```
WAG-7206-Left#show controllers Serial 1/0 | include tx_limited
tx_underrun_err=0, tx_soft_underrun_err=0, tx_limited=1(64)
WAG-7206-Left#
```

The value within the parentheses following the **tx_limited** keyword reflects the value of the Tx-ring. In this particular example, the Tx-ring is set to 64 packets. This value can be tuned to the recommended setting of 3 on T1/E1 (or slower) links using the command shown in Example 13-2.

Example 13-2 *Tuning the Tx-ring*

```
WAG-7206-Left(config)#interface Serial 1/0
WAG-7206-Left(config-if)#tx-ring-limit 3
```

The new setting quickly can be verified with the same **show controllers** command, as shown in Example 13-3.

Example 13-3 *Verifying Tx-ring Changes*

```
WAG-7206-Left#show controllers ser 1/0 | include tx_limited
Tx_underrun_err=0, tx-soft-underru_rr=0, tx-limited=1(3)
WAG-7206_Left#
```

NOTE   In ATM, the length of the Tx-ring is defined in (576-byte) particles, not packets, and is tuned on a per-PVC basis. On some non-ATM interfaces, the Tx-ring even can be tuned to a minimum of 1 (packet). In either case, the Tx-ring can be tuned (on ≤ 768 kbps links) to approximately 1500 bytes, which is the MTU of Ethernet.

PAK_priority

Chapter 5 introduced PAK_priority, the internal Cisco IOS mechanism for protecting routing and control traffic. The design implications of PAK_priority are summarized in the following list:

- Layer 2 and Layer 3 control traffic on moderately congested WAN links typically is protected adequately with the default PAK_priority treatment within the router and the IP ToS byte markings of IPP6/CS6.

- On heavily congested links, it might be necessary to explicitly provision a CBWFQ bandwidth class for routing/control traffic, as identified by either IPP or CS6.

- Although IS-IS traffic receives PAK_priority within the router, it cannot be marked to IPP6/CS6 because IS-IS uses a CLNS protocol. (It does not use IP, so there are no IPP or DSCP fields to mark.) This is important to keep in mind if explicit bandwidth provisioning is required for IS-IS traffic because it cannot be matched against IPP6/CS6 like most other IGPs. However, NBAR can be used within a class map to match IS-IS traffic (for example, **match protocol clns_is**).

- Although BGPs (both eBGPs and iBGPs) are marked to IPP6/CS6, they do not receive PAK_priority treatment within the routers. Therefore, it may be necessary to provision a separate bandwidth class to protect BGP sessions, even on moderately congested links where the underlying IGPs are stable.

- On Catalyst 6500 switches running Cisco IOS Software on both the supervisors and MSFC, IGP packets marked internally with PAK_priority additionally are marked with IPP6/CS6 and the Layer 2 CoS value of 6. This is because scheduling and congestion avoidance within Cisco Catalyst switches is performed against Layer 2 CoS values.

Link Speeds

In the context of WAN links, there are three main groupings of link speeds. These link speeds and their respective design implications are summarized in the following list:

- Slow (link speed ≤ 768 kbps):
  - Deployment of Interactive-Video generally is not recommended on these links because of serialization implications.
  - These links require LFI to be enabled if VoIP is to be deployed over them.

— cRTP is recommended (with a watchful eye on CPU levels).

— Check Tx-ring sizes (especially on slow-speed ATM PVCs); tune to 3, if needed.

— Three- to five-class traffic models are recommended.

- Medium (768 kbps ≤ link speed ≤ T1/E1):

— VoIP or Interactive-Video can be assigned to the LLQ (usually, there is not enough bandwidth to do both and still keep the LLQ provisioned at less than 33 percent—alternatively, Interactive-Video can be placed in a CBWFQ queue).

— LFI is not required.

— cRTP is optional.

— Three- to five-class traffic models are recommended.

- High (≥ T1/E1 link speeds):

— LFI is not required.

— cRTP generally is not recommended (because the cost of increased CPU levels typically offsets the benefits of the amount of bandwidth saved).

— Five- to 11-class traffic models are recommended.

Distributed Platform QoS and Consistent QoS Behavior

It is important to keep in mind that minor differences might exist between QoS configurations on distributed platforms (such as the Cisco 7500 series with VIPs) and those on nondistributed platforms (such as the Cisco 7200 or 1700). The most common difference is the inclusion of the **distributed** keyword after commands such as **ip cef** on distributed platforms. Where more complicated differences exist, they are highlighted explicitly in this chapter.

An important initiative is under way within Cisco to port the QoS code from the Cisco 7500 series routers to the nondistributed router families. This initiative is called Consistent QoS Behavior and has as its objectives simplifying QoS and increasing QoS consistency between platforms. Consistent QoS Behavior code should remove most, if not all, configuration idiosyncrasies between distributed and nondistributed platforms.

WAN Edge Classification and Provisioning Models

One of the most common questions raised when planning a QoS deployment over the WAN is "How many classes of traffic should be provisioned for?" The following considerations should be kept in mind when arriving at an appropriate traffic class model for a given enterprise.

Slow/Medium Link-Speed QoS Class Models

Slow-speed ($\leq$ 768 kbps) links have very little bandwidth to carve up, to begin with. When the serialization implications of sending Interactive-Video into the LLQ are taken into consideration, it becomes generally impractical to deploy more than five classes of traffic over slow-speed links.

Medium-speed ($\leq$ T1/E1) links do not have serialization restrictions and can accommodate either VoIP or Interactive-Video in their LLQs. However, typically both types of traffic cannot be provisioned at the same time without oversubscribing the LLQ (provisioning more than 33 percent of the traffic for the LLQ). Although this might be possible to configure (the parser will accept the policy and attach it to the interface), the administrator should remember the trade-off of significantly adverse data application response times when LLQs exceed one-third of the link. An alternative approach might be to provision Interactive-Video in a CBWFQ on medium-speed links.

Three-Class (Voice and Data) Model

If the business objective is simply to deploy VoIP over the existing data network, the Voice and Data WAN Edge Model is appropriate. Although it might seem that this is a two-class model, it is actually three: Voice, Call-Signaling, and (generic) data.

Voice is identified by DSCP EF, which is set by default on Cisco IP phones. When identified, VoIP is admitted into the LLQ, which, in this example, is set to the maximum recommended value of 33 percent of the link. Call admission control (CAC) correspondingly should be assigned to this link by dividing the allocated bandwidth by the voice codec (including Layer 2 overhead) to determine how many calls can be permitted simultaneously over this link. Because class-based cRTP is used in this example to compress voice traffic, it also should be factored into the CAC calculation.

Call-Signaling traffic also is marked on the IP phones (to AF31 currently, but it will be migrated to CS3, per the QoS Baseline) and requires a relatively small but dedicated bandwidth guarantee. All other data is fair-queued within class-default. This Three-class WAN Edge Model is illustrated in Figure 13-2 and detailed in Example 13-4.

Figure 13-2 *Three-Class WAN Edge Model Migration Strategy Example*

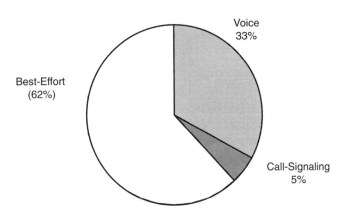

Example 13-4 *Three-Class WAN Edge Model*

```
!
 class-map match-all Voice
   match ip dscp ef              ! IP Phones mark Voice to EF
 class-map match-any Call Signaling
   match ip dscp cs3             ! Future Call-Signaling marking
   match ip dscp af31            ! IP Phones mark Call-Signaling to AF31
 !
 policy-map WAN-EDGE
   class Voice
     priority percent 33         ! Maximum recommended LLQ value
     compress header ip rtp      ! Optional: Enables Class-Based cRTP
   class Call Signaling
     bandwidth percent 5         ! BW guarantee for Call-Signaling
   class class-default
     fair-queue                  ! All other data gets fair-queuing
 !
```

NOTE   Sometimes administrators explicitly create a class map that functions as the MQC class-default. For instance, an administrator might create a class along the lines of that shown in the following code:

```
class-map match-all BEST-EFFORT
      match any
```

or even:

```
class-map match-all BEST-EFFORT
   match access-group 101
...
access-list 101 permit ip any any
```

These additional configurations are superfluous and inefficient for the router to process. The MQC implicit **class-default** should be used instead.

Another advantage of using the MQC implicit **class-default** is that (currently, before Consistent QoS Behavior code) on nondistributed platforms, class-default is the only class that supports fair queuing within it.

Verification command:

* **show policy**

Verification Command: **show policy**

The preceding three-class policy, like any other MQC policy, can be verified using the **show policy** command, as shown in Example 13-5.

Example 13-5 *Verification of Three-Class WAN Edge Policy*

```
RBR-2691-Right#show policy WAN-EDGE
   Policy Map WAN-EDGE
      Class VOICE
         Strict Priority       ! Voice will get LLQ
         Bandwidth 33 (%)      ! LLQ is provisioned to 33%
         compress:
             header ip rtp     ! cRTP is enabled
      Class CALL-SIGNALING
         Bandwidth 5 (%) Max Threshold 64 (packets) ! Call-Signaling gets 5% BW
      Class class-default
         Flow based Fair Queueing                    ! Data will get FQ
         Bandwidth 0 (kbps) Max Threshold 64 (packets)
RBR-2691-Right#
```

The Five-Class WAN Edge Model builds on the previous Three-Class WAN Edge Model and includes a provision for a Critical Data class and a Scavenger class.

The new Critical Data class requires Transactional Data traffic to be marked to DSCP AF21 (or AF22, in the case of dual-rate policers deployed within the campus). Additionally, IGP routing (marked by the routers as CS6) and Network-Management traffic (recommended to be marked to CS2) are protected within this class. In this example, the Critical Data class is provisioned to 36 percent of the link and DSCP-based WRED is enabled on it.

The Scavenger class constrains any traffic marked to DSCP CS1 to 1 percent of the link; this allows class-default to use the remaining 25 percent. However, to constrain Scavenger to 1 percent, an explicit bandwidth guarantee (of 25 percent) must be given to the Best-Effort class. Otherwise, if class-default is not explicitly assigned a minimum bandwidth guarantee, the Scavenger class still can rob it of bandwidth. This is because of the way the CBWFQ algorithm has been coded: If classes protected with a **bandwidth** statement are offered more traffic than their minimum bandwidth guarantee, the algorithm tries to protect such excess traffic at the direct expense of robbing bandwidth from class-default (if class-default is configured with **fair-queue**), *unless* class-default itself has a **bandwidth** statement (providing itself with a minimum bandwidth guarantee). However, assigning a **bandwidth** statement to class-default (on nondistributed platforms) currently precludes the enabling of fair queuing (**fair-queue**) on this class and forces FIFO queuing on class-default (this limitation is to be removed with the release of Consistent QoS Behavior code).

NOTE	An additional implication of using a **bandwidth** statement on class-default is that even though 25 percent of the link is reserved explicitly for class-default, the parser will not attach the policy to an interface unless the **max-reserved-bandwidth 100** command is entered on the interface before the **service-policy output** statement. This is because the parser adds the sum of the **bandwidth** statements (regardless of whether one of these is applied to the class-default) and, if the total is in excess of 75 percent of the link's bandwidth, rejects the application of the policy to the interface. This is shown in the following code:

```
!
interface Multilink1
 description T1 to Branch#60
 ip address 10.1.112.1 255.255.255.252
 max-reserved-bandwidth 100        ! overrides the default 75% BW limit
 service-policy output WAN-EDGE    ! attaches the MQC policy
 ppp multilink
 ppp multilink group 1
!
```

Furthermore, WRED can be enabled on the Best-Effort class to provide congestion management. Because all traffic assigned to the default class is to be marked to the same DSCP value (of 0), it would be superfluous to enable DSCP-based WRED on such a class; WRED (technically, RED, in this case because all the [IP Precedence] weights are the same) would suffice.

This Five-Class WAN Edge Model is illustrated in Figure 13-3 and detailed in Example 13-6.

Figure 13-3 *Five-Class WAN Edge Model Bandwidth Allocation Example*

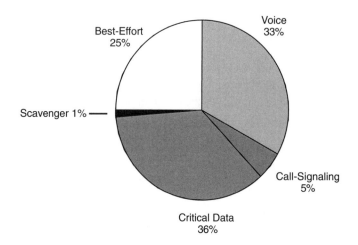

Example 13-6 *Five-Class WAN Edge Model*

```
!
class-map match-all Voice
  match ip dscp ef                     ! IP Phones mark Voice to EF
class-map match-any Call Signaling
  match ip dscp cs3                    ! Future Call-Signaling marking
  bandwidth percent 1                  ! Current Call-Signaling marking
class-map match-any Critical Data
  match ip dscp cs6                    ! Routers mark Routing traffic to CS6
  match ip dscp af21 af22              ! Recommended markings for Transactional-Data
  match ip dscp cs2                    ! Recommended marking for Network Management
class-map match-all Scavenger
  match ip dscp cs1                    ! Scavenger marking
!
 policy-map WAN-EDGE
  class Voice
    priority percent 33                ! Voice gets 33% of LLQ
  class Call Signaling
    bandwidth percent 5                ! BW guarantee for Call-Signaling
  class Critical Data
    bandwidth percent 36               ! Critical Data class gets 36% BW guarantee
    random-detect dscp-based           ! Enables DSCP-WRED for Critical-Data class
  class Scavenger
    bandwidth percent 1                ! Scavenger class is throttled
  class class-default
    bandwidth percent 25               ! Default class gets a 25% BW guarantee
    random-detect                      ! Enables WRED for class-default
!
```

Verification command:

- **show policy**

High Link Speed QoS Class Models

High-speed links (such as multiple T1/E1 or above speeds) allow for the provisioning of Voice, Interactive-Video, and multiple classes of data, according to the design rules presented in this chapter (for example, 25 percent for Best Effort class and ≤ 33 percent for all LLQs).

Enabling QoS only optimizes the efficiency of bandwidth utilization; it does not create bandwidth. Therefore, it is important to have adequate bandwidth for all the applications being provisioned. Furthermore, as WAN bandwidth is becoming less expensive, higher-speed links are becoming more popular.

Even if adequate bandwidth exists for up to 11 classes of traffic, as outlined by the QoS Baseline Model, not all enterprises are comfortable with deploying such complex QoS policies at this time. Therefore, it is recommended to start simple, but with room to grow into more complex models. Figure 13-4 illustrates a simple migration strategy showing which classes are good candidates for subdivision into more granular classes as future needs arise.

Figure 13-4 *Number of QoS Classes Migration Strategy Example*

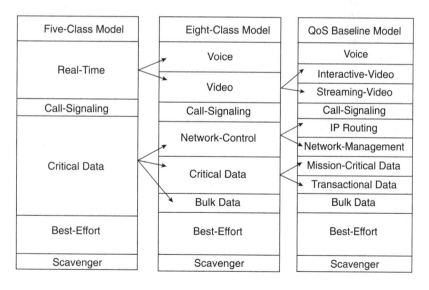

If the enterprises' QoS requirements exceed that which the Five-Class Model can provision for (such as requiring service guarantees for Interactive-Video and requiring Bulk Data to be controlled during busy periods), they might consider migrating to the Eight-Class Model.

Eight-Class Model

The Eight-Class Model introduces a dual-LLQ design: one for Voice and another for Interactive-Video.

As pointed out in Chapter 5, the LLQ has an implicit policer that allows for time-division multiplexing of the single priority queue. This implicit policer abstracts the fact that there is essentially a single LLQ within the algorithm and, thus, allows for the "provisioning" of multiple LLQs.

Interactive-video (or IP videoconferencing, known also as IP/VC) is recommended to be marked AF41 (which can be marked down to AF42 in the case of dual-rate policing at the campus access edge). It is recommended to overprovision the LLQ by 20 percent of the IP/VC rate. This takes into account IP/UDP/RTP headers as well as Layer 2 overhead.

Additionally, Cisco IOS Software automatically includes a 200-ms burst parameter (defined in bytes) as part of the **priority** command. On dual-T1 links, this has proven sufficient for protecting a single 384-kbps IP/VC stream; on higher-speed links (such as triple T1s), the default burst parameter has shown to be insufficient for protecting multiple IP/VC streams. However, multiple-stream IP/VC quality tested well with the burst set to 30,000 bytes (for example, **priority 920 30000**). Our testing did not arrive at a clean formula for predicting the required size of the burst parameters as IP/VC streams continually were added; however, given the variable packet sizes and rates of these Interactive-Video streams, this is not surprising. The main point is that the default LLQ burst parameter might require tuning as multiple IP/VC streams are added (which likely will be a trial-and-error process).

Optionally, DSCP-based WRED can be enabled on the Interactive-Video class, but testing has shown negligible performance difference in doing so (because, as already has been noted, WRED is more effective on TCP-based flows than UDP-based flows, such as Interactive-Video).

In these designs, WRED is not enabled on classes such as Call-Signaling, IP Routing, or Network-Management because WRED would take effect only if such classes were filling their queues nearly to their limits. Such conditions would indicate a provisioning problem that would better be addressed by increasing the minimum bandwidth allocation for the class than by enabling WRED.

Additionally, the Eight-Class Model subdivides the preferential data class to separate control plane traffic (IP routing and Network-Management applications) from business-critical data traffic. Interior Gateway Protocol (such as RIP, EIGRP, OSPF, and IS-IS) packets are protected through the PAK_priority mechanism within the router. However,

EGP protocols, such as BGP, do not get PAK_priority treatment and might need explicit bandwidth guarantees to ensure that peering sessions do not reset during periods of congestion. Additionally, administrators might want to protect network-management access to devices during periods of congestion.

The other class added to this model is for bulk traffic (Bulk Data class), which is also spun away from the Critical Data class. Because TCP continually increases its window sizes, which is especially noticeable in long sessions (such as large file transfers), constraining Bulk Data to its own class alleviates other data classes from being dominated by such large file transfers. Bulk Data is identified by DSCP AF11 (or AF12, in the case of dual-rate policing at the campus access edges). DSCP-based WRED can be enabled on the Bulk Data class (and also on the Critical Data class).

Figure 13-5 shows sample bandwidth allocations of an Eight-Class Model (for a dual-T1 link example). Figure 13-5 also shows how this model can be derived from the Five-Class Model in a manner that maintains respective bandwidth allocations as consistently as possible, which increases the overall end-user transparency of such a migration.

Figure 13-5 *Eight-Class WAN Edge Model Bandwidth Allocations Example*

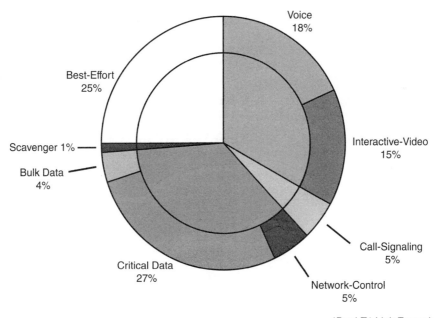

Example 13-7 shows the corresponding configuration (over a dual-T1 link) for the Eight-Class Model.

Example 13-7 *Eight-Class WAN Edge Model*

```
!
class-map match-all Voice
  match ip dscp ef                       ! IP Phones mark Voice to EF
class-map match-all Interactive Video
  match ip dscp af41 af42                ! Recommended markings for IP/VC
class-map match-any Call Signaling
  match ip dscp cs3                      ! Future Call-Signaling marking
  match ip dscp af31                     ! Current Call-Signaling marking
class-map match-any Network Control
  match ip dscp cs6                      ! Routers mark Routing traffic to CS6
  match ip dscp cs2                      ! Recommended marking for Network Management
class-map match-all Critical Data
  match ip dscp af21 af22                ! Recommended markings for Transactional-Data
class-map match-all Bulk Data
  match ip dscp af11 af12                ! Recommended markings for Bulk-Data
class-map match-all Scavenger
  match ip dscp cs1                      ! Scavenger marking
!
 policy-map WAN-EDGE
  class Voice
   priority percent 18                   ! Voice gets 552 kbps of LLQ
  class Interactive Video
   priority percent 15                   ! 384 kbps IP/VC needs 460 kbps of LLQ
  class Call Signaling
   bandwidth percent 5                   ! BW guarantee for Call-Signaling
  class Network Control
   bandwidth percent 5                   ! Routing and Network Management get min 5% BW
  class Critical Data
   bandwidth percent 27                  ! Critical Data gets min 27% BW
   random-detect dscp-based              ! Enables DSCP-WRED for Critical-Data class
  class Bulk Data
   bandwidth percent 4                   ! Bulk Data gets min 4% BW guarantee
   random-detect dscp-based              ! Enables DSCP-WRED for Bulk-Data class
  class Scavenger
   bandwidth percent 1                   ! Scavenger class is throttled
  class class-default
   bandwidth percent 25                  ! Fair-queuing is sacrificed for BW guarantee
   random-detect                         ! Enables WRED on class-default
 !
 !
```

NOTE	The Consistent QoS Behavior initiative will enable the configuration of a **bandwidth** statement along with **fair-queue** on any class, including class-default, on all platforms.

Verification command:

* **show policy**

QoS Baseline (11-Class) Model

As mentioned in the overview, the QoS Baseline is a guiding model for addressing the QoS needs of today and the foreseeable future. The QoS Baseline is not a mandate dictating what enterprises must deploy today; instead, this strategic document offers standards-based recommendations for marking and provisioning traffic classes that will allow for greater interoperability and simplified future expansion.

Building on the previous model, the Network-Control class is subdivided into the IP Routing and Network-Management classes.

The Critical Data class also is subdivided further into the Mission-Critical Data and Transactional Data classes. Although DSCP-based WRED is enabled on the Transactional Data class, because packets for this class can be marked AF21 (or AF22, as in the case of dual-rate policers being deployed in the campus), it would be superfluous to enable DSCP-based WRED on the Mission-Critical Data class (WRED will suffice because all Mission-Critical Data class packets are marked to the same value: DSCP 25).

Finally, a new class is provisioned for Streaming-Video. Testing has shown that there is a negligible difference in enabling WRED on this UDP-based traffic class, so, although it remains an option, WRED is not enabled in these design examples.

Figure 13-6 shows a sample WAN edge bandwidth allocation for a QoS Baseline Model (over a dual-T1 link) and also shows how this model can be derived from the Five- and Seven-Class Models in a manner that maintains respective bandwidth allocations as consistently as possible. This increases the overall end-user transparency of such a migration.

Figure 13-6 *QoS Baseline WAN Edge Model Bandwidth Allocations Example*

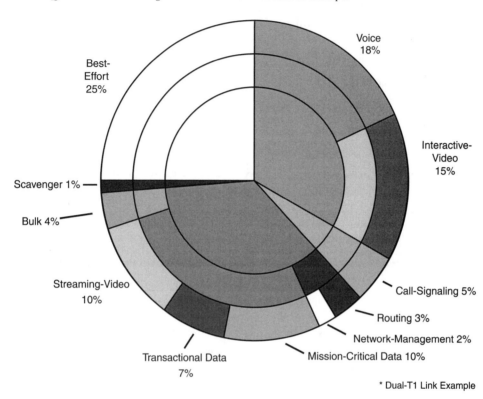

Example 13-8 shows the corresponding configuration for an 11-Class QoS Baseline WAN Edge Model (over a dual-T1 link).

Example 13-8 *QoS Baseline WAN Edge Model*

```
!
class-map match-all Voice
  match ip dscp ef                    ! IP Phones mark Voice to EF
class-map match-all Interactive Video
  match ip dscp af41 af42             ! Recommended markings for IP/VC
class-map match-any Call Signaling
  match ip dscp cs3                   ! Future Call-Signaling marking
  match ip dscp af31                  ! Current Call-Signaling marking
class-map match-all Routing
  match ip dscp cs6                   ! Routers mark Routing traffic to CS6
class-map match-all Net Mgmt
  match ip dscp cs2                   ! Recommended marking for Network Management
class-map match-all Mission-Critical Data
  match ip dscp 25                    ! Interim marking for Mission-Critical Data
class-map match-all Transactional Data
  match ip dscp af21 af22             ! Recommended markings for Transactional-Data
```

Example 13-8 *QoS Baseline WAN Edge Model (Continued)*

```
class-map match-all Bulk Data
  match ip dscp af11 af12              ! Recommended markings for Bulk-Data
class-map match-all Streaming Video
  match ip dscp cs4                    ! Recommended marking for Streaming-Video
class-map match-all Scavenger
  match ip dscp cs1                    ! Recommended marking for Scavenger traffic
!
 policy-map WAN-EDGE
  class Voice
    priority percent 18                ! Voice gets 552 kbps of LLQ
  class Interactive Video
    priority percent 15                ! 384 kbps IP/VC needs 460 kbps of LLQ
  class Call Signaling
    bandwidth percent 5                ! BW guarantee for Call-Signaling
  class Routing
    bandwidth percent 3                ! Routing class gets explicit BW guarantee
  class Net Mgmt
    bandwidth percent 2                ! Net-Mgmt class gets explicit BW guarantee
  class Mission-Critical Data
    bandwidth percent 10               ! Mission-Critical class gets 10% BW guarantee
    random-detect                      ! Enables WRED for Mission-Critical Data class
  class Transactional Data
    bandwidth percent 7                ! Transactional-Data class gets 7% BW guarantee
    random-detect dscp-based           ! Enables DSCP-WRED for Transactional-Data class
  class Bulk Data
    bandwidth percent 4                ! Bulk Data remains at 4% BW guarantee
    random-detect dscp-based           ! Enables DSCP-WRED for Bulk-Data class
  class Streaming Video
    bandwidth percent 10               ! Streaming-Video class gets 10% BW guarantee
  class Scavenger
    bandwidth percent 1                ! Scavenger class is throttled
  class class-default
    bandwidth percent 25               ! Class-Default gets 25% min BW guarantee
    random-detect                      ! Enables WRED on class-default
!
```

Verification command:

- **show policy**

Again, a **bandwidth** statement is used on class-default (currently), precluding the use of **fair-queue** on the class for all nondistributed platforms. Also, a **max-reserved-bandwidth 100** statement must be applied to the interface before the **service-policy output** statement.

Distributed-Platform/Consistent QoS Behavior—QoS Baseline Model

One of the current advantages of the Cisco 7500 (distributed platform) QoS code is that it can support **bandwidth** commands in conjunction with **fair-queue** on any given class, including class-default. This functionality will become available to nondistributed platforms with the release of Consistent QoS Behavior code. (As of this writing, this initiative does not have a fixed target delivery date.) When **fair-queue** is enabled on the main data classes, the resulting configuration becomes as shown in Example 13-9.

Example 13-9 *Distributed-Platform/Consistent QoS Behavior—QoS Baseline WAN Edge Model*

```
!
ip cef distributed        ! 'distributed' keyword required on 7500 for ip cef
!
class-map match-all Voice
  match ip dscp ef                   ! IP Phones mark Voice to EF
class-map match-all Interactive Video
  match ip dscp af41 af42            ! Recommended markings for IP/VC
class-map match-any Call Signaling
  match ip dscp cs3                  ! Future Call-Signaling marking
  match ip dscp af31                 ! Current Call-Signaling marking
class-map match-all Routing
  match ip dscp cs6                  ! Routers mark Routing traffic to CS6
class-map match-all Net Mgmt
  match ip dscp cs2                  ! Recommended marking for Network Management
class-map match-all Mission-Critical Data
  match ip dscp 25                   ! Interim marking for Mission-Critical Data
class-map match-all Transactional Data
  match ip dscp af21 af22            ! Recommended markings for Transactional-Data
class-map match-all Bulk Data
  match ip dscp af11 af12            ! Recommended markings for Bulk-Data
class-map match-all Streaming Video
  match ip dscp cs4                  ! Recommended marking for Streaming-Video
class-map match-all Scavenger
  match ip dscp cs1                  ! Recommended marking for Scavenger traffic
!
policy-map WAN-EDGE
  class Voice
    priority percent 18     ! Voice gets 552 kbps of LLQ
  class Interactive Video
    priority percent 15     ! 384 kbps IP/VC needs 460 kbps of LLQ
  class Call Signaling
    bandwidth percent 5     ! Bandwidth guarantee for Call-Signaling
  class Routing
    bandwidth percent 3     ! Bandwidth guarantee for Routing
  class Net Mgmt
    bandwidth percent 2     ! Bandwidth guarantee for Network Management
  class Mission-Critical Data
    bandwidth percent 10    ! Mission-Critical data gets min 10% BW guarantee
    fair-queue              ! Applies FQ to Mission-Critical Data class
    random-detect           ! Enables WRED on Mission-Critical Data class
  class Transactional Data
    bandwidth percent 7     ! Transactional Data gets min 7% BW guarantee
    fair-queue              ! Applies FQ to Transactional Data class
    random-detect dscp-based ! Enables DSCP-WRED on Transactional Data class
  class Bulk Data
    bandwidth percent 4     ! Bulk Data gets min 4% BW guarantee
    fair-queue              ! Applies FQ to Bulk Data class
```

Example 13-9 *Distributed-Platform/Consistent QoS Behavior—QoS Baseline WAN Edge Model (Continued)*

```
   random-detect dscp-based      ! Enables DSCP-WRED on Bulk Data class
  class Streaming Video
   bandwidth percent 10          ! Streaming-Video gets min 10% BW guarantee
  class Scavenger
   bandwidth percent 1           ! Scavenger class is throttled
  class class-default
   bandwidth percent 25          ! Class-Default gets min 25% BW guarantee
   fair-queue                    ! Applies FQ to Class-Default
   random-detect                 ! Enables WRED on Class-Default
 !
```

WAN Edge Link-Specific QoS Design

The most popular WAN media in use today are leased lines, Frame Relay, and ATM (including ATM-to-Frame Relay Service Interworking). Each of these media can be deployed in three broad categories of link speeds: slow speed ($\leq$ 768 kbps), medium speed ($\leq$ T1/E1), and high speed (multiple T1/E1 or greater). The following sections detail specific designs for each medium at each speed category. Additionally, ISDN QoS design is discussed in the context of a backup WAN link.

Leased Lines

Leased lines, or point-to-point links, can be configured with HDLC, PPP, or MLP encapsulation. MLP offers the network administrator the most flexibility and deployment options. For example, MLP is the only leased-line protocol that supports LFI on slow-speed links (through MLP LFI). Additionally, as bandwidth requirements grow over time, MLP requires the fewest modifications to accommodate the addition of multiple T1/E1 lines to a WAN link bundle. Furthermore, MLP supports all of the security options of PPP (such as CHAP authentication).

Slow-Speed ($\leq$ 768 kbps) Leased Lines

Recommendation: Use MLP LFI and cRTP.

For slow-speed leased lines (as illustrated in Figure 13-7), LFI is required to minimize serialization delay. MLP, therefore, is the only encapsulation option on slow-speed leased lines because MLP LFI is the only mechanism available for fragmentation and interleaving on such links. Optionally, cRTP can be enabled either as part of the MQC policy map (as shown in Example 13-10) or under the multilink interface (using the **ip rtp header-compression** command). Ensure that MLP LFI and cRTP, if enabled, are configured on both ends of the point-to-point link, as shown in Example 13-14.

Figure 13-7 *Slow-Speed Leased Lines*

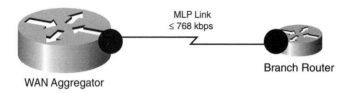

MLP Link
≤ 768 kbps

WAN Aggregator

Branch Router

Example 13-10 *Slow-Speed (≤ 768 kbps) Leased-Line QoS Design Example*

```
!
policy-map WAN-EDGE
  class Voice
    priority percent 33         ! Maximum recommended LLQ value
    compress header ip rtp      ! Enables Class-Based cRTP
  class Call Signaling
    bandwidth percent 5         ! BW guarantee for Call-Signaling
  …                             ! A 3 to 5 Class Model can be used
!
interface Multilink1
 description 768 kbps Leased-Line to RBR-3745-Left
 ip address 10.1.112.1 255.255.255.252
 service-policy output WAN-EDGE  ! Attaches the MQC policy to Mu1
 ppp multilink
 ppp multilink fragment delay 10  ! Limits serialization delay to 10 ms
 ppp multilink interleave        ! Enables interleaving of Voice with Data
 ppp multilink group 1
!
…
!
interface Serial1/0
 bandwidth 786
 no ip address
 encapsulation ppp
 ppp multilink
 ppp multilink group 1           ! Includes interface Ser1/0 into Mu1 group
!
```

Verification commands:

- **show policy**
- **show interface**
- **show policy interface**
- **show ppp multilink**

Verification Command: **show interface**

The **show interface** command indicates whether drops are occurring on an interface (an indication of congestion). Additionally, on a multilink interface with LFI enabled, the command displays interleaving statistics, as shown in Example 13-11.

Example 13-11 **show interface** *Verification of MLP LFI on a Slow-Speed Leased Line*

```
WAG-7206-Left#show interface multilink 1
Multilink1 is up, line protocol is up
  Hardware is multilink group interface
  Description: 768 kbps Leased-Line to RBR-3745-Left
  Internet address is 10.1.112.1/30
  MTU 1500 bytes, BW 768 Kbit, DLY 100000 usec,
      reliability 255/255, txload 233/255, rxload 1/255
  Encapsulation PPP, LCP Open, multilink Open
  Open: CDPCP, IPCP, loopback not set
  DTR is pulsed for 2 seconds on reset
  Last input 00:00:01, output never, output hang never
  Last clearing of "show interface" counters 00:16:15
  Input queue: 0/75/0/0 (size/max/drops/flushes);
  Total output drops: 49127
  Queueing strategy: weighted fair
  Output queue: 54/1000/64/49127/185507
  (size/max total/threshold/drops/interleaves)
```

In Example 13-11, 49,127 drops have occurred on the multilink interface (because of congestion), and LFI has engaged with 185,507 interleaves of voice with data.

Verification Command: **show policy interface** (Three-Class Policy)

The **show policy interface** command is probably the most useful **show** command for MQC-based QoS policies. It displays a wide array of dynamic statistics, including the number of matches on a class map as a whole, the number of matches against each discrete **match** statement within a class map, the number of queued or dropped packets (either tail dropped or WRED dropped), and many other relevant QoS statistics. Example 13-12 shows example output of the **show policy interface** command.

Example 13-12 **show policy interface** *Verification of a Three-Class Policy on a Slow-Speed Leased Line*

```
WAG-7206-Left#show policy interface multilink 1
 Multilink1
  Service-policy output: WAN-EDGE
    Class-map: Voice (match-all)
      68392 packets, 4377088 bytes
      30 second offered rate 102000 bps, drop rate 0 bps
      Match: ip dscp ef
      Queueing
        Strict Priority
```

continues

Example 13-12 **show policy interface** *Verification of a Three-Class Policy on a Slow-Speed Leased Line (Continued)*

```
              Output Queue: Conversation 264
              Bandwidth 33 (%)
              Bandwidth 253 (kbps) Burst 6325 (Bytes)
              (pkts matched/bytes matched) 68392/2043848
              (total drops/bytes drops) 0/0
            compress:
                header ip rtp
                UDP/RTP compression:
                Sent: 68392 total, 68388 compressed,
                      2333240 bytes saved, 1770280 bytes sent
                      2.31 efficiency improvement factor
                      99% hit ratio, five minute miss rate 0 misses/sec,0 max
                      rate 41000 bps
    Class-map: Call Signaling (match-any)
      251 packets, 142056 bytes
      30 second offered rate 3000 bps, drop rate 0 bps
      Match: ip dscp cs3
        0 packets, 0 bytes
        30 second rate 0 bps
      Match: ip dscp af31
        251 packets, 142056 bytes
        30 second rate 3000 bps
      Queueing
        Output Queue: Conversation 265
        Bandwidth 5 (%)
        Bandwidth 38 (kbps) Max Threshold 64 (packets)
        (pkts matched/bytes matched) 255/144280
        (depth/total drops/no-buffer drops) 0/0/0
    Class-map: class-default (match-any)
      51674 packets, 28787480 bytes
      30 second offered rate 669000 bps, drop rate 16000 bps
      Match: any
      Queueing
        Flow Based Fair Queueing
        Maximum Number of Hashed Queues 256
        (total queued/total drops/no-buffer drops) 36/458/0
WAG-7206-Left#
```

In Example 13-12, the Voice class map and Call-Signaling class map are receiving matches on their classification criteria (DSCP EF and DSCP CS3/AF31, respectively). However, because Cisco IP Telephony products currently mark Call-Signaling traffic to DSCP AF31, Call-Signaling traffic is matching only on DSCP AF31 in this example.

The last line of every class map output is important because this line indicates whether any drops are occurring on this traffic class. In this example, there are no drops in the Voice or Call-Signaling classes, which is the desired behavior. A few drops are occurring in class-default, but this is expected when the interface is congested (which is the trigger to engage queuing).

Also of note, and specific to this particular configuration, are the cRTP statistics included under the Voice class map. These cRTP statistics are displayed because class-based cRTP was enabled in this example (instead of enabling cRTP on the interface). Remember, cRTP must be enabled on both ends of the links for compression to occur; otherwise, these counters will never increment.

Medium-Speed (≤ T1/E1) Leased Lines

Recommendation: MLP LFI is not required; cRTP is optional.

Medium-speed leased lines (as shown in Figure 13-8) can use HDLC, PPP, or MLP encapsulation. An advantage of using MLP encapsulation is that future growth (to multiple T1/E1 links) will be easier to manage. Also, MLP includes all the security options of PPP (such as CHAP).

Figure 13-8 *Medium-Speed Leased Lines*

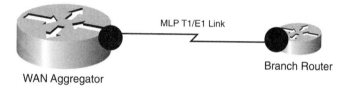

MLP T1/E1 Link

WAN Aggregator   Branch Router

However, MLP LFI is not required at these speeds, and cRTP is optional. Example 13-13 shows an example configuration for medium-speed leased lines.

Example 13-13 *Medium-Speed Leased-Line QoS Design Example*

```
!
interface Multilink1
 description T1 Leased-Line to RBR-3745-Left
 ip address 10.1.112.1 255.255.255.252
 service-policy output WAN-EDGE      ! Attaches the MQC policy to Mu1
 ppp multilink
 ppp multilink group 1         ! Identifies Mu1 as logical Int for Mu1 group
!
…
!
interface Serial1/0
 bandwidth 1536
 no ip address
 encapsulation ppp
 load-interval 30
 ppp multilink
 ppp multilink group 1          ! Includes interface Ser1/0 into Mu1 group
!
```

Verification commands:

- **show policy**
- **show interface**
- **show policy interface**

High-Speed (Multiple T1/E1 or Greater) Leased Lines

Recommendation: Use MLP bundling, but keep an eye on CPU levels. When enterprises have multiple T1/E1-speed leased lines to individual branches, three options exist for load sharing:

- IP CEF per-destination load balancing
- IP CEF per-packet load balancing
- Multilink PPP bundles

Cisco Technical Marketing testing has shown that IP CEF per-destination load balancing does not meet the SLAs required for Voice and Interactive-Video over multiple T1/E1 links, as shown in Figure 13-9.

Figure 13-9 *High-Speed Leased Lines*

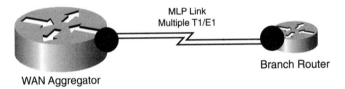

MLP Link
Multiple T1/E1

Branch Router

WAN Aggregator

On the other hand, IP-CEF per-packet load balancing did meet the required SLAs, but not quite as well as MLP bundling.

MLP bundling attained the best overall SLA values for delay and jitter, but it required more CPU resources than IP CEF per-packet load balancing. If CPU levels are kept under the recommended 75 percent, it is recommended to use MLP bundling for multiple T1/E1 links.

Also, if policy maps that require bandwidth statements on class-default are being attached to the multilink interface, the **max-reserved-bandwidth 100** command is required on the interface before the **service-policy output** statement can be applied, as shown in Example 13-14.

Example 13-14 *High-Speed (≥ Multiple T1/E1) Leased Line QoS Design Example*

```
!
interface Multilink1
 description Dual-T1 to RBR-3745-Left
 ip address 10.1.112.1 255.255.255.252
 max-reserved-bandwidth 100        ! Overrides the default 75% BW limit
 service-policy output WAN-EDGE     ! Attaches the MQC policy to Mu1
 ppp multilink
 ppp multilink group 1             ! Identifies Mu1 as logical int for Mu1 group
!
...
!
interface Serial1/0
 bandwidth 1536           ! defined on physical interface only
 no ip address
 encapsulation ppp
 ppp multilink
 ppp multilink group 1          ! includes interface Ser1/0 into Mu1 group
!
interface Serial1/1
 bandwidth 1536           ! defined on physical interface only
 no ip address
 encapsulation ppp
 ppp multilink
 ppp multilink group 1          ! includes interface Ser1/1 into Mu1 group
!
```

NOTE   Interface **bandwidth** commands (not to be confused with policy map CBWFQ **bandwidth** commands) should be defined only on the physical interfaces, not on multilink interfaces. This way, if any physical interfaces go down, the Cisco IOS Software will reflect the change in the multilink interface's bandwidth for routing and QoS purposes. This change can be verified by the **show interface** command. However, if a bandwidth statement is configured under the multilink interface, the bandwidth value for the interface will be static even if an underlying physical interface is lost.

Verification commands:

- **show policy**
- **show interface**
- **show policy interface**
- **show ppp multilink**

Verification Command: **show policy interface** (QoS Baseline Policy)

A more complex example of the **show policy interface** command is given in Example
13-15, where a QoS Baseline WAN edge policy is being applied to a dual-T1 (high-speed)
leased line.

Example 13-15 **show policy interface** *Verification of a QoS Baseline Policy on a High-Speed Leased*
Line

```
WAG-7206-Left#show policy interface multilink 1
 Multilink1
  Service-policy output: WAN-EDGE
    Class-map: Voice (match-all)
      444842 packets, 28467338 bytes
      30 second offered rate 434000 bps, drop rate 0 bps
      Match: ip dscp ef
      Queueing
        Strict Priority
        Output Queue: Conversation 264
        Bandwidth 18 (%)
        Bandwidth 552 (kbps) Burst 13800 (Bytes)
        (pkts matched/bytes matched) 444842/28467338
        (total drops/bytes drops) 0/0
    Class-map: Interactive Video (match-all)
      32685 packets, 25977946 bytes
      30 second offered rate 405000 bps, drop rate 0 bps
      Match: ip dscp af41
      Queueing
        Strict Priority
        Output Queue: Conversation 264
        Bandwidth 15 (%)
        Bandwidth 460 (kbps) Burst 11500 (Bytes)
        (pkts matched/bytes matched) 32843/26097186
        (total drops/bytes drops) 0/0
    Class-map: Call Signaling (match-any)
      1020 packets, 537876 bytes
      30 second offered rate 7000 bps, drop rate 0 bps
      Match: ip dscp cs3
        0 packets, 0 bytes
        30 second rate 0 bps
      Match: ip dscp af31
        1020 packets, 537876 bytes
        30 second rate 7000 bps
      Queueing
        Output Queue: Conversation 265
        Bandwidth 5 (%)
        Bandwidth 153 (kbps) Max Threshold 64 (packets)
        (pkts matched/bytes matched) 1022/538988
        (depth/total drops/no-buffer drops) 0/0/0
    Class-map: Routing (match-all)
      1682 packets, 112056 bytes
      30 second offered rate 0 bps, drop rate 0 bps
      Match: ip dscp cs6
      Queueing
```

Example 13-15 **show policy interface** *Verification of a QoS Baseline Policy on a High-Speed Leased Line (Continued)*

```
                      Output Queue: Conversation 266
                      Bandwidth 3 (%)
                      Bandwidth 92 (kbps) Max Threshold 64 (packets)
                      (pkts matched/bytes matched) 1430/95844
                      (depth/total drops/no-buffer drops) 0/0/0
                Class-map: Net Mgmt (match-all)
                   32062 packets, 2495021 bytes
                   30 second offered rate 41000 bps, drop rate 0 bps
                   Match: ip dscp cs2
                   Queueing
                      Output Queue: Conversation 267
                      Bandwidth 2 (%)
                      Bandwidth 61 (kbps) Max Threshold 64 (packets)
                      (pkts matched/bytes matched) 32256/2510284
                      (depth/total drops/no-buffer drops) 0/0/0
                Class-map: Mission-Critical Data (match-all)
                   56600 packets, 40712013 bytes
                   30 second offered rate 590000 bps, drop rate 0 bps
                   Match: ip dscp 25
                   Queueing
                      Output Queue: Conversation 268
                      Bandwidth 12 (%)
                      Bandwidth 368 (kbps)
                      (pkts matched/bytes matched) 57178/41112815
                      (depth/total drops/no-buffer drops) 10/0/0
                       exponential weight: 9
                       mean queue depth: 10
                class  Transmitted     Random drop     Tail drop    Minimum Maximum  Mark
                       pkts/bytes      pkts/bytes      pkts/bytes   thresh  thresh   prob
                0         0/0             0/0             0/0          20      40     1/10
                1         0/0             0/0             0/0          22      40     1/10
                2         0/0             0/0             0/0          24      40     1/10
                3      57178/41112815     0/0             0/0          26      40     1/10
                4         0/0             0/0             0/0          28      40     1/10
                5         0/0             0/0             0/0          30      40     1/10
                6         0/0             0/0             0/0          32      40     1/10
                7         0/0             0/0             0/0          34      40     1/10
                rsvp      0/0             0/0             0/0          36      40     1/10
                Class-map: Transactional Data (match-all)
                   31352 packets, 31591979 bytes
                   30 second offered rate 435000 bps, drop rate 10000 bps
                   Match: ip dscp af21
                   Queueing
                      Output Queue: Conversation 269
                      Bandwidth 8 (%)
                      Bandwidth 245 (kbps)
                      (pkts matched/bytes matched) 31741/32008133
                      (depth/total drops/no-buffer drops) 29/954/0
                       exponential weight: 9
                       mean queue depth: 26
```

continues

Example 13-15 **show policy interface** *Verification of a QoS Baseline Policy on a High-Speed Leased Line (Continued)*

class	Transmitted pkts/bytes	Random drop pkts/bytes	Tail drop pkts/bytes	Minimum thresh	Maximum thresh	Mark prob
0	0/0	0/0	0/0	20	40	1/10
1	0/0	0/0	0/0	22	40	1/10
2	30787/31019741	954/988392	0/0	24	40	1/10
3	0/0	0/0	0/0	26	40	1/10
4	0/0	0/0	0/0	28	40	1/10
5	0/0	0/0	0/0	30	40	1/10
6	0/0	0/0	0/0	32	40	1/10
7	0/0	0/0	0/0	34	40	1/10
rsvp	0/0	0/0	0/0	36	40	1/10

```
    Class-map: Streaming Video (match-all)
      23227 packets, 19293728 bytes
      30 second offered rate 291000 bps, drop rate 0 bps
      Match: ip dscp cs4
      Queueing
        Output Queue: Conversation 271
        Bandwidth 10 (%)
        Bandwidth 307 (kbps) Max Threshold 64 (packets)
        (pkts matched/bytes matched) 23683/19672892
        (depth/total drops/no-buffer drops) 2/0/0

    Class-map: Scavenger (match-all)
      285075 packets, 129433625 bytes
      30 second offered rate 2102000 bps, drop rate 2050000 bps
      Match: ip dscp cs1
      Queueing
        Output Queue: Conversation 272
        Bandwidth 1 (%)
        Bandwidth 30 (kbps) Max Threshold 64 (packets)
        (pkts matched/bytes matched) 291885/132532775
        (depth/total drops/no-buffer drops) 64/283050/0
    Class-map: class-default (match-any)
      40323 packets, 35024924 bytes
      30 second offered rate 590000 bps, drop rate 0 bps
      Match: any
      Queueing
        Output Queue: Conversation 273
        Bandwidth 25 (%)
        Bandwidth 768 (kbps)
        (pkts matched/bytes matched) 41229/35918160
        (depth/total drops/no-buffer drops) 12/268/0
        exponential weight: 9
        mean queue depth: 4
```

class	Transmitted pkts/bytes	Random drop pkts/bytes	Tail drop pkts/bytes	Minimum thresh	Maximum thresh	Mark prob
0	40961/35700528	268/217632	0/0	20	40	1/10
1	0/0	0/0	0/0	22	40	1/10
2	0/0	0/0	0/0	24	40	1/10

Example 13-15 **show policy interface** *Verification of a QoS Baseline Policy on a High-Speed Leased Line (Continued)*

3	0/0	0/0	0/0	26	40	1/10
4	0/0	0/0	0/0	28	40	1/10
5	0/0	0/0	0/0	30	40	1/10
6	0/0	0/0	0/0	32	40	1/10
7	0/0	0/0	0/0	34	40	1/10
rsvp	0/0	0/0	0/0	36	40	1/10

Important items to note for a given class are the **pkts matched** statistics (which verify that classification has been configured correctly and that the packets have been assigned to the proper queue) and the **total drops** statistics (which indicate whether adequate bandwidth has been assigned to the class).

Extremely few drops, if any, are desired in the Voice, Interactive-Video, Call-Signaling, and Routing classes.

NOTE   The Routing class is a special case because of the statistics that it displays.

On nondistributed platforms, the classification counter (the first line under the class map) shows any IGP traffic matched by the Routing class (identified by DSCP CS6). But remember that IGP protocols queue separately (because these are handled by the PAK_priority mechanism) and, therefore, do not register queuing statistics within the MQC counters for the Routing class. EGP protocols (such as BGP), on the other hand, do register queuing/dropping statistics within such an MQC class.

The situation is different on distributed platforms, where all routing packets (IGP or EGP) are matched and queued within a provisioned Routing class (complete with queuing/ dropping statistics through the **show policy interface** verification command).

Few drops are expected in the Mission-Critical Data class. WRED (essentially RED because all packets are marked to the same IPP/DSCP value) is enabled to avoid congestion on this class. Some drops are expected for the Transactional Data class, yet, in this particular example, WRED is minimizing tail drops for this class.

It is normal for the Bulk Data class to show drops (both WRED and tail). This is because the Bulk Data class is being constrained from dominating bandwidth by its large and sustained TCP sessions. The Scavenger class should show very aggressive dropping during periods of congestion. Finally, it is normal for drops to appear in the default class.

Verification Command: **show ppp multilink**

The **show ppp multilink** command is useful to verify that multiple physical links are correctly associated and included in the MLP bundle, as shown in Example 13-16. Also, the load (which might not quite hit 255/255) indicates congestion on the link.

Example 13-16 **show ppp multilink** *Verification of a High-Speed Leased Line*

```
WAG-7206-Left#show ppp multilink
Multilink1, bundle name is RBR-3745-Left
  Bundle up for 00:28:33, 254/255 load
  Receive buffer limit 24384 bytes, frag timeout 1000 ms
    0/0 fragments/bytes in reassembly list
    0 lost fragments, 2 reordered
    0/0 discarded fragments/bytes, 0 lost received
    0xE8F received sequence, 0x9A554 sent sequence
  Member links: 2 active, 0 inactive (max not set, min not set)
    Se1/0, since 00:28:35, 1920 weight, 1496 frag size
    Se1/1, since 00:28:33, 1920 weight, 1496 frag size
```

Frame Relay

Recommendation: For the latest feature combinations and management options, use class-based Frame Relay traffic shaping whenever possible.

Frame Relay networks are the most popular WANs in use today because of the low costs associated with them. Frame Relay is a nonbroadcast multiaccess (NBMA) technology that frequently utilizes oversubscription to achieve cost savings (similar to airlines overselling seats on flights to achieve maximum capacity and profitability).

To manage oversubscription and potential speed mismatches between senders and receivers, a traffic-shaping mechanism must be used with Frame Relay. Either Frame Relay traffic shaping (FRTS) or class-based FRTS can be used. The primary advantage of using class-based FRTS is management because shaping statistics and queuing statistics are displayed jointly with the **show policy interface** verification command and are included in the SNMPv2 Cisco class-based QoS Management Information Base (MIB).

FRTS and class-based FRTS require the following parameters to be defined:

- Committed information rate (CIR)
- Committed burst rate (Bc)
- Excess burst rate (Be)
- Minimum CIR
- Fragment size (required only on slow-speed links)

Committed Information Rate

Recommendation: Set the CIR to 95 percent of the PVC contracted speed.

In most Frame Relay networks, a central site's high-speed links connect to lower-speed links to/from many remote offices. For example, consider a central site that sends out data at 1.536 Mbps, while a remote branch might have only a 56-kbps circuit into it. This speed mismatch can cause congestion delays and drops. In addition, there is typically a many-to-one ratio of remote branches to central hubs, making it possible for many remote sites to send traffic at a rate that can overwhelm the T1 at the hub. Both scenarios can cause frame buffering in the provider network, which introduces jitter, delay, and loss.

The only solution to guarantee service-level quality is to use traffic shaping at both the central and remote routers and to define a consistent CIR at both ends of the Frame Relay PVC. Because the FRTS mechanism does not take Frame Relay overhead (headers and cyclic redundancy checks [CRCs]) into account in its calculations, it is recommended that the CIR be set slightly below the contracted speed of the PVC. Cisco Technical Marketing testing has shown that setting the CIR to 95 percent of the contracted speed of the PVC engages the queuing mechanism (LLQ/CBWFQ) slightly early and improves service levels for Real-Time applications, like Voice.

Committed Burst Rate

Recommendation: Set the Bc to CIR/100 on nondistributed platforms and to CIR/125 on distributed platforms.

With Frame Relay networks, you also need to consider the amount of data that a node can transmit at any given time. A 56-kbps PVC can transmit a maximum of 56 kbps of traffic in 1 second. Traffic is not sent during the entire second, however, but only during a defined window called the interval (Tc). The amount of traffic that a node can transmit during this interval is called the committed burst (Bc) rate. By default, Cisco IOS Software sets the Bc to CIR/8. This formula is used for calculating the Tc follows:

$$Tc = Bc / CIR$$

For example, a CIR of 56 kbps is given a default Tc of 125 ms (7000 / 56,000). If the 56-kbps CIR is provisioned on a WAN aggregator that has a T1 line-rate clock speed, every time the router sends its allocated 7000 bits, it has to wait 120.5 ms before sending the next batch of traffic. Although this is a good default value for data, it is a bad choice for voice.

By setting the Bc value to a much lower number, you can force the router to send less traffic per interval, but over more frequent intervals per second. This results in significant reduction in shaping delays.

The optimal configured value for Bc is CIR/100, which results in a 10-ms interval $(Tc = B / CIR)$.

On distributed platforms, the Tc must be defined in 4-ms increments. The nearest multiple of 4 ms within the 10-ms target is 8 ms. This interval can be achieved by configuring the Bc to equal CIR/125.

Excess Burst Rate

Recommendation: Set the Be to 0.

If the router does not have enough traffic to send all of its Bc (1000 bits, for example), it can "credit" its account and send more traffic during a later interval. The maximum amount that can be credited to the router's traffic account is called the excess burst (Be) rate. The problem with Be in converged networks is that this can create a potential for buffering delays within a Frame Relay network (because the receiving side can "pull" the traffic from a circuit only at the rate of Bc, not Bc + Be). To remove this potential for buffering delays, it is recommended to set the Be to 0.

Minimum Committed Information Rate

Recommendation: Set the minCIR to CIR.

The minimum CIR is the transmit value that a Frame Relay router will "rate down" to when backward-explicit congestion notifications (BECNs) are received. By default, Cisco IOS Software sets the minimum CIR to CIR/2. However, to maintain consistent service levels, it is recommended that adaptive shaping be disabled and that the minimum CIR be set equal to the CIR (which means there is no "rating down"). An exception to this rule would occur if a tool such as Frame Relay voice-adaptive traffic shaping was deployed (for more information and recommendations on using FR-VATS, refer to Chapter 4, "Policing and Shaping Tools").

Slow-Speed (≤ 768 kbps) Frame Relay Links

Recommendation: Enable FRF.12 and set the fragment size for 10 ms maximum serialization delay. Enable cRTP.

As with all slow-speed links, slow Frame Relay links (as illustrated in Figure 13-10) require a mechanism for fragmentation and interleaving. In the Frame Relay environment, the tool for accomplishing this is FRF.12.

Figure 13-10 *Slow-Speed Frame Relay Links*

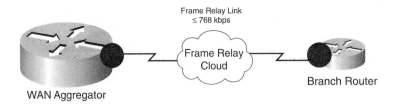

Frame Relay Link
≤ 768 kbps

Frame Relay
Cloud

WAN Aggregator

Branch Router

Unlike MLP LFI, which takes the maximum serialization delay as a parameter, FRF.12 requires the actual fragment sizes to be defined manually. This requires some additional calculations because the maximum fragment sizes vary by link speed. These fragment sizes can be calculated by multiplying the provisioned line-clocking speed by the recommended maximum serialization delay target (10 ms), and converting the result from bits to bytes (which is done by dividing the result by 8):

Fragment Size in Bytes = (Link Speed in kbps * Maximum Allowed Jitter in ms) / 8

For example, the calculation for the maximum fragment size for a 56-kbps circuit is as follows:

Fragment Size = (56 kbps * 10 ms) / 8 = 70 Bytes

Table 13-1 shows the recommended values for FRF.12 fragment sizes, CIR, and Bc for slow-speed Frame Relay links.

Table 13-1   *Recommended Fragment Sizes, CIR, and Bc Values for Slow-Speed Frame Relay Links*

PVC Speed	Maximum Fragment Size (for 10-ms Delay)	Recommended CIR Values	Recommended Bc Values
56 kbps	70 bytes	53,200 bps	532 bits per Tc
64 kbps	80 bytes	60,800 bps	608 bits per Tc
128 kbps	160 bytes	121,600 bps	1216 bits per Tc
256 kbps	320 bytes	243,200 bps	2432 bits per Tc
512 kbps	640 bytes	486,400 bps	4864 bits per Tc
768 kbps	960 bytes	729,600 bps	7296 bits per Tc

Both FRTS and class-based FRTS require a Frame Relay map class to be applied to the DLCI. Also in both cases, the **frame-relay fragment** command is applied to the map class. However, unlike FRTS, class-based FRTS does not require **frame-relay traffic-shaping** to be enabled on the main interface. This is because MQC-based/class-based FRTS requires a hierarchal (or nested) QoS policy to accomplish both shaping and queuing. This hierarchical policy is attached to the Frame Relay map class, which is bound to the DLCI.

As with slow-speed leased-line policies, cRTP can be enabled within the MQC queuing policy under the Voice class. Example 13-17 shows an example of slow-speed Frame Relay link-specific configuration.

Example 13-17   *Slow-Speed (≤ 768 kbps) Frame Relay QoS Design Example*

```
!
policy-map MQC-FRTS-768
  class class-default
    shape average 729600 7296 0       ! Enables MQC-Based FRTS
    service-policy WAN-EDGE           ! Queues packets headed to the shaper
```

continues

Example 13-17 *Slow-Speed (≤ 768 kbps) Frame Relay QoS Design Example (Continued)*

```
!
...
!
interface Serial2/0
 no ip address
 encapsulation frame-relay
!
interface Serial2/0.12 point-to-point
 ip address 10.1.121.1 255.255.255.252
 description 768kbps FR Circuit to RBR-3745-Left
 frame-relay interface-dlci 102
  class FR-MAP-CLASS-768              ! Binds the map-class to the FR DLCI
!
...
!
map-class frame-relay FR-MAP-CLASS-768
  service-policy output MQC-FRTS-768   ! Attaches nested MQC policies to map-class
  frame-relay fragment 960             ! Enables FRF.12
!
```

Verification commands:

- **show policy map**
- **show policy-map interface**
- **show frame-relay fragment**

Verification Command: **show frame-relay fragment**

The **show frame-relay fragment** command, shown in Example 13-18, provides verification of the fragment size, regardless of whether regular FRF.12 fragmentation or Frame Relay voice-adaptive traffic shaping (and fragmentation) is configured for a DLCI. Additionally, dynamic counters monitor how many frames required fragmentation in either direction.

Example 13-18 **show frame-relay fragment** *Verification of a Slow-Speed Frame Relay Link*

```
WAG-7206-Left#show frame-relay fragment 102
interface        dlci  frag-type   frag-size  in-frag   out-frag dropped-frag
Serial2/0.12     102   end-to-end  960        5476      2035     0
WAG-7206-Left#
```

Medium-Speed (≤ T1/E1) Frame Relay Links

Recommendation: FRF.12 is not required. cRTP is optional.

The configuration for medium-speed Frame Relay links, illustrated in Figure 13-11 and detailed in Example 13-19, is identical to that for slow-speed Frame Relay links, with the exception that enabling FRF.12 no longer is required.

Figure 13-11 *Medium-Speed Frame Relay Links*

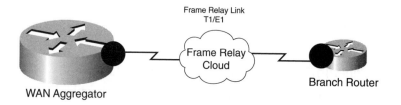

NOTE

In some cases, however, administrators have chosen to enable FRF.12 on T1/E1 speed links, even though the fragment size for a 10-ms maximum serialization delay at such speeds is greater than the MTU of Ethernet (1500 bytes). The rationale behind doing so is to retain the Frame Relay dual-FIFO queuing mechanism at Layer 2 (discussed in Chapter 5, "Congestion-Management Tools"), which can provide slightly superior service levels under certain conditions. Generally, this is not required, however.

Example 13-19 *Medium-Speed (T1/E1) Frame Relay QoS Design Example*

```
!
policy-map MQC-FRTS-1536
  class class-default
    shape average 1460000 14600 0      ! Enables MQC-Based FRTS
    service-policy WAN-EDGE            ! Queues packets headed to the shaper
 !
...
 !
interface Serial2/0
 no ip address
 encapsulation frame-relay
 !
interface Serial2/0.12 point-to-point
 ip address 10.1.121.1 255.255.255.252
 description 1536kbps FR Circuit to RBR-3745-Left
 frame-relay interface-dlci 102
  class FR-MAP-CLASS-1536              ! Binds the map-class to the FR DLCI
 !
...
 !
map-class frame-relay FR-MAP-CLASS-1536
  service-policy output MQC-FRTS-1536  ! Attaches nested MQC policies to map-class
 !
```

Verification commands:

- **show policy map**
- **show policy-map interface**

High-Speed (Multiple T1/E1 and Greater) Frame Relay Links

Recommendation: Use IP CEF per-packet load balancing for load sharing across multiple physical Frame Relay links.

When multiple Frame Relay circuits exist between a central WAN aggregation router and a remote branch router, as illustrated in Figure 13-12, it is recommended that IP CEF per-packet load balancing be used to load-share between the links. Multilink PPP over Frame Relay (MLPoFR) bundles are complex to configure and difficult to manage, whereas IP CEF per-packet load balancing is not and has the lowest CPU impact of the load-sharing mechanisms. Therefore, IP CEF per-packet load balancing is recommended across multiple Frame Relay links to the same branch.

Figure 13-12 *High-Speed Frame Relay Links*

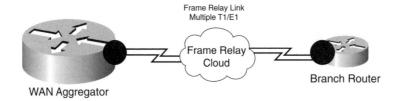

WAN Aggregator

Frame Relay Link
Multiple T1/E1

Frame Relay
Cloud

Branch Router

NOTE It is important to keep in mind that providers might have geographically dispersed paths to the same sites; therefore, the delay on one T1 FR link might be slightly higher or lower than the delay on another. This could cause TCP sequencing issues and slightly reduce effective data application throughput. Network administrators should keep these factors in mind when planning their WAN topologies.

The **max-reserved-bandwidth 100** command is not required on the interfaces because the queuing policy is not applied directly to the interface; instead, it is applied to another policy (the MQC-based Frame Relay traffic-shaping policy). Example 13-20 shows the configuration for a high-speed Frame Relay link.

Example 13-20 *High-Speed (≥ Multiple T1/E1) Frame Relay QoS Design Example*

```
!
policy-map MQC-FRTS-1536
  class class-default
    shape average 1460000 14600 0      ! Enables MQC-Based FRTS
    service-policy WAN-EDGE            ! Queues packets headed to the shaper
  !
  …
  !
interface Serial2/0
 no ip address
 encapsulation frame-relay
 no fair-queue
 frame-relay traffic-shaping
 !
interface Serial2/0.12 point-to-point
 description 1536kbps FR Circuit to RBR-3745-Left
 ip address 10.1.121.1 255.255.255.252
 ip load-sharing per-packet            ! Enables IP CEF Per-Packet Load-Sharing
 frame-relay interface-dlci 102
  class FR-MAP-CLASS-1536              ! Binds the map-class to FR DLCI 102
 !
interface Serial2/1
 no ip address
 encapsulation frame-relay
 serial restart_delay 0
 !
interface Serial2/1.12 point-to-point
 description 1536kbps FR Circuit to RBR-3745-Left
 ip address 10.1.121.5 255.255.255.252
 ip load-sharing per-packet            ! Enables IP CEF Per-Packet Load-Sharing
 frame-relay interface-dlci 112
  class FR-MAP-CLASS-1536              ! Binds the map-class to FR DLCI 112
 !
 …
 !
map-class frame-relay FR-MAP-CLASS-1536
 service-policy output MQC-FRTS-1536 ! Attaches nested MQC policies to map-class
 !
```

Verification commands:

- **show policy map**
- **show policy-map interface**

ATM

As with Frame Relay, ATM is an NBMA medium that permits oversubscription and speed mismatches, and thus requires shaping to guarantee service levels. In ATM, however, shaping is included as part of the PVC definition.

Two options exist for carrying voice traffic over slow-speed ATM PVCs: either Multilink PPP over ATM (MLPoATM), in conjunction with MLP LFI, or ATM PVC bundling. ATM PVC bundling is a legacy technique that has drawbacks such as inefficient bandwidth utilization and classification limitations (IP precedence versus DSCP). But sometimes service providers make ATM PVC bundles economically attractive to enterprise customers, so both approaches are discussed.

Slow-Speed (≤ 768 kbps) ATM Links: MLPoATM

Recommendation: Use MLP LFI. Tune the ATM PVC Tx-ring to 3. cRTP can be used only in Cisco IOS Release 12.2(2)T or later.

Serialization delays on slow-speed ATM links, as shown in Figure 13-4, necessitate a fragmentation and interleaving mechanism. The most common ATM adaptation layers (such as AAL5) do not have sequence numbers in the cell headers and, thus, require cells to arrive in the correct order. This requirement makes interleaving a problem that cannot be solved at these ATM adaptation layers and thus must be solved at a higher layer.

Figure 13-14 *Slow-Speed MLPoATM Links*

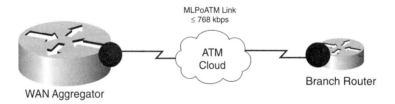

A solution to this problem is to run MLPoATM and let MLP LFI handle any necessary fragmentation and interleaving so that such operations are completely transparent to the lower ATM layer. As far as the ATM layer is concerned, all cells arrive in the same order they were sent.

MLPoATM functionality is enabled through the use of virtual-access interfaces. Virtual-access interfaces are built on demand from virtual-template interfaces and inherit their configuration properties from the virtual templates they are built from. Thus, the IP address, **service-policy** statement, and LFI parameters all are configured on the virtual template, as shown in Example 13-22.

cRTP is supported only on ATM PVCs (through MLPoATM), as of Cisco IOS Release 12.2(2)T.

Additionally, as discussed previously in this chapter and in Chapter 5, it is recommended that the value of the final output buffer, the Tx-ring, be tuned on slow-speed ATM PVCs to a value of three particles to minimize serialization delay.

Example 13-22 *Slow-Speed (≤ 768 kbps) MLPoATM QoS Design Example*

```
!
interface ATM4/0
 bandwidth 768
 no ip address
 no atm ilmi-keepalive
!
interface ATM4/0.60 point-to-point
 pvc BRANCH#60 0/60
  vbr-nrt 768 768               ! ATM PVC definition
  tx-ring-limit 3              ! Per-PVC Tx-ring is tuned to 3 particles
  protocol ppp Virtual-Template60   ! PVC is bound to the Virtual-Template
 !
interface Virtual-Template60
 bandwidth 768
 ip address 10.200.60.1 255.255.255.252
 service-policy output WAN-EDGE        ! Attaches MQC policy to Virtual-Template
 ppp multilink
 ppp multilink fragment-delay 10       ! Enables MLP Fragmentation
 ppp multilink interleave             ! Enables MLP Interleaving
 !
```

NOTE   When using virtual templates for low-speed ATM links, keep the following in mind:

- The dynamic nature of virtual-template interfaces might make network management unwieldy.

- MLPoATM can be supported only on hardware that supports per-VC traffic shaping.

Verification commands:

- **show policy map**
- **show policy-map interface**
- **show atm pvc**

Verification Command: **show atm pvc**

In ATM, the length of the Tx-ring is defined in particles, not packets. The size of a particle varies according to hardware. For example, on a Cisco 7200 PA-A3, particles are 580 bytes (including a 4-byte ATM core header). This means that a 1500-byte packet would require three particles of buffering. Furthermore, ATM defines Tx-rings on a per-PVC basis, as shown in Examples 13-23 and 13-24.

Example 13-23 *Basic ATM PVC Configuration Example*

```
!
interface ATM3/0.1 point-to-point
 ip address 10.2.12.1 255.255.255.252
 pvc 0/12
  vbr-nrt 768 768      ! ATM PVC definition
 !
!
```

The size of a default Tx-ring can be ascertained using the **show atm pvc** command (an output modifier is used to focus on the relevant portion of the output), as shown in Example 13-28.

Example 13-24 **show atm pvc** *Verification of Tx-ring Setting*

```
WAG-7206-Left#show atm pvc 0/12 | include TxRingLimit
VC TxRingLimit: 40 particles
```

The output shows that the Tx-ring is set, in this instance, to a default value of 40 particles. The Tx-ring for the PVC can be tuned to the recommended setting of 3 using the **tx-ring-limit** command under the PVC's definition, as shown in Example 13-25.

Example 13-25 *Tuning an ATM PVC Tx-ring*

```
WAG-7206-Left(config)#interface atm 3/0.1
WAG-7206-Left(config-subif)#pvc 0/12
WAG-7206-Le(config-if-atm-vc)#tx-ring-limit 3
```

The new setting can be verified quickly with the same **show atm pvc** command variation, as shown in Example 13-25 (see Example 13-26).

Example 13-26 **show atm pvc** *Verification of Tx-ring Setting After Tuning*

```
WAG-7206-Left#show atm pvc 0/12 | include TxRingLimit
VC TxRingLimit: 3 particles
```

Slow-Speed (≤ 768 kbps) ATM Links: ATM PVC Bundles

Recommendation: Queuing policies for voice are not required (because voice uses a dedicated ATM PVC). Tune the ATM PVC Tx-ring to 3.

An alternative option to provisioning QoS on slow-speed ATM PVCs is to use PVC bundles, as illustrated in Figure 13-15. PVC bundles consist of two (or more) PVCs with different ATM traffic contracts, grouped together in a logical association in which IPP levels determine the PVC to which the packet will be directed. The decision to use PVC bundles instead of MLPoATM for slow-speed ATM links is usually a matter of economics (because service providers often offer attractive pricing for PVC bundles) and configuration/management complexity comfort levels.

Figure 13-15 *Slow-Speed ATM PVC Bundles*

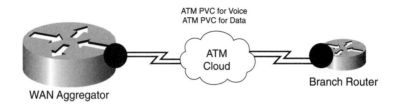

In Example 13-27, one PVC (for voice) has a variable bit rate, non-real-time (VBR-nrt) ATM traffic contract and an admission criterion of IPP 5, while another PVC (for data) has an unspecified bit rate (UBR) ATM traffic contract and accepts all other precedence levels.

Again, it is also recommended that the TX-ring be tuned to 3 on such slow-speed ATM PVCs.

Example 13-27 *Slow-Speed (≤ 768 kbps) ATM PVC Bundles QoS Design Example*

```
!
class-map match-any Call Signaling
  match ip dscp cs3
match ip dscp af31
class-map match-any Critical Data
  match ip dscp cs6
  match ip dscp af21
  match ip dscp cs2
!
!
 policy-map WAN-EDGE-DATA-PVC      ! Only data queuing is required (no voice)
  class Call Signaling
   bandwidth percent 5
  class Critical Data
   bandwidth percent 40
  class class-default
   fair-queue
!
vc-class atm VOICE-PVC-256         ! Voice PVC-class definition
  vbr-nrt 256 256                  ! Voice ATM PVC definition
  tx-ring-limit 3                  ! Per-PVC Tx-ring is tuned to 3 particles
  precedence 5                     ! Only IPP5 traffic (voice) can use this PVC
  no bump traffic                  ! Traffic will not be accepted from other PVCs
  protect vc                       ! Optional: Protects VC status of Voice PVC
```

continues

Example 13-27 *Slow-Speed (≤ 768 kbps) ATM PVC Bundles QoS Design Example (Continued)*

```
!
vc-class atm DATA-PVC-512       ! Data PVC-class definition
  ubr 512                       ! Data ATM PVC definition
  tx-ring-limit 3               ! Per-PVC Tx-ring is tuned to 3 particles
  precedence other              ! All other IPP values (data) use this PVC
!
…
!
interface ATM3/0
 no ip address
 no atm ilmi-keepalive
!
interface ATM3/0.60 point-to-point
 ip address 10.200.60.1 255.255.255.252
 bundle BRANCH#60
  pvc-bundle BRANCH60-DATA 0/60
   class-vc DATA-PVC-512                     ! Assigns PVC to data-class
   service-policy output WAN-EDGE-DATA-PVC:  ! Attaches (data) MQC policy to PVC
  pvc-bundle BRANCH60-VOICE 0/600
   class-vc VOICE-PVC-256                    ! Assigns PVC to voice-class
 !
```

A major drawback to PVC bundling is that data never can get access to the voice PVC, even if there is available bandwidth in it. This forces suboptimal consumption of WAN bandwidth.

Verification commands:

- **show policy map**
- **show policy-map interface**
- **show atm pvc**
- **show atm vc**
- **show atm bundle**

Verification Command: **show atm vc**

The **show atm vc** command details the configured ATM PVCs and highlights their encapsulation, ATM traffic contracts (or service contracts), status, and activity, as shown in Example 13-28.

Example 13-28 **show atm vc** *Verification of ATM PVC Definitions and Activity*

```
WAN-AGG-7200#show atm vc
              VCD /                             Peak  Avg/Min Burst
Interface     Name        VPI VCI Type  Encaps  SC   Kbps  Kbps    Cells  Sts
3/0.60        BRANCH60-DATA  0  60 PVC   SNAP    UBR  512   512     1145   UP
3/0.60        BRANCH60-VOICE 0 600 PVC   SNAP    VBR  256   256     94     UP
WAN-AGG-7200#
```

Verification Command: **show atm bundle**

The **show atm bundle** command provides details on the configured and current admission criteria for individual ATM PVCs. In Example 13-29, PVC 0/600 (the voice PVC) accepts only traffic that has been marked to IPP 5 (voice). All other IPP values (0 to 4 and 6 to 7) are assigned to PVC 0/60 (the data PVC). This command also shows the activity for each PVC.

Example 13-29 show atm bundle *Verification of ATM PVC Bundle Definitions and Activity*

```
WAN-AGG-7200#show atm bundle
BRANCH#60 on ATM3/0.60: UP
                        Config    Current   Bumping   PG/ Peak Avg/Min Burst
VC Name        VPI/ VCI Prec/Exp  Prec/Exp  PrecExp/  PV  Kbps  kbps  Cells Sts
                                            Accept
BRANCH60-DATA  0/60     7-6, 4-0  7-6, 4-0  - / Yes   -    512  512   1145  UP
BRANCH60-VOICE 0/600    5         5         - / No    PV   256  256   94    UP
WAN-AGG-7200#
```

Medium-Speed (≤ T1/E1) ATM Links

Recommendation: Use ATM inverse multiplexing over ATM (IMA) to keep future expansion easy to manage. No LFI is required. cRTP is optional.

ATM IMA is a natural choice for medium-speed ATM links, as shown in Figure 13-16. Although the inverse-multiplexing capabilities are not used at these speeds, IMA interfaces make future expansion to high-speed links easy to manage (as will be demonstrated between Example 13-30 and the high-speed ATM link in Example 13-35).

Figure 13-16 *Medium-Speed ATM Links*

ATM T1/E1 IMA Link
(Only One Group Member Is Active)

ATM Cloud

WAN Aggregator

Branch Router

Example 13-30 *Medium-Speed (T1/E1) ATM IMA QoS Design Example*

```
!
interface ATM3/0
 no ip address
 no atm ilmi-keepalive
 ima-group 0              ! ATM3/0 added to ATM IMA group 0
 no scrambling-payload
```

continues

Example 13-30 *Medium-Speed (T1/E1) ATM IMA QoS Design Example (Continued)*

```
!
...
!
interface ATM3/IMA0
 no ip address
 no atm ilmi-keepalive
!
interface ATM3/IMA0.12 point-to-point
 ip address 10.200.60.1 255.255.255.252
 description T1 ATM-IMA to Branch#60
 pvc 0/100
  vbr-nrt 1536 1536              ! ATM PVC defined under ATM IMA sub-int
  max-reserved-bandwidth 100     ! Overrides the default 75% BW limit
  service-policy output WAN-EDGE ! Attaches MQC policy to PVC
 !
!
```

Verification commands:

- **show policy map**
- **show policy-map interface**
- **show atm pvc**
- **show ima interface atm**

High-Speed (Multiple T1/E1) ATM Links

Recommendation: Use ATM IMA and add members to the IMA group, as needed.

Previous options for accommodating multiple T1/E1 links were software-based load-sharing solutions (MLP bundling and IP CEF per-packet load sharing). As such, these methods require additional CPU cycles to accommodate load-sharing multiple physical links. However, with ATM IMA, inverse multiplexing over multiple T1/E1 links, illustrated in Figure 13-17, is done in hardware on the port adaptor/network module. Therefore, ATM IMA scales much more efficiently.

Figure 13-17 *High-Speed ATM Links*

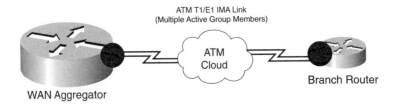

ATM T1/E1 IMA Link
(Multiple Active Group Members)

ATM
Cloud

WAN Aggregator

Branch Router

As mentioned, ATM IMA makes bandwidth expansion easy to manage. For example, all that is required to add another T1 line to the previous example is to add an **ima-group** statement to the next ATM interface and increase the PVC speed, as shown in Example 13-31.

Example 13-31 *High-Speed (Multiple T1/E1 and Greater) ATM IMA QoS Design Example*

```
!
interface ATM3/0
 no ip address
 no atm ilmi-keepalive
 ima-group 0          ! ATM3/0 added to ATM IMA group 0
 no scrambling-payload
!
interface ATM3/1
 no ip address
 no atm ilmi-keepalive
 ima-group 0          ! ATM3/1 added to ATM IMA group 0
 no scrambling-payload
!
…
!
interface ATM3/IMA0
 no ip address
 no atm ilmi-keepalive
!
interface ATM3/IMA0.12 point-to-point
 ip address 10.6.12.1 255.255.255.252
 pvc 0/100
  vbr-nrt 3072 3072           ! ATM PVC speed expanded
  max-reserved-bandwidth 100  ! Overrides the default 75% BW limit
  service-policy output WAN-EDGE  ! Attaches MQC policy to PVC
  !
!
```

Verification commands:

- **show policy map**
- **show policy-map interface**
- **show atm pvc**
- **show ima interface atm**

Verification Command: **show ima interface atm**

The **show ima interface atm** command is useful for verifying that all members of an ATM IMA group are active. See Example 13-32.

Example 13-32 **show ima interface atm** *Verification of ATM IMA Group*

```
WAG-7206-Left#show ima interface atm 3/ima0
Interface ATM3/IMA0 is up
        Group index is 1
        Ne state is operational, failure status is noFailure
        Active links bitmap 0x3
    IMA Group Current Configuration:
        Tx/Rx configured links bitmap 0x3/0x3
        Tx/Rx minimum required links 1/1
        Maximum allowed diff delay is 25ms, Tx frame length 128
        Ne Tx clock mode CTC, configured timing reference link ATM3/0
        Test pattern procedure is disabled
    IMA Group Current Counters (time elapsed 257 seconds):
        0 Ne Failures, 0 Fe Failures, 0 Unavail Secs
    IMA Group Total Counters (last 5 15 minute intervals):
        0 Ne Failures, 0 Fe Failures, 0 Unavail Secs
    IMA link Information:
        Link    Physical Status         NearEnd Rx Status    Test Status
        ----    ---------------         -----------------    -----------
        ATM3/0  up                      active               disabled
        ATM3/1  up                      active               disabled
        ATM3/2  administratively down   unusableInhibited    disabled
        ATM3/3  administratively down   unusableInhibited    disabled
```

Very-High-Speed (DS3-OC3+) ATM Links

Recommendation: Use newer hardware platforms and keep an eye on CPU levels.

Major site-to-site interconnections drift slightly away from the traditional WAN aggregator/ remote branch router models. In site-to-site scenarios, as illustrated in Figure 13-18, the WAN edge routers usually support only one or two links, as opposed to dozens or hundreds of links that typical WAN aggregators support. However, in a site-to-site scenario, the interconnecting links are running at far higher speeds than most remote branch links.

Figure 13-18 *Very High-Speed (DS3-OC3+) ATM Links*

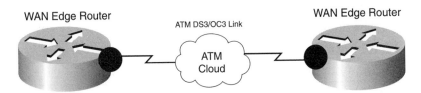

The policies and design principles do not change for site-to-site scenarios. The main consideration is the performance of the WAN edge router. Although newer platforms handle complex policies more efficiently, it is still highly recommended that proof-of-concept

testing of the platforms involved be performed before implementing policies at such critical junctions in the network. Example 13-33 illustrates a site-to-site QoS policy applied to a very-high-speed ATM (OC3) link.

Example 13-33 *Very High-Speed (DS3-OC3+) ATM Link QoS Design Example*

```
 !
 interface ATM3/0
  no ip address
  load-interval 30
  no atm ilmi-keepalive
 !
 interface ATM3/0.1 point-to-point
  ip address 10.2.12.1 255.255.255.252
  pvc 0/12
   vbr-nrt 149760 149760               ! ATM OC3 PVC definition
   max-reserved-bandwidth 100          ! Overrides the default 75% BW limit
   service-policy output WAN-EDGE      ! Attaches MQC policy to PVC
  !
 !
```

Verification commands:

- **show policy map**
- **show policy-map interface**
- **show atm pvc**

ATM-to-Frame Relay Service Interworking

Many enterprises are deploying converged networks that use ATM at the central site and Frame Relay at the remote branches. The media conversion is accomplished through ATM-to-Frame Relay Service Interworking (SIW or FRF.8) in the carrier network.

FRF.12 cannot be used because, currently, no service provider supports FRF.12 termination in the Frame Relay cloud. In fact, no Cisco WAN switching devices support FRF.12. Tunneling FRF.12 through the service provider's network does no good because there is no FRF.12 standard on the ATM side. This is a problem because fragmentation is a require-ment if any of the remote Frame Relay sites uses a circuit speed of 768 kbps or below. However, MLPoATM and MLPoFR provide an end-to-end, Layer 2 fragmentation and interleaving method for low-speed ATM to Frame Relay FRF.8 SIW links.

FRF.8 SIW is a Frame Relay Forum standard for connecting Frame Relay networks with ATM networks. SIW provides a standards-based solution for service providers, enterprises, and end users. In service interworking translation mode, Frame Relay PVCs are mapped to

ATM PVCs without the need for symmetric topologies. FRF.8 supports two modes of operation of the interworking function (IWF) for upper-layer user protocol encapsulation:

- **Translation mode**—Maps between ATM (AAL) and Frame Relay (IETF) encapsulation. It also supports interworking of routed or bridged protocols.

- **Transparent mode**—Does not map encapsulations, but sends them unaltered. This mode is used when translation is impractical because encapsulation methods do not conform to the supported standards for service interworking.

MLP for LFI on ATM and Frame Relay SIW networks is supported for transparent-mode VCs and translational-mode VCs that support PPP translation (FRF 8.1).

To make MLPoATM and MLPoFR SIW possible, the service provider's interworking switch must be configured in transparent mode, and the end routers must be capable of recognizing both MLPoATM and MLPoFR headers. This is accomplished with the **protocol ppp** command for ATM and the **frame-relay interface-dlci** *dlci* **ppp** command for Frame Relay.

When an ATM cell is sent from the ATM side of an ATM-to-Frame Relay SIW connection, the following must happen for interworking to be possible:

1 The sending router encapsulates a packet in the MLPoATM header by the sending router.

2 In transparent mode, the carrier switch prepends a 2-byte Frame Relay DLCI field to the received packet and sends the packet to its Frame Relay interface.

3 The receiving router examines the header of the received packet. If the first 4 bytes after the 2-byte DLCI field of the received packet are 0xfefe03cf, it treats it as a legal MLPoFR packet and sends it to the MLP layer for further processing.

When a frame is sent from the Frame Relay side of an ATM-to-Frame Relay SIW connection, the following must happen for interworking to be possible:

1 The sending router encapsulates a packet in the MLPoFR header.

2 In transparent mode, the carrier switch strips off the 2-byte Frame Relay DLCI field and sends the rest of the packet to its ATM interface.

3 The receiving router examines the header of the received packet. If the first 2 bytes of the received packet are 0x03cf, it treats it as a legal MLPoATM packet and sends it to MLP layer for further processing.

A new ATM-to-Frame Relay SIW standard, FRF.8.1, supports MLPoATM and Frame Relay SIW, but it could be years before all switches are updated to this new standard.

When using MLPoATM and MLPoFR, keep the following in mind:

- MLPoATM can be supported only on platforms that support per-VC traffic shaping.

- MLPoATM relies on per-VC queuing to control the flow of packets from the MLP bundle to the ATM PVC.

- MLPoATM requires the MLP bundle to classify the outgoing packets before they are sent to the ATM VC. It also requires the per-VC queuing strategy for the ATM VC to be FIFO because the MLP bundle handles queuing.

- MLPoFR relies on the FRTS engine to control the flow of packets from the MLP bundle to FR VC.

- cRTP is supported only over ATM links (through MLPoATM), as of Cisco IOS Release 12.2(2)T.

Slow-Speed (≤ 768 kbps) ATM-FR SIW Links

Recommendation: Use MLPoATM and MLPoFR. Use MLP LFI and optimize fragment sizes to minimize cell padding. cRTP can be used only in Cisco IOS Release 12.2(2)T or later. Tune the ATM PVC Tx-ring to 3.

As with any slow-speed WAN media, serialization delay must be addressed with a fragmentation and interleaving mechanism. As previously mentioned, FRF.12 is not an option for SIW links. Therefore, MLP LFI must be used. Generally, MLP LFI requires no additional calculations to configure, but a special case exists when interworking ATM and FR (as illustrated in Figure 13-19) because of the nature of ATM's fixed cell lengths.

Figure 13-19 *Slow-Speed ATM-FR SIW Links*

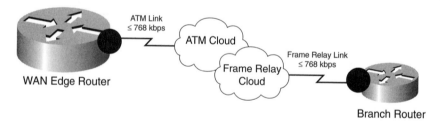

When enabling MLPoATM, the fragment size should be optimized so that it fits into an integral number of cells. Otherwise, the bandwidth required could double because of cell padding. For example, if a fragment size of 49 bytes is configured, this fragment would require 2 cells to transmit (because ATM cells have 48-byte payloads). This would generate 57 bytes of overhead (2 cell headers plus 47 bytes of cell padding), which is more than double the fragment itself.

Table 13-3 provides a summary of the optimal fragment-delay parameters for MLPoATM.

Table 13-3 *Optimal Fragment-Delay Values for MLP LFI for MLPoATM*

PVC Speed	Optimal Fragment Size	ATM Cells (Rounded Up)	ppp multilink fragment-delayvalue
56 kbps	84 bytes	2	12 ms
64 kbps	80 bytes	2	10 ms
128 kbps	176 bytes	4	11 ms
256 kbps	320 bytes	7	10 ms
512 kbps	640 bytes	14	10 ms
768 kbps	960 bytes	21	10 ms

A slow-speed ATM-to-Frame Relay SIW configuration is shown next, in two parts:

- The central site WAN aggregator MLPoATM configuration (see Example 13-34)
- The remote branch router MLPoFR configuration (see Example 13-39)

Example 13-34 *MLPoATM WAN Aggregator ATM-FR SIW QoS Design Example*

```
!
interface ATM4/0
 no ip address
 no atm ilmi-keepalive
!
interface ATM4/0.60 point-to-point
 pvc BRANCH#60 0/60
  vbr-nrt 256 256                    ! ATM PVC definition
  tx-ring-limit 3                    ! Per-PVC
 Tx-ring is tuned to 3 particles
  protocol ppp Virtual-     Template60      ! Enables MLPoATM
 !
interface Virtual-Template60
 bandwidth 256
 ip address 10.200.60.1 255.255.255.252
 service-policy output WAN-EDGE      ! Attaches MQC policy to Virtual-Template
 ppp multilink
 ppp multilink fragment-delay 10    ! Enables MLP fragmentation
 ppp multilink interleave           ! Enables MLP interleaving
 !
```

Verification commands:

- **show policy map**
- **show policy-map interface**
- **show atm pvc**
- **show ppp multilink**

Example 13-35 *MLPoFR Remote-Branch Router ATM-FR SIW QoS Design Example*

```
!
interface Serial6/0
 description Parent FR Link for BRANCH#60
 no ip address
 encapsulation frame-relay
 frame-relay traffic-shaping
!
interface Serial6/0.60 point-to-point
 description FR Sub-Interface for BRANCH#60
 bandwidth 256
 frame-relay interface-dlci 60 ppp Virtual-Template60      ! Enables MLPoFR
  class FRTS-256kbps                      ! Binds the map-class to the FR DLCI
!
interface Virtual-Template60
 bandwidth 256
 ip address 10.200.60.2 255.255.255.252
 service-policy output WAN-EDGE        ! Attaches MQC policy to map-class
 ppp multilink
 ppp multilink fragment-delay 10       ! Enables MLP fragmentation
 ppp multilink interleave              ! Enables MLP interleaving
!
...
!
map-class frame-relay FRTS-256kbps
 frame-relay cir 243200                ! CIR is set to 95% of FR DLCI rate
 frame-relay bc 2432                   ! Bc is set to CIR/100
 frame-relay be 0                      ! Be is set to 0
 frame-relay mincir 243200             ! MinCIR is set to CIR
!
```

Verification commands:

- **show policy map**
- **show policy-map interface**
- **show ppp multilink**

ISDN

When designing VoIP over ISDN networks, special consideration needs to be given to the following issues:

- Link bandwidth varies as B channels are added or dropped.
- RTP packets might arrive out of order when transmitted across multiple B channels.
- CallManager has limitations with locations-based CAC.

Variable Bandwidth

ISDN allows B channels to be added or dropped in response to the demand for bandwidth. The fact that the bandwidth of a link varies over time presents a special challenge to the LLQ/CBWFQ mechanisms of Cisco IOS Software. Before Cisco IOS Release 12.2(2)T, a policy map implementing LLQ could be assigned only a fixed amount of bandwidth. On an ISDN interface, Cisco IOS Software assumes that only 64 kbps is available, even though the interface has the potential to provide 128 kbps, 1.544 Mbps, or 2.408 Mbps of bandwidth. By default, the maximum bandwidth assigned must be less than or equal to 75 percent of the available bandwidth. Hence, before Cisco IOS Release 12.2(2)T, only 75 percent of 64 kbps, or 48 kbps, could be allocated to an LLQ on any ISDN interface. If more was allocated, an error message was generated when the policy map was applied to the ISDN interface. This severely restricted the number of VoIP calls that could be carried.

The solution to this problem was introduced in Cisco IOS Release 12.2(2)T with the **priority percent** command. This command allows the reservation of a variable bandwidth percentage to be assigned to the LLQ.

MLP Packet Reordering Considerations

MLP LFI is used for fragmentation and interleaving voice and data over ISDN links. LFI segments large data packets into smaller fragments and transmits them in parallel across all the B channels in the bundle. At the same time, voice packets are interleaved between the fragments, thereby reducing their delay. The interleaved packets are not subject to MLP encapsulation; they are encapsulated as regular PPP packets. Hence, they have no MLP sequence numbers and cannot be reordered if they arrive out of sequence.

The packets probably will need to be reordered. The depth of the various link queues in the bundle might differ, causing RTP packets to overtake each other as a result of the difference in queuing delay. The various B channels also might take different paths through the ISDN network and might end up with different transmission delays.

This reordering of packets is not generally a problem for RTP packets. The buffers on the receiving VoIP devices reorder the packets based on the RTP sequence numbers. However, reordering becomes a problem if cRTP is used. The cRTP algorithm assumes that RTP packets are compressed and decompressed in the same order. If they get out of sequence, decompression does not occur correctly.

Multiclass Multilink PPP (MCMP) offers a solution to the reordering problem. With MCMP, the interleaved packets are given a small header with a sequence number, which allows them to be reordered by the far end of the bundle before cRTP decompression takes place. MCMP is supported as of Cisco IOS Release 12.2(13)T.

CallManager CAC Limitations

IP telephony in branch networks typically is based on the centralized call-processing model and uses locations-based CAC to limit the number of calls across the WAN. Locations-based CAC currently does not have any mechanism for tracking topology changes in the network. Therefore, if the primary link to a branch goes down and ISDN backup engages, the CallManager remains ignorant of the occurrence. For this reason, it is critical that the ISDN backup link be capable of handling the same number of VoIP calls as the main link. Otherwise, CAC ultimately could oversubscribe the backup link.

The actual bandwidth of the primary link and the backup link do not need to be identical. They just need to be capable of carrying the same number of VoIP calls. For example, the backup link might use cRTP while the primary link does not, in which case, less bandwidth is required on the backup link to carry the same number of calls as the primary link.

Because of these limitations, it is recommended that the 33 percent LLQ recommendation be relaxed in this kind of dial-backup scenario. The LLQ could be provisioned as high as 70 percent (leaving 5 percent for Voice control traffic over the ISDN link and 25 percent for Best-Effort traffic).

Voice and Data on Multiple ISDN B Channels

The Voice and Data design model over ISDN, illustrated in Figure 13-20, allows a service policy to be applied to a bundle with multiple B channels. It takes advantage of the fact that LLQ bandwidth can be expressed as a percentage instead of an absolute number. If cRTP is enabled, MCMP is required on the ISDN links.

Figure 13-20 *Voice and Data over ISDN*

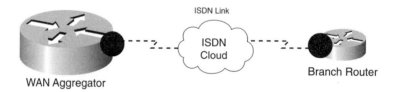

Cisco IOS provides two mechanisms for controlling how channels are added in response to demand.

The first mechanism commonly is referred to as dial-on-demand routing (DDR). With DDR, a load threshold must be specified (as a fraction of available bandwidth). When the traffic load exceeds this number, an additional channel is added to the bundle. The threshold is calculated as a running average. As a result, there is a certain delay in bringing up additional

B channels when the load increases. This delay does not present a problem with data, but it is unacceptable with voice. This delay can be reduced to around 30 seconds by adding the **load-interval** command to the physical ISDN interface, but even 30 seconds is too long.

The second mechanism is a more robust solution, which is simply to bring up all B channels immediately and keep them up as long as the ISDN service is required. This is achieved by using the **ppp multilink links minimum** command.

With two B channels available, the service policy can reserve (approximately) 90 kbps (70 percent of 128 kbps) for voice traffic. The total number of calls that can be transmitted depends on the codec and sampling rates used.

Example 13-36 illustrates the configuration for enabling voice and data over multiple ISDN B channels.

Example 13-36 *Voice and Data over Multiple ISDN B Channels QoS Design Example*

```
!
class-map match-all Voice
  match ip dscp ef
!
class-map match-any Call Signaling
  match ip dscp cs3
  match ip dscp af31
!
...
!
policy-map WAN-EDGE-ISDN
  class Voice
    priority percent 70          ! LLQ 33% Rule is relaxed for DDR scenarios
    compress header ip rtp       ! Enables Class-Based cRTP
  class Call Signaling
    bandwidth percent 5          ! Bandwidth guarantee for Call-Signaling
    class class-default
      fair-queue
!
interface BRI0/0
 encapsulation ppp
 dialer pool-member 1
!
interface Dialer1
 encapsulation ppp
 dialer pool 1
 dialer remote-name routerB-dialer1
 dialer-group 1
 dialer string 12345678
 service-policy output WAN-EDGE-ISDN    ! Attaches MQC policy to Dialer interface
 ppp multilink
 ppp multilink fragment-delay 10        ! Enables MLP fragmentation
 ppp multilink interleave               ! Enables MLP interleaving
 ppp multilink links minimum 2          ! Activates both B Channels immediately
 ppp multilink multiclass               ! Enables MCMP
!
```

Verification commands:

- **show policy map**
- **show policy-map interface**
- **show ppp multilink**

Case Study: WAN Aggregation Router QoS Design

A fictitious company, ABC, Inc., already correctly is classifying and marking (at Layer 3 via DSCP) all 11 classes of traffic from the QoS Baseline Model within its campus. It wants to provision QoS policies for each of these application classes over its WANs as well.

ABC, Inc., selected ATM as its primary Layer 2 medium because of its ease of expansion for future bandwidth needs. Each remote branch is connected to the main campus by dual-T1 links (at a minimum), with some larger sites using three or four T1s for connectivity. Most remote branches are connected using Frame Relay links (through ATM-to-FR SIW); however, some remote sites are using ATM IMA.

ABC, Inc., has selected the Cisco 7500-VIP6-80 for the WAN aggregation platform and is provisioning sites so that the CPU utilization of any given WAN aggregator is no more than 75 percent; it is running Cisco IOS Release 12.3 mainline code.

WAN edge QoS designs for one of the WAN aggregation routers are shown in Figure 13-22 and Example 13-37.

Figure 13-21 *Case Study: QoS Baseline Policies on WAN Aggregation Router with High-Speed ATM Links*

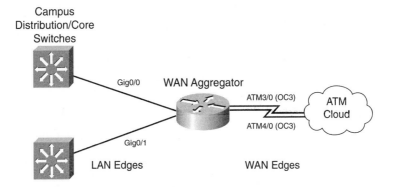

Example 13-37   *Case Study: QoS Baseline Policies on WAN Aggregation Router with Dual-T1 ATM IMA*
Links

```
!
ip cef distributed                      ! Required for C7500-VIP
!
class-map match-all Voice
  match ip dscp ef                      ! IP Phones mark Voice to EF
class-map match-all Interactive Video
  match ip dscp af41 af42               ! Recommended markings for IP/VC
class-map match-any Call Signaling
  match ip dscp cs3                     ! Future Call-Signaling marking
  match ip dscp af31                    ! Current Call-Signaling marking
class-map match-all Routing
  match ip dscp cs6                     ! Routers mark Routing traffic to CS6
class-map match-all Net Mgmt
  match ip dscp cs2                     ! Recommended marking for Network Management
class-map match-all Mission-Critical Data
  match ip dscp 25                      ! Interim marking for Mission-Critical Data
class-map match-all Transactional Data
  match ip dscp af21 af22               ! Recommended markings for Transactional-Data
class-map match-all Bulk Data
  match ip dscp af11 af12               ! Recommended markings for Bulk-Data
class-map match-all Streaming Video
  match ip dscp cs4                     ! Recommended marking for Streaming-Video
class-map match-all Scavenger
  match ip dscp cs1                     ! Recommended marking for Scavenger traffic
!
policy-map WAN-EDGE
  class Voice
    priority percent 18                 ! Voice gets 552 kbps of LLQ
  class Interactive Video
    priority percent 15                 ! 384 kbps IP/VC needs 460 kbps of LLQ
  class Call Signaling
    bandwidth percent 5                 ! Bandwidth guarantee for Call-Signaling
  class Routing
    bandwidth percent 3                 ! Bandwidth guarantee for Routing
  class Net Mgmt
    bandwidth percent 2                 ! Bandwidth guarantee for Network Management
  class Mission-Critical Data
    bandwidth percent 10                ! Mission-Critical data gets min 10% BW guarantee
    fair-queue                          ! Applies FQ to MC-Data class (VIP Only)
    random-detect                       ! Enables WRED on Mission-Critical Data class
  class Transactional Data
    bandwidth percent 7                 ! Transactional Data gets min 7% BW guarantee
    fair-queue                          ! Applies FQ to Trans-Data class (VIP Only)
    random-detect dscp-based            ! Enables DSCP-WRED on Transactional Data class
  class Bulk Data
    bandwidth percent 4                 ! Bulk Data gets min 4% BW guarantee
    fair-queue                          ! Applies FQ to Bulk Data class (VIP Only)
    random-detect dscp-based            ! Enables DSCP-WRED on Bulk Data class
  class Streaming Video
    bandwidth percent 10                ! Streaming-Video gets min 10% BW guarantee
  class Scavenger
```

Example 13-37 *Case Study: QoS Baseline Policies on WAN Aggregation Router with Dual-T1 ATM IMA Links (Continued)*

```
   bandwidth percent 1          ! Scavenger class is throttled
  class class-default
   bandwidth percent 25         ! Class-Default gets min 25% BW guarantee
   fair-queue                   ! Applies FQ to Class-Default (VIP Only)
   random-detect                ! Enables WRED on Class-Default
 !
 …
 !
 interface ATM3/0
  no ip address
  no atm ilmi-keepalive
 !
 interface ATM3/0.60 point-to-point
  ip address 10.2.60.1 255.255.255.252
  description Dual-T1 ATM PVC to Branch#60
  pvc 0/60
   vbr-nrt 3072 3072            ! Dual-T1 ATM PVC definition
   max-reserved-bandwidth 100   ! Overrides the default 75% BW limit
   service-policy output WAN-EDGE   ! Attaches MQC policy to PVC
  !
 !
```

Verification commands:

- **show policy map**
- **show policy-map interface**
- **show atm pvc**

Summary

This chapter discussed the QoS requirements of routers performing the role of a WAN aggregator. Specifically, it addressed the need for queuing policies on the WAN edges, combined with shaping policies when NBMA media (such as Frame Relay or ATM) are being used, and link-specific policies, such as LFI/FRF.12 and cRTP, for slow-speed (≤ 768 kbps) links.

For the WAN edges, bandwidth-provisioning guidelines were considered, such as leaving 25 percent of the bandwidth for the Best-Effort class and limiting the sum of all LLQs to 33 percent.

Three categories of WAN link speeds and their design implications were presented:

- Slow-speed (≤ 768 kbps) links, which can support only Three- to Five-Class QoS models and require LFI mechanisms and cRTP.
- Medium-speed (≤ T1/E1) links, which, likewise, can support only Three- to Five-Class QoS Models but no longer require LFI mechanisms. cRTP becomes optional.

- High-speed (multiple T1/E1 or greater) links, which can support 5- to 11-Class QoS Models. No LFI is required on such links. cRTP likely would have a high CPU cost (compared to realized bandwidth savings) and, as such, generally is not recommended for such links. Additionally, some method of load sharing, bundling, or inverse multiplexing is required to distribute the traffic across multiple physical links.

These principles then were applied to certain WAN media designs—specifically, for leased lines, Frame Relay, ATM, and ATM-to-Frame Relay SIW. The corner case of ISDN as a backup WAN link also was considered.

Finally, a case study was presented, illustrating a complex scenario to show how these designs can be put together.

Further Reading

Layer 3 queuing:

- Class-based weighted fair queuing (Cisco IOS Release 12.0.5T): http://www.cisco.com/univercd/cc/td/doc/product/software/ios120/120newft/120t/120t5/cbwfq.htm.

- Low-latency queuing (Cisco IOS Release 12.0.7T): http://www.cisco.com/univercd/cc/td/doc/product/software/ios120/120newft/120t/120t7/pqcbwfq.htm.

- Distributed low-latency queuing (Cisco IOS Release 12.1.5T): http://www.cisco.com/univercd/cc/td/doc/product/software/ios121/121newft/121t/121t5/dtllqvip.htm.

- Low-latency queuing with priority percentage support (Cisco IOS Release 12.2.2T): http://www.cisco.com/univercd/cc/td/doc/product/software/ios122/122newft/122t/122t2/ftllqpct.htm.

Congestion avoidance:

- MQC-based WRED (Cisco IOS Release 12.0.5T): http://www.cisco.com/univercd/cc/td/doc/product/software/ios120/120newft/120t/120t5/cbwfq.htm.

- DiffServ-compliant weighted random early detection (Cisco IOS Release 12.1.5T): http://www.cisco.com/univercd/cc/td/doc/product/software/ios121/121newft/121t/121t5/dtdswred.htm.

- Distributed class-based weighted fair queuing and distributed weighted random early detection (Cisco IOS Release 12.1.5T): http://www.cisco.com/univercd/cc/td/doc/product/software/ios121/121newft/121t/121t5/dtcbwred.htm.

Frame Relay traffic shaping:

- Class-based shaping (Cisco IOS Release 12.1.2T): http://www.cisco.com/univercd/cc/td/doc/product/software/ios121/121newft/121t/121t2/clsbsshp.htm.

- MQC-based Frame Relay traffic shaping (Cisco IOS Release 12.2.13T): http://www.cisco.com/univercd/cc/td/doc/product/software/ios122/122newft/122t/122t13/frqosmqc.htm.

- Distributed traffic shaping (Cisco IOS Release 12.1.5T): http://www.cisco.com/univercd/cc/td/doc/product/software/ios121/121newft/121t/121t5/dtdts.htm.

ATM PVC traffic parameters:

- Configuring ATM traffic parameters: http://www.cisco.com/univercd/cc/td/doc/product/software/ios122/122cgcr/fwan_c/wcfatm.htm#1001126.

Link fragmentation and interleaving:

- MLP interleaving and queuing for Real-Time traffic (Cisco IOS Release 12.0): http://www.cisco.com/univercd/cc/td/doc/product/software/ios120/12cgcr/dial_c/dcppp.htm#4550.

- FRF.12 (Cisco IOS Release 12.0.4T): http://www.cisco.com/univercd/cc/td/doc/product/software/ios120/120newft/120t/120t4/120tvofr/index.htm.

- Link fragmentation and interleaving for Frame Relay and ATM virtual circuits (Cisco IOS Release 12.1.5T): http://www.cisco.com/univercd/cc/td/doc/product/software/ios121/121newft/121t/121t5/dtlfifra.htm.

- Distributed link fragmentation and interleaving over leased lines (Cisco IOS Release 12.2.8T): http://www.cisco.com/univercd/cc/td/doc/product/software/ios122/122newft/122t/122t8/ftdlfi2.htm.

- Distributed link fragmentation and interleaving for Frame Relay and ATM interfaces (Cisco IOS Release 12.2.4T): http://www.cisco.com/univercd/cc/td/doc/product/software/ios122/122newft/122t/122t4/ftdlfi.htm.

Compressed Real-Time Protocol:

- RTP and TCP header compression (Cisco IOS Release 12.0.7T): http://www.cisco.com/univercd/cc/td/doc/product/software/ios120/120newft/120t/120t7/rtpfast.htm.

- Class-based RTP and TCP header compression (Cisco IOS Release 12.2.13T): http://www.cisco.com/univercd/cc/td/doc/product/software/ios122/122newft/122t/122t13/fthdrcmp.htm.

Tx-ring:

- Tx-ring tuning: http://www.cisco.com/en/US/tech/tk39/tk824/technologies_tech_note09186a00800fbafc.shtml.

PAK_priority:

- Understanding how routing updates and Layer 2 control packets are queued on an interface with a QoS service policy: http://www.cisco.com/warp/public/105/rtgupdates.html.

ISDN:

- Multiclass Multilink PPP (Cisco IOS Release 12.2.13T) http://www.cisco.com/ univercd/cc/td/doc/product/software/ios122/122newft/122t/122t13/ftmmlppp.htm.

Marking:

- Class-based marking (Cisco IOS Release 12.1.5T): http://www.cisco.com/univercd/ cc/td/doc/product/software/ios121/121newft/121t/121t5/cbpmark2.htm.

- Enhanced packet marking (Cisco IOS Release 12.2.13T): http://www.cisco.com/ univercd/cc/td/doc/product/software/ios122/122newft/122t/122t13/ftenpkmk.htm.

This chapter discusses Branch QoS considerations and designs, including the following:

- Unidirectional applications
- Branch LAN edge ingress classification
- Branch NBAR policies for worm identification and policing

CHAPTER 14

Branch Router QoS Design

Chapter 13, "WAN Aggregator QoS Design," discussed the QoS design recommendations for WAN aggregators in detail. For the most part, theses designs also apply to branch routers located at the far end of the WAN links. However, at least three unique considerations must be made for branch router QoS design. This chapter examines in detail these considerations and their related designs.

The first consideration is that of unidirectional applications. Some applications, such as Streaming-Video (whether unicast or multicast), require bandwidth allocation only on the WAN aggregator's WAN edge, not on the branch router's WAN edge. Therefore, bandwidth allocated to unidirectional applications on the WAN aggregator WAN edge can be redistributed among other preferential classes on the branch router's WAN edge.

Another characteristic common to branches is that traffic destined to the campus might not be correctly marked on the branch access switches. These switches, which are usually lower-end switches, might or might not have the capabilities to classify by Layer 3 or 4 parameters and mark DSCP values for data applications. Therefore, classification and marking might need to be performed on the branch router's LAN edge in the ingress direction. Furthermore, branch routers provide the capability to use NBAR to classify and mark flows that require stateful packet inspection.

Related to classification and NBAR, another unique consideration to branch QoS design is that branch routers are a strategic place to deploy NBAR policies for worm identification and policing. NBAR policies can be used to identify and drop Code Red, NIMDA, SQL Slammer, RPC DCOM/W32/MS Blaster, Sasser, and other worms.

Figure 14-1 shows the QoS policies required on a remote branch router.

Figure 14-1 *Branch Router QoS Policies*

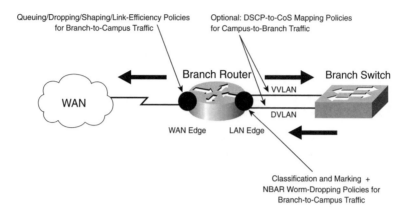

Branch WAN Edge QoS Design

WAN edge considerations discussed in Chapter 13 apply also to the branch router's WAN edge. This includes the following:

- Link-speed categories (slow, medium, and high) and their respective design implications

- Bandwidth-provisioning guidelines (at least 25 percent for Best-Effort traffic and no more than 33 percent for Real-Time applications)

- Link-specific caveats (such as the fact that tools such as LFI and cRTP, when enabled, must be enabled on both ends of the WAN link for them to function correctly)

Distributed platform idiosyncrasies are not as relevant for branch router designs because these platforms rarely are deployed at remote sites (although they can be used for site-to-site links, as discussed in Chapter 13).

Unidirectional Applications

Some applications are completely symmetrical and require identical bandwidth provisioning on both ends of the WAN link. For example, if 100 kbps of LLQ are assigned to voice in one direction, 100 kbps of LLQ also must be provisioned for voice in the opposite direction (assuming that the same VoIP codecs are being used in both directions, and putting aside for a moment multicast Music-on-Hold [MoH] provisioning). Furthermore, having symmetrical polices on both sides of the WAN links greatly simplifies QoS policy deployment and management, which is an important aspect of large-scale designs.

However, certain applications, such as Streaming-Video and multicast MoH, most often are unidirectional. Therefore, it might be unnecessary and even inefficient to provision any bandwidth guarantees for such traffic on the branch router for the branch-to-campus direction of traffic flow.

Most applications lie somewhere in the middle of the scale, between the extremes of being fully bidirectional and being completely unidirectional. Most client/server applications lie closer to the unidirectional end of the scale because these applications usually consist of small amounts of client-to-server traffic coupled with larger amounts of server-to-client traffic. Such behavior can be reflected in the asymmetrical bandwidth provisioning for such types of applications.

For purely unidirectional applications, it is recommended that provisioning be removed from the WAN edge policies on branch routers and the allocated bandwidth be redistributed among other classes.

Branch Router WAN Edge (10-Class) QoS Baseline Model

The inclusion or exclusion of the Streaming-Video class affects only those enterprises deploying complex QoS class models, such as the 11-Class QoS Baseline Model. When the Streaming-Video class is removed from this model (for branch router WAN edges), the bandwidth previously allocated to this class can be reallocated among the other preferential data classes, as illustrated in Figure 14-2. Notice that no class is provisioned for Streaming-Video in this model, and the bandwidth assigned to it from the 11-Class WAN edge model (from Figure 13-6 in the previous chapter) has been reassigned to the Mission-Critical Data class and the Transactional Data class.

The configuration for such a branch router (10-class) QoS Baseline policy on a dual-T1 interface is shown in Example 14-1. Notice that there is no Streaming-Video class and that the bandwidth for it has been distributed equally between the Mission-Critical Data class (now at 15 percent instead of 10 percent) and the Transactional Data class (now at 12 percent instead of 7 percent).

A **bandwidth** statement is used on class-default, precluding the use of **fair-queue** on the class for all nondistributed platforms. Also, a **max-reserved-bandwidth 100** command must be issued on the interface before the **service-policy output** command.

Figure 14-2   *Branch Router (10-Class) QoS Baseline WAN Edge Model Bandwidth Allocations Example*
(Dual-T1 Link Example)

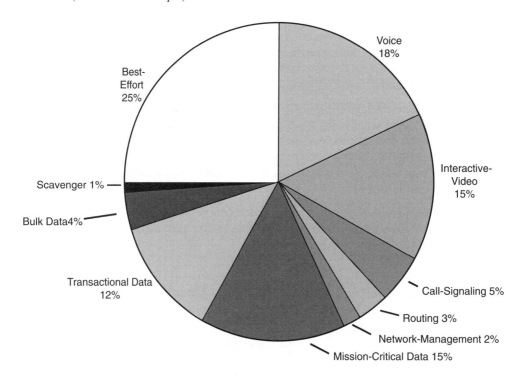

Example 14-1   *Branch Router (10-Class) QoS Baseline WAN Edge Model*

```
!
class-map match-all VOICE
   match ip dscp ef              ! IP Phones mark Voice to EF
class-map match-all INTERACTIVE-VIDEO
   match ip dscp af41 af42       ! Recommended markings for IP/VC
class-map match-any CALL-SIGNALING
   match ip dscp cs3             ! Future Call-Signaling marking
   match ip dscp af31            ! Current Call-Signaling marking
class-map match-all ROUTING
   match ip dscp cs6             ! Routers mark Routing traffic to CS6
class-map match-all NET-MGMT
   match ip dscp cs2             ! Recommended marking for Network Management
class-map match-all MISSION-CRITICAL-DATA
   match ip dscp 25              ! Interim marking for Mission-Critical Data
class-map match-all TRANSACTIONAL-DATA
   match ip dscp af21 af22       ! Recommended markings for Transactional Data
class-map match-all BULK-DATA
```

Example 14-1 *Branch Router (10-Class) QoS Baseline WAN Edge Model (Continued)*

```
     match ip dscp af11 af12      ! Recommended markings for Bulk Data
 class-map match-all SCAVENGER
     match ip dscp cs1            ! Recommended marking for Scavenger traffic
 !
 policy-map BRANCH-WAN-EDGE
   class VOICE
     priority percent 18          ! Voice gets 552 kbps of LLQ
   class INTERACTIVE-VIDEO
     priority percent 15          ! 384 kbps IP/VC needs 460 kbps of LLQ
   class CALL-SIGNALING
     bandwidth percent 5          ! Minimal BW guarantee for Call-Signaling
   class ROUTING
     bandwidth percent 3          ! Routing class gets 3% explicit BW guarantee
   class NET-MGMT
     bandwidth percent 2          ! Net-Mgmt class gets 2% explicit BW guarantee
   class MISSION-CRITICAL-DATA
     bandwidth percent 15         ! Mission-Critical class gets min 15% BW guarantee
     random-detect                ! Enables WRED on Mission-Critical Data class
   class TRANSACTIONAL-DATA
     bandwidth percent 12         ! Transactional-Data class gets min 12% BW guarantee
     random-detect dscp-based     ! Enables DSCP-WRED on Transactional-Data class
   class BULK-DATA
     bandwidth percent 4          ! Bulk Data class gets 4% BW guarantee
     random-detect dscp-based     ! Enables DSCP-WRED on Bulk-Data class
   class SCAVENGER
     bandwidth percent 1          ! Scavenger class is throttled
   class class-default
     bandwidth percent 25         ! Default class gets min 30% BW guarantee
     random-detect                ! Enables WRED on the default class
 !
```

Verification commands:

- **show policy**
- **show policy interface**

Now that considerations and designs for the WAN edge of the branch router have been addressed, the next section discusses the LAN edge.

Branch Router LAN Edge QoS Design

The LAN edge of the branch router can have egress and ingress policies. Because you have been dealing with egress policies since the WAN/branch discussion began, and because the egress policies are not only optional, but also considerably simpler, they are discussed first.

As previously mentioned, it is better to mark at Layer 3 (DSCP) instead of Layer 2 whenever possible because Layer 2 markings are lost when the transmission medium changes. This is the case with any Ethernet 802.1Q/p CoS values that have been set within the campus and are carried over a WAN (or VPN). In some cases, network administrators prefer to have these markings restored at the branch; DSCP-to-CoS mapping then can be performed on the branch router's LAN edge.

In the ingress direction, the branch router might be required to perform classification and marking of branch-to-campus traffic. This might be because the branch switch lacks the capability to classify and mark traffic, or because the traffic consists of stateful flows that require NBAR for classification. NBAR classification also is required at branch LAN ingress edges to identify (and immediately drop) known worm traffic.

Each of these types of polices is discussed in more detail in the following sections.

DSCP-to-CoS Remapping

DSCP-to-CoS remapping is optional. Newer Catalyst switches perform QoS based on internal DSCP values that are generated either by trusted DSCP markings or by trusted CoS markings (coupled with CoS-to-DSCP mappings). In the case of legacy switches at the branch that perform QoS strictly by preset CoS values, CoS might need to be remapped on the branch router's LAN edge.

Enhanced packet marking (Cisco IOS Release 12.2[13]T or higher) is the optimal tool for resetting CoS values because it uses a table. In this manner, a default DSCP-to-CoS mapping can be used without having to configure explicitly a class-based marking policy that matches every DiffServ class and performs a corresponding **set cos** function.

In both cases, keep in mind that only Ethernet trunking protocols, such as 802.1Q, carry CoS information. Therefore, the policy works correctly only when applied to a trunked subinterface, not to a main Ethernet interface.

Example 14-2 presents an enhanced packet marking DSCP-to-CoS configuration for a branch LAN edge. Note that this DSCP-to-CoS remapping policy requires application to both the voice VLAN (VVLAN) subinterface and the data VLAN (DVLAN) subinterface on the branch router's LAN edge.

Example 14-2 *Branch LAN Edge Enhanced Packet Marking for DSCP-to-CoS Remapping Example*

```
!
ip cef                                  ! IP CEF is Required for Packet Marking
!
policy-map BRANCH-LAN-EDGE-OUT
  class class-default
    set cos dscp                        ! Enables default DSCP-to-CoS Mapping
!
!
interface FastEthernet0/0
 no ip address
 speed auto
 duplex auto
 !
```

Example 14-2 *Branch LAN Edge Enhanced Packet Marking for DSCP-to-CoS Remapping Example (Continued)*

```
interface FastEthernet0/0.60
 description DVLAN SUBNET 10.1.60.0
 encapsulation dot1Q 60
 ip address 10.1.60.1 255.255.255.0
 service-policy output BRANCH-LAN-EDGE-OUT        ! Restores CoS for Data VLAN
!
interface FastEthernet0/0.160
 description VVLAN SUBNET 10.1.160.0
 encapsulation dot1Q 160
 ip address 10.1.160.1 255.255.255.0
 service-policy output BRANCH-LAN-EDGE-OUT        ! Restores CoS on Voice VLAN
!
```

Verification commands:

- **show policy**
- **show policy interface**

Branch-to-Campus Classification and Marking

In keeping with the unofficial Differentiated Services design principle of marking traffic as close to its source as possible, IP phones mark voice-bearer traffic (to DSCP EF) and Call-Signaling traffic (currently, to DSCP AF31, but this will soon change to DSCP CS3) on the phones themselves. Some IP/VC devices mark Interactive-Video traffic to AF41 on their network interface cards (NICs).

However, as has already been discussed, it is not recommended that end-user PCs be trusted to set their CoS/DSCP markings correctly because users easily can abuse this (either unintentionally or deliberately). Therefore, application traffic that originates from untrusted hosts should be marked on branch access switches. However, in some circumstances, this might not be possible:

- The branch access switch does not have Layer 3 or Layer 4 awareness for traffic classification or does not support marking.
- Classification needs to be performed at the application layer (through NBAR).

In such cases, DSCP classification must be performed at the ingress interface of the branch router.

Administrators can identify and then mark application traffic based on the following criteria:

- **Source or destination IP address (or subnet)**—Typically, destination subnets are used when setting branch QoS policies. For example, the destination subnet for a group of application servers can be used to identify a particular type of client-to-server application traffic.

- **Well-known TCP/UDP ports**—It is important to know whether the well-known port is a source port or a destination port from the branch router's perspective.

- **NBAR protocol (for example, Citrix or KaZaa) or application subparameter (for example, HTTP URL)**—NBAR Packet Description Language Modules (PDLMs) also can be configured to identify stateful or proprietary applications, as well as worms.

Regardless of the method used to identify the application traffic, the inbound classification and marking policy needs to be applied only to the DVLAN subinterface. This is because only trusted IP Telephony applications, which mark their voice traffic correctly, are admitted onto the voice VLAN.

NOTE   If the branch access switches support access-edge policers (as described in Chapter 12, "Campus QoS Design"), these likewise should be enabled on them. This adds another layer of defense to the network, mitigating DoS/worm traffic that originates from the branch through Scavenger-class QoS.

If the branch access switches do not support such policing, compatible policers could be placed at the branch router access edge. This is in harmony with the principle of policing as close to the source as possible.

Whenever possible, though, such policing should be done in Catalyst hardware rather than Cisco IOS Software.

Although it might be tempting to use the same class-map names (such as MISSION-CRITICAL, TRANSACTIONAL-DATA, or BULK-DATA) for ingress LAN edge classification and marking policies as are in use for egress WAN edge queuing policies, this might cause confusion in policy definition and troubleshooting. Therefore, for management and troubleshooting simplicity, it is beneficial to have similar yet descriptive names for these new classes (for example, branch-originated traffic might have class-map names prepended with "BRANCH-"). A description can also be added to the class maps with the **description** command.

Source or Destination IP Address Classification

Example 14-3 shows how traffic destined to a specific subnet (10.200.200.0/24)—which, in this case, represents a server farm of proprietary Mission-Critical Data application servers—can be identified and marked on ingress on the branch router's LAN edge.

Example 14-3 *Branch LAN Edge Destination IP Classification and Marking Example*

```
!
ip cef                                           ! Required for Packet Marking
!
class-map match-all BRANCH-MISSION-CRITICAL
  match access-group name MISSION-CRITICAL-SERVERS    ! ACL to reference
!
 policy-map BRANCH-LAN-EDGE-IN
  class BRANCH-MISSION-CRITICAL
   set ip dscp 25   ! (Interim) Recommended marking for Mission-Critical traffic
!
...
!
interface FastEthernet0/0
 no ip address
 speed auto
 duplex auto
!
interface FastEthernet0/0.60
 description DVLAN SUBNET 10.1.60.0
 encapsulation dot1Q 60
 ip address 10.1.60.1 255.255.255.0
 service-policy output BRANCH-LAN-EDGE-OUT  ! Restores CoS on Data VLAN
 service-policy input BRANCH-LAN-EDGE-IN    ! Marks MC Data on ingress
!
...
!
ip access-list extended MISSION-CRITICAL-SERVERS
 permit ip any 10.200.200.0 0.0.0.255    ! MC Data Server-Farm Subnet
!
```

Verification commands:

- **show policy**
- **show policy interface**
- **show ip access-list**

Verification Command: **show ip access-list**

When access lists are used as the filtering criteria for a class map, the **show ip access-list** command is helpful in identifying whether the access list is registering matches, especially for ACLs that have multiple lines of match criteria. This command provides granular visibility into which lines of an access list are registering matches. In Example 14-4, 464 matches are registered against the access list.

Example 14-4 show ip access-list *Verification of Remote Branch LAN Edge Destination IP Classification Example*

```
BRANCH#60-C3745#show ip access-list MISSION-CRITICAL-SERVERS
Extended IP access list MISSION-CRITICAL-SERVERS
    10 permit ip any 10.200.200.0 0.0.0.255 (464 matches)
BRANCH#60-C3745#
```

Well-Known TCP/UDP Port Classification

Most applications can be identified by their well-known TCP/UDP ports. Some of these ports have keywords within Cisco IOS Software to identify them when defining access lists.

NOTE   The Internet Assigned Numbers Authority (IANA) lists registered well-known and registered application ports at http://www.iana.org/assignments/port-numbers.

Building on Example 14-4, Example 14-5 classifies and marks branch-originated FTP and e-mail traffic, both POP3 and IMAP (TCP port 143), as Bulk Data (DSCP AF11).

Example 14-5 *Branch LAN Edge Well-Known Port Classification Example*

```
!
ip cef                                    ! Required for Packet Marking
!
class-map match-all BRANCH-MISSION-CRITICAL
  match access-group name MISSION-CRITICAL-SERVERS
class-map match-all BRANCH-BULK-DATA
  match access-group name BULK-DATA-APPS      ! ACL to reference
!
 policy-map BRANCH-LAN-EDGE-IN
  class BRANCH-MISSION-CRITICAL
   set ip dscp 25
  class BRANCH-BULK-DATA
   set ip dscp af11                       ! Bulk data apps are marked to AF11
!
!
interface FastEthernet0/0
 no ip address
 speed auto
 duplex auto
!
interface FastEthernet0/0.60
 description DVLAN SUBNET 10.1.60.0
 encapsulation dot1Q 60
 ip address 10.1.60.1 255.255.255.0
 service-policy output BRANCH-LAN-EDGE-OUT      ! Restores CoS on Data VLAN
 service-policy input BRANCH-LAN-EDGE-IN        ! Marks Data on ingress
!
...
```

Example 14-5 *Branch LAN Edge Well-Known Port Classification Example (Continued)*

```
 !
 ip access-list extended MISSION-CRITICAL-SERVERS
  permit ip any 10.200.200.0 0.0.0.255
 !
 ip access-list extended BULK-DATA-APPS
  permit tcp any any eq ftp              ! Identifies FTP Control traffic
  permit tcp any any eq ftp-data         ! Identifies FTP Data traffic
  permit tcp any any eq pop3             ! Identifies POP3 E-mail traffic
  permit tcp any any eq 143              ! Identifies IMAP E-mail traffic
 !
```

Verification commands:

- **show policy**
- **show policy interface**
- **show ip access-list**

NBAR Application Classification

At the time of this writing, Cisco IOS Software included NBAR PDLMs for 98 of the most common network applications, with the capability to define an additional 10 applications using custom PDLMs.

Of these protocols, 15 require stateful packet inspection for positive identification. Because NBAR operates in the IP Cisco Express Forwarding (CEF) switching path, only the first packet within a flow requires stateful packet inspection, and the policy is applied to all packets belonging to the flow. NBAR stateful packet inspection requires more CPU processing power than simple access control lists (ACLs). However, on newer branch router platforms, such as the Cisco 3745 or 2691, Cisco Technical Marketing testing has shown the overhead of enabling NBAR classification at dual-T1 rates to be quite minimal (typically 2 to 5 percent, depending on the traffic mix).

Building again on the previous example, Example 14-6 uses NBAR to identify several types of Transactional Data applications, Network-Management applications, and Scavenger applications.

In Example 14-6, Transactional Data applications include Citrix, LDAP, Oracle SQL*NET, and HTTP web traffic with "SalesReport" in the URL. In addition, a custom PDLM is defined to identify SAP traffic (by TCP ports 3200 through 3203 and 3600), and SAP also is included as a Transactional Data application.

Additionally, Network-Management applications, such as SNMP, Syslog, Telnet, NFS, DNS, ICMP, and TFTP, are identified through NBAR and marked to DSCP CS2.

Furthermore, Scavenger applications, such as Napster, Gnutella, KaZaa (versions 1 and 2), Morpheus, Grokster, and many other peer-to-peer file-sharing applications, are identified by NBAR and marked to DSCP CS1.

Example 14-6 *Branch LAN Edge NBAR Classification Example*

```
!
ip nbar port-map custom-01 tcp 3200 3201 3202 3203 3600    ! PDLM Mapping for SAP
!
ip cef    ! IP CEF is required for both Class-Based Marking and for NBAR
!
class-map match-all BRANCH-MISSION-CRITICAL
  match access-group name MISSION-CRITICAL-SERVERS
class-map match-any BRANCH-TRANSACTIONAL-DATA! Must use "match-any"
  match protocol citrix                      ! Identifies Citrix traffic
  match protocol ldap                      ! Identifies LDAP traffic
  match protocol sqlnet                    ! Identifies Oracle SQL*NET traffic
  match protocol http url "*SalesReport*"  ! Identifies "SalesReport" URLs
  match protocol custom-01          ! Identifies SAP traffic via Custom-01 PDLM Port-Map
class-map match-all BRANCH-BULK-DATA
  match access-group name BULK-DATA-APPS
class-map match-any BRANCH-NET-MGMT
  match protocol snmp                        ! Identifies SNMP traffic
  match protocol syslog                      ! Identifies Syslog traffic
  match protocol telnet                      ! Identifies Telnet traffic
  match protocol nfs                         ! Identifies NFS traffic
  match protocol dns                         ! Identifies DNS traffic
  match protocol icmp                        ! Identifies ICMP traffic
  match protocol tftp                        ! Identifies TFTP traffic
class-map match-any BRANCH-SCAVENGER
  match protocol napster                     ! Identifies Napster traffic
  match protocol gnutella                    ! Identifies Gnutella traffic
  match protocol fasttrack                   ! Identifies KaZaa (v1) traffic
  match protocol kazaa2                      ! Identifies KaZaa (v2) traffic
!
policy-map BRANCH-LAN-EDGE-IN
  class BRANCH-MISSION-CRITICAL
    set ip dscp 25
  class BRANCH-TRANSACTIONAL-DATA
    set ip dscp af21            ! Transactional Data apps are marked to DSCP AF21
  class BRANCH-NET-MGMT
    set ip dscp cs2             ! Network Management apps are marked to DSCP CS2
  class BRANCH-BULK-DATA
    set ip dscp af11
  class BRANCH-SCAVENGER
    set ip dscp cs1             ! Scavenger apps are marked to DSCP CS1
!
...
!
interface FastEthernet0/0
 no ip address
 speed auto
 duplex auto
```

Example 14-6 *Branch LAN Edge NBAR Classification Example (Continued)*

```
!
interface FastEthernet0/0.60
 description DVLAN SUBNET 10.1.60.0
 encapsulation dot1Q 60
 ip address 10.1.60.1 255.255.255.0
 service-policy output BRANCH-LAN-EDGE-OUT   ! Restores CoS on Data VLAN
 service-policy input BRANCH-LAN-EDGE-IN     ! Input Marking policy on DVLAN only
!
...
!
ip access-list extended MISSION-CRITICAL-SERVERS
 permit ip any 10.200.200.0 0.0.0.255
!
!
ip access-list extended BULK-DATA-APPS
 permit tcp any any eq ftp
 permit tcp any any eq ftp-data
 permit tcp any any eq pop3
 permit tcp any any eq 143
!
```

NOTE   The NBAR **fasttrack** PDLM identifies KaZaa (version 1), Morpheus, Grokster, and other applications. The NBAR **gnutella** PDLM identifies Gnutella, BearShare, LimeWire, and other peer-to-peer applications.

Verification commands:

- **show policy**
- **show policy interface**
- **show ip access-list**
- **show ip nbar port-map**

Verification Command: **show ip nbar port-map**

When NBAR custom PDLMs are used to identify applications, it is useful to verify that the ports bound to the PDLM have been entered correctly. This information is obtained with the **show ip nbar port-map** command. In this (filtered) example, Example 14-7, the TCP ports given for SAP (3200 through 3203 and 3600) were bound correctly to the Custom-01 NBAR PDLM.

Example 14-7 *show ip nbar port-map Verification Custom-PDLM TCP/UDP Port-Mapping Example*

```
BRANCH#60-C3745#show ip nbar port-map | include custom-01
port-map custom-01          tcp 3200 3201 3202 3203 3600
BRANCH#60-C3745#
```

NBAR Known-Worm Classification and Policing

Worms are nothing new. They've been around almost as long as the Internet itself (one of the first Internet worms was the Morris worm, released in November 1988). Typically, worms are self-contained programs that attack a system and try to exploit a vulnerability in the target. Upon successfully exploiting the vulnerability, the worm copies its program from the attacking host to the newly exploited system to begin the cycle again.

NOTE   A virus, which is slightly different from a worm, requires a vector to carry the virus code from one system to another. The vector can be either a word-processing document, an e-mail, or an executable program.

The main element that distinguishes a worm from a virus is that a computer virus requires human intervention to facilitate its spreading, whereas worms (once released) propagate without requiring additional human intervention.

Worms are comprised of three primary components (as illustrated in Figure 14-3):

- **The enabling exploit code**—The enabling exploit code is used to exploit a vulnerability on a system. Exploitation of this vulnerability provides access to the system and the capability to execute commands on the target system.

- **A propagation mechanism**—When access has been obtained through the enabling exploit, the propagation mechanism is used to replicate the worm to the new target. The method used to replicate the worm can be achieved through the use of the Trivial File Transfer Protocol (TFTP), FTP, or another communication method. When the worm code is brought to the new host, the cycle of infection can be started again.

- **A payload**—Some worms also contain payloads, which might include additional code to further exploit the host, modify data on the host, or change a web page. A payload is not a required component, and, in many cases, the worm's enabling exploit code itself can be considered the payload.

Figure 14-3 *Anatomy of an Internet Worm*

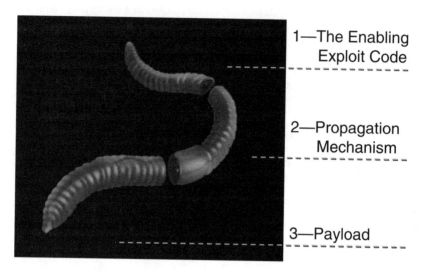

1—The Enabling
    Exploit Code

2—Propagation
    Mechanism

3—Payload

Some worms use unique TCP/UDP ports to propagate. These types of worms are fairly simple to block using access lists (when the ports are known). Such ACLs can be configured on the branch switch (whenever supported) or on the branch router's LAN edge.

Other worms hijack legitimate TCP/UDP ports to carry their harmful payloads. For these latter types of worms, NBAR can be used at the branch LAN edge to perform deep-packet analysis and drop any packets that are carrying the payloads of known worms. Some of these known worms include Code Red, NIMDA, SQL Slammer, RPC DCOM/W32/MS Blaster, and Sasser. The following sections discuss how NBAR can be used for each of these types of worms.

NBAR Versus Code Red

First released in July 2001, Code Red targeted Microsoft Internet Information Server (IIS) using a vulnerability in the IIS Indexing Service. Although the first variant of this worm did little damage because of a flaw in the random number–generator code used to generate addresses of hosts to exploit, a second variant appeared with the flaw fixed.

This worm, CodeRedv2, spread quickly and became the most widespread and damaging worm to hit the Internet since the Morris worm. CodeRedv2's success as a worm relied on the fact that the worm exploited the vulnerability in the IIS Indexing Service only as a means of gaining access to the host. This, coupled with the wide deployment of IIS as well as the large number of unpatched IIS web servers, contributed to the quick and wide-ranging spread of the worm. An estimated 360,000 hosts were infected within a period of 14 hours.

CodeRedv2 temporarily replaced the home page of the web servers that it struck with a new page. Additionally, the code of the worm indicated that it was programmed to begin a packet-flooding DoS attack against a hard-coded IP address. (At the time, this was the IP address of the White House web server at http://www.whitehouse.gov.)

The original Code Red payload is shown in Example 14-8. The initial infection attempt sends a large HTTP GET request to the target IIS server.

Example 14-8 *Original Code Red Payload*

```
2001-08-04 16:32:23 24.101.17.216 - 10.1.1.75 80 GET /default.ida
NNNNNNNNNNNNNNNNNNNNNNNNNNNNNNNNNNNNNNNNNNNNNNNNNNNNNNNNNNNNNNNNNNNN
NNNNNNNNNNNNNNNNNNNNNNNNNNNNNNNNNNNNNNNNNNNNNNNNNNNNNNNNNNNNNNNNNNNNN
NNNNNNNNNNNNNNNNNNNNNNNNNNNNNNNNNNNNNNNNNNNNNNNNNNNNNNNNNNNNNNNNNNNNN
NNNNNNNNNNNNNNNNNNNNNNNNNNNNN%u9090%u6858%ucbd3%u7801%u9090%u6858%ucbd
3%u7801%u9090%u6858%ucbd3%u7801%u9090%u9090%u8190%u00c3%u0003%u8b00%u
531b%u53ff%u0078%u0000%u00=a 403
```

The CodeRedv2 payload is shown in Example 14-9.

Example 14-9 *CodeRedv2 Payload*

```
2001-08-04 15:57:35 64.7.35.92 - 10.1.1.75 80 GET /default.ida
XXXXXXXXXXXXXXXXXXXXXXXXXXXXXXXXXXXXXXXXXXXXXXXXXXXXXXXXXXXXXXXXXX
XXXXXXXXXXXXXXXXXXXXXXXXXXXXXXXXXXXXXXXXXXXXXXXXXXXXXXXXXXXXXXXXXXXX
XXXXXXXXXXXXXXXXXXXXXXXXXXXXXXXXXXXXXXXXXXXXXXXXXXXXXXXXXXXXXXXXXXXX
XXXXXXXXXXXXXXXXXXXXXXXXXXXXXXXXXXXXX%u9090%u6858%ucbd3%u7801%u
9090%u6858%ucbd3%u7801%u9090%u6858%ucbd3%u7801%u9090%u9090%u
8190%u00c3%u0003%u8b00%u531b%u53ff%u0078%u0000%u00=a 403 -
```

Notice that the GET request in both cases is looking for a file named default.ida. However, this filename changes in newer variants of Code Red, such as CodeRedv3/CodeRed.C, as shown in Example 14-10.

Example 14-10 *CodeRedv3 Payload*

```
2001-08-06 22:24:02 24.30.203.202 - 10.1.1.9 80 GET /x.ida
AAAAAAAAAAAAAAAAAAAAAAAAAAAAAAAAAAAAAAAAAAAAAAAAAAAAAAAAAAAAAAAAA
AAAAAAAAAAAAAAAAAAAAAAAAAAAAA
AAAAAAAAAAAAAAAAAAAAAAAAAAAAAAAAAAAAAAAAAAAAAAAAAAAAAAAAAAAAAAAAA
AAAAAAAAAAAAAAAAAAAAAAAAAAAAAAAAAAAAAAAAAAAAAAAAAAAAAAAAAAAAAAAAA
AAAAAAAAAAAAAAA=X 403 HTTP/1.1 -
```

Although the filename has changed, the .ida suffix remains the same.

Code Red variants can include payloads that execute cmd.exe or root.exe functions to program scripts within the IIS scripts directory, thus providing a ready-made back door to the server for any attacker to use.

Therefore, to combat Code Red, NBAR policies can be configured to check the payload of HTTP packets for these criteria (.ida, cmd.exe, and root.exe), as shown in Example 14-11.

Example 14-11 *NBAR Policies to Identify Code Red*

```
!
class-map match-any CODE-RED
  match protocol http url "*.ida*"      ! Identifies HTTP GET .ida requests
  match protocol http url "*cmd.exe*"   ! Identifies HTTP with cmd.exe
  match protocol http url "*root.exe*"  ! Identifies HTTP with root.exe
!
```

Verification command:

- **show policy**

NBAR Versus NIMDA

Two months after Code Red struck the Internet, another large-scale worm, NIMDA, was released. Unlike Code Red, NIMDA was a hybrid worm because it contained the characteristics of both a worm and a virus. NIMDA spread using several vectors:

- Through e-mail as an attachment (virus vector)
- Through network shares (worm vector)
- Through JavaScript by browsing compromised websites (virus vector)
- Through infected hosts actively scanning for additional exploitable hosts (worm vector)
- Through infected hosts actively scanning for back doors created by Code Red (worm vector)

NIMDA did not appear to exhibit intentional destructive capabilities; to date, NIMDA's activities have been restricted to its self-propagation, which has the side effect of a DoS (flooding) attack.

NIMDA propagates itself by copying, downloading, or executing a file called readme.eml. Therefore, NBAR can be used to check the payload of HTTP packets to see if they are propagating this file, as shown in Example 14-12.

Example 14-12 *NBAR Policies to Identify NIMDA*

```
!
class-map match-any NIMDA
  match protocol http url "*readme.eml*"   ! Identifies HTTP with "readme.eml"
!
```

Verification command:

- **show policy**

NBAR Versus SQL Slammer

After the NIMDA infection subsided, the Internet saw the appearance of smaller infectious worms. In January 2003, a new worm infected the Internet at such a high rate that it was categorized as a flash worm. This worm, termed SQL Slammer, once again targeted Microsoft Windows servers; specifically, this worm targeted servers running Microsoft Structured Query Language (SQL) Server software. The vulnerability exploited by SQL Slammer had been published in July 2002, and a patch from Microsoft was available at that time as well. Even though this patch was available for almost six months, SQL Slammer spread with incredibly high efficiency.

SQL slammer is a 376-byte User Datagram Protocol (UDP)–based worm that infects Microsoft SQL servers through UDP port 1434. Example 14-13 shows a signature string from the SQL Slammer worm.

Example 14-13 *SQL Slammer Worm Signature String*

```
\x04\x01\x01\x01\x01\x01.*[.][Dd][Ll][Ll]
```

Because of its small size, the SQL Slammer worm is contained in a single packet. The fast scanning rate of SQL Slammer is achieved not only because of this small size, but also because the worm is UDP based. The worm does not have to complete a handshake (necessary with TCP-based worms) to connect with a target system.

SQL Slammer reached its full scanning rate of 55 million scans per second within 3 minutes of the start of the infection and infected the majority of vulnerable hosts on the Internet within 10 minutes of the start of the infection, with an estimated 300,000 infected hosts overall. A major consequence of such a fast scanning rate was that edge networks were overwhelmed by the amount of traffic generated by the worm. SQL Slammer's doubling rate was approximately 8.5 seconds. In contrast, CodeRedv2's doubling rate was about 37 minutes.

SQL Slammer does not carry an additional harmful payload (beyond its enabling exploit code), and its primary purpose is to cause DoS through exponential self propagation.

NBAR can be used to detect the SQL Slammer worm by mapping a custom PDLM to UDP port 1434 and matching on the packet length (376-byte worm + 8 bytes of UDP header + 20 bytes of IP header = 404 bytes). This is shown in Example 14-14.

Example 14-14 *NBAR Policies to Identify SQL Slammer*

```
!
ip nbar port-map custom-02 udp 1434          ! Maps a custom PDLM to UDP 1434
!
class-map match-all SQL-SLAMMER
   match protocol custom-02                   ! Matches the custom Slammer PDLM
   match packet length min 404 max 404        ! Matches the packet length (376+28)
!
```

Verification commands:

- **show policy**
- **show ip nbar port-map**

NOTE   Because NBAR custom-01 PDLM has been used in previous examples to identify SAP traffic, another custom PDLM (custom-02) is used in this example. Subsequent examples similarly are defined with the next-available custom PDLM.

NBAR Versus RPC DCOM/W32/MS Blaster

First released in August 2003, the Remote Procedure Call (RPC) Distributed Component Object Model (DCOM) worm exploited a flaw in a section of Microsoft's RPC code dealing with message exchange over TCP/IP, resulting in the incorrect handling of malformed messages. This flaw was a stack-based buffer overflow occurring in a low-level DCOM interface within the RPC process listening on TCP ports 135, 139, and 445.

The DCOM protocol enables Microsoft software components to communicate with one another. This is a core function of the Windows kernel and cannot be disabled. The vulnerability results because the Windows RPC service does not properly check message inputs under certain circumstances. By sending a malformed RPC message, an attacker can cause the RPC service on a device to fail in such a way that arbitrary code could be executed. The typical exploit for this vulnerability launches a reverse-telnet back to the attacker's host to gain complete access to the target.

Successful exploitation of this vulnerability enables an attacker to run code with local system privileges. This enables an attacker to install programs; view, change, or delete data; and create new accounts with full privileges. Because RPC is active by default on all versions of the Windows operating system, any user who can deliver a malformed TCP request to an RPC interface of a vulnerable computer could attempt to exploit the vulnerability. It is even possible to trigger this vulnerability through other means, such as logging into an affected system and exploiting the vulnerable component locally.

A variant of the RPC DCOM worm is termed W32 Blaster or MS Blaster. When MS Blaster successfully exploits a host, it attempts to upload a copy of the worm program to the newly exploited host. MS Blaster uses TFTP to copy the worm program from the attacking host to the target system. MS Blaster also starts up a cmd.exe process and binds it to TCP port 4444 of the newly exploited system. This provides any attacker with direct command-line access at the local system privilege level, as discussed previously.

To access the system, the attacker needs only to telnet to TCP port 4444 on the exploited host. If the worm is successful in copying the MS Blaster program to the target, the worm exploit code modifies the system registry to ensure that the worm is restarted if the system reboots. It then launches the worm program on the newly exploited host to begin the cycle again, starting with scanning for more exploitable hosts. MS Blaster also contained code for a DoS attack. This particular attack was targeted at www.windowsupdate.com.

NBAR can be used to combat the RPC DCOM/W32/MS Blaster worm by identifying communications on TCP/UDP ports 135, 139, and 445.

By default, the NBAR **exchange** PDLM is mapped to TCP port 135; therefore, this PDLM can be used as part of the MS Blaster worm policy definition. Similarly, the NBAR **netbios** PDLM is bound by default to TCP/UDP port 139 (in addition to TCP port 137 and UDP ports 137 and 138), so this PDLM also can be used within the policy definition; specifically, the **netbios** PDLM can have its port mapping expanded to include TCP port 445 and UDP ports 135, 139, and 445, as shown in Example 14-15.

NOTE   Alternatively, a custom PDLM can be defined for these ports (TCP/UDP 135, 139, and 445), but before this could be done, you would have to map the **exchange** and **netbios** PDLMs ports away from their defaults, to avoid conflicting PDLM port mappings.

Example 14-15 *NBAR Policies to Identify RPC DCOM/W32/MS Blaster*

```
!
ip nbar port-map netbios tcp 137 139 445            ! Matches TCP 137/139/445
ip nbar port-map netbios udp 135 137 138 139 445    ! Matches UDP 135/137-139/445
!
class-map match-any MS-BLASTER
   match protocol exchange                 ! Matches TCP port 135
   match protocol netbios                  ! Matches MS Blaster NetBIOS PDLM
!
```

Verification commands:

- **show policy**
- **show ip nbar port-map**

NBAR Versus Sasser

The next major worm after MS Blaster was the Sasser worm (and variants Sasser.A/B/C/D), which was released in late April 2004. Sasser exploits a flaw in the Windows Local Security Authority Service Server (LSASS) that can cause systems to crash and continually reboot, or allow a remote attacker to execute arbitrary code with local system privileges.

Sasser is very efficient in scanning: It can scan 1024 separate IP addresses simultaneously (on TCP port 445). When scanning reveals a vulnerable system, the worm exploits the

LSASS vulnerability and creates a remote shell (RSH) session on TCP port 9996 back to the infecting system. Then Sasser starts an FTP server on TCP port 5554 to retrieve a copy of the worm.

Sasser can be identified through a custom NBAR PDLM listening for communication on TCP ports 445, 5554, and 9996, as shown in Example 14-16.

NOTE   If TCP port 445 already has been bound to the **netbios** NBAR PDLM (as recommended previously in the MS Blaster worm definition), it is not necessary to include this port in the Sasser custom PDLM port mapping (because it will cause a conflict).

Example 14-16 *NBAR Policies to Identify Sasser*

```
!
ip nbar port-map custom-03 tcp 445 5554 9996   ! Matches on TCP 445/5554/9996
!
class-map match-all SASSER
   match protocol custom-03                     ! Matches Sasser custom PDLM
!
```

Verification commands:

- **show policy**
- **show ip nbar port-map**

NBAR Versus Future Worms

There is every reason to believe that new worms will be released in the future. These worms will be not only more complex, but also more efficient in their propagation, and thus more damaging in their scope.

A new NBAR feature (introduced in Cisco IOS Release 12.3[4]T) enables network administrators to extend the capability of NBAR to classify (and monitor) additional static port applications or to allow NBAR to classify unsupported static port traffic. Specifically, it enables administrators to define the strings that they want to search for in the application payload (for any application, not just HTTP URLs) to identify a given application.

This functionality can be used to identify proprietary applications that otherwise could not be matched. However, it also can be very useful in plugging holes that future worms might open.

For example, consider the example of a fictitious worm called Moonbeam. Moonbeam scans and propagates itself on randomly generated TCP ports within the range of 21000 through 21999. Furthermore, the worm carries the word Moonbeam within the payload, beginning with the ninth ASCII character of the string. Moonbeam's (fictitious) payload is shown in Example 14-17.

Example 14-17 *Moonbeam Worm Payload*

```
\x04\x01Moonbeam\x01\x01\x01\x01.*[.][Dd][L1][L1]u9090%u6858%ucbd3%
u7801%u9090%u6858%ucbd3%u7801%u9090%u6858%ucbd3%u7801%u9090%u9090%
u8190%u00c3%u0003%u8b00%u531b%u53ff%u0078%u0000%u00=a 403 ...
```

Moonbeam could be identified by a custom NBAR PDLM that examines TCP packets within the range of 21000 through 21999, ignores the first eight ASCII values, and checks for the string "Moonbeam" (case sensitive), as shown in Example 14-18.

Example 14-18 *NBAR Policies to Identify Moonbeam*

```
!
ip nbar custom MOONBEAM 8 ascii Moonbeam tcp range 21000 21999  ! "Moonbeam" PDLM
!
class-map match-all MOONBEAM-WORM
 match protocol MOONBEAM          ! Matches the "Moonbeam" custom PDLM
!
```

Verification commands:

- **show policy**
- **show ip nbar port-map**

Policing Known Worms

These are just a few examples of known worms that can be identified using NBAR. After traffic generated by known worms has been positively identified, it should not be re-marked or limited; rather, it should be dropped immediately. This can be done on ingress on branch LAN edges, as shown in Example 14-19, which combines the policies for Code Red, NIMDA, SQL Slammer, RPC DCOM/W32/MS Blaster, and Sasser. Additionally, the fictitious worm Moonbeam has been included in the policy.

NOTE   A recursive classification is required in this policy for SQL Slammer. This is because SQL Slammer requires a **match-all** criteria for its initial classification, but for policy-management purposes, it is desired that this initial classification of SQL Slammer be lumped under a single policy (with a **match-any** criteria) to identify and drop all known worms.

Example 14-19 *NBAR Branch LAN Edge Ingress Policy for Known Worms*

```
!
ip nbar port-map custom-02 udp 1434            ! SQL Slammer custom PDLM
ip nbar port-map custom-03 tcp 5554 9996       ! Sasser custom PDLM
ip nbar port-map netbios tcp 137 139 445       ! MS Blaster TCP 137/139/445
ip nbar port-map netbios udp 135 137 138 139 445 ! MS Blaster UDP 135/137-139/445
ip nbar custom MOONBEAM 8 ascii Moonbeam tcp range 21000 21999  ! "Moonbeam" PDLM
!
class-map match-all SQL-SLAMMER
   match protocol custom-02                     ! Matches the SQL Slammer PDLM
   match packet length min 404 max 404          ! Matches the packet length (376+28)
!
class-map match-any WORMS
   match protocol http url "*.ida*"             ! CodeRed
   match protocol http url "*cmd.exe*"          ! CodeRed
   match protocol http url "*root.exe*"         ! CodeRed
   match protocol http url "*readme.eml*"       ! NIMDA
   match class-map SQL-SLAMMER                  ! SQL Slammer class-map
   match protocol exchange                      ! MS Blaster (TCP 135)
   match protocol netbios                       ! MS Blaster NetBIOS PDLM
   match protocol custom-03                     ! Sasser custom PDLM
   match protocol MOONBEAM                      ! "Moonbeam" PDLM
!
policy-map WORM-DROP
 class WORMS
   drop                                         ! Drops all known worms
!
...
!
interface FastEthernet0/0
 no ip address
 speed auto
 duplex auto
!
interface FastEthernet0/0.60
 description DVLAN SUBNET 10.1.60.0
 encapsulation dot1Q 60
 ip address 10.1.60.1 255.255.255.0
 service-policy input WORM-DROP                 ! Drops known worms (DVLAN only)
!
```

Case Study: Branch Router QoS Design

Continuing the example from the previous chapters, the fictitious company ABC, Inc.,
already is correctly classifying and marking all 11 classes of traffic from the QoS Baseline
Model within its campus. Such marking is being performed at Layer 3 via DSCP. Furthermore, dual-rate policing is used within the campus so that certain AF classes of traffic can
be marked down to a second level of drop preference (for example, AF21 can be marked

down to AF22). Additionally, the WAN aggregator is provisioning LLQ and CBWFQ policies (with WRED on major data classes) for all 11 classes of traffic over the preferred Layer 2 WAN medium: ATM.

Every quarter, ABC, Inc., multicasts company meetings to all its branches and provides each branch with on-demand (unicast) e-learning content. However, because all the IP/TV servers belonging to ABC, Inc., are located at the central campus, they see no need to provision a class for Streaming-Video in both directions on the WAN links. Therefore, the company has chosen to eliminate this class from the branch router WAN edge configurations and redistribute the bandwidth between the Mission-Critical Data class and the Transactional Data class.

Currently, the branch access switches do not have the capability to classify and mark traffic, although they plan to eventually deploy switches in their branches with such capabilities (including dual-rate policing and marking). In the meantime, ABC, Inc., will mark all branch-to-campus traffic on the branch router's LAN edge on ingress. When the budget enables them to upgrade their branch switches, marking policies dependent on Layer 3 or Layer 4 criteria will be pushed out to the branch access switch (based on designs covered in Chapter 12). However, policies will remain on the branch router's LAN edge to classify and mark applications that require stateful packet inspection (using NBAR).

ABC, Inc., also has been hit with a number of worms over the past few years and wants to do everything possible to limit and mitigate such attacks. The company has provisioned Scavenger-class QoS within the campus and WAN edges. Furthermore, ABC, Inc., has chosen to deploy NBAR policies to identify and drop known worms that might originate within their branches. These policies are included in the branch router's ingress QoS policies.

QoS designs for the WAN and LAN edges of one of ABC, Inc.'s, branch routers is illustrated in Figure 14-4 and detailed in Example 14-20.

Figure 14-4 *Case Study: Branch Router with 10-Class QoS Baseline WAN Edge Policies and DSCP-to-CoS Remapping and NBAR Classification Plus Worm-Dropping LAN Edge Policies*

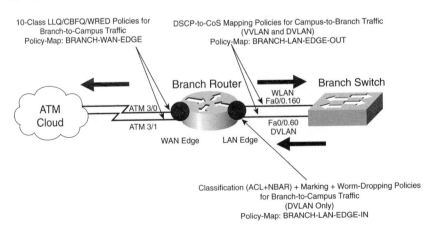

Example 14-20 *Case Study: Branch Router with 10-Class QoS Baseline WAN Edge Policies, DSCP-to-CoS Remapping, and NBAR Classification Plus Worm-Dropping LAN Edge Policies*

```
 !
 ip nbar port-map custom-01 tcp 3200 3201 3202 3203 3600        ! SAP custom PDLM
 ip nbar port-map custom-02 udp 1434                            ! SQL Slammer PDLM
 ip nbar port-map custom-03 tcp 5554 9996                       ! Sasser PDLM
 ip nbar port-map netbios tcp 137 139 445                       ! MS Blaster NetBIOS
 ip nbar port-map netbios udp 135 137 138 139 445              ! MS Blaster NetBIOS
 ip nbar custom MOONBEAM 8 ascii Moonbeam tcp range 21000 21999  ! "Moonbeam" PDLM
 !
 !
 class-map match-all BRANCH-MISSION-CRITICAL
    match access-group name MISSION-CRITICAL-SERVERS   ! MC Data ACL to reference
 !
 class-map match-any BRANCH-TRANSACTIONAL-DATA
    match protocol citrix                    ! Identifies Citrix traffic
    match protocol ldap                      ! Identifies LDAP traffic
    match protocol sqlnet                    ! Identifies Oracle SQL*NET traffic
    match protocol http url "*SalesReport*"   ! Identifies "SalesReport" URLs
    match protocol custom-01                 ! Identifies SAP traffic via PDLM
 !
 class-map match-any BRANCH-NET-MGMT
    match protocol snmp                      ! Identifies SNMP traffic
    match protocol syslog                    ! Identifies Syslog traffic
    match protocol telnet                    ! Identifies Telnet traffic
    match protocol nfs                       ! Identifies NFS traffic
    match protocol dns                       ! Identifies DNS traffic
    match protocol icmp                      ! Identifies ICMP traffic
    match protocol tftp                      ! Identifies TFTP traffic
 !
 class-map match-all BRANCH-BULK-DATA
    match access-group name BULK-DATA-APPS   ! Reference ACL for Bulk Data apps
 !
 class-map match-any BRANCH-SCAVENGER
    match protocol napster                   ! Identifies Napster traffic
    match protocol gnutella                  ! Identifies Gnutella traffic
    match protocol fasttrack                 ! Identifies KaZaa (v1) traffic
    match protocol kazaa2                    ! Identifies KaZaa (v2) traffic
 !
 class-map match-all SQL-SLAMMER
    match protocol custom-02                 ! Matches the custom Slammer PDLM
    match packet length min 404 max 404      ! Matches the packet length (376+28)
 !
 class-map match-any WORMS
    match protocol http url "*.ida*"         ! CodeRed
    match protocol http url "*cmd.exe*"      ! CodeRed
    match protocol http url "*root.exe*"     ! CodeRed
    match protocol http url "*readme.eml*"   ! NIMDA
    match class-map SQL-SLAMMER              ! SQL Slammer class-map
    match protocol exchange                  ! MS Blaster (TCP 135)
    match protocol netbios                   ! MS Blaster NetBIOS PDLM
```

continues

Example 14-20 *Case Study: Branch Router with 10-Class QoS Baseline WAN Edge Policies, DSCP-to-CoS Remapping, and NBAR Classification Plus Worm-Dropping LAN Edge Policies (Continued)*

```
   match protocol custom-03              ! Sasser custom PDLM
   match protocol MOONBEAM               ! "Moonbeam" PDLM
 !
 !
class-map match-all VOICE
   match ip dscp ef                ! IP Phones mark Voice to EF
class-map match-all INTERACTIVE-VIDEO
   match ip dscp af41 af42         ! Recommended markings for IP/VC
class-map match-any CALL-SIGNALING
   match ip dscp cs3               ! Future Call-Signaling marking
   match ip dscp af31              ! Current Call-Signaling marking
class-map match-all ROUTING
   match ip dscp cs6               ! Routers mark Routing traffic to CS6
class-map match-all NET-MGMT
   match ip dscp cs2               ! Net-Mgmt apps are marked via NBAR ingress policy
class-map match-all MISSION-CRITICAL-DATA
   match ip dscp 25                ! MC Data apps are marked via ACL ingress policy
class-map match-all TRANSACTIONAL-DATA
   match ip dscp af21 af22         ! Transactional apps are marked via NBAR policy
class-map match-all BULK-DATA
   match ip dscp af11 af12         ! Bulk Data apps are marked via ACL ingress policy
class-map match-all SCAVENGER
   match ip dscp cs1               ! Scavenger apps are marked via NBAR ingress policy
 !
 !
policy-map BRANCH-LAN-EDGE-OUT    ! Enhanced Packet Marking DSCP-to-CoS policy
   class class-default
     set cos dscp                 ! Default DSCP-to-CoS marking
 !
 !
policy-map BRANCH-LAN-EDGE-IN     ! BRANCH LAN Edge Ingress Marking Policy
   class BRANCH-MISSION-CRITICAL
     set ip dscp 25               ! Marks Mission-Critical apps to DSCP 25
   class BRANCH-TRANSACTIONAL-DATA
     set ip dscp af21             ! Marks Transactional Data apps to DSCP AF21
   class BRANCH-NET-MGMT
     set ip dscp cs2              ! Marks Net Mgmt apps to DSCP CS2
   class BRANCH-BULK-DATA
     set ip dscp af11             ! Marks Bulk Data apps to DSCP AF11
   class BRANCH-SCAVENGER
     set ip dscp cs1              ! Marks Scavenger apps to DSCP CS1
   class WORMS
     drop                         ! Drops all known worms
   class class-default
     set ip dscp default          ! Marks everything else to DSCP 0
 !
 !
policy-map BRANCH-WAN-EDGE
   class VOICE
     priority percent 18          ! Voice gets 552 kbps of LLQ
   class INTERACTIVE-VIDEO
```

Example 14-20 *Case Study: Branch Router with 10-Class QoS Baseline WAN Edge Policies, DSCP-to-CoS Remapping, and NBAR Classification Plus Worm-Dropping LAN Edge Policies (Continued)*

```
      priority percent 15            ! 384 kbps IP/VC needs 460 kbps of LLQ
     class CALL-SIGNALING
      bandwidth percent 5            ! Minimal BW guarantee for Call-Signaling
     class ROUTING
      bandwidth percent 3            ! Routing class gets 3% explicit BW guarantee
     class NET-MGMT
      bandwidth percent 2            ! Net-Mgmt class gets 2% explicit BW guarantee
     class MISSION-CRITICAL-DATA
      bandwidth percent 15           ! Mission-Critical class gets min 15% BW guarantee
      random-detect                  ! Enables WRED on Mission-Critical Data class
     class TRANSACTIONAL-DATA
      bandwidth percent 12           ! Transactional-Data class gets min 12% BW guarantee
      random-detect dscp-based       ! Enables DSCP-WRED on Transactional-Data class
     class BULK-DATA
      bandwidth percent 4            ! Bulk Data class gets 4% BW guarantee
      random-detect dscp-based       ! Enables DSCP-WRED on Bulk-Data class
     class SCAVENGER
      bandwidth percent 1            ! Scavenger class is throttled
     class class-default
      bandwidth percent 25           ! Default class gets min 30% BW guarantee
      random-detect                  ! Enables WRED on the default class
     !
     ...
     !
     interface FastEthernet0/0
      no ip address
      speed auto
      duplex auto
     !
     interface FastEthernet0/0.60
      description DVLAN SUBNET 10.1.60.0
      encapsulation dot1Q 60
      ip address 10.1.60.1 255.255.255.0
      service-policy output BRANCH-LAN-EDGE-OUT      ! Restores CoS on Data VLAN
      service-policy input BRANCH-LAN-EDGE-IN        ! Marks data and drops worms
     !
     interface FastEthernet0/0.160
      description VVLAN SUBNET 10.1.160.0
      encapsulation dot1Q 160
      ip address 10.1.160.1 255.255.255.0
      service-policy output BRANCH-LAN-EDGE-OUT      ! Restores CoS on Voice VLAN
     !
     ...
     !
     interface ATM3/0
      no ip address
      no atm ilmi-keepalive
      ima-group 0                                    ! ATM3/0 added to ATM IMA group 0
      no scrambling-payload
```

continues

Example 14-20 *Case Study: Branch Router with 10-Class QoS Baseline WAN Edge Policies, DSCP-to-CoS Remapping, and NBAR Classification Plus Worm-Dropping LAN Edge Policies (Continued)*

```
 !
 interface ATM3/1
  no ip address
  no atm ilmi-keepalive
  ima-group 0                                ! ATM3/1 added to ATM IMA group 0
  no scrambling-payload
 !
 ...
 !
 interface ATM3/IMA0
  no ip address
  no atm ilmi-keepalive
 !
 interface ATM3/IMA0.12 point-to-point
  ip address 10.6.12.1 255.255.255.252
  pvc 0/100
   vbr-nrt 3072 3072                         ! ATM PVC speed set for Dual-T1
   max-reserved-bandwidth 100                ! Overrides the default 75% BW limit
   service-policy output BRANCH-WAN-EDGE     ! Attaches MQC policy to the ATM PVC
  !
 !
 ...
 !
 ip access-list extended MISSION-CRITICAL-SERVERS
  permit ip any 10.200.200.0 0.0.0.255       ! MC Data Server-Farm Subnet
 !
 ip access-list extended BULK-DATA-APPS
  permit tcp any any eq ftp                  ! Identifies FTP Control traffic
  permit tcp any any eq ftp-data             ! Identifies FTP Default traffic
  permit tcp any any eq pop3                 ! Identifies POP3 E-mail traffic
  permit tcp any any eq 143                  ! Identifies IMAP E-mail traffic
 !
```

Verification commands:

- **show policy map**
- **show policy-map interface**
- **show ip nbar port-map**
- **show atm pvc**
- **show ima interface atm**

Summary

Although the QoS design recommendations for branch routers are very similar to and are related to the QoS recommendations for WAN aggregators, this chapter examined three unique considerations of branch routers.

The first consideration is whether applications provisioned over the WAN are bidirectional or unidirectional. Some unidirectional applications, such as Streaming-Video, provisioned on the WAN aggregator WAN edge do not need to be provisioned correspondingly on the branch router's WAN edge. Bandwidth from unidirectional application classes can be redistributed among other preferential application classes on the branch router's WAN edge.

The second consideration unique to branch routers is that ingress marking might need to be performed on branch-to-campus traffic. This might be because the remote branch access switch does not have the capability to classify and mark traffic, or it might be because some applications require stateful packet inspection (NBAR) to identify them correctly. In either case, ingress marking policies would be required on the branch router's LAN edge, on the data VLAN's subinterface (the voice VLAN traffic markings are trusted). Branch-to-campus traffic can be identified by Layer 3 parameters (such as destination subnet), Layer 4 parameters (such as well-known TCP/UDP ports), or NBAR PDLMs. An example of each type of classification is provided. Additionally, optional DSCP-to-CoS mapping policies (for restoring 802.1p CoS markings that were lost when campus-originated traffic traversed the WAN media) can be set on the branch router's LAN edge.

A third unique consideration in branch QoS design is that branch router ingress LAN edges are a strategic place to deploy NBAR policies for worm identification and policing. NBAR policies can be used to identify and drop Code Red, NIMDA, SQL Slammer, RPC DCOM/W32/MS Blaster, Sasser, and other worms. This chapter discussed an extension of the NBAR feature that enables administrators to program the strings that they want NBAR to search packet payloads for; this feature enables NBAR policies to be used to identify new worms that undoubtedly will be released in the future.

Finally, a case study was presented illustrating how these three unique considerations could be combined in a complex branch router design.

Further Reading

Cisco IOS documentation:

- Class-based marking (Cisco IOS Release 12.1.5T): http://www.cisco.com/univercd/cc/td/doc/product/software/ios121/121newft/121t/121t5/cbpmark2.htm.

- Enhanced packet marking (Cisco IOS Release 12.2.13T): http://www.cisco.com/univercd/cc/td/doc/product/software/ios122/122newft/122t/122t13/ftenpkmk.htm.

- NBAR overview (Cisco IOS Release 12.3): http://www.cisco.com/univercd/cc/td/doc/product/software/ios122/122cgcr/fqos_c/fqcprt1/qcfclass.htm#1003102.

- Network-Based Application Recognition (Cisco IOS Release 12.1.5T): http://www.cisco.com/univercd/cc/td/doc/product/software/ios122/122cgcr/fqos_c/fqcprt1/qcfnbar.htm.

- Network-Based Application Recognition (Cisco IOS Release 12.2.8T): http://www.cisco.com/univercd/cc/td/doc/product/software/ios122/122newft/122t/122t8/dtnbarad.htm.

- Network-Based Application Recognition (Cisco IOS Release 12.3[4]T): http://www.cisco.com/univercd/cc/td/doc/product/software/ios122/122newft/122t/122t8/dtnbarad.htm.

Cisco SAFE whitepapers:

- SAFE worm mitigation: http://www.cisco.com/en/US/netsol/ns340/ns394/ns171/ns128/networking_solutions_white_paper09186a00801e120c.shtml.

- Using Network-Based Application Recognition and ACLs for blocking the Code Red worm: http://www.cisco.com/en/US/products/hw/routers/ps359/products_tech_note09186a00800fc176.shtml.

- How to protect your network against the NIMDA virus: http://www.cisco.com/en/US/products/sw/iosswrel/ps1835/products_tech_note09186a0080110d17.shtml.

- SAFE SQL Slammer worm attack mitigation: http://www.cisco.com/en/US/netsol/ns340/ns394/ns171/ns128/networking_solutions_white_paper09186a00801cd7f5.shtml.

- SAFE RPC DCOM/W32/Blaster attack mitigation: http://www.cisco.com/en/US/netsol/ns340/ns394/ns171/ns128/networking_solutions_white_paper09186a00801b2391.shtml.

- Combating the Internet worm Sasser: http://www.cisco.com/application/pdf/en/us/guest/netsol/ns441/c664/cdccont_0900aecd800f613b.pdf.

VPN QoS Design

Part V of this book provides an in-depth discussion of QoS considerations and designs for both MPLS and IPSec VPNs. MPLS VPN QoS design is examined from both the enterprise subscriber's perspective, covering important considerations and designs for mapping into service-provider models, and also from the service provider's perspective, including MPLS DiffServ Tunneling modes and MPLS Traffic Engineering (in brief). IPSec VPN designs are considered for both site-to-site scenarios and telecommuter scenarios.

The chapters in this part of the book are as follows:

MPLS VPN QoS design typically is viewed from two distinct perspectives:

- The enterprise customer subscribing to the MPLS VPN service
- The service provider provisioning edge and core QoS within the MPLS VPN service

To achieve end-to-end service levels, enterprise and service-provider QoS policies must be consistent and complimentary. Therefore, QoS considerations and design recommendations for both the enterprise and service provider are presented in this chapter. The following topics are discussed:

- Enterprise-to-service provider mapping models
- Service provider-to-enterprise models
- MPLS DiffServ tunneling modes
- DiffServ in the backbone
- MPLS traffic engineering

CHAPTER 15

MPLS VPN QoS Design

MPLS is a combination of routing and switching technologies that can provide scalable VPNs with end-to-end quality of service.

Many customers are turning to service providers that offer MPLS VPN services as private WAN alternatives. One of the main reasons for this is the any-to-any connectivity capabilities of MPLS VPNs. However, this full-mesh nature in itself poses significant QoS implications to enterprise customers and service providers alike—namely, that they both need to comanage QoS in a cooperative and complementary fashion to achieve end-to-end service levels.

This chapter examines in detail QoS considerations that enterprise customers need to bear in mind when subscribing to MPLS VPNs, including how best to map into various service-provider MPLS VPN QoS models.

Service provider-edge QoS considerations are reviewed in depth, including egress queuing models and MPLS DiffServ tunneling modes (Uniform, Short Pipe, and Pipe). Furthermore, service-provider core QoS considerations are reviewed, including aggregate bandwidth provisioning and DiffServ in the backbone. MPLS traffic engineering as it relates to QoS is covered, along with two detailed examples: MPLS per-VPN traffic engineering and MPLS DiffServ traffic engineering.

This chapter concludes with a case study that shows how these designs can be combined in a complex MPLS VPN end-to-end scenario.

NOTE   This chapter addresses QoS design for MPLS VPNs, not the theory and operation of MPLS VPNs themselves. It is assumed that the reader is familiar with basic MPLS VPN architectures and technologies. For a detailed discussion of MPLS VPNs, refer to the Cisco Press books *MPLS and VPN Architectures*, Volumes I and II, by Ivan Pepelnjak and Jim Guichard; *Traffic Engineering with MPLS*, by Eric Osborne and Ajay Simha; and *Advanced MPLS Design and Implementation*, by Vivek Alwayn.

Where Is QoS Needed over an MPLS VPN?

MPLS VPN architectures are comprised of customer edge (CE) routers, provider-edge (PE) routers, and provider (P) routers. MPLS VPNs provide fully meshed Layer 3 virtual WAN services to all interconnected CE routers, as outlined by RFC 2547. This fully meshed characteristic of MPLS VPNs presents a significant design implication to traditional Layer 2 WAN QoS design.

Because of cost, scalability, and manageability constraints, traditional private WAN designs rarely use full-mesh models. Instead, most Layer 2 WAN designs revolve around a hub-and-spoke model, implementing either a centralized hub design or the more efficient regional hub design. Under such hub-and-spoke designs, QoS primarily is administered at the hub router by the enterprise. As long as the service provider meets the contracted service levels, the packets received at remote branches will reflect the scheduling policies of the hub router (sometimes referred to as a *WAN aggregator*). The WAN aggregator controls not only campus-to-branch traffic, but also branch-to-branch traffic (which is homed through the hub). Under traditional hub-and-spoke models, QoS principally is administered by the enterprise customer, as shown in Figure 15-1.

Figure 15-1   *QoS Administration in Traditional Hub-and-Spoke Layer 2 WAN Design*

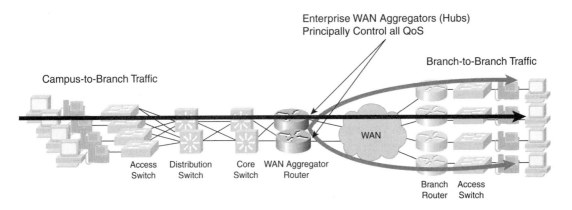

However, with the advent of MPLS VPN service offerings that inherently offer full-mesh connectivity, the QoS administration paradigm shifts. Under a full-mesh design, the hub router still administers QoS for all campus-to-branch traffic, but it no longer fully controls the QoS for branch-to-branch traffic. Although it might appear that the only required workaround for this new scenario is to ensure that QoS is provisioned on all branch routers, this is insufficient because it addresses only part of the issue.

For example, consider the case of provisioning any-to-any videoconferencing. As with a traditional Layer 2 WAN design, a scheduling policy to prioritize IP/VC on the WAN aggregator is required. Then the enterprise must properly provision similar priority scheduling for IP/VC on the branch routers also. In this manner, any videoconferencing calls from the campus to the branch (and also from branch to branch) are protected against traffic of lesser importance flowing between the *same* sites. The complexity of the fully meshed model arises when considering that contending traffic might not always come for the same sites, but could come from *any* site. Furthermore, the enterprise no longer fully controls QoS for branch-to-branch traffic because this traffic no longer is homed through a hub. Continuing the example, if a videoconferencing call is set up between two branches and a user from one of the branches also initiates a large FTP download from the central site, the potential for oversubscription of the PE-to-CE link from the fully meshed MPLS VPN cloud into one of the branches becomes very real, likely causing drops from the IP/VC call.

The only way to guarantee service levels in such a scenario is for the service provider to provision QoS scheduling that is compatible with the enterprise's policies on all PE links to remote branches. This is what creates the paradigm shift in QoS administration for fully meshed topologies. Namely, enterprises and service providers must cooperate to jointly administer QoS over MPLS VPNs, as shown in Figure 15-2.

Figure 15-2 *QoS Administration in Fully Meshed MPLS VPN Design*

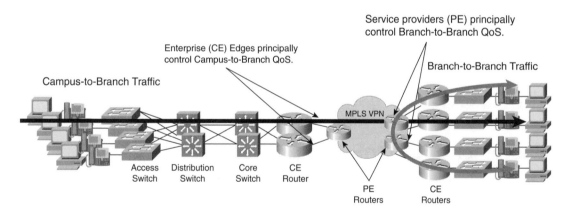

Queuing policies are mandatory on CE and PE routers because of the full-mesh implications of MPLS VPNs. PE routers also typically have policing (and markdown) policies on ingress to enforce SLAs.

QoS policies on P routers are optional. Such policies are optional because some service providers overprovision their MPLS core networks and, as such, do not require any additional QoS policies within their backbones; on the other hand, other providers might implement simplified DiffServ policies within their cores or might even deploy MPLS traffic engineering (MPLS TE) to handle congestion scenarios within their backbones. Figure 15-3 summarizes the points where QoS policies can be provisioned within MPLS VPN architectures.

Figure 15-3 *Where QoS Is Required in MPLS VPN Architectures*

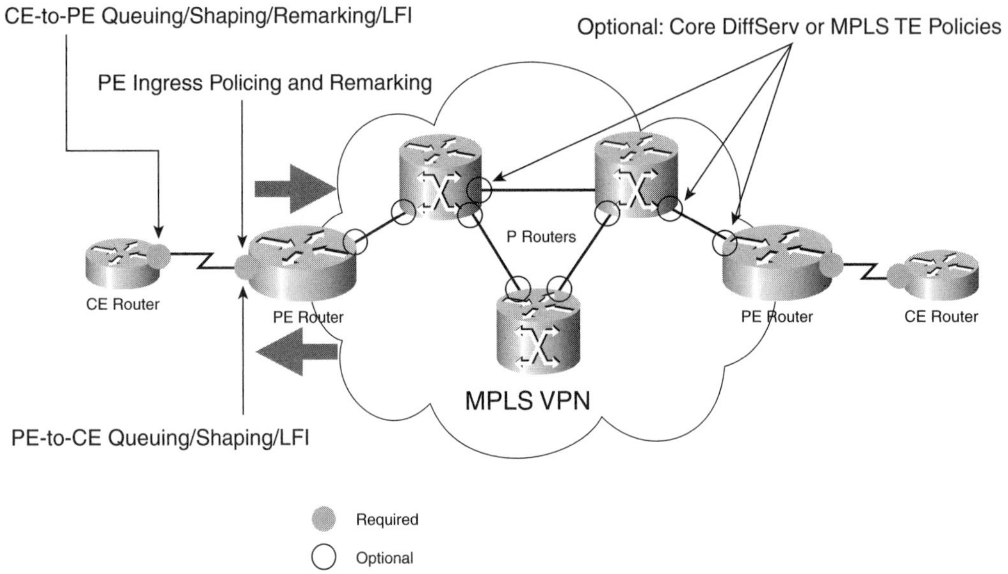

This design chapter first examines CE and PE QoS designs; then it overviews MPLS VPN core QoS options and designs.

Customer Edge QoS Design Considerations

In addition to the full-mesh implication of MPLS VPNs, these considerations should be kept in mind when considering MPLS VPN CE QoS design:

- Layer 2 access (link-specific) QoS design
- Service-provider service-level agreements (SLA)
- Enterprise-to-service provider mapping models

The following sections examine these considerations in more detail.

Layer 2 Access (Link-Specific) QoS Design

Although MPLS VPNs are essentially Layer 3 WANs, a Layer 2 access medium to connect to the MPLS VPN service provider is an obvious requirement. Most providers support Frame Relay and ATM as access media because this makes migration from Layer 2 WANs to Layer 3 MPLS VPNs easier and cheaper to manage; customers are not forced to convert hardware on hundreds (or, in some cases, thousands) of remote branch routers to connect to MPLS VPN providers.

It is important to recognize that Layer 2 QoS link-specific issues and designs remain the same with regular Layer 2 WAN edges or with Layer 3 MPLS VPN CE/PE edges. For example, shaping and LFI recommendations for slow-speed FR links are identical whether the link is used for a Layer 2 WAN or for a Layer 3 MPLS VPN access link. Again, this makes migration easier to manage because link-specific QoS designs do not need to be changed (although the service policy itself might require minor modification, which is discussed in more detail shortly).

In addition to FR and ATM for access, some service providers support Ethernet/Fast Ethernet as access media but usually guarantee a CIR of only subline rate. In such cases, hierarchical shaping and queuing policies on the CE edges are recommended, as illustrated later in this chapter.

Service-Provider Service-Level Agreements

End-to-end QoS is like a chain that is only as strong as the weakest link. Therefore, it's essential for enterprises (with converged networks) subscribing to MPLS VPN services to choose service providers that can provide the required SLAs for their converged networks. For example, these are the end-to-end SLA requirements of voice and interactive video:

- No more than 150 ms of one-way latency from mouth to ear (per ITU G.114 standard)
- No more than 30 ms of jitter
- No more than 1 percent loss

As a subset of the trip, the service provider's component of the SLA must be considerably tighter. These SLAs are defined for Cisco-Powered Networks (CPN)–IP Multiservice Service Providers:

- No more than 60 ms of one-way latency from edge to edge
- No more than 20 ms of jitter
- No more than 0.5 percent loss

Figure 15-4 illustrates the interrelationship of these SLAs.

CPN-IP Multiservice Service Providers that meet these SLAs can be found at http://www.cisco.com/pcgi-bin/cpn/cpn_pub_bassrch.pl; choose the IP VPN Multiservice option.

To achieve such end-to-end SLAs, enterprise customers (managing CEs) and service providers (managing PEs and core Ps) must cooperate and be consistent in classifying, provisioning, and integrating their respective QoS designs. To this end, various mapping models have been developed to integrate enterprise requirements into service-provider solutions.

Figure 15-4 *CPN-IP Multiservice Service-Provider SLAs*

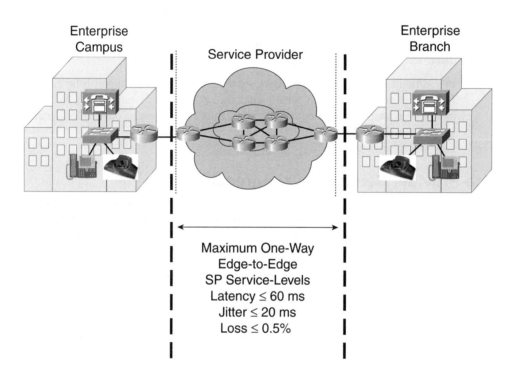

Maximum One-Way End-to-End Service-Levels
Latency ≤ 150 ms / Jitter ≤ 30 ms / Loss ≤ 1%

Enterprise
Campus

Service Provider

Enterprise
Branch

Maximum One-Way
Edge-to-Edge
SP Service-Levels
Latency ≤ 60 ms
Jitter ≤ 20 ms
Loss ≤ 0.5%

Enterprise-to-Service Provider Mapping Models

Although Cisco is adopting its new QoS Baseline initiative and designing tools such as
Cisco AutoQoS Enterprise to facilitate and simplify the deployment of advanced QoS
traffic models within the enterprise, to date, very few enterprises have deployed more than
a handful of traffic classes. Therefore, most service providers offer only a limited number
of classes within their MPLS VPN clouds. At times, this might require enterprises to
collapse the number of classes that they have provisioned to integrate into their service
provider's QoS models. The following caveats should be remembered when deciding how
best to collapse and integrate enterprise classes into various service-provider QoS models.

Voice and Video

Service providers typically offer only one Real-Time class or Priority class of service. If an enterprise wants to deploy both Voice and Interactive-Video (each of which is recommended to be provisioned with strict priority treatment) over their MPLS VPN, they might be faced with a dilemma. Which one should be assigned to the Real-Time class? Are there any implications about assigning both to the Real-Time class?

Keep in mind that voice and video should never both be assigned low-latency queuing on link speeds where serialization is a factor (≤ 768 kbps). Packets offered to the LLQ typically are not fragmented; thus, large IP/VC packets can cause excessive delays for VoIP packets on slow-speed links.

An alternative is to assign IP/VC to a nonpriority class, which entails not only the obvious caveat of lower service levels, but also possible traffic-mixing concerns, as discussed shortly.

Call-Signaling

VoIP requires provisioning not only of RTP bearer traffic, but also of Call-Signaling traffic, which is very lightweight and requires only a moderate amount of guaranteed bandwidth. Because the service levels applied to Call-Signaling traffic directly affect delay to the dial tone, it is important from the end user's expectations that Call-Signaling be protected. Service providers might not always offer a suitable class just for call signaling traffic itself, leading to the question of which other traffic classes Call-Signaling should be mixed with.

On links where serialization is not an issue (> 768 kbps), Call-Signaling could be provisioned into the Real-Time class, along with voice.

However, this is not recommended on slow-speed links where serialization *is* a factor. On such slow-speed links, Call-Signaling is best assigned to one of the preferential data classes for which the service provider provides a bandwidth guarantee.

It is important to realize that a guarantee applied to a service-provider class as a whole does not itself guarantee adequate bandwidth for an individual enterprise applications within the class.

Mixing TCP with UDP

It is a general best practice to not mix TCP-based traffic with UDP-based traffic (especially Streaming-Video) within a single service-provider class because of the behaviors of these protocols during periods of congestion. Specifically, TCP transmitters throttle back flows when drops are detected. Although some UDP applications have application-level windowing, flow control, and retransmission capabilities, most UDP transmitters are completely oblivious to drops and, thus, never lower transmission rates because of dropping.

When TCP flows are combined with UDP flows within a single service-provider class and the class experiences congestion, TCP flows continually lower their transmission rates, potentially giving up their bandwidth to UDP flows that are oblivious to drops. This effect is called TCP starvation/UDP dominance.

TCP starvation/UDP dominance likely occurs if (TCP-based) Mission-Critical Data is assigned to the same service-provider class as (UDP-based) Streaming-Video and the class experiences sustained congestion. Even if WRED is enabled on the service-provider class, the same behavior would be observed because WRED (for the most part) manages congestion only on TCP-based flows.

Granted, it is not always possible to separate TCP-based flows from UDP-based flows, but it is beneficial to be aware of this behavior when making such application-mixing decisions within a single service-provider class.

Marking and Re-Marking

Most service providers use Layer 3 marking attributes (IPP or DSCP) of packets offered to them to determine which service provider class of service the packet should be assigned to. Therefore, enterprises must mark or re-mark their traffic consistent with their service provider's admission criteria to gain the appropriate level of service. Additionally, service providers might re-mark at Layer 3 out-of-contract traffic within their cloud, which might affect enterprises that require consistent end-to-end Layer 3 markings.

A general DiffServ principle is to mark or trust traffic as close to the source as administratively and technically possible. However, certain traffic types might need to be re-marked before handoff to the service provider to gain admission to the correct class. If such re-marking is required, it is recommended that the re-marking be performed at the CE's egress edge, not within the campus. This is because service-provider service offerings likely will evolve or expand over time, and adjusting to such changes will be easier to manage if re-marking is performed only at the CE egress edge.

Additionally, in some cases, multiple types of traffic are required to be marked to the same DiffServ code point value to gain admission to the appropriate queue. For example, on high-speed links, it might be desired to send Voice, Interactive-Video, and Call-Signaling to the service provider's Real-Time class. If this service-provider class admits only DSCP EF and CS5, two of these three applications would be required to share a common code point. The class-based marking configuration in Example 15-1 shows how this can be done (in this example, both Interactive-Video and Call-Signaling are re-marked to share DSCP CS5).

Example 15-1 *CE (Egress) Enterprise-to-Service Provider Re-Marking Example*

```
!
class-map match-any VOICE
 match ip dscp ef
class-map match-all INTERACTIVE-VIDEO
```

Example 15-1 *CE (Egress) Enterprise-to-Service Provider Re-Marking Example (Continued)*

```
 match ip dscp af41
class-map match-any CALL-SIGNALING
 match ip dscp af31
 match ip dscp cs3
!
policy-map CE-EGRESS-EDGE
 class VOICE
  priority percent 18
 class INTERACTIVE-VIDEO
  priority percent 15
  set ip dscp cs5              ! Interactive-Video is remarked to CS5
 class CALL-SIGNALING
  priority percent 2           ! Call-Signaling gets LLQ for this scenario
  set ip dscp cs5              ! Call-Signaling is also remarked to CS5
 !
 !
 interface Serial1/0
  service-policy output CE-EGRESS-EDGE
 !
```

Verification commands:

- **show policy**
- **show policy interface**

Service providers might re-mark traffic at Layer 3 to indicate whether certain flows are out of contract. Although this is consistent with DiffServ standards, such as RFC 2597, it might present minor difficulties to enterprises that require consistent end-to-end Layer 3 marking (typically, for management or accounting purposes). In such cases, the enterprise can choose to apply re-marking policies as traffic is received back from the service provider's MPLS VPN (on the ingress direction of the enterprise's CE).

Class-based marking can be used again because it supports not only access lists for classification, but also Network-Based Application Recognition (NBAR).

Continuing and expanding on the previous example, the enterprise wants to restore the original markings that it set for Interactive-Video and Call-Signaling. Additionally, it wants to restore original markings for Oracle traffic (which it originally marked DSCP 25 and is using TCP port 9000 with) and DLSw+ traffic (originally marked AF21). Both of these data applications were handed off to the service provider marked as AF21, but they might have been marked down to AF22 within the service-provider cloud. Example 15-2 shows a configuration that enables such re-marking from the MPLS VPN. The "match-all" criteria of the class maps performs a logical AND operation against the potential markings and re-markings, and the access list (or NBAR-supported protocol) that sifts the applications apart. The policy is applied on the same CE link, but in the ingress direction.

Example 15-2 *CE (Ingress) Service Provider-to-Enterprise Re-Marking Example*

```
!
class-map match-all REMARKED-INTERACTIVE-VIDEO
  match ip dscp cs5
  match access-group 101          ! Interactive-Video must be CS5 AND UDP
!
class-map match-all REMARKED-CALL-SIGNALING
  match ip dscp cs5
  match access-group 102          ! Call-Signaling must be CS5 AND TCP
!
class-map match-all REMARKED-ORACLE
  match ip dscp af21  af22         ! Oracle may have been remarked to AF22
  match access-group 103          ! Oracle uses TCP port 9000
!
class-map match-all REMARKED-DLSW+
  match ip dscp af21  af22         ! DLSw+ may have been remarked to AF22
  match protocol dlsw             ! DLSw+ is identified by NBAR
!
policy-map CE-INGRESS-EDGE
 class REMARKED-INTERACTIVE-VIDEO
  set ip dscp af41              ! Restores Interactive-Video marking to AF41
 class REMARKED-CALL-SIGNALING
  set ip dscp af31              ! Restores Call-Signaling marking to AF31
 class REMARKED-ORACLE
  set ip dscp 25               ! Restores Oracle marking to DSCP 25
 class REMARKED-DLSW+
  set ip dscp af21             ! Restores DLSw+ marking to AF21
 !
 !
interface serial 1/0
 service-policy output CE-EGRESS-EDGE
 service-policy input  CE-INGRESS-EDGE        ! Marking restoration on ingress
 !
 !
access-list 101 permit udp any any          ! Identifies UDP traffic
access-list 102 permit tcp any any          ! Identifies TCP traffic
access-list 103 permit tcp any eq 9000 any  ! Identifies Oracle on TCP 9000
!
```

Verification commands:

- **show policy**
- **show policy interface**

Three-Class Provider-Edge Model: CE Design

In this model, the service provider offers three classes of service: Real-Time (strict priority, available in 5-percent increments), Critical Data (guaranteed bandwidth), and Best-Effort. The admission criterion for the Real-Time class is either DSCP EF or CS5; the admission criterion for Critical Data is DSCP CS6, AF31, or CS3. All other code points are re-marked to 0. Additionally, out-of-contract AF31 traffic can be marked down within the service provider's MPLS VPN cloud to AF32.

Under such a model, there is no recommended provision for protecting Streaming-Video (following the "Don't mix TCP with UDP" guideline), nor is there a service-provider class suitable for bulk data, which consists of large, nonbursty TCP sessions that could drown out smaller data transactions. Figure 15-5 shows a re-marking diagram for a three-class service-provider model.

Figure 15-5 *Three-Class Provider-Edge Model Re-Marking Diagram*

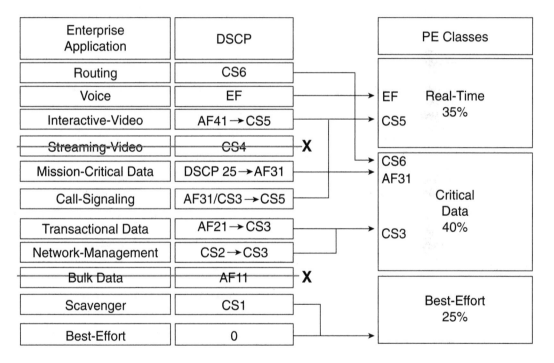

Example 15-3 shows an example CE configuration for an advanced enterprise model mapping (over a dual-T1 link) into a three-class service-provider model.

Example 15-3 *CE Configuration for Three-Class Provider-Edge Model*

```
!
class-map match-all ROUTING
 match ip dscp cs6
class-map match-all VOICE
 match ip dscp ef
```

continues

Example 15-3 *CE Configuration for Three-Class Provider-Edge Model (Continued)*

```
class-map match-all INTERACTIVE-VIDEO
 match ip dscp af41
class-map match-all MISSION-CRITICAL-DATA
 match ip dscp 25
class-map match-any CALL-SIGNALING
 match ip dscp af31
 match ip dscp cs3
class-map match-all TRANSACTIONAL-DATA
 match ip dscp af21
class-map match-all NETWORK-MANAGEMENT
 match ip dscp cs2
class-map match-all SCAVENGER
 match ip dscp cs1
!
!
policy-map CE-THREE-CLASS-SP-MODEL
 class ROUTING
  bandwidth percent 3   ! Routing is assigned (by default) to Critical SP class
 class VOICE
  priority percent 18   ! Voice is admitted to Realtime SP class
 class INTERACTIVE-VIDEO
  priority percent 15
  set ip dscp cs5        ! Interactive-Video is assigned to the Realtime SP class
 class CALL-SIGNALING
  priority percent 2     ! Call-Signaling gets LLQ for this scenario
  set ip dscp cs5        ! Call-Signaling is assigned to the Realtime SP class
 class MISSION-CRITICAL-DATA
  bandwidth percent 20
  random-detect
  set ip dscp af31       ! MC Data is assigned to the Critical SP class
 class TRANSACTIONAL-DATA
  bandwidth percent 15
  random-detect
  set ip dscp cs3        ! Transactional Data is assigned to Critical SP class
 class NETWORK-MANAGEMENT
  bandwidth percent 2
  set ip dscp cs3        ! Net Mgmt is assigned to Critical SP class
 class SCAVENGER
  bandwidth percent 1
 class class-default
  bandwidth percent 24
  random-detect
 !
```

Verification commands:

- **show policy**
- **show policy interface**

The **max-reserved-bandwidth** command might be required on the interface to which the previously discussed policy is applied.

Four-Class Provider-Edge Model: CE Design

Building on the previous model, a fourth class is added that can be used for either Bulk Data or Streaming-Video. The admission criterion for this new class is either DSCP AF21 or CS2. The re-marking diagram shown in Figure 15-6 illustrates how this new class can be used for Streaming-Video and (primarily UDP-based) Network-Management traffic.

Figure 15-6 *Four-Class Provider-Edge Model Re-Marking Diagram*

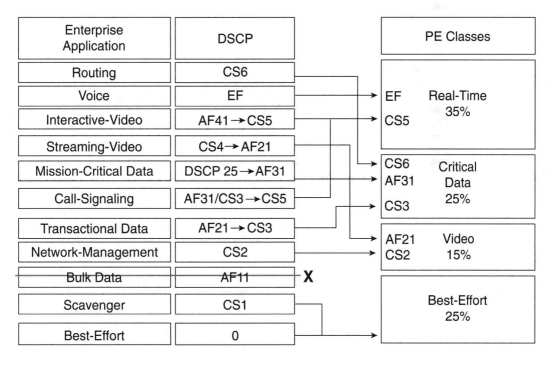

Example 15-4 shows an example CE configuration for an advanced enterprise model mapping (over a dual-T1 link) into a four-class service-provider model.

Example 15-4 *CE Configuration for Four-Class Provider-Edge Model*

```
!
class-map match-all ROUTING
 match ip dscp cs6
class-map match-all VOICE
 match ip dscp ef
class-map match-all INTERACTIVE-VIDEO
 match ip dscp af41
class-map match-all STREAMING-VIDEO
 match ip dscp cs4
class-map match-all MISSION-CRITICAL-DATA
 match ip dscp 25
class-map match-any CALL-SIGNALING
 match ip dscp af31
 match ip dscp cs3
class-map match-all TRANSACTIONAL-DATA
 match ip dscp af21
class-map match-all NETWORK-MANAGEMENT
 match ip dscp cs2
class-map match-all SCAVENGER
 match ip dscp cs1
!
!
policy-map CE-FOUR-CLASS-SP-MODEL
 class ROUTING
  bandwidth percent 3  ! Routing is assigned (by default) to Critical SP class
 class VOICE
  priority percent 18  ! Voice is admitted to Realtime SP class
 class INTERACTIVE-VIDEO
  priority percent 15
  set ip dscp cs5       ! Interactive-Video is assigned to the Realtime SP class
 class STREAMING-VIDEO
  bandwidth percent 13
  set ip dscp af21      ! Streaming-Video is assigned to the Video SP class
 class CALL-SIGNALING
  priority percent 2   ! Call-Signaling gets LLQ for this scenario
  set ip dscp cs5       ! Call-Signaling is assigned to the Realtime SP class
 class MISSION-CRITICAL-DATA
  bandwidth percent 12
  random-detect
  set ip dscp af31      ! MC Data is assigned to the Critical SP class
 class TRANSACTIONAL-DATA
  bandwidth percent 10
  random-detect
  set ip dscp cs3       ! Transactional Data is assigned to Critical SP class
 class NETWORK-MANAGEMENT
  bandwidth percent 2 ! Net Mgmt (mainly UDP) is admitted to Video SP class
 class SCAVENGER
  bandwidth percent 1
 class class-default
  bandwidth percent 24
  random-detect
!
```

Verification commands:

- **show policy**
- **show policy interface**

The **max-reserved-bandwidth** command might be required on the interface to which the previously discussed policy is applied.

Five-Class Provider-Edge Model: CE Design

Building again on the previous model, a fifth class is added that also can be used for either Bulk Data or Streaming-Video (whichever wasn't used under the four-class model). The admission criterion for this new class is either DSCP AF11 or CS1, which necessitates the previously unrequired re-marking of the Scavenger class to DSCP 0 (so that it will not be admitted into the Bulk Data class, but will fall into the Best-Effort class). Figure 15-7 illustrates the re-marking required when using this new class for Bulk Data.

Figure 15-7 *Five-Class Provider-Edge Model Re-Marking Diagram*

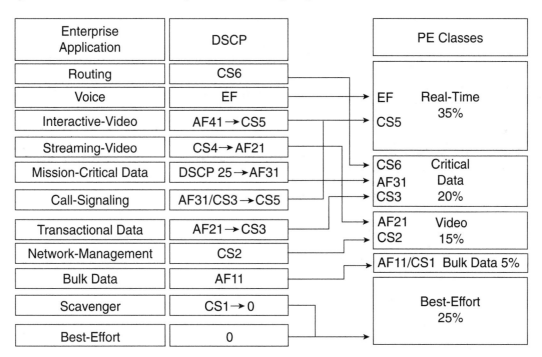

Example 15-5 shows an example CE configuration for a QoS Baseline enterprise model mapping (over a dual-T1 link) into a five-class service-provider model.

Example 15-5 *CE Configuration for Five-Class Provider-Edge Model*

```
!
class-map match-all ROUTING
 match ip dscp cs6
class-map match-all VOICE
 match ip dscp ef
class-map match-all INTERACTIVE-VIDEO
 match ip dscp af41
class-map match-all STREAMING-VIDEO
 match ip dscp cs4
class-map match-all MISSION-CRITICAL-DATA
 match ip dscp 25
class-map match-any CALL-SIGNALING
 match ip dscp af31
 match ip dscp cs3
class-map match-all TRANSACTIONAL-DATA
 match ip dscp af21
class-map match-all BULK-DATA
 match ip dscp af11
class-map match-all NETWORK-MANAGEMENT
 match ip dscp cs2
class-map match-all SCAVENGER
 match ip dscp cs1
!
!
policy-map CE-FIVE-CLASS-SP-MODEL
 class ROUTING
  bandwidth percent 3  ! Routing is assigned (by default) to Critical SP class
 class VOICE
  priority percent 18  ! Voice is admitted to Realtime SP class
 class INTERACTIVE-VIDEO
  priority percent 15
  set ip dscp cs5       ! Interactive-Video is assigned to the Realtime SP class
 class STREAMING-VIDEO
  bandwidth percent 13
  set ip dscp af21      ! Streaming-Video is assigned to the Video SP class
 class CALL-SIGNALING
  priority percent 2  ! Call-Signaling gets LLQ for this scenario
  set ip dscp cs5       ! Call-Signaling is assigned to the Realtime SP class
 class MISSION-CRITICAL-DATA
  bandwidth percent 12
  random-detect
  set ip dscp af31      ! MC Data is assigned to the Critical SP class
 class TRANSACTIONAL-DATA
  bandwidth percent 5
  random-detect
  set ip dscp cs3       ! Transactional Data is assigned to Critical SP class
 class NETWORK-MANAGEMENT
  bandwidth percent 2  ! Net Mgmt (mainly UDP) is admitted to Video SP class
 class BULK-DATA
  bandwidth percent 5  ! Bulk Data is assigned to Bulk SP class
  random-detect
 class SCAVENGER
```

Example 15-5 *CE Configuration for Five-Class Provider-Edge Model (Continued)*

```
    bandwidth percent 1
    set ip dscp 0              ! Scavenger is re-marked to 0
  class class-default
    bandwidth percent 24
    random-detect
!
```

Verification commands:

- **show policy**
- **show policy interface**

The **max-reserved-bandwidth** command might be required on the interface to which the preceding policy is applied.

Provider-Edge QoS Considerations

PE designs are relevant for service providers (and for enterprises that are self-managing their own MPLS VPNs). Two unique considerations for PE QoS design are discussed next:

- Service provider-to-enterprise models
- MPLS DiffServ tunneling modes

These considerations are examined in more detail in the following sections.

Service Provider-to-Enterprise Models

The PE edges facing customer CEs are complementary to the enterprise-to-service provider mapping models discussed previously. The PE designs for each class model (three, four, and five) are detailed in the following sections.

Three-Class Provider-Edge Model: PE Design

As outlined previously (and illustrated in Figure 15-5), in this model, the service provider offers three classes of service: Real-Time (strict priority, available in 5-percent increments), Critical Data (guaranteed bandwidth), and Best-Effort. The admission criterion for the Real-Time class is either DSCP EF or CS5; the admission criterion for Critical Data is DSCP CS6 (for customer routing traffic), AF31, or CS3. All other code points are re-marked to 0 by an ingress policer (not shown in this configuration example, but detailed later under the MPLS DiffServ tunneling examples). Additionally, service-provider policers can re-mark out-of-contract AF31 traffic down to AF32, which results in a higher drop preference because DSCP-based WRED is enabled on this class. As in previous examples, Example 15-6 is based on an access link of more than 3 Mbps.

Example 15-6 *PE Configuration for Three-Class Provider-Edge Model*

```
!
class-map match-any REALTIME
 match ip dscp ef
 match ip dscp cs5
class-map match-any CRITICAL-DATA
 match ip dscp cs6
 match ip dscp af31
 match ip dscp cs3
!
policy-map PE-THREE-CLASS-SP-MODEL
 class REALTIME
  priority percent 35          ! Realtime class gets 35% LLQ
 class CRITICAL-DATA
  bandwidth percent 40         ! Critical-Data SP class gets 40% CBWFQ
  random-detect dscp-based     ! DSCP-based WRED enabled on class
 class class-default
  fair-queue                   ! Best Effort SP class gets FQ
  random-detect                ! WRED enabled on Best Effort SP class
 !
```

Verification commands:

- **show policy**
- **show policy interface**

Four-Class Provider-Edge Model: PE Design

Building on the previous model (and as illustrated in Figure 15-6), a fourth class is added to this SP model, which can be used for either Bulk Data or Streaming-Video. The admission criterion for this new class is either DSCP AF21 or CS2. Out-of-contract AF21 traffic offered to this class can be marked down to AF22. In this particular example, the class is being called Video, but it is important to keep in mind that the customer can offer any traffic desired to this class, provided that it is marked appropriately. For this reason (although it normally is not required on UDP-based flows such as Streaming-Video), DSCP-based WRED is enabled on this class to aggressively drop out-of-contract traffic as needed. As in previous examples, Example 15-7 is based on an access link of more than 3 Mbps.

Example 15-7 *PE Configuration for Four-Class Provider-Edge Model*

```
!
class-map match-any REALTIME
 match ip dscp ef
 match ip dscp cs5
class-map match-any CRITICAL-DATA
 match ip dscp cs6
 match ip dscp af31
 match ip dscp cs3
```

Example 15-7 *PE Configuration for Four-Class Provider-Edge Model (Continued)*

```
class-map match-any VIDEO
 match ip dscp af21
 match ip dscp cs2
!
policy-map PE-FOUR-CLASS-SP-MODEL
 class REALTIME
  priority percent 35          ! Realtime SP class gets 35% LLQ
 class CRITICAL-DATA
  bandwidth percent 25         ! Critical-Data SP class gets 40% CBWFQ
  random-detect dscp-based     ! DSCP-based WRED enabled on class
 class VIDEO
  bandwidth percent 15         ! Video SP class gets 15% CBWFQ
  random-detect dscp-based     ! DSCP-based WRED enabled on "Video" SP class
 class class-default
  fair-queue                   ! Best Effort SP class gets FQ
  random-detect                ! WRED enabled on Best Effort SP class
!
```

Verification commands:

- **show policy**
- **show policy interface**

Five-Class Provider-Edge Model: PE Design

Building again on the previous model (and as illustrated in Figure 15-7), a fifth class is added that can be used for either Bulk Data or Video (whichever wasn't used under the four-class model). In this example, the new class is used for Bulk Data. The admission criterion for this new class is either DSCP AF11 or CS1. Out-of-contract AF11 traffic offered to this class can be re-marked to AF12 and can be discarded earlier by the DSCP-based WRED algorithm operating on the output queue for this class.

To prevent long TCP sessions of the Bulk Data SP class from dominating bandwidth intended for the Best-Effort class, a bandwidth guarantee is offered to the Best-Effort class. This guarantee might require the use of the **max-reserved-bandwidth** override under the applied interface configuration. As in the previous examples, an access link of more than 3 Mbps is assumed in Example 15-8.

Example 15-8 *PE Configuration for Five-Class Provider-Edge Model*

```
!
class-map match-any REALTIME
 match ip dscp ef
 match ip dscp cs5
class-map match-any CRITICAL-DATA
 match ip dscp cs6
 match ip dscp af31
```

continues

Example 15-8 *PE Configuration for Five-Class Provider-Edge Model*

```
  match ip dscp cs3
 class-map match-any VIDEO
  match ip dscp af21
  match ip dscp cs2
 class-map match-any BULK-DATA
  match ip dscp af11
  match ip dscp cs1
 !
 policy-map PE-FIVE-CLASS-SP-MODEL
  class REALTIME
   priority percent 35          ! Realtime SP class gets 35% LLQ
  class CRITICAL-DATA
   bandwidth percent 20         ! Critical-Data SP class gets 40% CBWFQ
   random-detect dscp-based     ! DSCP-based WRED enabled on class
  class VIDEO
   bandwidth percent 15         ! Video SP class gets 15% CBWFQ
   random-detect dscp-based     ! DSCP-based WRED enabled on "Video" SP class
  class BULK-DATA
   bandwidth percent 5          ! Bulk Data SP class gets 15% CBWFQ
   random-detect dscp-based     ! DSCP-based WRED enabled on Bulk Data SP class
  class class-default
   bandwidth percent 25         ! Best Effort SP class gets 25% CBWFQ
   random-detect                ! WRED enabled on Best Effort SP class
 !
```

Verification commands:

- **show policy**
- **show policy interface**

MPLS DiffServ Tunneling Modes

As described in previous examples, some service providers re-mark packets at Layer 3 to indicate whether traffic is in contract or out-of-contract. Although this conforms to DiffServ standards, such as RFC 2597, this is not always desirable from an enterprise customer's standpoint.

Because MPLS labels include 3 bits that commonly are used for QoS marking, it is possible to "tunnel DiffServ"—that is, preserve Layer 3 DiffServ markings through a service provider's MPLS VPN cloud while still performing re-marking (via MPLS EXP bits) within the cloud to indicate in- or out-of-contract traffic.

RFC 3270 defines three distinct modes of MPLS DiffServ tunneling; each is discussed in detail in the following sections:

- Uniform Mode
- Short Pipe Mode
- Pipe Mode

Uniform Mode

Uniform Mode generally is utilized when the customer and service provider share the same DiffServ domain, as in the case of an enterprise deploying its own MPLS VPN core.

In Uniform Mode, which is the default mode, the first 3 bits of the IP ToS field (IP Precedence bits) automatically are mapped to the MPLS EXP bits on the ingress PE as labels are pushed onto the packets.

If policers or any other mechanisms re-mark the MPLS EXP values within the MPLS core, these marking changes are propagated to lower-level labels and eventually are propagated to the IP ToS field (MPLS EXP bits are mapped to IP Precedence values on the egress PE).

Figure 15-8 shows the behavior of Uniform Mode MPLS DiffServ tunneling.

Figure 15-8 *MPLS DiffServ Uniform Tunneling Mode Operation*

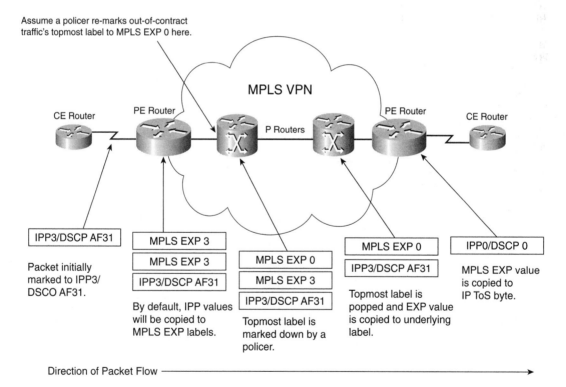

The mapping of IP Precedence to MPLS EXP is performed by default on PEs for customer-to-provider traffic.

However, for provider-to-customer egress traffic (from the MPLS VPN cloud), additional configuration is required on the PE to achieve mapping of MPLS EXP to IP Precedence. This is because the final label is popped (and discarded) when it is received from the MPLS VPN cloud and, therefore, cannot be used as a match criterion for policies applied to the egress interface of the final PE router (facing the destination CE). The solution is to copy the final MPLS EXP bit values to a temporary placeholder on PE ingress from the MPLS core (before the label is discarded) and then use these temporary placeholder values for setting the IP Precedence bits on egress to the customer CE.

Cisco IOS provides two such temporary placeholders, the QoS Group and the Discard Class. For Uniform Mode scenarios, it is recommended to copy the MPLS EXP values to QoS Group values on ingress from the MPLS VPN cloud. (The Discard Class is recommended for use in Pipe Mode scenarios only.) Then QoS Group values can be copied to IP Precedence values (on egress to the customer CE). Figure 15-9 illustrates the policies required for a single direction for Uniform Mode MPLS DiffServ tunneling. (This policy also would be required on the complementary interfaces for the reverse traffic direction.)

Figure 15-9 *MPLS DiffServ Uniform Tunneling Mode Policies*

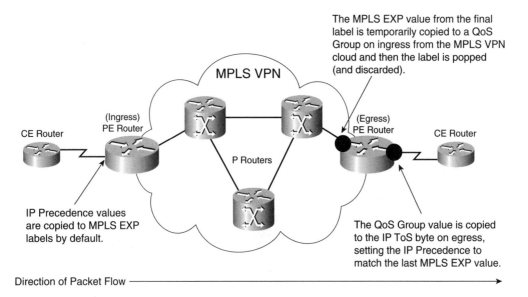

Example 15-9 shows the configuration for Uniform Mode operation on a PE.

Example 15-9 *PE Configuration for MPLS DiffServ Uniform Mode Tunneling*

```
!
policy-map MPLSEXP-TO-QOSGROUP
  class class-default
    set qos-group mpls experimental topmost  ! Copies MPLS EXP to QoS Group
!
 policy-map QOSGROUP-TO-IPP
  class class-default
    set precedence qos-group                 ! Copies QoS Group to IPP
!
...
!
interface ATM2/0
 no ip address
 no atm ilmi-keepalive
!
interface ATM2/0.1 point-to-point
 description ATM-OC3 TO MPLS VPN CORE        ! Link to/from MPLS VPN Core
 ip address 20.2.34.4 255.255.255.0
 pvc 0/304
  vbr-nrt 149760 149760
  service-policy input MPLSEXP-TO-QOSGROUP   ! MPLS EXP to QoS Group on ingress
 !
 tag-switching ip
!
...
!
interface FastEthernet1/0
 description FE TO CUSTOMER RED CE           ! Link to/from CE
 ip vrf forwarding RED
 ip address 10.1.45.4 255.255.255.0
 service-policy output QOSGROUP-TO-IPP       ! QoS Group to IPP on egress to CE
 !
```

Verification commands:

- **show policy**
- **show policy interface**

Of course, additional QoS policies (to these Uniform Mode tunneling policies), such as queuing or WRED, can be applied on the PE-to-CE egress link (as detailed earlier in the previous section).

Short Pipe Mode

Short Pipe Mode is utilized when the customer and service provider are in different DiffServ domains. (The service provider's DiffServ domain begins at the ingress PE's ingress interface and terminates on the egress PE's ingress interface.)

This mode is useful when the service provider wants to enforce its own DiffServ policy and the customer requests that its DiffServ information be preserved through the MPLS VPN cloud. Short Pipe Tunneling Mode provides DiffServ transparency through the service provider network (as does Pipe Mode).

The outmost label is utilized as the single most meaningful information source as it relates to the service provider's QoS PHB. On MPLS label imposition, the IP classification is not copied into the outermost label's EXP. Instead, the value for the MPLS EXP is set explicitly on the ingress PE's ingress interface, according to the service provider's administrative policies.

In the case of any re-marking occurrence within the service provider's MPLS VPN cloud, changes are limited to MPLS EXP re-marking only and are not propagated down to the underlying IP packet's ToS byte. Figure 15-10 shows the operation of Short Pipe Mode MPLS DiffServ tunneling.

Figure 15-10 *MPLS DiffServ Short Pipe Mode Tunneling Operation*

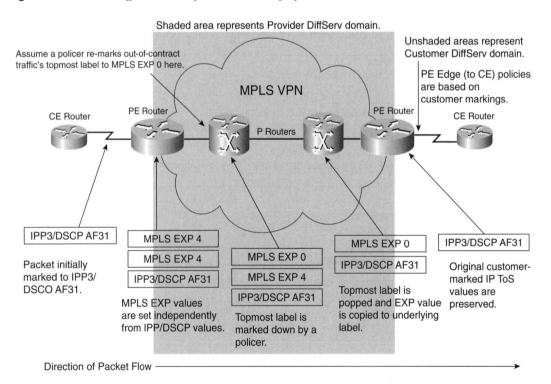

MPLS EXP values can be marked in any way that the provider wants to provide local significance. Figure 15-11 shows an example use of MPLS EXP markings to indicate in- or out-of-contract traffic for a five-class service-provider model.

Figure 15-11 *Five-Class Service Provider Model Short Pipe Mode Re-Marking Diagram*

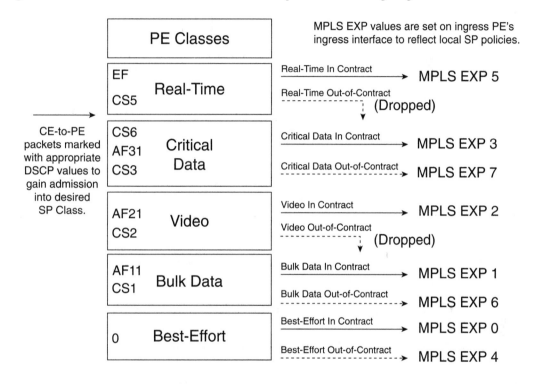

Figure 15-12 shows the ingress PE ingress interface re-marking policies for Short Pipe Mode, based on the re-marking diagram provided in Figure 15-11. No mapping from MPLS EXP to QoS Group is needed on the egress PE's ingress interface (as was required for Uniform Mode) because the MPLS EXP value loses relevance beyond this interface.

Any egress policies on the egress PE's egress interface (facing the customer's destination CE), are based on IP Precedence or DSCP values (which have remained untouched). This is the main difference between Short Pipe Mode and Pipe Mode.

Figure 15-12 shows the interfaces in which explicit policy configuration is required for Short Pipe Mode MPLS DiffServ tunneling.

Figure 15-12 *MPLS DiffServ Short Pipe Mode Tunneling Policies*

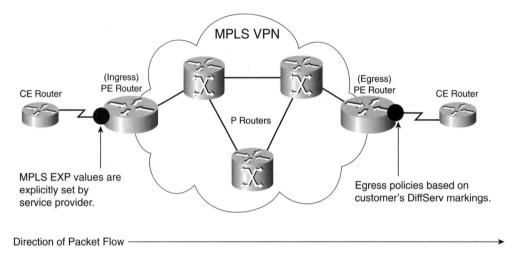

Direction of Packet Flow

Example 15-10 shows the configuration for Short Pipe Mode operation on a PE. Traffic received from CEs is marked explicitly (through MPLS EXP values) to reflect the service provider's policies. In this example, the customer is given a 3-Mbps CIR through an FE access link. The provider is using a five-class model with 35 percent for Real-Time traffic, 20 percent for Critical Data traffic, 15 percent for Video traffic, 5 percent for Bulk Data traffic, and 25 percent for Best-Effort traffic. On PE-to-CE links (in the egress direction), queuing and dropping policies based on customer IP DiffServ markings also are recommended (as was discussed previously).

Example 15-10 *PE Configuration for MPLS DiffServ Short Pipe Mode Tunneling*

```
!
class-map match-any REALTIME
  match ip dscp ef
  match ip dscp cs5
class-map match-any CRITICAL-DATA
  match ip dscp cs6
  match ip dscp af31
  match ip dscp cs3
class-map match-any VIDEO
  match ip dscp af21
  match ip dscp cs2
class-map match-any BULK-DATA
  match ip dscp af11
  match ip dscp cs1
!
!
  policy-map PE-FIVE-CLASS-SHORT-PIPE-MARKING
```

Example 15-10 *PE Configuration for MPLS DiffServ Short Pipe Mode Tunneling (Continued)*

```
    class REALTIME
     police cir 1050000
       conform-action set-mpls-exp-topmost-transmit 5   ! Conforming RT set to 5
       exceed-action drop                               ! Excess Realtime is dropped
    class CRITICAL-DATA
     police cir 600000
       conform-action set-mpls-exp-topmost-transmit 3   ! Critical Data set to 3
       exceed-action set-mpls-exp-topmost-transmit 7    ! Excess Critical set 7
    class VIDEO
     police cir 450000
       conform-action set-mpls-exp-topmost-transmit 2   ! Conforming Video set to 2
       exceed-action drop                               ! Excess Video dropped
    class BULK-DATA
     police cir 150000
       conform-action set-mpls-exp-topmost-transmit 1   ! Conforming Bulk set to 1
       exceed-action set-mpls-exp-topmost-transmit 6    ! Excess Bulk set to 6
    class class-default
     police cir 750000
       conform-action set-mpls-exp-topmost-transmit 0   ! Conforming BE set to 0
       exceed-action set-mpls-exp-topmost-transmit 4    ! Excess BE set to 4
 !
 …
 !
interface FastEthernet1/0
 description FE TO CUSTOMER RED CE                       ! Link to/from CE
 ip vrf forwarding RED
 ip address 10.1.12.2 255.255.255.0
 service-policy input PE-FIVE-CLASS-SHORT-PIPE-MARKING
 !
```

Verification commands:

* **show policy**
* **show policy interface**

Pipe Mode

The main difference between Short Pipe Mode and Pipe Mode MPLS DiffServ tunneling is that the PE egress policies (toward the customer CEs) are provisioned according to the *service provider's* explicit markings and re-markings, not the enterprise customer's IP DiffServ markings (although these are preserved). As with Short Pipe Mode, any changes to label markings that occur within the service provider's cloud do not get propagated to the IP ToS byte when the packet leaves the MPLS network.

Because egress PE-to-CE QoS policies in Pipe Mode are dependent on the last MPLS EXP value, this value must be preserved before the final label is popped. A temporary place-holder (as used in Uniform Mode operation) is again required. On the final PE router in a given path, the MPLS EXP value is copied to the QoS Group value. Optionally, a Discard Class value also might set drop preference at the same time. Thereafter, egress queuing or dropping policies are performed based on these QoS Group/Discard Class values. Figure 15-13 illustrates the Pipe Mode MPLS DiffServ tunneling operation.

Figure 15-13 *MPLS DiffServ Pipe Mode Tunneling Operation*

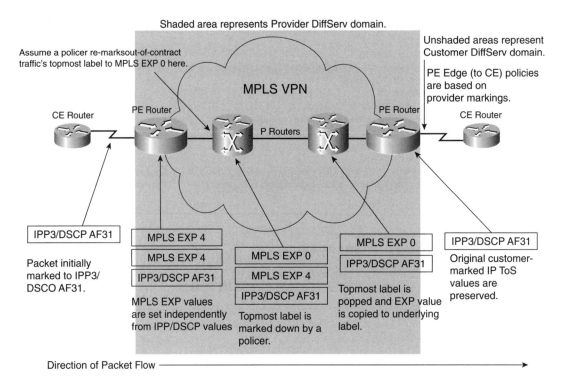

QoS Groups and Discard Classes can be combined to provide virtual DiffServ PHB classification. For example, RFC 2597 assured-forwarding PHBs can be mimicked using QoS Group values 1 through 4 (to represent the AF class) coupled with Discard Class values 1 through 3 (to represent the drop preference). In general, QoS Group and Discard Class values are arbitrary and have only local significance. However, an exception is found when WRED is configured to selectively drop based on Discard Class values, in which case the lower Discard Class values are dropped first (by default). If no Discard Class value is assigned explicitly, the value defaults to 0.

Figure 15-14 shows the points where policies are required for Pipe Mode MPLS DiffServ tunneling.

Figure 15-14 *MPLS DiffServ Pipe Mode Tunneling Policies*

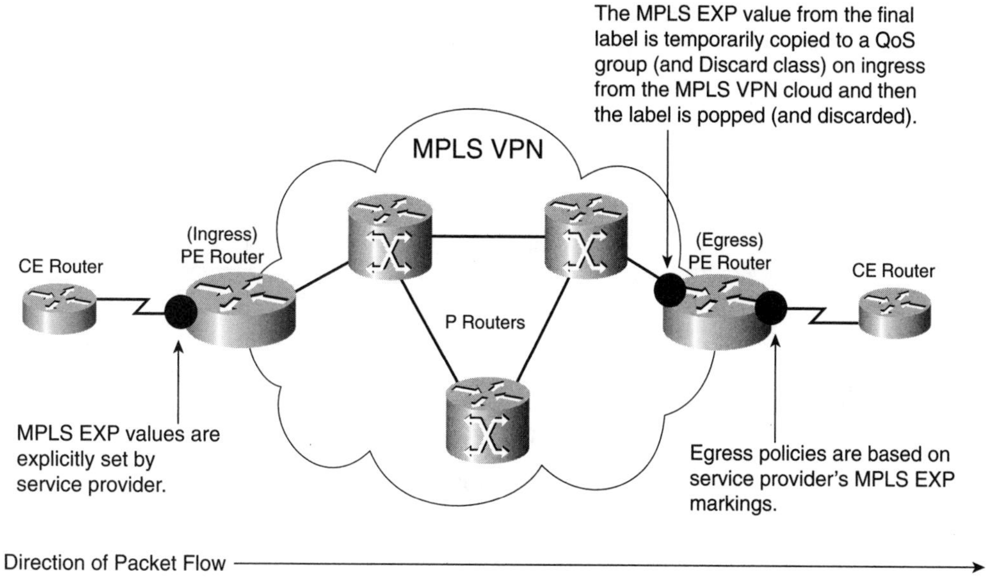

The MPLS EXP value from the final label is temporarily copied to a QoS group (and Discard class) on ingress from the MPLS VPN cloud and then the label is popped (and discarded).

MPLS EXP values are explicitly set by service provider.

Egress policies are based on service provider's MPLS EXP markings.

Direction of Packet Flow

Figure 15-15 illustrates adapting the five-class service provider model to Pipe Mode. The first set of re-markings shows ingress PE re-marking from DSCP to MPLS EXP values, depending on whether the traffic is in contract or out-of-contract. The second set of markings shows how these MPLS EXP values can be mapped to QoS Groups (QG) and Discard Classes (DC) to provide PHB classification and provisioning on PE-to-CE links (without altering the IP DSCP values of the tunneled packets).

Example 15-11 shows the configuration for bidirectional re-marking on a PE router to support Pipe Mode operation. Traffic received from CEs is marked explicitly (through MPLS EXP values) to reflect the service provider's policies. Then traffic (traversing in the opposite direction) received from the MPLS VPN core is mapped to QoS Groups and Discard Classes so that PE-to-CE PHB egress policies can be performed against provider re-markings. In this example, the customer has contracted for 3-Mbps service over an FE link. Hierarchical policies are used to achieve queuing within (3 Mbps) shaping over this (100-Mbps) link. Additionally, Discard-class WRED is enabled on the output queues so that dropping decisions are based on Discard-class values (not IP ToS or DSCP values). Furthermore, Discard-class dropping thresholds are tuned so that Discard-Class 1 (indicating out-of-contract traffic) is dropped more aggressively than Discard-Class 0 (mimicking DSCP-based WRED behavior), which is more consistent with RFC 2597 Assured-Forwarding PHBs.

Figure 15-15 *Five-Class Service Provider Model Pipe Mode Ingress and Egress Re-Marking Diagram*

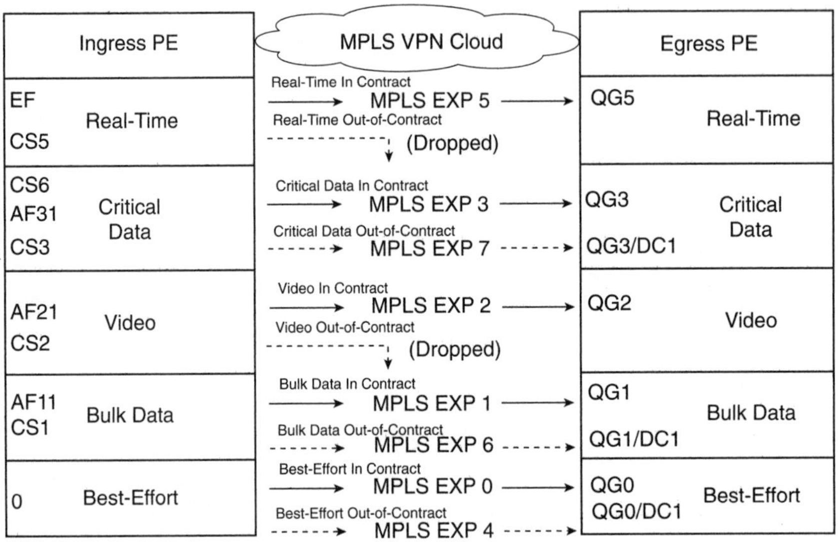

Example 15-11 *PE Configuration for MPLS DiffServ Pipe Mode Tunneling*

```
!
class-map match-any REALTIME
  match ip dscp ef
  match ip dscp cs5
class-map match-any CRITICAL-DATA
  match ip dscp cs6
  match ip dscp af31
  match ip dscp cs3
class-map match-any VIDEO
  match ip dscp af21
  match ip dscp cs2
class-map match-any BULK-DATA
  match ip dscp af11
  match ip dscp cs1
!
!
 class-map match-all MPLS-EXP-7
  match mpls experimental topmost 7        ! Matches MPLS EXP 7
 class-map match-all MPLS-EXP-6
  match mpls experimental topmost 6        ! Matches MPLS EXP 6
 class-map match-all MPLS-EXP-5
  match mpls experimental topmost 5        ! Matches MPLS EXP 5
 class-map match-all MPLS-EXP-4
  match mpls experimental topmost 4        ! Matches MPLS EXP 4
```

Example 15-11 *PE Configuration for MPLS DiffServ Pipe Mode Tunneling (Continued)*

```
class-map match-all MPLS-EXP-3
 match mpls experimental topmost 3        ! Matches MPLS EXP 3
class-map match-all MPLS-EXP-2
 match mpls experimental topmost 2        ! Matches MPLS EXP 2
class-map match-all MPLS-EXP-1
 match mpls experimental topmost 1        ! Matches MPLS EXP 1
class-map match-all MPLS-EXP-0
 match mpls experimental topmost 0        ! Matches MPLS EXP 0
!
!
class-map match-all QOSGROUP5
 match qos-group 5                        ! Matches QoS Group 5
class-map match-all QOSGROUP3
 match qos-group 3                        ! Matches QoS Group 3
class-map match-all QOSGROUP2
 match qos-group 2                        ! Matches QoS Group 2
class-map match-all QOSGROUP1
 match qos-group 1                        ! Matches QoS Group 1
class-map match-all QOSGROUP0
 match qos-group 0                        ! Matches QoS Group 0
!
!
policy-map PIPE-MARKING                   ! Sets MPLS EXP Values
 class REALTIME
  police cir 1050000
   conform-action set-mpls-exp-topmost-transmit 5 ! Conforming RT set to 5
   exceed-action drop                             ! Excess Realtime is dropped
 class CRITICAL-DATA
  police cir 600000
   conform-action set-mpls-exp-topmost-transmit 3 ! Critical Data set to 3
   exceed-action set-mpls-exp-topmost-transmit 7  ! Excess Critical set 7
 class VIDEO
  police cir 450000
   conform-action set-mpls-exp-topmost-transmit 2 ! Conforming Video set to 2
   exceed-action drop                             ! Excess Video dropped
 class BULK-DATA
  police cir 150000
   conform-action set-mpls-exp-topmost-transmit 1 ! Conforming Bulk set to 1
   exceed-action set-mpls-exp-topmost-transmit 6  ! Excess Bulk set to 6
 class class-default
  police cir 750000
   conform-action set-mpls-exp-topmost-transmit 0 ! Conforming BE set to 0
   exceed-action set-mpls-exp-topmost-transmit 4  ! Excess BE set to 4
!
!
policy-map MPLSEXP-QOSGROUP-DISCARDCLASS   ! Maps MPLS EXP to QG/DC values
 class MPLS-EXP-5
  set qos-group 5                ! Conforming Realtime is set to QG 5
 class MPLS-EXP-3
  set qos-group 3                ! Conforming Critical Data is set to QG 3
```

continues

Example 15-11 *PE Configuration for MPLS DiffServ Pipe Mode Tunneling (Continued)*

```
     class MPLS-EXP-7
      set qos-group 3          ! Excess Critical Data is set to QG3
      set discard-class 1      ! Excess Critical Data has DC set to 1
     class MPLS-EXP-2
      set qos-group 2          ! Conforming Video is set to QG 2
     class MPLS-EXP-1
      set qos-group 1          ! Conforming Bulk is set to QG 1
     class MPLS-EXP-6
      set qos-group 1          ! Excess Bulk is set to QG 1
      set discard-class 1      ! Excess Bulk has DC set to 1
     class MPLS-EXP-0
      set qos-group 0          ! Conforming Best Effort is set to QG 0
     class MPLS-EXP-4
      set qos-group 0          ! Excess Best Effort is set to QG 0
      set discard-class 1      ! Excess Best Effort has DC set to 1
    !
    !
    policy-map PE-CE-QUEUING    ! Queuing policy for PE to CE link
     class QOSGROUP5
      priority percent 35       ! Voice class gets 35% LLQ
     class QOSGROUP3
      bandwidth percent 20        ! Critical Data class gets 20% CBWFQ
      random-detect discard-class-based         ! DC-Based WRED is enabled
      random-detect discard-class 0   30   40    10   ! DC 0 is tuned for WRED
      random-detect discard-class 1   20   40    10   ! DC 1 is tuned for WRED
     class QOSGROUP2
      bandwidth percent 15        ! Video class gets 15% CBWFQ
     class QOSGROUP1
      bandwidth percent 5         ! Bulk class gets 5% CBWFQ
      random-detect discard-class-based         ! DC-Based WRED is enabled
      random-detect discard-class 0   30   40    10   ! DC 0 is tuned for WRED
      random-detect discard-class 1   20   40    10   ! DC 1 is tuned for WRED
     class QOSGROUP0
      bandwidth percent 25        ! Best Effort class gets 25% CBWFQ
      random-detect discard-class-based         ! DC-Based WRED is enabled
      random-detect discard-class 0   30   40    10   ! DC 0 is tuned for WRED
      random-detect discard-class 1   20   40    10   ! DC 1 is tuned for WRED
    !
    !
    policy-map PE-CE-SHAPING-QUEUING     ! Customer has 3 Mbps CIR over FE
      class class-default
       shape average 3000000           ! Shaping policy for 3 Mbps CIR
       service-policy PE-CE-QUEUING     ! Nested queuing policy
    !
    interface ATM2/0
     no ip address
     no atm ilmi-keepalive
    !
```

Example 15-11 *PE Configuration for MPLS DiffServ Pipe Mode Tunneling (Continued)*

```
interface ATM2/0.1 point-to-point
 description ATM-OC3 TO MPLS VPN CORE        ! Link to/from MPLS VPN Core
 ip address 20.2.34.4 255.255.255.0
 pvc 0/304
  vbr-nrt 149760 149760
  service-policy input MPLSEXP-QOSGROUP-DISCARDCLASS ! MPLS EXP to QG/DC
 !
 tag-switching ip
!
!
interface FastEthernet1/0
 description FE TO CUSTOMER RED CE                ! Link to/from CE
 ip vrf forwarding RED
 ip address 10.1.12.2 255.255.255.0
 service-policy input PIPE-MARKING                ! Pipe marking policy
 service-policy output PE-CE-SHAPING-QUEUING      ! Shaping/Queuing policy
 !
```

Verification commands:

- **show policy**
- **show policy interface**

Pipe Mode with an Explicit Null LSP

When CEs are provider managed, some providers prefer to offload the ingress MPLS EXP marking of customer traffic from the PE and push these policies out to the ingress interface of the CE. However, because the CE-to-PE link is regular IP (not MPLS), a difficulty arises as to how to set the provider's marking without affecting the IP DiffServ markings that the customer has set (because, again, these are to be preserved and untouched through the MPLS VPN cloud in Pipe Mode operation). Therefore, a solution to this scenario was introduced in Cisco IOS Release 12.2(13)T, with the Pipe Mode MPLS DiffServ tunneling with an Explicit Null LSP feature.

This feature prepends an Explicit Null LSP label for customer traffic headed from the CE to the PE. This label is not used for MPLS switching; it is used only to preserve the provider's MPLS EXP markings over the CE-to-PE link. On the PE, the MPLS EXP values are copied to regular MPLS labels that are pushed onto the packet (which are used for MPLS switching), and the explicit null label is discarded.

Thus, the ingress marking policies from the PE are pushed to the managed CE. This expands the provider's DiffServ domain to include the (managed) CEs. All other aspects of Pipe Mode operation and configuration, however, remain the same.

Figure 15-16 *MPLS DiffServ Pipe Mode with an Explicit Null LSP Tunneling Operation*

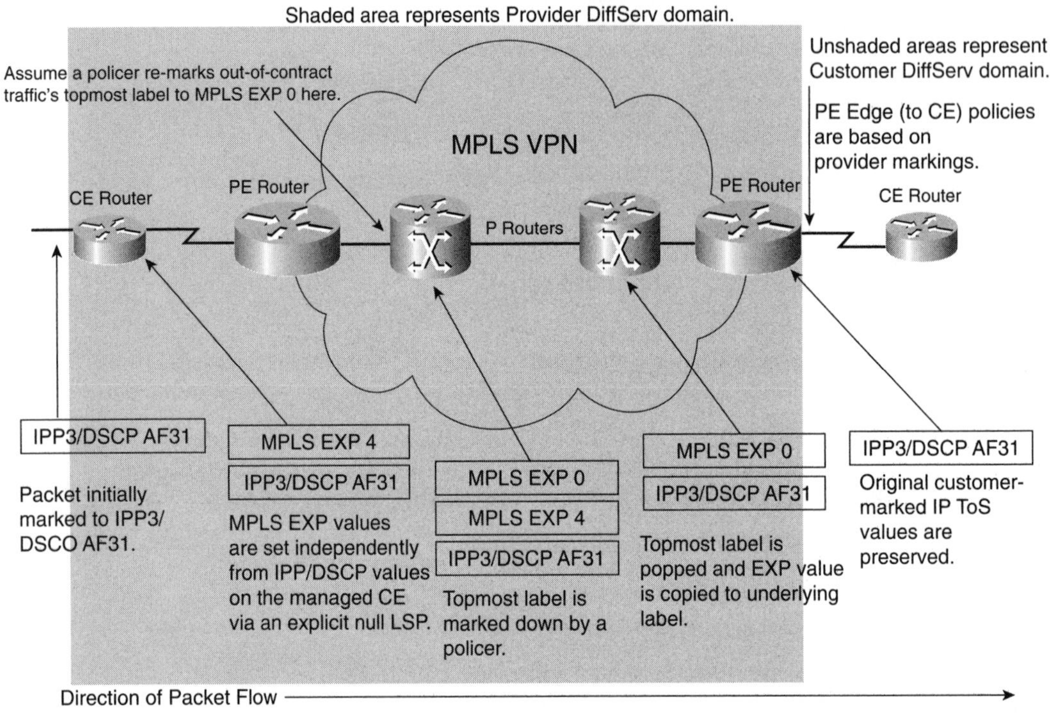

Figure 15-17 shows the points where policies are required for Pipe Mode with Explicit Null LSP MPLS DiffServ tunneling.

As noted, PE configurations remain the same as with normal Pipe Mode, with the exception that ingress MPLS EXP marking policies have been removed. These policies now are set on the managed CE, as shown in Example 15-12. As with Example 15-13, the provider has contracted for a CIR of 3 Mbps in a five-class model. All ingress traffic is policed on the customer edge of the CE and is marked (through MPLS EXP values) to indicate whether it is in contract or out-of-contract. Then an Explicit Null LSP is pushed onto the packet to carry these MPLS EXP markings from the CE to the PE. Optionally, queuing policies can be added on the CE-to-PE link, but for simplicity, these have been omitted from this example because they already have been covered.

Figure 15-17 *MPLS DiffServ Pipe Mode with an Explicit Null LSP Tunneling Policies*

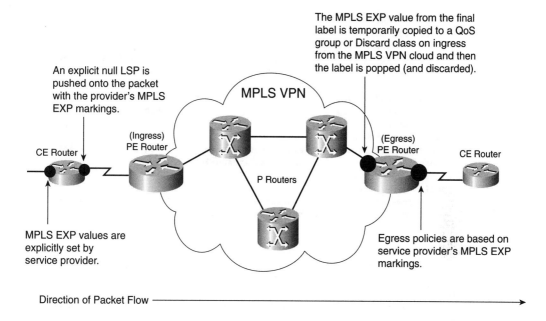

Example 15-12 *Managed CE Configuration for MPLS DiffServ Pipe Mode with an Explicit Null LSP Tunneling*

```
!
class-map match-any REALTIME
  match ip dscp ef
  match ip dscp cs5
class-map match-any CRITICAL-DATA
  match ip dscp cs6
  match ip dscp af31
  match ip dscp cs3
class-map match-any VIDEO
  match ip dscp af21
  match ip dscp cs2
class-map match-any BULK-DATA
  match ip dscp af11
  match ip dscp cs1
!
!
 policy-map PIPE-EXPLICIT-NULL-MARKING
  class REALTIME
   police cir 1050000
     conform-action set-mpls-exp-topmost-transmit 5   ! Conforming RT set to 5
     exceed-action drop                                ! Excess Realtime is dropped
```

continues

Example 15-12 *Managed CE Configuration for MPLS DiffServ Pipe Mode with an Explicit Null LSP Tunneling (Continued)*

```
 class CRITICAL-DATA
  police cir 600000
   conform-action set-mpls-exp-topmost-transmit 3   ! Critical Data set to 3
   exceed-action set-mpls-exp-topmost-transmit 7    ! Excess Critical set 7
 class VIDEO
  police cir 450000
   conform-action set-mpls-exp-topmost-transmit 2   ! Conforming Video set to 2
   exceed-action drop                               ! Excess Video dropped
 class BULK-DATA
  police cir 150000
   conform-action set-mpls-exp-topmost-transmit 1   ! Conforming Bulk set to 1
   exceed-action set-mpls-exp-topmost-transmit 6    ! Excess Bulk set to 6
 class class-default
  police cir 750000
   conform-action set-mpls-exp-topmost-transmit 0   ! Conforming BE set to 0
   exceed-action set-mpls-exp-topmost-transmit 4    ! Excess BE set to 4
!
...
!
interface FastEthernet0/0
 description FE to Customer Network                 ! Link to/from customer
 ip address 10.1.1.1 255.255.255.0
 service-policy input PIPE-EXPLICIT-NULL-MARKING    ! MPLS EXP set on ingress
!
!
interface FastEthernet0/1
 description FE TO PE                               ! Link to/from PE
 ip address 10.1.12.1 255.255.255.0
 duplex auto
 speed auto
 mpls ip encapsulate explicit-null                 ! Explicit Null LSP is added
!
```

Verification commands:

- **show policy**
- **show policy interface**

Core QoS Considerations

Several options exist to meet strict SLA considerations for loss, delay, and jitter in the service-provider MPLS VPN core:

- Aggregate bandwidth overprovisioning
- DiffServ in the backbone
- MPLS traffic engineering (which might or might not be used in conjunction with DiffServ in the backbone)

Aggregate Bandwidth Overprovisioning

Aggregate bandwidth overprovisioning is a common trend in the service-provider backbone because of its simplicity and ease of design, deployment, and operation. Although DiffServ domain characteristics are assumed at the provider edges for traffic aggregation, studies have shown that designing the service provider backbone for low delay, jitter, or loss can be a matter of simply overprovisioning the network by approximately two times the maximum of the aggregate traffic load.

Caveats to overprovisioning include capacity planning failures, network failure situations, and unexpected traffic demands or patterns. For instance, because this strategy does not differentiate between Real-Time traffic and Best-Effort traffic, real-time service levels can be degraded if network failure or congestion occurs. Furthermore, this approach is relatively expensive and inefficient, compared to alternative options such as Core DiffServ and MPLS TE.

DiffServ in the Backbone

Deploying a simplified DiffServ policy in the backbone allows the service provider to support multiple classes of traffic with different overprovisioning and underprovisioning ratios on a per-class basis.

DiffServ in the backbone allows for more aggregate traffic to be supported for the same provisioned network bandwidth, as compared to the non-DiffServ backbone. Also, Real-Time traffic can be serviced preferentially, even if failure or congestion occurs.

The main caveat to this solution is that it adds complexity to the core network design and operations.

In a DiffServ backbone, it might not be necessary to assume the same number of classes that exist at the edge in the PE-to-CE link, as long as provision is made for a Real-Time traffic class (which is associated to a PQ) and Critical Data is protected over Best-Effort traffic.

Three-Class Provider-Core Model: PE-to-P or P-to-P Design

It is not necessary to ensure that the backbone supports the same number of DiffServ classes as the edge, assuming that proper design principles are in place to support the given SLAs.

Figure 15-18 gives an example of how a five-class provider-edge model can be collapsed into a three-class provider-core model.

Figure 15-18 *Five-Class Provider-Edge Model Short Pipe/Pipe Mode Mapping to Three-Class Provider-Core Model Example*

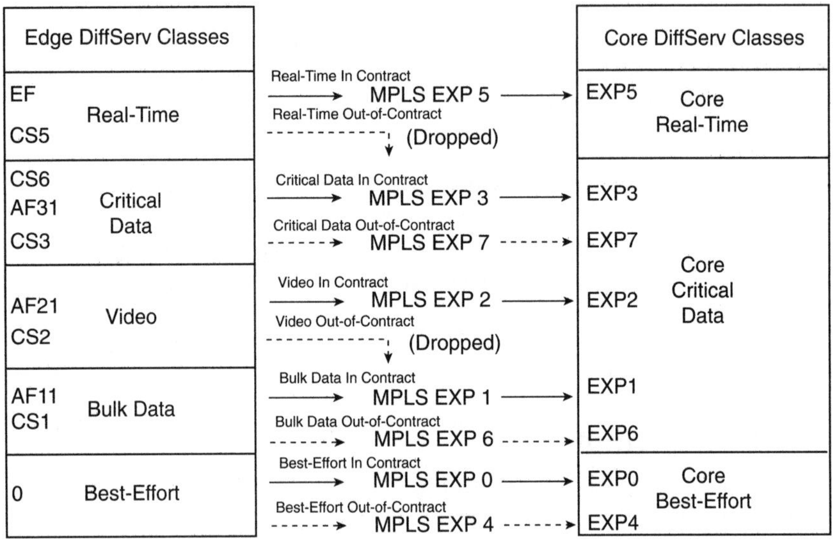

Detailed definitions of the core classes used in this figure follow:

- **Core Real-Time**—This class targets applications such as Voice and Interactive-Video, which require low loss (less than 0.25 percent), low delay, and low jitter (typically 5 ms within the backbone), and have a defined availability. This class also supports per-flow sequence preservation. This class always should be engineered for the worst-case delay, to support Real-Time traffic. Excess traffic in this class typically is dropped. This class should be associated with MPLS EXP 5 with a PQ, to ensure that the delay and jitter contracts are met. Between 25 and 35 percent of link capacity should be allocated to the PQ. WRED typically is not required on this queue.

- **Core Critical Data**—This class represents business-critical interactive applications. Round-trip time (RTT) should be less than 250 ms (the threshold for human delay perception), and loss should be less than 0.5 percent. Throughput is derived from loss and RTT. Jitter is not important for this service class and is not defined. Excess traffic within this class typically is re-marked with an out-of-contract identifier (re-marking of either DSCP or MPLS EXP values) and transmitted. This class also supports per-flow sequence preservation. This class should be associated with an AF class-based queue or MPLS EXP-based queue (depending on the MPLS DiffServ tunneling mode in use). WRED could be configured here to optimize TCP throughput and to accommodate a drop policy for out-of-profile traffic.

- **Core Best-Effort**—This class represents all other customer traffic that has not been classified as Real-Time or Critical Data. It is defined in terms of a loss rate with availability; throughput is derived from loss. Delay and jitter are not important for this service and are not defined.

Example 15-13 shows the configuration of a three-class provider-core model. If DiffServ is implemented within the core, the policies should be kept as simple as possible, to reduce the CPU utilization for QoS to an absolute minimum.

Example 15-13 *Three-Class Provider Core Model Example*

```
!
class-map match-all CORE-REALTIME
  match mpls experimental topmost 5    ! Identifies in-contract Realtime
class-map match-all CORE-CRITICAL-DATA
  match mpls experimental topmost 3    ! Identifies in-contract Critical-Data
  match mpls experimental topmost 7    ! Identifies out-of-contract Critical Data
  match mpls experimental topmost 2    ! Identifies in-contract Video
  match mpls experimental topmost 1    ! Identifies in-contract Bulk
  match mpls experimental topmost 6    ! Identifies out-of-contract Bulk
!
!
 policy-map CORE-THREE-CLASS-SP-MODEL
  class CORE-REALTIME
    priority percent 35                 ! CORE-REALTIME gets 35% LLQ
  class CORE-CRITICAL-DATA
    bandwidth percent 55                ! CORE-CRITICAL gets 55% CBWFQ
  class class-default
    fair-queue                          ! CORE-BEST-EFFORT gets FQ
!
```

Verification commands:

- **show policy**
- **show policy interface**

The **max-reserved-bandwidth** command might be required on the interface to which the policy is applied.

Platform-Specific Considerations—Cisco 12000 GSR MDRR Example

Because of the highly specialized role of core routers, not all previously discussed QoS features are supported by each platform/line card combination. It is beyond the scope of this chapter to enumerate all platform/line card caveats; however, an example of the Cisco 12000 GSR can illustrate the point.

The Cisco 12000 series router platforms support queuing through a modified-deficit round-robin (MDRR) algorithm. MDRR works in much the same manner as CBWFQ and allows for up to eight queues to be provisioned; non-empty queues are serviced in a round-robin fashion, depending on the bandwidth assigned to them.

Within these eight queues, MDRR maintains a priority queue, which can be serviced in strict priority or alternate priority.

With MDRR strict priority, the priority queue always is serviced exhaustively, as long as there are packets in this queue. An important distinction between MDRR priority queuing and LLQ is that MDRR priority queuing does not have an implicit policer. However, the MQC syntax does support configuring MDRR strict priority in conjunction with class-based policing to enforce a limit on the amount of traffic that can be given strict priority.

To prevent starvation scenarios that could exist with the lack of a policer, an alternative to MDRR strict-priority servicing exists in the option of MDRR alternate-priority queuing. When alternate-priority queuing is configured, the priority queue is serviced alternately with all other queues. For example, one priority packet is serviced, followed by a packet from any one of the other queues (depending on how they are configured). Then another priority packet is serviced and again is followed by a nonpriority packet. In this manner, priority servicing does not starve other traffic as strict-priority queuing could.

MDRR can be applied to an inbound interface or an outbound interface.

Example 15-14 shows how to adapt the previous three-class provider-core policy to a Cisco 12000 GSR router. In this example, the LLQ is policed to approximately 35 percent of the Packet-over-SONET (POS) line rate of OC3 (155 Mbps). Because the Cisco 12000 GSR does not support WFQ, no explicit configuration is required for the Best-Effort class.

Example 15-14   *Three-Class Provider Core Model Adapted for a Cisco 12000 GSR with Line Card 3 Example*

```
!
class-map match-all CORE-REALTIME
  match mpls experimental  5
class-map match-all CORE-CRITICAL-DATA
  match mpls experimental  3
  match mpls experimental  7
  match mpls experimental  2
  match mpls experimental  1
  match mpls experimental  6
!
!
policy-map CORE-THREE-CLASS-SP-MODEL-GSR
  class CORE-REALTIME
    police cir 54248000 bc 4470 be 4470       ! Voice is explicitly policed to 33%
    conform-action transmit
    exceed-action drop
    priority                       ! Voice is assigned strict-priority MDRR
  class CORE-CRITICAL-DATA
    bandwidth percent 40
!
! WFQ is not supported - so no default-class polices are required
!
```

Example 15-14 *Three-Class Provider Core Model Adapted for a Cisco 12000 GSR with Line Card 3 Example (Continued)*

```
interface POS0/0
 ip address 10.131.160.233 255.255.255.252
 no ip directed-broadcast
 tag-switching ip
 crc 16
 service-policy output CORE-THREE-CLASS-SP-MODEL-GSR
 !
```

NOTE   The implementation of the priority command on the Cisco 12000 series differs from the implementation on other routers running Cisco IOS Software. On this platform, the priority traffic is not limited to the configured kbps value during periods of congestion. Thus, you also must configure the **police** command to limit how much bandwidth a priority class can use and to ensure adequate bandwidth for other classes. At this time, the **police** command is supported on only Engine 3 line cards. On the other engine line cards, only class-default is allowed when you configure a priority class.

Verification commands:

* **show policy**
* **show policy interface**

MPLS Traffic Engineering

Traffic engineering enables service providers to route network traffic efficiently to offer the optimal service levels, in terms of throughput and delay. Such effective use of network resources allows providers to offer more granular services and, at the same time, reduce the cost of their network.

Currently, many service providers base their services on an overlay model. In the overlay model, transmission facilities are managed by Layer 2 switching. The routers see only a fully meshed virtual topology, making most destinations appear one hop away. MPLS traffic engineering (MPLS TE) provides a way to achieve the same traffic-engineering benefits of the overlay model without needing to run a separate network and without needing a nonscalable, full mesh of router interconnects. Furthermore, MPLS TE enables administrators to use complex metrics in determining the optimal path of a given flow.

MPLS traffic engineering does the following:

* Replaces the need to manually configure the network devices to set up explicit routes. Instead, you can rely on the MPLS traffic engineering functionality to understand the backbone topology and the automated signaling process.

- Accounts for link bandwidth and for the size of the traffic flow when determining explicit routes across the backbone.

- Has a dynamic adaptation mechanism that enables the backbone to be resilient to failures, even if several primary paths are precalculated offline.

MPLS TE automatically establishes and maintains a tunnel across the backbone, using RSVP. The path used by a given tunnel at any point in time is determined based on the tunnel resource requirements and network resources, such as bandwidth.

Available resources are flooded through extensions to a link state–based Interior Gateway Protocol (IGP), such as OSPF or IS-IS.

Tunnel paths are calculated at the tunnel head based on a fit between required and available resources (constraint-based routing). The IGP automatically routes the traffic into these tunnels. Typically, a packet crossing the MPLS TE backbone travels on a single tunnel that connects the ingress point to the egress point.

MPLS TE is built on the following Cisco IOS mechanisms:

- Label-switched path (LSP) tunnels, which are signaled through RSVP, with traffic engineering extensions. LSP tunnels are represented as tunnel interfaces, have a configured destination, and are unidirectional.

- A link-state IGP (such as OSPF or IS-IS) with extensions for the global flooding of resource information, and extensions for the automatic routing of traffic onto LSP tunnels, as appropriate.

- An MPLS TE path-calculation module that determines paths to use for LSP tunnels.

- An MPLS TE link-management module that does link admission and bookkeeping of the resource information to be flooded.

One approach to engineer a backbone is to define a mesh of tunnels from every ingress device to every egress device. The IGP, operating at an ingress device, determines which traffic should go to which egress device, and steers that traffic into the tunnel from ingress to egress. The MPLS traffic-engineering path-calculation and signaling modules determine the path taken by the LSP tunnel, subject to resource availability and the dynamic state of the network. For each tunnel, counts of packets and bytes sent are kept.

Sometimes a flow is so large that it cannot fit over a single link, so it cannot be carried by a single tunnel. In this case, multiple tunnels between a given ingress and egress can be configured, and the flow is load-shared among them.

Basic MPLS TE

Basic MPLS TE configuration requires you to do the following:

- Enable IP CEF globally:

```
Router(config)#ip cef
```

- Enable MPLS TE globally:

```
Router(config)#mpls traffic-eng tunnels
```

- Enable MPLS TE on every interface that might be part of a tunnel, and configure the amount of bandwidth that can be reserved (through RSVP) for all tunnels traversing the link:

```
Router(config)#interface POS5/0
Router(config-if)#mpls traffic-eng tunnels
Router(config-if)#ip rsvp bandwidth 77500 77500
```

- Define a loopback interface to be used as an MPLS TE Router ID (RID):

```
Router(config)#interface loopback 0
Router(config-if)#ip address 20.1.1.1 255.255.255.255
```

- Configure a link-state Interior Gateway Protocol (IGP) for MPLS TE, either OSPF or IS-IS:

  — OSPF

```
Router(config)#router ospf 100
Router(config-router)# mpls traffic-eng router-id loopback 0
Router(config-router)# mpls traffic-eng area 0
```

  — IS-IS

```
Router(config)#router isis
Router(config-router)#net 49.0000.0000.0000.0010.00
Router(config-router)#metric-style wide
Router(config-router)#mpls traffic-eng level-1
Router(config-router)#mpls traffic-eng router-id loopback 0
```

- Define a tunnel interface configured with MPLS TE, with an amount of bandwidth that can be reserved (through RSVP) for the tunnel:

```
Router(config)#interface Tunnel0
Router(config-if)# description BLUE-TUNNEL (PE1=>PE2)
Router(config-if)# ip unnumbered loopback 0
Router(config-if)# tunnel destination 20.2.2.2
Router(config-if)# tunnel mode mpls traffic-eng
Router(config-if)# tunnel mpls traffic-eng bandwidth  77500
```

- Set a priority for the tunnel interface (lower is preferred):

```
Router(config-if)# tunnel mpls traffic-eng priority 7 7
```

- Select a path option for the tunnel—dynamic, explicit, or a combination:

  — **Dynamic path option**—The software calculates the best path to the destination, based on tunnel constraints.

```
Router(config-if)#tunnel mpls traffic-eng path-option 10 dynamic
```

  — **Explicit path option**—Each hop is defined statically.

```
Router(config-if)# tunnel mpls traffic-eng path-option1 explicit name BLUE-TUNNEL
   Router(config-if)#exit
Router(config)#ip explicit-path name BLUE-TUNNEL enable
Router(cfg-ip-expl-path)# next-address 20.1.12.2
Explicit Path name BLUE-TUNNEL:
       1: next-address 20.1.12.2
Router(cfg-ip-expl-path)#
```

— **Combination path options**—When the first option cannot be met, the algorithm attempts the second, and so on.

```
Router(config-if)# tunnel mpls traffic-eng path-option 1 explicit name  BLUE-
TUNNEL
Router(config-if)# tunnel mpls traffic-eng path-option 2 dynamic
        Router(config-if)#exit
Router(config)#ip explicit-path name BLUE-TUNNEL enable
Router(cfg-ip-expl-path)# next-address 20.1.12.2
Explicit Path name BLUE-TUNNEL:
        1: next-address 20.1.12.2
Router(cfg-ip-expl-path)#
```

- Select a forwarding option to direct traffic down the tunnel—static routes, policy routing, or AutoRoute:

  — Static routes

```
Router(config)#ip route 16.16.16.16 255.255.255.255 Tunnel0
```

  — Policy-based routing

```
Router(config)#interface FastEthernet 1/0
Router(config-if)#ip policy route-map TUNNEL-ASSIGNMENT
Router(config-if)#exit
Router(config)#route-map TUNNEL-ASSIGNMENT
Router(config-route-map)#match ip address 100
Router(config-route-map)#set interface Tunnel 0
Router(config-route-map)#exit
Router(config)#access-list 100 permit ip any 10.2.2.0 0.0.0.255
```

  — AutoRoute (enabled on the tunnel headend)

```
Router(config)#interface Tunnel0
Router(config-if)#tunnel mpls traffic-eng autoroute announce
```

NOTE   As stated at the opening of the chapter, it is simply beyond the scope of this book to go into detail on MPLS traffic engineering. Many MPLS TE features, such as attribute flags, affinity, administrative weights, flooding thresholds, and FastReroute, have been omitted from this overview. For a comprehensive technical discussion on these and other MPLS TE features and operation, refer to the Cisco Press book *Traffic Engineering with MPLS*, by Eric Osborne and Ajay Simha.

Two examples of QoS-related MPLS TE scenarios are presented in this chapter. The first is the use of MPLS per-VPN traffic engineering; the second is the use of MPLS DiffServ traffic engineering (MPLS DS-TE).

MPLS Per-VPN TE

MPLS VPNs provide the route isolation necessary for data privacy and support of private IP address allocation overlapping, while RSVP-signaled MPLS-TE provides optimal path selection, per-VPN SLAs, and path resiliency.

The notion of integrating these two MPLS applications is pretty straightforward. Where it gets interesting is in the actual binding process of an MPLS VPN to the TE tunnel. Today this can be achieved by taking advantage of next-hop route recursion at the PE; however, this is a less than elegant interim solution. Cisco IOS innovations in policy-based routing (PBR) and QoS-based routing (QBR) will allow for a more scalable way to integrate MPLS VPN and TE in the near future.

In this simplified example scenario, the service provider has Packet over SONET (POS) links from each PE to the core, and also direct PE-to-PE POS links for geographically adjacent PEs. Furthermore, the service provider has two customers, Blue and Red. Customer Blue has contracted with the provider for a premium service so that Blue traffic that is destined for geographically adjacent CEs is tunneled over the direct PE-to-PE links. However, Red traffic always is switched through the MPLS core, even when there is a shorter path to the destination CEs through the direct PE-to-PE links. Figure 15-19 illustrates the desired operation of this scenario. Because MPLS TE is unidirectional, separate tunnels would be required for the same behavior in the return direction.

Figure 15-19 *MPLS Per-VPN TE Operation Example*

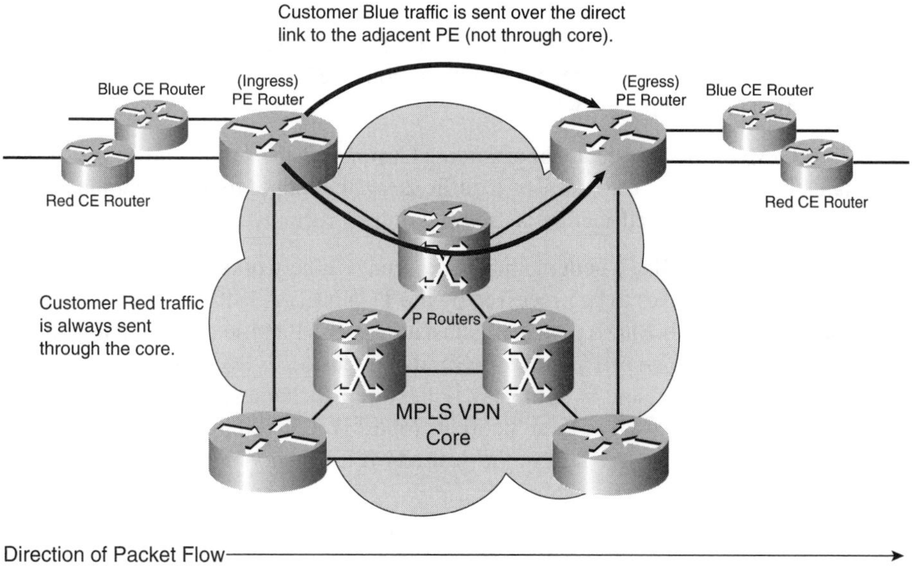

Figure 15-20 zooms in on the relevant subsection of the previous diagram and provides specific addressing detail for this example.

Figure 15-20 *MPLS Per-VPN TE Example Details*

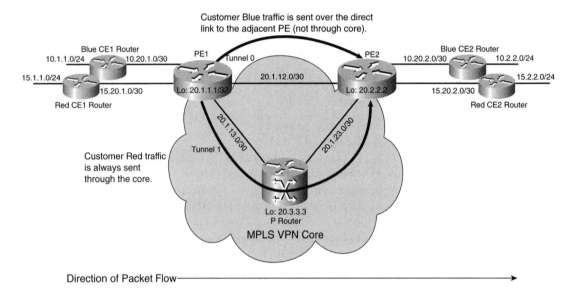

The configuration for this example of MPLS per-VPN TE spans three routers: PE1 configuration (see Example 15-15), PE2 configuration (see Example 15-16), and the P-router configuration (see Example 15-17).

To achieve the desired behavior of forcing Customer Blue's traffic down the shorter MPLS tunnel and forcing Customer Red's traffic down the longer tunnel, a combination of static and BGP policy-based routing is used (relying on recursive routing on each PE).

When Customer Blue's geographically adjacent CE networks are received at the PE, BGP directs these prefixes to be processed by the TUNNEL-ASSIGNMENT route map. This route map matches Blue's prefixes against access-list 1 and sets the BGP next-hop attribute to the fictitious route of 16.16.16.16. Similarly, Customer Red's prefixes are matched against access-list 2 and have their BGP next-hop attribute set to the fictitious route of 17.17.17.17. Then each of these fictitious routes is resolved through static-routing statements that direct the flow to the desired MPLS tunnel interface. This is detailed in Example 15-15.

Example 15-15 *PE1 MPLS Per-VPN TE Example Configuration*

```
!
hostname PE1
!
```

Example 15-15 *PE1 MPLS Per-VPN TE Example Configuration (Continued)*

```
!
ip vrf BLUE                            ! BLUE MPLS VPN definition
 rd 100:1
 route-target export 100:1
 route-target import 100:1
!
ip vrf RED                             ! RED MPLS VPN definition
 rd 150:1
 route-target export 150:1
 route-target import 150:1
!
ip cef                                 ! IP CEF is required for MPLS and MPLS TE
mpls ldp logging neighbor-changes
mpls traffic-eng tunnels               ! MPLS TE is enabled globally
!
!
interface Loopback0                    ! Loopback interface for MPLS TE RID
 ip address 20.1.1.1 255.255.255.255
!
interface Tunnel0
 description BLUE-TUNNEL (PE1=>PE2)
 ip unnumbered Loopback0
 tunnel destination 20.2.2.2
 tunnel mode mpls traffic-eng                  ! MPLS TE is enabled on Tunnel int
 tunnel mpls traffic-eng priority 7 7          ! Lower value is preferred
 tunnel mpls traffic-eng bandwidth  77500      ! 77.5 Mbps can be reserved
 tunnel mpls traffic-eng path-option 1 explicit name BLUE-TUNNEL   ! BLUE Path
!
interface Tunnel1
 description RED-TUNNEL (PE1=>P=>PE2)
 ip unnumbered Loopback0
 tunnel destination 20.2.2.2
 tunnel mode mpls traffic-eng                  ! MPLS TE is enabled on Tunnel int
 tunnel mpls traffic-eng priority 7 7          ! Lower value is preferred
 tunnel mpls traffic-eng bandwidth  77500      ! 77.5 Mbps can be reserved via RSVP
 tunnel mpls traffic-eng path-option 1 explicit name RED-TUNNEL       ! RED Path
!
!
interface FastEthernet1/0
 description FE to Customer Blue CE1
 ip vrf forwarding BLUE                         ! Interface to Blue CE1
 ip address 10.20.1.2 255.255.255.252
!
interface FastEthernet1/1
 description FE to Customer Red CE1
 ip vrf forwarding RED                          ! Interface to Blue CE1
 ip address 15.20.1.2 255.255.255.252
!
interface POS5/0
 ip address 20.1.12.1 255.255.255.252
 description PE1=>PE2 POS Link
```

continues

Example 15-15 *PE1 MPLS Per-VPN TE Example Configuration (Continued)*

```
 mpls traffic-eng tunnels                  ! MPLS TE enabled on int
 tag-switching ip                          ! MPLS enabled on int
 ip rsvp bandwidth 77500 77500             ! RSVP enabled on int for 77.5 Mbps
 !
 interface POS6/0
  description PE1=>P-Router (Core) POS Link
  ip address 20.1.13.1 255.255.255.252
  mpls traffic-eng tunnels                 ! MPLS TE enabled on int
  tag-switching ip                         ! MPLS enabled on int
  ip rsvp bandwidth 77500 77500            ! RSVP enabled on int for 77.5 Mbps
 !
 router ospf 100
  mpls traffic-eng router-id Loopback0     ! MPLS TE RID
  mpls traffic-eng area 0                  ! Enables OSPF area 0 for MPLS TE
  log-adjacency-changes
  redistribute connected subnets
  network 20.1.12.0 0.0.0.3 area 0
  network 20.1.13.0 0.0.0.3 area 0
 !
 router bgp 100
  no synchronization
  bgp log-neighbor-changes
  redistribute connected
  neighbor 20.2.2.2 remote-as 100
  neighbor 20.2.2.2 update-source Loopback0
  no auto-summary
  !
  address-family vpnv4
   neighbor 20.2.2.2 activate                 ! MPLS VPN neighbor (PE2)
   neighbor 20.2.2.2 send-community extended
   neighbor 20.2.2.2 route-map TUNNEL-ASSIGNMENT in  ! Applies BGP PBR
  exit-address-family
  !
  address-family ipv4 vrf BLUE
   redistribute connected
   neighbor 10.20.1.1 remote-as 10            ! EBGP peer with Customer Blue CE1
   neighbor 10.20.1.1 activate
   neighbor 10.20.1.1 default-originate
   no auto-summary
   no synchronization
   exit-address-family
  !
  address-family ipv4 vrf RED
   redistribute connected
   neighbor 15.20.1.1 remote-as 15            ! EBGP peer with Customer Red CE1
   neighbor 15.20.1.1 activate
   neighbor 15.20.1.1 default-originate
   no auto-summary
   no synchronization
   exit-address-family
```

Example 15-15 *PE1 MPLS Per-VPN TE Example Configuration (Continued)*

```
!
ip classless
ip route 16.16.16.16 255.255.255.255 Tunnel0 ! Static Route for BLUE Tunnel
ip route 17.17.17.17 255.255.255.255 Tunnel1 ! Static Route for RED Tunnel
!
ip bgp-community new-format
!
ip explicit-path name BLUE-TUNNEL enable     ! Explicit Path for BLUE Tunnel
 next-address 20.1.12.2                       ! Direct to PE2
!
ip explicit-path name RED-TUNNEL enable      ! Explicit Path for RED Tunnel
 next-address 20.1.13.2                        ! First to P-Router (Core)
 next-address 20.1.23.1                        ! Then to PE2
!
access-list 1 permit 10.2.2.0 0.0.0.255      ! Adjacent Customer Blue subnets
access-list 1 permit 10.20.2.0 0.0.0.3       ! Adjacent Customer Blue subnets
access-list 2 permit 15.2.2.0 0.0.0.255      ! Adjacent Customer Red subnets
access-list 2 permit 15.20.2.0 0.0.0.3       ! Adjacent Customer Red subnets
!
route-map TUNNEL-ASSIGNMENT permit 10        ! BGP Inbound Route-Map
 match ip address 1                           ! Identifies Customer Blue subnets
 set ip next-hop 16.16.16.16                  ! Sets BGP Next-Hop to 16.16.16.16
!
route-map TUNNEL-ASSIGNMENT permit 20
 match ip address 2                           ! Identifies Customer Red subnets
 set ip next-hop 17.17.17.17                  ! Sets BGP Next-Hop to 17.17.17.17
!
!
```

Because all tunnels are unidirectional, the same logic is applied in the reverse direction, where the fictitious addresses are 18.18.18.18 (for Blue) and 19.19.19.19 (for Red), as detailed in Example 15-16.

Example 15-16 *PE2 MPLS Per-VPN TE Example Configuration*

```
!
hostname PE2
!
!
ip vrf BLUE                         ! BLUE MPLS VPN definition
 rd 100:1
 route-target export 100:1
 route-target import 100:1
!
ip vrf RED                          ! RED MPLS VPN definition
 rd 150:1
 route-target export 150:1
 route-target import 150:1
!
```

continues

Example 15-16 *PE2 MPLS Per-VPN TE Example Configuration (Continued)*

```
ip cef                                  ! IP CEF is required for MPLS and MPLS TE
mpls ldp logging neighbor-changes
mpls traffic-eng tunnels                ! MPLS TE is enabled globally
!
!
interface Loopback0                     ! Loopback interface for MPLS TE RID
 ip address 20.2.2.2 255.255.255.255
!
interface Tunnel0
 description BLUE-TUNNEL (PE2=>PE1)
 ip unnumbered Loopback0
 tunnel destination 20.1.1.1
 tunnel mode mpls traffic-eng           ! MPLS TE is enabled on Tunnel int
 tunnel mpls traffic-eng priority 7 7   ! Lower value is preferred
 tunnel mpls traffic-eng bandwidth  77500   ! 77.5 Mbps can be reserved
 tunnel mpls traffic-eng path-option 1 explicit name BLUE-TUNNEL ! BLUE Path
!
interface Tunnel1
 description RED-TUNNEL (PE2=>P=>PE1)
 ip unnumbered Loopback0
 tunnel destination 20.1.1.1
 tunnel mode mpls traffic-eng           ! MPLS TE is enabled on Tunnel int
 tunnel mpls traffic-eng priority 7 7   ! Lower value is preferred
 tunnel mpls traffic-eng bandwidth  77500   ! 77.5 Mbps can be reserved via RSVP
 tunnel mpls traffic-eng path-option 1 explicit name RED-TUNNEL   ! RED Path
!
!
interface FastEthernet1/0
 description FE to Customer Blue CE2
 ip vrf forwarding BLUE                 ! Interface to Blue CE2
 ip address 10.20.2.2 255.255.255.252
!
interface FastEthernet1/1
 description FE to Customer Red CE2
 ip vrf forwarding RED                  ! Interface to Red CE2
 ip address 15.20.2.2 255.255.255.252
!
interface POS5/0
 description PE2=>PE1 POS Link
 ip address 20.1.12.2 255.255.255.252
 mpls traffic-eng tunnels               ! MPLS TE enabled on int
 tag-switching ip                       ! MPLS enabled on int
 ip rsvp bandwidth 77500 77500          ! RSVP enabled on int for 77.5 Mbps
!
interface POS6/0
 description PE2=>P-Router (Core) POS Link
 ip address 20.1.23.1 255.255.255.252
 mpls traffic-eng tunnels               ! MPLS TE enabled on int
 tag-switching ip                       ! MPLS enabled on int
 ip rsvp bandwidth 77500 77500          ! RSVP enabled on int for 77.5 Mbps
!
router ospf 100
```

Example 15-16 *PE2 MPLS Per-VPN TE Example Configuration (Continued)*

```
 mpls traffic-eng router-id Loopback0        ! MPLS TE RID
 mpls traffic-eng area 0                     ! Enables OSPF area 0 for MPLS TE
 log-adjacency-changes
 redistribute connected subnets
 network 20.1.12.0 0.0.0.3 area 0
 network 20.1.23.0 0.0.0.3 area 0
!
router bgp 100
 no synchronization
 bgp log-neighbor-changes
 redistribute connected
 neighbor 20.1.1.1 remote-as 100
 neighbor 20.1.1.1 update-source Loopback0
 no auto-summary
 !
 address-family vpnv4
 neighbor 20.1.1.1 activate                         ! MPLS VPN neighbor (PE1)
 neighbor 20.1.1.1 send-community extended
 neighbor 20.1.1.1 route-map TUNNEL-ASSIGNMENT in   ! Applies BGP PBR
 exit-address-family
 !
 address-family ipv4 vrf BLUE
 redistribute connected
 neighbor 10.20.2.1 remote-as 10     ! EBGP peer with Customer Blue CE2
 neighbor 10.20.2.1 activate
 neighbor 10.20.2.1 default-originate
 no auto-summary
 no synchronization
 exit-address-family
 !
 address-family ipv4 vrf RED
 redistribute connected
 neighbor 15.20.2.1 remote-as 15     ! EBGP peer with Customer Red CE2
 neighbor 15.20.2.1 activate
 neighbor 15.20.2.1 default-originate
 no auto-summary
 no synchronization
 exit-address-family
 !
ip classless
ip route 18.18.18.18 255.255.255.255 Tunnel0  ! Static Route for BLUE Tunnel
ip route 19.19.19.19 255.255.255.255 Tunnel1  ! Static Route for RED Tunnel
!
ip bgp-community new-format
!
ip explicit-path name BLUE-TUNNEL enable        ! Explicit Path for BLUE Tunnel
 next-address 20.1.12.1                          ! Direct to PE1
!
ip explicit-path name RED-TUNNEL enable         ! Explicit Path for RED Tunnel
 next-address 20.1.23.2                          ! First to P-Router (Core)
 next-address 20.1.13.1                          ! Then to PE1
```

continues

Example 15-16 *PE2 MPLS Per-VPN TE Example Configuration (Continued)*

```
!
access-list 1 permit 10.1.1.0 0.0.0.255      ! Adjacent Customer Blue subnets
access-list 1 permit 10.20.1.0 0.0.0.3       ! Adjacent Customer Blue subnets
access-list 2 permit 15.1.1.0 0.0.0.255      ! Adjacent Customer Red subnets
access-list 2 permit 15.20.1.0 0.0.0.3       ! Adjacent Customer Red subnets
!
route-map TUNNEL-ASSIGNMENT permit 10        ! BGP Inbound Route-Map
 match ip address 1                          ! Identifies Customer Blue subnets
 set ip next-hop 18.18.18.18                 ! Sets BGP Next-Hop to 18.18.18.18
!
route-map TUNNEL-ASSIGNMENT permit 20
 match ip address 2                          ! Identifies Customer Red subnets
 set ip next-hop 19.19.19.19                 ! Sets BGP Next-Hop to 19.19.19.19
!
```

A sample P-router configuration is shown in Figure 15-17 to illustrate the MPLS TE commands required in the core.

Example 15-17 *P-Router MPLS Per-VPN TE Example Configuration*

```
!
hostname P-Router
!
!
ip cef                      ! IP CEF is required for MPLS and MPLS TE
mpls ldp logging neighbor-changes
mpls traffic-eng tunnels    ! MPLS TE is enabled globally
!
!
!
interface Loopback0         ! Loopback interface for MPLS TE RID
 ip address 20.3.3.3 255.255.255.255
!
!
interface POS5/0
 description P-Router (Core) => PE1 POS Link
 ip address 20.1.13.2 255.255.255.252
 mpls traffic-eng tunnels                     ! MPLS TE enabled on int
 tag-switching ip                             ! MPLS enabled on int
 ip rsvp bandwidth 77500 77500                ! RSVP enabled on int for 77.5 Mbps
!
interface POS6/0
 description P-Router (Core) => PE2 POS Link
 ip address 20.1.23.2 255.255.255.252
 mpls traffic-eng tunnels                     ! MPLS TE enabled on int
 tag-switching ip                             ! MPLS enabled on int
 ip rsvp bandwidth 77500 77500                ! RSVP enabled on int for 77.5 Mbps
```

Example 15-17 *P-Router MPLS Per-VPN TE Example Configuration (Continued)*

```
!
router ospf 100
  mpls traffic-eng router-id Loopback0       ! MPLS TE RID
  mpls traffic-eng area 0                     ! Enables OSPF area 0 for MPLS TE
  log-adjacency-changes
  redistribute connected subnets
  network 20.1.13.0 0.0.0.3 area 0
  network 20.1.23.0 0.0.0.3 area 0
!
```

Verification commands:

- **show ip rsvp interface**
- **show ip rsvp neighbor**
- **show mpls interface**
- **show mpls traffic-eng tunnels summary**
- **show mpls traffic-eng tunnels show mpls traffic-eng topology**
- **show ip bgp vpnv4 all**
- **ping vrf** with **show interface tunnel**

Verification Command: **show ip rsvp interface**

The **show ip rsvp interface** command is useful to verify whether all physical interfaces that can participate in tunnels have been configured with an amount of reservable bandwidth. If the command **ip rsvp bandwidth** is omitted from the interface configuration, the amount of reservable bandwidth for that interface defaults to 0. A common cause of tunnels not coming up is the oversight of configuring RSVP reservations on the physical interface. See Example 15-18.

Example 15-18 *Verification of RSVP Configuration on Local Router*

```
PE1#show ip rsvp interface
interface      allocated  i/f max  flow max sub max
PO5/0          77500K     77500K   77500K   0
PO6/0          77500K     77500K   77500K   0
PE1#
```

Verification Command: **show ip rsvp neighbor**

A similar command for checking whether RSVP has been enabled properly on physical interfaces is the **show ip rsvp neighbor** command, which reports whether RSVP has been enabled on neighboring router interfaces. See Example 15-19.

Example 15-19 *Verification of RSVP Configuration on Neighboring Routers*

```
PE1#show ip rsvp neighbor
   20.1.12.2       RSVP
   20.1.13.2       RSVP
PE1#
```

Verification Command: **show mpls interface**

The **show mpls interface** command is a useful command to verify whether tag switching has been configured properly on local interfaces. This command also lists which interfaces may participate in tunnels. Notice that tag switching is not configured explicitly on tunnel interfaces, although they are advertised through the link-state IGP. See Example 15-20.

Example 15-20 *Verification of Tag-Switching Configuration*

```
PE1#show mpls interfaces
Interface          IP            Tunnel   Operational
POS5/0             Yes (tdp)     Yes      Yes
POS6/0             Yes (tdp)     Yes      Yes
Tunnel0            No            No       Yes
Tunnel1            No            No       Yes
PE1#
```

Verification Command: **show mpls traffic-eng tunnels summary**

A quick way to check whether MPLS TE has been enabled globally and has been configured properly is to use the **show mpls traffic-eng tunnels summary** command. Example 15-21 shows an example of this command: Two tunnel heads and two tunnel tails have been configured correctly and are active.

Example 15-21 *Verification of MPLS TE Global Configuration*

```
PE1#show mpls traffic-eng tunnels summary
Signalling Summary:
    LSP Tunnels Process:            running
    RSVP Process:                   running
    Forwarding:                     enabled
    Head: 2 interfaces, 2 active signalling attempts, 2 established
           3 activations, 1 deactivations
    Midpoints: 0, Tails: 2
    Periodic reoptimization:        every 3600 seconds, next in 1712 seconds
    Periodic auto-bw collection:    disabled
PE1#
```

Verification Command: **show mpls traffic-eng tunnels**

Additional per-tunnel detail is shown by the **show mpls traffic-eng tunnels** command. See Example 15-22.

Example 15-22 *Verification of MPLS Tunnel Details*

```
PE1#show mpls traffic-eng tunnels tunnel 0
Name: BLUE-TUNNEL (PE1=>PE2)                (Tunnel0) Destination: 20.2.2.2
  Status
    Admin: up          Oper: up       Path: valid        Signalling: connected
    path option 1, type explicit BLUE-TUNNEL (Basis for Setup, path weight 1)
  Config Parameters:
    Bandwidth: 77500    kbps (Global) Priority: 7  7   Affinity: 0x0/0xFFFF
    Metric Type: TE (default)
    AutoRoute: disabled LockDown: disabled Loadshare: 77500    bw-based
    auto-bw: disabled
  InLabel  :  -
  OutLabel : POS5/0, implicit-null
  RSVP Signalling Info:
      Src 20.1.1.1, Dst 20.2.2.2, Tun_Id 0, Tun_Instance 7
    RSVP Path Info:
      My Address: 20.1.1.1
      Explicit Route: 20.1.12.2 20.2.2.2
      Record Route:  NONE
      Tspec: ave rate=77500 kbits, burst=1000 bytes, peak rate=77500 kbits
    RSVP Resv Info:
      Record Route:  NONE
      Fspec: ave rate=77500 kbits, burst=1000 bytes, peak rate=77500 kbits
  Shortest Unconstrained Path Info:
    Path Weight: 1 (TE)
    Explicit Route: 20.1.12.2 20.2.2.2
  History:
    Tunnel:
      Time since created: 2 hours, 34 minutes
      Time since path change: 2 hours, 34 minutes
    Current LSP:
      Uptime: 2 hours, 34 minutes
PE1#
```

Verification Command: **ping vrf** with **show interface tunnel**

Verification of the MPLS TE solution can be performed with a **ping vrf** command coupled with a **show interface tunnel** command to demonstrate that traffic for each VPN is being sent over the proper tunnel. The interface counters can be cleared with the **clear counters** command before these tests. See Example 15-23.

Example 15-23 *Solution Verification with* **ping vrf** *and* **show interface tunnel** *Commands*

```
PE1#ping vrf BLUE 10.2.2.2
Type escape sequence to abort.
Sending 5, 100-byte ICMP Echos to 10.2.2.2, timeout is 2 seconds:
!!!!!
Success rate is 100 percent (5/5), round-trip min/avg/max = 1/2/4 ms
PE1#ping vrf RED 15.2.2.2
Type escape sequence to abort.
```

continues

Example 15-23 *Solution Verification with* **ping vrf** *and* **show interface tunnel** *Commands (Continued)*

```
Sending 5, 100-byte ICMP Echos to 15.2.2.2, timeout is 2 seconds:
!!!!!
Success rate is 100 percent (5/5), round-trip min/avg/max = 1/1/4 ms
PE1#ping vrf RED 15.2.2.2
Type escape sequence to abort.
Sending 5, 100-byte ICMP Echos to 15.2.2.2, timeout is 2 seconds:
!!!!!
Success rate is 100 percent (5/5), round-trip min/avg/max = 1/1/4 ms
PE1#ping vrf RED 15.2.2.2
Type escape sequence to abort.
Sending 5, 100-byte ICMP Echos to 15.2.2.2, timeout is 2 seconds:
!!!!!
Success rate is 100 percent (5/5), round-trip min/avg/max = 1/1/4 ms
PE1#
PE1#show interface tunnel 0
Tunnel0 is up, line protocol is up
  Hardware is Tunnel
  Description: BLUE-TUNNEL (PE1=>PE2)
  Interface is unnumbered. Using address of Loopback0 (20.1.1.1)
  MTU 1514 bytes, BW 9 Kbit, DLY 500000 usec,
     reliability 255/255, txload 1/255, rxload 1/255
  Encapsulation TUNNEL, loopback not set
  Keepalive not set
  Tunnel source UNKNOWN, destination 20.2.2.2
  Tunnel protocol/transport Label Switching, key disabled, sequencing disabled
  Checksumming of packets disabled,  fast tunneling enabled
  Last input never, output never, output hang never
  Last clearing of "show interface" counters 00:00:28
  Input queue: 0/75/0/0 (size/max/drops/flushes); Total output drops: 0
  Queueing strategy: fifo
  Output queue: 0/0 (size/max)
  5 minute input rate 0 bits/sec, 0 packets/sec
  5 minute output rate 0 bits/sec, 0 packets/sec
     0 packets input, 0 bytes, 0 no buffer
     Received 0 broadcasts, 0 runts, 0 giants, 0 throttles
     0 input errors, 0 CRC, 0 frame, 0 overrun, 0 ignored, 0 abort
     5 packets output, 500 bytes, 0 underruns
     0 output errors, 0 collisions, 0 interface resets
     0 output buffer failures, 0 output buffers swapped out
PE1#
PE1#show interface tunnel 1
Tunnel1 is up, line protocol is up
  Hardware is Tunnel
  Description: RED-TUNNEL (PE1=>P=>PE2)
  Interface is unnumbered. Using address of Loopback0 (20.1.1.1)
  MTU 1514 bytes, BW 9 Kbit, DLY 500000 usec,
     reliability 255/255, txload 1/255, rxload 1/255
  Encapsulation TUNNEL, loopback not set
  Keepalive not set
  Tunnel source UNKNOWN, destination 20.2.2.2
  Tunnel protocol/transport Label Switching, key disabled, sequencing disabled
  Checksumming of packets disabled,  fast tunneling enabled
```

Example 15-23 *Solution Verification with* **ping vrf** *and* **show interface tunnel** *Commands (Continued)*

```
         Last input never, output never, output hang never
         Last clearing of "show interface" counters 00:00:37
         Input queue: 0/75/0/0 (size/max/drops/flushes); Total output drops: 0
         Queueing strategy: fifo
         Output queue: 0/0 (size/max)
         5 minute input rate 0 bits/sec, 0 packets/sec
         5 minute output rate 0 bits/sec, 0 packets/sec
            0 packets input, 0 bytes, 0 no buffer
            Received 0 broadcasts, 0 runts, 0 giants, 0 throttles
            0 input errors, 0 CRC, 0 frame, 0 overrun, 0 ignored, 0 abort
            15 packets output, 1500 bytes, 0 underruns
            0 output errors, 0 collisions, 0 interface resets
            0 output buffer failures, 0 output buffers swapped out
    PE1#
```

MPLS DS-TE

MPLS traffic engineering allows constraint-based routing (CBR) of IP traffic. One of the constraints satisfied by CBR is the availability of required bandwidth over a selected path. DiffServ-aware traffic engineering extends MPLS traffic engineering to enable you to perform constraint-based routing of "guaranteed" traffic, which satisfies a more restrictive bandwidth constraint than that required for regular traffic. The more restrictive bandwidth is termed a subpool, and the regular TE tunnel bandwidth is called the global pool (the subpool is a portion of the global pool). This capability to satisfy a more restrictive bandwidth constraint translates into a capability to achieve higher quality of service performance (in terms of delay, jitter, or loss) for the guaranteed traffic.

For example, DS-TE can be used to ensure that traffic is routed over the network so that, on every link, there is never more than 35 percent (or any assigned percentage) of the link capacity of guaranteed traffic (for example, voice), while there can be up to 100 percent of the link capacity of regular traffic. Assuming that QoS mechanisms also are used on every link to queue guaranteed traffic separately from regular traffic, it then becomes possible to enforce separate "overbooking" ratios for guaranteed and regular traffic.

Also, through the capability to enforce a maximum percentage of guaranteed traffic on any link, the network administrator directly can control the end-to-end QoS performance parameters without having to rely on overengineering or on expected shortest-path routing behavior. This is essential for transport of applications that have very high QoS requirements (such as real-time voice, virtual IP leased line, and bandwidth trading), where overengineering cannot be assumed everywhere in the network.

DS-TE involves extending the IGP link-state protocols so that the available subpool bandwidth at each preemption level is advertised in addition to the available global pool bandwidth at each preemption level. DS-TE modifies constraint-based routing to take this more complex advertised information into account during path computation.

DiffServ-aware traffic engineering enables service providers to perform separate admission control and separate route computation for discrete subsets of traffic (for example, voice and data traffic). Remember, as with expedited forwarding, PHBs can protect voice from data, but only admission-control mechanisms can protect voice from voice.

For example, a service provider might sell voice services to two customers, both with a strict-priority servicing requirement. However, if congestion is occurring on a node to the point that not enough bandwidth is available for both customers' voice traffic, MPLS DS-TE can signal this condition back to the headend so that additional voice traffic can be rerouted along a different path where adequate priority bandwidth still exists.

In short, MPLS DS-TE offers additional granularity and guarantees to traffic engineering scenarios, which are suited especially to Real-Time applications such as Voice and Interactive-Video.

These incremental steps are required for enabling MPLS DS-TE:

- Provision per-link DiffServ policies:

```
PE1(config)#class-map match-all CORE-REALTIME
PE1(config-cmap)#match mpls experimental topmost 5
PE1(config-cmap)#class-map match-all CORE-CRITICAL-DATA
PE1(config-cmap)#match mpls experimental topmost 6
PE1(config-cmap)#match mpls experimental topmost 3
PE1(config-cmap)#policy-map CORE-THREE-CLASS-SP-MODEL
PE1(config-pmap)#class CORE-REALTIME
PE1(config-pmap-c)#priority percent 35
PE1(config-pmap-c)#class CORE-CRITICAL-DATA
PE1(config-pmap-c)#bandwidth percent 55
PE1(config-pmap-c)#class class-default
PE1(config-pmap-c)#interface pos 5/0
PE1(config-if)# max-reserved-bandwidth 100
PE1(config-if)# service-policy output CORE-THREE-CLASS-SP-MODEL
PE1(config)#interface pos 6/0
PE1(config-if)# max-reserved-bandwidth 100
PE1(config-if)# service-policy output CORE-THREE-CLASS-SP-MODEL
PE1(config-if)#exit
```

- Assign per-link reservable subpool bandwidth allotments on all physical interfaces that are participating in DS-TE tunnels (including links on midpoint routers):

```
PE1(config)#interface pos 5/0
PE1(config-if)# ip rsvp bandwidth 77500 sub-pool 54250
```

- Assign a reservable subpool bandwidth to each MPLS DS-TE tunnel headend:

```
PE1(config)#interface tunnel 0
PE1(config-if)#tunnel mpls traffic-eng bandwidth sub-pool 54250
```

- Lower the priority (remember lower is better) of the MPLS DS-TE tunnel so that it can preempt reservations, as needed:

```
PE1(config)#interface tunnel 0
PE1(config-if)# tunnel mpls traffic-eng priority 0 0
```

- Tighten down on the MPLS DS-TE headend tunnel admission control criteria (via static routes and/or policy-based routing).

Example 15-24 *PE1 MPLS DS-TE Example Configuration (Continued)*

```
 tunnel mode mpls traffic-eng
 tunnel mpls traffic-eng priority 0 0                    ! Lower value is preferred
 tunnel mpls traffic-eng bandwidth sub-pool 54250   ! MPLS DS-TE sub-pool
 tunnel mpls traffic-eng path-option 1 explicit name TUNNEL0
!
interface Tunnel1
 description TUNNEL0 (PE1=>P=>PE2)
 ip unnumbered Loopback0
 tunnel destination 20.2.2.2
 tunnel mode mpls traffic-eng
 tunnel mpls traffic-eng priority 7 7
 tunnel mpls traffic-eng bandwidth  77500
 tunnel mpls traffic-eng path-option 1 explicit name TUNNEL1
!
!
interface FastEthernet1/0
 description FE to Customer Blue CE1
 ip vrf forwarding BLUE                        ! Interface to Blue CE1
 ip address 10.20.1.2 255.255.255.252         ! Same IP address as Red
!
interface FastEthernet1/1
 description FE to Customer Red CE1
 ip vrf forwarding RED                         ! Interface to Red CE1
 ip address 10.20.1.2 255.255.255.252         ! Same IP address as Blue
!
interface POS5/0
 description PE1=>PE2 POS Link
 ip address 20.1.12.1 255.255.255.252
 max-reserved-bandwidth 100
 service-policy output CORE-THREE-CLASS-SP-MODEL    ! Scheduling applied
 mpls traffic-eng tunnels
 tag-switching ip
 ip rsvp bandwidth 77500 sub-pool 54250        ! Sub-pool defined on int
!
interface POS6/0
 description PE1=>P-Router (Core) POS Link
 ip address 20.1.13.1 255.255.255.252
 max-reserved-bandwidth 100
 service-policy output CORE-THREE-CLASS-SP-MODEL    ! Scheduling applied
 mpls traffic-eng tunnels
 tag-switching ip
 ip rsvp bandwidth 77500 77500                 ! No change to PE-P RSVP
!
router ospf 100
 mpls traffic-eng router-id Loopback0
 mpls traffic-eng area 0
 log-adjacency-changes
 redistribute connected subnets
 network 20.1.12.0 0.0.0.3 area 0
 network 20.1.13.0 0.0.0.3 area 0
```

continues

Example 15-24 *PE1 MPLS DS-TE Example Configuration (Continued)*

```
!
router bgp 100
 no synchronization
 bgp log-neighbor-changes
 redistribute connected
 neighbor 20.2.2.2 remote-as 100
 neighbor 20.2.2.2 update-source Loopback0
 no auto-summary
 !
 address-family vpnv4
 neighbor 20.2.2.2 activate
 neighbor 20.2.2.2 send-community extended
 neighbor 20.2.2.2 route-map TUNNEL-ASSIGNMENT in  ! Applies BGP PBR
 exit-address-family
 !
 address-family ipv4 vrf RED
 redistribute connected
 neighbor 10.20.1.1 remote-as 15
 neighbor 10.20.1.1 activate
 neighbor 10.20.1.1 default-originate
 no auto-summary
 no synchronization
 exit-address-family
 !
 address-family ipv4 vrf BLUE
 redistribute connected
 neighbor 10.20.1.1 remote-as 10
 neighbor 10.20.1.1 activate
 neighbor 10.20.1.1 default-originate
 no auto-summary
 no synchronization
 exit-address-family
 !
ip classless
ip route 16.16.16.16 255.255.255.255 Tunnel0  ! Static route for Tunnel 0
ip route 17.17.17.17 255.255.255.255 Tunnel1 ! Static route for Tunnel 1
!
ip extcommunity-list 1 permit rt 100:1        ! Identifies Blue VPN by RT
ip extcommunity-list 2 permit rt 150:1        ! Identifies Red VPN by RT
ip bgp-community new-format
!
ip explicit-path name TUNNEL0 enable
 next-address 20.1.12.2
 !
ip explicit-path name TUNNEL1 enable
 next-address 20.1.13.2
 next-address 20.1.23.1
 !
access-list 1 permit 10.2.102.0 0.0.0.255     ! Identifies (Blue) Voice-VLAN
access-list 2 permit 10.2.2.0 0.0.0.255       ! Identifies (Blue) Data-VLAN
access-list 2 permit 10.20.2.0 0.0.0.3        ! Identifies (Blue) PE-CE link
access-list 3 permit 10.2.102.0 0.0.0.255     ! Identifies (Red) Voice-VLAN
```

Example 15-24 *PE1 MPLS DS-TE Example Configuration (Continued)*

```
access-list 3 permit 10.2.2.0 0.0.0.255      ! Identifies (Red) Data-VLAN
access-list 3 permit 10.20.2.0 0.0.0.3       ! Identifies (Red) PE-CE Link
!
route-map TUNNEL-ASSIGNMENT permit 10
 match ip address 1                          ! Matches Voice-VLAN subnet
 match extcommunity 1                        ! Matches Blue VPN RT
 set ip next-hop 16.16.16.16                 ! Sets BGP Next-Hop to 16.16.16.16
 !
route-map TUNNEL-ASSIGNMENT permit 20
 match ip address 2                          ! Matches other (Blue) subnets
 match extcommunity 1                        ! Matches Blue VPN RT
 set ip next-hop 17.17.17.17                 ! Sets BGP Next-Hop to 17.17.17.17
 !
route-map TUNNEL-ASSIGNMENT permit 30
 match ip address 3                          ! Matches all (Red) subnets
 match extcommunity 2                        ! Matches Red VPN RT
 set ip next-hop 17.17.17.17                 ! Sets BGP Next-Hop to 17.17.17.17
 !
```

The second/complementary PE router's configuration for this MPLS DS-TE example is shown in Example 15-25.

Example 15-25 *PE2 MPLS DS-TE Example Configuration*

```
!
hostname PE2
!
!
ip vrf BLUE                     ! BLUE MPLS VPN definition
 rd 100:1
 route-target export 100:1
 route-target import 100:1
 !
ip vrf RED                      ! RED MPLS VPN definition
 rd 150:1
 route-target export 150:1
 route-target import 150:1
 !
ip cef                          ! IP CEF is required for MPLS and MPLS TE
mpls ldp logging neighbor-changes
mpls traffic-eng tunnels        ! MPLS TE is enabled globally
 !
 !
class-map match-all CORE-REALTIME
  match mpls experimental topmost 5
class-map match-all CORE-CRITICAL-DATA
  match mpls experimental topmost 6
  match mpls experimental topmost 3
 !
```

continues

Example 15-25 *PE2 MPLS DS-TE Example Configuration (Continued)*

```
!
policy-map CORE-THREE-CLASS-SP-MODEL              ! Per-link scheduling policy
  class CORE-REALTIME
   priority percent 35
  class CORE-CRITICAL-DATA
   bandwidth percent 55
  class class-default
   fair-queue
!
!
interface Loopback0            ! Loopback interface for MPLS TE RID
 ip address 20.2.2.2 255.255.255.255
!
interface Tunnel0
 description TUNNEL0 (PE2=>PE1)
 ip unnumbered Loopback0
 tunnel destination 20.1.1.1
 tunnel mode mpls traffic-eng
 tunnel mpls traffic-eng priority 0 0              ! Lower value is preferred
 tunnel mpls traffic-eng bandwidth sub-pool 54250  ! MPLS DS-TE sub-pool
!
interface Tunnel1
 description TUNNEL1 (PE2=>P=>PE1)
 ip unnumbered Loopback0
 tunnel destination 20.1.1.1
 tunnel mode mpls traffic-eng
 tunnel mpls traffic-eng priority 7 7
 tunnel mpls traffic-eng bandwidth  77500
 tunnel mpls traffic-eng path-option 1 explicit name TUNNEL1
!
!
interface FastEthernet1/0
 description FE to Customer Blue CE2
 ip vrf forwarding BLUE                   ! Interface to Blue CE2
 ip address 10.20.2.2 255.255.255.252     ! Same IP address as Red
!
interface FastEthernet1/1
 description FE to Customer Red CE2
 ip vrf forwarding RED                    ! Interface to Red CE2
 ip address 10.20.2.2 255.255.255.252     ! Same IP address as Blue
!
interface POS5/0
 description PE2=>PE1 POS Link
 ip address 20.1.12.2 255.255.255.252
 max-reserved-bandwidth 100
 service-policy output CORE-THREE-CLASS-SP-MODEL   ! Scheduling applied
 mpls traffic-eng tunnels
 tag-switching ip
 ip rsvp bandwidth 77500 sub-pool 54250            ! Sub-pool defined on int
!
interface POS6/0
 description PE2=>P-Router (Core) POS Link
```

Example 15-25 *PE2 MPLS DS-TE Example Configuration (Continued)*

```
ip address 20.1.23.1 255.255.255.252
max-reserved-bandwidth 100
service-policy output CORE-THREE-CLASS-SP-MODEL       ! Scheduling applied
mpls traffic-eng tunnels
tag-switching ip
ip rsvp bandwidth 77500 77500                 ! No change to PE-P RSVP
!
router ospf 100
mpls traffic-eng router-id Loopback0
mpls traffic-eng area 0
log-adjacency-changes
redistribute connected subnets
network 20.1.12.0 0.0.0.3 area 0
network 20.1.23.0 0.0.0.3 area 0
!
router bgp 100
no synchronization
bgp log-neighbor-changes
redistribute connected
neighbor 20.1.1.1 remote-as 100
neighbor 20.1.1.1 update-source Loopback0
no auto-summary
!
address-family vpnv4
neighbor 20.1.1.1 activate
neighbor 20.1.1.1 send-community extended
neighbor 20.2.2.2 route-map TUNNEL-ASSIGNMENT in    ! Applies BGP PBR
exit-address-family
!
address-family ipv4 vrf RED
redistribute connected
neighbor 10.20.2.1 remote-as 15
neighbor 10.20.2.1 activate
neighbor 10.20.2.1 default-originate
no auto-summary
no synchronization
exit-address-family
!
address-family ipv4 vrf BLUE
redistribute connected
neighbor 10.20.2.1 remote-as 10
neighbor 10.20.2.1 activate
neighbor 10.20.2.1 default-originate
no auto-summary
no synchronization
exit-address-family
!
ip classless
ip route 18.18.18.18 255.255.255.255 Tunnel0 ! Static route for Tunnel 0
ip route 19.19.19.19 255.255.255.255 Tunnel1 ! Static route for Tunnel 1
!
```

continues

Example 15-25 *PE2 MPLS DS-TE Example Configuration (Continued)*

```
ip extcommunity-list 1 permit rt 100:1    ! Identifies Blue VPN by RT
ip extcommunity-list 2 permit rt 150:1    ! Identifies Red VPN by RT
ip bgp-community new-format
!
ip explicit-path name TUNNEL0 enable
 next-address 20.1.12.1
!
ip explicit-path name TUNNEL1 enable
 next-address 20.1.23.2
 next-address 20.1.13.1
!
access-list 1 permit 10.1.101.0 0.0.0.255    ! Identifies (Blue) Voice-VLAN
access-list 1 access-list 2 permit 10.1       ! Identifies (Blue) Data-VLAN
access-list 2 permit 10.20.1.0 0.0.0.3        ! Identifies (Blue) PE-CE link
access-list 3 permit 10.1.101.0 0.0.0.255     ! Identifies (Red) Voice-VLAN
access-list 3 permit 10.1.1.0 0.0.0.255       ! Identifies (Red) Data-VLAN
access-list 3 permit 10.20.1.0 0.0.0.3        ! Identifies (Red) PE-CE Link
!
route-map TUNNEL-ASSIGNMENT permit 10
 match ip address 1                       ! Matches Voice-VLAN subnet
 match extcommunity 1                     ! Matches Blue VPN RT
 set ip next-hop 18.18.18.18              ! Sets BGP Next-Hop to 18.18.18.18
!
route-map TUNNEL-ASSIGNMENT permit 20
 match ip address 2                       ! Matches other (Blue) subnets
 match extcommunity 1                     ! Matches Blue VPN RT
 set ip next-hop 19.19.19.19              ! Sets BGP Next-Hop to 19.19.19.19
!
route-map TUNNEL-ASSIGNMENT permit 30
 match ip address 3                       ! Matches all (Red) subnets
 match extcommunity 2                     ! Matches Red VPN RT
 set ip next-hop 19.19.19.19              ! Sets BGP Next-Hop to 19.19.19.19
!
```

A P router's configuration for this MPLS DS-TE example is shown in Example 15-26 to highlight the MPLS DS-TE configurations required in the core.

Example 15-26 *P-Router MPLS DS-TE Example Configuration*

```
!
hostname P-Router
!
!
ip cef                        ! IP CEF is required for MPLS and MPLS TE
mpls ldp logging neighbor-changes
mpls traffic-eng tunnels      ! MPLS TE is enabled globally
!
!
class-map match-all CORE-REALTIME
  match mpls experimental topmost 5
```

Example 15-26 *P-Router MPLS DS-TE Example Configuration (Continued)*

```
class-map match-all CORE-CRITICAL-DATA
  match mpls experimental topmost 6
  match mpls experimental topmost 3
!
!
policy-map CORE-THREE-CLASS-SP-MODEL                ! Per-link scheduling policy
  class CORE-REALTIME
   priority percent 35
  class CORE-CRITICAL-DATA
   bandwidth percent 55
  class class-default
   fair-queue
!
!
interface Loopback0        ! Loopback interface for MPLS TE RID
 ip address 20.3.3.3 255.255.255.255
!
interface POS5/0
 description P-Router (Core) => PE1 POS Link
 ip address 20.1.13.2 255.255.255.252
 max-reserved-bandwidth 100
 service-policy output CORE-THREE-CLASS-SP-MODEL    ! Scheduling applied
 mpls traffic-eng tunnels
 tag-switching ip
 ip rsvp bandwidth 77500 77500                      ! RSVP enabled on int for 77.5 Mbps
!
interface POS6/0
 description P-Router (Core) => PE2 POS Link
 ip address 20.1.23.2 255.255.255.252
 max-reserved-bandwidth 100
 service-policy output CORE-THREE-CLASS-SP-MODEL    ! Scheduling applied
 mpls traffic-eng tunnels
 tag-switching ip
 ip rsvp bandwidth 77500 77500                      ! RSVP enabled on int for 77.5 Mbps
!
router ospf 100
 mpls traffic-eng router-id Loopback0      ! MPLS TE RID
 mpls traffic-eng area 0                   ! Enables OSPF area 0 for MPLS TE
 log-adjacency-changes
 redistribute connected subnets
 network 20.1.13.0 0.0.0.3 area 0
 network 20.1.23.0 0.0.0.3 area 0
!
```

Verification commands:

- **show ip rsvp interface**
- **show ip rsvp neighbor**
- **show mpls interface**

- show mpls traffic-eng tunnels summary
- show mpls traffic-eng tunnels
- show mpls traffic-eng topology
- show ip bgp vpnv4 all
- ping vrf with show interface tunnel

Verification Command: **show mpls traffic-eng topology**

The **show mpls traffic-eng topology** command details (among other things) the amount of allocated bandwidth for reservations on a per-priority basis. Example 15-27 shows the details of the 54.25 Mbps (or 35 percent of the link) to be reserved in a subpool of priority 0 (best priority) on the PE-to-PE tunnel (Tunnel0). Furthermore, because the total reservable bandwidth on the PE-to-PE links is 77.5 Mbps, there remains 23.35 Mbps (77.5 – 54.25 Mbps) available to be reserved over the same link by global-pool traffic.

The command also shows that 77.5 Mbps of global-pool traffic has been allocated over the PE-to-P tunnel (Tunnel1).

Example 15-27 *Verification of Subpool and Global-Pool RSVP Reservations for DS-TE*

```
PE1#show mpls traffic-eng topology 20.1.1.1
IGP Id: 20.1.1.1, MPLS TE Id:20.1.1.1 Router Node   id 1
      link[0 ]:Nbr IGP Id: 20.2.2.2, nbr_node_id:2, gen:30
          frag_id 0, Intf Address:20.1.12.1, Nbr Intf Address:20.1.12.2
          TE metric:1, IGP metric:1, attribute_flags:0x0
          physical_bw: 155000 (kbps), max_reservable_bw_global: 77500 (kbps)
          max_reservable_bw_sub: 54250 (kbps)
                                          Global Pool     Sub Pool
                        Total Allocated   Reservable      Reservable
                        BW (kbps)         BW (kbps)       BW (kbps)
                        ---------------   -----------     ----------
          bw[0]:            54250            23250                0
          bw[1]:                0            23250                0
          bw[2]:                0            23250                0
          bw[3]:                0            23250                0
          bw[4]:                0            23250                0
          bw[5]:                0            23250                0
          bw[6]:                0            23250                0
          bw[7]:                0            23250                0
      link[1 ]:Nbr IGP Id: 20.3.3.3, nbr_node_id:3, gen:32
          frag_id 1, Intf Address:20.1.13.1, Nbr Intf Address:20.1.13.2
          TE metric:1, IGP metric:1, attribute_flags:0x0
          physical_bw: 155000 (kbps), max_reservable_bw_global: 77500 (kbps)
          max_reservable_bw_sub: 0 (kbps)
```

Example 15-27 *Verification of Subpool and Global-Pool RSVP Reservations for DS-TE (Continued)*

```
                                 Global Pool      Sub Pool
                  Total Allocated Reservable       Reservable
                  BW (kbps)       BW (kbps)        BW (kbps)
                  --------------- ----------       ----------
          bw[0]:             0        77500                 0
          bw[1]:             0        77500                 0
          bw[2]:             0        77500                 0
          bw[3]:             0        77500                 0
          bw[4]:             0        77500                 0
          bw[5]:             0        77500                 0
          bw[6]:             0        77500                 0
          bw[7]:         77500            0                 0
PE1#
```

Verification Command: **show ip bgp vpnv4 all**

The **show ip bgp vpnv4 all** command displays the BGP next-hop (and other) attributes of all prefixes from all VRFs. In Example 15-28, the next-hop attribute of the prefix representing Customer Blue's adjacent CE's voice VLAN (10.1.102.0/24) is shown to be set to the fictitious address of 16.16.16.16, which is resolved recursively to point to Tunnel0 (the premium DS-TE tunnel for voice). Although Customer Red has the same IP address prefix, its next hop is set to the fictitious address of 17.17.17.17, which is resolved recursively to point to Tunnel1 (the default tunnel).

Example 15-28 *Verification of BGP Next-Hop Policies*

```
PE1#show ip bgp vpnv4 all
BGP table version is 78, local router ID is 20.1.1.1
Status codes: s suppressed, d damped, h history, * valid, > best, i - internal,
              r RIB-failure, S Stale
Origin codes: i - IGP, e - EGP, ? - incomplete
   Network          Next Hop            Metric LocPrf Weight Path
Route Distinguisher: 100:1 (default for vrf BLUE)
*> 10.1.1.0/24      10.20.1.1                0              0 10 ?
*> 10.1.101.0/24    10.20.1.1                0              0 10 ?
*>i10.2.2.0/24      17.17.17.17              0    100       0 10 ?
*>i10.2.102.0/24    16.16.16.16              0    100       0 10 ?
*  10.20.1.0/30     10.20.1.1                0              0 10 ?
*>                  0.0.0.0                  0          32768 ?
*>i10.20.2.0/30     17.17.17.17              0    100       0 ?
Route Distinguisher: 150:1 (default for vrf RED)
*> 10.1.1.0/24      10.20.1.1                0              0 15 ?
*> 10.1.101.0/24    10.20.1.1                0              0 15 ?
*>i10.2.2.0/24      17.17.17.17              0    100       0 15 ?
*>i10.2.102.0/24    17.17.17.17              0    100       0 15 ?
*  10.20.1.0/30     10.20.1.1                0              0 15 ?
*>                  0.0.0.0                  0          32768 ?
*>i10.20.2.0/30     17.17.17.17              0    100       0 ?
PE1#
```

Case Study: MPLS VPN QoS Design (CE/PE/P Routers)

Continuing the example from the previous design chapters, the fictitious company ABC, Inc., has been growing and expanding, both geographically and technologically. It has multiple data centers in geographically diverse regions to which its field needs to connect efficiently. Additionally, to increase collaboration and simultaneously reduce travel expenses, ABC, Inc., plans to roll out any-to-any videoconferencing. For these business reasons, ABC, Inc., has decided to migrate from its private WAN to an MPLS VPN, managed by service provider XYZ (SP XYZ).

To minimize the costs of migration, SP XYZ supports both Frame Relay and ATM Layer 2 access (including ATM IMA, which has been ABC, Inc.'s, primary choice for branch WAN media).

Furthermore, SP XYZ is a leader in MPLS VPN services and supports a five-class provider-edge model. Real-time service can be purchased in 5 percent increments, as can the amounts of the three other levels of preferred service (Critical Data, Video, and Bulk Data). ABC Inc. wants its WAN migration to MPLS VPN to be as transparent to end users as possible, so it agrees to purchase these services in amounts that closely match the current QoS Baseline WAN edge model, without causing traffic class-mixing issues.

Additionally, ABC, Inc., monitors network utilization (particularly videoconferencing traffic) and performs traffic accounting and department bill-back based on the DSCP markings of traffic flows. ABC, Inc., views it as essential that the SP *not* re-mark any traffic at Layer 3 as it traverses the MPLS VPN, but rather preserve the DSCP markings intact. Again, SP XYZ can accommodate ABC, Inc., because it deploys the popular Short Pipe Mode of MPLS DiffServ tunneling.

SP XYZ also offers the option of premium service for voice traffic to geographically adjacent sites (through MPLS DS-TE). Because ABC, Inc., is a heavy IP telephony user, it elects to purchase this premium service for voice traffic (thus, from SP XYZ's perspective, ABC, Inc., is considered a "BLUE" class customer).

Figure 15-22 illustrates the combined enterprise and service-provider nodes where QoS policies are required for this complex MPLS VPN scenario.

In Example 15-29, it is assumed that traffic has been marked correctly on campus/branch switches before it arrives at the CE LAN edges. Where such an assumption is invalid, ingress LAN edge marking policies, discussed in Chapter 14, "Branch Router QoS Design," can be applied to the CE LAN edges. Additionally, it has been assumed that there are no unidirectional applications in this example.

Queuing and marking policies for a five-class provider-edge model have been applied on CE edges.

Figure 15-22   *Case Study: MPLS VPN QoS Design Example Details*

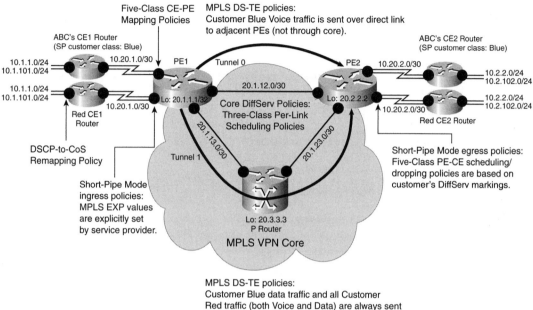

On ingress, SP XYZ applies a five-class short pipe MPLS DiffServ tunneling mode policer to identify (through MPLS EXP values) traffic that is in contract or out-of-contract. DiffServ policies are applied throughout the MPLS VPN core, and MPLS DS-TE also is provisioned for voice traffic to geographically adjacent CEs. On egress, SP XYZ applies a five-class provider-edge model, which is based on the customer's DiffServ markings. In this example, company ABC, Inc., fits service provider XYZ's customer Blue profile.

The configuration for this example spans six routers: Blue-CE1, Blue-CE2, Red-CE1, Red-CE2, PE1, PE2, and P router. However, because CE configurations are virtually identical, only one is presented here (Blue-CE1—see Example 15-29), along with the configurations for PE1 (see Example 15-30), PE2 (see Example 15-31), and the P router (see Example 15-32).

Example 15-29   *Blue-CE1 Case Study MPLS VPN QoS Design Example*

```
!
hostname CE1-BLUE
!
ip cef                          ! IP CEF is required for Packet Marking
!
class-map match-all ROUTING
 match ip dscp cs6
```

continues

Example 15-29 *Blue-CE1 Case Study MPLS VPN QoS Design Example (Continued)*

```
class-map match-all VOICE
 match ip dscp ef
class-map match-all INTERACTIVE-VIDEO
 match ip dscp af41
class-map match-all STREAMING-VIDEO
 match ip dscp cs4
class-map match-all MISSION-CRITICAL-DATA
 match ip dscp 25
class-map match-any CALL-SIGNALING
 match ip dscp af31
 match ip dscp cs3
class-map match-all TRANSACTIONAL-DATA
 match ip dscp af21
class-map match-all BULK-DATA
 match ip dscp af11
class-map match-all NETWORK-MANAGEMENT
 match ip dscp cs2
class-map match-all SCAVENGER
 match ip dscp cs1
!
!
policy-map CE-FIVE-CLASS-SP-MODEL
 class ROUTING
  bandwidth percent 3  ! Routing is assigned (by default) to Critical SP class
 class VOICE
  priority percent 18  ! Voice is admitted to Realtime SP class
 class INTERACTIVE-VIDEO
  priority percent 15
  set ip dscp cs5      ! Interactive-Video is assigned to the Realtime SP class
 class STREAMING-VIDEO
  bandwidth percent 13
  set ip dscp af21     ! Streaming-Video is assigned to the Video SP class
 class CALL-SIGNALING
  priority percent 2   ! Call-Signaling gets LLQ for this scenario
  set ip dscp cs5      ! Call-Signaling is assigned to the Realtime SP class
 class MISSION-CRITICAL-DATA
  bandwidth percent 12
  random-detect
  set ip dscp af31     ! MC Data is assigned to the Critical SP class
 class TRANSACTIONAL-DATA
  bandwidth percent 5
  random-detect
  set ip dscp cs3      ! Transactional Data is assigned to Critical SP class
 class NETWORK-MANAGEMENT
  bandwidth percent 2  ! Net Mgmt (mainly UDP) is admitted to Video SP class
 class BULK-DATA
  bandwidth percent 5  ! Bulk Data is assigned to Bulk SP class
  random-detect
 class SCAVENGER
  bandwidth percent 1
  set ip dscp 0
```

Example 15-29 *Blue-CE1 Case Study MPLS VPN QoS Design Example (Continued)*

```
 class class-default
  bandwidth percent 24
  random-detect
 !
 !
 policy-map CE-LAN-EDGE-OUT
  class class-default
   set cos dscp                    ! Enables default DSCP-to-CoS Mapping
 !
 !
interface FastEthernet0/0
 description TO CAT3500 BRANCH ACCESS-SWITCH
 no ip address
 !
interface FastEthernet0/0.11
 description DLVAN SUBNET 10.1.1.0
 encapsulation dot1Q 11
 ip address 10.1.1.1 255.255.255.0
 service-policy output CE-LAN-EDGE-OUT       ! Restores CoS for Data VLAN
 !
 !
interface FastEthernet0/0.101
 description VVLAN SUBNET 10.1.101.0
 encapsulation dot1Q 101
 ip address 10.1.101.1 255.255.255.0
 service-policy output CE-LAN-EDGE-OUT       ! Restores CoS on Voice VLAN
 !
 !
interface ATM1/0
 no ip address
 no atm ilmi-keepalive
 ima-group 1
 no scrambling-payload
 !
interface ATM1/1
 no ip address
 no atm ilmi-keepalive
 ima-group 1
 no scrambling-payload
 !
 !
interface ATM1/IMA1
 no ip address
 no atm ilmi-keepalive
 !
interface ATM1/IMA1.20 point-to-point
 description Dual-T1 ATM IMA Link to PE1
 ip address 10.20.1.1 255.255.255.252
 pvc 0/120
  vbr-nrt 3072 3072
```

continues

Example 15-29 *Blue-CE1 Case Study MPLS VPN QoS Design Example (Continued)*

```
 max-reserved-bandwidth 100                    ! Overrides 75% BW limit
 service-policy output CE-FIVE-CLASS-SP-MODEL  ! Applies 5-Class CE-PE Model
 !
!
router bgp 10
 no synchronization
 bgp log-neighbor-changes
 redistribute connected
 neighbor 10.20.1.2 remote-as 100
 no auto-summary
 !
 !
```

The configuration for the first PE router for this MPLS VPN QoS design case study example is shown in Example 15-30.

Example 15-30 *PE1 Case Study MPLS VPN QoS Design Example*

```
!
hostname PE1
!
!
ip vrf BLUE                       ! BLUE MPLS VPN Definition
 rd 100:1
 route-target export 100:1
 route-target import 100:1
 !
ip vrf RED                        ! RED MPLS VPN Definition
 rd 150:1
 route-target export 150:1
 route-target import 150:1
 !
ip cef
mpls ldp logging neighbor-changes
mpls traffic-eng tunnels          ! Enables MPLS TE globally
 !
 !
 !
class-map match-any REALTIME
 match ip dscp ef
 match ip dscp cs5
class-map match-any CRITICAL-DATA
 match ip dscp cs6
 match ip dscp af31
 match ip dscp cs3
class-map match-any VIDEO
 match ip dscp af21
 match ip dscp cs2
class-map match-any BULK-DATA
 match ip dscp af11
 match ip dscp cs1
```

Example 15-30 *PE1 Case Study MPLS VPN QoS Design Example (Continued)*

```
class-map match-all CORE-REALTIME
  match mpls experimental topmost 5  ! Identifies in-contract Realtime
class-map match-all CORE-CRITICAL-DATA
  match mpls experimental topmost 3  ! Identifies in-contract Critical-Data
  match mpls experimental topmost 7  ! Identifies out-of-contract Critical Data
  match mpls experimental topmost 2  ! Identifies in-contract Video
  match mpls experimental topmost 1  ! Identifies in-contract Bulk
  match mpls experimental topmost 6  ! Identifies out-of-contract Bulk
!
!
policy-map PE-FIVE-CLASS-SHORT-PIPE-MARKING
  claexceed-action set-mpls-exp-topmost-transmit 7
   police cir 1050000
     conform-action set-mpls-exp-topmost-transmit 5  ! Conforming RT set to 5
     exceed-action drop                              ! Excess Realtime is dropped
   class CRITICAL-DATA
    police cir 600000
     conform-action set-mpls-exp-topmost-transmit 3  ! Critical Data set to 3
     exceed-action set-mpls-exp-topmost-transmit 7   ! Excess Critical set 7
   class VIDEO
    police cir 450000
     conform-action set-mpls-exp-topmost-transmit 2  ! Conforming Video set to 2
     exceed-action drop                              ! Excess Video dropped
   class BULK-DATA
    police cir 150000
     conform-action set-mpls-exp-topmost-transmit 1  ! Conforming Bulk set to 1
     exceed-action set-mpls-exp-topmost-transmit 6   ! Excess Bulk set to 6
   class class-default
    police cir 750000
     conform-action set-mpls-exp-topmost-transmit 0  ! Conforming BE set to 0
     exceed-action set-mpls-exp-topmost-transmit 4   ! Excess BE set to 4
!
!
policy-map PE-FIVE-CLASS-SP-MODEL
 class REALTIME
  priority percent 35          ! Realtime SP class gets 35% LLQ
 class CRITICAL-DATA
  bandwidth percent 20         ! Critical-Data SP class gets 40% CBWFQ
  random-detect dscp-based     ! DSCP-based WRED enabled on class
 class VIDEO
  bandwidth percent 15         ! Video SP class gets 15% CBWFQ
  random-detect dscp-based     ! DSCP-based WRED enabled on "Video" SP class
 class BULK-DATA
  bandwidth percent 5          ! Bulk Data SP class gets 15% CBWFQ
  random-detect dscp-based     ! DSCP-based WRED enabled on Bulk Data SP class
 class class-default
  bandwidth percent 25         ! Best Effort SP class gets 25% CBWFQ
  random-detect                ! WRED enabled on Best Effort SP class
!
```

continues

Example 15-30 *PE1 Case Study MPLS VPN QoS Design Example (Continued)*

```
!
policy-map CORE-THREE-CLASS-SP-MODEL
  class CORE-REALTIME
    priority percent 35                ! CORE-REALTIME gets 35% LLQ
  class CORE-CRITICAL-DATA
    bandwidth percent 55               ! CORE-CRITICAL gets 55% CBWFQ
  class class-default
    fair-queue                         ! CORE-BEST-EFFORT gets FQ
!
!
interface Loopback0           ! Loopback interface for MPLS TE RID
 ip address 20.1.1.1 255.255.255.255
!
interface Tunnel0
 description TUNNEL0 (PE1=>PE2)
 ip unnumbered Loopback0
 tunnel destination 20.2.2.2
 tunnel mode mpls traffic-eng                ! Enables MPLS TE on tunnel
 tunnel mpls traffic-eng priority 0 0        ! Best priority
 tunnel mpls traffic-eng bandwidth sub-pool 54250  ! Assigns sub-pool
 tunnel mpls traffic-eng path-option 1 explicit name TUNNEL0
!
interface Tunnel1
 description TUNNEL1 (PE1=>P=>PE2)
 ip unnumbered Loopback0
 tunnel destination 20.2.2.2
 tunnel mode mpls traffic-eng                ! Enables MPLS TE
 tunnel mpls traffic-eng priority 7 7        ! Worst priority
 tunnel mpls traffic-eng bandwidth  77500    ! Assigns global pool
 tunnel mpls traffic-eng path-option 1 explicit name TUNNEL1
!
!
interface ATM2/0
 no ip address
 ima-group 1
!
interface ATM2/1
 no ip address
 ima-group 1
!
interface ATM2/ima1
 no ip address
 no atm ilmi-keepalive
!
interface ATM2/ima1.20 point-to-point
 description Dual-T1 ATM IMA Link to Blue CE1
 ip vrf forwarding BLUE
 ip address 10.20.1.2 255.255.255.252
 pvc 0/120
  vbr-nrt 3072 3072
  max-reserved-bandwidth 100                           ! Overrides 75% BW
```

Example 15-30 *PE1 Case Study MPLS VPN QoS Design Example (Continued)*

```
     service-policy input PE-FIVE-CLASS-SHORT-PIPE-MARKING        ! Short Pipe Marking
     service-policy output PE-FIVE-CLASS-SP-MODEL                 ! Egress policy to CE
 !
!
interface ATM2/2
 no ip address
 ima-group 2
!
interface ATM2/ima2
 no ip address
 no atm ilmi-keepalive
!
interface ATM2/ima2.20 point-to-point
 description Dual-T1 ATM IMA Link to Red CE1
 ip vrf forwarding RED
 ip address 10.20.1.2 255.255.255.252
 pvc 0/220
  vbr-nrt 3072 3072
  max-reserved-bandwidth 100                                     ! Overrides 75% BW
  service-policy input PE-FIVE-CLASS-SHORT-PIPE-MARKING          ! Short Pipe Marking
  service-policy output PE-FIVE-CLASS-SP-MODEL                   ! Egress policy to CE
  !
 !
interface ATM2/3
 no ip address
 ima-group 2
!
!
interface POS5/0
 description PE1=>PE2 POS Link
 ip address 20.1.12.1 255.255.255.252
 max-reserved-bandwidth 100                                      ! Overrides 75% BW limit
 service-policy output CORE-THREE-CLASS-SP-MODEL                 ! Applies Core DS policies
 mpls traffic-eng tunnels                                        ! Enables MPLS TE on int
 tag-switching ip
 ip rsvp bandwidth 77500 sub-pool 54250                          ! Assigns sub-pool BW
!
interface POS6/0
 description PE1=>P-Router (Core) POS Link
 ip address 20.1.13.1 255.255.255.252
 max-reserved-bandwidth 100                                      ! Overrides 75% BW limit
 service-policy output CORE-THREE-CLASS-SP-MODEL                 ! Applies Core DS policies
 mpls traffic-eng tunnels                                        ! Enables MPLS TE on int
 tag-switching ip
 ip rsvp bandwidth 77500 77500                                   ! Assigns global-pool BW
!
router ospf 100
 mpls traffic-eng router-id Loopback0          ! MPLS TE RID
 mpls traffic-eng area 0                        ! Enables OSPF area 0 for MPLS TE
 log-adjacency-changes
```

continues

Example 15-30 *PE1 Case Study MPLS VPN QoS Design Example (Continued)*

```
 redistribute connected subnets
 network 20.1.12.0 0.0.0.3 area 0
 network 20.1.13.0 0.0.0.3 area 0
!
router bgp 100
 no synchronization
 bgp log-neighbor-changes
 redistribute connected
 neighbor 20.2.2.2 remote-as 100
 neighbor 20.2.2.2 update-source Loopback0
 no auto-summary
 !
 address-family vpnv4
 neighbor 20.2.2.2 activate
 neighbor 20.2.2.2 send-community extended
 neighbor 20.2.2.2 route-map TUNNEL-ASSIGNMENT in   ! Applies BGP PBR
 exit-address-family
 !
 address-family ipv4 vrf RED
 redistribute connected
 neighbor 10.20.1.1 remote-as 15
 neighbor 10.20.1.1 activate
 neighbor 10.20.1.1 default-originate
 no auto-summary
 no synchronization
 exit-address-family
 !
 address-family ipv4 vrf BLUE
 redistribute connected
 neighbor 10.20.1.1 remote-as 10
 neighbor 10.20.1.1 activate
 neighbor 10.20.1.1 default-originate
 no auto-summary
 no synchronization
 exit-address-family
ip extcommunity-list 2 permit rt 150:1
ip classless
ip route 16.16.16.16 255.255.255.255 Tunnel0 ! Static route for Tunnel 0
ip route 17.17.17.17 255.255.255.255 Tunnel1 ! Static route for Tunnel 1
 !
ip extcommunity-list 1 permit rt 100:1      ! Identifies Blue VPN by RT
ip extcommunity-list 2 permit rt 150:1      ! Identifies Red VPN by RT
ip bgp-community new-format
 !
ip explicit-path name TUNNEL0 enable        ! Defines explicit path for Tu0
 next-address 20.1.12.2
 !
ip explicit-path name TUNNEL1 enable        ! Defines explicit path for Tu1
 next-address 20.1.13.2
 next-address 20.1.23.1
 !
```

Example 15-30 *PE1 Case Study MPLS VPN QoS Design Example (Continued)*

```
access-list 1 permit 10.2.102.0 0.0.0.255    ! Identifies (Blue) Voice-VLAN
access-list 2 permit 10.2.2.0 0.0.0.255      ! Identifies (Blue) Data-VLAN
access-list 2 permit 10.20.2.0 0.0.0.3       ! Identifies (Blue) PE-CE link
access-list 3 permit 10.2.102.0 0.0.0.255    ! Identifies (Red) Voice-VLAN
access-list 3 permit 10.2.2.0 0.0.0.255      ! Identifies (Red) Data-VLAN
access-list 3 permit 10.20.2.0 0.0.0.3       ! Identifies (Red) PE-CE Link
!
route-map TUNNEL-ASSIGNMENT permit 10
 match ip address 1                          ! Matches Voice-VLAN subnet
 match extcommunity 1                        ! Matches Blue VPN RT
 set ip next-hop 16.16.16.16                 ! Sets BGP Next-Hop to 16.16.16.16
!
route-map TUNNEL-ASSIGNMENT permit 20
 match ip address 2                          ! Matches other (Blue) subnets
 match extcommunity 1                        ! Matches Blue VPN RT
 set ip next-hop 17.17.17.17                 ! Sets BGP Next-Hop to 17.17.17.17
!
route-map TUNNEL-ASSIGNMENT permit 30
 match ip address 3                          ! Matches all (Red) subnets
 match extcommunity 2                        ! Matches Red VPN RT
 set ip next-hop 17.17.17.17                 ! Sets BGP Next-Hop to 17.17.17.17
!
!
```

Example 15-31 shows the configuration for the second PE router for this MPLS VPN QoS design case study example.

Example 15-31 *PE2 Case Study MPLS VPN QoS Design Example*

```
!
hostname PE2
!
!
ip vrf BLUE                     ! BLUE MPLS VPN Definition
 rd 100:1
 route-target export 100:1
 route-target import 100:1
!
ip vrf RED                      ! RED MPLS VPN Definition
 rd 150:1
 route-target export 150:1
 route-target import 150:1
!
ip cef
mpls ldp logging neighbor-changes
mpls traffic-eng tunnels        ! Enables MPLS TE globally
!
!
```

continues

Example 15-31 *PE2 Case Study MPLS VPN QoS Design Example (Continued)*

```
 !
 class-map match-any REALTIME
  match ip dscp ef
  match ip dscp cs5
 class-map match-any CRITICAL-DATA
  match ip dscp cs6
  match ip dscp af31
  match ip dscp cs3
 class-map match-any VIDEO
  match ip dscp af21
  match ip dscp cs2
 class-map match-any BULK-DATA
  match ip dscp af11
  match ip dscp cs1
 class-map match-all CORE-REALTIME
   match mpls experimental topmost 5  ! Identifies in-contract Realtime
 class-map match-all CORE-CRITICAL-DATA
   match mpls experimental topmost 3  ! Identifies in-contract Critical-Data
   match mpls experimental topmost 7  ! Identifies out-of-contract Critical Data
   match mpls experimental topmost 2  ! Identifies in-contract Video
   match mpls experimental topmost 1  ! Identifies in-contract Bulk
   match mpls experimental topmost 6  ! Identifies out-of-contract Bulk
 !
 !
 policy-map PE-FIVE-CLASS-SHORT-PIPE-MARKING
   class REALTIME
    police cir 1050000
      conform-action set-mpls-exp-topmost-transmit 5  ! Conforming RT set to 5
      exceed-action drop                              ! Excess Realtime is dropped
   class CRITICAL-DATA
    police cir 600000
      conform-action set-mpls-exp-topmost-transmit 3  ! Critical Data set to 3
      exceed-action set-mpls-exp-topmost-transmit 7   ! Excess Critical set 7
   class VIDEO
    police cir 450000
      conform-action set-mpls-exp-topmost-transmit 2  ! Conforming Video set to 2
      exceed-action drop                              ! Excess Video dropped
   class BULK-DATA
    police cir 150000
      conform-action set-mpls-exp-topmost-transmit 1  ! Conforming Bulk set to 1
      exceed-action set-mpls-exp-topmost-transmit 6   ! Excess Bulk set to 6
   class class-default
    police cir 750000
      conform-action set-mpls-exp-topmost-transmit 0  ! Conforming BE set to 0
      exceed-action set-mpls-exp-topmost-transmit 4   ! Excess BE set to 4
 !
 !
 policy-map PE-FIVE-CLASS-SP-MODEL
  class REALTIME
   priority percent 35         ! Realtime SP class gets 35% LLQ
  class CRITICAL-DATA
   bandwidth percent 20        ! Critical-Data SP class gets 40% CBWFQ
```

Example 15-31 *PE2 Case Study MPLS VPN QoS Design Example (Continued)*

```
   random-detect dscp-based      ! DSCP-based WRED enabled on class
  class VIDEO
   bandwidth percent 15          ! Video SP class gets 15% CBWFQ
   random-detect dscp-based      ! DSCP-based WRED enabled on "Video" SP class
  class BULK-DATA
   bandwidth percent 5           ! Bulk Data SP class gets 15% CBWFQ
   random-detect dscp-based      ! DSCP-based WRED enabled on Bulk Data SP class
  class class-default
   bandwidth percent 25          ! Best Effort SP class gets 25% CBWFQ
   random-detect                 ! WRED enabled on Best Effort SP class
 !
 !
 policy-map CORE-THREE-CLASS-SP-MODEL
   class CORE-REALTIME
     priority percent 35                 ! CORE-REALTIME gets 35% LLQ
   class CORE-CRITICAL-DATA
     bandwidth percent 55                ! CORE-CRITICAL gets 55% CBWFQ
   class class-default
     fair-queue                          ! CORE-BEST-EFFORT gets WFQ
 !
 !
 interface Loopback0             ! Loopback interface for MPLS TE RID
  ip address 20.2.2.2 255.255.255.255
 !
 interface Tunnel0
  description TUNNEL0 (PE2=>PE1)
  ip unnumbered Loopback0
  tunnel destination 20.1.1.1
  tunnel mode mpls traffic-eng               ! Enables MPLS TE on tunnel
  tunnel mpls traffic-eng priority 0 0       ! Best priority
  tunnel mpls traffic-eng bandwidth sub-pool 54250   ! Assigns sub-pool
  tunnel mpls traffic-eng path-option 1 explicit name TUNNEL0
 !
 interface Tunnel1
  description TUNNEL1 (PE2=>P=>PE1)
  ip unnumbered Loopback0
  tunnel destination 20.1.1.1
  tunnel mode mpls traffic-eng               ! Enables MPLS TE
  tunnel mpls traffic-eng priority 7 7       ! Worst priority
  tunnel mpls traffic-eng bandwidth 77500    ! Assigns global pool
  tunnel mpls traffic-eng path-option 1 explicit name TUNNEL1
 !
 !
 interface ATM2/0
  no ip address
  ima-group 1
 !
 interface ATM2/1
  no ip address
  ima-group 1
```

continues

Example 15-31 *PE2 Case Study MPLS VPN QoS Design Example (Continued)*

```
!
interface ATM2/ima1
 no ip address
 no atm ilmi-keepalive
!
interface ATM2/ima1.20 point-to-point
 description Dual-T1 ATM IMA Link to Blue CE2
 ip vrf forwarding BLUE
 ip address 10.20.2.2 255.255.255.252
 pvc 0/120
  vbr-nrt 3072 3072
  max-reserved-bandwidth 100                          ! Overrides 75% BW
  service-policy input PE-FIVE-CLASS-SHORT-PIPE-MARKING  ! Short Pipe Marking
  service-policy output PE-FIVE-CLASS-SP-MODEL         ! Egress policy to CE
 !
!
interface ATM2/2
 no ip address
 ima-group 2
!
interface ATM2/ima2
 no ip address
 no atm ilmi-keepalive
!
interface ATM2/ima2.20 point-to-point
 description Dual-T1 ATM IMA Link to Red CE2
 ip vrf forwarding RED
 ip address 10.20.2.2 255.255.255.252
 pvc 0/220
  vbr-nrt 3072 3072
  max-reserved-bandwidth 100                          ! Overrides 75% BW
  service-policy input PE-FIVE-CLASS-SHORT-PIPE-MARKING  ! Short Pipe Marking
  service-policy output PE-FIVE-CLASS-SP-MODEL         ! Egress policy to CE
 !
!
interface POS5/0
 description PE2=>PE1 POS Link
 ip address 20.1.12.2 255.255.255.252
 max-reserved-bandwidth 100                           ! Overrides 75% BW limit
 service-policy output CORE-THREE-CLASS-SP-MODEL      ! Applies Core DS policies
 mpls traffic-eng tunnels                             ! Enables MPLS TE on int
 tag-switching ip
 ip rsvp bandwidth 77500 sub-pool 54250               ! Assigns sub-pool BW
!
interface POS6/0
 description PE2=>P-Router (Core) POS Link
 ip address 20.1.23.1 255.255.255.252
 max-reserved-bandwidth 100                           ! Overrides 75% BW limit
 service-policy output CORE-THREE-CLASS-SP-MODEL      ! Applies Core DS policies
 mpls traffic-eng tunnels                             ! Enables MPLS TE on int
 tag-switching ip
 ip rsvp bandwidth 77500 77500                        ! Assigns global-pool BW
```

Example 15-31 *PE2 Case Study MPLS VPN QoS Design Example (Continued)*

```
!
router ospf 100
 mpls traffic-eng router-id Loopback0          ! MPLS TE RID
 mpls traffic-eng area 0                       ! Enables OSPF area 0 for MPLS TE
 log-adjacency-changes
 redistribute connected subnets
 network 20.1.12.0 0.0.0.3 area 0
 network 20.1.23.0 0.0.0.3 area 0
!
router bgp 100
 no synchronization
 bgp log-neighbor-changes
 redistribute connected
 neighbor 20.1.1.1 remote-as 100
 neighbor 20.1.1.1 update-source Loopback0
 no auto-summary
 !
 address-family vpnv4
 neighbor 20.1.1.1 activate
 neighbor 20.1.1.1 send-community extended
 neighbor 20.1.1.1 route-map TUNNEL-ASSIGNMENT in   ! Applies BGP PBR
 exit-address-family
 !
 address-family ipv4 vrf RED
 redistribute connected
 neighbor 10.20.2.1 remote-as 15
 neighbor 10.20.2.1 activate
 neighbor 10.20.2.1 default-originate
 no auto-summary
 no synchronization
 exit-address-family
 !
 address-family ipv4 vrf BLUE
 redistribute connected
 neighbor 10.20.2.1 remote-as 10
 neighbor 10.20.2.1 activate
 neighbor 10.20.2.1 default-originate
 no auto-summary
 no synchronization
 exit-address-family
!
ip classless
ip route 18.18.18.18 255.255.255.255 Tunnel0 ! Static route for Tunnel 0
ip route 19.19.19.19 255.255.255.255 Tunnel1 ! Static route for Tunnel 1
!
ip extcommunity-list 1 permit rt 100:1        ! Identifies Blue VPN by RT
ip extcommunity-list 2 permit rt 150:1        ! Identifies Red VPN by RT
ip bgp-community new-format
!
```

continues

Example 15-31 *PE2 Case Study MPLS VPN QoS Design Example (Continued)*

```
ip explicit-path name TUNNEL0 enable        ! Defines explicit path for Tu0
 next-address 20.1.12.1
!
ip explicit-path name TUNNEL1 enable        ! Defines explicit path for Tu1
 next-address 20.1.23.2
 next-address 20.1.13.1
!
access-list 1 permit 10.1.101.0 0.0.0.255   ! Identifies (Blue) Voice-VLAN
access-list 2 permit 10.1.1.0 0.0.0.255     ! Identifies (Blue) Data-VLAN
access-list 2 permit 10.20.1.0 0.0.0.3      ! Identifies (Blue) PE-CE link
access-list 3 permit 10.1.101.0 0.0.0.255   ! Identifies (Red) Voice-VLAN
access-list 3 permit 10.1.1.0 0.0.0.255     ! Identifies (Red) Data-VLAN
access-list 3 permit 10.20.1.0 0.0.0.3      ! Identifies (Red) PE-CE Link
!
route-map TUNNEL-ASSIGNMENT permit 10
 match ip address 1                         ! Matches Voice-VLAN subnet
 match extcommunity 1                       ! Matches Blue VPN RT
 set ip next-hop 18.18.18.18                ! Sets BGP Next-Hop to 18.18.18.18
!
route-map TUNNEL-ASSIGNMENT permit 20
 match ip address 2                         ! Matches other (Blue) subnets
 match extcommunity 1                       ! Matches Blue VPN RT
 set ip next-hop 19.19.19.19                ! Sets BGP Next-Hop to 19.19.19.19
!
route-map TUNNEL-ASSIGNMENT permit 30
 match ip address 3                         ! Matches all (Red) subnets
 match extcommunity 2                       ! Matches Red VPN RT
 set ip next-hop 19.19.19.19                ! Sets BGP Next-Hop to 19.19.19.19
!
!
```

The configuration for the P router for this MPLS VPN QoS design case-study example is shown in Example 15-32.

Example 15-32 *P-Router Case Study MPLS VPN QoS Design Example*

```
!
hostname P-Router
!
!
ip cef
mpls ldp logging neighbor-changes
mpls traffic-eng tunnels                   ! MPLS TE is enabled globally
!
!
class-map match-all CORE-REALTIME
  match mpls experimental topmost 5        ! Identifies in-contract Realtime
class-map match-all CORE-CRITICAL-DATA
  match mpls experimental topmost 3        ! Identifies in-contract Critical-Data
  match mpls experimental topmost 7        ! Identifies out-of-contract Critical Data
  match mpls experimental topmost 2        ! Identifies in-contract Video
```

Example 15-32 *P-Router Case Study MPLS VPN QoS Design Example (Continued)*

```
   match mpls experimental topmost 1   ! Identifies in-contract Bulk
   match mpls experimental topmost 6   ! Identifies out-of-contract Bulk
 !
 !
policy-map CORE-THREE-CLASS-SP-MODEL
  class CORE-REALTIME
    priority percent 35               ! CORE-REALTIME gets 35% LLQ
  class CORE-CRITICAL-DATA
    bandwidth percent 55              ! CORE-CRITICAL gets 55% CBWFQ
  class class-default
    fair-queue                        ! CORE-BEST-EFFORT gets WFQ
 !
 !
interface Loopback0                   ! Loopback interface for MPLS TE RID
 ip address 20.3.3.3 255.255.255.255
 !
 !
interface POS5/0
 description P-Router (Core) => PE1 POS Link
 ip address 20.1.13.2 255.255.255.252
 max-reserved-bandwidth 100                    ! Overrides 75% BW limit
 service-policy output CORE-THREE-CLASS-SP-MODEL  ! Applies Core DS policies
 mpls traffic-eng tunnels                      ! Enables MPLS TE on int
 tag-switching ip
 ip rsvp bandwidth 77500 77500                 ! Assigns global-pool BW
 !
interface POS6/0
 description P-Router (Core) => PE2 POS Link
 ip address 20.1.23.2 255.255.255.252
 max-reserved-bandwidth 100                    ! Overrides 75% BW limit
 service-policy output CORE-THREE-CLASS-SP-MODEL  ! Applies Core DS policies
 mpls traffic-eng tunnels                      ! Enables MPLS TE on int
 tag-switching ip
 ip rsvp bandwidth 77500 77500                 ! Assigns global-pool BW
 !
router ospf 100
 mpls traffic-eng router-id Loopback0          ! MPLS TE RID
 mpls traffic-eng area 0                       ! Enables OSPF area 0 for MPLS TE
 log-adjacency-changes
 redistribute connected subnets
 network 20.1.13.0 0.0.0.3 area 0
 network 20.1.23.0 0.0.0.3 area 0
 !
 !
```

Verification commands:

- **show ip rsvp interface**
- **show ip rsvp neighbor**
- **show mpls interface**

- **show mpls traffic-eng tunnels summary**
- **show mpls traffic-eng tunnels**
- **show mpls traffic-eng topology**
- **show ip bgp vpnv4 all**
- **ping vrf** with **show interface tunnel**

Summary

MPLS VPNs are rapidly gaining popularity as private WAN alternatives. This chapter presented QoS design principles and designs to achieve end-to-end service levels over MPLS VPNs.. The foremost design principle is that enterprise subscribers and service providers have to cooperatively deploy QoS over MPLS VPNs in a consistent and complementary manner.

Enterprise (customer) considerations, such as class-collapsing guidelines and traffic-mixing principles, were overviewed along with re-marking examples.

Service-provider edge QoS policies were presented for three-, four-, and five-class edge models. Additionally, details on how RFC 3270 tunneling modes (Uniform, Short Pipe, and Pipe) can be implemented within Cisco IOS Software were provided.

Service provider core QoS options, such as aggregate bandwidth overprovisioning or deploying DiffServ in the backbone, were considered along with platform-specific considerations, such as MDRR on the 12000 GSR.

MPLS traffic engineering was introduced in brief, and two examples of MPLS TE for QoS were presented (MPLS per-VPN TE and MPLS DS-TE).

The chapter concluded with a case-study continuation from previous chapters, showing how an enterprise that is compliant with the QoS Baseline can migrate its private WAN to an MPLS VPN. The service provider's QoS designs also were detailed within the case study.

Further Reading

Standards:

- RFC 2547, "BGP/MPLS VPNs": http://www.ietf.org/rfc/rfc2547.txt.
- RFC 2597, "Assured Forwarding PHB Group": http://www.ietf.org/rfc/rfc2597.txt.
- RFC 2702, "Requirements for Traffic Engineering over MPLS": http://www.ietf.org/rfc/rfc2702.txt.
- RFC 2917, "A Core MPLS IP VPN Architecture": http://www.ietf.org/rfc/rfc2917.txt.

- RFC 3270, "Multiprotocol Label Switching (MPLS) Support of Differentiated Services": http://www.ietf.org/rfc/rfc3270.txt.
- RFC 3564, "Requirements for Support of Differentiated Services-Aware MPLS Traffic Engineering": http://www.ietf.org/rfc/rfc3564.txt.

Books:

- Alwayn, Vivek. *Advanced MPLS Design and Implementation.* Indianapolis: Cisco Press, 2001.
- Pepelnjak, Ivan, and Jim Guichard. *MPLS and VPN Architectures.* Cisco Press, 2002.
- Pepelnjak, Ivan, Jim Guichard, and Jeff Apcar. MPLS and VPN Architectures. Cisco Press, 2003.
- Osborne, Eric, and Ajay Simha. *Traffic Engineering with MPLS.* Cisco Press, 2003.

Cisco MPLS features:

- Configuring MPLS and MPLS traffic engineering (Cisco IOS Release 12.2): http://www.cisco.com/univercd/cc/td/doc/product/software/ios122/122cgcr/fswtch_c/swprt3/xcftagc.htm.
- MPLS VPNS (Cisco IOS Release 12.2.13T): http://www.cisco.com/univercd/cc/td/doc/product/software/ios122/122newft/122t/122t13/ftvpn13.htm.
- MPLS DiffServ tunneling modes (Cisco IOS Release 12.2.13T): http://www.cisco.com/univercd/cc/td/doc/product/software/ios122/122newft/122t/122t13/ftdtmode.htm.
- MPLS DiffServ-Aware Traffic Engineering (DS-TE) (Cisco IOS Release 12.2.4T): http://www.cisco.com/univercd/cc/td/doc/product/software/ios122/122newft/122t/122t4/ft_ds_te.htm.
- MPLS Cisco IOS documentation main link (Cisco IOS Release 12.3): http://www.cisco.com/univercd/cc/td/doc/product/software/ios123/123cgcr/swit_vcg.htm#999526.

IPSec VPNs are the most widely deployed VPNs and are found in three main contexts:

- Site-to-site IPSec VPNs
- Teleworker IPSec VPNs
- Remote-access client (mobility) IPSec VPNs

QoS considerations for site-to-site and teleworker IPSec VPNs are examined in this design chapter (as QoS is rarely—if ever—deployed in remote-access client IPSec VPN scenarios). These considerations include the following:

- IPSec modes of operation
- Bandwidth and delay increases because of encryption
- IPSec and cRTP incompatibility
- IP ToS byte preservation through IPSec encryption
- QoS and Anti-Replay interaction implications

Following a discussion of these considerations, design recommendations for site-to-site and teleworker (DSL and cable) solutions are presented in detail.

IPSec VPN QoS Design

Whereas MPLS technologies provide VPN services, such as network segregation and privacy, by maintaining independent virtual router forwarding tables, IPSec achieves such VPN services through encryption.

As defined in RFCs 2401 through 2412, IPSec protocols provide mechanisms to enable remote sites to cost effectively connect to enterprise intranets or extranets using the Internet (or a service provider's shared IP networks). Because of IPSec protocol encryption, such VPNs can provide the same management and security policies as private networks.

IPSec VPN services are built by overlaying a point-to-point mesh over the Internet using Layer 3–encrypted tunnels. This architecture requires security appliances, such as (hardware or software) firewalls or routers that support IPSec tunnels, to be installed at both ends of each tunnel. Encryption/decryption is performed at these tunnel endpoints, and the protected traffic is carried across the shared network.

Three main design contexts for IPSec VPNs exist, as shown in Figure 16-1:

- **Site-to-site VPNs**—Tunnels are maintained by hardware devices to connect multiple users at remote branches to (one or more) central sites.

- **Teleworker VPNs**—Tunnels are maintained by hardware devices to connect (typically) a single user at his or her residence to a central site.

- **Remote-access clients**—Tunnels are established by software to connect mobile users at airports, hotels, or similar places to a central site using WLAN hotspots, LAN ports, or modems.

Figure 16-1 *IPSec VPN Design Contexts*

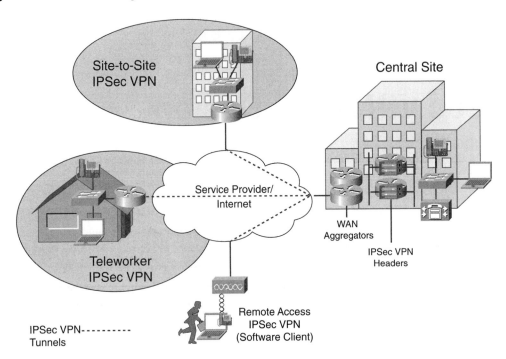

Enabling converged services, such as voice and video, on an IPSec VPN has been dubbed V3PN. V3PN is essentially the overlaying of QoS technologies over IPSec VPNs to provide the required service levels to voice and video applications. As such, V3PN solutions relate to only two of the three IPSec VPN design contexts: site-to-site VPNs and telecommuter VPNs. (Little, if any, QoS is available in remote-access client networks.)

This chapter discusses QoS design considerations and recommendations for both site-to-site and telecommuter V3PN solutions.

NOTE   It is beyond the scope of this chapter to detail IPSec encryption operation and configuration; a working knowledge of IPSec is assumed.

Site-to-Site V3PN QoS Considerations

Attractive pricing is usually the driver behind deploying site-to-site IPSec VPNs as an alternative to private WAN technologies. Many of the same considerations required by private WANs need to be taken into account for IPSec VPN scenarios because they usually are deployed over the same Layer 2 WAN access media.

IPSec VPNs also share some similar concerns with MPLS VPNs. For instance, the enterprise's end-to-end delay and jitter budgets depend significantly on the service provider's SLAs. Therefore, enterprises deploying V3PN solutions are recommended to utilize Cisco Powered Network IP Multiservice service providers, as discussed in Chapter 15, "MPLS VPN QoS Design."

However, IPSec VPNs present many unique considerations for QoS design, including the following (each is discussed in detail throughout the rest of the chapter):

- IPSec VPN modes of operation
- Packet overhead increases because of encryption
- cRTP and IPSec incompatibility
- Prefragmentation
- Bandwidth provisioning
- Logical topologies
- Delay budget increases because of encryption
- ToS byte preservation
- QoS Pre-Classify feature
- Pre-encryption queuing
- Anti-Replay implications
- Control plane provisioning

IPSec VPN Modes of Operation

Three principal modes of IPSec VPN operation exist:

- **IPSec tunnel mode**—No IP GRE tunnel
- **IPSec transport mode**—Encrypting an IP GRE tunnel
- **IPSec tunnel mode**—Encrypting an IP GRE tunnel

The advantages, disadvantages, features, and limitations of these options are discussed next.

IPSec Tunnel Mode (No IP GRE Tunnel)

This option does not utilize an IP GRE tunnel. With this option, only IPSec unicast traffic can be transported. (IP multicast traffic cannot be transported between IPSec peers without configuring an IP GRE tunnel.)

This configuration might be sufficient to support application requirements; its advantage lies in lower CPU overhead (primarily at the headend IPSec VPN router) compared with alternative IPSec design options.

IPSec security associations (SAs) are created for each access list line matched. An access list must be specified in the crypto map to designate packets that are to be encrypted. Such an access list typically entails several lines to define the application(s) to be encrypted by the five ACL tuples: source/destination IP address, protocol, and source/destination port numbers. When not encrypting a GRE tunnel, it is possible to create a separate SA for each application or access-list line match or to create an SA that carries all traffic that matches an ACL range (which is recommended). Each SA has its own Encryption Security Protocol (ESP) or Authentication Header (AH) sequence number.

Anti-Replay drops can be eliminated or minimized by constructing access lists that create a separate security association for each class of traffic being influenced by per-hop QoS policies. (Anti-Replay is an IPSec standard feature that discards packets that fall outside a receiver's 64-byte sliding window because such packets are considered suspect or potentially compromised—it is discussed in greater detail later in this chapter.)

The Cisco IOS feature of prefragmentation for IPSec VPNs (also discussed later in this chapter) is supported in IPSec tunnel mode (no IP GRE tunnel) as of Cisco IOS Release 12.2(12)T.

IPSec Transport Mode (Encrypting an IP GRE Tunnel)

IPSec transport mode (encrypting an IP GRE tunnel) is a commonly deployed option because it provides all the advantages of using IP GRE, such as IP Multicast protocol support (and, thus, also the support of routing protocols that utilize IP Multicast) and multiprotocol support. Furthermore, this option saves 20 bytes per packet over IPSec tunnel mode (encrypting an IP GRE tunnel) because an additional IP header is not required. Figure 16-2 illustrates IPSec transport mode versus tunnel mode when encryption is performed in an IP GRE tunnel.

The IPSec peer IP addresses and the IP GRE peer address must match for transport mode to be negotiated; if they do not match, tunnel mode is negotiated.

Figure 16-2 *IPSec Transport Mode Versus Tunnel Mode for a G.729 VoIP Packet*

IPSec ESP Transport Mode 120 Bytes	IPSec Hdr	ESP Hdr	ESP IV	GRE	IP Hdr	UDP	RTP	Voice	ESP Pad/NH	ESP Auth
	20	8	8	4	20	8	12	20	2-257	12

IPSec ESP Tunnel Mode 140 Bytes	IPSec Hdr	ESP Hdr	ESP IV	GRE IP Hdr	GRE	IP Hdr	UDP	RTP	Voice	ESP Pad/NH	ESP Auth
	20	8	8	20	4	20	8	12	20	2-257	12

The Cisco IOS prefragmentation feature for IPSec VPNs (discussed later in the chapter) is *not* supported for transport mode because the decrypting router cannot determine whether the fragmentation was done before or after encryption (for example, by a downstream router between the encrypting and decrypting routers).

Although IPSec transport mode saves a small to moderate amount of link bandwidth, it does not provide any reduction in packets per second switched by the router. Therefore, because the number of packets per second primarily affects CPU performance, no significant CPU performance gain is realized by using IPSec transport mode.

IPSec tunnel mode is the default configuration option. To configure transport mode, it must be specified under the IPSec transform set, as shown in Example 16-1.

Example 16-1 *Enabling IPSec Transport Mode*

```
!
crypto ipsec transform-set ENTERPRISE esp-3des esp-sha-hmac
 mode transport                ! Enables IPSec Transport mode
 !
```

IPSec Tunnel Mode (Encrypting an IP GRE Tunnel)

IPSec tunnel mode (encrypting an IP GRE tunnel) is the primarily recommended IPSec VPN design option. Although it incurs the greatest header overhead of the three options, it is capable of supporting IP Multicast (with the capability to run a dynamic routing protocol within the IP GRE tunnel for failover to an alternative path), and it supports prefragmentation for IPSec VPNs.

When configured with a routing protocol running within an IP GRE tunnel, the routing protocol's Hello packets maintain the security associations between the branch and both (assuming a redundant configuration) headend routers. There is no need to create a security association with a backup headend peer if the primary peer fails.

NOTE   The design principles in this chapter were proven by scalability testing in the Cisco
        Enterprise Solutions Engineering labs. These large-scale testing methods were designed to
        test worst-case scenarios. From a design standpoint, these entailed enabling the following:

- Strong Triple-Digital Encryption Standard (3DES) encryption for both Internet Key Exchange (IKE) and IPSec

- IP GRE with IPSec tunnel mode

- Diffie-Hellman Group 2 (1024 bit) for IKE

- Secure Hash Algorithm (SHA) 160-bit RFC 2104 Keyed-Hashing for Message Authentication (HMAC) with RFC 1321 Message Digest 5 (MD5)

- (MD5)-HMAC (both hash algorithms truncated to 12 bytes in the ESP packet trailer)

- Preshared keys

If an enterprise chooses to implement less stringent security parameters, to use IPSec transport mode instead of tunnel mode, or to not implement IP GRE tunnels, the designs continue to be applicable from functional and scalability standpoints.

Packet Overhead Increases

The addition of tunnel headers and encryption overhead increases the packet sizes of all encrypted applications: voice, video, and data. This needs to be taken into account when provisioning LLQ or CBWFQ bandwidth to a given class.

For example, consider voice. The two most widely deployed codecs for voice are G.711 and G.729. Each codec typically is deployed at 50 pps (generating 20-ms packetization intervals).

The Layer 3 data rate for a G.711 call (at 50 pps) is 80 kbps. IP Generic Routing Encapsulation (GRE) tunnel overhead adds 24 bytes per packet. The IPSec Encapsulating Security Payload (ESP) adds another 56 bytes. The combined additional overhead increases the rate from 80 kbps (clear voice) to 112 kbps (IPSec ESP tunnel-mode encrypted voice).

The calculation is as follows:

$$
\begin{array}{r}
200 \text{ bytes per packet (G.711 voice)} \\
24 \text{ bytes per packet (IP GRE overhead)} \\
+ \quad \underline{56 \text{ bytes per packet (IPSec ESP overhead)}} \\
280 \text{ bytes per packet} \\
\times \quad \underline{8 \text{ bits per byte}} \\
2240 \text{ bits per packet} \\
\times \quad \underline{50 \text{ packets per second}} \\
112{,}000 \text{ bits per second}
\end{array}
$$

The additional overhead represents a 40 percent increase in the bandwidth required for an encrypted G.711 call.

The 280-byte packet's header, data, and trailer fields for an IPSec tunnel-mode ESP encrypted G.711 call are shown in Figure 16-3.

Figure 16-3 *Anatomy of an IPSec-Encrypted G.711 Packet*

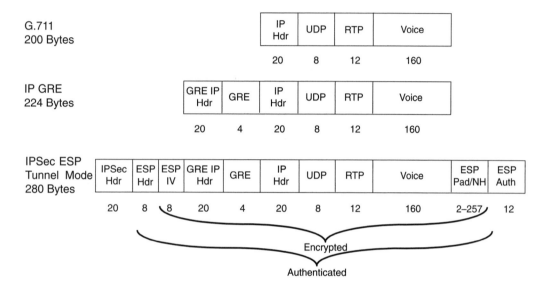

The Layer 3 data rate for a G.729 call (at 50 pps) is 24 kbps. IP GRE tunnel overhead adds 24 bytes per packet. IPSec ESP adds another 52 bytes. The combined additional overhead increases the rate from 24 kbps (clear voice) to just less than 56 kbps (IPSec ESP tunnel-mode encrypted voice).

The calculation is as follows:

$$
\begin{array}{rl}
& 60 \text{ bytes per packet (G.729 voice)} \\
& 24 \text{ bytes per packet (IP GRE overhead)} \\
+ & \underline{52 \text{ bytes per packet (IPSec ESP overhead)}} \\
& 136 \text{ bytes per packet} \\
\times & \underline{8 \text{ bits per byte}} \\
& 1088 \text{ bits per packet} \\
\times & \underline{50 \text{ packets per second}} \\
& 54{,}400 \text{ bits per second}
\end{array}
$$

The additional overhead represents a 227 percent increase in the bandwidth required for an encrypted G.729 call.

The 136-byte packet's header, data, and trailer fields for an IPSec tunnel-mode ESP encrypted G.729 call are shown in Figure 16-4.

Figure 16-4 *Anatomy of an IPSec-Encrypted G.729 Packet*

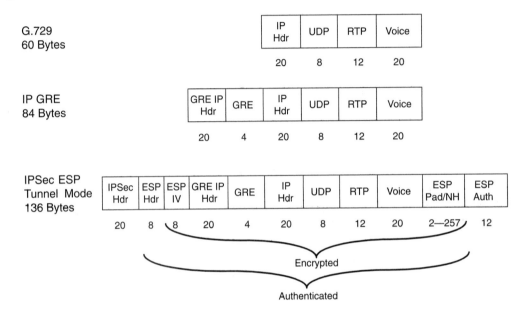

It is important to note that these bandwidth allocations are Layer 3 bandwidth requirements and *do not include* Layer 2 overhead (which is media dependent). Therefore, Layer 2 overhead needs to be added on top of the Layer 3 requirements in provisioning LLQ and CBWFQ bandwidth. This is illustrated in Figure 16-5, where Ethernet overhead (Ethernet plus 802.1Q trunking) and Frame Relay overhead are added and removed from the packet in transit.

Key Layer 2 overhead values are reiterated in Table 16-1.

Table 16-1 *Layer 2 Encapsulation Overhead*

L2 Encapsulation	Overhead
Ethernet	14 bytes (+ 4 for 802.1Q)
Frame Relay	4 bytes (+ 4 for FRF.12)
MLP	10 bytes (+ 3 for MLP LFI)
ATM	5 bytes per 53-byte cell + cell padding (variable)

Figure 16-5 *Packet Size Changes of a G.729 IPSec-Encrypted Packet*

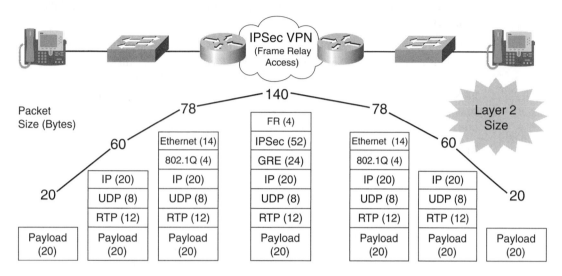

Therefore, the calculation, inclusive of Layer 2 overhead, is as follows. This example assumes that a G.729 call will be encrypted over a slow speed (≤ 768-kbps Frame Relay link), which requires FRF.12 fragmentation and interleaving.

> 60 bytes per packet (G.729 voice)
> 24 bytes per packet (IP GRE overhead)
> 52 bytes per packet (IPSec ESP overhead)
> 4 bytes per packet (FR overhead)
> + ____ 4 bytes per packet (FRF.12 overhead)
>
> 44 bytes per packet
> × ____ 8 bits per byte
>
> 1152 bits per packet
> × ____ 50 packets per second
>
> 57,600 bits per second (rounded up to 58 kbps)

In summary, it is important always to include Layer 2 overhead in accurate bandwidth provisioning for IPSec-encrypted applications.

cRTP and IPSec Incompatibility

The significant increases in bandwidth required by IPSec encryption lead many administrators to consider the use of IP RTP header compression (cRTP) to offset these increases.

However, one of the caveats of encryption is that key portions of the original IP packet that could be referenced for QoS (and other) purposes are no longer readable. Such is the case with cRTP.

cRTP and IPSec are inherently incompatible standards. The original IP/UDP/RTP header already is encrypted by IPSec by the time the RTP compressor is called upon to perform the compression. Therefore, because cRTP cannot associate the encrypted IP/UDP/RTP packet with a known media stream, compression cannot occur and cRTP bandwidth savings cannot be realized. The encrypted IP/UDP/RTP packet simply bypasses the compression process and continues (uncompressed) to the transmit queue.

This is illustrated in Figure 16-6.

Figure 16-6 *IPSec and cRTP Incompatibility*

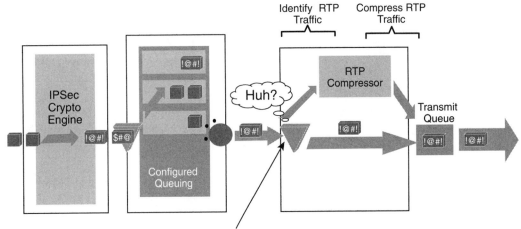

The RTP compression engine cannot identify the stream as RTP,
(since it has been encrypted) and, thus, cannot compress the stream.

It is important to recognize that cRTP functions on a hop-by-hop basis, whereas IPSec can span multiple intermediate (Layer 3) hops between IPSec endpoints. This distinction further exacerbates incompatibility between the features.

Although developments are under way to address these incompatibilities, at the time of this writing, cRTP cannot be utilized to achieve bandwidth savings in an IPSec VPN environment.

Prefragmentation

A problem arises when a packet is nearly the size of the maximum transmission unit (MTU) of the outbound link of the encrypting router and then is encapsulated with IPSec headers.

The resulting packet is likely to exceed the MTU of the outbound link. This causes packet fragmentation after encryption, which makes the decrypting router reassemble in the process path.

Cisco IOS Release 12.2(13)T introduced a new feature: prefragmentation for IPSec VPNs. Prefragmentation increases the decrypting router's performance by enabling it to operate in the high-performance CEF path instead of the process path.

This feature enables an encrypting router to predetermine the encapsulated packet size from information available in transform sets, which are configured as part of the IPSec security association. If it is predetermined that the packet will exceed the MTU of the output interface, the packet is fragmented before encryption. This function avoids process-level reassembly before decryption and helps improve decryption performance and overall IPSec traffic throughput.

Prefragmentation for IPSec VPNs is enabled globally by default for Cisco VPN routers running Cisco IOS Release 12.2(13)T or higher.

Bandwidth Provisioning

Chapter 2, "QoS Design Overview," presented the 33 Percent LLQ Rule, along with the design rationale behind the recommendation. Furthermore, the rule was expressed as a conservative design recommendation that might not be valid under all constraints. Provisioning for VoIP over IPSec on slow links sometimes poses constraints that might preclude applying the 33 Percent LLQ Rule.

As shown in Table 16-2, the percentage of LLQ required on 64-, 128-, and 256-kbps links for a single encrypted G.729 call exceeds the recommended 33 percent LLQ limit. Enterprises considering such deployments must recognize the impact on data traffic traversing such links when encrypted voice calls were made—specifically, data applications would slow down significantly. If that is considered an acceptable trade-off, not much can be said or done. Otherwise, it is recommended to increase bandwidth to the point that encrypted VoIP calls can be made and still fall within the 33 percent bandwidth recommendation for priority queuing.

When planning the bandwidth required for a branch office, consider the number of concurrent calls traversing the IPSec VPN that the branch is expected to make during peak call periods. This varies based on the job function of the employees located at a branch. For example, an office of software engineers would be expected to make fewer calls than an office of telemarketers. A typical active call ratio may be one active call for every six people (1:6), but this could range from 1:4 or 1:10, depending on the job function of the employees. Given the 512-kbps link from Table 16-2 as an example, with a target of 3 G.729 calls, this link theoretically could support a branch office of between 12 and 30 people. As with all other topologies, call admission control must be administered properly to correspond to the QoS policies deployed within the network infrastructure.

Table 16-2 *G.729 Calls by Link Speeds (FRF.12 Is Enabled on Link Speeds ≤ 768 kbps Only)*

Line Rate (kbps)	Maximum Number of G.729 Calls	LLQ Bandwidth (kbps)	LLQ Bandwidth (Percentage)
64 (FRF.12)	1 (58 kbps)	58	**91%**
128 (FRF.12)	1 (58 kbps)	58	**46%**
256 (FRF.12)	2 (58 kbps)	116	**46%**
512 (FRF.12)	3 (58 kbps)	174	34%
768 (FRF.12)	4 (58 kbps)	232	31%
1024	6 (56 kbps)	336	33%
1536	9 (56 kbps)	504	33%
2048	12 (56 kbps)	672	33%

NOTE   Although VoIP has been discussed as a primary example of bandwidth provisioning considerations when deploying QoS over IPSec VPNs, it is important to recognize that VoIP is not the only application that might require such considerations; this exercise needs to be performed for *any* application that is being encrypted.

Unlike VoIP, however, other applications—such as video and data—have varying packet rates and sizes. Therefore, crisp provisioning formulas might not apply. Moderate traffic analysis and best guesses, along with trial-and-error tuning, are usually the only options for factoring bandwidth provisioning increases for non-VoIP applications.

Logical Topologies

Similar to private WANs, but unlike fully meshed MPLS VPNs, IPSec VPNs typically are deployed in a (logical) hub-and-spoke topology.

The QoS implications of hub-and-spoke topologies include that access rates to remote sites need to be constrained and shaped at the hub, to avoid delays and drops within the provider's cloud. Shaping at the IPSec VPN hub is done in a manner similar to that of private WAN NBMA media, such as Frame Relay or ATM. Refer to the "Headend VPN Edge QoS Options for Site-to-Site V3PNs" section, later in this chapter, and also to Chapter 13, "WAN Aggregator QoS Design," for additional details.

IPSec VPNs are not limited to hub-and-spoke designs. They also can be deployed in partial-mesh or even fully meshed topologies. In such cases, shaping is recommended on any links where speed mismatches occur (similar to private WAN scenarios).

Another alternative is to deploy IPSec VPNs via Dynamic Multipoint Virtual Private Networks (DMVPN), which establish site-to-site IPSec tunnels as needed and tear them down when they no longer are required. As with the previously discussed logical topologies, shaping is required on DMVPN NBMA links with speed mismatches. Specifically, shapers are required to be created dynamically and applied to *logical* DMVPN tunnels to offset any speed mismatches attributed to *physical* NMBA links. However, as of the time of this writing, no shaping or queuing solution exists to guarantee QoS SLAs over DMVPN topologies (although Cisco IOS solutions currently are being evaluated and are in development).

Delay Budget Increases

As previously discussed, the delay budget for a typical IP Telephony implementation includes fixed and variable components. The ITU G.114 specification's target value for one-way delay is 150 ms. In an IPSec VPN deployment, however, two additional delay components must be factored into the overall delay budget:

* Encryption delay at the origination point of the IPSec VPN tunnel

* Decryption delay at the termination point of the IPSec VPN tunnel

Performance and scalability testing results suggest that, in most cases, the additional delay caused by encryption and decryption is approximately 4 to 10 ms (combined). These incremental delays are shown in Figure 16-7.

Figure 16-7 *IPSec Encryption/Decryption Incremental Delays*

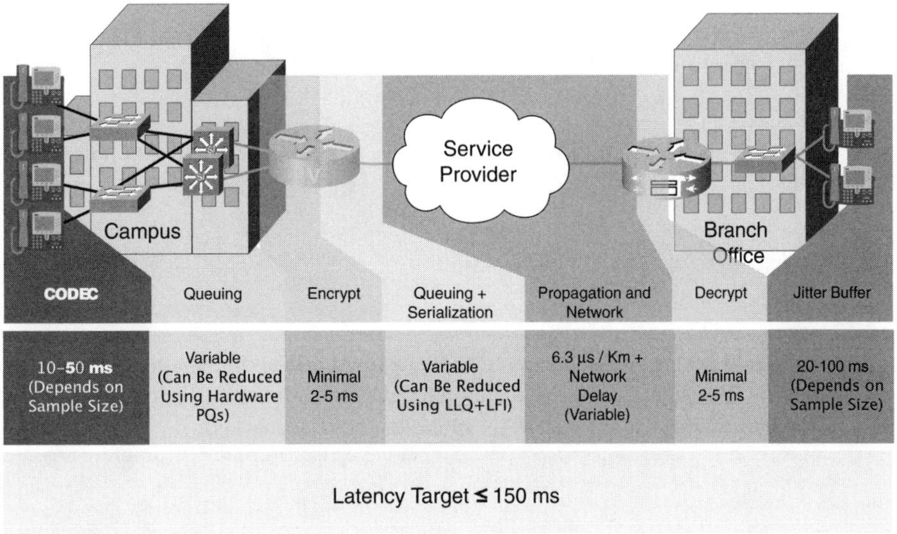

A conservative planning estimate would be 10 ms for encryption delay and 10 ms for decryption delay.

This delay might not seem significant for a campus-to-branch call (hub-to-spoke), but the delay might be more relevant in branch-to-branch (spoke-to-spoke) scenarios because encryption and decryption might occur twice (depending on the logical topology of the VPN). This is illustrated in Figure 16-8.

Figure 16-8 *IPSec VPN Spoke-to-Spoke Encryption/Decryption Delays*

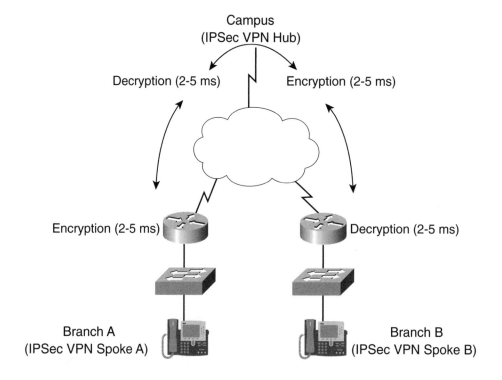

NOTE Not only do encryption delays need to be factored into spoke-to-spoke IPSec VPN scenarios, but queuing and serialization delays for both legs of the tunnel do as well (as they also would in private WAN spoke-to-spoke scenarios).

ToS Byte Preservation

For the majority of QoS designs discussed thus far, classification is performed based on DSCP markings in the ToS byte of the IP packet. However, when an IP packet is encrypted through IPSec, the original ToS byte values also are encrypted and, thus, unusable by QoS mechanisms that process the packet (post encryption).

To overcome this predicament, the IPSec protocol standards inherently have provisioned the capability to preserve the ToS byte information of the original IP header by copying it to the IP headers added by the tunneling and encryption process.

As shown in Figure 16-9, the original IP ToS byte values are copied initially to the IP header added by the GRE encapsulation. Then these values are copied again to the IP header added by IPSec encryption.

Figure 16-9 *IP ToS Byte Preservation*

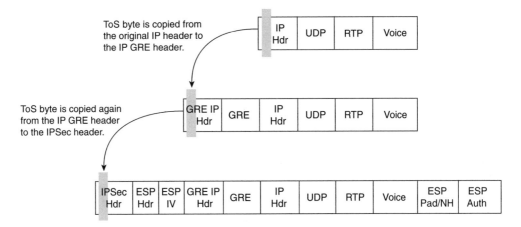

This process compensates for the fact that the original IP header (including the ToS byte) is actually unreadable (because of encryption) and allows the packet to be processed by (post encryption) QoS mechanisms in the same manner as any other packet.

Additionally, this process underscores the importance of ensuring that the encrypted traffic is marked properly (at Layer 3) before encryption.

QoS Pre-Classify

The QoS Pre-Classify feature often is confused with ToS byte preservation. QoS Pre-Classify is a Cisco IOS feature that allows for packets to be classified on header parameters other than ToS byte values after encryption.

Because all original packet header fields are encrypted, including source or destination IP addresses, Layer 4 protocol, and source or destination port addresses, post-encryption QoS mechanisms cannot perform classification against criteria specified within any of these fields.

A solution to this constraint is to create a clone of the original packet's headers before encryption. The crypto engine encrypts the original packet, and then the clone is associated with the newly encrypted packet and sent to the output interface. At the output interface, any QoS decisions based on header criteria, except for ToS byte values—which have been preserved—can be performed by matching on any or all of the five access-list tuple values of the clone. In this manner, advanced classification can be administered even on encrypted packets. The process is illustrated in Figure 16-10.

Figure 16-10 *QoS Pre-Classify Feature Operation*

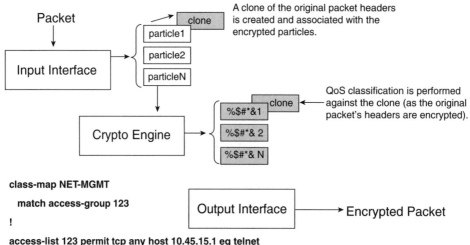

A key point to remember regarding QoS Pre-Classify is that it is applicable only at the encrypting router's output interface. The fields preserved by QoS Pre-Classify are not available to any routers downstream; the clone never leaves the router performing the encryption, thus ensuring the integrity and security of the IPSec VPN tunnel.

QoS Pre-Classify is supported in all Cisco IOS switching paths and is recommended to be enabled on some platforms even when only the ToS byte values are being used for classification. Testing has shown that when hardware-based encryption cards are combined with QoS, the Cisco IOS Software implementation of the QoS Pre-Classify feature slightly enhances performance, even when matching only on ToS byte values. Furthermore, enabling QoS Pre-Classify by default eliminates the possibility that its configuration will be overlooked if the QoS policy later is changed to include matching on IP addresses, ports, or protocols.

Design recommendations for the QoS Pre-Classify feature can be summarized as follows:

- Enable QoS Pre-Classify on all branch IPSec VPN routers that support the feature.
- Enable QoS Pre-Classify on headend IPSec VPN routers only when both the VPN termination and QoS policies reside on the same device.

Pre-Encryption Queuing

The hardware crypto engine within a Cisco VPN router's chassis can be viewed as an internal interface that processes packets for encryption or decryption.

Before Cisco IOS Release 12.2(13)T, packets to be encrypted were handed off to the crypto engine in a *first-in-first-out* (FIFO) basis. No distinction was made between voice packets and data packets. The FIFO queuing for crypto engines is illustrated in Figure 16-11.

Figure 16-11 *FIFO Crypto Engine QoS*

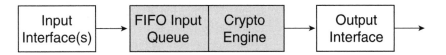

Consider a Cisco 2651XM router deployed at a branch site configured with a full-duplex Fast Ethernet interface, a Serial E1 interface (also full duplex), and an AIM-BP encryption accelerator. The Fast Ethernet interface connects to the branch's LAN, and the serial interface connects to the Internet. These factors could limit throughput (causing a bottleneck) in this scenario:

- The clock rate of the slowest interface (in bits per second—in this case, 2 Mbps transmitted or 2 Mbps received over the E1 interface)
- The packet-forwarding rate of the router's main CPU (in packets per second)
- The crypto engine encryption/decryption rate (in packets per second)

The performance characteristics of these items further are influenced by the traffic mix, including the rates and sizes of the IP packets being switched through the router and the configured Cisco IOS switching path (process-switched, fast-switched, or CEF-switched).

NOTE   In most hardware platforms, the packets-per-second capabilities of the router are more important for planning purposes than bits per second switched through the router. For example, if the average packet size of packets switched through the router increases from 128 bytes to 256 bytes, the packet-per-second capabilities of the main CPU are not necessarily cut in half.

The control plane requirements also factor into the CPU's utilization. These requirements are determined by the routing protocol(s) in use, the number of routes in the routing table, the overall network stability, and any redistribution requirements. Management requirements such as NTP and SNMP also add to the CPU tax. Additionally, Cisco IOS HA, QoS, multicast, and security features all consume CPU resources and must be taken into account.

Another factor in the equation is the ratio of packets switched through (and originated by) the router in relation to the number of packets selected by the crypto map's access list for encryption or decryption. If an IP GRE tunnel is being encrypted, this tends to be a large percentage of encrypted packets to total packets; if an IP GRE tunnel is not being encrypted, the ratio could be quite small.

Hardware crypto engines can become congested when their packet-processing capabilities are less than those of the router's main CPU and interface clock speeds. In such a case, the crypto engine becomes a bottleneck, or a congestion point. The crypto engine might be oversubscribed on either a momentary or (worse case) sustained basis. Such internal precrypto congestion could affect the quality of real-time applications, such as VoIP.

Cisco internal testing and evaluation has shown it to be extremely difficult for conditions to arise that cause hardware crypto engine congestion. In nearly all cases, the Cisco VPN router platform's main CPU is exhausted before reaching the limit of the crypto engine's packet-processing capabilities.

Nevertheless, Cisco provides a solution to this potential case of congestion in the rare event that a hardware crypto engine is overwhelmed so that VoIP quality will be preserved. This feature, low-latency queuing (LLQ) for IPSec encryption engines, was introduced in Cisco IOS Release 12.2(13)T.

The LLQ for Crypto Engine feature provides a dual-input queuing strategy for packets being sent to the crypto engine:

- A priority or low-latency queue
- A best-effort queue

This feature is targeted at alleviating any effects of momentary or sustained oversubscription of the hardware crypto engines that could result in priority traffic (such as voice and video) experiencing quality issues. This feature is illustrated in Figure 16-12.

NOTE   Because software-based crypto adds unacceptable latency and jitter, there are no plans to incorporate this feature for software crypto. Hardware accelerators for IPSec encryption are highly recommended.

Figure 16-12 *LLQ (Dual-FIFO) Crypto Engine QoS*

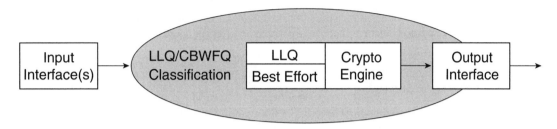

The classification component to segregate traffic between the priority (LLQ) queue and the best-effort queue is based on the MQC service policy on the output interface(s).

No additional configuration is required to enable LLQ for crypto engines; it is enabled internally by the presence of a service policy with an LLQ **priority** command that is applied to an output interface of an IPSec VPN router.

Traffic specified in the service policy to be assigned to the interface's priority queue (LLQ) automatically is sent to the crypto engine's LLQ. Traffic included in any CBWFQ band-width classes (including the default class) automatically is assigned to the crypto engine's best-effort queue.

It is possible to configure different service policies, each with different traffic assigned to an LLQ, on different interfaces. For example, perhaps voice is assigned to the LLQ of Serial1/0 and video is assigned to the LLQ of an ATM PVC. Assuming that both voice and video are to be encrypted, the question arises, which type of traffic (voice or video) will be assigned to the crypto engine's LLQ?

Because the crypto engine acts like a single interface inside the VPN router, encrypting and decrypting all outbound and inbound traffic streams for each interface on which crypto is applied, in the case of multiple service policies (on different interfaces) the crypto engine maps *all* interface priority queues (LLQ) to its LLQ and all other queues to its best-effort queue. Therefore, *both* voice and video would be assigned to the crypto engine's LLQ.

In short, the LLQ for Crypto Engine feature ensures that if packets are dropped by momentary or sustained congestion of the crypto engine, the dropped packets will be of appropriately lower priority (not VoIP packets).

Although the feature is enabled by the presence of a service policy with an LLQ **priority** statement, as with interface queuing itself, crypto-engine queuing does not actually engage prioritization through the dual-FIFO queuing strategy until the crypto engine itself experiences congestion.

The LLQ for Crypto Engine feature in Cisco IOS Software is not a prerequisite for deploying QoS for IPSec VPN implementations in a high-quality manner. As indicated previously, internal Cisco evaluations have found it extremely difficult to produce network traffic conditions that resulted in VoIP quality suffering because of congestion of the hardware crypto engine.

In general, the LLQ for Crypto Engine feature offers the most benefit under one of the following conditions:

- When implementing Cisco IOS VPN router platforms that have a relatively high amount of main CPU resources relative to crypto engine resources (these vary depending on the factors outlined earlier in this discussion).

- When the network experiences a periodic or sustained burst of large packets (for example, for video applications).

To summarize, high-quality IPSec VPN deployments are possible today without the LLQ for Crypto Engine feature in Cisco IOS software. The addition of this feature in Cisco IOS software further ensures that high-priority applications, such as voice and video, can operate in a high-quality manner even under harsh network conditions.

Anti-Replay Implications

IPSec offers inherent message-integrity mechanisms to provide a means to identify whether an individual packet is being replayed by an interceptor or hacker. This concept is called connectionless integrity. IPSec also provides for a partial sequence integrity, preventing the arrival of duplicate packets. These concepts are outlined in RFC 2401, "Security Architecture for the Internet Protocol."

When ESP authentication (**esp-sha-hmac**) is configured in an IPSec transform set, for each security association, the receiving IPSec peer verifies that packets are received only once. Because two IPSec peers can send millions of packets, a 64-packet sliding window is implemented to bound the amount of memory required to tally the receipt of a peer's packets. Packets can arrive out of order, but they must be received within the scope of the window to be accepted. If they arrive too late (outside the window), they are dropped.

The operation of the Anti-Replay window protocol is as follows:

1 The sender assigns a unique sequence number (per security association) to encrypted packets.

2 The receiver maintains a 64-packet sliding window, the right edge of which includes the highest sequence number received. In addition, a Boolean variable is maintained to indicate whether each packet in the current window was received.

3 The receiver evaluates the received packet's sequence number:

— If a received packet's sequence number falls within the window and was not received previously, the packet is accepted and marked as received.

— If the received packet's sequence number falls within the window and previously was received, the packet is dropped and the replay error counter is incremented.

— If the received packet's sequence number is greater than the highest sequence in the window, the packet is accepted and marked as received, and the sliding window is moved "to the right."

— If the received packet's sequence number is less than the lowest sequence in the window, the packet is dropped and the replay error counter is incremented.

In a converged IPSec VPN implementation with QoS enabled, lower-priority packets are delayed so that higher-priority packets receive preferential treatment. This has the unfortunate side effect of reordering the packets to be out of sequence from an IPSec Anti-Replay sequence number perspective. Therefore, there is a concern that through the normal QoS prioritization process, the receiver might drop packets as Anti-Replay errors, when, in fact, they are legitimately sent or received packets.

Figure 16-13 provides a visualization of the process. In this example, voice packets 4 through 67 have been received, and data packet 3 was delayed and transmitted following voice packet 68. When the Anti-Replay logic is called to process packet 3, it is dropped because it is outside the left edge of the sliding window. Packets can be received out of order, but they must fall within the window to be accepted.

Figure 16-13 *Anti-Replay Operation*

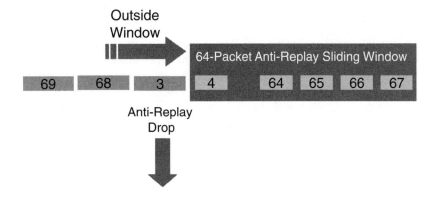

Anti-Replay drops can be eliminated in a pure IPSec tunnel design (no encrypted IP GRE tunnel) by creating separate security associations for voice and data; voice and data packets must match a separate line in the access list referenced by the crypto map. This is implemented easily if the IP phones are addressed by network addresses (such as private RFC 1918 addresses) separate from the workstations.

However, if IPSec tunnel mode (with an encrypted IP GRE tunnel) is used for a converged network of voice and data, Anti-Replay drops impact data packets instead of voice packets because the QoS policies prioritize voice over data.

Consider the effect of packet loss on a TCP-based application: TCP is connection oriented and incorporates a flow-control mechanism within the protocol. The TCP application cannot see why a packet was dropped. A packet dropped by a service policy on a congested output interface is no different to the application than a packet lost by an Anti-Replay drop. From a *network perspective*, however, it would be more efficient to drop the packet *before* sending it over the WAN link (where bandwidth is the most expensive, only to have it dropped by the Anti-Replay mechanism on the receiving IPSec VPN router), but the location or nature of the packet loss is immaterial to the TCP driver.

Anti-Replay drops of data traffic flows are usually in the order of 1 percent to 1.5 percent on IPSec VPN links that experience sustained congestion and have queuing engaged (without any additional policy tuning).

Output drops on the output WAN interface, however, tend to be few, if any, and certainly are far fewer than those dropped by Anti-Replay. This is because Anti-Replay triggers packet drops more aggressively than the output service policy, which is a function of the size of the output queues and the number of defined classes.

By default, each CBWFQ class receives a queue with a length of 64 packets. This can be verified with the **show policy interface** verification command. Meanwhile, the receiving IPSec peer has a *single* 64-packet Anti-Replay window (per IPSec Security Association) with which to process all packets from all LLQ and CBWFQ bandwidth classes.

So, it stands to reason that the Anti-Replay mechanism on the receiving VPN router will be more aggressive at dropping packets delayed by QoS mechanisms preferential to VoIP than the service policy at the sending router. This is because of the size mismatch of the queue depth on the sender's output interface (multiple queues of 64 packets each) compared to the width of the receiver's Anti-Replay window (a single sliding window of 64 packets per SA). As more bandwidth classes are defined in the policy map, this mismatch increases. As mentioned, this is an inefficient use of expensive WAN/VPN bandwidth because packets are transmitted only to be dropped before decryption.

The default value of 64 packets per CBWFQ queue is designed to absorb bursts of data traffic and delay rather than drop those packets. This is optimal behavior in a non-IPSec–enabled network.

When IPSec authentication is configured (**esp-sha-hmac**) in the network, the scenario can be improved by reducing the queue limit (max threshold) of the bandwidth classes of the sender's output service policy so that it becomes more aggressive at dropping packets than buffering or delaying them. Extensive lab testing has shown that such queue-limit tuning can reduce the number of Anti-Replay drops from 1 percent to less than a tenth of percent (< 0.1 percent). This is because decreasing the service policy queue limits causes the sender's output service policy to become more aggressive in dropping instead of significantly delaying packets (which occurs with large queue depths). This, in turn, decreases the number of Anti-Replay drops.

As a rule of thumb, the queue limits should be reduced in descending order of application priority. For example, the queue limit for Scavenger should be set lower than the queue limit for a Transactional Data class, as is shown later in Examples 16-3 through 16-6.

NOTE   In many networks, the default queue limits and IPSec Anti-Replay performance are considered acceptable. A modification of queue-limit values entails side effects on the QoS service policy and related CPU performance. When queue limits are tuned, a careful eye should be kept on CPU levels.

Control Plane Provisioning

As discussed in Chapter 13, Cisco IOS Software has an internal mechanism for protecting control traffic, such as routing updates, called PAK_priority.

PAK_priority marks routing protocols to DSCP CS6, but it currently does not protect IPSec control protocols, such as ISAKMP (UDP port 500). Therefore, it is recommended to provision an explicit CBWFQ bandwidth class for control plane traffic, including ISAKMP, as shown in Example 16-2.

Example 16-2 *Protecting IPSec Control Plane Traffic*

```
!
class-map match-any INTERNETWORK-CONTROL
  match ip dscp cs6
  match access-group name IKE                 ! References ISAKMP ACL
!
!
policy-map V3PN
  ...
  class INTERNETWORK-CONTROL
    bandwidth percent 5                       ! Control Plane provisioning
  ...
!
ip access-list extended IKE
  permit udp any eq isakmp any eq isakmp      ! ISAKMP ACL
!
```

Site-to-Site V3PN QoS Designs

As with WAN and MPLS VPN QoS models, site-to-site V3PN QoS models can range from a basic number of classes (in this case, the minimum number of recommended classes is 6) to a complex QoS Baseline model (11 classes). Each enterprise must determine present needs and comfort level of QoS complexity, along with future needs, to more easily migrate to progressively more complex QoS models, as required.

Six-Class Site-to-Site V3PN Model

The six-class V3PN model technically should be referred to as V2PN because it includes provisioning for only voice (not for video) over an IPSec VPN. Voice is protected explicitly with LLQ; call signaling and control plane traffic also explicitly are protected through CBWFQ classes. This model includes a preferential data class (Transactional Data) and a deferential class (Scavenger, which is squelched to the minimum configurable amount: 1 percent). If the queue limits are tuned to minimize Anti-Replay drops, the queue limit for Transactional Data should be set higher than the queue limit for class default.

An example six-class V3PN model, which is suitable for link speeds up to and including T1/E1 speeds, is illustrated in Figure 16-14 and detailed in Example 16-3.

Figure 16-14 *Six-Class Site-to-Site V3PN Model*

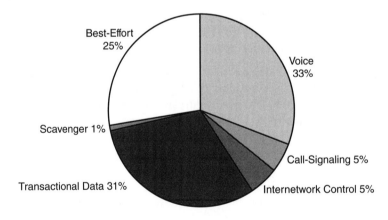

Example 16-3 *Six-Class Site-to-Site V3PN Model Configuration Example*

```
 !
 class-map match-all VOICE
   match ip dscp ef                            ! VoIP
 class-map match-any CALL-SIGNALING
   match ip dscp cs3                           ! New Call-Signaling
   match ip dscp af31                          ! Old Call-Signaling
 class-map match-any INTERNETWORK-CONTROL
   match ip dscp cs6                           ! IP Routing
   match access-group name IKE                 ! References ISAKMP ACL
 class-map match-all TRANSACTIONAL-DATA
   match ip dscp af21 af22                      ! Transactional-Data
 class-map match-all SCAVENGER
   match ip dscp cs1                           ! Scavenger
 !
 !
 policy-map SIX-CLASS-V3PN-EDGE
   class VOICE
     priority percent 33                       ! VoIP gets 33% LLQ
   class CALL-SIGNALING
     bandwidth percent 5                       ! Call-Signaling provisioning
   class INTERNETWORK-CONTROL
     bandwidth percent 5                       ! Control Plane provisioning
   class TRANSACTIONAL-DATA
     bandwidth percent 31                      ! Transactional-Data provisioning
     queue-limit 20                            ! Optional: Anti-Replay tuning
   class SCAVENGER
     bandwidth percent 1                       ! Scavenger class is throttled
     queue-limit 1                             ! Optional: Anti-Replay tuning
   class class-default
     bandwidth percent 25                      ! Best Effort needs BW guarantee
     queue-limit 16                            ! Optional: Anti-Replay Tuning
   !
   !
 ip access-list extended IKE
   permit udp any eq isakmp any eq isakmp      ! ISAKMP ACL
 !
```

NOTE   Currently, only distributed platforms support the **queue-limit** command in conjunction with WRED commands. However, this command combination will be available on nondistributed platforms with the release of Consistent QoS Behavior, as discussed in Chapter 13.

Verification commands:

- **show policy**
- **show policy interface**

Eight-Class Site-to-Site V3PN Model

With the addition of a class for Interactive-Video, this model more accurately lives up to its V3PN name. Interactive-Video (as with VoIP) must be provisioned adequately to include IPSec encryption overhead, but (unlike VoIP) there are no clean formulas for calculating the required incremental bandwidth. This is because video packet sizes and packet rates vary significantly and are largely a function of the degree of motion within the video images being transmitted.

On an unencrypted topology, the guideline for provisioning for Interactive-Video is to overprovision the LLQ by 20 percent. Although this conservative guideline holds true in most videoconferencing scenarios, which usually consist of relatively minor motion (meetings, conferences, talking heads, and so on), in some cases this rule proves inadequate over an IPSec VPN. In such cases, the LLQ might need to be provisioned to the stream's rate plus 25 percent or more. The need to increase the bandwidth for Interactive-Video's LLQ will be apparent if drops (in excess of 1 percent) appear under this class when using the verification command **show policy interface**.

The other class added to this model is a separate class for Bulk Data applications (which will be constrained if congestion occurs, to prevent long sessions of TCP-based flows from dominating the link). Notice that the queue limit of the Bulk Data class has been reduced to below the queue limit of the Best-Effort class. This is because of the relative ranking of application priority: During periods of congestion, the Bulk Data class (large TCP-based file operations that operate mainly in the background) is prevented from dominating bandwidth away from the Best-Effort class (as a whole).

This policy is suitable for link speeds of 3 Mbps or higher. However, in an IPSec environment, it is good to remember that load-sharing GRE tunnels over multiple physical interfaces exacerbate Anti-Replay drops. Whenever possible, a single physical interface should be used to achieve these higher speeds. Another consideration to bear in mind is that higher-end platforms, such as the 2691 and 3700- or 7200-series routers, are required to perform crypto at higher speeds. The Eight-Class Site-to-Site V3PN model is illustrated in Figure 16-15 and detailed in Example 16-4.

Figure 16-15 *Eight-Class Site-to-Site V3PN Model*

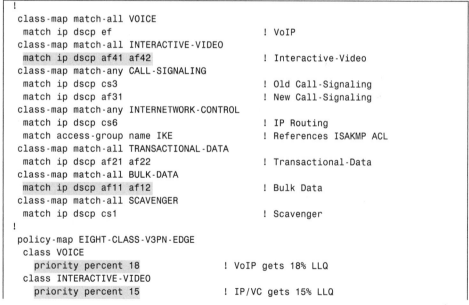

Example 16-4 *Eight-Class Site-to-Site V3PN Model Configuration Example*

```
!
class-map match-all VOICE
 match ip dscp ef                           ! VoIP
class-map match-all INTERACTIVE-VIDEO
 match ip dscp af41 af42                     ! Interactive-Video
class-map match-any CALL-SIGNALING
 match ip dscp cs3                           ! Old Call-Signaling
 match ip dscp af31                          ! New Call-Signaling
class-map match-any INTERNETWORK-CONTROL
 match ip dscp cs6                           ! IP Routing
 match access-group name IKE                 ! References ISAKMP ACL
class-map match-all TRANSACTIONAL-DATA
 match ip dscp af21 af22                     ! Transactional-Data
class-map match-all BULK-DATA
 match ip dscp af11 af12                     ! Bulk Data
class-map match-all SCAVENGER
 match ip dscp cs1                           ! Scavenger
!
policy-map EIGHT-CLASS-V3PN-EDGE
 class VOICE
   priority percent 18              ! VoIP gets 18% LLQ
 class INTERACTIVE-VIDEO
   priority percent 15              ! IP/VC gets 15% LLQ
```

continues

Example 16-4 *Eight-Class Site-to-Site V3PN Model Configuration Example*

```
     class CALL-SIGNALING
       bandwidth percent 5                  ! Call-Signaling provisioning
     class INTERNETWORK-CONTROL
       bandwidth percent 5                  ! Control Plane provisioning
     class TRANSACTIONAL-DATA
       bandwidth percent 27                 ! Transactional-Data provisioning
       queue-limit 18                       ! Optional: Anti-Replay tuning
     class BULK-DATA
       bandwidth percent 4                  ! Bulk-Data provisioning
       queue-limit 3                        ! Optional: Anti-Replay tuning
     class SCAVENGER
       bandwidth percent 1                  ! Scavenger class is throttled
       queue-limit 1                        ! Optional: Anti-Replay tuning
     class class-default
       bandwidth percent 25                 ! Best Effort needs BW guarantee
       queue-limit 16                       ! Optional: Anti-Replay Tuning
     !
   ip access-list extended IKE
    permit udp any eq isakmp any eq isakmp     ! ISAKMP ACL
    !
```

Verification commands:

- **show policy**
- **show policy interface**

QoS Baseline (11-Class) Site-to-Site V3PN Model

Building on the previous model, three new classes are added: Network-Management, Mission-Critical Data, and Streaming-Video.

This model also is suitable only for high-speed (3 Mbps and above) links, with the same caveats regarding multiple physical links aggravating Anti-Replay drops and the requirement of using newer platforms to perform crypto at these speeds. The queue limits have been tuned to reflect relative application priority.

The QoS Baseline V3PN model, suitable for 3-Mbps link speeds and higher, is illustrated in Figure 16-16 and detailed in Example 16-5.

Figure 16-16 *QoS Baseline (Eleven-Class) Site-to-Site V3PN Model*

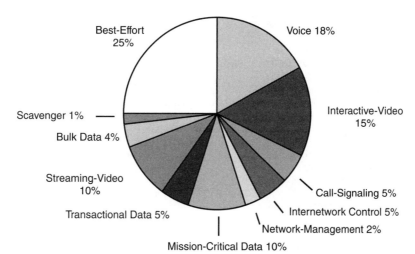

Example 16-5 *QoS Baseline (Eleven-Class) Site-to-Site V3PN Model Configuration Example*

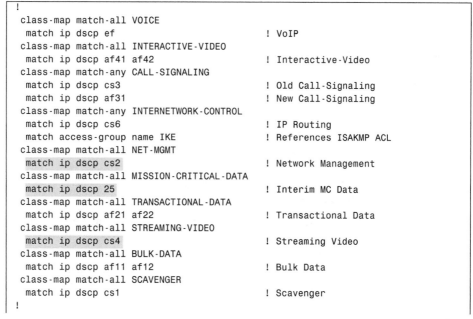

```
!
class-map match-all VOICE
  match ip dscp ef                        ! VoIP
class-map match-all INTERACTIVE-VIDEO
  match ip dscp af41 af42                 ! Interactive-Video
class-map match-any CALL-SIGNALING
  match ip dscp cs3                       ! Old Call-Signaling
  match ip dscp af31                      ! New Call-Signaling
class-map match-any INTERNETWORK-CONTROL
  match ip dscp cs6                       ! IP Routing
  match access-group name IKE             ! References ISAKMP ACL
class-map match-all NET-MGMT
  match ip dscp cs2                       ! Network Management
class-map match-all MISSION-CRITICAL-DATA
  match ip dscp 25                        ! Interim MC Data
class-map match-all TRANSACTIONAL-DATA
  match ip dscp af21 af22                 ! Transactional Data
class-map match-all STREAMING-VIDEO
  match ip dscp cs4                       ! Streaming Video
class-map match-all BULK-DATA
  match ip dscp af11 af12                 ! Bulk Data
class-map match-all SCAVENGER
  match ip dscp cs1                       ! Scavenger
!
```

continues

Example 16-5 *QoS Baseline (Eleven-Class) Site-to-Site V3PN Model Configuration Example (Continued)*

```
!
policy-map QOSBASELINE-V3PN-EDGE
  class VOICE
    priority percent 18                ! VoIP gets 18% LLQ
  class INTERACTIVE-VIDEO
    priority percent 15                ! IP/VC gets 15% LLQ
  class CALL-SIGNALING
    bandwidth percent 5                ! Call-Signaling provisioning
  class INTERNETWORK-CONTROL
    bandwidth percent 5                ! Control Plane provisioning
  class NET-MGMT
    bandwidth percent 2                ! Network Management provisioning
  class MISSION-CRITICAL-DATA
    bandwidth percent 10               ! Mission-Critical Data provisioning
    queue-limit 6                      ! Optional: Anti-Replay tuning
  class TRANSACTIONAL-DATA
    bandwidth percent 5                ! Transactional-Data provisioning
    queue-limit 3                      ! Optional: Anti-Replay tuning
  class STREAMING-VIDEO
    bandwidth percent 10               ! Streaming-Video provisioning
    queue-limit 6                      ! Optional: Anti-Replay tuning
  class BULK-DATA
    bandwidth percent 4                ! Bulk-Data provisioning
    queue-limit 3                      ! Optional: Anti-Replay tuning
  class SCAVENGER
    bandwidth percent 1                ! Scavenger throttling
    queue-limit 1                      ! Optional: Anti-Replay tuning
  class class-default
    bandwidth percent 25               ! Best Effort needs BW guarantee
    queue-limit 16                     ! Optional: Anti-Replay tuning
 !
 !
ip access-list extended IKE
 permit udp any eq isakmp any eq isakmp      ! ISAKMP ACL
 !
```

Verification commands:

- **show policy**

- **show policy interface**

At remote sites, these policies can be applied to the physical interfaces connecting them to the service provider (provided that the SLAs are for line rates—otherwise, shapers must be used). For example, if the service provider guarantees a full T1 rate to a remote site and the access medium is Frame Relay, the service policy can be applied directly to the main Frame Relay interface. If the service provider guarantees only ≤ 768 kbps across the same link, Frame Relay traffic shaping (either legacy or class-based FRTS) combined with FRF.12 must be used at the remote site.

For the central site(s) WAN aggregators, however, unique considerations exist. These are discussed in the next section.

Headend VPN Edge QoS Options for Site-to-Site V3PNs

IPSec V3PNs can be configured in various ways at the central sites. Some enterprises simply overlay V3PNs on top of their existing private WANs; others subscribe to service providers that offer classes of service within their clouds. Many enterprises deploy VPN headends behind WAN aggregation routers to distribute CPU loads, while some perform encryption and QoS on the same box. Each of these options presents considerations on how V3PN policies optimally are applied on WAN aggregation routers.

For enterprises that have overlaid IPSec VPNs on top of their private WAN topologies, the V3PN policies should be applied to the leased lines or Frame Relay/ATM PVCs, as described in Chapter 13.

For enterprises that are subscribing to service providers that offer PE-to-CE QoS classes (including enterprises that are deploying IPSec VPNs *over* MPLS VPNs), V3PN policies need to be applied on the CE-to-PE links (complete with any re-marking that the service provider requires to map into these service provider classes), as described in Chapter 15, "MPLS VPN QoS Design."

For enterprises that are subscribing to service providers that do not offer explicit QoS (beyond an SLA) within their cloud and are using VPN headends behind WAN aggregation routers, the V3PN service policies would be applied to the WAN aggregator's (CE-to-PE) physical links. This prioritizes packets (by applications) and relies on the service provider's SLA to ensure that the delivery largely reflects the priority of the packets as they are handed off to the service provider. Such a configuration would require only a single QoS policy for a WAN aggregator (albeit, on a high-speed interface), but at the same time, it would involve an increased dependence on the service provider's SLA to deliver the desired QoS service levels.

When the VPN headend routers have adequate CPU cycles to perform QoS, another option exists: hierarchical MQC policies that shape and queue (within the shaped rate) and are applied on a per-tunnel basis. A sample of per-tunnel hierarchal QoS policies is shown in Example 16-6. As with previous shaping design recommendations, the shaper is configured to shape to 95 percent of the remote site's line rate.

NOTE   It is critical to keep an eye on CPU levels when IPSec VPN encryption *and* per-tunnel QoS policies are applied on the same router. CPU levels, in general, should not exceed 75 percent during normal operating conditions. Configuring hierarchical shaping and queuing policies on a per-tunnel (per-SA) basis to a large number of sites could be very CPU intensive, especially when such sites experience periods of sustained congestion.

Example 16-6 *Per-Tunnel Hierarchical Shaping and Queuing MQC Policy for VPN Headends/WAN Aggregators*

```
!
policy-map SHAPING-T1-TUNNEL
  class class-default
    shape average 1460000 14600 0      ! Shaped to 95% of T1 line-rate
    service-policy V3PN-EDGE           ! Nested queuing policy
!
!
interface Tunnel120
 description VPN Pipe to V3PN Site#120 (T1 Link)
 bandwidth 1536
 ip address 10.10.120.1 255.255.255.252
 ip mtu 1420
 service-policy output SHAPING-T1-TUNNEL    ! Policy applied to tunnel int
 qos pre-classify                           ! Performance recommandation
 tunnel source 192.168.1.1
 tunnel destination 192.168.2.2
 crypto map VPN
!
```

Teleworker V3PN QoS Considerations

Organizations constantly are striving to reduce costs and improve productivity and employee retention. Teleworker solutions address these organizational objectives by giving employees the ability to work from home with compatible quality, functionality, performance, convenience, and security, as compared to working in an office location. Teleworker solutions that provide such functionality have been branded "enterprise class" or "business ready" by Cisco Marketing and are illustrated in Figure 16-17.

Figure 16-17 *Business-Ready Teleworker Design*

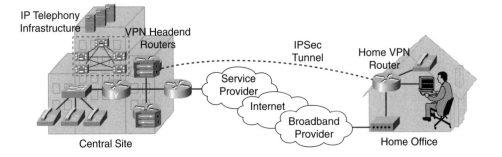

Telecommuter solutions include these main benefits:

- **Increased productivity**—On average, employees spend 60 percent of their time or less at their desks, yet this is where the bulk of investment is made in providing access to corporate applications. Providing similar services at an employee's residence, for a relatively minor investment, significantly can increase productivity gains.

- **Business resilience**—Employees can be displaced from their normal workplace by natural events (such as winter storms, hurricanes, or earthquakes), health alerts (such as SARS), man-made events (such as travel restrictions or traffic conditions), or simply family-related events, such as sick children or home repairs. These disruptions significantly can impact an organization's processes. Providing employees with central site–equivalent access to applications and services in geographically dispersed locations (such as home offices) creates a built-in back-up plan to keep business processes functioning in unforeseen circumstances.

- **Cost savings**—A traditional remote worker setup involves toll charges for dial-up and additional phone lines. Integrating services into a single, broadband-based connection can eliminate these charges while delivering superior overall connectivity performance.

- **Security**—Demands for access to enterprise applications outside the campus are stretching the limits of security policies. Teleworking over IPSec VPNs offers inherent security provided by encryption of all traffic, including data, voice, and video. Also critical is integrating firewall and intrusion-detection capabilities, along with finding ways to easily accommodate both corporate and personal users who share a single broadband connection (the "spouse-and-children" concern, which will be discussed shortly).

- **Employee recruitment and retention**—In the past, enterprises recruited employees in the locations where corporate offices were located. Today enterprises need the flexibility of hiring skilled employees wherever the skills exist and need to integrate remote workers into geographically dispersed teams with access to equivalent corporate applications.

Although QoS designs for IPSec V3PN teleworker scenarios share many of the same concerns of site-to-site V3PN scenarios, additional specific considerations relating to teleworker deployment models and broadband access technologies need to be taken into account.

Teleworker Deployment Models

Business-ready teleworker deployment models must provide the following services:

- **Basic services**—These include NAT, DHCP, IP routing, and multiple Ethernet connections for home office devices and broadband connection (attachment to the WAN circuit cable, DSL, ISDN, or wireless network).

- **QoS services**—These include classification, prioritization, and, in some cases, shaping of traffic.
- **VPN/security services**—These include encryption of traffic to the main site and firewall functionality for the home office.

Given these requirements, there are three main deployment models for business-ready teleworker V3PN solutions, as illustrated in Figure 16-18. These include the Integrated Unit Model, the Dual-Unit Model, and the Integrated Unit + Access Model.

Figure 16-18 *Business-Ready Teleworker Deployment Models*

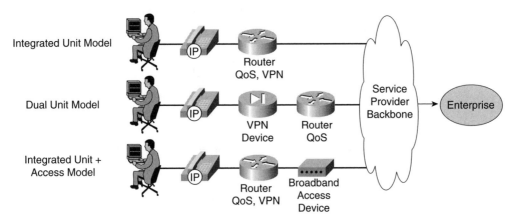

Integrated Unit Model

In the Integrated Unit Model, a single device (such as a Cisco 837 or 1700-series router) provides basic services, QoS services, and VPN/security services. Furthermore, the device connects directly to the broadband media.

NOTE   The Cisco routers used in these scenarios require an IP/FW/PLUS 3DES Cisco IOS Software feature set. This feature set would include support for LLQ/CBWFQ with class-based hierarchical traffic shaping, and also support for Easy VPN (EZVPN), PKI, IDS, AES, URL filtering, and EIGRP.

Advantages include the following:

- Single-device deployment and management
- Adaptability for service provider fully managed services (transport, QoS, IP Telephony application)
- Potential cost savings

Disadvantages include the following:

- Availability of a single device at an appropriate cost with the features and performance required
- No single unit for some broadband access circuit types

The Integrated Model is a preferred model for service providers offering a fully managed V3PN teleworker service.

From a QoS design perspective, this model is highly similar to a site-to-site V3PN, except that it interfaces with a broadband media instead of a traditional WAN access media.

Dual-Unit Model

In this model, one device (such as a Cisco 831, 837, or 1700-series router) provides basic services and QoS, and a second device (a Cisco router or a PIX 501 or even a VPN 3002) performs security/VPN services.

Advantages include the following:

- **Granularity of managed services**—Service providers can manage broadband access while enterprises manage VPN/security and private network addressing because these are two different units.
- **Media independence**—Because the VPN/security device is separate from the router connecting to the broadband circuit, the same VPN device can be used for cable, DSL, wireless, and ISDN by changing the router model or module in the router. This is especially valuable if one enterprise must support teleworkers with different broadband circuit types (such as DSL, cable, and ISDN).

Disadvantages include the following:

- Two units packaged for deployment
- Ongoing management of two devices
- The cost for two devices

From a QoS design perspective, this model is no different from the previous (Integrated Unit) model.

Integrated Unit + Access Model

In this third model, a single router (such as a Cisco 831 or 1700-series router) provides basic services, QoS services, and VPN/security services. However, the router does not connect directly to the broadband access media; it connects (through Ethernet) to a broadband access device (such as a DSL or cable modem).

Advantages include the following:

- Cost savings realized by using existing broadband-access devices

- Simplified provisioning because one size fits all, regardless of broadband access media

- Solution support even when no router interface for a specific broadband circuit type is available

Disadvantages include the following:

- Increased troubleshooting complexity because most broadband-access devices (modem) are not intelligent and, therefore, cannot be queried, managed, or controlled.

- Additional QoS complexity because, in this model, the router does not control the broadband circuit and, thus, must perform hierarchical shaping, as shown in Figure 16-19.

Figure 16-19 *Hierarchical QoS Requirements for Integrated Unit + Access Teleworker Deployment Model*

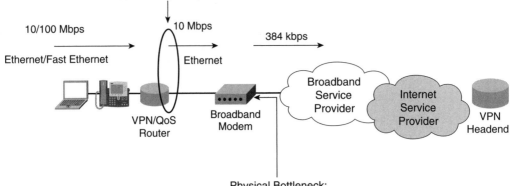

Because of the media-specific encapsulation overhead requirements (discussed in the following sections), it is recommended to shape to 95 percent of broadband link for cable and 70 percent of the uplink rate for DSL.

A hierarchical shaping policy that forces queuing to engage for a 384-kbps cable broadband connection is shown in Example 16-7.

Example 16-7 *Hierarchical Shaping and Queuing MQC Policy for a 384-kbps Cable Connection*

```
!
policy-map SHAPE-384-CABLE
  class class-default
    shape average 364800 3640          ! Shapes to 95% of 384 kbps cable link
    service-policy V3PN-TELEWORKER     ! Nested V3PN Teleworker queuing policy
  !
  ...
  !
interface Ethernet0
  service-policy output SHAPE-384-CABLE     ! Shaper applied to LAN interface
  !
```

The Integrated Unit + Access Model is a preferred model for enterprise V3PN teleworker deployments because it completely abstracts any service provider– or access media–specific requirements (a one-size-fits-all solution).

Broadband-Access Technologies

In North America, there are four main broadband-access technology options for telecommuter scenarios: DSL, cable, ISDN, and wireless. DSL and cable are by far the dominant broadband technologies.

Because of per-minute costs, ISDN is used considerably less; however, ISDN flat rate is becoming available and will make ISDN a good option for areas where DSL or cable is not available. Last-mile wireless is a new option that is being piloted in certain areas to determine viability.

The minimum recommended broadband data rate for most deployments is 160 kbps (uplink)/860 kbps (downlink). Data rates below this speed require more troubleshooting by support staff and are less likely to provide acceptable voice quality. The recommended data rate for V3PN teleworker deployments is 256 kbps (uplink)/1.4 Mbps (downlink) or higher rates. Although V3PN can be deployed at rates less than 160 kbps/860 kbps, generally the voice quality at that service level is in the cell phone quality range, and support costs are higher.

Because QoS design for ISDN was discussed in Chapter 13, and because wireless as a last-mile broadband technology has yet to gain wide deployment, this section focuses only on DSL and cable broadband technologies.

DSL and cable topologies are illustrated in Figure 16-20. Cable is a shared medium between the teleworker's cable modem and the broadband provider's cable headend router. DSL is a dedicated circuit between the teleworker's DSL modem (bridge) and the DSL Access Multiplexer (DSLAM). Both cable and DSL offerings utilize shared uplinks between these aggregation devices and the service provider's core network. QoS typically is not provisioned within the broadband service provider's cloud in either medium. This lack of QoS within the broadband cloud underscores the requirement of adequate QoS provisioning at the endpoints of the VPN tunnels.

Figure 16-20 *DSL and Cable Topologies*

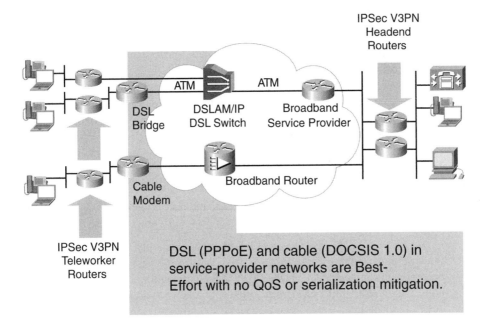

Digital Subscriber Line

DSL service features a dedicated access circuit and offers a service similar to Frame Relay or Asynchronous Transfer Mode (ATM), in which a single permanent virtual circuit (PVC) is provisioned from the home office to the service provider aggregation point. DSL has a variety of speeds and encoding schemes.

Most service providers today offer residential Asynchronous Digital Subscriber Line (ADSL). ADSL provides for asymmetric speeds (with the downstream rate greater than the upstream rate). Asymmetrical links are a better choice and benefit for the telecommuter because the greater the downlink bandwidth is, the less the need is for QoS. (Slower-speed uplinks slow TCP sender transmission rates to more manageable levels.) Because QoS is not generally available by broadband service providers, such uplink/downlink speed mismatches are desirable.

Residential access speeds are generally 128 to 384 kbps upstream and 608 kbps to 1.5 Mbps downstream. For ADSL circuits with upstream speeds less than 256 kbps, G.729 VoIP codecs are recommended.

ADSL also utilizes a single best-effort PVC using RFC 2516–based PPP over Ethernet (PPPoE) encapsulation. In DSL networks, delay and jitter are very low but are not guaranteed. Because PPPoE is used, no LFI is available in service provider DSL networks. In the future, QoS at Layer 2 might be available across service provider networks using familiar ATM variable bit-rate (VBR) definitions.

Single-pair high bit-rate DSL (G.SHDSL) is the new high-speed standard for business DSL. Most residences will continue to be served by ADSL, while small business and branch offices likely will use G.SHDSL. G.SHDSL offers varying rates controlled by the service provider; the upstream and downstream rates are the same speed (symmetric). G.SHDSL is seen as an eventual replacement for T1s in the United States and will become increasingly available from more service providers.

The telecommuter deployment options for DSL circuits include all three teleworker deployment models: Integrated Unit, Dual-Unit, and Integrated Unit + Access, as shown in Figure 16-21.

Figure 16-21 *Teleworker Deployment Models for DSL*

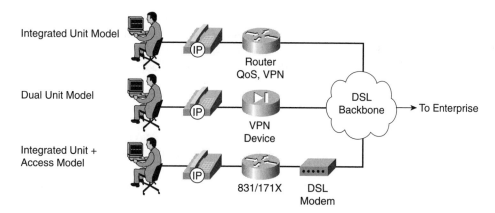

Cable

Cable offers a shared service with symmetric speeds varying from 100 kbps to 4 Mbps. In the past, delay and jitter varied too greatly over cable, making it unsuitable for VoIP.

The common installed base of cable services today is made up of Data-over-Cable Service Interface Specifications (DOCSIS) 1.0. No LFI is available with DOCSIS 1.0, although DOCSIS 1.1 defines fragmentation and interleaving mechanisms.

DOCSIS 1.1 also provides the capabilities to shape traffic at Layer 2 before transmission over the cable network. Although the circuit and frequencies physically are shared, access to the medium can be controlled by the headend so that a device can be guaranteed specified bandwidth.

At the time of this writing, the only recommended deployment model for cable is the Integrated Unit + Access Model, as shown in Figure 16-22.

Figure 16-22 *Teleworker Deployment Model for Cable*

Bandwidth Provisioning

A few key differences with respect to bandwidth provisioning need to be taken into account for broadband teleworker scenarios, as compared to site-to-site VPNs.

The first is that usually only a single call needs to be provisioned for (unless two teleworkers share a single residential broadband connection, which is rarely the case). If bandwidth is low, G.729 codecs are recommended. The second key bandwidth-provisioning consideration is the inclusion of the overhead required by the broadband access technologies, whether DSL or cable.

NOTE   Sometimes multicast support is not required in a teleworker environment. For example, routing protocols (which depend on multicast support) might not be required by teleworkers (because default gateways are usually sufficient in this context). In such cases, IPSec tunnel mode (no encrypted IP GRE tunnel) can be used to achieve additional bandwidth savings of 24 bytes per packet.

For the remainder of this chapter, IPSec tunnel mode (no encrypted IP GRE tunnel) is the assumed mode of operation.

NAT Transparency Feature Overhead

Beginning in Cisco IOS Release 12.2(13)T, NAT transparency was introduced and is enabled by default, provided that both peers support the feature. It is negotiated in the IKE exchange between the peers. This feature addresses the environment in which IPSec packets must pass through a NAT/pNAT device, and it adds 16 bytes to each voice and data packet. The overhead that this feature adds is shown in Figure 16-23.

Figure 16-23 *NAT Transparency Feature (Layer 3) Overhead*

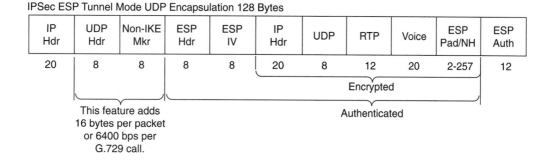

No additional overhead is caused by NAT transparency on a G.729 call over DSL (PPPoE/ AAL5) because there is enough AAL5 cell padding to absorb the 16 additional bytes per packet (discussed in more detail in the following section). In cable implementations, these additional 16 bytes increase the number of bits on the wire and, thus, the overall bandwidth consumption. At the headend, NAT transparency increases the bandwidth consumption of VoIP traffic by 1 Mbps for approximately every 82 concurrent G.729 calls; on the teleworker router, NAT transparency increases the bandwidth required by 6.4 kbps per G.729 call.

Unless there is a need to implement this feature, the recommendation is to disable it when bandwidth conservation is a requirement. This feature can be disabled with the **no crypto ipsec nat-transparency udp-encapsulation** global configuration command.

DSL (AAL5 + PPPoE) Overhead

For DSL broadband connections, PPPoE is the most commonly implemented deployment. Given the 112-byte, Layer 3 size of an IPSec (only) encrypted G.729 VoIP call, 40 bytes of PPP, PPPoE, Ethernet, and ATM AAL5 headers and trailers are added. Additionally, the pre-ATM Software Segmentation and Reassembly (SAR) engine is required to pad the resulting 152-byte packet to the nearest multiple of 48 (each fixed-length ATM cell can transport only a 48-byte payload). Figure 16-24 shows the resulting 192-byte pre-ATM packet.

Figure 16-24 *IPSec-Encrypted G.729 Packet Size Through AAL5 + PPPoE Encapsulation*

LLC Snap	802.3 Hdr	PPP oE PPP	IPSec Hdr	ESP Hdr	ESP IV	IP Hdr	UDP	RTP	Voice	ESP Pad/NH	ESP Auth	AAL5 Pad	AAL5 Trail
10	14	8	20	8	8	20	8	12	20	4	12	40	8

PPPoE + AAL5 Frame - 192 Bytes

The 192 bytes of cell payload are incorporated through ATM SAR into the (48-byte) payloads of four 53-byte ATM cells (192 / 48 = 4 cells).

Therefore, the bandwidth required for an IPSec (only) encrypted G.729 VoIP call over DSL is calculated as follows:

$$53 \text{ bytes per cell}$$
$$\times \quad 4 \text{ cells per IPSec-encrypted VoIP packet}$$
$$212 \text{ bytes per (192-byte) AAL5/PPPoE IPSec VoIP packet}$$
$$\times \quad 50 \text{ packets per second}$$
$$10,600 \text{ bytes per second}$$
$$\times \quad 8 \text{ bits per byte}$$
$$84,800 \text{ bits per second}$$

Thus, an encrypted G.729 call requires 85 kbps of bandwidth, while an encrypted G.711 requires seven ATM cells or 148,400 bps on the wire.

This results in the LLQ configuration values of 85 kbps (**priority 85**) for a G.729 VoIP call and 150 kbps for a G.711 (**priority 150**) VoIP call, respectively, for DSL.

Cable Overhead

For cable deployments, the Layer 2 overhead is less than that for DSL. The IPSec packet is encapsulated in an Ethernet header (and trailer) that includes a 6-byte DOCSIS header, as shown in Figure 16-25.

Figure 16-25 *IPSec-Encrypted G.729 Packet Size Through Ethernet and DOCSIS Encapsulation*

DOC SIS Hdr	802.3 Hdr	IPSec Hdr	ESP Hdr	ESP IV	IP Hdr	UDP	RTP	Voice	ESP Pad/NH	ESP Auth	802.3 CRC
6	14	20	8	8	20	8	12	20	4	12	4

Ethernet + DOCSIS Frame - 136 Bytes

If baseline privacy is enabled (baseline privacy encrypts the payload between a cable modem and the headend), the extended header is used, adding another 5 bytes.

The packet size of a G.729 call (with a zero-length extended header) is 136 bytes or 54,400 bps (at 50 pps); a G.711 call is 280 bytes or 112,000 bps (at 50 pps).

To simplify configuration and deployment, the values of 64 kbps (for G.729) and 128 kbps (for either G.729 or G.711) can be used for priority queue definition for cable.

Asymmetric Links and Unidirectional QoS

With both DSL and cable, the uplink connection can be enabled with QoS, either in the form of a service policy on the DSL (ATM PVC) interface or through a hierarchical MQC service policy that shapes the uplink and prioritizes packets within the shaped rate on the Ethernet interface. This half of the link is under the enterprise's control and easily can be configured.

The downlink connection is under the control of the broadband service provider, and any QoS policy must be configured by the service provider; however, most service providers do not offer QoS-enabled broadband services. This is usually because DSL providers often have implemented non-Cisco equipment (DSLAM or other ATM concentration devices) that typically have few or no QoS features available. Cable providers, on the other hand, might have an option to enable QoS as DOCSIS 1.1 becomes more widely deployed.

Fortunately, most service offerings are asymmetrical. For example, consider a circuit with a 256-kbps uplink and 1.5-Mbps downlink. The downlink rarely is congested to the point of degrading voice quality.

Testing in the Cisco Enterprise Solutions Engineering labs has shown that when congestion is experienced on the uplink, the resulting delay of (TCP) data packet acknowledgments automatically decreases the arrival rate of downlink data traffic so that downlink congestion does not occur. To summarize the results of these tests: Asymmetrical links are preferred (over symmetrical links) as long as QoS is enabled on the uplink, provided that the lower of the two speeds (the uplink) is adequate for transporting both voice and data.

Some service providers for business-class services offer symmetrical links in an effort to compete with Frame Relay providers; 384 kbps/384 kbps and 768 kbps/768 kbps are examples. With no QoS enabled on the service provider edge, this offering is not optimal for the enterprise. An asymmetrical link such as 384 kbps/1.5 kbps is a better choice for the V3PN networks.

Broadband Serialization Mitigation Through TCP Maximum Segment Size Tuning

The majority of broadband deployments are DSL with PPPoE and cable with DOCSIS 1.0. As previously noted, neither of these technologies includes any mechanisms to fragment data packets and interleave voice packets at Layer 2 to minimize the impact of serialization and blocking delay on voice packets (which is a recommended requirement on link speeds ≤ 768 kbps).

The DOCSIS 1.1 specification for cable includes fragmentation and interleaving support, and DSL providers can implement MLP over ATM (which includes MLP LFI support). However, these do not represent the majority of the currently deployed base of broadband networks.

An alternative way to mitigate serialization delay on broadband circuits is provided by adjusting the TCP Maximum Segment Size (MSS). The TCP MSS value influences the resulting size of TCP packets and can be adjusted with the **ip tcp adjust-mss** interface command. Because the majority of large data packets on a network are TCP (normal UDP application packets, such as DNS and NTP, average less than 300 bytes and do not create a significant serialization delay issue), this command effectively can reduce serialization delay in most teleworker scenarios when no Layer 2 fragmentation and interleaving mechanism is available.

NOTE   It is not recommended to run UDP-based video applications on broadband links ≤ 768 kbps that do not support Layer 2 LFI in a V3PN teleworker scenario. This is because such applications regularly generate large UDP packets that, obviously, are not subject to TCP MSS and thus can cause significant and unmitigatable serialization delays to VoIP packets.

The recommended TCP MSS value of 542 was calculated to eliminate the IPSec crypto algorithm (3DES) padding and the ATM AAL5 padding in DSL implementations (cable implementations have 3DES padding but no AAL5). Therefore, a TCP MSS value of 542 bytes is valid for cable but is optimized for DSL. Figure 16-26 illustrates a TCP packet with an MSS size of 542.

NOTE   Both the ESP and AAL5 pad lengths are 0. A TCP packet with a TCP MSS value of 542 fits exactly into 14 ATM cells, with no wasted bytes because of cell padding.

Figure 16-26 *Optimized TCP MSS Value for DSL (542 Bytes)*

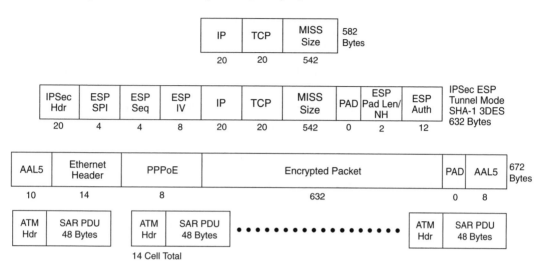

The evident negative aspect of using this technique to minimize the impact of serialization delay is the decreased efficiency of large data transfers, coupled with an increase in the number of packets per second that the router must switch. The higher packets-per-second rate is not as much of an issue at the remote router as at the headend, where hundreds or thousands of remote connections are concentrated. However, adjusting the TCP MSS value provides a means for the network manager to deploy voice over broadband connections, which do not support any LFI mechanism at rates less than 768 kbps.

Split Tunneling

The teleworker is usually not the only user of the residential broadband connection. The worker's spouse and children also might utilize this link from other devices, such as additional PCs or laptops or even gaming units. In such cases, only "work-related" traffic would require encryption and could be given a preferential treatment, through QoS, over general Internet traffic.

In this situation, prioritization could be made based on the destination address of the traffic. One method to accomplish this would be to create a separate bandwidth class (for example, named CORPORATE) and provision this class with a dedicated CBWFQ queue.

Given the sample topology illustrated in Figure 16-27, a suitable QoS configuration is broken down as follows:

- **VOICE**—A single call's VoIP packets assigned to an LLQ, with the bandwidth allocation based on codec and broadband media (DSL or cable).

- **CALL-SIGNALING**—Call-Signaling traffic in a CBWFQ queue, allocated 5 percent.

- **INTERNETWORK**—Internetwork-Control traffic, such as routing protocol updates and IKE keepalives, in a CBWFQ queue, allocated 5 percent.

- **CORPORATE**—All other traffic that is destined to the enterprise through the IPSec tunnel, in a CBWFQ queue, allocated 25 percent.

- **INTERNET/Class-Default**—Traffic to the Internet (outside the IPSec tunnel) defaults to this fair-queued class.

Figure 16-27 *Split Tunnel Example Topology*

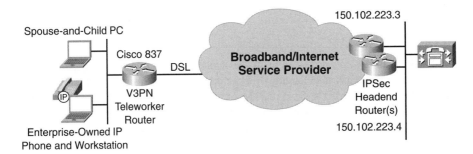

The following configuration fragment provides a means to implement this policy. It assumes that the headend IPSec crypto peers reside on network 150.102.223.0/29. In this example environment, two peers are configured at 150.102.223.3 and 150.102.223.4. Packets within the IPSec tunnel—those matching the CORP-INTRANET access control list (identifying RFC 1918 private addresses that are assumed in this example to represent the intranets behind the headends)—will be encapsulated in an ESP (IPSec-IP protocol 50) IP header. A class-map CORPORATE is configured that references the CORPORATE extended access list, pointing to the VPN headend subnet.

A policy map named V3PN-SPLIT-TUNNEL is created that includes classes for VOICE, INTERNETWORK-CONTROL, and CALL-SIGNALING, along with a bandwidth class for CORPORATE.

In this example, the VOICE class is provisioned for a G.711 codec over a (384-kbps) DSL uplink, allocating 150 kbps (or 40 percent, whichever syntax is preferred) for VoIP. Example 16-8 shows the relevant configuration fragment.

Example 16-8 *V3PN-SPLIT-TUNNEL Policy Example*

```
!
crypto map SPLIT-TUNNEL-CRYPTO-MAP 1 ipsec-isakmp
 set peer 150.102.223.3
 set peer 150.102.223.4
 set transform-set TS
 match address CORP-INTRANET                ! References CORP-INTRANET ACL
 qos pre-classify                           ! Enables QoS Pre-Classify
 !
 !
class-map match-all VOICE
  match ip dscp ef                          ! VoIP
 class-map match-any INTERNETWORK-CONTROL
  match ip dscp cs6                         ! IP Routing
  match access-group name IKE               ! References ISAKMP ACL
 class-map match-any CALL-SIGNALING
  match ip dscp cs3                         ! New Call-Signaling
  match ip dscp af31                        ! Old Call-Signaling
 class-map match-all CORPORATE
  match access-group name CORPORATE         ! References CORPORATE ACL
 !
policy-map V3PN-SPLIT-TUNNEL
  class VOICE
    priority 150                            ! Encrypted G.711 over DSL (PPPoE/AAL5)
  class INTERNETWORK-CONTROL
    bandwidth percent 5                     ! Control Plane provisioning
  class CALL-SIGNALING
    bandwidth percent 5                     ! Call-Signaling provisioning
  class CORPORATE
    bandwidth percent 25                    ! "Work-related" traffic provisioning
    queue-limit 15                          ! Optional: Anti-Replay Tuning
  class class-default
    fair-queue
    queue-limit 15                          ! Optional: Anti-Replay Tuning
 !
 ...
 !
ip access-list extended CORP-INTRANET       ! CORP-INTRANET ACL (RFC 1918)
 permit ip any 10.0.0.0 0.255.255.255
 permit ip any 172.16.0.0 0.15.255.255
 permit ip any 192.168.0.0 0.0.255.255
 !
ip access-list extended IKE
 permit udp any eq isakmp any eq isakmp     ! ISAKMP ACL
 !
ip access-list extended CORPORATE           ! CORPORATE ACL (VPN Head-ends)
 permit esp any 150.102.223.0 0.0.0.7
 !
```

Teleworker V3PN QoS Designs

To review, three deployment models exist for teleworker V3PN scenarios:

- Integrated Unit Model
- Dual-Unit Model
- Integrated Unit + Access Model

Furthermore, there are two main broadband deployment media: DSL and cable. DSL supports all three teleworker deployment models, but cable supports (at the time of writing) only the Integrated Unit + Access Model.

Integrated Unit/Dual-Unit Models—DSL Design

The key point to remember when provisioning QoS for V3PN over DSL (PPPoE/ATM AAL5) is the significant bandwidth overhead required by these protocols (85 kbps is needed per G.729 call, and 150 kbps is needed per G.711 call).

Some additional points to keep in mind are that since the service policy is being applied to a low-speed ATM PVC, the Tx-ring should be tuned to 3 (as discussed in Chapter 13) and also that because no LFI mechanism exists for DSL, TCP-MSS tuning can be done on the dialer interface to mitigate serialization delay. An Integrated Unit/Dual-Unit V3PN teleworker example for a 384-kbps DSL circuit is illustrated in Figure 16-28 and detailed in Example 16-9.

Figure 16-28 *Integrated Unit/Dual-Unit V3PN Teleworker Model for 384-kbps DSL Uplink*

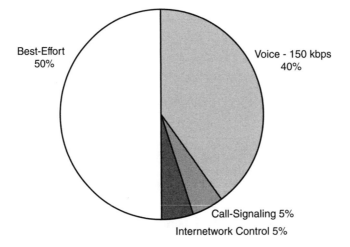

Example 16-9 *Integrated Unit/Dual-Unit V3PN Teleworker QoS Design Example for a 384-kbps (PPPoE/ATM) DSL Uplink*

```
 !
  class-map match-all VOICE
   match ip dscp ef                        ! VoIP
  class-map match-any INTERNETWORK-CONTROL
   match ip dscp cs6                        ! IP Routing
   match access-group name IKE              ! References ISAKMP ACL
  class-map match-any CALL-SIGNALING
   match ip dscp cs3                        ! New Call-Signaling
   match ip dscp af31                       ! Old Call-Signaling
  !
  !
  policy-map V3PN-TELEWORKER
   class VOICE
     priority 150                           ! Encrypted G.711 over DSL (PPPoE/AAL5)
   class INTERNETWORK-CONTROL
     bandwidth percent 5                    ! Control Plane provisioning
   class CALL-SIGNALING
     bandwidth percent 5                    ! Call-Signaling provisioning
   class class-default
     fair-queue
     queue-limit 30                         ! Optional: Anti-Replay Tuning
  !
  ...
  !
 interface ATM0
  no ip address
  no atm ilmi-keepalive
  dsl operating-mode auto
  dsl power-cutback 0
  !
 interface ATM0.35 point-to-point
  description Outside PPPoE/ATM DSL Link
  bandwidth 384
  pvc dsl 0/35
   vbr-nrt 384 384
   tx-ring-limit 3                          ! Tx-Ring tuned to 3
   pppoe max-sessions 5
   service-policy output V3PN-TELEWORKER    ! MQC policy applied to PVC
   pppoe-client dial-pool-number 1
  !
  ...
  !
 interface Dialer1
  description Dialer for PPPoE
  ip address negotiated
  ip mtu 1492
  encapsulation ppp
  ip tcp adjust-mss 542                     ! TCP MSS value tuned for slow-link
  !
```

continues

Example 16-9 *Integrated Unit/Dual-Unit V3PN Teleworker QoS Design Example for a 384-kbps (PPPoE/ATM) DSL Uplink (Continued)*

```
...
!
ip access-list extended IKE
 permit udp any eq isakmp any eq isakmp       ! ISAKMP ACL
!
```

Verification commands:

- **show policy**
- **show policy interface**
- **show atm pvc**

Integrated Unit + Access Model—DSL/Cable Designs

Hierarchical MQC policies are required for Integrated Unit + Access Models to shape and queue (within the shaped rate) on the outbound Ethernet interface. For cable, the shaped rate should be 95 percent of the broadband link's speed (as detailed in Chapter 13 in the "Frame Relay" section ["Committed Information Rate" subsection]). For DSL, the shaped rate should be 70 percent of the uplink's speed (to account for the increased bandwidth overhead required by DSL). Furthermore, on slow-speed (≤ 768 kbps) links, TCP-MSS should be tuned on both the inbound and outbound Ethernet interfaces. An Integrated Unit + Access Model for a 384-kbps cable teleworker uplink is shown in Figure 16-29 and detailed in Example 16-10.

Figure 16-29 *Integrated Unit + Access V3PN Teleworker Model for 384-kbps Cable Uplink*

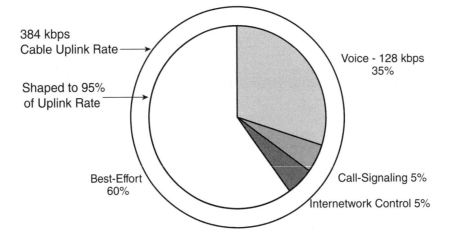

Example 16-10 *Integrated Unit + Access Model—Cable Design Example*

```
!
class-map match-all VOICE
 match ip dscp ef                       ! VoIP
class-map match-any INTERNETWORK-CONTROL
 match ip dscp cs6                      ! IP Routing
 match access-group name IKE            ! References ISAKMP ACL
class-map match-any CALL-SIGNALING
 match ip dscp cs3                      ! Old Call-Signaling
 match ip dscp af31                     ! New Call-Signaling
!
!
policy-map V3PN-TELEWORKER
 class VOICE
   priority 128                         ! Encrypted G.711 over Cable
 class INTERNETWORK-CONTROL
   bandwidth percent 5                  ! Control Plane provisioning
 class CALL-SIGNALING
   bandwidth percent 5                  ! Call-Signaling provisioning
 class class-default
   fair-queue
   queue-limit 30                       ! Optional: Anti-Replay Tuning
!
!
policy-map SHAPE-384-CABLE
 class class-default
   shape average 364800 3640            ! Shapes to 95% of 384 kbps cable link
   service-policy V3PN-TELEWORKER       ! Nested V3PN Teleworker queuing policy
!
...
!
interface Ethernet0
 description Inside Ethernet Interface
 ip tcp adjust-mss 542                           ! TCP MSS value tuned for slow-link
!
interface Ethernet1
 description Outside Ethernet Interface
 ip address dhcp
 ip tcp adjust-mss 542                           ! TCP MSS value tuned for slow-link
 service-policy output SHAPE-384-CABLE           ! Shaper applied to LAN interface
!
```

Verification commands:

- **show policy**
- **show policy interface**

Case Study: IPSec VPN QoS Design

ABC, Inc., is continuing to expand in its operations. Recently, it acquired a new subsidiary, DEF Group, and wants to incorporate this new group within its existing network infrastructure.

DEF already has provisioned its wide-area networking needs to its more than 100 branches through IPSec VPNs. However, it has provisioned only for data networking needs. ABC, Inc., wants to deploy IP Telephony to all of DEF's remote sites immediately. At this point in time, DEF's branches are running full T1s, with Frame Relay as the access medium. ABC also plans to deploy IP videoconferencing to these sites in the future, after the access links have been upgraded to higher-speed ATM PVCs.

At the same time, ABC, Inc.'s, management has received numerous requests from employees who want to relocate away from the company's central campus because the cost of living in other areas is more attractive. ABC is concerned that it will lose much of its top talent and has decided to deploy a business-ready teleworker solution for any approved employees.

This teleworker solution is to be tailored to work with either DSL or cable residential broadband options through the Integrated Unit + Access Teleworker deployment model.

The combined set of V3PN solutions is illustrated in Figure 16-30.

In this example, ABC, Inc., is continuing to partner with a Cisco IP Multiservice Service Provider (Service Provider XYZ) who offers them tight service-level agreements, such as 60-ms edge-to-edge delay, 10-ms edge-to-edge jitter, and 0.5 percent packet loss. However, for this particular service (namely, the interconnect of DEF's remote sites), XYZ is not offering explicit classes of service or QoS (beyond the edge-to-edge SLA).

For scalability and availability reasons, ABC, Inc., has decided to decouple IPSec VPN encryption and QoS at its central site: one pair of routers (Cisco 7200 VXR NPE-G1s with dual VPN Acceleration Modules, or VAMs) will provide IPSec VPN encryption, and another pair of routers (Cisco 7500 with VIP6-80s) will perform WAN aggregation QoS. As ABC continues to expand its operations, it plans to migrate its VPN headends to the Catalyst 6500 with the VPN Services Module (VPNSM) to achieve even higher scalability.

Because ABC, Inc., plans to support IP videoconferencing in the future—and, therefore, will be expanding the link speeds to its branches—it has decided to upgrade its branch routers to Cisco 3725s and Cisco 3745s (both with AIM-II hardware crypto engines), with the 3745s being deployed at the busiest sites.

For the telecommuter solution, ABC, Inc., has chosen a Cisco 831 router to perform the basic, VPN/security, and QoS services required by teleworkers. It has decided to support split-tunneling so that Internet traffic belonging to a spouse or child will not tax network resources.

Figure 16-30 *Case Study IPSec VPN QoS Design Example*

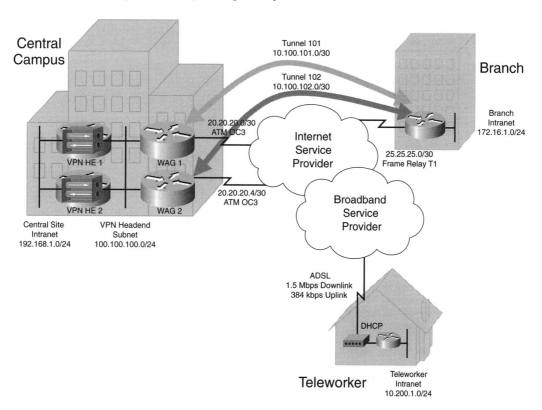

The configuration solution for this example spans multiple routers: VPN headend routers (see Example 16-11), WAN aggregators (see Example 16-12), branch routers (see Example 16-13), and telecommuter routers (see Example 16-14). To minimize redundancy, only a single example of each router type is presented.

A key point to notice in the VPN headend designs, as detailed in Example 16-11, is that QoS Pre-Classify is not required because encryption and QoS are being performed on separate routers at the central site.

Example 16-11 *Case Study Example: Part 1, VPN Headend Design*

```
!
hostname VPN-HEADEND-1
!
ip cef
!
```

continues

Example 16-11 *Case Study Example: Part 1, VPN Headend Design (Continued)*

```
!
crypto isakmp policy 1
 encr 3des
 authentication pre-share
 group 2
crypto isakmp key SECRETKEY address 25.25.25.1
!
!
crypto ipsec transform-set V3PN-TS esp-3des esp-sha-hmac
!
crypto map V3PN-CM 10 ipsec-isakmp
 set peer 25.25.25.1
 set transform-set V3PN-TS
 match address V3PN-SITE1
 [REPEAT CRYPTO MAP ENTRIES FOR EVERY REMOTE SITE, INCLUDING TELEWORKER SITES]
!
crypto map static-map local-address GigabitEthernet0/1
!
...
!
interface Tunnel101
 ip address 10.100.101.1 255.255.255.252
 tunnel source 100.100.100.1
 tunnel destination 25.25.25.1
 crypto map V3PN-CM         ! Applies crypto-map to tunnel interface
!
 [REPEAT TUNNEL INTERFACES FOR EVERY REMOTE SITE, INCLUDING TELEWORKER SITES]
!
interface GigabitEthernet0/1
 description CENTRAL SITE DATA SUBNET
 ip address 192.168.1.1 255.255.255.0
 duplex auto
 speed auto
 media-type rj45
 no negotiation auto
!
!
interface GigabitEthernet0/2
 description VPN HEADEND SUBNET
 ip address 100.100.100.1 255.255.255.0
 duplex auto
 speed auto
 media-type rj45
 no negotiation auto
 crypto map V3PN-CM             ! Applies crypto map to GE 0/2
!
...
!
ip access-list extended V3PN-SITE1
 permit gre host 100.100.100.1 host 25.25.25.1
!
```

Verification commands:

- **show policy**
- **show policy interface**

Some key points to notice in the WAN aggregator designs, as detailed in Example 16-12, include these:

- IP CEF is required to be run in distributed mode on this platform (Cisco 7500).
- A six-class V3PN policy has been deployed on the WAN aggregators edge.
- WRED in conjunction with queue-limit tuning is supported on distributed platforms (such as the Cisco 7500), although it currently is not supported on nondistributed platforms (until the release of Consistent QoS Behavior, as described in Chapter 13).
- Because the central site's link to the ISP is a (very) high-speed ATM PVC (OC3), no tuning of the Tx-ring is required.
- ISAKMP traffic is not encrypted and thus can be classified by a simple ACL (UDP port 500).

Example 16-12 *Case Study Example: Part 2, WAN Aggregator QoS Design*

```
!
hostname WAG-1
!
ip cef distributed                          ! Distributed platform
!
class-map match-all VOICE
  match ip dscp ef                          ! VoIP
 class-map match-any CALL-SIGNALING
  match ip dscp cs3                         ! New Call-Signaling
  match ip dscp af31                        ! Old Call-Signaling
 class-map match-any INTERNETWORK-CONTROL
  match ip dscp cs6                         ! IP Routing
  match access-group name IKE               ! References ISAKMP ACL
 class-map match-all TRANSACTIONAL-DATA
  match ip dscp af21 af22                   ! Transactional-Data
 class-map match-all SCAVENGER
  match ip dscp cs1                         ! Scavenger
 !
 !
 policy-map SIX-CLASS-V3PN-EDGE
  class VOICE
    priority percent 33                     ! VoIP gets 33% LLQ
  class CALL-SIGNALING
    bandwidth percent 5                     ! Call-Signaling provisioning
  class INTERNETWORK-CONTROL
    bandwidth percent 5                     ! Control Plane provisioning
```

continues

Example 16-12 *Case Study Example: Part 2, WAN Aggregator QoS Design (Continued)*

```
  class TRANSACTIONAL-DATA
    bandwidth percent 31              ! Transactional-Data provisioning
    random-detect dscp-based          ! WRED + QL tuning supported on 7500
    queue-limit 20                    ! Optional: Anti-Replay tuning
  class SCAVENGER
    bandwidth percent 1               ! Scavenger class is throttled
    queue-limit 1                     ! Optional: Anti-Replay tuning
  class class-default
    bandwidth percent 25              ! Best Effort needs BW guarantee
    random-detect dscp-based          ! WRED + QL tuning supported on 7500
    queue-limit 16                    ! Optional: Anti-Replay Tuning
 !
 ...
 !
interface GigabitEthernet1/0/0
 description VPN HEADEND SUBNET
 ip address 100.100.100.3 255.255.255.0
 duplex auto
 speed auto
 media-type rj45
 no negotiation auto
 !
 ...
 !
interface ATM1/1/0
 no ip address
 no atm ilmi-keepalive
 !
interface ATM1/1/0.100 point-to-point
 description ATM OC3 TO ISP
 ip address 20.20.20.1 255.255.255.252
 pvc 0/100
   vbr-nrt 149760 149760
   service-policy out SIX-CLASS-V3PN-EDGE        ! MQC policy applied to PVC
  !
 !
 ...
 !
ip access-list extended IKE                      ! ISAKMP ACL
  permit udp any eq isakmp any eq isakmp
 !
```

Verification commands:

- **show policy**
- **show policy interface**

Some key points to notice in the V3PN branch router designs, as detailed in Example 16-13, include these:

- A six-class V3PN policy has been deployed on the branch VPN access edge.

- WRED is not supported in conjunction with queue-limit tuning (for Anti-Replay) on these nondistributed platforms.

- Even though Frame Relay is being used as the access medium, no shaping is required because all sites are running at full (T1) port speeds.

- QoS Pre-Classify is enabled on both crypto map entries and tunnel interfaces, to enhance performance.

- The delay parameter has been tuned on the tunnel interfaces to influence the routing protocol's (EIGRP, in this instance) choice for primary and secondary tunnels.

Example 16-13 *Case Study Example: Part 3, V3PN Branch Router Design*

```
!
hostname V3PN-BRANCH-1
!
ip cef
!
!
crypto isakmp policy 1
 encr 3des
 authentication pre-share
 group 2
crypto isakmp key SECRETKEY address 100.100.100.1
crypto isakmp key SECRETKEY address 100.100.100.2
!
!
crypto ipsec transform-set V3PN-TS esp-3des esp-sha-hmac
!
crypto map V3PN-CM 10 ipsec-isakmp
 set peer 100.100.100.1
 set transform-set V3PN-TS
 match address V3PN-HE1
 qos pre-classify                           ! Enables QoS Pre-Classify
crypto map V3PN-CM 20 ipsec-isakmp
 set peer 100.100.100.2
 set transform-set V3PN-TS
 match address V3PN-HE2
 qos pre-classify                           ! Enables QoS Pre-Classify
!
crypto map static-map local-address Serial0/0
!
```

continues

Example 16-13 *Case Study Example: Part 3, V3PN Branch Router Design (Continued)*

```
!
class-map match-all VOICE
 match ip dscp ef                          ! VoIP
class-map match-any CALL-SIGNALING
 match ip dscp cs3                         ! New Call-Signaling
 match ip dscp af31                        ! Old Call-Signaling
class-map match-any INTERNETWORK-CONTROL
 match ip dscp cs6                         ! IP Routing
 match access-group name IKE               ! References ISAKMP ACL
class-map match-all TRANSACTIONAL-DATA
 match ip dscp af21 af22                   ! Transactional-Data
class-map match-all SCAVENGER
 match ip dscp cs1                         ! Scavenger
!
!
policy-map SIX-CLASS-V3PN-EDGE
 class VOICE
  priority percent 33                      ! VoIP gets 33% LLQ
 class CALL-SIGNALING
  bandwidth percent 5                      ! Call-Signaling provisioning
 class INTERNETWORK-CONTROL
  bandwidth percent 5                      ! Control Plane provisioning
 class TRANSACTIONAL-DATA
  bandwidth percent 31                     ! Transactional-Data provisioning
  queue-limit 20                           ! Optional: Anti-Replay tuning
 class SCAVENGER
  bandwidth percent 1                      ! Scavenger class is throttled
  queue-limit 1                            ! Optional: Anti-Replay tuning
 class class-default
  bandwidth percent 25                     ! Best Effort needs BW guarantee
  queue-limit 16                           ! Optional: Anti-Replay Tuning
!
!
...
!
interface Tunnel101
 ip address 10.100.101.2 255.255.255.252
 delay 50000
 qos pre-classify                         ! Enables QoS Pre-Classify
 tunnel source 25.25.25.1
 tunnel destination 100.100.100.1
 crypto map V3PN-CM
!
interface Tunnel102
 ip address 10.100.102.2 255.255.255.252
 delay 60000
 qos pre-classify                         ! Enables QoS Pre-Classify
 tunnel source 25.25.25.1
 tunnel destination 100.100.100.2
 crypto map V3PN-CM
!
!
```

Example 16-13 *Case Study Example: Part 3, V3PN Branch Router Design (Continued)*

```
interface FastEthernet0/0
 description V3PN-BRANCH-1 INTRANETS
 ip address 172.16.1.1 255.255.255.0
 duplex auto
 speed auto
!
...
!
interface Serial0/0
 description FRAME RELAY T1 TO ISP
 bandwidth 1536
 ip address 25.25.25.1 255.255.255.252
 service-policy output SIX-CLASS-V3PN-EDGE ! MQC policy applied to T1 int
 encapsulation frame-relay
 frame-relay interface-dlci 100
 crypto map V3PN-CM
!
...
!
ip access-list extended IKE                ! ISAKMP ACL
 permit udp any eq isakmp any eq isakmp
!
ip access-list extended V3PN-HE1
 permit gre host 25.25.25.1 host 100.100.100.1
!
ip access-list extended V3PN-HE2
 permit gre host 25.25.25.1 host 100.100.100.2
!
```

Verification commands:

- **show policy**
- **show policy interface**

Some key points to notice in the V3PN teleworker router designs, as detailed in Example 16-14, include these:

- In this example, an ADSL link (of 1536 kbps downlink and 384 kbps uplink) is provisioned for V3PN. Because of the overhead of DSL, VoIP bandwidth is provisioned for 150 kbps (which can support either G.711 or G.729).

- A hierarchical QoS policy is set to shape (and queue within the shaped rate) to 70 percent of the uplink's rate and is applied to the Ethernet interface facing the DSL modem.

- WRED is not supported in conjunction with queue-limit tuning (for Anti-Replay) on these nondistributed platforms.

- NAT transparency is disabled globally to reduce bandwidth overhead.

- QoS Pre-Classify is enabled on the crypto map to enhance performance.
- A split-tunneling policy is provisioned on teleworker routers, determining "work-related" traffic as being destined to private intranet addresses.
- TCP MSS is adjusted on both Ethernet interfaces to mitigate serialization delay.

Example 16-14 *Case Study Example: Part 4, Telecommuter Router*

```
!
hostname TELEWORKER-V3PN-1
!
ip cef
ip inspect name CBAC tcp
ip inspect name CBAC udp
ip inspect name CBAC ftp
!
crypto isakmp policy 1
 encr 3des
 group 2
!
!
crypto ipsec transform-set V3PN-TELEWORKER-TS esp-3des esp-sha-hmac
no crypto ipsec nat-transparency udp-encaps   ! Disables NAT Transparency
!
crypto map V3PN-TELEWORKER-CM 1 ipsec-isakmp
 set peer 100.100.100.1
 set peer 100.100.100.2
 set transform-set V3PN-TELEWORKER-TS
 match address CORP-INTRANET
 qos pre-classify                      ! Enables QoS Pre-Classify
!
!
class-map match-all VOICE
  match ip dscp ef                     ! VoIP
class-map match-any INTERNETWORK-CONTROL
  match ip dscp cs6                    ! IP Routing
  match access-group name IKE          ! References ISAKMP ACL
class-map match-any CALL-SIGNALING
  match ip dscp cs3                    ! New Call-Signaling
  match ip dscp af31                   ! Old Call-Signaling
class-map match-all CORPORATE
  match access-group name CORPORATE    ! References CORPORATE ACL
!
!
policy-map V3PN-SPLIT-TUNNEL
  class VOICE
    priority 150                       ! Encrypted G.711 over DSL (PPPoE/AAL5)
  class INTERNETWORK-CONTROL
    bandwidth percent 5                ! Control Plane provisioning
  class CALL-SIGNALING
    bandwidth percent 5                ! Call-Signaling provisioning
```

Example 16-14 *Case Study Example: Part 4, Telecommuter Router (Continued)*

```
   class CORPORATE
     bandwidth percent 25               ! "Work-related" traffic provisioning
     queue-limit 15                     ! Optional: Anti-Replay Tuning
   class class-default
     fair-queue
     queue-limit 15                     ! Optional: Anti-Replay Tuning
 !
 !
policy-map SHAPE-384-ADSL-UPLINK
 class class-default
   shape average 268800 2688           ! Shapes to 70% of 384 kbps ADSL uplink
   service-policy V3PN-SPLIT-TUNNEL    ! Nested V3PN split-tunnel policy
 !
 ...
 !
interface Ethernet0
 description TELEWORKER 1 INTRANET
 ip address 10.200.1.1 255.255.255.248
 ip inspect CBAC in
 ip tcp adjust-mss 542                 ! TCP MSS value tuned for slow-link
 !
interface Ethernet1
 description ETHERNET LINK TO DSL MODEM
 ip address dhcp
 service-policy output SHAPE-384-ADSL-UPLINK        ! Shaping + Queuing
 ip tcp adjust-mss 542                 ! TCP MSS value tuned for slow-link
 duplex auto
 no cdp enable
 crypto map V3PN-TELEWORKER-CM
 !
 !
ip access-list extended CORP-INTRANET              ! CORP-INTRANET ACL (RFC 1918)
 permit ip 10.200.1.0 0.0.0.7 10.0.0.0 0.255.255.255
 permit ip 10.200.1.0 0.0.0.7 172.16.0.0 0.15.255.255
 permit ip 10.200.1.0 0.0.0.7 192.168.0.0 0.0.255.255
 !
ip access-list extended IKE
 permit udp any eq isakmp any eq isakmp            ! ISAKMP ACL
 !
ip access-list extended CORPORATE                  ! CORPORATE ACL (VPN Head-ends)
 permit esp any 100.100.100.0 0.0.0.3
 !
```

Verification commands:

- **show policy**
- **show policy interface**

Summary

IPSec VPNs, the most commonly deployed VPN solutions today, are found in three main contexts: site-to-site VPNs, teleworker VPNs, and remote-access VPNs. The overlaying of QoS technologies on top of IPSec VPNs is dubbed V3PN, for voice- and video-enabled Virtual Private Networks. This chapter presented considerations and design recommendations for V3PN deployments in site-to-site and teleworker contexts. A summary of the design recommendations for encryption and QoS for site-to-site and teleworker IPSec V3PNs is illustrated in Figure 16-31.

Figure 16-31 *IPSec V3PN Site-to-Site and Teleworker Design Summary Comparison*

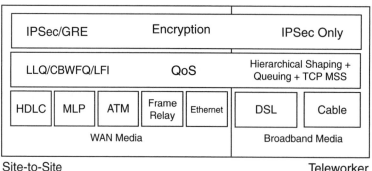

Some site-to-site considerations that were discussed include the bandwidth implications of various IPSec modes of operations and the incompatibility of cRTP and IPSec. The interrelation of IPSec VPN logical hub-and-spoke topologies and the effect these have on spoke-to-spoke delay budgets also were examined. Subsequently, the ToS byte preservation mechanism was overviewed along with the QoS Pre-Classify Cisco IOS Software feature, which allows for the classification of packets already encrypted (on the same router) through ACLs. QoS and Anti-Replay implications then were discussed, illustrating how QoS policies that reorder packets potentially can exacerbate Anti-Replay drops (an IPSec message-integrity mechanism). Techniques for minimizing such undesired QoS/Anti-Reply interaction effects, such as reducing the queue length of data queues, were presented. Next, the need for control plane provisioning was highlighted, along with basic designs for doing so.

Several site-to-site QoS models were detailed, ranging from a six-class V3PN QoS model to a complex 11-class V3PN QoS Baseline model. WAN aggregator considerations specific to IPSec VPN deployments were examined next, including QoS provisioning for IPSec over private WANs, per-tunnel hierarchical shaping and queuing, and recommendations for decoupled VPN headend/WAN aggregation deployment models, where encryption and QoS are performed on different routers.

Attention then shifted to teleworker scenarios and the three main teleworker deployment models: the Integrated Unit Model, the Dual-Unit Model, and the Integrated Unit + Access Model. The two main broadband media types, DSL and cable, were broken down to ascertain the bandwidth-provisioning implications of each media. Neither DSL nor (DOCSIS 1.0) cable includes any mechanism for serialization delay mitigation, so TCP maximum segment-size tuning was considered as an alternative mechanism to achieve this. Split-tunneling designs, to address spouse-and-child requirements, were introduced.

Teleworker V3PN designs then were detailed for Integrated Unit and Dual-Unit models over DSL, in addition to an Integrated Unit + Access Model solution for cable.

The chapter concluded with a case study (which, likewise, concluded the case studies presented in each previous design chapter) highlighting how an enterprise could overlay QoS on top of an existing site-to-site IPSec VPN to enable a V3PN. Additionally, a solution was presented for a business-ready teleworker.

Further Reading

Standards:

- RFC 1321, "The MD5 Message-Digest Algorithm": http://www.ietf.org/rfc/rfc1321.txt.
- RFC 1918, "Address Allocation for Private Internets": http://www.ietf.org/rfc/rfc1918.txt.
- RFC 2104, "HMAC: Keyed-Hashing for Message Authentication": http://www.ietf.org/rfc/rfc2104.txt.
- RFC 2401, "Security Architecture for the Internet Protocol": http://www.ietf.org/rfc/rfc2401.txt.
- RFC 2402, "IP Authentication Header": http://www.ietf.org/rfc/rfc2402.txt.
- RFC 2403, "The Use of HMAC-MD5-96 Within ESP and AH": http://www.ietf.org/rfc/rfc2403.txt.
- RFC 2404, "The Use of HMAC-SHA-1-96 within ESP and AH": http://www.ietf.org/rfc/rfc2404.txt.
- RFC 2405, "The ESP DES-CBC Cipher Algorithm with Explicit IV": http://www.ietf.org/rfc/rfc2405.txt.
- RFC 2406, "IP Encapsulating Security Payload (ESP)": http://www.ietf.org/rfc/rfc2406.txt.
- RFC 2407, "The Internet IP Security Domain of Interpretation for ISAKMP": http://www.ietf.org/rfc/rfc2407.txt.
- RFC 2408, "Internet Security Association and Key Management Protocol (ISAKMP)": http://www.ietf.org/rfc/rfc2408.txt.

- RFC 2409, "The Internet Key Exchange (IKE)": http://www.ietf.org/rfc/rfc2409.txt.

- RFC 2410, "The NULL Encryption Algorithm and Its Use with IPSec": http://www.ietf.org/rfc/rfc2410.txt.

- RFC 2411, "IP Security Document Roadmap": http://www.ietf.org/rfc/rfc2411.txt.

- RFC 2412, "The OAKLEY Key Determination Protocol": http://www.ietf.org/rfc/rfc2412.txt.

Books:

- Kaeo, Merike. *Designing Network Security*. Indianapolis: Cisco Press, 2003.

- Malik, Saadat. *Network Security Principles and Practices*. Indianapolis: Cisco Press, 2002.

- Mason, Andrew. *Cisco Secure Virtual Private Networks*. Indianapolis: Cisco Press, 2001.

Cisco IOS documentation:

- IP Security and Encryption overview (Cisco IOS Release 12.2): http://www.cisco.com/univercd/cc/td/doc/product/software/ios122/122cgcr/fsecur_c/fipsenc/scfencov.htm.

- Configuring IPSec network security (Cisco IOS Release 12.2): http://www.cisco.com/univercd/cc/td/doc/product/software/ios122/122cgcr/fsecur_c/fipsenc/scfipsec.htm.

- Configuring Internet Key Exchange Security Protocol (Cisco IOS Release 12.2): http://www.cisco.com/univercd/cc/td/doc/product/software/ios122/122cgcr/fsecur_c/fipsenc/scfike.htm.

- Prefragmentation for IPSec VPNs (Cisco IOS Release 12.2[13]T): http://www.cisco.com/univercd/cc/td/doc/product/software/ios122/122newft/122t/122t13/ftprefrg.htm.

- Quality of service for Virtual Private Networks (Cisco IOS Release 12.2[2]T): http://www.cisco.com/univercd/cc/td/doc/product/software/ios122/122newft/122t/122t2/ftqosvpn.htm.

- Low-latency queuing (LLQ) for IPSec encryption engines (Cisco IOS Release 12.2[13]T): http://www.cisco.com/univercd/cc/td/doc/product/software/ios122/122newft/122t/122t13/llqfm.htm.

- IPSec NAT transparency (Cisco IOS Release 12.2[13]T): http://www.cisco.com/univercd/cc/td/doc/product/software/ios122/122newft/122t/122t13/ftipsnat.htm.

- IPSec and quality of service feature (Cisco IOS Release 12.3[8]T): http://www.cisco.com/univercd/cc/td/doc/product/software/ios123/123newft/123t/123t_8/gtqosips.htm.

- Configuring broadband access (Cisco IOS Release 12.2): http://www.cisco.com/
  univercd/cc/td/doc/product/software/ios122/122cgcr/fwan_c/wcfppp.htm.

- PPP over Ethernet Client (Cisco IOS Release 12.2[2]T): http://www.cisco.com/
  univercd/cc/td/doc/product/software/ios122/122newft/122t/122t2/ftpppoec.htm.

QoS "At-A-Glance" Summaries

QoS Tools

QoS is the measure of transmission quality and service availability of a network (or internetworks). The transmission quality of the network is determined by the following factors: Latency, Jitter, and Loss.

QoS technologies refer to the set of tools and techniques to manage network resources and are considered the key enabling technologies for the transparent convergence of voice, video, and data networks. Additionally, QoS tools can play a strategic role in significantly mitigating DoS/worm attacks.

The Cisco QoS toolset consists of the following:

- Classification and Marking tools
- Policing and Markdown tools
- Scheduling tools
- Link-specific tools
- AutoQoS tools

Classification can be done at Layers 2-7 via the following tools:

- Layer 2—MAC access lists
- Layer 3/4—IP access lists
- Layer7—Network-Based Application Recognition

Marking can be done at Layers 2 or Layer 3:
Layer 2: 802.1Q/p CoS, MPLS EXP
Layer 3: IP Precedence, DSCP, and/or IP ECN

Layer 3 (IP ToS Byte) Marking Options:

7	6	5	4	3	2	1	0
IP Precedence					*Un*		
DiffServ Code Point (DSCP)						IP ECN	

RFC 2474 DiffServ Extensions	RFC 3168 IP ECN Bits

Cisco recommends end-to-end marking at Layer 3 with standards-based DSCP values.

Policing tools can complement marking tools by marking metering flows and marking-down out-of-contract traffic.

Policers meter traffic into three categories:

- Conform: Traffic is within the defined rate (green light)
- Exceed: Moderate bursting is allowed (yellow light)
- Violate: No more traffic is allowed beyond this upper-limit (red light)

Scheduling tools reorder and selectively-drop packets whenever congestion occurs.

Link-specific tools are useful on slow-speed WAN/VPN links and include shaping, compression, fragmentation, and interleaving.

AutoQoS features automatically configure Cisco-recommended QoS on Catalyst switches and IOS routers with just one or two commands.

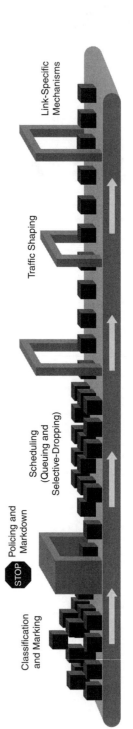

Classification and Marking

STOP Policing and Markdown

Scheduling (Queuing and Selective-Dropping)

Traffic Shaping

Link-Specific Mechanisms

The Cisco QoS Baseline

The QoS Baseline is a strategic document designed to unify QoS within Cisco. The QoS Baseline provides uniform, standards-based recommendations to help ensure that QoS products, designs, and deployments are unified and consistent.

The QoS Baseline defines up to 11 classes of traffic that may be viewed as critical to a given enterprise. A summary these classes and their respective standards-based markings and recommended QoS configurations are shown below.

Cisco products that support QoS features use these QoS Baseline recommendations for marking and scheduling and admission control.

The QoS Baseline recommendations are intended as a standards-based guideline for customers—not as a mandate.

Application	L3 Classification PHB	DSCP	Referencing Standard (12)	Recommended Configuration (13)
1 IP Routing	CS6	48	RFC 2474-4.2.2	Rate-Based Queuing + RED
2 Voice	EF	46	RFC 3246	RSVP Admission Control + Priority Queuing
3 Interactive-Video	AF41	34	RFC 2597	RSVP + Rate-Based Queuing + DSCP-WRED
4 Streaming-Video	CS4	32	RFC 2474-4.2.2	RSVP + Rate-Based Queuing + RED
5 Mission-Critical Data	AF31	26	RFC 2597	Rate-Based Queuing + DSCP-WRED
6 Call-Signaling	CS3	24	RFC 2474-4.2.2	Rate-Based Queuing + RED
7 Transactional Data	AF21	28	RFC 2597	Rate-Based Queuing + DSCP-WRED
8 Network-Management	CS2	16	RFC 2474-4.2.2	Rate-Based Queuing + RED
9 Bulk Data	AF11	10	RFC 2597	Rate-Based Queuing + DSCP-WRED
10 Scavenger	CS1	8	Internet 2	No BW Guarantee + RED
11 Best-Effort	0	0	RFC 2474-4.1	BW Guarantee Rate-Based Queuing + RED

❶ The IP Routing class is intended for IP Routing protocols, such as BGP, OSPF, etc.

❷ Voice refers to VoIP bearer traffic only (and does not include Call-Signaling traffic).

❸ Interactive-Video refers to IP Video-Conferencing.

❹ Streaming-Video is either unicast or multicast unidirectional video.

❺ The (Locally-Defined) Mission-Critical Data class is intended for a subset of Transactional Data applications that contribute most significantly to the business objectives (this is a non-technical assessment).

❻ The Call-Signaling class is intended for voice and/or video signaling traffic, such as Skinny, SIP, H.323, etc.

❼ The Transactional Data class is intended for foreground, user-interactive applications, such as database access, transaction services, interactive messaging, and preferred data services.

❽ The Network-Management class is intended for network management protocols, such as SNMP, Syslog, DNS, etc.

❾ The Bulk Data class is intended for background, non-interactive traffic flows, such as large file transfers, content distribution, database synchronization, backup operations, and e-mail.

❿ The Scavenger class is based on an Internet 2 draft that defines a less-than best-effort service. In the event of link congestion, this class will be dropped the most aggressively.

⓫ The Best-Effort class is also the default class. Unless an application has been assigned for preferential/deferential service, it remains in this default class. Most enterprises have hundreds—if not thousands—of applications on their networks; the majority of which will remain in the Best-Effort service class.

⓬ Standards-based marking recommendations allow for better integration with service-provider offerings as well as other internetworking scenarios.

⓭ In Cisco IOS, rate-based queuing translates to CBWFQ; priority queuing is LLQ.DSCP-Based WRED (based on RFC 2597) drops AFx3 before AFx2 and in turn drops AFx2 before AFx1. RSVP is recommended (whenever supported) for Voice and/or Interactive-Video admission control

QoS Best-Practices

A successful QoS deployment includes three key phases:

- Strategically defining the business objectives to be achieved via QoS.
- Analyzing the service-level requirements of the traffic classes.
- Designing and testing QoS policies

1 Strategically defining the business objectives to be achieved by QoS.

Business QoS objectives need to be defined:

- Is the objective to enable VoIP only or is video also required?
- If so, is video-conferencing required or streaming video? Or both?
- Are there applications that are considered mission-critical? If so, what are they?
- Does the organization wish to squelch certain types of traffic? If so, what are they?
- Does the business want to use QoS tools to mitigate DoS/worm attacks?
- How many classes of service are needed to meet the business objectives?

Because QoS introduces a system of managed unfairness, most QoS deployments inevitably entail political and organizational repercussions when implemented. This is typically because disagreement often arises over which applications are to be considered "mission-critical," which is a non-technical, subjective evaluation (Mission-Critical applications are foreground, interactive applications that most directly contribute to the main business objective of the enterprise).

To minimize the effects of these non-technical obstacles to deployment, address these political and organizational issues as early as possible, garnering executive endorsement whenever possible.

2 Analyzing the application service-level requirements.

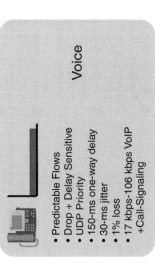

Voice

- Predictable Flows
- Drop + Delay Sensitive
- UDP Priority
- 150-ms one-way delay
- 30-ms jitter
- 1% loss
- 17 kbps-106 kbps VoIP +Call-Signaling

Video

- Unpredictable Flows
- Drop + Delay Sensitive
- UDP Priority
- 150-ms one-way delay
- 30-ms jitter
- 1% loss
- Overprovision stream by 20% to account for headers + bursts

Data

- No "one-size fits all"
- Smooth/Bursty
- Benign/Greedy
- TCP retransmits/ UDP does not

3 Designing and testing the QoS policies.

Classify, mark, and police as close to the traffic-sources as possible; following Differentiated Services standards, such as RFCs 2474, 2475, 2597, 2698, and 3246.

Application	L3 Classification PBH	DSCP
Routing	CS6	48
Voice	EF	46
Interactive-Video	AF41	34
Streaming-Video	CS4	32
Mission-Critical Data	AF31	26
Call-Signaling	CS3	24
Transactional Data	AF21	18
Network-Management	CS2	16
Bulk Data	AF11	10
Scavengor	CS1	8
Best-Effort	0	0

Provision queuing in a consistent manner (according to platform capabilities). For example, in the campus (inner circle) there may be only four hardware queues available; however, on the WAN/VPN (outer circle), eleven software queues may be used. The point is to keep the respective bandwidth allocations consistent.

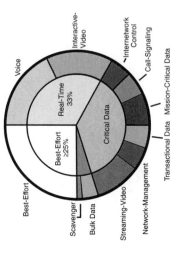

Thoroughly test QoS policies prior to production-network deployment.

Scavenger-Class QoS Strategy for DoS/Worm Attack Mitigation

DoS and worm attacks are exponentially increasing in frequency, complexity, and scope of damage.

QoS tools and strategic designs can mitigate the effects of worms and keep critical applications available during DoS attacks.

One such strategy, referred to as Scavenger-class QoS, uses a two-step tactical approach to provide first- and second-order anomaly detection and reaction to DoS/worm attack-generated traffic.

The first step in deploying Scavenger-class QoS is to profile applications to determine what constitutes a normal versus abnormal flow (within a 95% confidence interval).

Application traffic exceeding this normal rate is subject to first-order anomaly detection at the Campus Access-Edge: specifically, excess traffic is marked down to Scavenger (DSCP CS1/8).

Note that anomalous traffic is not dropped or penalized at the edge; it is simply re-marked.

Only traffic in excess of the normal/abnormal threshold is re-marked to Scavenger.

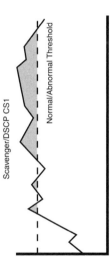

Scavenger/DSCP CS1

Normal/Abnormal Threshold

Campus Access-Edge policing policies are coupled with Scavenger-class queuing policies on the uplinks to the Campus Distribution Layer.

Queuing policies only engage when links are congested. Therefore, only if uplinks become congested does traffic begin to be dropped.

Anomalous traffic—previously marked to Scavenger—is dropped the most aggressively (only after all other traffic types have been fully-serviced).

A key point of this strategy is that legitimate traffic flows which temporarily exceed thresholds are not penalized by Scavenger-class QoS.

Only sustained, abnormal streams generated simultaneously by multiple hosts (highly-indicative of DoS/worm attacks) are subject to aggressive dropping—and such dropping only occurs *after* legitimate traffic has been fully-serviced.

The Campus uplinks are not the only points in the network infrastructure that congestion can occur. Typically WAN and VPN links are the first to congest.

Therefore, Scavenger-class less-than best-effort queuing should be provisioned on all network devices in a consistent manner (according to platform capabilities).

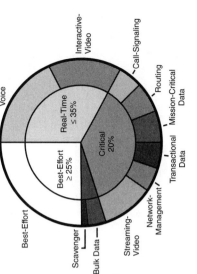

Thoroughly test QoS policies prior to production-network deployment.

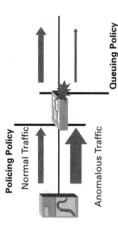

Policing Policy

Normal Traffic

Anomalous Traffic

Policing Policy

Normal Traffic

Anomalous Traffic

Queuing Policy

Campus QoS Design

QoS policies should always be enabled in Catalyst switch hardware—rather than router software—whenever a choice exists.

Three main types of QoS policies are required within the campus:
- Classification and Marking
- Policing and Markdown
- Queuing

Classification, marking, and policing should be performed as close to the traffic sources as possible, specifically at the Campus Access-Edge. Queuing, on the other hand, needs to be provisioned at all campus layers (access, distribution, core) due to oversubscription ratios.

Classify and mark as close to the traffic sources as possible following the Cisco QoS Baseline marking recommendations, which are based on Differentiated Services standards, such as: RFC, 2474, 2597, and 3246.

Queuing policies will vary by platform:
e.g., 1P3Q1T   P = Priority Queue
                Q = Non-Priority Queue
                T = WRED Threshold

Access-Edge policers, such as this one, detect anomalous flows and re-mark these to Scavenger (DSCP CS1).

The diagram below shows *what* QoS policies are needed *where* in the Campus.

VVLAN = Voice VLAN
DVLAN = Data VLAN

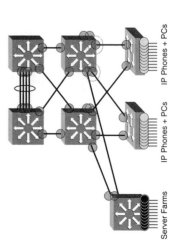

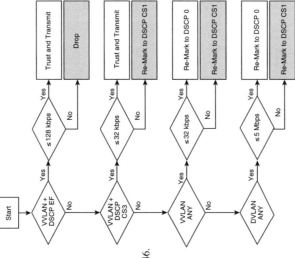

Application	L3 Classification PBH	DSCP
Routing	CS6	48
Voice	EF	46
Interactive-Video	AF41	34
Streaming-Video	CS4	32
Mission-Critical	AF31	26
Call-Signaling	CS3	24
Transactional Data	AF21	28
Network-Management	CS2	16
Bulk Data	AF11	10
Scavenger	CS1	8
Best-Effort	0	0

DSCP	CoS
-	CoS 7
CS6	CoS 6
EF	CoS 5
AF41	CoS 4
CS4	CoS 4
DSCP 25	CoS 3
AF31/CS3	CoS 3
AF21	CoS 2
CS2	CoS 2
AF11	CoS 1
CS1	CoS 1
0	0

1P3Q1T
- Q4 Priority Queue — CoS 5
- Queue 3 (70%) — CoS 7, CoS 6, CoS 4, CoS 3
- Queue 2 (25%) — CoS 0
- Queue 1 (5%) — CoS 1

Legend:
- Trust-DSCP + Queuing
- Conditional Trust + Policing + Queuing
- Untrusted + Policing + Queuing
- Per-User Microflow Policing

Flowchart:
- Start → VVLAN + DSCP EF → Yes → ≤128 kbps → Yes → Trust and Transmit / No → Drop
- VVLAN + DSCP EF → No → VVLAN + DSCP CS3 → Yes → ≤32 kbps → Yes → Trust and Transmit / No → Re-Mark to DSCP CS1
- VVLAN + DSCP CS3 → No → VVLAN ANY → Yes → ≤32 kbps → Yes → Re-Mark to DSCP 0 / No → Re-Mark to DSCP CS1
- VVLAN ANY → No → DVLAN ANY → Yes → ≤5 Mbps → Yes → Re-Mark to DSCP 0 / No → Re-Mark to DSCP CS1

IP Phones + PCs   IP Phones + PCs   Server Farms

cut here

WAN QoS Design

In an enterprise network infrastructure, bandwidth is scarcest—and thus most expensive—over the WAN. Therefore, the business case for efficient bandwidth optimization via QoS technologies is strongest over the WAN.

WAN QoS policies need to be configured on the WAN edges of WAN Aggregator (WAG) routers and Branch routers. WAN-edge QoS policies include queuing, shaping, selective dropping, and link-specific policies.

The number of WAN classes of traffic is determined by the business objectives and may be expanded over time.

Queuing model examples for 5/8/11 classes of service are shown below:

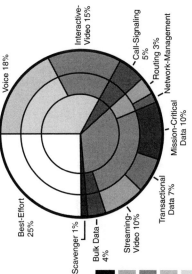

- Voice 18%
- Interactive-Video 15%
- Call-Signaling 5%
- Routing 3%
- Network-Management 2%
- Mission-Critical Data 10%
- Transactional Data 7%
- Streaming-Video 10%
- Bulk Data 4%
- Scavenger 1%
- Best-Effort 25%

WAN QoS tools: RTP Header Compression (cRTP)

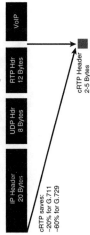

IP Header 20 Bytes | UDP Hdr 8 Bytes | RTP Hdr 12 Bytes | VoIP

cRTP Header 2–5 Bytes | VoIP

cRTP saves:
~20% for G.711
~60% for G.729

WAN QoS tools: Link Fragmentation and Interleaving

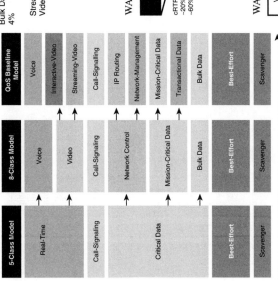

VoIP | Data

Data | Data | Data | VoIP | Data

LFI tools (MLP LFI or FRF.12) fragment large data packets and interleave these with high-priority VoIP.

WAN links can be categorized into three main speed groups:
Slow-Speed (≤ 768 kbps)
Medium-Speed (> 768 kbps & ≤ T1/E1)
High-Speed (≥ T1/E1)

5-Class Model	8-Class Model	QoS Baseline Model
Real-Time	Voice	Voice
		Interactive-Video
	Video	Streaming-Video
Call-Signaling	Call-Signaling	Call-Signaling
	Network Control	IP Routing
		Network-Management
Critical Data	Mission-Critical Data	Mission-Critical Data
		Transactional Data
	Bulk Data	Bulk Data
Best-Effort	Best-Effort	Best-Effort
Scavenger	Scavenger	Scavenger

Time

Link-Specific Design Recommendations:

Leased-Line (MLP) Link

Use MLP LFI and cRTP on ≤768-kbps links

Frame-Relay Link

- Use Frame-Relay traffic shaping
- Set CIR to 95% of guaranteed rate
- Set Committed Burst to CIR/100
- Set Excess Burst to 0
- Use FRF.12 and cRTP on ≤768-kbps links

ATM Link

- Use MLP LFI (via MLPoATM) and cRTP on slow-speed links
- Set the ATM PVC Tx-ring to 3 for ≤768-kbps links

ATM-to-FR SIW Link

- Use MLP LFI (via MLPoATM and MLPoFR) for ≤768-kbps links
- Optimize fragment sizes to minimize ATM cell-padding

Branch QoS Design

Branch routers are connected to central sites via private-WAN or VPN links, which often prove to be the bottlenecks for traffic flows. QoS policies at these bottlenecks align expensive WAN/VPN bandwidth utilization with business objectives.

QoS designs for Branch routers are—for the most part—identical to WAN Aggregator QoS designs. However, Branch routers require three unique QoS considerations:

1) Unidirectional applications
2) Ingress classification requirements
3) NBAR policies for worm policing

Each of these Branch router QoS design considerations is reviewed.

❶ Unidirectional Applications

Some applications (like Streaming-Video) usually only traverse the WAN/VPN in the campus-to-branch direction and, therefore, do not require provisioning in the branch-to-campus direction on the branch router's WAN edge.

Bandwidth for such unidirectional application classes can be reassigned to other critical classes, as shown in the following diagram. Notice that no Streaming-Video class is provisioned and the bandwidth allocated to it (on the campus side of the WAN link) is reallocated to the Mission-Critical and Transactional Data classes.

An example 10-Class QoS Baseline Branch Router WAN Edge Queuing Model:

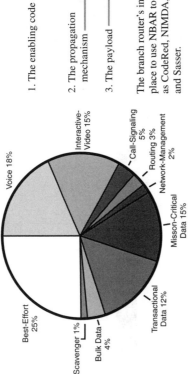

- Voice 18%
- Interactive-Video 15%
- Call-Signaling 5%
- Routing 3%
- Network-Management 2%
- Mission-Critical Data 15%
- Transactional Data 12%
- Bulk Data 4%
- Scavenger 1%
- Best-Effort 25%

❷ Ingress Classification

Branch-to-campus traffic may not be correctly marked on the branch access-layer switch.

These switches—which are usually lower-end switches—may or may not have the capabilities to classify and mark application traffic. Therefore, classification and marking may need to be performed on the branch router's LAN edge (in the ingress direction).

Furthermore, branch routers offer the ability to use NBAR to classify and mark traffic flows that require stateful packet inspection.

❸ NBAR for Known Worm Policing

Worms are nothing new, but they have increased exponentially in frequency, complexity and scope of damage in recent years.

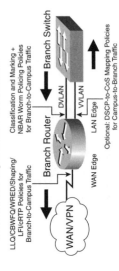

1. The enabling code
2. The propagation mechanism
3. The payload

The branch router's ingress LAN edge is a strategic place to use NBAR to identify and drop worms, such as CodeRed, NIMDA, SQL Slammer, MS-Blaster, and Sasser.

L2 Frame	L3 IP Packet	L4 Segment	L7 Data Payload
			Worm

NBAR extensions allow for custom Packet Data Language Modules (PDLMs) to be defined for future worms.

Where is QoS required on Branch routers?

LLQ/CBWFQ/WRED/Shaping/ LFI/cRTP Policies for Branch-to-Campus Traffic

Classification and Marking + NBAR Worm Policing Policies for Branch-to-Campus Traffic

Branch Router

Branch Switch

WAN/VPN

WAN Edge

LAN Edge

DVLAN

VVLAN

Optional: DSCP-to-CoS Mapping Policies for Campus-to-Branch Traffic

QoS Design for MPLS VPN Subscribers

QoS design for an enterprise subscribing to an MPLS VPN requires a major paradigm shift from private-WAN QoS design.

This is because with private-WAN design, the enterprise principally controlled QoS. The WAN Aggregator (WAG) provisioned QoS for not only campus-to-branch traffic, but also for branch-to-branch traffic, which was hmed through the WAG.

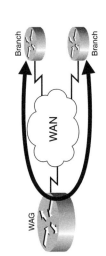

However, due to the any-to-any/full-mesh nature of MPLS VPNs, branch-to-branch traffic is no longer homed through the WAG. While branch-to-MPLS VPN QoS is controlled by the enterprise (on their Customer Edge [CE] routers), MPLS VPN-to-branch QoS is controlled by the service provider (on their Provider Edge [PE] routers).

MPLS VPN service providers offer classes of service to enterprise subscribers.

Admission criteria for these classes is the DSCP markings of enterprise traffic. Thus, enterprises may have to re-mark application traffic to gain admission into the required service-provider class.

Some best practices to consider when assigning enterprise traffic to service-provider classes of service include:

- Don't put Voice and Interactive-Video into the Real-Time class on slow-speed (≤ 768 kbps) CE-to-PE links.

- Don't put Call-Signaling into the Real-Time class on slow-speed CE-to-PE links.

- Don't mix TCP applications with UDP applications within a single service-provider class (whenever possible); UDP applications may dominate the class when congested.

- Enterprises should be aware of which RFC 3270 MPLS DiffServ Tunneling Mode their service provider is using (Uniform Mode, Pipe Mode, or Short Pipe Mode). If Uniform Mode is being used, the service provider may re-mark customer traffic at Layer 3 (overriding the customer's DSCP markings). If such is the case, the enterprise subscriber may need to restore such DSCP markings on ingress (from the MPLS VPN).

Therefore, to guarantee end-to-end QoS, enterprises must comanage QoS with their MPLS VPN service providers; their policies must be both consistent and complementary.

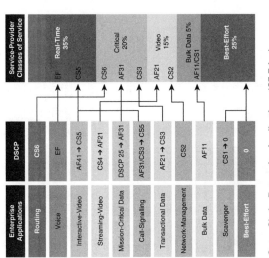

Example enterprise subscriber DSCP Remarking Diagram and CE Edge Bandwidth Allocation Diagram.

Enterprise Applications	DSCP	Service-Provider Classes of Service
Routing	CS6	EF — Real-Time 35%
Voice	EF	CS5 — Real-Time 35%
Interactive-Video	AF41 → CS5	CS6 — Critical 20%
Streaming-Video	CS4 → AF21	AF31 — Critical 20%
Mission-Critical Data	DSCP 25 → AF31	CS3 — Video 15%
Call-Signaling	AF31/CS3 → CS5	AF21 — Video 15%
Transactional Data	AF21 → CS3	CS2 — Bulk Data 5% AF11/CS1
Network-Management	CS2	Best-Effort 25%
Bulk Data	AF11	
Scavenger	CS1 → 0	
Best-Effort	0	

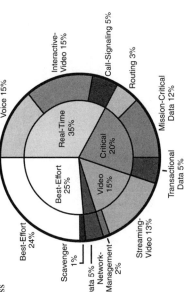

Outer-Circle: Enterprise Applications (CE Edge)
Inner-Circle: Service-Provider Classes of Service (PE Edge)

QoS Design for MPLS VPN Service Providers

In order to support enterprise-subscriber voice, video and data networks, service providers must include QoS provisioning within their MPLS VPN service offerings.

This is due to the any-to-any/full-mesh nature of MPLS VPNs, where enterprise subscribers depend on their service providers to provision Provider-Edge (PE) to Customer-Edge (CE) QoS policies consistent with their CE-to-PE policies.

In addition to these PE-to-CE policies, service providers will likely implement ingress policers on their PEs to identify whether traffic flows are in or out-of-contract. Optionally, service providers may also provision QoS policies within their core networks, using Differentiated Services and/or MPLS Traffic Engineering (TE).

To guarantee end-to-end QoS, enterprises must comanage QoS with their MPLS VPN service providers; their policies must be both consistent and complementary.

Service providers can mark at Layer 2 (MPLS EXP) or at Layer 3 (DSCP).

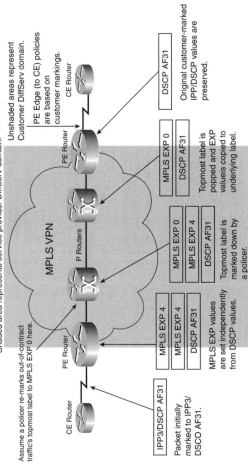

Direction of Packet Flow

RFC 3270 presents three modes of MPLS/DiffServ marking for service providers:
- **Uniform Mode:** Service provider can re-mark customer DSCP values
- **Pipe Mode:** Service provider does not re-mark customer DSCP values (service provider uses independent MPLS EXP markings); final PE-to-CE policies are based on *service provider's* markings
- **Short Pipe Mode (shown above):** Service provider does not re-mark customer DSCP values (service provider uses independent MPLS EXP markings); final PE-to-CE policies are based on *customer's* markings

Service providers can guarantee service levels within their core by:
- **Aggregate Bandwidth Overprovisioning:** Adding redundant links when utilization hits 50%(simple to implement, but expensive and inefficient)
- **Core DiffServ policies:** Simplified DiffServ policies for core links
- **MPLS TE:** TE provides granular policy-based control over traffic flows within the core

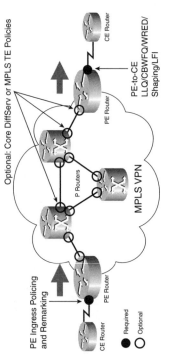

QoS Design for IPSec VPNs

IPSec VPNs achieve network segregation and privacy via encryption. IPSec VPNs are built by overlaying a point-to-point mesh over the Internet using Layer 3-encrypted tunnels. Encryption/ decryption is performed at these tunnel endpoints and the protected traffic is carried across the shared network.

Three main QoS considerations specific to IPSec VPNs are

• The additional bandwidth required by IPSec encryption and authentication
• The marginal time element required at each point where encryption/decryption takes place
• Anti-Replay interactions

❶ IPSec Bandwidth Overhead

The additional bandwidth required to encrypt and authenticate a packet needs to be factored into account when provisioning QoS policies.

This is especially important for VoIP, where IPSec could more than double the size of a G.729 voice packet, as shown below.

❷ Encryption/Decryption Delays

A marginal time element for encryption and decryption should be factored into the end-to-end delay budget for Real-Time applications, such as VoIP. Typically these processes require 2–10 ms per hop but may be doubled in the case of spoke-to-spoke VoIP calls that are homed through a central VPN headend hub.

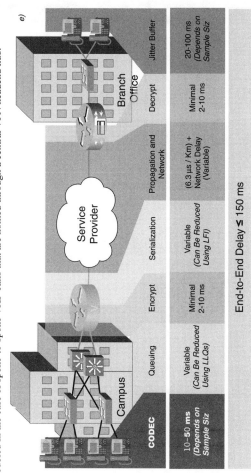

CODEC	Queuing	Encrypt	Serialization	Propagation and Network	Decrypt	Jitter Buffer
10–50 ms *(Depends on Sample Siz)*	Variable *(Can Be Reduced Using LLQs)*	Minimal 2-10 ms	Variable *(Can Be Reduced Using LFI)*	(6.3 us / Km) + Network Delay (Variable)	Minimal 2-10 ms	20-100 ms *(Depends on Sample Siz)*

End-to-End Delay ≤ 150 ms

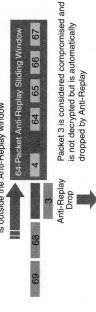

e)

❸ Anti-Replay Interactions

Anti-Relay is a standards-defined mechanism to protect IPSec VPNs from hackers. If packets arrive outside of a 64-byte window, they are considered compromised and are dropped prior to decryption. QoS queuing policies may reorder packets such that they fall outside of the Anti-Replay window. Therefore, IPSec VPN QoS policies need to be properly tuned to minimize Anti-Replay drops.

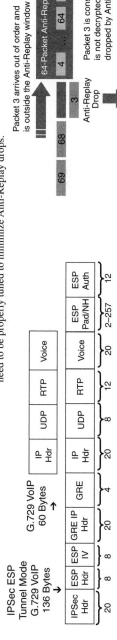

Packet 3 arrives out of order and is outside the Anti-Replay window

64-Packet Anti-Replay Sliding Window

Anti-Replay Drop

Packet 3 is considered compromised and is not decrypted but is automatically dropped by Anti-Replay

IPSec ESP
Tunnel Mode
G.729 VoIP
136 Bytes

IPSec Hdr	ESP Hdr	ESP IV	GRE	GRE IP Hdr	IP Hdr	UDP	RTP	Voice	ESP Pad/NH	ESP Auth
20	8	8	4	20	20	8	12	20	2–257	12

G.729 VoIP
60 Bytes

GRE IP Hdr	IP Hdr	UDP	RTP	Voice
20	20	8	12	20

Numerics

M

Q

S

T

U

CISCO SYSTEMS

Cisco Press

FUNDAMENTALS SERIES
ESSENTIAL EXPLANATIONS AND SOLUTIONS

Voice over IP Fundamentals

A systematic approach to understanding the basics of Voice over IP

Jonathan Davidson, CCIE° No. 2560
James Peters

ciscopress.com

When you need an authoritative introduction to a key networking topic, **reach for a Cisco Press Fundamentals book**. Learn about network topologies, deployment concepts, protocols, and management techniques and **master essential networking concepts and solutions**.

Look for Fundamentals titles at your favorite bookseller

802.11 Wireless LAN Fundamentals
ISBN: 1-58705-077-3

Cisco CallManager Fundamentals:
A Cisco AVVID Solution
ISBN: 1-58705-008-0

Data Center Fundamentals
ISBN: 1-58705-023-4

IP Addressing Fundamentals
ISBN: 1-58705-067-6

IP Routing Fundamentals
ISBN: 1-57870-071-X

Voice over IP Fundamentals
ISBN: 1-57870-168-6

Visit **www.ciscopress.com/series** for details about the Fundamentals series and a complete list of titles.

Learning is serious business.
Invest wisely.

CISCO SYSTEMS

Cisco Press

NETWORKING TECHNOLOGY GUIDES
MASTER THE NETWORK

Turn to Networking Technology Guides whenever you need **in-depth knowledge of complex networking technologies**. Written by leading networking authorities, these guides offer theoretical and practical knowledge for **real-world networking applications and solutions**.

Look for Networking Technology Guides at your favorite bookseller

**Cisco Access Control Security:
AAA Administration Services**
ISBN: 1-58705-124-9

**Cisco CallManager Best Practices:
A Cisco AVVID Solution**
ISBN: 1-58705-139-7

Designing Network Security,
Second Edition
ISBN: 1-58705-117-6

Network Security Architectures
ISBN: 1-58705-115-X

**Optical Network Design
and Implementation**
ISBN: 1-58705-105-2

Top-Down Network Design, Second Edition
ISBN: 1-58705-152-4

Troubleshooting Virtual Private Networks
ISBN: 1-58705-104-4

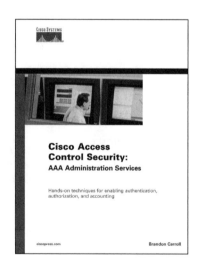

Visit **www.ciscopress.com/series** for details about Networking Technology Guides and a complete list of titles.

Learning is serious business.
Invest wisely.

SEARCH THOUSANDS OF BOOKS FROM LEADING PUBLISHERS

Safari® Bookshelf is a searchable electronic reference library for IT professionals that features more than 2,000 titles from technical publishers, including Cisco Press.

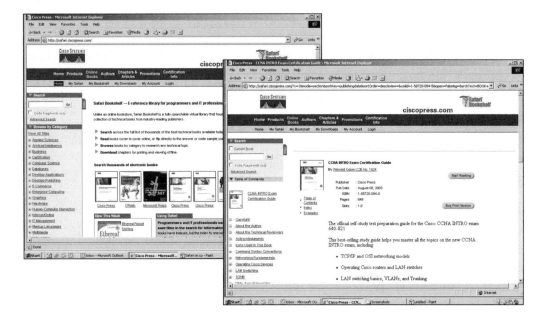

With Safari Bookshelf you can

- **Search** the full text of thousands of technical books, including more than 70 Cisco Press titles from authors such as Wendell Odom, Jeff Doyle, Bill Parkhurst, Sam Halabi, and Karl Solie.

- **Read** the books on My Bookshelf from cover to cover, or just flip to the information you need.

- **Browse** books by category to research any technical topic.

- **Download** chapters for printing and viewing offline.

With a customized library, you'll have access to your books when and where you need them—and all you need is a user name and password.

TRY SAFARI BOOKSHELF FREE FOR 14 DAYS!

You can sign up to get a 10-slot Bookshelf free for the first 14 days.
Visit **http://safari.ciscopress.com** to register.

CISCO SYSTEMS

Cisco Press

3 STEPS TO LEARNING

STEP 1

First-Step

STEP 2

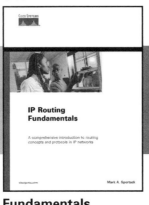

Fundamentals

STEP 3

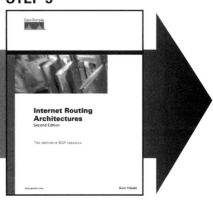

**Networking
Technology Guides**

STEP 1 **First-Step**—Benefit from easy-to-grasp explanations.
No experience required!

STEP 2 **Fundamentals**—Understand the purpose, application,
and management of technology.

STEP 3 **Networking Technology Guides**—Gain the knowledge
to master the challenge of the network.

NETWORK BUSINESS SERIES

The Network Business series helps professionals tackle the
business issues surrounding the network. Whether you are a
seasoned IT professional or a business manager with minimal
technical expertise, this series will help you understand the
business case for technologies.

Justify Your Network Investment.

Look for Cisco Press titles at your favorite bookseller today.

Visit **www.ciscopress.com/series** for details on each of these book series.